COMPLETE SCIENCE

BOOK TWO

P.A. HOBSON G.W. MURPHY G.P. WHEELER

Scholarstown Educational Publishers, London

First Published 1987
by Scholarstown Educational Publishers Ltd.,
London House, 26-40 Kensington High Street,
London W8 4PF.

Artwork by Michael Phillips

ISBN 1 85276 002 8

Contents

1 — Atomic Structure and the Periodic Table

1.1 Introduction

In *Book 1*, we discussed the meaning of the terms **element** and **atom**. We said that all matter is made up of approximately ninety elements. These elements are themselves made up of very small particles called **atoms**. In the early nineteenth century, an English chemist, John Dalton, put forward some ideas about atoms. He said that atoms were extremely small particles which were indivisible, i.e. could not be broken up into other particles. Dalton's theory was accepted up to the 1890s when a number of scientists began to explore atoms in more detail and found some unexpected results. They discovered that atoms are made up of even smaller particles. These particles, found inside an atom, are called **sub-atomic particles**.

1.2 Sub-Atomic Particles

The atom is made up of three sub-atomic particles called the **proton**, the **neutron**, and the **electron**. The story of the discovery of these particles is a fascinating one. It is not possible to cover the details of the discoveries at this stage but you will be studying these details in your G.C.S.E. Chemistry course.

Table 1.1 Summary of the Properties of the Sub-Atomic Particles

Name of Particle	*Its situation in the atom*	*Relative mass*	*Relative charge*
Proton	Nucleus	1 unit	+1 unit
Neutron	Nucleus	1 unit	0
Electron	Electron cloud	1/1850 unit	−1 unit

The properties of protons, neutrons and electrons are summarised in *Table 1.1.* The masses of these particles are so small that, if expressed in grams, there would be about 23 zeros after the decimal point before the first digit of the number (mass of proton = 1.6×10^{-24}g). Therefore, we use a new unit of mass called the **atomic mass unit** (a.m.u.). On this scale, the mass of the proton or neutron is 1 a.m.u. The mass of the electron is only 1/1850 of the mass of the proton, *Fig. 1.1*

The proton and the electron have another property called **charge**. Charge exerts a force of attraction between the particles and holds the atom together. No particle has been

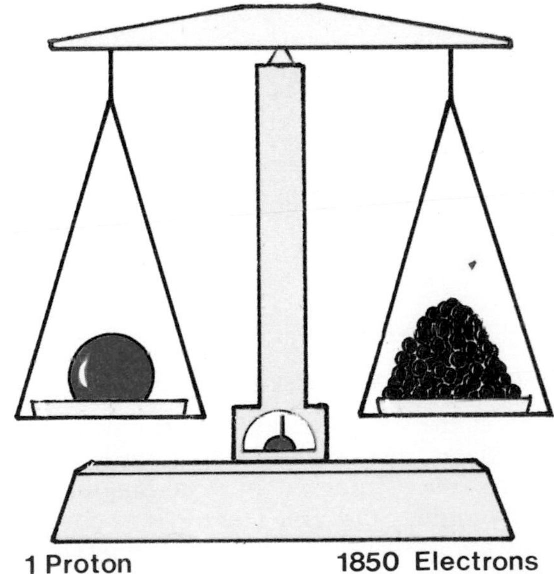

Fig. 1.1 Neutron and Protons have the same mass

discovered which carries a smaller charge of electricity than the electron. We say that the electron carries unit negative charge or a charge of -1. The proton also carries unit electrical charge but in this case the charge is positive, $+1$.

1.3 Structure of the Atom

Fig. 1.2 Ernest Rutherford proposed the idea of atoms having a central nucleus

In 1910, Ernest Rutherford, *Fig. 1.2*, discovered that the atom consists of a small central part called the **nucleus**. The protons and neutrons are concentrated in the nucleus and the electrons revolve around it rather like the planets move around the sun. This is illustrated in *Fig. 1.3.* The movement of electrons around the nucleus gives rise to what is often called an **electron cloud**.

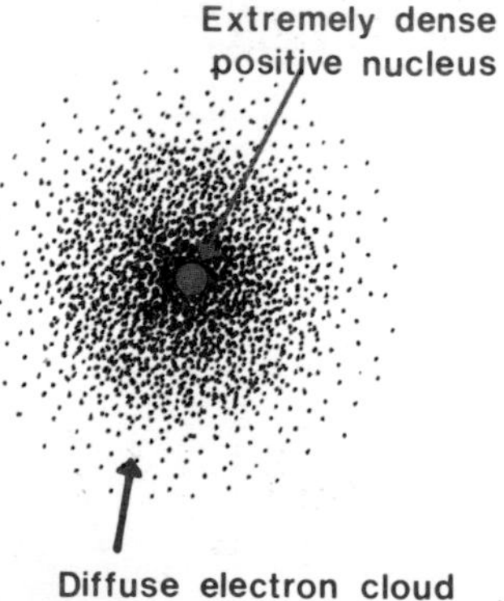

Fig. 1.3 The movement of electrons around the nucleus

If one compares the size of an atom to the size of the sub-atomic particles, one concludes that **most of the atom consists of empty space**. Imagine an atom magnified until it is the size of Wembley Stadium. The nucleus could be represented by a marble at the centre of the pitch. The electrons would be like specks of dust at various parts of the stands. Everything in between would be just empty space. The electrons are free to move in this space. (For this reason, any diagrams drawn in this text to indicate the structure of the atom are purely descriptive and not to scale).

1.4 Atomic Structure of the First Twenty Elements

Although it was Rutherford who put forward the idea of the nucleus, it was the Danish scientist, Niels Bohr, who gave a clearer picture of the structure of the atom. Bohr, *Fig. 1.4*, proposed that electrons move around the nucleus in fixed paths called **shells** or **orbits**.

Fig. 1.4 Niels Bohr put forward the idea of electrons moving round the nucleus in fixed paths called shells or orbits.

Before we can study the atomic structure of some elements, we must be clear on the meaning of the terms **atomic number** and **mass number**. Although an atom contains electrically charged particles, the atom itself is electrically neutral. Therefore, the number of protons in the nucleus must be balanced by an equal number of electrons moving around the nucleus. The number of protons in the nucleus of an atom is given a special name and is called the **atomic number** of the atom.

The atomic number of an atom is the number of protons in the nucleus of that atom.

Each element has a different atomic number, e.g. the atomic number of carbon is 6 (6 protons in the nucleus) while the atomic number of copper is 29 (29 protons in the nucleus).

The **mass number**, as the name implies, gives us information about the mass of an atom. Since the mass of an electron is very small compared to that of a proton or neutron, its mass may be ignored for most purposes.

The mass number of an atom is the sum of the number of protons and neutrons.

For example, the mass number of an atom of aluminium is 27. This means that if we add up the number of protons and neutrons in the nucleus of an atom of aluminium, our answer will be 27.

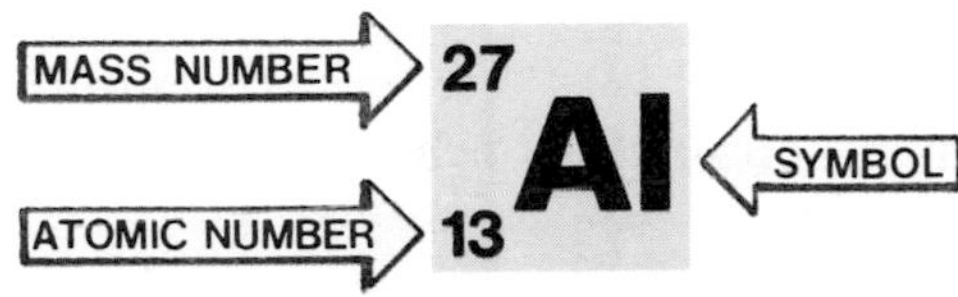

Fig. 1.5 Writing the nuclear formula

The atomic number and the mass number are often written with the symbol of the element as shown in *Fig. 1.5.* This shorthand method of expressing the atomic number and the mass number of an atom is called the **nuclear formula**. For example, an atom of aluminium may be written as $^{27}_{13}$Al. This gives us the following information:

* Atomic number of aluminium = 13, i.e. an atom of aluminium contains 13 protons and 13 electrons.
* Aluminium is the thirteenth element in the Periodic Table.
* Mass number of aluminium = 27, i.e. sum of protons plus neutrons = 27.
* Number of neutrons = 27 − 13 = 14 since, in general, the atomic number subtracted from the mass number tells us the number of neutrons.

Number of neutrons = mass number — atomic number.

The nuclear formulae for the first ten elements are given in *Table 1.2.* It is left as an exercise to the student to complete his table up to element number 20.

In drawing how the electrons are arranged around the nucleus, we use the symbol n to indicate the shells or orbits*. Thus, the first shell is the $n = 1$ shell, the second shell is the $n = 2$ shells, etc. Bohr deduced that the maximum number of electrons which may occupy each shell is given by the formula $2 \times n^2$. Therefore, the $n = 1$ shell may hold a maximum of 2 electrons, the $n = 2$ shell may hold a maximum of 8 electrons, the $n = 3$ shell may hold a maximum of 18 electrons, etc. Some examples of diagrams representing the atomic structures of various elements are shown in *Fig. 1.6.* There is no need to learn off any of these structures as all information may be deduced from the Periodic Table.

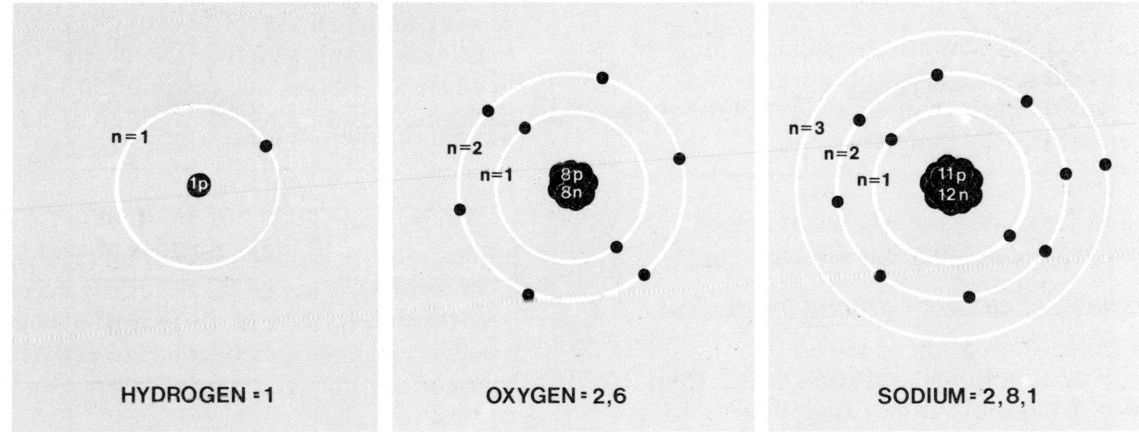

Fig. 1.6 This diagram shows the atomic structure and arrangement of electrons of some elements. Although the shells are represented as circles, it should be remembered that, in reality, the electrons move within a sphere rather than in a circle

Table 1.2 The Structure of Atoms of the first 10 Elements

Element	*Atomic number*	*Number of protons*	*Number of electrons*	*Mass number*	*Number of neutrons* *
H	1	1	1	1	0
He	2	2	2	4	4 — 2 = 2
Li	3	3	3	7	7 — 3 = 4
Be	4	4	4	9	9 — 4 = 5
B	5	5	5	11	11 — 5 = 6
C	6	6	6	12	12 — 6 = 6
N	7	7	7	14	14 — 7 = 7
O	8	8	8	16	16 — 8 = 8
F	9	9	9	19	19 — 9 = 10
Ne	10	10	10	20	20 — 10 = 10

* (mass number — atomic number)

1.5 Isotopes

All atoms of the same element contain the same number of protons. However, they do not always contain the same number of neutrons. Atoms of the same element that have a different number of neutrons are called **isotopes**.

> **Isotopes are forms of the same element, the atoms of which have the same atomic number but different mass number.**

Isotopes are named by giving the mass number after the name of the element, e.g. two isotopes of carbon are ${}^{12}_{6}C$ and ${}^{14}_{6}C$ which are called carbon – 12 and carbon – 14 respectively.

Naturally occurring chlorine is found to consist of two isotopes of chlorine: ${}^{35}_{17}Cl$ and ${}^{37}_{17}Cl$. These are illustrated in

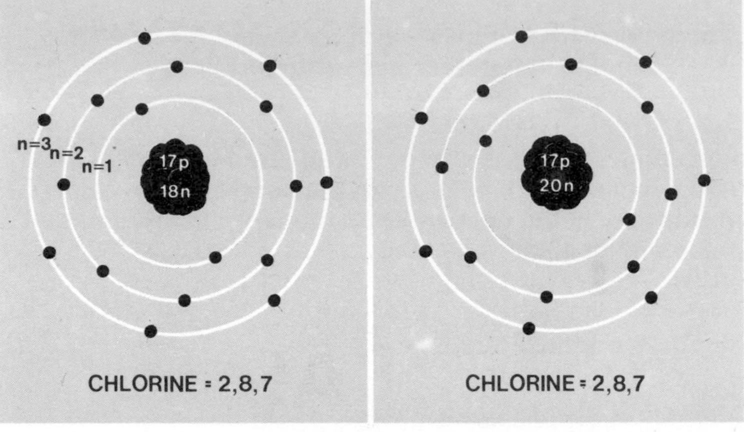

*Fig 1.7 Chlorine consists normally of a mixture of two kinds of atoms, one with a mass of 35 a.m.u. and the other with a mass of 37 a.m.u. Both **isotopes** contain the same number of protons and electrons but differ in the number of neutrons*

By experiment, it is found that in a sample of chlorine gas there are about three times as many ${}^{35}_{17}Cl$ atoms as there are ${}^{37}_{17}Cl$ atoms. Therefore, the approximate average mass of chlorine atom is

$$\frac{(3 \times 35) + (1 \times 37)}{4} = 35.5$$

This average mass is given a special name and is called the **relative atomic mass**. (The old name for relative atomic mass was **atomic weight**.) The word "relative" is used because all masses are compared to the mass of the carbon-12 isotope which is taken as having a mass of 12 a.m.u.

> **The relative atomic mass of an element is the average mass of an atom of the naturally occurring element measured relative to the carbon – 12 isotope, whose mass is taken as exactly 12 units.**

If one examines the values of relative atomic mass of the various elements *(Periodic Table inside back cover)*, it is clear that very few of the values are whole numbers. This means that practically all elements contain isotopes. The fact that the relative atomic mass of carbon is given as 12.010 must mean that by far the largest proportion of naturally occurring carbon is made up of $^{12}_{6}C$ and very little of the $^{13}_{6}C$ and $^{14}_{6}C$ isotopes are present.

Note: When drawing out the structures of atoms it is normal to bring the relative atomic mass to the nearest whole number and this gives the mass number of that isotope. For example, in drawing the structure of an atom of sodium, the relative atomic mass of 22.997 is changed to 23 and the structure of $^{23}_{11}Na$ is drawn.

1.6 Classifying the Elements

Elements could be divided into solids, liquids and gases but this division would not be very useful. Another way would be to divide them into metals and non-metals.

This could be done quite easily because many metals have physical properties in common and the same applies to non-metals.

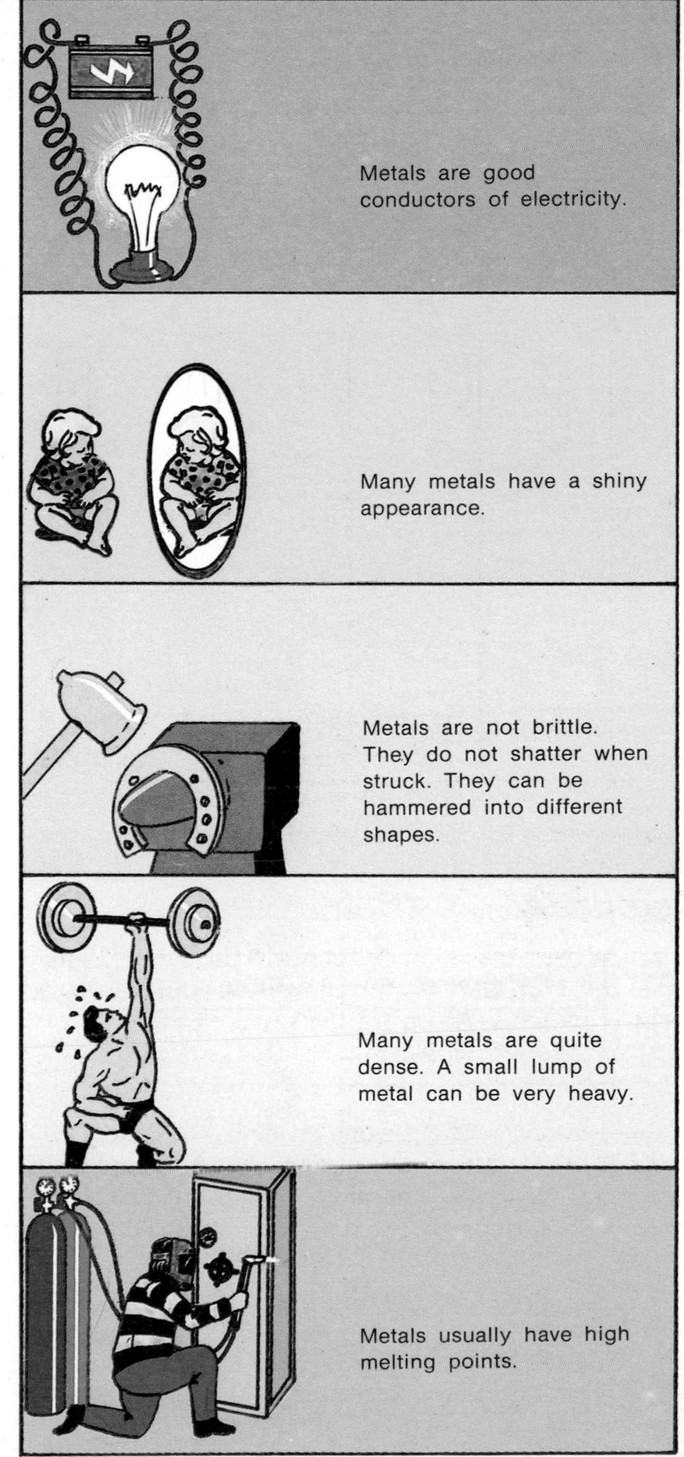

Properties of metals

1. Malleable — can be hammered into shape without breaking
2. Ductile — can be drawn into wires.
3. Shiny.
4. High melting point.
5. Usually heavy.
6. Good conductors of heat.
7. Good conductors of electricity.
8. React with oxygen to form basic oxides *(Section 4.4)*.

Properties of non-metals

1. Brittle — easily broken when solid.
2. Brittle — when crushed.
3. Dull when solid.
4. Usually low melting point.
5. Light.
6. Poor conductors of heat.
7. Usually poor conductors of electricity.
8. React with oxygen to form acidic oxides.

Experiment 1.1 To show that metals conduct electricity

Method

Take pieces of each of the following elements:— Copper, sulphur (roll), iron (nail), magnesium, carbon as charcoal and as graphite (rod), iodine (a flake), zinc (foil) and lead (foil).

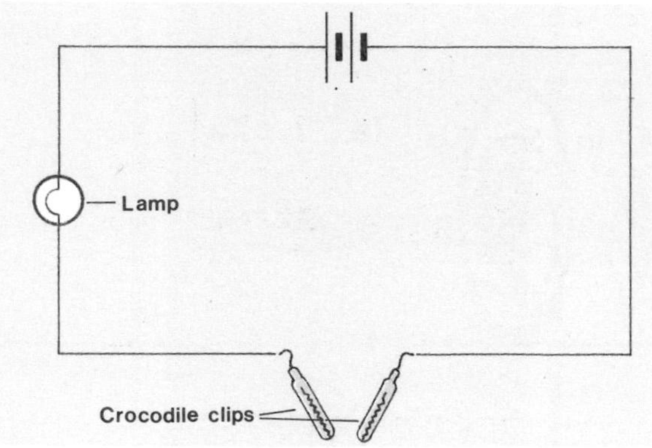

Fig. 1.9

1. Set up the circuit as shown and check that the bulb lights when the crocodile clips touch.
2. Take the pieces of different elements in turn and use them to bridge the circuit.
3. Record your results in a chart as follows:—

Element	Bulb Lights

If the bulb lights mark Yes if not mark No.

4. Draw a conclusion from your results.

The division of the elements into metals and non-metals is not completely reliable because there are exceptions. Can you think of a metal which is a liquid? Can you think of a non-metal which conducts electricity? Because of this a different way of grouping the elements had to be found. That way is the Periodic Table.

1.7 The Periodic Table

What is the Periodic Table?

The Periodic Table is an arrangement of elements in order of increasing **atomic number**. This type of table was first drawn up in 1869 by a Russian chemist, Mendeleef. In the Periodic Table *(see inside back cover)* elements are arranged in such a way that those elements with the same number of electrons in their outermost shells are placed under one another. These vertical columns are called **groups** and, from a study of the Periodic Table, it is clear that there are essentially eight groups in the Periodic Table — we ignore, for the moment, the presence of the elements in the centre of the Periodic Table. The horizontal rows of elements are called **periods** and there are seven periods in the Table.

The main uses of the Periodic Table may be listed under the following headings.

1. **Studying Chemistry**
   Instead of studying the chemical reactions of over one hundred elements, it is far easier to study the reactions of a small number of groups of elements. All elements in the one group have similar chemical properties — we shall see the reason for this at a later stage. Therefore, knowing the chemical properties of one element in a group, we may deduce that the other elements in the group behave similarly, e.g. knowing that sodium reacts vigorously with water implies that potassium does likewise, since both are found in *Group I.*

2. **Classifying elements into metals and non-metals**
   It is useful to divide the elements of the Periodic Table into metals and non-metals as shown in *Fig. 1.10.* We shall be studying the properties of these at a later stage.

3. **Writing Electron Configurations**
   The **electron configuration** of an element may easily be deduced from its position in the Periodic Table. Electron configuration means the electron arrangement which an element has, i.e. the number of electrons in each shell. A shorthand method of indicating the electron configuration is shown in *Table 1.3.* The electron configuration for carbon is given as 2,4. This means that there are two electrons in the $n = 1$ shell and 4 electrons in the $n = 2$ shell.

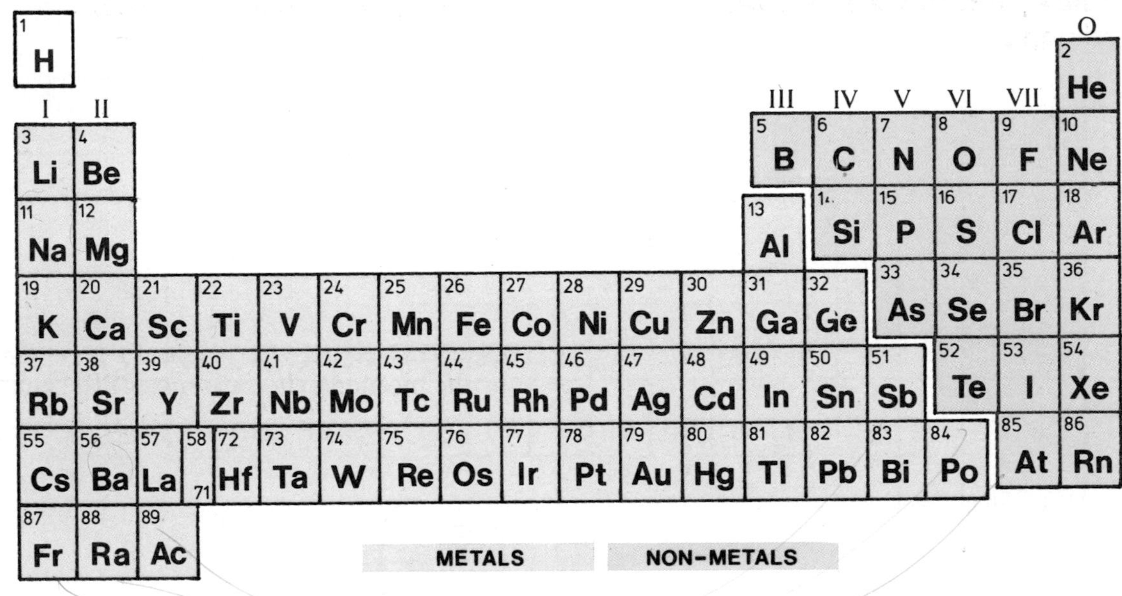

Fig. 1.10 The elements of the Periodic Table may be divided into metals and non-metals by the "steps of stairs" going from boron to astatain

Table 1.3 The Electron Arrangement of Some Elements

Element	*Atomic Number*	*Electrons in each shell* $n = 1$	$n = 2$	$n = 3$	Shorthand method of writing electron configuration
Hydrogen	1	1			1
Helium	2	2			2
Lithium	3	2	1		2,1
Beryllium	4	2	2		2,2
Boron	5	2	3		2,3
Carbon	6	2	4		2,4
Nitrogen	7	2	5		2,5
Oxygen	8	2	6		2,6
Fluorine	9	2	7		2,7
Neon	10	2	8		2,8
Sodium	11	2	8	1	2,8,1
Magnesium	12	2	8	2	2,8,2

Suppose we wish to write the electron configuration for sulphur, then we proceed as follows:

(a) Locate the position of the element in the Periodic Table. Sulphur is element number 16.

(b) Note the group number and the period number. Sulphur is in group six (i.e. six electrons in the outer shell) and period number three i.e. these six electrons are in the $n = 3$ shell and all inner shells are completely filled.

(c) From the above information you can now write the electron configuration of sulphur as S = 2,8,6. Check that this is correct by adding up these numbers $2+8+6$ and this sum should be equal to the atomic number of sulphur given on the Periodic Table.

(d) If required, draw out the atomic structures as indicated in *Fig. 1.11.* The atomic number and mass number are obtained from the Periodic Table.

Note: We have already stated *(Section 1.4)* that the $n = 3$ shell may hold a maximum of 18 electrons. However, it is clear from the Periodic Table that the electron configuration of K = 2,8,8,1 (*not* 2,8,9) and that of Ca =

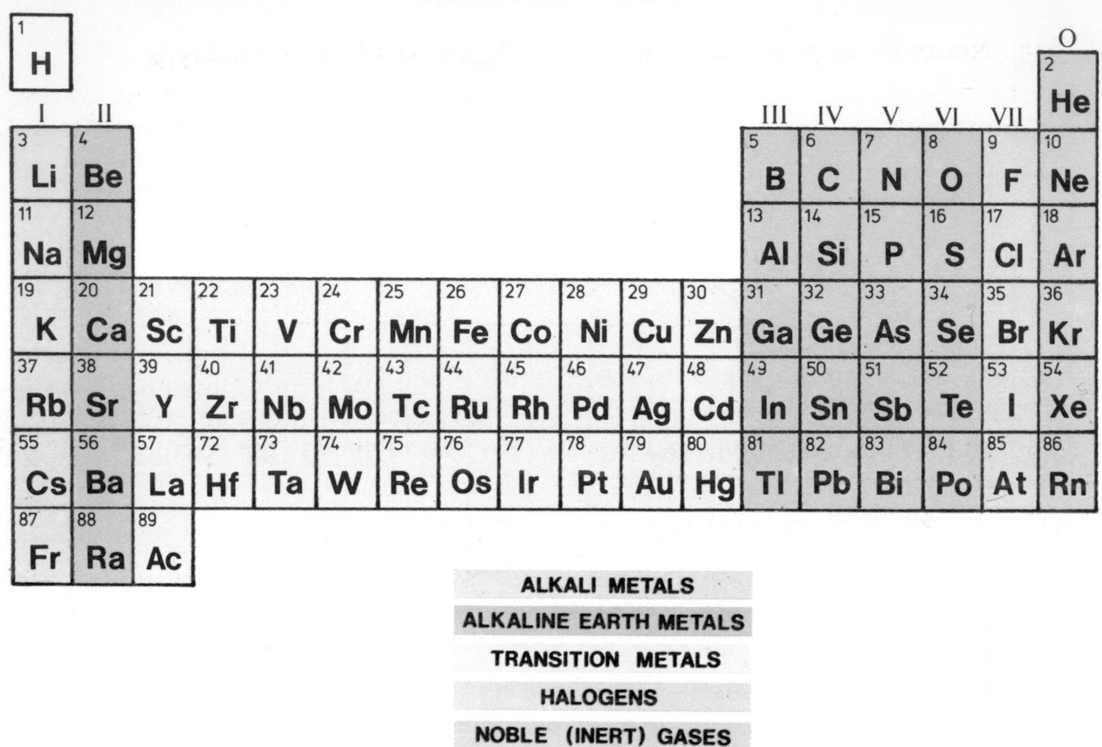

Fig. 1.11 Some groups in the Periodic Table are given special names

2,8,8,2 (*not* 2,8,10). The reason for this apparent contradiction will be given in your G.C.S.E. course.

4. Predicting chemical bonding
The use of the Periodic Table to deduce information about the type of forces holding molecules together will be covered in *Chapter 2.*

A closer look at some of the Groups

Group I The alkali metals

These are: Lithium Li, Sodium Na, Potassium K, Rubidium Rb, Caesium Cs, Francium Fr

These are:				
	Lithium	Li	Rubidium	Rb
	Sodium	Na	Caesium	Cs
	Potassium	K	Francium	Fr

Experiment 1.2 To show similarities in Group I elements

(This experiment may only be done by the teacher)

Method

Using lithium, sodium and potassium.

1. Remove the metal from the jar. Notice how it is stored.

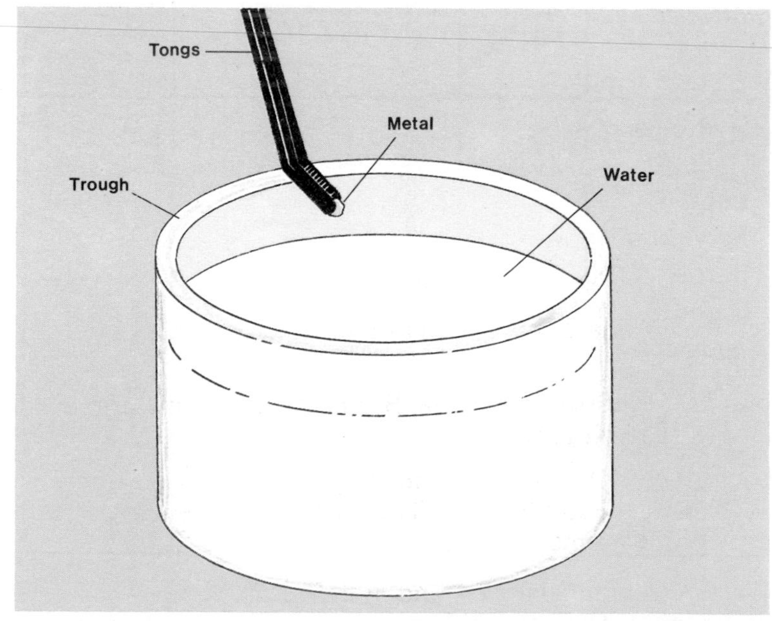

Fig. 1.12

2. Cut a small piece of metal. Notice the appearance of the freshly cut part.
3. Add a small piece of metal to the water in a trough.
   Does the metal sink?
   Does the metal change its shape?
   Does the metal burn?
4. At the end of the experiment add a piece of universal indicator paper to the water in the trough. What colour does it go?

Make a list of all the similarities and say which you think was the most reactive and which was the least reactive.

Group I elements, the alkali metals react in a similar way because **their atoms have the same number of outer electrons** and this number is the **same as the group number** which is **ONE**.

Group II, Beryllium, Magnesium, Calcium, Strontium, Barium are known as the alkaline earth metals because these elements are found combined with other elements in rocks and soils, for example, magnesium sulphate is commonly known as Epsom Salts.

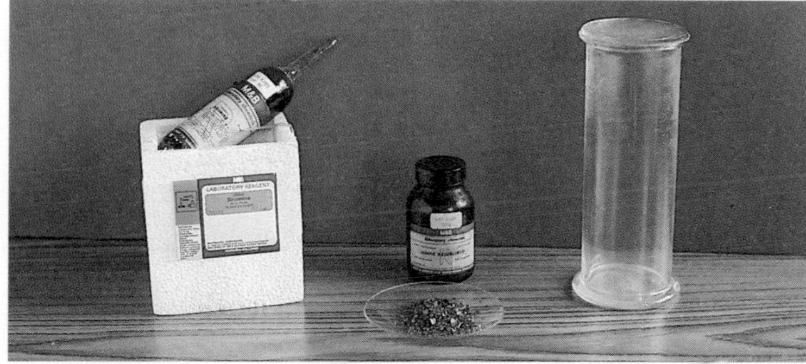

Fig. 1.13

Calcium carbonates are found as limestone, chalk and marble.

Group VII, Fluorine, Chlorine, Bromine and Iodine are known as the halogens.

Group VIII, or O Helium, Neon, Argon, Krypton, Xenon are known as the noble gases. These are very **unreactive** and exist as single atoms.

The Transition metals are found in the centre of the Periodic table. They resemble each other. They are heavy metals with high melting point. They form **coloured compound**.

Some Final Points

1. In an introductory chemistry course, elements 58-71 and those beyond element 89 are not included in the Periodic Table. The reason for this is because many of these elements are quite rare and their chemistry is complex.
2. The properties of hydrogen are quite unique. For convenience, hydrogen is often placed with the alkali metals but it shows little resemblance to these elements. It is more correct to keep it separate from the rest of the table as shown in the preceding diagrams. A similar problem exists with helium. Although helium has only two electrons in its outer shell, it shows such a remarkable resemblance to the noble gases in all its properties, that it is normally placed with them in the Periodic Table.

Summary

* Atoms contain protons, neutrons and electrons.
* Protons and neutrons are found in the nucleus of the atom. Electrons move about the nucleus in paths called shells or orbits.
* Protons and neutrons have a mass of 1 a.m.u. Electrons have a mass of 1/1850 a.m.u.
* Protons carry a charge of +1, electrons carry a charge of −1, neutrons carry no charge.
* There are equal numbers of protons and electrons in an atom of an element.
* The atomic number of an atom is the number of protons in the nucleus of that atom.
* The mass number of an atom is the sum of the number of protons and neutrons.
* The number of neutrons in an atom is calculated by subtracting the atomic number from the mass number.
* Isotopes are atoms of the same element which have the same atomic number but different mass number.
* The relative atomic mass of an element is the average mass of an atom of the naturally occurring element and measured relative to the carbon – 12 isotope, whose mass is taken as being exactly 12 units.
* The Periodic Table is an arrangement of elements in order of increasing atomic number.
* The Periodic Table is very useful for deducing atomic structure and electron configuration of an element.
* Elements of similar chemical properties appear in the same group of the Periodic Table.

Questions

Section A

1. The particles inside an atom are referred to as a ....
2. Protons and neutrons are found in the ....
3. The electrons orbit the nucleus in paths called ....
4. A proton has a .... charge but an electron has a .... charge.
5. The neutron is so called because it is a .... particle.
6. The maximum number of electrons which any shell can accommodate may be calculated from the formula .....
7. Both the proton and the neutron have a mass of .... but the mass of the electron is only .... of the mass of the proton.
8. List two items of information which the atomic number gives us about the atoms of an element ....
9. In a neutral atom the number of .... is always equal to the number of ....
10. The only element in the Periodic Table which has no neutron in its nucleus is ....
11. The nuclear formula of potassium is $^{39}_{19}K$. This tells us that there are .... protons and ...... neutrons in the nucleus of an atom.
12. What are isotopes?
13. $^{12}_{6}Ca$ and $^{14}_{6}C$ are two isotopes of carbon. Carbon-12 has .... neutrons but carbon-14 has .... neutrons in the nucleus.
14. Write down the electronic structures of (i) Sodium .... (ii) Potassium ....
15. In the Periodic Table the vertical columns are called ... and the horizontal rows are called ....
16. Unerline the non-metals in the following list:

    sodium carbon iron oxygen copper.
17. Elements of similar properties are found in the same ...
18. The elements of Group 1 are commonly known as .....
19. To what family of elements do chlorine and bromine belong? ....
20. The elements in the centre of the Periodic Table are commonly called the ....
21. Which of the following statements are correct:—
    (a) All elements in the same group have the same number of outer electrons.
    (b) Metals in Group I are heavy.
    (c) The noble gases exist as single atoms.
    (d) The compounds of the transition metals are always white.

Section B

1. Discuss the properties of protons, neutrons and electrons under the following headings: (i) charge; (ii) mass; (iii) location. Explain what is meant by the terms **mass number** and **relative atomic mass (atomic weight).**
   "The mass number of an atom is always a whole number but the relative atomic mass is rarely a whole number". Explain this statement.
2. Explain clearly the meaning of the term **isotope**. Hydrogen has three isotopes: $^{1}_{1}H$ (protium), $^{2}_{1}H$ (deuterium) and $^{3}_{1}H$ (tritium). Draw the structures of each of these isotopes and point out the difference between them.
   Given that the relative atomic mass (atomic weight) of hydrogen is 1.0080, which of the above isotopes is present in the greatest amount? Explain your answer.
3. Draw diagrams to show the structures of the following atoms:

   $^{20}_{10}Ne$, $^{23}_{11}Na$, $^{40}_{18}Ar$, $^{40}_{20}Ca$.

   "The position of an element in the Periodic Table gives us much information about its electronic structure". Explain this statement. Write down the electron configurations of lithium, sulphur and potassium. Sodium and potassium belong to the same family of elements. Name this family and give the name of any other member of the family.
4. Describe the difference between metals and non-metals by referring to:—
   (i) their appearance
   (ii) physical properties
   (iii) electrical properties.

2 — Chemical Bonding and Shapes of Molecules

2.1 Introduction

We have already seen that elements combine to form a very large number of compounds *(Book 1, Chapter 2)*. In this chapter we shall study the forces of attraction which hold atoms together in a compound. These forces of attraction are called **chemical bonds**. Chemical bonding involves the rearrangement of the electrons of the atoms involved in forming the bond.

Our study of chemical bonding will be greatly simplified if we first consider a very simple rule called the *Octet Rule.*

2.2 The Octet Rule

The octet rule is *not* a strict chemical law* but rather a useful guide to understanding bonding.

Octet Rule: When bonding occurs, atoms tend to reach an electron arrangement with eight electrons in the outermost shell.

***There are some exceptions to the octet rule, the main ones being hydrogen and lithium which tend to reach the electron configuration of helium when chemical bonding occurs. Also, the transition metals do not usually obey the octet rule.**

Fig. 2.1 The noble gas is used in lighting

Atoms try to attain eight electrons in the outermost shell because, by experiment, it is found that this is a very stable arrangement. The noble or inert gases have eight electrons in their outer shell. These gases are very unreactive (hence the name inert) and form practically no compounds. A sample of neon gas, *Fig. 2.1*, consists entirely of neon atoms — neon molecules do not exist.

There are two main types of chemical bond — the **ionic bond** and the **covalent bond**.

2.3 Ionic Bond

Ionic bonding involves the complete transfer of one or more electrons from one atom to another. The name ionic bond comes from the fact that *ions* are always formed when a neutral atom gains or loses one or more electrons.

An ion is a charged atom or group of atoms.

Some examples of common ions are given in *Table 2.1.*

Table 2.1

Positive ions	*Negative ions*
Li^+, Na^+, K^+ Mg^{2+}, Ca^{2+} Cu^{2+}, Al^{3+}	F^-, Cl^-, Br^-, I^- O^{2-}, S^{2-}

An atom (neutral) which gains an extra electron becomes a negatively charged ion which has one more negative charge than it has positive charges. Likewise, an atom which loses an electron becomes a positively charged ion which has one more proton than electrons.

Note that when an ion is formed the atom usually attains an octet of electrons in its outer shell. There is a strong electrical attraction between positive ions and negative ions and the ions are held together by the force of this attraction. This force of attraction is called an **ionic bond** or **electrovalent bond**.

An ionic bond is the force of attraction between oppositely charged ions in a compound.

The following examples of ionic bond formation should be studied carefully.

Example 1 Sodium Chloride, NaCl

We have already seen *(Book 1, Chapter 2)* that when sodium metal is burned in chlorine gas, a white crystalline material is formed. This compound is called sodium chloride or common salt. Let us consider this reaction in a little more detail.

Electron configuration of Na = 2,8,1

Electron configuration of Cl = 2,8,7

It is clear that the sodium atom could attain eight electrons in its outer shell by simply losing its one outer electron. If the chlorine atom were to accept this one electron, then chlorine would have eight electrons in its outer shell. Thus, the formation of the ionic bond involves the complete transfer of an electron from an atom of sodium to an atom of chlorine. This is shown in *Fig. 2.2.* The formation of this bond can be represented more simply as

Na Cl = Na+ Cl

Example 2 Magnesium Oxide MgO

Magnesium burns brightly in oxygen to form a white powder called magnesium oxide. On closer examination, this white powder is found to consist of Mg^{2+} ions and O^{2-} ions. If we consider the electron configuration of both elements, it becomes obvious what is actually happening.

Mg = 2,8,2

O = 2,6

Each Mg atom donates its two outer electrons to an oxygen atom. As the Mg atom has lost two electrons it is written as Mg^{2+} and as the oxygen atom has gained *two* electrons it is written as O^{2-}. The formation of this ionic bond is shown in *Fig. 2.3.*

$$\mathrm{Mg} \longrightarrow \mathrm{O} = \mathrm{Mg}^{2+}\ \mathrm{O}^{2-}$$

Fig. 2.3 Simplied diagram of the formation of the ionic bond in magnesium oxide. Only the outer electrons are shown

Note that both the Mg^{2+} ion and the O^{2-} ion have the same electron configuration as that of neon.

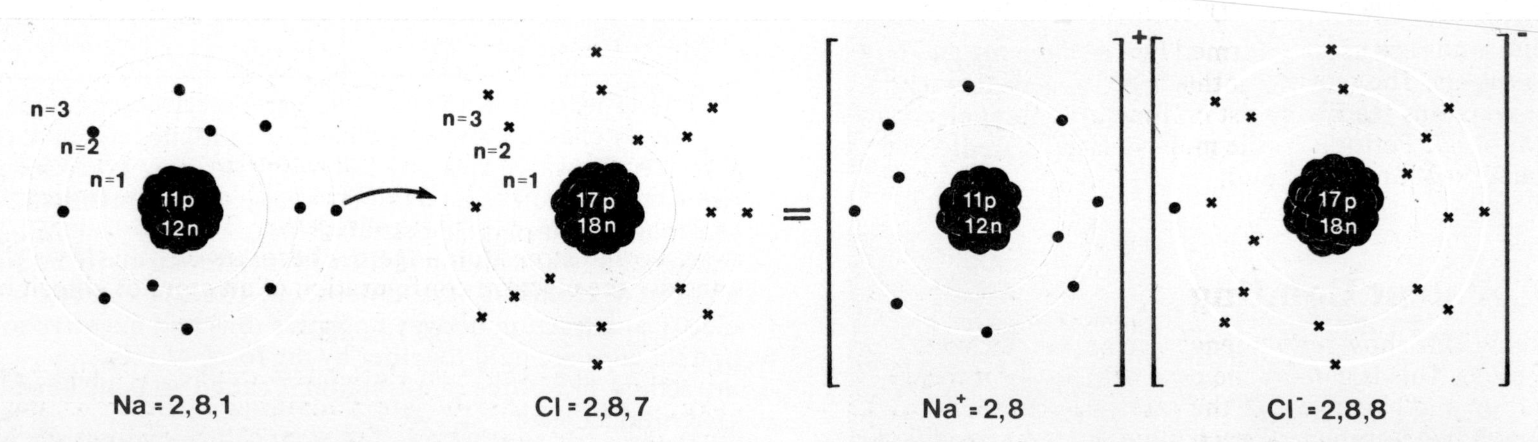

Fig. 2.2 A sodium atom gives an electron to a chlorine atom to form sodium chloride. In this diagram ● symbols are used to represent an electron on an atom of sodium than on an atom of chlorine. This, of course, is not accurate since all electrons are identical but it is helpful, at times, to indicate the origin of the electrons

The following generalisations should be noted.

1. Ionic compounds are usually solid due to the large force of attraction between the millions of ions present.
2. The ions are usually packed together in a regular arrangement. *Fig. 2.4* illustrates how the Na^+ and Cl^- ions are arranged in a crystal of NaCl.

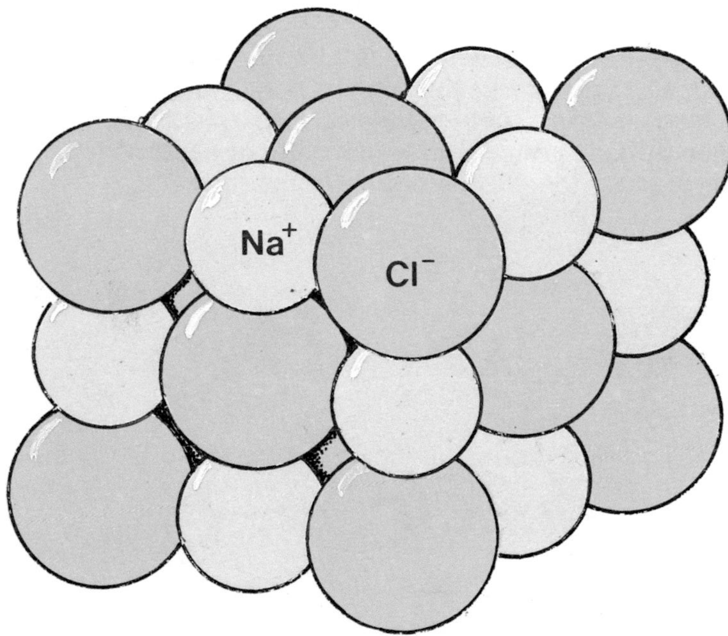

Fig. 2.4 Structure of a crystal of sodium chloride

3. Ionic bonds are usually formed between metals and non-metals. The reason for this is because metals tend to lose electrons readily whilst non-metals accept electrons readily. The Periodic Table may be used to predict the formation of an ionic bond.

2.4 Covalent Bonding

Some elements show no tendency to transfer electrons one to the other. This is usually the case with two non-metals, e.g. carbon and hydrogen. In the case of a compound containing two non-metals, each atom attempts to achieve eight electrons in its outer shell by **sharing** electrons with one or more other atoms. The electrons shared between two atoms are generally shared in pairs. A **shared pair** forms a bond between the two atoms. This particular type of bond is called a **covalent bond**.

A covalent bond is a bond which consists of shared electrons.

In general, covalent bonds are found in elements which are non-metals e.g. hydrogen (H_2), oxygen (O_2), chlorine (Cl_2), etc.; and in compounds which contain only non-metals, e.g. water (H_2O), ammonia (NH_3), methane (CH_4), etc.

The following examples of covalent bond formation should be studied carefully.

Example 1 **The chlorine molecule**

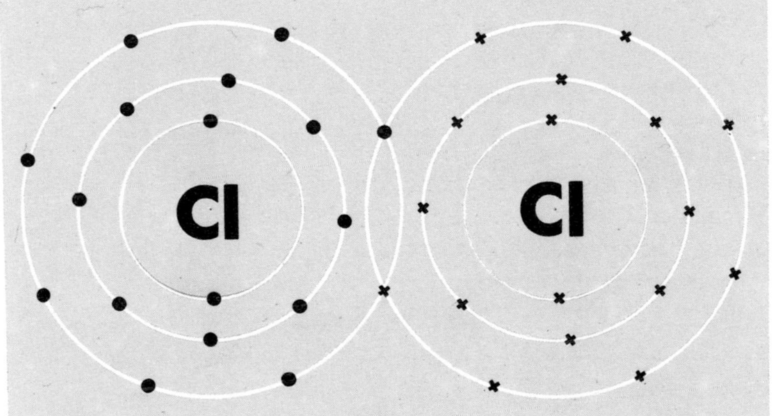

Fig. 2.5 Covalent bond formation in a molecule of chlorine

or more simply $:\ddot{\underset{\cdot\cdot}{Cl}}\cdot\!\!-\!\!{}_{x}\overset{xx}{\underset{xx}{Cl}}\,{}^{x}_{x}$

A sample of chlorine gas does not contain any individual chlorine atoms. Rather, it consists of chlorine molecules, i.e. two chlorine atoms joined together. The reason why two chlorine atoms join together becomes obvious if we consider the electron configuration of an atom of chlorine.

$$Cl = 2,8,7$$

By sharing one of its own electrons with one from another chlorine atom, a chlorine atom attains eight electrons in its outer shell. This attraction of the two chlorine atoms for the same pair of electrons forms the bond between them. This is shown in *Fig. 2.5.* A covalent bond is often simply represented by a dash, e.g. Cl-Cl.

Example 2 **The methane molecule**

A molecule of methane (natural gas) consists of one atom of carbon joined to four atoms of hydrogen. It is easy to understand how the CH_4 molecule is formed if we consider the electron configuration of the atoms involved in bonding.

C = 2,4 H = 1

The carbon atom and four hydrogen atoms share electrons in order to fill their outer shells. This is illustrated in *Fig. 2.6.* We shall be meeting many more examples of covalent bonding in this chemistry course.

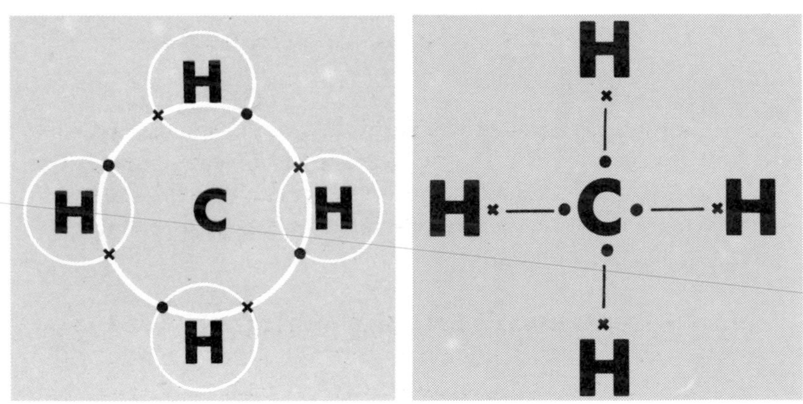

Fig. 2.6 The methane molecule.

2.5 Double and Triple Covalent Bonds

In the covalent bonds which we have studied so far, a pair of electrons is shared between two atoms. In some molecules, two atoms may be held together by sharing *two* or even *three* pairs of electrons.

A single bond is formed when one pair of electrons is shared. A double bond is formed when two pairs of electrons are shared. A triple bond is formed when three pairs of electrons are shared.

An example of an element which contains a double bond is oxygen, O_2. From a study of *Fig. 2.7*, it may be seen how each oxygen atom attains eight electrons in its outer shell. Carbon dioxide is an example of a compound in which the atoms are held together by double bonds, *Fig. 2.7.*

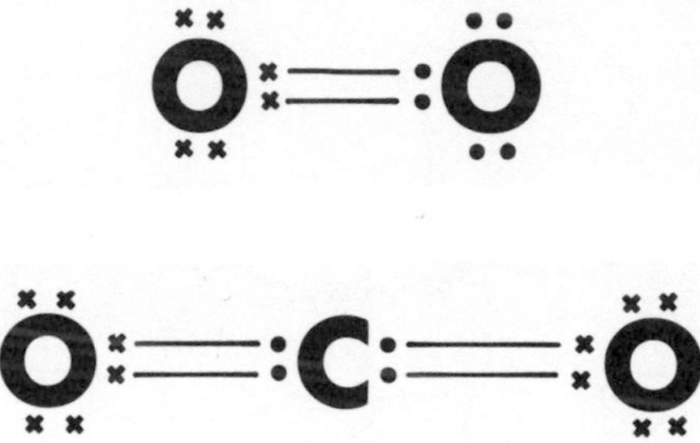

Fig. 2.7 Both the oxygen molecule and the carbon dioxide molecule contain double bands

An example of an element whose molecules contain a triple bond is nitrogen, N_2. This is illustrated in *Fig. 2.8.*

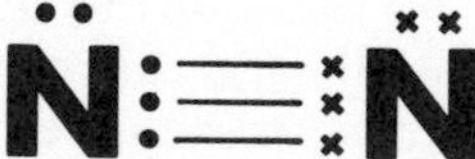

Fig. 2.8 The nitrogen molecule

2.6 Properties of Ionic and Covalent Compounds

An ionic (electrovalent) compound is one in which the bonds between the constituent ions are ionic (electrovalent) bonds. Ionic compounds usually consist of millions of ions packed together to form a crystal. This orderly packing of ions is demonstrated in *Fig. 2.9.* If one examines a series of ionic compounds, it is possible to identify several common characteristics.

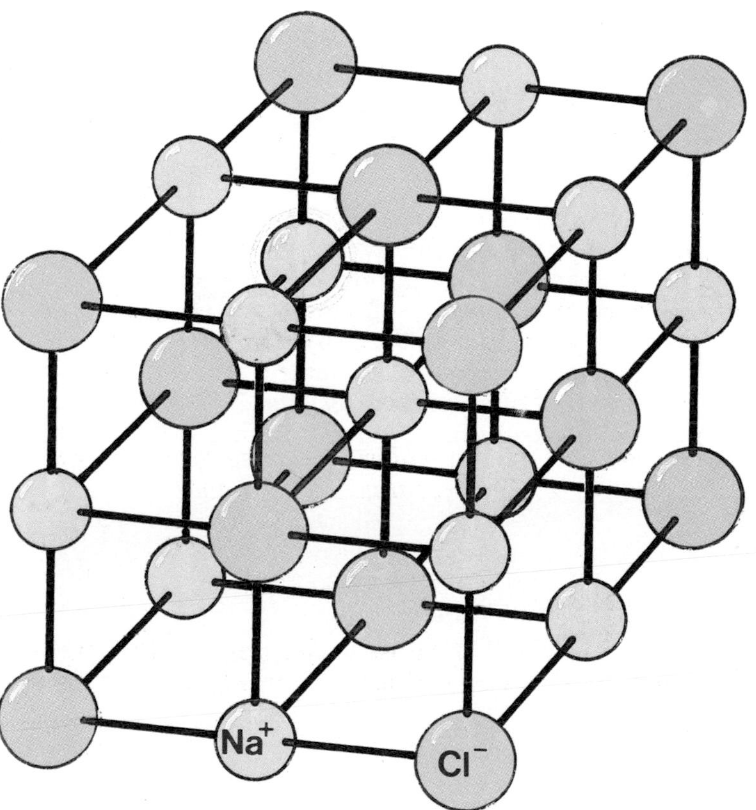

Fig. 2.9 The arrangement of ions in a crystal of NaCl

Table 2.2 The Properties of Ionic (electrovalent) and Covalent Compounds.

Ionic compounds	*Covalent Compounds*
1. Usually solid at room temperature.	Usually liquid or gas at room temperature.
2. Usually high melting points and boiling points.	Usually low melting points and boiling points.
3. Usually soluble in water.	Usually insoluble in water.
4. Conduct electricity when melted or when dissolved in water.	Do not conduct electricity.

General Properties of Ionic Compounds

1. **Ionic compounds are usually solid at room temperature.** This is because of the strong attraction between the millions of oppositely charged ions in the crystal. This strong attraction holds the crystal together giving it a definite shape, *Fig. 2.9.*

2. **Ionic compounds usually have high melting points and boiling points.** This is because there is a strong attraction between the ions and therefore a lot of heat energy is needed to separate them from each other, e.g. the melting point of sodium chloride is over 800 °C and its boiling point is almost 1500 °C.

3. **Ionic compounds usually dissolve in water**. The reason for this is because water molecules are attracted to ions. The ions are pulled away from the crystal lattice and go into solution.

4. **Ionic compounds usually conduct electricity when molten (melted) or when dissolved in water**. The reason for this is because when the ionic material is molten or dissolved in water, the ions are free to move and carry the electric current.

General Properties of Covalent Compounds

1. **Covalent compounds are usually either liquids or gases at room temperature.** The reason for this is that there are no strong forces of attraction between the separate molecules.

2. **Covalent compounds usually have low melting points and boiling points**. This is because the attractive forces between covalent molecules are not very strong and therefore not much heat energy is needed to separate them from each other, e.g. the melting point of ice is 0 °C and the boiling point of water is 100 °C.

3. **Many covalent compounds (but not all) do not dissolve in water**. The reason for this is because covalent compounds do not contain ions. Water molecules are not normally attracted to covalent molecules. However, there are many exceptions to this generalisation.

4. **Covalent compounds do not conduct electricity**. Covalent compounds cannot conduct electricity because there are no ions present. However, in some cases the covalent compound may react with the water and form ions, e.g. HCl dissolves in water and the resulting solution conducts electricity. The apparatus used to study if compounds conduct electricity is shown in *Fig. 2.10.*

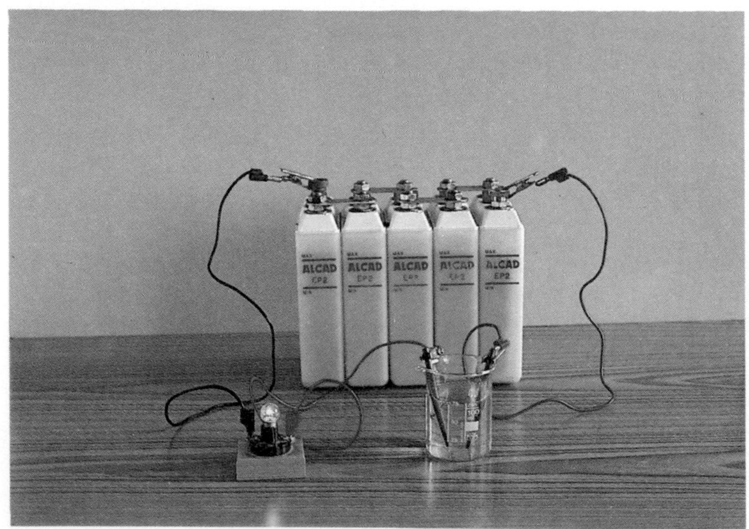

Fig. 2.10 The bulb lights if ions are present

2.7 Shapes of Molecules

Ionic compounds, because they consist of a network of positive and negative ions, do not contain individual molecules. However, covalent compounds do consist of separate molecules each of which has a definite shape, i.e. the atoms are arranged at definite angles to each other.

Any molecule with only two atoms (called a diatomic molecule) must, of course, be linear. Examples of linear molecules are shown in *Fig. 2.11.*

H—H Cl—Cl H—Cl

Fig. 2.11 All diatomic molecules are linear

For molecules with more than two atoms, their approximate shape may be predicted by counting the number of electron pairs around the central atom. **These electron pairs repel each other and always arrange themselves so as to be as far apart as possible**. Any molecule with four bond pairs of electrons around the central atom will have a shape similar to that of a **tetrahedron**, *Fig. 2.12.* A bond pair is a pair of electrons involved in bonding.

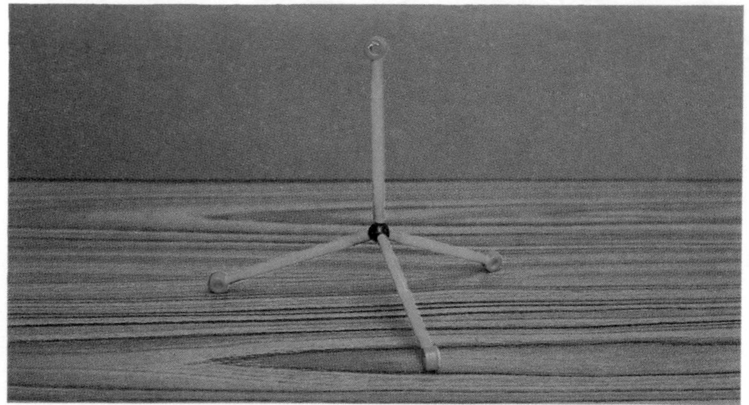

Fig. 2.12 Four pairs of electrons arrange themselves in the shape of a tetrahedron to minimise repulsion

For your G.C.S.E., you need to have a knowledge of the shapes of certain molecules. These molecular shapes are illustrated in *Fig. 2.13(a).*

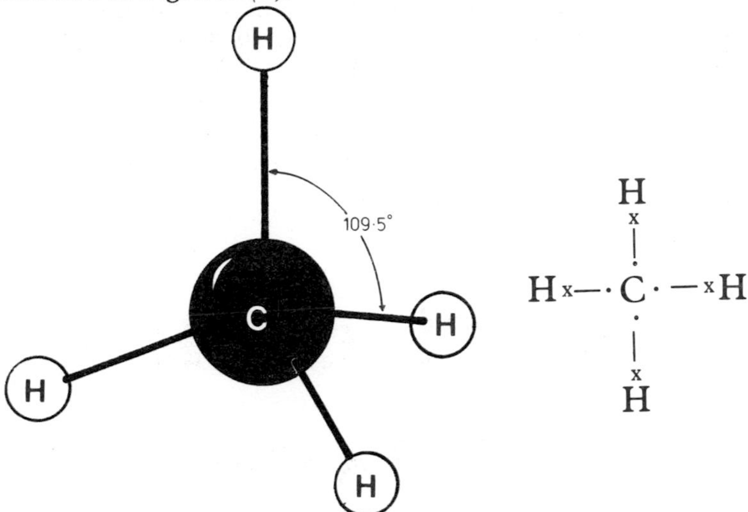

Fig. 2.13 (a) the methane molecule

Shape of Methane Molecule

The methane molecule has the shape of a tetrahedron with all bond angles of 109½°.

Shape of Ammonia Molecule

By experiment, it is found that the shape of the ammonia molecule is that of a pyramid with a bond angle of 107°. As shown in *Fig. 2.13 (b)*, there are four pairs of electrons around the central nitrogen atom. Three of these pairs are **bond pairs** because they are involved in bonding to the three hydrogen atoms. The fourth pair is not used in bonding and is called a **lone pair** or non-bonding pair. If all four pairs of electrons were bond pairs, the ammonia molecule would be tetrahedral with a bond angle of 109°. However, the presence of the lone pair causes the shape of the ammonia molecule to be pyramidal with a bond angle of 107°.

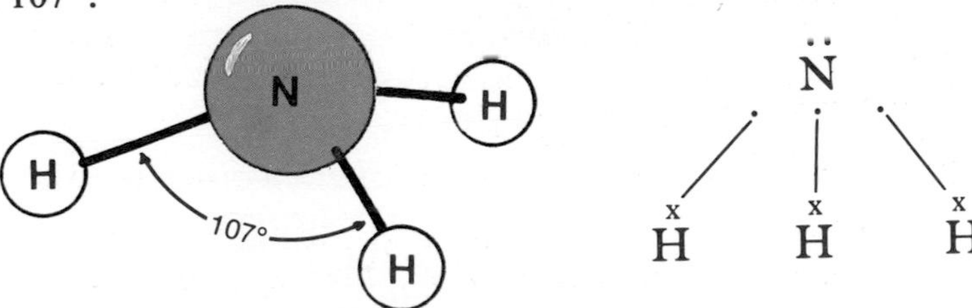

Fig. 2.13 (b) The ammonia molecule is pyramidal and contains 1 lone pair and 3 bond pairs

Shape of Water Molecule

By experiment, it is found that the water molecule is V-shaped with a bond angle of approximately 105°. There are four pairs of electrons around the central atom — two bond pairs and two lone pairs *(see Fig. 2.13 (c))*. The extra repulsion between the two lone pairs causes the bond angle to decrease from that of a regular tetrahedron to an angle of 105°.

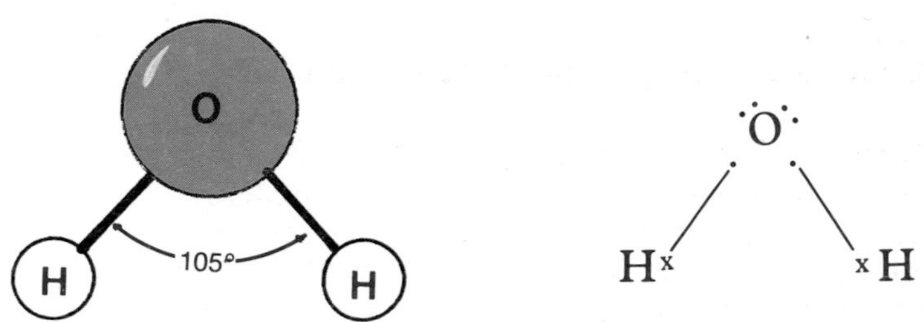

Fig. 2.13 (c) The water molecule is V-shaped and contains 2 lone pairs and 2 bond pairs

Summary

* A chemical bond is the force of attraction holding atoms or ions together in a compound.
* The Octet Rule helps us to understand chemical bonding. This rule states that when bonding occurs, atoms tend to reach an electron arrangement with eight electrons in the outermost shell.
* The ionic bond (electrovalent bond) and the covalent bond are the two main types of chemical bond.
* An ion is a charged atom or group of atoms.
* An ionic bond is the force of attraction between oppositely charged ions in a compound.
* Ionic compounds are usually formed between metals and non-metals.
* A covalent bond is a bond which consists of a shared pair of electrons
* A double bond is formed when two pairs of electrons are shared and a triple bond is formed when three pairs of electrons are shared.

* Ionic compounds are usually solid at room temperature, have high melting points and boiling points, dissolve in water and conduct electricity in the molten state or when dissolved in water.
* Covalent compounds are usually either liquids or gases at room temperature, have low melting and boiling points, most do not dissolve in water and they do not conduct electricity.
* The methane molecule has the shape of a tetrahedron, the ammonia molecule has the shape of a pyramid and the water molecule is V-shaped with a bond angle of 105°.

Questions

Section A

1. The forces of attraction which hold atoms together in a compound are called ....
2. A useful rule which helps us in our study of chemical bonding is the .... rule.
3. Neon is a very unreactive element due to the fact that it has .... electrons in its outer shell.
4. Another name for an ionic bond is an .... bond.
5. In the formation of an ionic bond electrons are always .... from one atom to another.
6. Potassium and fluorine combine to form potassium fluoride. Underline which of the following statements are correct: (i) each potassium atom loses one electron; (ii) each potassium atom gains one electron; (iii) the potassium and fluorine atoms share electrons.
7. The two main types of bond are ionic and .... bonds.
8. Covalent bonds are formed when electrons are .... between atoms.
9. The type of bond formed in the hydrogen molecule is a .... bond.
10. Two examples of covalent compounds are .... and ....
11. The chlorine molecule is said to be diatomic because it contains .... atoms.
12. Helium is an example of a monatomic element. Write down the name of another example of monatomic element ....
13. A covalent bond in which two pairs of electrons are shared is called a .... bond and one in which three pairs of electrons are shared is called a .... bond.
14. The chemical name for natural gas is ....
15. In the following list underline which of the compounds are ionic: carbon dioxide, potassium chloride, sulphur dioxide, lithium fluoride.
16. Covalent compounds are good conductors of electricity. True or false? ....
17. Ionic compounds conduct electricity when .... or when dissolved in ....
18. A four-sided figure with a bond angle of 109 ° is called a ....
19. An example of a linear molecule is ....
20. The water molecule may be described as being V-shaped with a bond angle of ....

Section B

1. Explain what is meant by a covalent bond and an electrovalent (ionic) bond. State the type of bond in each of the following: (i) hydrogen chloride; (ii) potassium chloride and (iii) water. Compare covalent and electrovalent compounds under the following headings: (a) melting and boiling points; (b) solubility; (c) electrical conductivity.
2. Draw a simple diagram showing the arrangement of electrons in an atom of sodium. Show also the arrangement of electrons in an atom of chlorine. Describe, in terms of electrons, what happens when sodium reacts with chlorine. Name the type of bond formed. Give one difference between this type of bond and the type of bond formed between the two chlorine atoms in a molecule of chlorine.
3. *"Four electron pairs around a central atom give rise to a basically tetrahedral shape".* Explain the reason for this. Every diatomic molecule must be linear. Why is this so? Describe, with the aid of diagrams, the shape of a molecule of ammonia and of water.

3 — Chemical Formulae

3.1 What is a Chemical Formula?

We have already seen that an element is represented by a chemical **symbol**, e.g. carbon is represented by C and sodium is represented by Na. A symbol may also be used to indicate one atom of an element. When a symbol is followed by a small number, this represents a **molecule** of that element, e.g. H_2 represents a molecule of hydrogen which consists of two atoms. A **chemical formula** is used to represent a compound or a molecule of a compound. A chemical formula consists of the symbols of the elements in this compound, e.g. the chemical formula for magnesium oxide is MgO and for iron sulphide is FeS. A chemical formula also indicates the ratio of the different atoms in a compound, e.g. in magnesium oxide, MgO, there are equal numbers of magnesium and oxygen atoms but in water, H_2O, there are twice as many hydrogen atoms as oxygen atoms.

Every compound has a chemical formula. Using our knowledge of bonding and of the Periodic Table, it is quite an easy task to write down the chemical formula of most compounds.

3.2 Writing Chemical Formulae of Ionic Compounds

In studying ionic bonding *(Section 2.3)*, we learned that ionic compounds are formed by the transfer of electrons from metals to non-metals. *Fig. 3.1* illustrates which of the first twenty elements form ions and the charges which these ions have.

From this diagram it is clear that, except for the noble gases, the elements which form ions are mainly on the left or right hand side of the Periodic Table. The reason for this is because these elements have only a few electrons to lose or gain in order to achieve eight electrons in their outer shell. (The elements of groups IV and V do not tend to form ions as it costs too much energy. These elements tend to share electrons.)

From a knowledge of the type and number of charges on each ion, it is possible to deduce the formula of any ionic compound which you will meet in this course.

Example 1 *Write down the formula of lithium chloride*

Step 1 Write the charge of each ion: Li^+Cl^-

Step 2 If necessary, adjust the number of ions so that the positive charge is equal to the total negative charge: in Li^+Cl^-, there are the same number of positive and negative charges so there is no need to adjust.

Step 3 Write down the formula without the charges: LiCl.

Example 2 *Write the formula of sodium oxide*

Step 1 Charge on each ion: Na^+O^{2-}

Step 2 Adjust number of ions: $Na^+_2O^{2-}$

Step 3 Write formula: Na_2O

Example 3 *Write the formula of magnesium chloride*

Step 1 Charge on each ion: $Mg^{2+}Cl^-$

Step 2 Adjust number of ions: $Mg^{2+}Cl^-_2$

Step 3 Write formula: $MgCl_2$

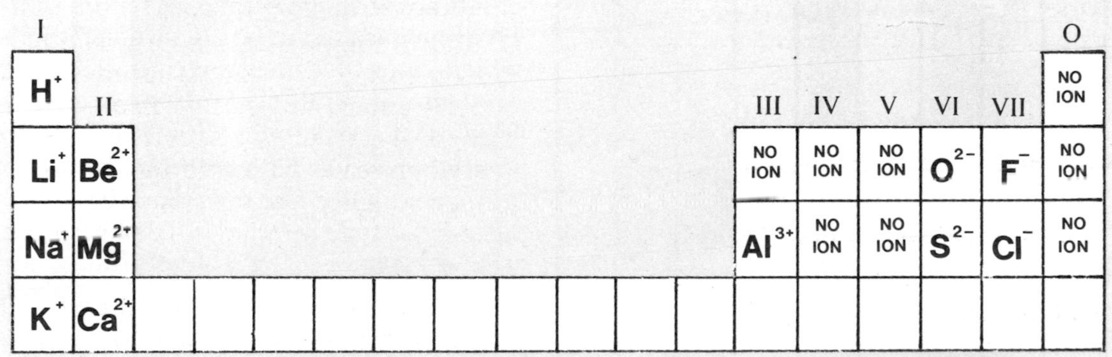

Fig. 3.1 The ions of the first 20 elements may be deduced from the Periodic Table

Example 4 *Write the formula of aluminium oxide*

Step 1 Charge on each ion: $Al^{3+}O^{2-}$
Step 2 Adjust number of ions: $Al_2^{3+}\ O_3^{2-}$
(total positive charge = + 6
total negative charge = — 6)
Step 3 Write formula: Al_2O_3

All of the above examples contain simple ions, i.e. charged atoms. However, an ion may also be a **group** of charged atoms. A group of atoms bonded together and carrying a charge is also called a **radical**. A list of the most common radicals is given in *Table 3.1*

Table 3.1 Some Common Radicals (Group Ions)

	Name	*Formula*
One negative charge	Hydroxyl ion	OH^-
	Nitrate ion	NO_3^-
	Acetate ion (Ethanoate ion)	CH_3COO^-
	Permanganate ion	MnO_4^-
	Chlorate ion	ClO_3^-
Two negative charges	Sulphate ion	$SO_4{}^{2-}$
	Carbonate ion	$CO_3{}^{2-}$
Three negative charges	Phosphate ion	$PO_4{}^{3-}$
One positive charge	Ammonium ion	NH_4^+

The formulae of ionic compounds containing radicals may easily be written using the information given in *Table 3.1.* The same steps as in *Examples 1-4* above are used.

Example 5 *Write the formula of potassium nitrate*

Step 1 Charge on each ion: $K^+NO_3^-$
Step 2 Adjust number of ions — no need to do this in this example as there are the same number of positive and negative charges: $K^+NO_3^-$
Step 3 Write formula: KNO_3

Example 6 *Write the formula of sodium sulphate*

Step 1 Charge on each ion $Na^+SO_4{}^{2-}$
Step 2 Adjust number of ions — we have two negative charges, therefore we must have two positive charges.
i.e. $Na_2{}^+SO_4{}^{2-}$
Step 3 Write formula Na_2SO_4

Example 7 *Write the formula of calcium nitrate*

Step 1 Charge on each ion: $Ca^{2+}NO_3{}^-$
Step 2 Adjust number of ions $Ca^{2+}(NO^{-3})_2$. Note that the formula for the radical is put in brackets. When the number of radicals present is greater than one, brackets are always used to avoid confusion, i.e. $(NO^-{}_3)_2$ means two nitrate radicals are present.
Step 3 Write formula: $Ca(NO_3)_2$

Example 8 *Write the formula for magnesium phosphate*

Step 1 Charge on each ion $Mg^{2+}PO_4{}^{3-}$
Step 2 Adjust number of ions — in order to have equal numbers of positive and negative charges, we require three Mg^{2+} ions and two PO_4^{3-} ions, i.e. $Mg^{2+}{}_3\,(PO_4^{3-})_2$
Step 3 Write formula $Mg_3(PO_4)_2$

3.3 Valency

The word valency means **combining power**. The valency of hydrogen is taken as 1 since a hydrogen atom never combines with more than one atom of any other element. Hydrogen is said to be **monovalent** and is the standard by which valency is measured. An element is said to be **divalent** if it combines with two atoms of hydrogen; **trivalent** if it combines with three atoms of hydrogen. Examples of these types of elements are given in *Fig. 3.2.*

HCl	H_2O	NH_3	CH_4
Chlorine is monovalent	Oxygen is divalent	Nitrogen is trivalent	Carbon is tetravalent

Fig. 3.2 The Valencies of various elements

If an element does not combine with hydrogen, its valency may be determined by investigating how many atoms of any other monovalent element, e.g. chlorine, with which it combines.

> **The valency of an element may be defined as the number of atoms and hydrogen, or any other monovalent element, with which each atom of the element combines.**

The common valencies of most elements may easily be found from the Period Table, *Fig. 3.3.*

Note from the diagram that the common valencies of the elements in Groups I, II, III and IV are 1, 2, 3 and 4, respectively. The reason for this lies in the fact that these valency numbers are the number of electrons which these elements must lose or share in order to achieve noble gas configuration. Similarly, the valencies of the elements of Groups V, VI and VII are 3, 2 and 1 respectively since these are the number of electrons which must be gained or shared to achieve noble gas configuration.
In ionic compounds, the valency may be taken as being numerically equal to the charge on the ion, e.g. in magnesium chloride, $Mg^{2+}Cl^-_2$ the valency of magnesium is 2 and that of chlorine is 1.

Note: Many of the transition metals have more than one valency. They are said to exhibit **variable valency**, e.g. two compounds of copper and chlorine are known, CuCl and $CuCl_2$. The valency is normally indicated by Roman numerals. CuCl is known as copper(I) chloride and $CuCl_2$ is known as copper(II) chloride.

3.4 Writing Chemical Formulae of Covalent compounds

In general, covalent bonds are formed between two non-metallic elements. In this course, the most common elements which are found in covalent compounds are carbon, nitrogen, oxygen, sulphur and hydrogen. The formulae of some common covalent compounds are given in *Table 3.2.*

Table 3.2 Some Common Covalent Compounds

Name	*Formula*
Water	H_2O
Methane	CH_4
Ammonia	NH_3
Carbon dioxide	CO_2
Sulphur dioxide	SO_2
Hydrogen chloride (Hydrochloric acid)	HCl
Sulphuric acid	H_2SO_4
Nitric acid	HNO_3
Ethanoic acid	CH_3COOH

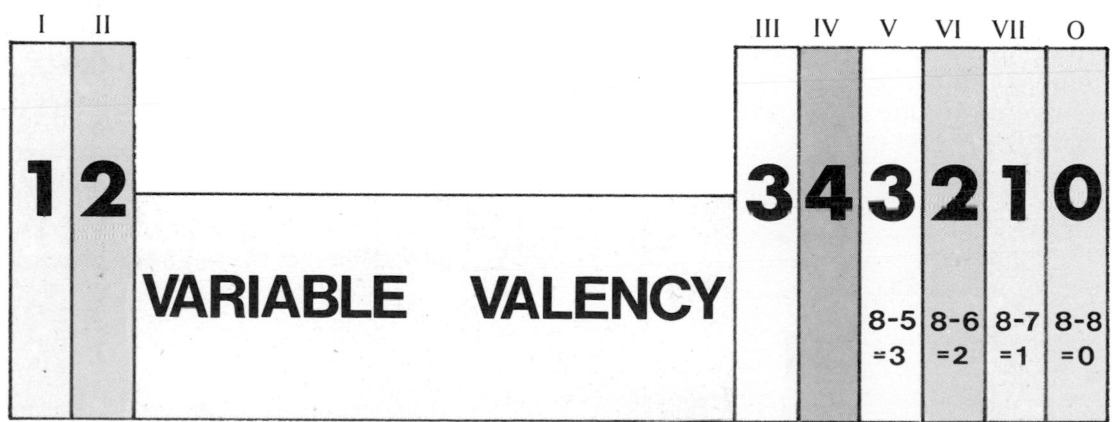

Fig. 3.3 The valencies of many elements may be deduced from the Periodic Table

Most of the formulae in this table may be predicted using our knowledge of valency. The method is illustrated in the following examples.

Example 9 *Write the formula of a compound which contains carbon and chlorine only*

Referring to the Periodic Table, we see that carbon has a valency of four and chlorine a valency of one. Therefore, four chlorine atoms will combine with one carbon atom, i.e. the formula of the compound is CCl_4, tetrachloromethane. The arrangement of the outer electrons in this molecule is shown in *Fig. 3.4.*

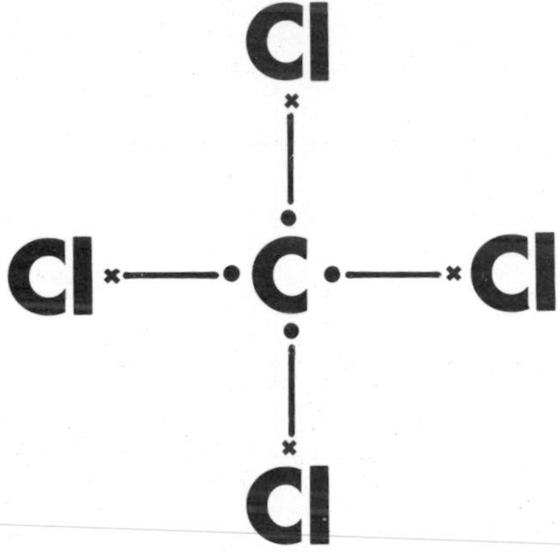

Fig. 3.4

Example 10 *Write the formula of a compound which contains sulphur and hydrogen only.*

Referring to the Period Table, we see that sulphur has a valency of two. Therefore, two atoms of hydrogen will combine with one atom of sulphur, i.e. the formula of the compound is H_2S, hydrogen sulphide. The arrangement of outer electrons is shown in *Fig. 3.5.*

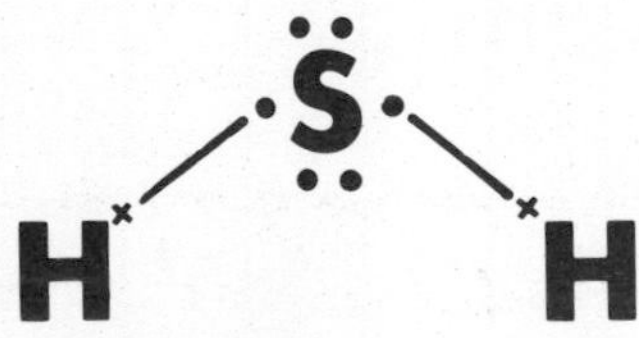

Fig. 3.5

The number of covalent compounds which you will meet in your course is quite small. It is recommended that *Table 3.2* be studied carefully.

Experiment 3.1 To Find the Formula of Magnesium Oxide

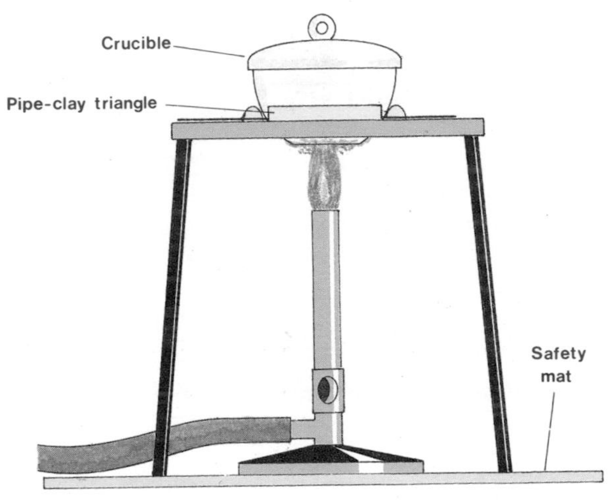

Fig. 3.6

Method

1. Weigh a crucible and lid. Record the mass as shown below.
2. Weigh a piece of magnesium ribbon. Record the mass.
3. Coil the magnesium and place in the crucible.
4. Heat the crucible with the lid on, occasionally lift the lid using tongs, try to stop the white smoke from escaping.
5. When the reaction appears to have finished, continue heating the crucible and contents without the lid.
6. Replace the lid and leave the crucible and contents to cool. When cool weigh the crucible and contents.

Results

Mass of magnesium = g.
Mass of crucible and lid = g.
Mass of crucible, lid and magnesium oxide = g.
Mass of magnesium oxide = g.
Mass of oxygen = g.

The relative atomic masses of magnesium and oxygen are 24 and 16 respectively.

	Magnesium	Oxygen
Mass	g.	g.
Number of atoms (divide mass by R.A.M.)	24	16
Simple Ratio of Atoms (Divide by the smallest number)		
Ratio of atoms		

What is the formula of magnesium oxide?

3.5 Balancing Chemical Equations

A chemical equation is a simple sentence written with chemical symbols. It gives information about what is reacting and what is being formed in a chemical reaction, e.g. the equation.

$$Fe + S \rightarrow FeS$$

tells us that iron reacts with sulphur to form iron II sulphide. So equations may be regarded as a sort of chemist's short-hand. When writing a chemical equation, the following rules must be obeyed:

1. The reactants always appear on the left hand side and the products on the right hand side of the equation.

   REACTANTS → PRODUCTS

   Sometimes, the arrow may be replaced by the "=" sign.

2. The correct formula for all reactants and products must be used.

3. **The equation must be balanced**, i.e. the total number of atoms of each element on the left hand side of the equation must equal the total number of atoms on the right hand side of the equation. This follows from the *Law of Conservation of Matter (Book 1, Chapter 6).*

State symbols *(Book 1, Chapter 2)* are usually included in equations

Let us now consider how to write balanced equations by studying some typical examples.

Example 1 *Magnesium burns in oxygen to form magnesium oxide.*

Write a balanced chemical equation to describe this reaction.

Step 1 Write the reaction in words.

Magnesium + oxygen → magnesium oxide

Step 2 Change the words into correct symbols and formulae.

$$Mg + O_2 \rightarrow MgO$$

Step 3 Balance the equation.

Left hand side	*Right hand side*	
1 Mg	1 Mg	Mg balanced
2 O atoms	1 O atom	O is not balanced

Adjust number of oxygen atoms on R.H.S.

$$Mg + O_2 \rightarrow 2MgO$$

Check if it is now balanced: O atoms balanced, but Mg atoms not.
Adjust number of Mg atoms on L.H.S.

$$\mathbf{2Mg_{(s)}} + O_{2(g)} \rightarrow 2MgO_{(s)}$$

The equation is now balanced.

Note one very important point about balancing chemical equations.

In balancing a chemical equation, only the numbers in front of the symbols or formulae may be changed. Formulae cannot be altered in any way.

***Example** 2 Balance the equation*

$$FeS_{(s)} + HCl_{(aq)} \rightarrow FeCl_{2(aq)} + H_2S_{(g)}$$

Proceed as in step 3 above.

L.H.S.	*R.H.S.*	
1 Fe	1 Fe	Fe balanced
1 S	1 S	S balanced
1 Cl	2 Cl	Cl not balanced
1H	2 H	H not balanced.

Adjust number of H atoms and Cl atoms on L.H.S.

$$FeS_{(s)} + 2HCl \rightarrow FeCl_{2(aq)} + H_2S_{(g)}$$

The equation is now balanced.

***Example** 3 Balance the following equation*

$$KC1O_{3(s)} \rightarrow KCl_{(s)} + O_{2(g)}$$

L.H.S.	*R.H.S.*	
1 K	1 K	K balanced
1 Cl	1 Cl	Cl balanced
3 O	2 O	O not balanced

Increase number of oxygen atoms on both sides to six.

$$2KClO_{3(s)} \rightarrow KCl^{+}_{(s)} + 3O_{2(g)}$$

Equation still not balanced — adjust K and Cl atoms on R.H.S.

$$2KClO_{3(s)} \rightarrow 2KCl_{(s)} + 3O_{2(g)}$$

The above method of balancing equations is known as **balancing by inspection**. This “trial-and-error” method is quite suitable for fairly simple chemical equations. By working through the examples below you will become quite familiar with this method. In the G.C.S.E. chemistry course, a more systematic method of balancing chemical equations will be studied.

Summary

* A chemical formula is used to represent the formula of a compound.
* When writing the formula of an ionic compound, always ensure that the number of positive ions is equal to the number of negative ions.
* An ion is a charged atom or a group of charged atoms.
* A group of charged atoms is also called a radical.
* The valency of an element is the number of atoms of hydrogen, or of any other monovalent element, with which each of its atoms combines.
* When writing the chemical formula of a covalent compound, ensure that the valency of each element is satisfied.
* A chemical equation must always be balanced, i.e. there must be the same number of each particular type of atom on each side of the equation.
* In balancing an equation, formulae may not be altered but may only be multiplied by an appropriate number.
* When the equation is balanced state symbols are added.

Questions

1. Write down the formula for each of the following compounds.

   (a) potassium chloride;
   (b) aluminium chloride;
   (c) calcium oxide;
   (d) sodium oxide;
   (e) sulphuric acid;
   (f) iron(II) chloride;
   (g) aluminium oxide;
   (h) lithium bromide;
   (i) magnesium chloride;
   (j) potassium sulphide;
   (k) potassium hydroxide;
   (l) calcium hydroxide;
   (m) sodium ethanote;
   (n) ammonium nitrate;
   (o) potassium chlorate;
   (p) ammonium carbonate;
   (q) sodium phosphate;
   (r) ethanoic (acetic) acid;
   (s) aluminium phosphate;
   (t) ammonia.

2. For each of the compounds in Question 1, state whether the bonding is ionic or covalent.

3. Write the following word equations as balanced chemical equations.

   (a) Hydrogen and oxygen react to form water.
   (b) Calcium oxide reacts with water to form calcium hydroxide.
   (c) Zinc reacts with sulphuric acid to form zinc sulphate and hydrogen.
   (d) Ammonia reacts with hydrogen chloride to form ammonium chloride.
   (e) Sodium reacts with water to form sodium hydroxide and hydrogen.
   (f) Calcium carbonate decomposes to form calcium oxide and carbon dioxide.
   (g) Calcium carbonate reacts with hydrochloric acid to form calcium chloride, carbon dioxide and water.
   (h) Sodium hydroxide reacts with hydrochloric acid to form sodium chloride and water.
   (i) Magnesium burns in carbon dioxide to form magnesium oxide and carbon.
   (j) Calcium chloride reacts with sodium carbonate to form calcium carbonate and sodium chloride.

4. Balance the following equations

   (a) $Na + Cl_2 = NaCl$
   (b) $H_2 + O_2 = H_2O$
   (c) $H_2 + Cl_2 = HCl$
   (d) $H_2SO_4 + Zn = ZnSO_4 + H_2$
   (e) $Na + O_2 = Na_2O$
   (f) $P + O_2 = P_2O_5$
   (g) $KClO_3 = KCl + O_2$
   (h) $NaOH + CO_2 = Na_2CO_3 + H_2O$
   (i) $KOH + CO_2 = K_2CO_3 + H_2O$

4 — Oxygen

4.1 Introduction

We have already seen that approximately one fifth of the air consists of oxygen. Oxygen was discovered in 1774 by Joseph Priestley, an English scientist, and Antoine Lavoisier, a French scientist. A sample of oxygen gas consists of O_2 molecules which contain a double bond as shown in *Fig. 4.1.*

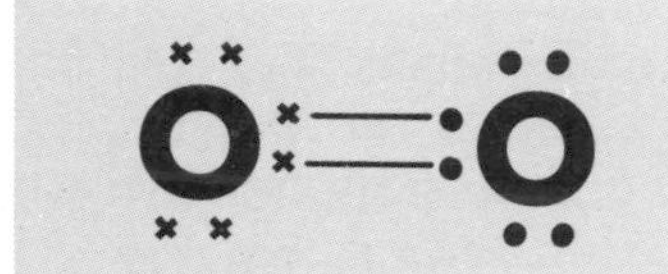

Fig. 4.1

Almost all of the oxygen used in industry is obtained by cooling the air to a liquid and then distilling it. However, we shall study a more convenient method of preparing oxygen in the laboratory.

4.2 Laboratory Preparation of Oxygen

One of the simplest methods of preparing oxygen in the laboratory is by decomposing (breaking down) **hydrogen peroxide**. Hydrogen peroxide, H_2O_2 is a colourless liquid which slowly decomposes to give off oxygen and form water according to the equation:

$$2H_2O_{2(aq)} \rightarrow 2H_2O_{(l)} + O_{2(g)}$$

A compound called manganese IV dioxide, MnO_2, is used to make the hydrogen peroxide decompose more quickly. The manganese IV oxide is not used up in the reaction and does not appear in the chemical equation — it is called a **catalyst**. We shall study this in more detail at a later stage.

An alternative method of preparing oxygen is to heat a mixture of potassium chlorate and manganese IV dioxide. The manganese dioxide acts as a catalyst

$$2KClO_3 \rightarrow 2KCl + 3O_2$$

This method of preparing oxygen is not recommended as potassium chlorate is a very dangerous compound. (See NB2 *Experiment 4.5*)

Method

1. Set up the apparatus as shown in *Fig. 4.2.*

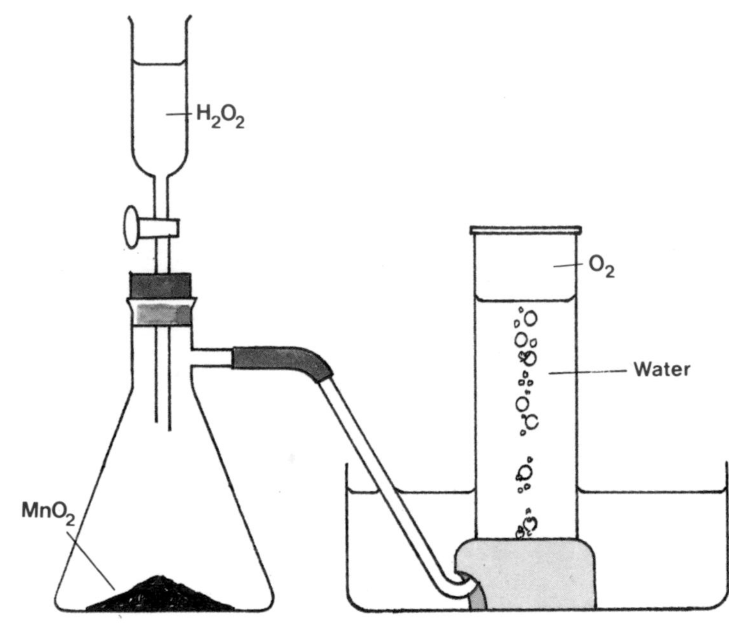

Fig. 4.2 Laboratory prep of oxygen

2. Allow the hydrogen peroxide to fall on the manganese IV dioxide so that evolution of oxygen occurs at a fairly brisk rate. Wait for about a half a minute before collecting the oxygen to allow for the air in the flask to be displaced.
3. Collect five jars of the gas.

4.3 Examination of the Properties of Oxygen

1. Note that the gas is colourless and odourless. Place pieces of moist red litmus paper and blue litmus paper into a jar of the gas. Note that there is no change in colour of the paper indicating that oxygen is a neutral gas.
2. Place a glowing splint into a gas jar of oxygen and note how the glowing splint is re-kindled and bursts into flames. This is a characteristic test for oxygen.

3. Heat a small piece of charcoal on a deflagrating spoon by holding it near the edge of a Bunsen flame — adjust the length of the deflagrating spoon if necessary, so that it will fit into the gas jar. When the charcoal begins to glow, quickly put the deflagrating spoon into a jar of oxygen, *Fig. 4.3.*

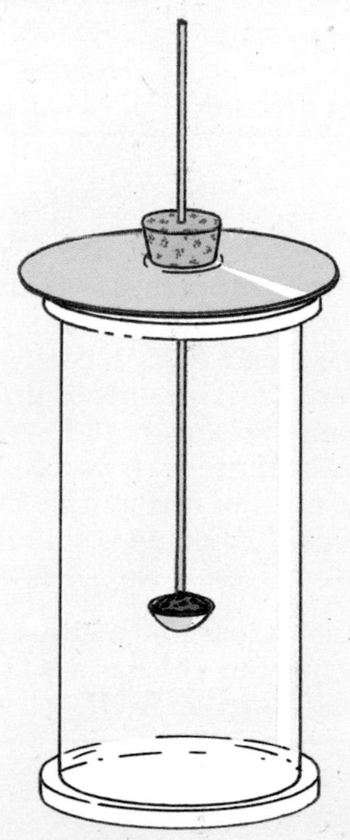

Fig. 4.3 The glowing carbon

Note that the carbon continues to glow brightly. Take out the deflagrating spoon and cover the jar with the gas jar cover. Add water to the gas jar and shake (with the cover on) to dissolve any gas formed. Add some blue litmus paper and note that it turns red.

4. If the laboratory is not well ventilated, it is advisable to carry out the following experiment in a fume cupboard. Heat a small amount of sulphur on a deflagrating spoon and, when it catches fire, plunge it into a gas jar of oxygen. Note that it burns with a blue flame forming white fumes. **Do not let these fumes escape as they are very poisonous**. Dissolve these fumes in water as described in 3 above and test the solution with blue litmus. Note that the paper turns red.

5. Using a tongs, heat a small piece of magnesium until it just begins to burn and then plunge it into a gas jar of oxygen.

   Caution: Do not look at the burning magnesium as the bright light could damage your eyes. Also, keep your free hand away from the jar as there is considerable heat generated which could cause the jar to crack.

   Note that there is a white powder formed inside the gas jar. Add some water and shake well to try and get the white powder dissolved. Test the solution with red litmus paper and note that it turns blue.

4.4 Oxides

An oxide is a compound containing two elements, one of which is oxygen. In the above experiments, the oxides were prepared by simply burning the elements in oxygen. The results of these experiments are summarised in *Table 4.1.*

Table 4.1 Oxides of Elements

Element	*Oxide formed*	*Balanced equation*
Non metals		
Sulphur	Sulphur dioxide	$S + O_2 \rightarrow SO_2$
Carbon	Carbon dioxide	$C + O_2 \rightarrow CO_2$
Phosphorus	Phosphorus pentoxide	$4P + 5O_2 \rightarrow 2P_2O_5$
Metals		
Magnesium	Magnesium oxide	$2Mg + O_2 \rightarrow 2MgO$
Sodium	Sodium oxide	$4Na + O_2 \rightarrow 2Na_2O$
Calcium	Calcium oxide	$2Ca + O_2 \rightarrow 2CaO$

From the results of our experiments with oxygen, we saw that the oxides of sulphur, carbon and phosphorus dissolve in water to form acidic solutions. Thus, these oxides are called **acidic oxides**. In general, the oxides of non-metals are acidic.

On the other hand, it is clear from the results of our experiments that the oxides of magnesium, sodium and calcium dissolve in water to form basic solutions. Thus, these oxides are called **basic oxides**. In general, the oxides of metals are basic.

The reactions of the oxides with water are summarised in *Table 4.2.*

Table 4.2 Reactions of Some Common Oxides with Water

Name of oxide	*Reaction with water*	*Equation*	*Effect on litmus*
Sulphur dioxide	Forms sulphurous acid, H_2SO_3	$SO_2 + H_2O \rightarrow H_2SO_3$	Blue → Red
Carbon dioxide	Forms carbonic acid H_2CO_3	$CO_2 + H_2O \rightarrow H_2CO_3$	Blue → Red
Phosphorus pentoxide	Forms phosphoric acid, H_3PO_4	$P_2O_5 + 3H_2O \rightarrow 2H_3PO_4$	Blue → Red
Magnesium oxide	Forms magnesium hydroxide, $Mg(OH)_2$	$MgO + H_2O \rightarrow Mg(OH)_2$	Red → Blue
Sodium oxide	Forms sodium hydroxide, NaOH	$Na_2O + H_2O \rightarrow 2 NaOH$	Red → Blue
Calcium oxide	Forms calcium hydroxide, $Ca(OH)_2$	$CaO + H_2O \rightarrow Ca(OH)_2$	Red → Blue

Note: Some oxides show both acidic and basic properties. These are called **amphoteric oxides**. Examples of amphoteric oxides are ZnO and Al_2O_3.

4.5 Properties of Oxygen

The main properties of oxygen are summarised in *Table 4.3.* The fact that oxygen is slightly soluble in water is an important property since fish breathe the oxygen dissolved in water. When water is heated, the bubbles which come out of it are mainly oxygen.

Table 4.3 The Properties of Oxygen

Physical properties	*Chemical properties*
1. Colourless, odourless, tasteless gas.	1. Supports combustion — substances which burn in air burn more vigorously in oxygen.
2. Slightly soluble in water.	2. Reacts with most elements to form oxides.
3. Slightly heavier than air.	3. No effect on litmus.

4.6 Catalysts

A solution of hydrogen peroxide slowly decomposes to release oxygen if it is left standing over a period of time. However, as we have seen when preparing oxygen, a small amount of manganese IV oxide speeds up the release of oxygen. If the amount of manganese IV oxide present before and after this experiment is carefully weighed, it is found that the same mass of manganese IV oxide is present. The manganese IV oxide is said to be a **catalyst**.

A catalyst is a substance which alters the speed of a chemical reaction but which is not used up in the reaction itself.

Fig. 4.4 In this reactor iron is used as a catalyst in the formation of ammonia

Catalysts are widely used in industry to bring about chemical reactions at a reasonable speed, *Fig. 4.4.* Normally catalysts are used to accelerate reactions but certain catalysts can be used to slow down reactions, e.g. glycerine is sometimes added to hydrogen peroxide as a negative catalyst in order to slow down its decomposition. Almost every chemical reaction in your body is controlled by catalysts — these biological catalysts are called **enzymes.**

4.7 Uses of Oxygen

1. **Breathing**. Oxygen stored in cylinders is used to support breathing, e.g. in hospitals it is used for patients suffering from lung disorders. These patients are put in oxygen tents. Cylinders of oxygen are also used in high altitude and underwater work.
2. **Manufacture of steel**. Oxygen is used in vast quantities in the manufacture of steel from iron, *Fig. 4.5.*

Fig. 4.5 When steel is being made, oxygen is used to remove the impurities from the molten iron.

3. **Burning and welding**. Acetylene gas burns in oxygen to produce an intensely hot flame of about 3000°C. This flame may be used to cut through metals or to melt metals and join them together (welding).

Summary

* Oxygen is made in the laboratory by decomposing hydrogen peroxide using manganese IV oxide as a catalyst.

$$2\,H_2O_2 \rightarrow 2H_2O + O_2$$

* An oxide is a compound containing two elements, one of which is oxygen.
* Oxides of non-metals are acidic; oxides of metal are basic.
* Oxygen is a colourless, odourless, tasteless gas, is slightly soluble in water and supports combustion very well.
* A catalyst is a substance which alters the speed of a chemical reaction but which is not used up in the reaction itself.
* Oxygen is used in respiration, manufacture of steel and burning and welding.

Questions

Section A

1. The symbol for a molecule of oxygen is ....
2. The chemicals used to prepare oxygen are .... and ....
3. One of the two chemicals used to prepare oxygen is only present to speed up the reaction. This chemical is . ...
4. Name the chemical formed when magnesium is burned in oxygen. ....
5. A chemical which helps to speed up a reaction but is not used up in the reaction is called a ....
6. Sulphur burns with a .... flame in oxygen and forms ....
7. Name an element which burns in oxygen with a dazzling white flame and forms a white powder........
8. Is the oxide of sulphur acidic or basic?...............
9. Name the compound formed when carbon burns in oxygen ....
10. Name any catalyst and mention a reaction which it catalyses ....
11. In general, the oxides of metals are .... and the oxides of non-metals are ....
12. Write a chemical equation for the reaction of carbon dioxide with water. ....
13. When sulphur dioxide dissolves in water it forms a compound called ....
14. A basic oxide is one which ....
15. Write the chemical equation for the reaction of magnesium oxide with water. ....
16. An oxide which shows both acidic and basic properties is called an .... oxide.
17. What is the source of oxygen for fish? ....
18. An element on burning in oxygen forms a compound which is a gas at room temperature. Which of the following elements could it be: magnesium, sulphur, carbon, phosphorus? ....
19. Oxygen is used in large quantities in the manufacture of ....
20. **Oxygen combines with .... to produce a very hot flame.**

Section B

1. Describe how you would prepare and collect a sample of oxygen gas in the laboratory. Give three physical properties and three chemical properties of oxygen. Give a characteristic test for the presence of oxygen. Explain what is meant by the term *catalyst* and give an example of one.
2. What is an oxide?
   Give the name and formula of the compound formed when (i) carbon; (ii) magnesium; (iii) sulphur is burned in oxygen. Describe the properties of each compound under the headings: state, colour, reaction with water. Give a balanced chemical equation for the reaction of each compound with water.

5 — Acids and Bases

5.1 Introduction

In the previous chapter we saw that certain substances like carbon dioxide and sulphur dioxide dissolve in water to produce solutions which turns litmus paper red. Such solutions are said to be **acidic**. The word **acid** comes from the Latin word *acidus* meaning sour.

Fig. 5.1

The sour taste of lemons and grapefruit is due to an acid called citric acid; vinegar has a similar sharp taste because it contains an acid (called ethanoic acid); the pain felt after an ant or nettle sting is caused by the presence of an acid called formic acid (methanoic acid). Examples of common substances containing acids are shown in *Fig. 5.1.*

5.2 Properties of acids

Although some acids are quite harmless, others are highly dangerous and corrosive, i.e. they "eat away" substances like metals and human flesh. Acid rain is causing the death of forests and lakes in many parts of Europe, *Fig. 5.2.*

The main properties of acids may be summarised as follows:

1. Acids have a sour taste.
2. Acids turn litmus red.

Survey reveals major Acid Rain destruction

DESTRUCTION of the European countryside by acid rain pollution has reached "catastrophic" levels, a conference was told today. A new survey among national parks throughout Europe has revealed what it says is major destruction from the menace.

Forests are dying, fish life is being blighted and buildings are crumbling away, says the survey.

Leaders of the national parks movement called for a major onslaught on the problem from governments and industry when the Federation of Nature and National Parks of Europe ended their conference at Castleton, Derbyshire.

Vice-President Dr. Hans Bibelreither said the new survey was "devastating".

He added: "There has been major destruction. Now is the time for prompt action by governments and industry to save other important forests and woodlands, rivers and lakes and the wildlife they support."

In Germany, pressure groups have calledfor research into the deaths of babies from respiratory linked illnesses which they fear could be related to the pollution problem.

In Sweden, the survey showed that 16 out of 47 water courses were affected by acid rain, a term covering not just rain but any airborne pollution from power stations, industry and car exhausts.

In parts of the Black Forest in West Germany, 80% of fir trees were affected and 46% of all trees in West Germany were blighted.

"These results reveal the size of the catastrophe", said Dr. Bibelreither. "Irreplaceable parts of the national heritage of this old continent that used to consist of large areas of forest will be ruined within a few years"

The call for action from the national park officials from 13 countries follows a report earlier this month from an all-party Commons Committee which said that acid rain was "one of the major environmental hazards faced by the industrialised world."

It said buildings damaged in Britain included Westminister Abbey, Lincoln and Liverpool Cathedrals, Yorkminster and the Palace of Westminister.

The four-day conference called on governments and political parties to act to restrict pollution.

It urged industry to acknowledge its responsibilities and asked motoring organisations to cease opposition to anti-air pollution measures.

The findings and call for action will be sent out to all European governments.

Newspaper extract 25/9/84

Fig. 5.2 Acid rain is a growing problem

3. Acids donate hydrogen ions (protons) when dissolved in water.

$$\begin{aligned} \text{e.g. } HCl &\rightarrow H^+ + Cl^- \\ H_2SO_4 &\rightarrow 2H^+ + SO_4^{2-} \\ HNO_3 &\rightarrow H^+ + NO_3^- \end{aligned}$$

4. Acids react with many metals to liberate hydrogen gas.

$$\text{e.g. } Zn_{(s)} + H_2SO_{4(aq)} \rightarrow ZnSO_{4(aq)} + H_{2(g)}$$

This type of reaction helps metals to corrode more quickly.

5. Acids react with carbonates to liberate carbon dioxide.

$$\underset{\text{Calcium carbonate}}{CaCO_{3(s)}} + \underset{\text{hydrochloric acid}}{2HCl_{(aq)}} \rightarrow \underset{\text{calcium chloride}}{CaCl_{2(aq)}} + \underset{\text{carbon dioxide}}{CO_{2(g)}} + \underset{\text{water}}{H_2O_{(l)}}$$

The most satisfactory definition of an acid was formulated by Bronsted and Lowry in 1923.

An acid is a proton donor.

Examples of acids donating protons are given in point 3 above.

A **strong acid** is one which dissociates (breaks up) almost completely in water, i.e. one which readily donates protons. For example, when nitric acid is dissolved in water it is almost 100% dissociated.

$$HNO_3 \rightarrow H^+ + NO_3^-$$

Therefore, nitric acid is said to be a strong acid. Similarly hydrochloric acid and sulphuric acid are strong acids also. However, when ethanoic acid is dissolved in water, only a small fraction (0.4% approx.) of the molecules dissociate.

$$CH_3COOH \rightleftharpoons H^+ + CH_3COO^-$$

Therefore, ethanoic acid is said to be a **weak acid**.

Note: The words "strong" and "weak" as applied to acids must not be confused with the words "concentrated" and "dilute", used to describe strength of solutions. A strong acid is always a strong acid whether it is in a concentrated or a dilute solution. One would make up a dilute solution of a strong acid by dissolving a small quantity of, say, nitric acid in a large quantity of water; a concentrated solution of a weak acid could be made up by dissolving a large quantity of, say, ethanoic in a small quantity of water. Think carefully about this.

WARNING: Care must be taken when handling acids in the laboratory. Keep them well away from the eyes, mouth and any cuts. Students should never handle concentrated solutions of acids in the laboratory without the permission of their teacher.

5.3 Indicators

We have already seen that litmus, a purple dye obtained from lichens, turns red when mixed with an acid. However, if litmus is added to a solution of sodium hydroxide, a blue colour is observed, *Fig. 5.3* A substance which has this effect on litmus is commonly called a **base**. A base is a metal oxide or metal hydroxide which reacts on acid to form a salt. The properties of these substances will be studied in more detail in the next section.

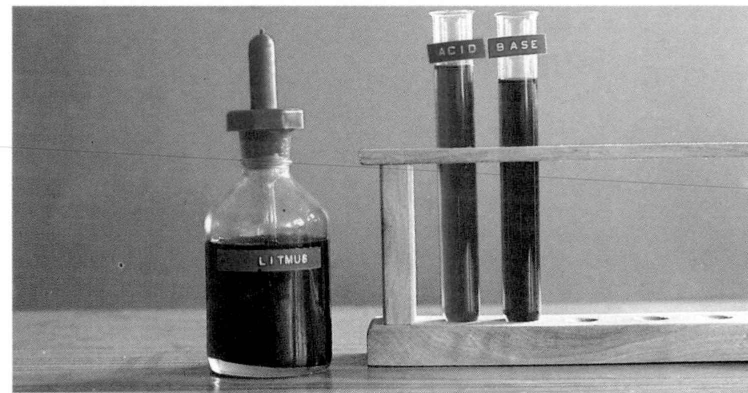

Fig. 5.3 Litmus is red in an acid and blue in a base.

A compound which shows whether a substance is acidic or basic is called an **indicator**. It shows this by means of some colour change.

An indicator is a compound which shows, by means of a colour change, whether a substance is acidic or basic.

Litmus is the best known indicator but other indicators commonly used in the laboratory are methyl orange and phenolphthalein, *Fig. 5.4*. Indicators may be used in liquid form or, as in the case of litmus, may be soaked onto paper and dried.

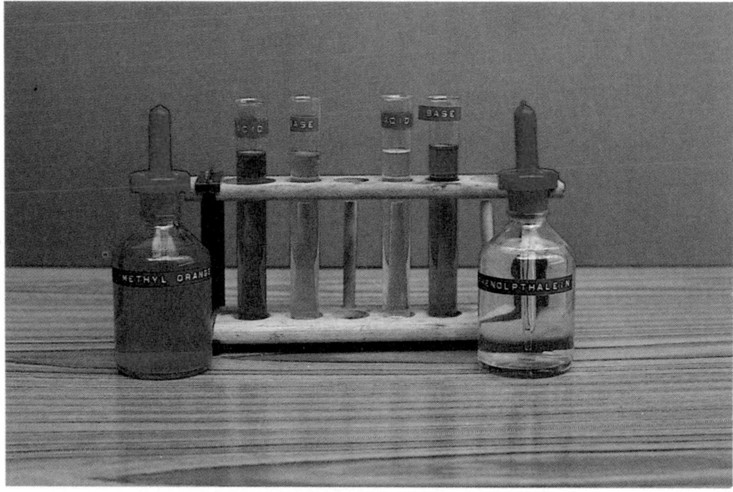

Fig. 5.4 Methyl orange and phenolphthalein are further examples of indicators.

Note: A base which dissolves in water is commonly called an **alkali**. The most common alkalis are sodium hydroxide. NaOH, potassium hydroxide, KOH, and calcium hydroxide, $Ca(OH)_2$. An example of a base which is not an alkali is zinc hydroxide, $Zn(OH)_2$.

5.4 Reactions of Acids with Bases — Neutralisation and Salt Formation

It is found that bases, like acids, have characteristic properties, i.e. they turn litmus blue, are corrosive and their solutions have a soapy feeling. The popular name for sodium hydroxide is **caustic soda because of the burning effect which it has on the skin. Some examples of common bases are shown in** *Fig. 5.5*.

Fig. 5.5 Some common bases

By experiment, it is found that when an acid and a base react with each other in the appropriate amounts, each substance loses its characteristic properties. This process is often called **neutralisation reaction** as the final product is often neutral (i.e. neither acidic nor basic). Neutralisation reactions are quite common in everyday life: excess hydrochloric acid in the stomach is neutralised by a base such as milk of magnesia, $Mg(OH)_2$; toothpaste is slightly alkaline to counteract the acids from food which cause tooth decay; vinegar is used to neutralise the alkaline sting of wasps and sodium bicarbonate (baking soda) is used to neutralise the acidic sting of bees; lime is spread on soil to neutralise the acid in the soil.

In general, a neutralisation reaction may be represented as:

Acid + Base → Salt + Water

e.g.

$$\underset{\text{hydrochloric acid}}{HCl} + \underset{\text{sodium hydroxide}}{NaOH} \rightarrow \underset{\text{sodium chloride}}{NaCl} + \underset{\text{water}}{H_2O}$$

Let us examine this reaction carefully and ignore the ions which are not changed in the reaction:

$$\underset{\text{From Acid}}{H^+} + Cl^- + Na^+ + \underset{\text{From Base}}{OH^-} \rightarrow Na^+ + Cl^- + H_2O$$

It is clear that a neutralisation reaction simply involves the transfer of a proton from the acid to the base, i.e. the base accepts the proton.

$$H^+ + OH^- \rightarrow H_2O$$

A base is a proton acceptor

When most people hear the name salt they probably think of ordinary table salt. Common salt, sodium chloride, is formed by the reaction of hydrochloric acid is just one of many salts which can be formed whenever an acid is neutralised by a base. A list of equations showing how some salts are formed is given in *Table 5.1*.

Table 5.1 A Salt is always formed when an acid and a base react

Acid		*Base*		*Salt*		*Water*
HCl	+	$NaOH$	→	$NaCl$ sodium chloride	+	H_2O
H_2SO_4	+	$2NaOH$	→	Na_2SO_4 sodium sulphate	+	$2H_2O$
HNO_3	+	$NaOH$	→	$NaNO_3$ sodium nitrate	+	H_2O
$2HCl$	+	$Ca(OH)_2$	→	$CaCl_2$ calcium chloride	+	$2H_2O$
HCl	+	NH_4OH	→	NH_4Cl ammonium chloride	+	H_2O
CH_3COOH	+	$NaOH$	→	CH_3COONa sodium ethanoate	+	H_2O

Note that each salt is made up of two ions. The first ion is a positive metal ion or an ammonium ion. This comes from the base. The second ion is a negative ion which comes from an acid. This leads us to a definition of salt.

A salt is the compound formed when the hydrogen in an acid is replaced by a metal or other positive ions.

Thus, if the hydrogen atoms in H_2SO_4 are replaced by copper we form copper II sulphate, $CuSO_4$. A list of some important salts and their uses is given in *Table 5.2.*

Table 5.2 Some important Salts and their uses

Salt	*Uses*
Copper II sulphate	Garden insecticide and fungicide
Potassium nitrate *(saltpetre)*	Making gunpowder, fertiliser, curing meat
Sodium carbonate *(washing soda)*	Soap powders
Sodium hydrogen-carbonate *(baking soda)*	Baking
Magnesium sulphate *(Epsom salts)*	Medicinal purposes
Calcium sulphate *(plaster of Paris)*	Holding injured limbs rigid.

Experiment 5.1 Preparation of Salt

Many salts may be prepared by reacting together an acid and alkali. In order to detect when the acid has been exactly neutralised, an indicator is used. The general procedure is that the acid (in a burette) is slowly added to the alkali (in a conical flask) until the indicator starts to change colour. This controlled addition of one solution to another is called a **titration**.

Suppose we wish to prepare sodium chloride, NaCl. We could use NaOH to supply the Na^+ part of the salt and HCl to supply the Cl^- part.

$$HCl + NaOH \rightarrow NaCl + H_2O$$

Method

1. Set up the apparatus as shown in *Fig. 5.6*.

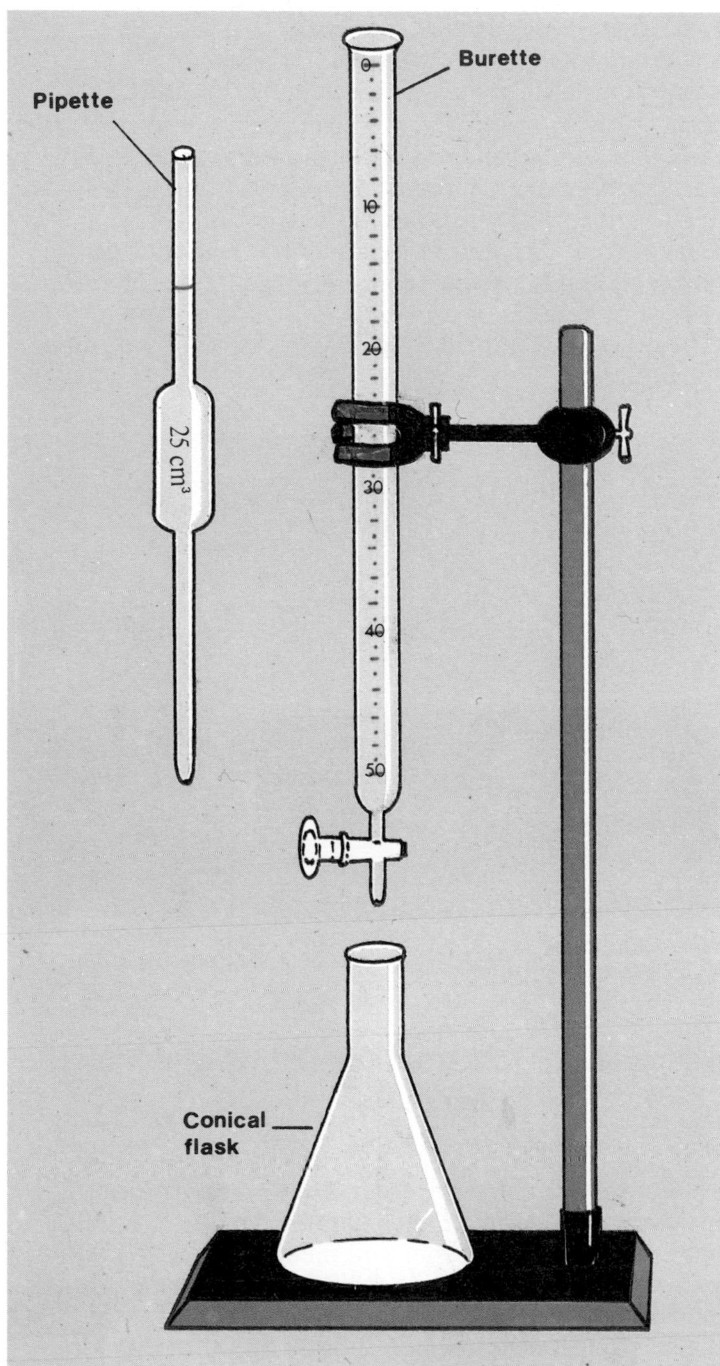

Fig. 5.6 Apparatus used in titration

2. Rinse out a pipette with water and with a small amount of sodium hydroxide solution. Using the pipette, place 20 cm^3 of the sodium hydroxide solution into a clean conical flask.
3. Wash out a burette with water and also with a small amount of hydrochloric acid. Use a funnel when pouring liquid into the burette.
4. Clamp the burette vertically in a retort stand and fill the burette to above the 0 cm^3 mark with hydrochloric acid.
5. Fill the part of the burette below the tap by allowing the HCl to run out until the level of liquid in the burette drops to the 0 cm^3 mark. Take care to read from the bottom of the meniscus.
6. Add about 3 drops of litmus indicator to the conical flask.
7. Place a white tile or paper underneath the conical flask (to assist in detecting the colour change) and allow the acid to run into the conical flask. Add about 2 cm^3 of the acid at a time, swirling the conical flask continuously.
8. When the red colour does not disappear almost immediately add in the acid a drop at a time until the litmus remains slightly pink. Note the burette reading. This is the amount of acid required to neutralise 20 cm^3 of sodium hydroxide solution. The conical flask now contains an almost neutral solution of sodium chloride but it is coloured pink.
9. Discard the contents of the conical flask and repeat the titration to get an average titration figure.
10. Again, discard the contents of the conical flask and repeat the experiment **without using an indicator**. Add the appropriate quantity of acid to neutralise the alkali.
11. Pour the contents of the conical flask into an evaporating dish and evaporate to dryness over a water bath. Crystals of NaCl are seen to form inside in the dish.

5.5 The pH Scale

In *Section 5.3* we used indicators to tell us whether a substance is acidic or basic. However, there are degrees of acidity and basicity and a special scale called the **pH scale** is used to measure the degree of acidity or basicity. The pH scale goes from 0 to 14, *Fig. 5.7*.

A pH of less than 7 indicates that a substance is acidic and the lower the pH value, the more strongly acidic the substance.* If the pH = 7, the substance is neutral. A pH

* The origin of the number 7 is outside the scope of this text.

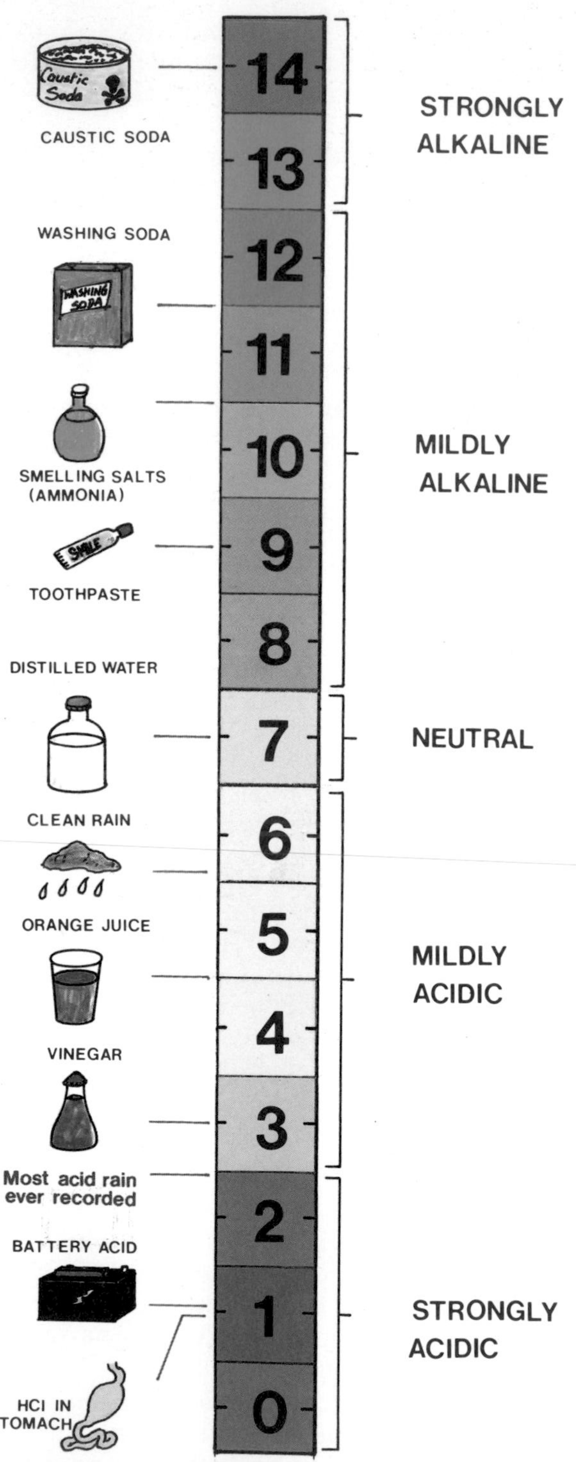

Fig. 5.7 The pH scale of acidity.

greater than 7 indicates that the substance is alkaline and the higher the pH value, the more alkaline is the substance.

> **A solution whose pH is 7 is neutral.**
> **A solution whose pH is less than 7 is acidic.**
> **A solution whose pH is greater than 7 is alkaline.**

The pH of a solution may be determined using pH paper or universal indicator. A piece of pH paper or a few drops of universal indicator are placed in the solution whose pH is to be measured. The colour assumed by the paper or indicator is then matched against a standard set of colours. The range of colours of universal indicator is shown in *Fig. 5.8.* Universal indicator is actually a mixture of a number of indicators.

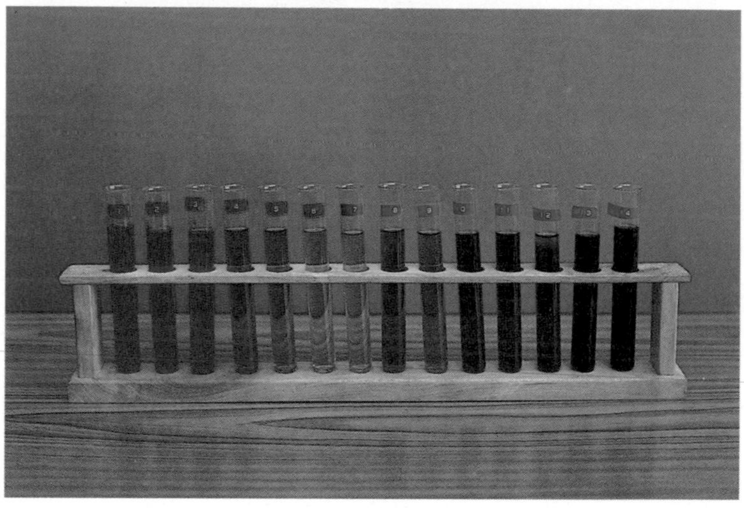

Fig. 5.8 Universal indicator shows a range of colours depending on the pH

Experiment 5.2 To Determine the pH of various Substances

Method

Use a wide-range universal indication paper to find the approximate pH value of each solution. Then choose a suitable narrow-range paper and measure each pH value more accurately by matching the colour obtained against the accompanying colour chart. The substances tested may be taken from the following: dilute hydrochloric acid, dilute sodium hydroxide solution, vinegar, sodium carbonate, lime water, household bleach **(caution!)**, tea, milk, detergent, baking soda, indigestion powder, lemonade, cola, acid drop sweets, ammonia solution.

Note: In the case of solid substances, these must first be dissolved in water.

Fig. 5.9 The three common laboratory acids.

5.6 Common Laboratory Acids

The acids which are commonly found in the laboratory are **sulphuric acid**, H_2SO_4, **hydrochloric acid**, HCl and **nitric acid**, HNO_3. These acids are often referred to as mineral acids because they used to be manufactured from minerals.

The main properties of these acids are summarised in *Table 5.3.*

	Sulphuric Acid	*Hydrochloric Acid*	*Nitric Acid*
Physical Properties	Colourless, oily liquid. Heavy: density = 1.83 g/cm³. Very corrosive — burns skin.	Colourless liquid, fumes giving off gas with pungent smell. It is a solution of hydrogen chloride gas in water.	Colourless or yellow liquid (due to presence of nitrogen dioxide). Very corrosive to rubber, wood, corks, etc. Pungent smell.
Chemical Properties	1. It is a strong acid. 2. Has a great attraction for water. 3. In dilute form reacts with metals to liberate H_2 e.g. $Zn + H_2SO_4 \rightarrow ZnSO_4 + H_2$ 4. Reacts with bases to form salts and water, e.g. $H_2SO_4 + 2NaOH \rightarrow Na_2SO_4 + H_2O$	1. It is a strong acid. 2. Fumes on contact with air — the HCl gas dissolves in water vapour in air. 3. Reacts with many metals to liberate hydrogen. $Zn + 2HCl \rightarrow ZnCl_2 + H_2$ 4. Reacts with bases to form salts and water, e.g. $HCl + NaOH \rightarrow NaCl + H_2O$	1. It is a strong acid. 2. Reacts with bases to form salts and water. $HNO_3 + NaOH \rightarrow NaNO_3 + H_2O$ 3. The dilute acid does *not* usually liberate H_2 gas on reaction with metals but rather nitrogen monoxide gas is formed, e.g. $8HNO_3 + 3Cu \rightarrow 3Cu(NO_3)_2 + 2NO + 4H_2O$
Uses	1. Car batteries. 2. As a drying agent. 3. Manufacture of fertilisers. **Note:** When sulphuric acid is added to water, a large quantity of heat is given off. The acid must always be added to the water.*	1. Industry, used for removing rust from steel sheets before galvanising. 2. Manufacture of chemicals.	1. Manufacture of explosives and fertilisers. 2. Etching and refining metals.

*"If you're doing what you oughter
Add the acid to the water.
May your rest be long and placid
Adding water to the acid.
The water must be in before
You add the H_2SO_4
Or else you may not feel too well
You may not even live to tell!"

Table 5.3 Properties of Sulphuric, Hydrochloric and Nitric Acid

Summary

* An acid is a proton donor.
* A base is a proton acceptor.
* A strong acid is one which readily donates protons.
* A weak acid is one which does not donate protons readily.
* An indicator is a compound which shows, by means of a colour change, whether a substance is acidic or basic.
* An alkali is a base which is soluble in water.
* Acid + Base → Salt + Water.
* The reaction of an acid and base is called a neutralisation reaction.
* A salt is the compound formed when the hydrogen in an acid is replaced by a metal or ammonium ion.
* The pH scale is used to measure degree of acidity or basicity.
* A solution whose pH = 7 is neutral.
* A solution whose pH is less than 7 is acidic.
* A solution whose pH is greater than 7 is basic.

1 2 3 4 5 6 7 8 9 10 11 12 13 14

Acidic *Neutral* *Basic*

* The three most common laboratory acids are sulphuric acid, hydrochloric acid, and nitric acid.

Questions

Section A

1. A Bronsted-Lowry acid is defined as . . . .
2. A Bronsted-Lowry base is defined as . . . .
3. The sour taste in lemons is due to an acid called . . . .
4. Acids react with metals to liberate . . . . gas.
5. A base which is soluble in water is called . . . .
6. Nitric acid is an example of a . . . . acid but ethanoic acid is an example of a . . . . acid.
7. An indicator is defined as . . . .
8. Litmus is and indicator which is coloured . . . . in an acid and . . . . in a base.
9. The common name for sodium hydroxide is . . . .
10. Complete the following: acid + base → . . . . . + ...
11. A salt is defined as the compound formed when . . . .
12. Name the chemicals which could be used to prepare potassium nitrate . . . .
13. The pH scale ranges from . . . . to . . . .
14. The pH of distilled water is . . . . Water is said to be . . . .
15. A solution whose pH acid is less than 7 is said to be . . . . and one whose pH is greater than 7 is said to be . . . .
16. Which is the more acidic solution, one with a pH of 2 or one with a pH of 6? . . . .
17. Give the name and formula of the acid used in car batteries. . . . .
18. Of the common laboratory acids, the one which is most dense is . . . .
19. When hydrogen chloride gas is dissolved in water, the acid formed is called . . . .

Section B

1. Explain what is meant by the terms
   (i) acid;
   (ii) base;
   (iii) salt.
   Describe how you would carry out a titration in the laboratory to prepare a salt. Name the acid and alkali used and write a balanced equation for the reaction. If this salt was dissolved in water, would you expect the resulting solution to be acidic, basic or neutral?
2. (a) What is meant by (i) an indicator; (ii) pH? How would you determine the pH of a solution? Name two acids and two alkalis which are found in the home.
   (b) Outline the principal properties of nitric acid. Why is nitric acid usually stored in dark bottles? Nitric acid should never be kept in a bottle with a cork or rubber stopper. Why is this?

6 — Preparation of Salts

Salts are ionic compounds containing positive metal ions and negative ions formed when an acid reacts.

Salts can either be soluble salts, ones which dissolve in water and form crystals from concentrated solution or insoluble salts which form as precipitates.

Methods of making soluble salts

1. Reacting an acid with a metal

Many metals react with dilute acids to form salts and hydrogen gas. However this method is not suitable for all metals. Sodium, potassium and calcium react violently with acids. Unreactive metals, for example lead and copper, do not react with dilute acids.

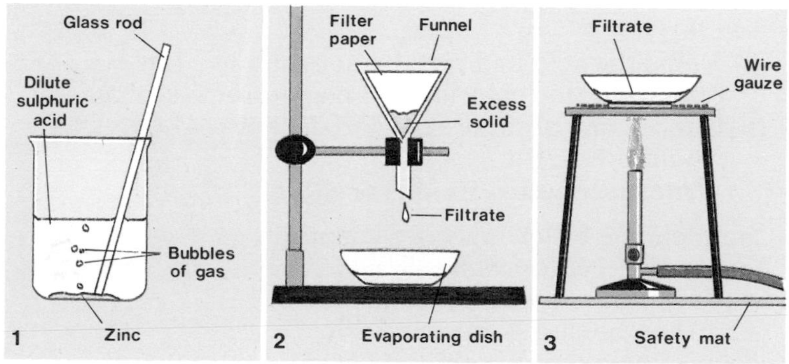

Fig. 6.1

Experiment 6.1 Preparation of Zinc Sulphate

1. Put 25 cm^3 dilute sulphuric acid in a small beaker. Add zinc until zinc remains on the bottom of the beaker, (it is present in excess). Reaction is finished when the bubbles stop because all acid has been used up.
2. Filter the solution to remove excess zinc.
3. Collect the filtrate, salt dissolved in water, and heat to concentrate the solution.
4. Cover the hot solution and leave to cool.
5. Filter off the crystals, wash with a small amount of distilled water and dry between filter paper.

Slow cooling produces large crystals

METAL + ACID → SALT + HYDROGEN

$$Zn_{(s)} + H_2SO_{4\,(aq)} \rightarrow ZnSO_{4\,(aq)} + H_{2(g)}$$

2. Reacting an Acid with an Insoluble Base

Experiment 6.2 Preparation of Copper II Sulphate

The method is the same as before only using Copper II oxide and dilute sulphuric acid.

ACID + BSE → SALT + WATER

$$H_2SO_{4(aq)} + Cu\,O_{(s)} \rightarrow CuSO_{4(aq)} + H_2O_{(l)}$$

3. Reacting an acid with a carbonate

Experiment 6.3 Preparation of Magnesium sulphate

The method is the same as before only using magnesium carbonate and dilute sulphuric acid.

ACID + CARBONATE → SALT + CARBON DIOXIDE + WATER

$$H_2SO_{4(aq)} + Mg\,CO_{3(s)} \rightarrow Mg\,SO_{4(aq)} + CO_{2(g)} + H_2O_{(l)}$$

Preparation of insoluble salts

Most salts are soluble but some are insoluble. These are formed by **precipitation**. A **precipitate** is a solid which is produced when two clear solutions are mixed.

In this type of preparation a solution containing the metal ion is mixed with a solution containing the negative ion.

Experiment 6.4 Preparation of Lead II oxide

Method

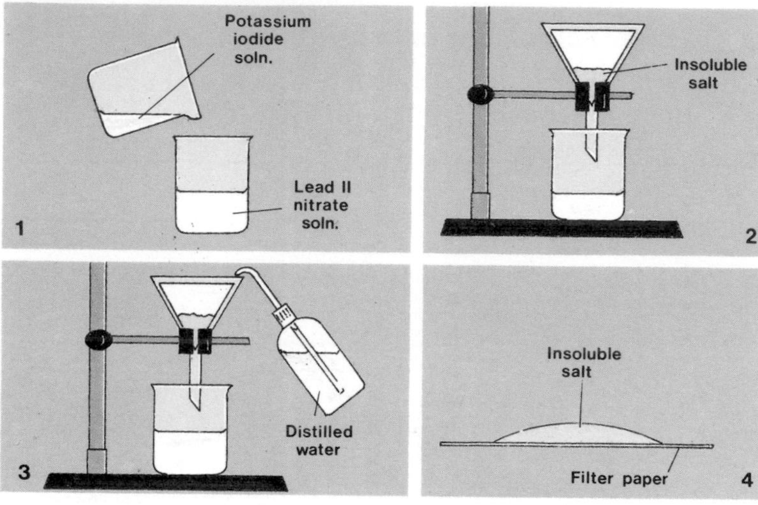

Fig. 6.2

1. Put about 15 cm^3 lead II nitrate solution in a small beaker.
2. Add potassium iodide solution until no more precipitate forms.
3. Filter the mixture.
4. Wash the insoluble salt in the filter paper with distilled water.
5. Leave the solid to dry.

Summary

* Salts are ionic compounds.
* There are two types of salts, soluble and insoluble.
* Acids react with metals to form salts and hydrogen.
* Acids react with insoluble bases to form salts.
* Acids react with carbonates to form salts.
* Excess react is used when making salts.
* Slow cooling produces large crystals.
* Insoluble salts form as precipitates.

Questions

Section A

1. Salts are .... compounds.
2. There are two types of salts. These are .... and ....
3. A metal which will not react with dilute acids to form a salt is ....
4. The filtered solution of the salt is heated to ....it.
5. Slow cooling produces .... crystals.
6. When an acid reacts with a carbonate bubbles of .... gas are seen.
7. .... solid is added to the acid to ensure that all the acid reacts.
8. When the bubbles stop the reaction is ....
9. Insoluble salts are prepared by.......................
10. The insoluble salt remains in the ....

Section B

1. (i) Name the acid and metal you would use for preparing zinc chloride and magnesium sulphate.
   (ii) Choose one of these salts and describe how you would prepare it.
   (iii) Write an equation for this reaction.
2. Complete the following word equations
   Zinc + hydrochloric acid →
   Lead II nitrate + sodium sulphate →
   Lead II carbonate + nitric acid →
   Magnesium oxide + sulphuric acid →
   Silver nitrate + sodium chloride →
3. Magnesium sulphate crystals can be prepared by adding excess magnesium oxide to dilute sulphuric acid.
   (a) Why is the magnesium oxide present in excess?
   (b) The diagram could be used to separate the excess magnesium oxide from the solution. Give the correct labels for the letters.
   (c) Describe how you would obtain large dry crystals of magnesium sulphate from magnesium sulphate solution.

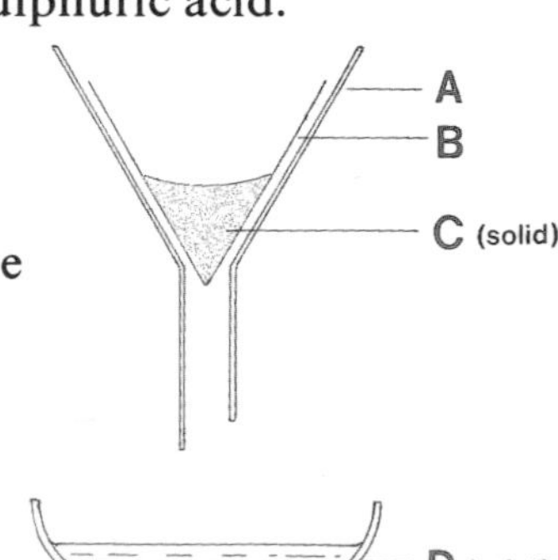

7 — Carbon and Carbon Dioxide

7.1 Introduction

The element carbon forms a very large number of compounds — several hundred thousand different carbon compounds are known. Carbon and its compounds are found in the air, the sea, in our bodies and in the food we eat. All living organisms contain carbon. Clothing, medicines, plastics and paper all consist mainly of carbon. The carbon content of materials becomes obvious to us if a piece of paper is burned or a slice of bread is toasted too much — the black substance which appears in both cases is carbon.

In this chapter we shall study the different forms in which carbon exists and shall consider the properties of one compound of carbon — carbon dioxide.

7.2 Allotropes of Carbon

Carbon is found in two distinct forms, diamond and graphite. It is difficult to believe that both these substances, which differ completely in their appearance, *Fig. 7.1*, consist of pure carbon. Graphite and diamond are said to be **allotropes** of carbon.

Fig. 7.1 Diamond and Graphite have completely different physical appearances.

> **Allotropes are different physical forms of the same element.**

It may easily be shown that diamond and graphite are pure carbon by burning the same weight of each of them in oxygen. The same quantity of carbon dioxide and nothing else is produced in each case. The differences in the physical properties of diamond and graphite may be explained by considering the arrangement in space of the carbon atoms in each substance.

Natural diamonds are formed when carbon in the ground is subjected to extremely high temperatures and pressures. The structure of diamond is shown in *Fig. 7.2.* Each carbon atom is covalently bonded to four other carbon atoms to form a large interlocking network of carbon atoms. This structure may be used to explain the properties of diamond.

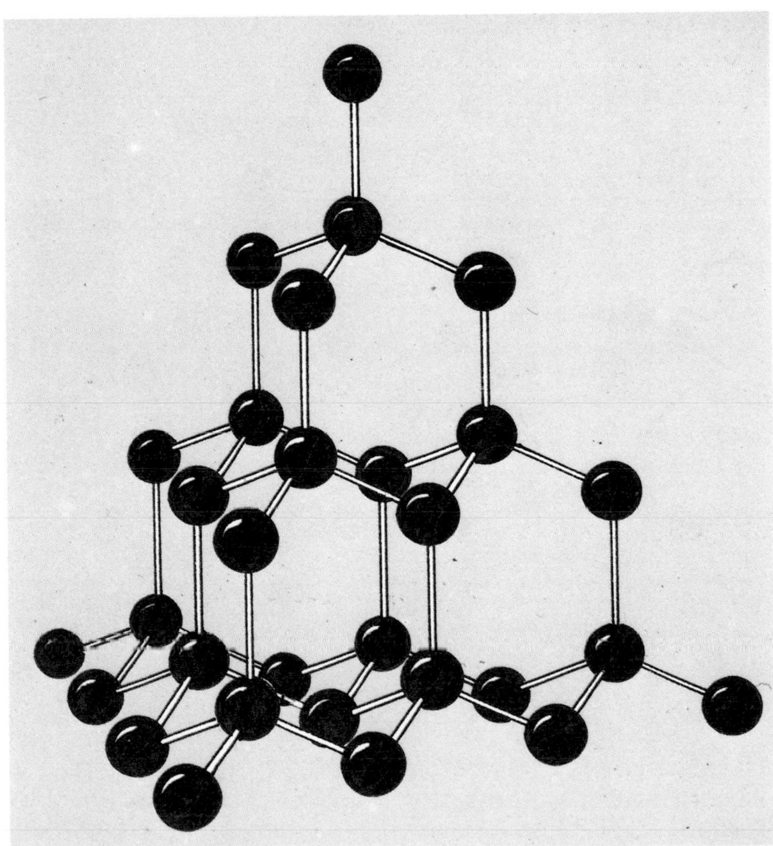

Fig. 7.2 The structure of diamond

1. **Diamond is the hardest naturally occurring substance known.** The reason for this is because the tetrahedral arrangement of carbon atoms and the even pull in four directions makes the structure very rigid. Because of its hardness, diamond-tipped drills are used when drilling for oil; and by dentists.
2. **Diamonds do not conduct electricity.** All the electrons in the outer shell of the carbon atoms are used in bonding and none are left to carry an electric current.
3. **Pure diamonds are colourless and sparkle in light.** This is because light entering the crystal is reflected a number of times from each face inside the crystal before being reflected out again.

Graphite consists of carbon atoms arranged in rings of six and joined together in large flat sheets, *Fig. 7.3.* These layers of carbon atoms have the ability to slide over one another. The structure of graphite may be used to explain its properties.

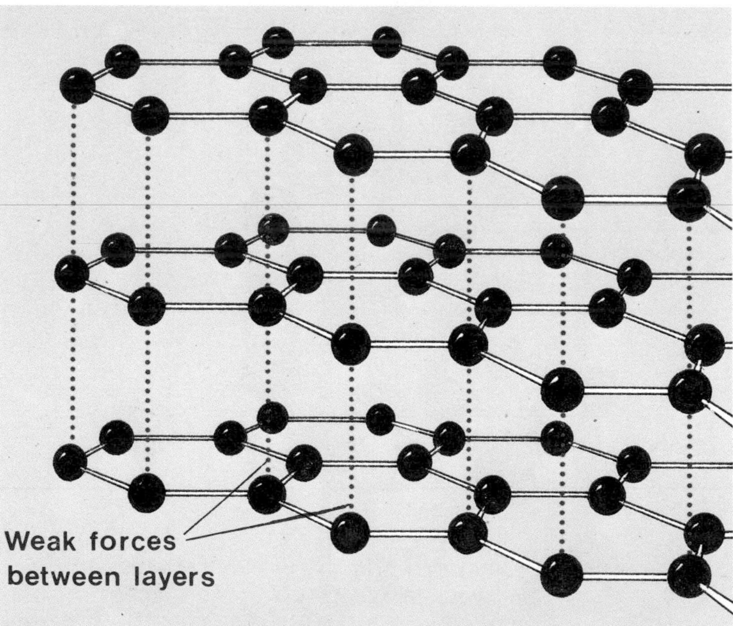

Fig. 7.3 The structure of graphite.

1. **Graphite is soft and greasy to touch.** This is because the flat sheets of carbon atoms can slide over each other. For this reason, graphite is often used as a lubricant. The "lead' of a pencil is, in fact, graphite and when you write it leaves thin layers of graphite on the paper.
2. **Graphite conducts electricity.** Of the four outer eletrons of carbon, only three are localised in bonding. The other electron is free to move and carry the electric current.
3. **Graphite is black.** The layers of carbon atoms are randomly stacked on top of each other and do not allow light to pass through.

Note: X-ray analysis of substances like soot, coke, coal and charcoal indicate that these contain carbon in the form of very small graphite crystals.

7.3 Laboratory Preparation of Carbon Dioxide

Carbon dioxide is usually prepared in the laboratory by the reaction between dilute hydrochloric acid and marble chips using the apparatus shown in *Fig. 7.4.*

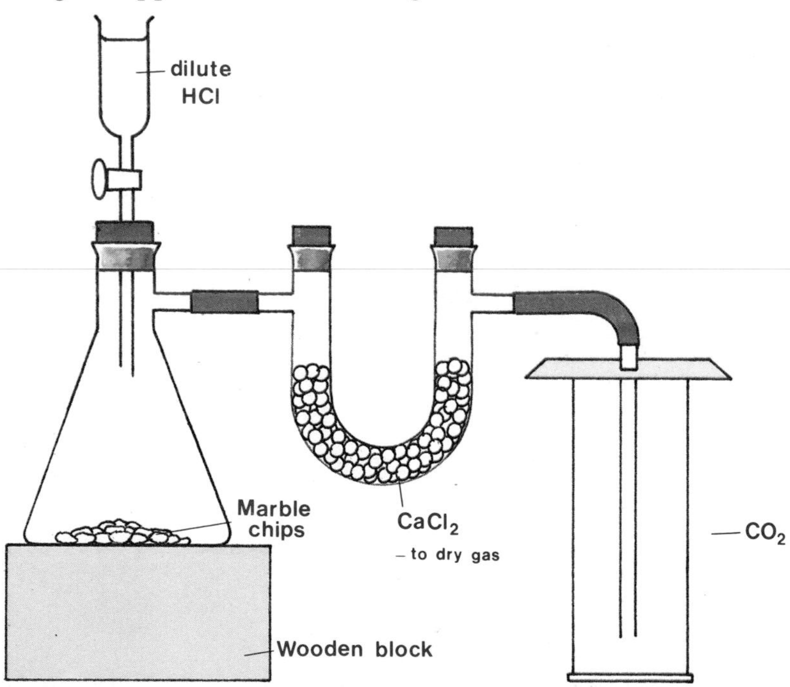

Fig. 7.4 Diagram

Marble chips are a reasonably pure form of calcium carbonate. The balanced equation for this reaction is:

$$CaCO_3 + 2HCl \rightarrow CaCl_2 + H_2O + CO_2$$

calcium carbonate + hydrochloric acid (dilute) → calcium chloride + water + carbon dioxide

The gas is collected by upward displacement of air. It may also be collected over water since it is not very soluble in water. If the gas is required dry it may be passed through a U-tube containing calcium chloride.

Method

1. Set up the appartus as shown in *Fig. 7.4.*
2. Allow the dilute hydrochloric acid to fall on the marble chips. Note that a brisk effervesence ("fizzing") begins as soon as the acid and marble come in contact.
3. Add a little hydrochloric acid from time to time to maintain the reaction.
4. Collect five jars of the gas. Check that each gas jar is full by slowly lowering a lighted taper into it. If the jar is full, the taper will be extinguished at the mouth.

7.4 Properties of Carbon Dioxide

1. **Carbon dioxide is a colourless, odourless and tasteless gas.**
2. **Carbon dioxide does not support combustion.** A lighted taper placed in a jar of the gas is extinguished.
3. **Carbon dioxide is heavier than air.** This may easily be shown by pouring carbon dioxide from one jar into another, *Fig. 7.5.* Each jar may be tested for the presence of carbon dioxide using a lighted taper. Alternatively, pour a jar of the gas down on a lighted candle and note that the candle is extinguished.
4. **Carbon dioxide turns limewater milky.** Bubble carbon dioxide through a test tube containing limewater. It is observed that the limewater turns milky, *Fig. 7.6.*

   This is a characteristic test for the presence of carbon dioxide. The milkiness is caused by the formation of calcium carbonate — a white compound which is insoluble in water. (An insoluble substance formed in this way by a chemical reaction is called a **precipitate**). The following is the reaction which occurs:

   $$Ca(OH)_2 + CO_2 \rightarrow CaCO_3 + H_2O$$

   calcium hydroxide + carbon dioxide → calcium carbonate + water

   If carbon dioxide continues to be bubbled through the limewater, it is found that the milkiness disappears. This is because the excess carbon dioxide reacts with the calcium carbonate and water to form calcium hydrogen carbonate which is a soluble in water.

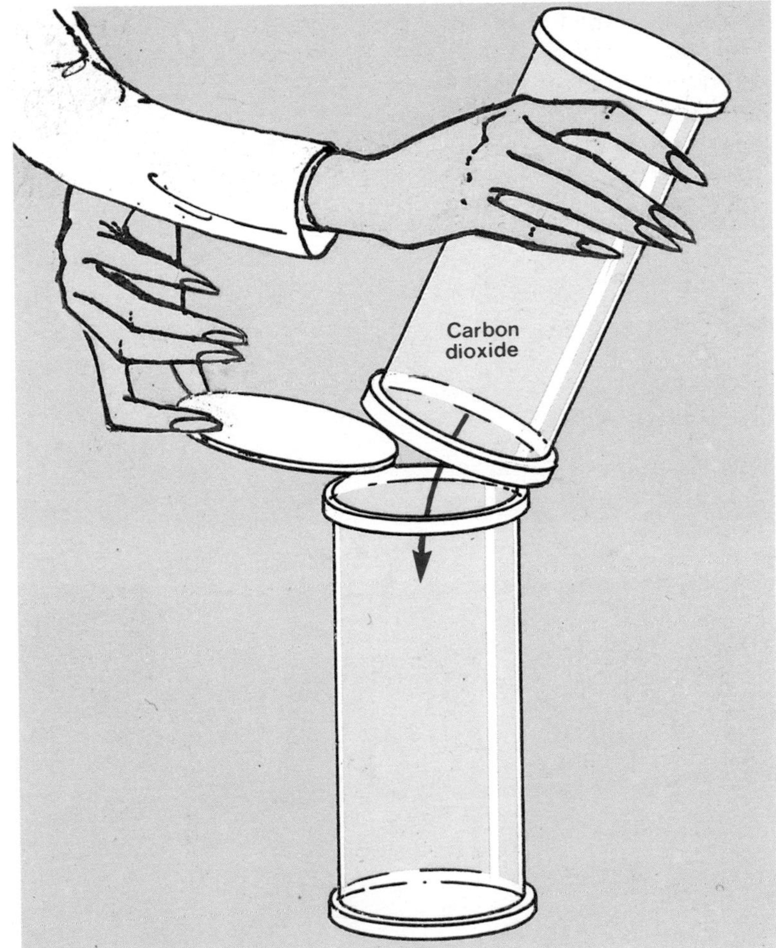

Fig. 7.5 Carbon dioxide is heavier than air.

$$CaCO_3 + CO_2 + H_2O \rightarrow Ca(HCO_3)_2$$

calcium carbonate + carbon dioxide + water → hydrogen carbonate (calcium bicarbonate)

5. **Carbon dioxide dissolves in water to form a weakly acidic solution.** Bubble some carbon dioxide into a solution of litmus and note that the litmus gradually turns red. This is because carbonic acid, a weak acid, is formed by the reaction of carbon dioxide and water.

   $$CO_2 + H_2O \rightarrow H_2CO_3$$

   carbon dioxide + water → carbonic acid

   Carbonic acid easily decomposes back into carbon dioxide

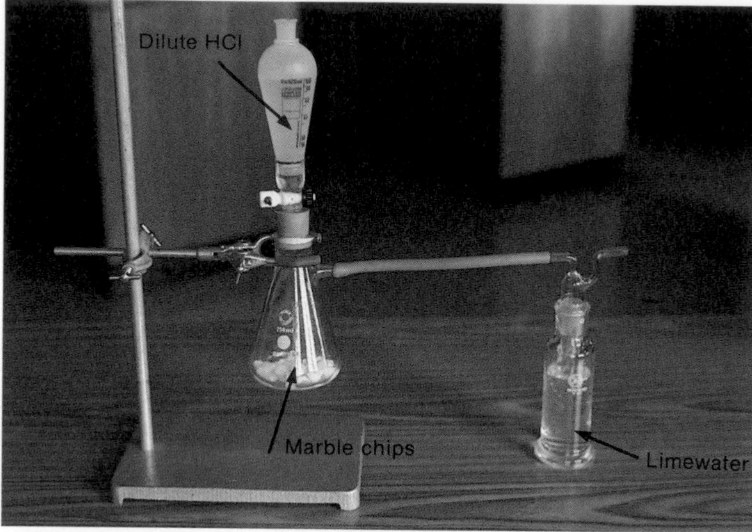

Fig. 7.6 (a)

Fig. 7.6 (b) Carbon dioxide turns limewater milky.

and water and therefore is not kept in bottles like other acids. However, the salts of carbonic acid, carbonates and hydrogencarbonates are quite stable.

6. **Magnesium burns in carbon dioxide**. Using a tongs, lower a piece of burning magnesium into a gas jar of carbon dioxide. The magnesium continues to burn with a crackling noise — this is because magnesium is reactive enough to take oxygen away from the carbon dioxide. Note that black specks of carbon are formed on the sides of the jar. The following is the reaction which takes place.

$$2Mg + CO_2 \rightarrow 2MgO + C$$

magnesium + carbon dioxide → magnesium oxide + carbon

Dissolve the white powder in water and test with litmus. What did you find? Is this what you expected? Explain.

The properties of carbon dioxide are summarised in *Table 7.1.*

Table 7.1 The Properties of Carbon Dioxide

Physical properties	*Chemical properties*
1. Colourless, odourless, tasteless gas.	1. Does not support combustion.
2. Slightly soluble in water.	2. Forms acidic solution when dissolved in water. Turns blue litmus paper dull red.
3. Heavier than air. Density of carbon dioxide is almost one and a half times that of air.	3. Turns limewater milky.

7.5 Uses of Carbon Dioxide

1. **Fizzy drinks**: carbon dioxide is present in all fizzy drinks, *Fig. 7.7.* These contain carbon dioxide under pressure — under normal conditions carbon dioxide is only moderately

Fig. 7.7 Fizzy drinks contain carbon dioxide under pressure

soluble in water but under pressure a much larger quantity of it may be dissolved. As the drink warms up in your mouth, the gas comes out of solution, forming carbon dioxide bubbles on your tongue giving the characteristic sharp taste. Soda water is water containing carbon dioxide under pressure.

2. **Fire extinguishers:** carbon dioxide is contained in many fire extinguishers because, being heavier than air, it can form a blanket over the fire. Thus, the fire is extinguished by preventing oxygen reaching the flames.

3. **Refrigeration:** carbon dioxide gas, under pressure, may be converted to a white solid. This solid is commonly referred to as **dry ice**, *(Fig. 7.8).*

Fig. 7.8 When dry ice, solid carbon dioxide, is warmed up, it changes into a cloudy gas

The Carbon Cycle

The amount of carbon dioxide in the air, although small, remains constant. The circulation of carbon into and out of the air is known as the carbon cycle.

The process of respiration occurs in plants and animals and puts carbon dioxide into the air. During daylight hours plants take in carbon dioxide by a process called photosynthesis and build up food stores. While plants take in carbon dioxide during photosynthesis, they give out oxygen and restore the balance of oxygen. (for more information see Chapter 27.)

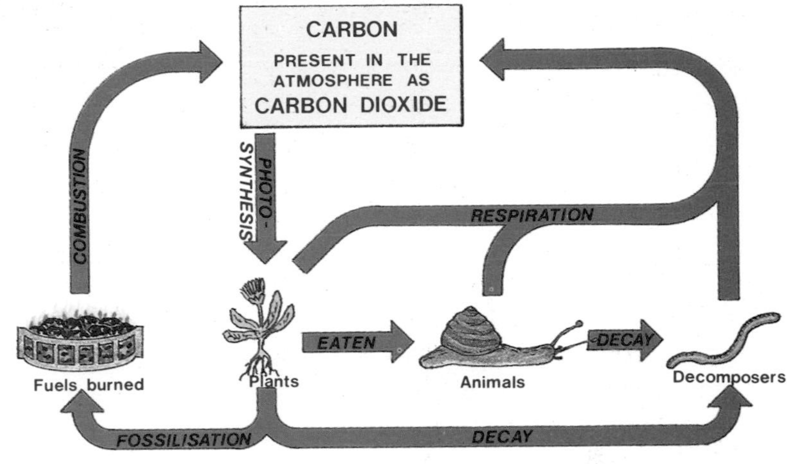

Fig. 7.9 The Carbon Cycle

Summary

* Allotropes are different physical forms of the same element.
* Diamond and graphite are allotropes of carbon.
* The structure of diamond consists of carbon atoms joined in a tetrahedral fashion to four others to form a giant molecule.
* Graphite consists of layers of carbon atoms in which each carbon atom is joined to three other carbon atoms.
* Carbon dioxide is prepared in the laboratory by the reaction between dilute hydrochloric acid and marble chips.
* $CaCO_3 + 2HCl \rightarrow CaCl_2 + H_2O + CO_2$
* Carbon dioxide is a colourless, odourless, tasteless gas which does not support combustion and which is heavier than air.
* The characteristic test for carbon dioxide is that it turns limewater milky.
* Carbon dioxide dissolves in water to form carbonic acid.
* Carbon dioxide is used in fizzy drinks, fire extinguishers and in refrigeration.
* The circulation of carbon in and out of the atmosphere is known as the carbon cycle.

Questions

Section A

1. Allotropes are different .... forms of the same element.
2. Name two allotropes of carbon ....
3. Give one common use of each of the above named allotropes. ....
4. In diamond the carbon atoms are arranged in a ....
5. In graphite each carbon atom is joined to .... other carbon atoms but in diamond each atom is joined to .... other atoms.
6. The allotrope of carbon used as a lubricant is ....
7. The two substances used to prepare carbon dioxide in the laboratory are .... and ....
8. Carbon dioxide may be collected by .... displacement of air because it is .... than air.
9. The chemical name for marble is ....
10. Carbon dioxide may be collected over water. True or false? ....
11. Complete the following: $CaCO_3 + 2HCl \rightarrow$ ....
12. How would you distinguish between carbon dioxide and nitrogen? ....
13. Write down the chemical equation for the reaction of carbon dioxide and water. ....
14. When carbon dioxide is bubbled through limewater the limewater turns .... This is because an insoluble compound .... is formed.
15. If the passage of carbon dioxide through the limewater is continued the solution becomes clear because the soluble compound .... is formed.
16. The chemical name for limewater is ....
17. The only element which burns in carbon dioxide is ....
18. Fizzy drinks contain carbon dioxide which is under ......
19. Give two uses for carbon dioxide ....
20. Solid carbon dioxide is commonly called ....
21. The amount of carbon dioxide in the atmosphere is constant. True or false?
22. Plants take in carbon dioxide by ....
23. Plants give out oxygen in the day time. True or false?
24. Plants and animals put carbon dioxide in the atmoshpere by ....

Section B

1. Distinguish between the terms isotope and allotrope. Draw the structure of two isotopes of carbon. Name two allotropes of carbon and give three properties of each allotrope. Account for each of these properties in terms of the structure of each allotrope.
2. Describe, with the aid of a diagram, a laboratory method of preparing carbon dioxide. Write down the balanced chemical equation for the preparation.

   List three physical and three chemical properties of carbon dioxide and describe how you would demonstrate these properties in the laboratory.

8 — Hardness of Water

8.1 Introduction

Approximately four-fifths of the surface of the earth is covered by water. However, it is very unusual to find absolutely pure water. The reason for this is because water is a very good solvent. Water dissolves a greater variety of substances than any other liquid. Rain water is one of the purest forms of water. However, even rain contains nitrogen, oxygen and carbon dioxide which dissolve in the raindrops passing through the atmosphere.

As streams and rivers flow over the land, substances from the soil and rocks are dissolved in the water. Eventually all water passes down to the sea. Over millions of years the dissolved solids have built up in the sea, giving sea water its salty taste. Before the water reaches the sea, some of it is collected in reservoirs. This water is used by us in our houses and factories before being eventually returned to the sea. These ideas are illustrated in *Fig. 8.1.* (See also the importance of water in biological systems *Chapter 6*)

One of the important uses of water is for washing. When

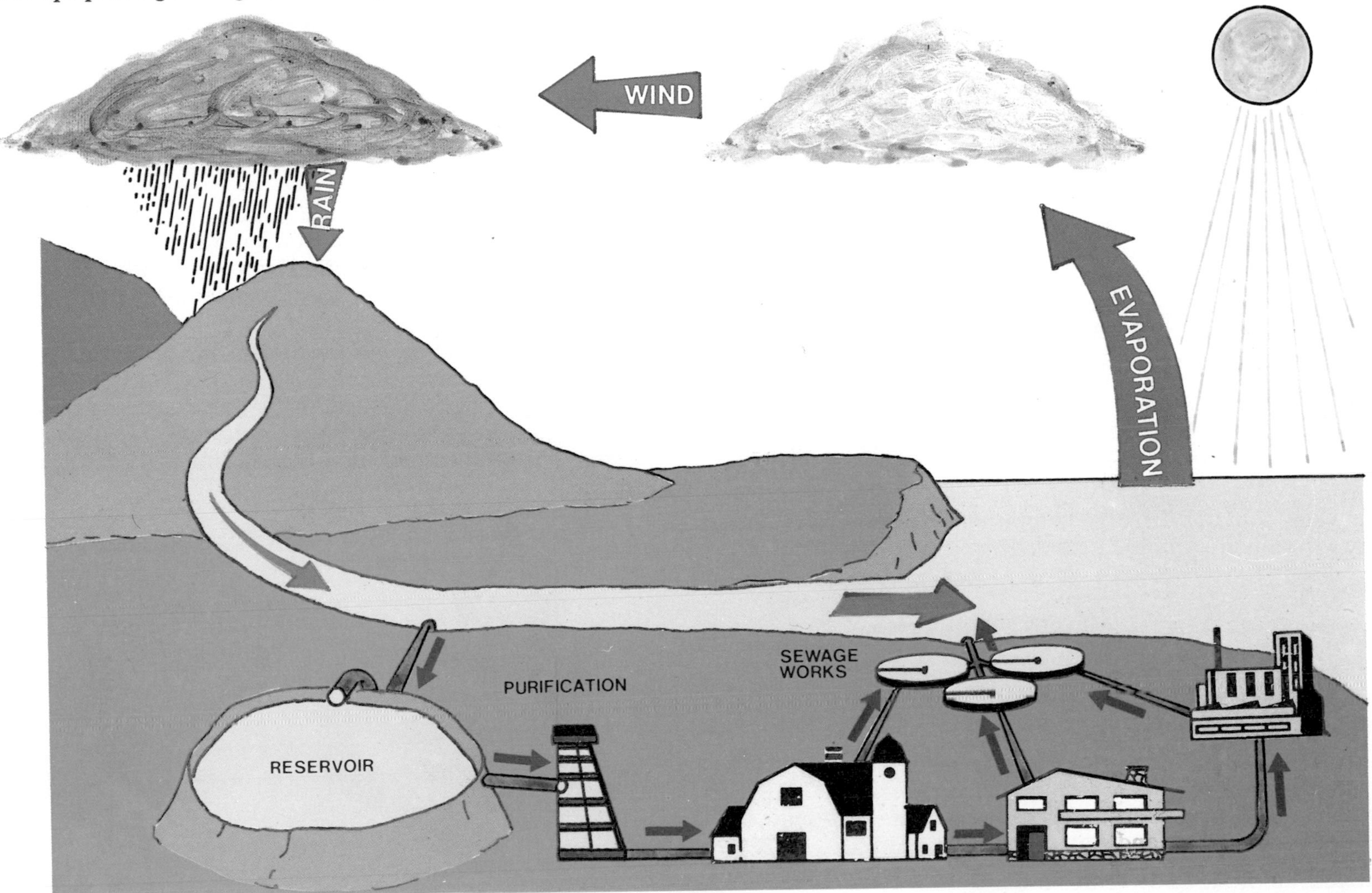

Fig. 8.1 The water cycle

soap dissolves in water it usually forms a lather. However, in some cases it is found that it is difficult to form a lather. Instead, a dirty scum is produced before the lather is formed. Water which does this is said to be **hard water.**

8.2 What is hard water?

Hard water is water which does not easily form a lather with soap.

Hardness in water is caused by the presence of calcium or magnesium compounds dissolved in the water. The Ca^{2+} ions and Mg^{2+} ions react with the negative ions of soap (called stearate ions) to form the scum.

Calcium ions + stearate ions → calcium stearate (scum)

It is only when the soap has removed these Ca^{2+} or Mg^{2+} ions that a lather begins to form. As a result, soap is wasted. The two main compounds which cause hardness in water are calcium hydrogencarbonate, $Ca(HCO_3)_2$ and calcium sulphate, $CaSO_4$. The corresponding salts of magnesium also cause hardness but to a lesser extent.

Calcium hydrogencarbonate becomes dissolved in water as a result of the reaction between rain water and limestone. Limestone is calcium carbonate and most of the surface of Ireland is limestone.

Rainwater contains dissolved carbon dioxide and this acidic solution of carbonic acid dissolves the limestone.

$$CaCO_{3(s)} + H_2CO_{3(aq)} \rightarrow Ca(HCO_{3(aq)})_2$$

limestone (calcium carbonate) (INSOLUBLE) → calcium hydrogencarbonate (SOLUBLE)

Many lakes and caves have been formed by this reaction of rainwater on limestone.

As the water containing calcium hydrogencarbonate drips through the cracks in the limestone in the caves, the calcium hydrogencarbonate changes to calcium carbonate and forms stalagmites and stalactites in the cave.

Calcium sulphate and various other salts become dissolved in water as it passes through the soil.

8.3 Temporary and Permanent Hardness

There are two types of hardness in water: temporary hardness and permanent hardness.

Temporary hardness is hardness which can be removed by boiling the water.

Temporary hardness is caused by the presence of calcium hydrogencarbonate dissolved in the water. When the water is boiled, the dissolved calcium hydrogencarbonate is changed to solid limestone (calcium carbonate).

$$Ca(HCO_3)_{2(aq)} \rightarrow CaCO_{3(s)} + CO_{2(g)} + H_2O_{(l)}$$

calcium hydrogencarbonate (soluble) → calcium carbonate (insoluble)

Thus, the calcium is removed from the water and cannot react with soap to form a scum. The water is said to have been softened. In limestone areas, it is found that a considerable amount of "fur" or "scale" (calcium carbonate) builds up in kettles, boilers, hot water pipes, etc. This is due to the above chemical reaction. This "fur" causes problems as it can eventually block pipes. Also, it is a bad conductor of heat and therefore causes fuel to be wasted. The problem of temporary hardness is illustrated in *Fig. 8.2.*

Fig. 8.2 Effects of hard water

When hardness is caused by the presence of calcium sulphate or magnesium sulphate dissolved in the water, this hardness cannot be removed by simply boiling the water. This type of hardness is known as **permanent hardness**.

> **Permanent hardness is hardness which cannot be removed by boiling the water.**

We shall study the removal of this type of hardness at a later stage.

Experiment 8.1 To Compare the Hardness of Different Water Samples

In this experiment the hardness of different samples of water is compared. This is done by adding soap flakes (or soap solution) to the water, a small amount at a time until the water gives a permanent lather. Hard water will need more soap flakes than soft water, *Fig. 8.3.*

Fig. 8.3 Which test-tube contains hard water?

Method

1. Fill some test-tubes to about one third their capacity with some or all of the following: rain water, tap water, sea water, distilled water, hard water.
2. Obtain a small quantity of soap flakes, e.g. *Lux* flakes.
3. Add a soap flake to each sample of water.
4. Put your thumb over the mouth of each test-tube and shake vigorously for a few seconds.
5. Put each test-tube back in the rack and wait for about 20 seconds. If a lather remains after this time, we can say that one soap flake was required.
6. If a lather does not remain, add another soap flake and shake again. Wait a further 20 seconds.
7. Continue on in this way and record the number of soap flakes required to produce a permanent lather in each sample of water. Can you now arrange the samples in order of increasing hardness?

Experiment 8.2 To Investigate Temporary and Permanent Hardness

Method

1. Fill two test-tubes to about one third their capacity with a solution of calcium hydrogencarbonate.
2. Add soap flakes to one of the test-tubes and count how many flakes are required to give a permanent lather.
3. Boil the solution of calcium hydrogencarbonate in the other test-tube (use a water bath).
4. Allow the latter solution to cool. Has any precipitate formed? Check the hardness of this solution by adding soap flakes. Explain your observations.
5. Repeat steps 1-4 above using a solution of calcium sulphate. Does boiling this solution have any effect on the hardness?

8.4 Removal of Hardness

A number of methods may be used to remove the hardness from water. All methods involve the removal from solution of the metal ions causing the hardness i.e. Ca^{2+} or Mg^{2+} ions.

1. Boiling

This removes temporary hardness only. As already stated, boiling the water converts the soluble calcium hydrogencarbonate into insoluble calcium carbonate. Thus, the Ca^{2+} ions are removed from the solution.

2. Addition of washing soda

Washing soda is a compound called sodium carbonate,

Na_2CO_3. Addition of crystals of washing soda to hard water removes both temporary and permanent hardness. The carbonate ions from the washing soda combine with the ions which cause the hardness and remove these ions from solution.

$$Ca^{2+} + CO_3^{2-} \rightarrow CaCO_{3(s)}$$

Fig. 8.4 Bath salts are crystals of sodium carbonate. They soften the water and help the soap to lather more easily

Bath salts are simply coloured and perfumed crystals of washing soda. Washing soda was used with soap for washing clothes before detergents* were invented.

3. Ion exchange

The calcium and magnesium ions in hard water may be replaced by ions which do not cause hardness. A substance which does this is known as an **ion exchange material**. There are two types of ion exchange materials: zeolites and resins.

(a) **Zeolites**: These are naturally occurring solids which contain sodium ions. They have the ability to "swop" their sodium ions for calcium or magnesium ions. If hard water is passed through a column of zeolites, the Ca^{2+} and Mg^{2+} ions are removed from the water and are replaced by Na^+ ions. Na^+ ions do not cause hardness. Thus, the water has been softened. Representing the zeolite as Na^+Z^-, the softening reaction may be expressed as follows:

$$2Na^+Z^- + Ca^{2+} \rightarrow Ca^{2+}Z_2^- + 2Na^+$$

$$2Na^+Z^- + Mg^{2+} \rightarrow Mg^{2+}Z_2^- + 2Na^+$$

*Modern detergents are soapless i.e. they do not form a scum with hard water. They are manufactured using vegetable oils or oils from petroleum. They have the same washing action as soap.

An illustration of a water softener which makes use of this type of ion exchange is given in *Fig. 8.5*.

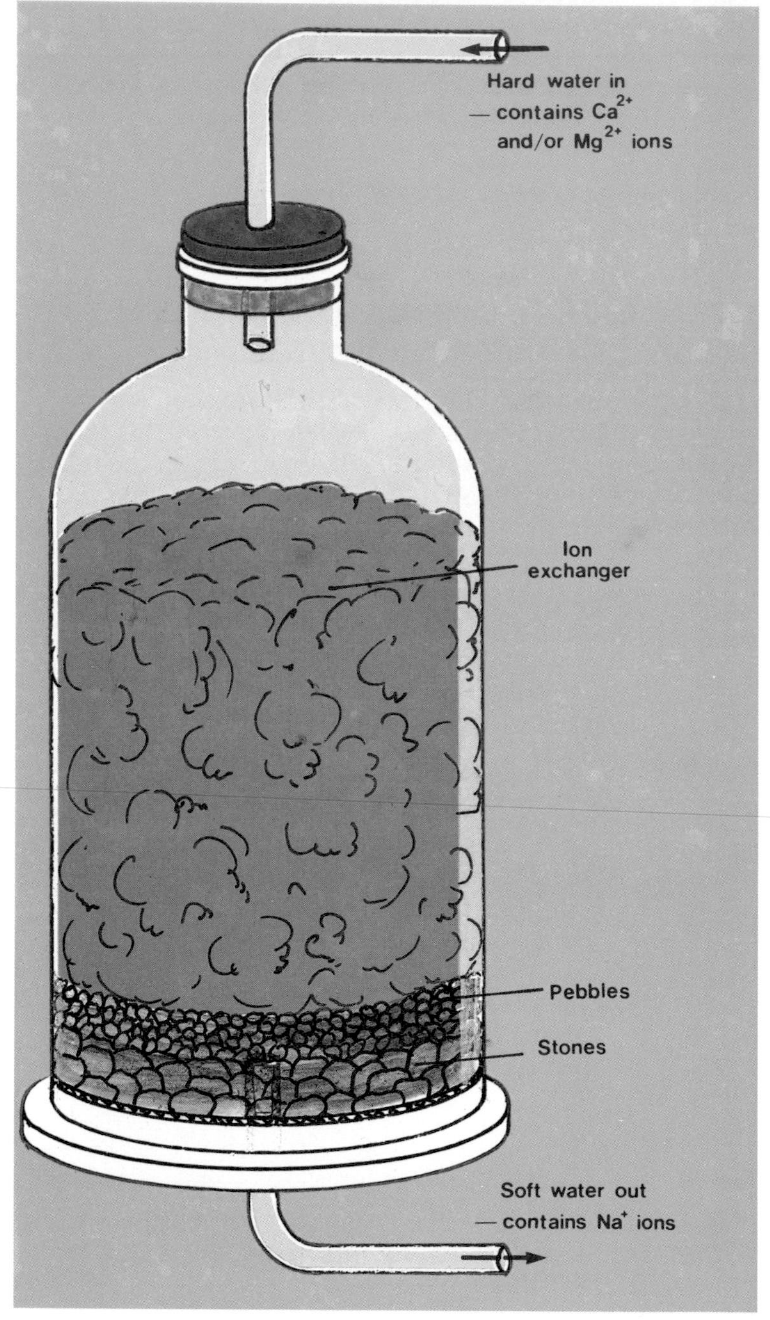

Fig. 8.5 A Water softener.

(b) **Resins**: This is the most modern way of softening water. Ion exchange resins are man-made materials which have the ability to swop H^+ ions for metal ions and OH^- ions for negative ions. Water which has passed through an ion exchange resin will have *all* ions removed. Such water is said to be **deionised**. This process is illustrated in *Fig. 8.6*.

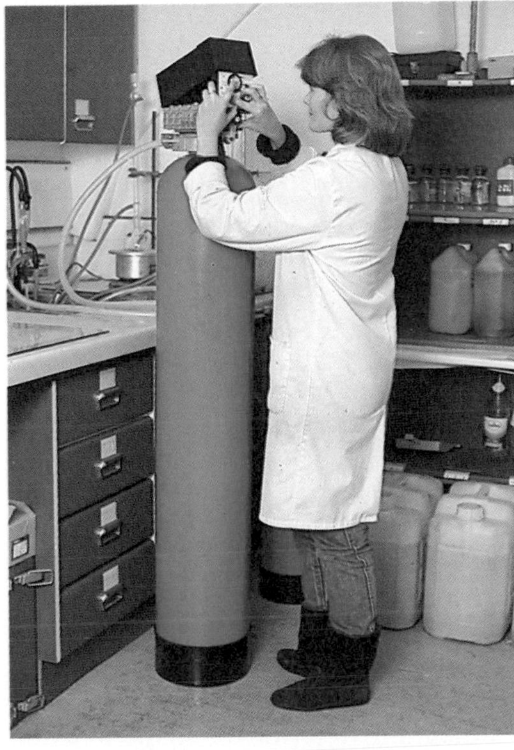

Fig. 8.6 This water deioniser contains two ion exchange resins — one to remove the positive ions from the water and the other to remove the negative ions from the water

4. Distillation

Distillation of water removes all dissolved material in it. Thus, hard water may be softened by this method. However, distilled water is expensive to prepare in large quantities because of the energy required to boil the water. Therefore, this method of softening water is not often used.

The advantages and disadvantages of hard water are summarised in *Table 8.1*.

Table 8.1 The advantages and disadvantages of hard water.

Advantages	*Disadvantages*
1. Provides calcium for teeth and bones.	1. Blocks pipes, leaves scale on kettles and boilers
2. Nicer taste.	2. Wastes soap.
3. Good for brewing beer.	3. Produces scum.

The chalk cycle

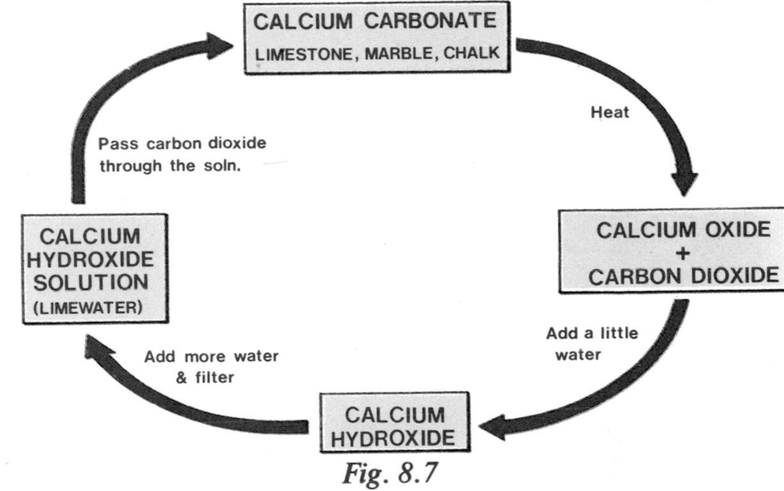

Fig. 8.7

Experiment 8.3 To Follow the Chalk Cycle

Method You must wear safety glasses for this experiment.

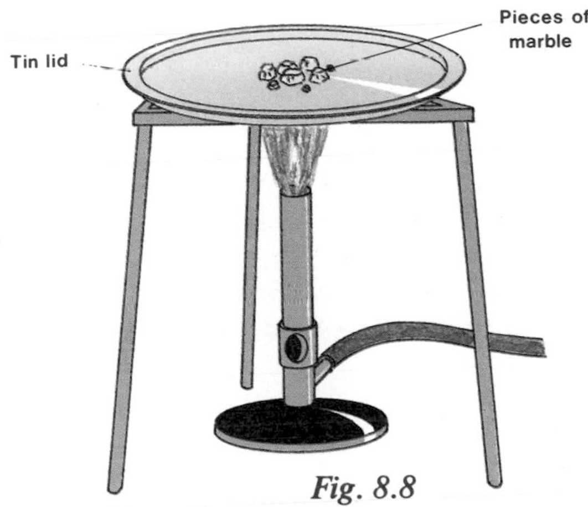

Fig. 8.8

1. Put some small pieces of marble in a crucible or on a tin lid.

2. Heat the marble strongly until it begins to crumble.
3. Leave the solid to cool. Record all your observations.
4. Add a small amount of water to the solid.
5. When the reaction has stopped add more water. This solution is called limewater.
6. Pass carbon dioxide through the limewater. The milky appearance of liquid is because calcium carbonate in the form of chalk is formed.

Summary

* Water is a very good solvent.
* Hard water is water which does not easily form a lather with soap.
* Hardness in water is caused by the presence of calcium or magnesium compounds dissolved in the water.
* Temporary hardness is hardness which can be removed by boiling.
* Temporary hardness is caused by the presence of calcium hydrogencarbonate.
* The calcium hydrogencarbonate is formed when limestone dissolves in rain water.
* Temporary hardness causes scale to build up in kettles, boilers, etc.
* Permanent hardness is hardness which cannot be removed by boiling.
* Permanent hardness is due to the presence of calcium sulphate or magnesium sulphate dissolved in the water.
* Temporary hardness is removed by boiling.
* Temporary and permanent hardness are removed by washing soda, ion exchange and distillation.
* Although hard water causes scale to build up in kettles and boilers and although it wastes soap, it is useful in that it provides a good supply of calcium in our diets and it has a nicer taste than soft water.
* Stalactites and stalagmites are caused by temporary hard water.

Questions

Section A

1. Hard water is water which does not easily form a .... with soap.
2. Hardness in water is caused mainly by the presence of .... ions and .... in the water.
3. Temporary hardness in water is caused by the presence of ....
4. Permanent hardness in water is caused by the presence of ....
5. Temporary hardness is so called because it can be removed by ....
6. The compound that forms on the inside of kettles in hard water areas is called ....
7. Permanent hardness is removed by adding .... to the water.
8. An ion exchange resin is so called because ....
9. Water from which all ions have been removed is called ....
10. Distillation is not widely used to soften water because ....

Section B

1. (a) Using a diagram, describe the shape of a molecule of water. What type of bond is present in this molecule? Why is it so difficult to obtain absolutely pure water?
   (b) What is meant by hard water? Why is hard water commonly found in limestone areas? Explain what is meant by temporary hardness and permanent hardness.
2. *"Boiling removes temporary hardness but does not remove permanent hardness".* Explain.
   Why is it necessary to remove hardness from water? Describe two methods of removing permanent hardness from water. Give two advantages of hard water.

9 — Oxidation and Reduction

9.1 Introduction

The word **oxidation** was originally used in chemistry to denote the reaction of a substance with oxygen. The substance which combined with oxygen was said to be **oxidised**. We have already studied some examples of oxidation reactions, e.g. the reaction between magnesium and oxygen to form magnesium oxide ($2Mg + O_2 \rightarrow 2MgO$) and the combination of iron with oxygen in the process of rusting, *Fig. 9.1.*

Fig. 9.1 Photo — The rusting of iron is an example of an oxidation reaction

The term **reduction** was first used when referring to the extraction of metals from their ores, i.e. the isolation of metals from their compounds in rocks and minerals. Since the element combined with the metal was usually oxygen, the word **reduction** became used generally to denote the removal of oxygen from *any* compound. We have already studied some examples of reduction reactions, e.g. copper II oxide loses its oxygen when it reacts with hydrogen *(Book 1, Chapter 7)* — this is commonly referred to as the reduction of copper II oxide to copper.

Fig. 9.2 The oxide coating on the coin is being removed by the hot chemical. This is an example of a reduction reaction

$$CuO + H_2 \rightarrow Cu + H_2O$$

A further example of a reduction reaction is shown in *Fig. 9.2.*

Thus, we see that reduction is the reverse of oxidation.

9.2 Oxidation and Reduction in terms of Electron Transfer

If we consider in more detail the reaction between magnesium and oxygen, it is clear that what is essentially happening is that electrons are being transferred from magnesium atoms to oxygen atoms:

$$2Mg + O_2 \rightarrow 2Mg^{2+}O^{2-}$$

(Mg → Mg^{2+}: loses two electrons)

OXIDATION

In general, when a metal combines with oxygen, the atoms of the metal lose electrons. This fact may be used to give a more general definition of oxidation.

> **Oxidation of an element takes place when it loses electrons.**

If we examine the reaction between copper II oxide and hydrogen, it is clear that in the reduction process each Cu^{2+} ion gains two electrons and becomes a neutral copper atom.

$$Cu^{2+}O^{2-} + H_2 \qquad Cu + H_2O$$

(Cu^{2+} → Cu: gains two electrons)

REDUCTION

This fact may be used to form a more general definition of reduction.

> **Reduction of an element takes place when it gains electrons.**

To help you remember these definitions, think of the words OIL RIG ("Oxidation is loss, reduction is gain").
Using the above definitions, it is clear that oxidation and reduction can occur without any oxygen being present at all. The following examples demonstrate this fact.

Example 1 *The reaction between sodium and chlorine.*

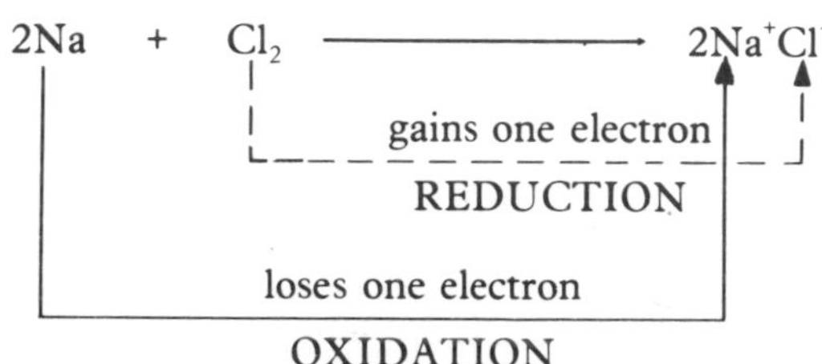

Each sodium atom loses an electron ($Na - e \rightarrow Na^+$) and each chlorine atom gains an electron ($Cl + e \rightarrow Cl^-$). Thus, the sodium has been oxidised and the chlorine has been reduced.

Example 2 *The reaction between iron and sulphur.*

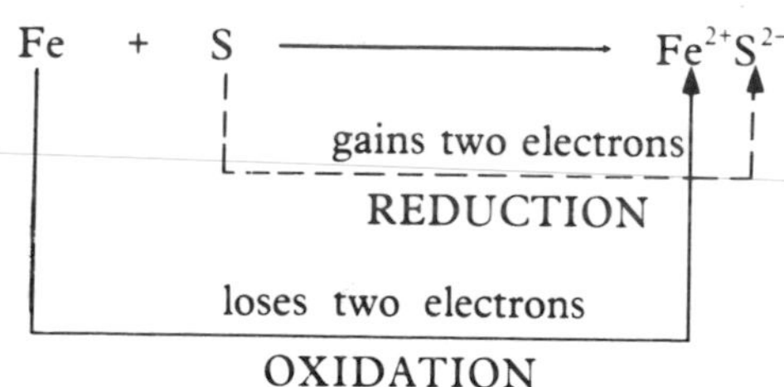

The iron is oxidised ($Fe - 2e \rightarrow Fe^{2+}$) and the sulphur is reduced ($S + 2e \rightarrow S^{2-}$).
If we think about the processes of oxidation and reduction, we realise that they must always occur simultaneously. If element A loses electrons (oxidation), there must be some other element, B, to accept these electrons (reduction). Any reaction involving the transfer of electrons from atoms of one element to those of another is called an **oxidation- reduction reaction** or **redox reaction.**

9.3 Oxidising and Reducing Agents

In the laboratory, it is often convenient to use specific chemicals to bring about oxidation-reduction reactions. A substance which brings about oxidation is called an **oxidising agent** and a substance which brings about reduction is called a **reducing agent**. One of the most commonly used oxidising agents is potassium permanganate, (potassium manganate VII) $KMnO_4$. This brings about oxidation by removing electrons from some other substance. These electrons are accepted by the oxidising agent, i.e. **the oxidising agent is itself reduced**. When potassium permanganate is reduced (in acidic solution) it becomes colourless, *Fig. 9.3.*

Fig. 9.3 An acidified solution of $KMnO_4$ is added to a solution of $FeSO_4$.

An oxidising agent is a substance which brings about oxidation by removing electrons from another substance.

One of the most commonly used reducing agents is carbon which is widely used in the extraction of metals from their ores, e.g. $C + 2ZnO \rightarrow 2Zn + CO_2$. In general, a reducing agent brings about reduction by donating electrons to another substance. Since the reducing agent loses these electrons, then **the reducing agent is itself oxidised**. Think carefully about this.

A reducing agent is a substance which brings about reduction by donating electrons to another substance.

A test for a reducing agent is that it will decolourise an acidified solution of potassium permanganate (potassium manganate VII). We shall be meeting many more examples of oxidising and reducing agents in our Chemistry course.

Summary

* Oxidation of an element takes place when it loses electrons.
* Reduction of an element takes place when it gains electrons.
* Oxidation and reduction always occur simultaneously.
* An oxidation-reduction reaction is also called a redox reaction.
* An oxidising agent is a substance which brings about oxidation by removing electrons from another substance.
* A reducing agent is a substance which brings about reduction by donating electrons to another substance.

Questions

Section A

1. Oxidation may be defined as the .... of electrons.
2. Reduction may be defined as the .... of electrons.
3. In the reaction between sodium and chlorine the .... is oxidised and the .... is reduced.
4. Mark X after the oxidation-reduction reactions in the following list:

   $CuO + H_2 \rightarrow Cu + H_2O$

   $HCl + NaOH \rightarrow NaCl + H_2O$

   $C + PbO \rightarrow Pb + CO$
5. An oxidation-reduction reaction is also called a .... reaction.
6. An oxidising agent ....electrons but a reducing agent.................................... electrons.
7. An example of an oxidising agent is .... and of a reducing agent is..................................
8. In redox reactions the oxidising agent is always .... and the reducing agent is ....
9. One of the most commonly used reducing agents in the extraction of metals from their ores is ....
10. A reducing agent may be detected by the fact that it will decolorise an acidified solution of ....

Section B

1. Define reduction in terms of transfer of electrons. Show that the reaction $Mg + S \rightarrow MgS$ is a redox reaction and state (i) what has been oxidised; (ii) what has been reduced; (iii) the oxidising agent; (iv) the reducing agent. Write down the names of one commonly used oxidising agent and one commonly used reducing agent. *"Oxidation cannot take place without reduction also taking place".* Explain this statement.
2. For each of the following reactions, write down (i) what species is oxidised; (ii) what species is reduced; (iii) the oxidising agent; (iv) the reducing agent.

   (a) $Zn + FeO \rightarrow Fe + ZnO$

   (b) $Mg + Cu^{2+} \rightarrow Mg^{2+} + Cu$

   (c) $2K + Br_2 \rightarrow 2KBr$

   (d) $Zn + 2H^+ \rightarrow Zn^{2+} + H_2$

   (e) $Cu + 2Ag^+ \rightarrow Cu^{2+} + 2Ag$

   (f) $Mg + ZnSO_4 \rightarrow Zn + MgSO_4$

   (g) $2Mg + CO_2 \rightarrow 2MgO + C$

   (h) $Cl_2 + 2I^- \rightarrow 2Cl^- + I_2$

   (i) $Zn + 2HCl \rightarrow ZnCl_2 + H_2$

   (j) $Cu + 2AgNO_3 \rightarrow Cu(NO_3)_2 + 2Ag$.

10 The Alkali Metals The Activity Series

10.1 Metals

We have already seen that elements are either metals or non-metals, *(Section 1.6 Book 2)*. The majority of the elements (approximately four-fifths) are metals. But what is a metal? Metals are used so often in our work and in the home that we rarely ask ourselves what the term "metal" actually means. We know that copper is used in electrical wiring and in water pipes, aluminium is used in the manufacture of windows and doors, iron, in the form of steel is used for reinforcing concrete, gold and silver are used for jewellery, etc. (**Note**: A mixture of metals is called an **alloy** e.g. brass is a mixture of copper and zinc, bronze is a mixture of copper and tin, and steel is a mixture of iron, carbon and various other elements.) Physical properties of metals can be found in *Section 1.6.*

In this chapter we shall study the properties of a wide range of metals and shall attempt to group together the properties of these metals in an organised fashion.

10.2 The Alkali Metals

The alkali metals are the elements of Group 1 of the Periodic Table. The name **alkali** comes from the fact that they form an alkaline solution when added to water. Our study of the alkali metals will be confined to lithium, sodium, and potassium as the remaining members of the group are not usually found in school laboratories.

Physical Properties

The alkali metals are soft silvery metals, which can easily be cut with a knife, they have low densities and float on water. They are good conductors of heat and electricity and have low melting points compared with other metals e.g. the melting point of sodium is 98°C but that of aluminium is 660 °C. Some alkali metals are shown in *Fig. 10.1.*

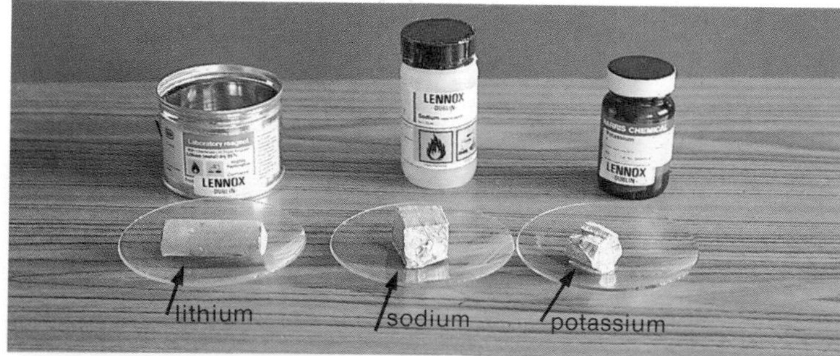

Fig. 10.1 Sodium and potassium are always stored under oil to prevent contact with oxygen and moisture.

Chemical Properties

The chemical properties of the alkali metals are governed by the fact that they all have a single electron in their outermost shell. When this electron is lost, the resulting ion has the stable electron configuration of a noble gas. Therefore, in all their chemical reactions the alkali metals tend to lose the single outer electron. Hence, the alkali metals are extremely reactive.

(a) **Reaction with oxygen**
All the alkali metals tarnish rapidly (lose their shiny appearance) when exposed to air. Also, when ignited they continue to burn in oxygen, for example.

$$4Na_{(s)} + O_{2(g)} \rightarrow \underset{\text{sodium oxide}}{2Na_2O_{(s)}}$$

(A considerable amount of sodium peroxide, Na_2O_2, is also formed i.e. $2Na + O_2 \rightarrow Na_2O_2$).

Lithium burns with a red flame, sodium with a yellow flame and potassium with a lilac flame. The yellow colour of sodium may also be achieved by passing an electric current through sodium.

Fig. 10.2

Sodium is used extensively in street lighting since the light emitted has a low dazzling effect, *Fig. 10.2.*

(b) **Reaction with water**
All of the alkali metals react vigorously with water to form hydrogen gas and a solution of an alkali e.g. when a piece of sodium is added to water, the metal floats on the surface

of the water, melts into a ball and the hydrogen generated pushes the metal about the surface of the water.

$$2Na + 2H_2O \rightarrow \underset{\text{sodium hydroxide}}{2NaOH} + H_2$$

This reaction is shown in *Fig. 10.3* and may be demonstrated by your teacher. Sodium hydroxide (caustic soda) is used in the manufacture of soap and paper. How could you test for the presence of the sodium hydroxide?

Fig. 10.3

Note: The alkali metals should never be handled directly. Always use a tongs.

(c) **Reaction with acids**
All of the alkali metals react violently with acids to liberate a large quantity of hydrogen gas. **WARNING**: Under no circumstances should this reaction be attempted.

$$2Na_{(s)} + 2HCl_{(aq)} \rightarrow 2NaCl_{(aq)} + H_{(g)}$$

(d) **Reaction with halogens**
As outlined in our study of chemical bonding, the alkali metals react with the halogens to form ionic compounds e.g. sodium burns vigorously in chlorine to form sodium chloride.

$$2Na_{(s)} + Cl_{2(g)} \rightarrow 2NaCl_{(s)}$$

Having studied the alkali metals, we are now in a position to define what is meant by the term **metal**.

Metals are substances which tend to lose electrons to form positive ions.

Obviously, the alkali metals have a great tendency to lose their outer electrons. We now investigate the tendency of other metals to do likewise.

10.3 The Activity Series

In the following experiment we shall investigate the properties of four typical metals.

Experiment 10.1 Investigation of Metals

Method

1. Take four test-tubes and fill them to about one-third their volume with water.
2. Into one test-tube place a piece of zinc, into another a piece of copper, into another a piece of calcium and into the fourth one a piece of magnesium (previously cleaned with sandpaper). Write down your observations.
3. Repeat steps 1 and 2 above but this time put dilute hydrochloric acid (or dilute sulphuric acid) in the test-tubes instead of water.

   WARNING: The addition of calcium to the acid should only be carried out under the direct supervision of your teacher. Safety glasses must be worn. Again, note your observations. If any gas is evolved collect a sample of it using the apparatus in *Fig. 10.4*. Test the gas with a lighted taper.

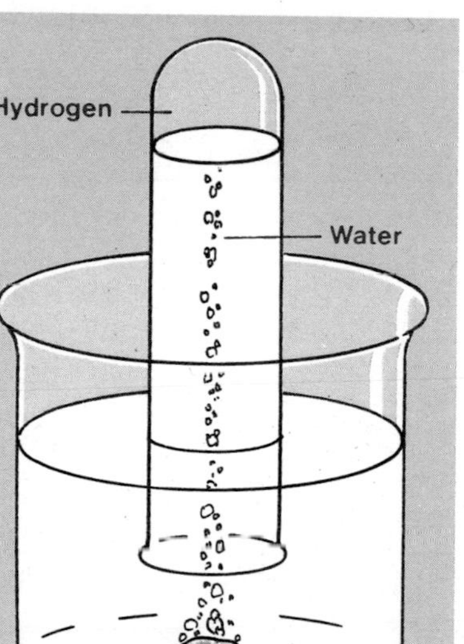

Fig. 10.4 Apparatus for collecting gas evolved when a metal reacts with a liquid.

4. Try to ignite a sample of each of the metals by holding them in the flame of a Bunsen burner. Use a deflagrating spoon for the calcium and a tongs for the other metals. Note your observations.

Experiment 10.2 To Find Order of Reactivity From Displacement Reactions

You will need solutions of zinc sulphate, copper II sulphate, magnesium sulphate, iron II sulphate and lead II nitrate and pieces of zinc, copper, magnesium, lead and iron.

Method

1. Take four test-tubes and put about 2 cm^3 of the same solution in each.
2. Then put a different piece of metal in each and notice if there is a change in appearance.
3. Wash the test-tubes, then repeat the experiment using a different solution.
4. Copy out the table below and fill in your results. If there is no change put X. If there is a change put✓.

	Zinc	Copper	Magnesium	Lead	Iron
Zinc sulphate					
Copper II sulphate					
Magnesium sulphate					
Lead II nitrate					
Lead II sulphate					

Put the metals in order of reactivity the one with the most✓ at the top as this is most reactive and continue down.

On the basis of these four experiments in Experiment 10.1, attempt to list the metals in order of reactivity starting with

Table 10.1

	Reaction with water	*Reaction with dilute HCl*	*Reaction with oxygen*
Potassium Sodium	Very vigorous. $2K + 2H_2O \rightarrow 2KOH + H_2$	Violent and dangerous reaction. $2Na + 2HCl \rightarrow 2NaCl + H_2$	React readily with oxygen. Must be stored under oil. $4Na + O_2 \rightarrow 2Na_2O$
Calcium	Less vigorous than alkali metals $Ca + 2H_2O \rightarrow Ca(OH)_2 + H_2$	Vigorous reaction but decrease in vigour of reaction. $Mg + 2HCl \rightarrow MgCl_2 + H_2$	React readily with oxygen if heated. Decreasing ease of reaction. $4Al + 3O_2 \rightarrow 2Al_2O_3$
Magnesium Aluminium Zinc, Iron, Lead	Heat and steam required. $Mg + H_2O \rightarrow MgO + H_2$		
Hydrogen			
Copper Mercury Silver	No Reaction.	No Reaction.	React slowly with oxygen on heating to form surface coating of oxide. $2Cu + O_2 \rightarrow 2CuO$
Gold			No Reaction.

one which reacts most readily. A table in which metals are listed according to their reactivity is called the **Activity Series**. Metals are given positions in this "league table" according to their reactivity with (a) water, (b) dilute acid and (c) oxygen. Thus, the position of a metal on this list gives an indication of its chemical reactivity. The Activity Series is listed in *Table 10.1.*

(a) **Reaction with water**

Potassium and sodium react vigorously with water, calcium less vigorously and magnesium hardly reacts at all. (It takes several days for a few cm^3 of hydrogen gas to be collected from the reaction of magnesium with water). Magnesium does react with steam in the apparatus shown in *Fig. 10.5,* as also do aluminium and zinc. The reaction of iron and lead with steam is slow and a high temperature is needed. Hydrogen is put into the Activity Series as a reference. Metals below hydrogen do not react with water or steam at all.

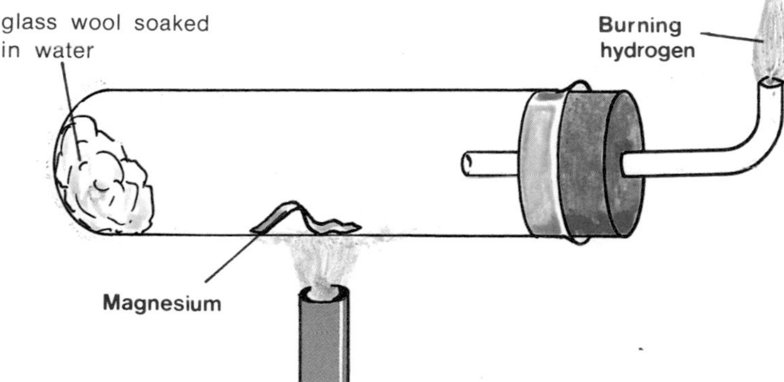

Fig. 10.5 Reacting Magnesium with steam

(b) **Reaction with dilute acid**

Potassium and sodium react violently with acid and hydrogen is evolved. The metals from calcium to iron all liberate hydrogen from dilute acid but there is a noticeable decrease in the vigour of the reaction as one proceeds downwards. The reaction with lead is very slow and the metals below hydrogen show no reaction with dilute hydrochloric or sulphuric acid.

(c) **Reaction with oxygen**

Lithium, sodium and potassium burn readily in oxygen, *Fig. 10.6.* Magnesium burns with a blinding white flame and aluminium powder when heated glows with a white flame which is less bright than that of magnesium. Zinc powder and iron filings burn slowly. Both copper and mercury react at the surface only: copper forms a black coating of copper II oxide and mercury forms a red coating of mercury II oxide. Neither silver nor gold reacts with oxygen.

Fig. 10.6 Burning lithium and sodium in oxygen.

The order of the common metals in the Activity Series may be remembered using some suitable mnemonic e.g. "**P**retty **S**ally **C**ould **M**arry **A** **Z**ulu **I**n **L**ovely **H**onolulu **C**ausing **M**any **S**trange **G**azes".

10.4 Uses of the Activity Series

1. Occurrence of metals

A knowledge of the Activity Series enables us to understand why some metals occur free in nature (i.e. as the metals themselves) and other metals are only found in compounds. Copper and gold were the very first elements discovered by man but potassium and sodium were not discovered until the nineteenth century. The reason for this is simple: copper and gold, being near the bottom of the Activity Series are very unreactive and lumps of these metals could be picked up from the beds of rivers where they had been washed free of earth by the water. However, potassium and sodium being so very reactive are only found in compounds and it took many years before it was discovered how to isolate these metals from their compounds.

Thus, metals near the bottom of the Activity Series are used for making jewellery, ornaments, coins, etc.

2. Displacement of metals

A metal higher up in the series will displace another metal which is below it from a solution of a salt of the latter e.g. if an iron nail is put into copper II sulphate solution, copper metal is formed and Fe^{2+} ions go into solution.

$$Fe_{(s)} + CuSO_{4(aq)} \rightarrow FeSO_{4(aq)} + Cu_{(s)}$$

This occurs because iron has a greater tendency than copper to lose electrons and the iron atoms force the Cu^{2+} ions to accept two electrons to form copper metal i.e.

$$Fe + Cu^{2+} \rightarrow Fe^{2+} + Cu$$

A knowledge of the Activity Series is useful in explaining certain processes like the Thermit reaction. A mixture of aluminium and iron oxide is ignited and the tremendous heat generated is sufficient to weld metals together. The original use of the Thermit reaction was in welding railway tracks, *Fig. 10.7.*

Fig. 10.7 The Thermit reaction

$$2Al + Fe_2O_3 \rightarrow Al_2O_3 + 2Fe$$

Note: Metals above hydrogen in the Activity Series displace hydrogen from dilute acids. Thus, zinc was used in the preparation of hydrogen (*Book 1, Chapter 7*) rather than a metal like copper which does not react with dilute sulphuric acid.

3. Metals in cells

The different ability of metals to donate electrons is utilised in voltaic cells. The further apart the metals in the Activity Series, the greater is the voltage obtained. This is covered in more detail in *(Physics Book 2, Chapter 12).*
Note: Metals which we have not listed in the Activity Series, *Table 10.1*, (e.g. tin, nickel, etc) generally fall into the section from calcium to copper.

Summary

* The alkali metals are the elements of Group I.
* The alkali metals are kept under oil to prevent them from reacting with either oxygen or water.
* The alkali metals tarnish rapidly in air, react vigorously with water and explosively with acids.
* Metals tend to lose electrons to form positive ions.
* The Activity Series is a list of metals according to their reactivity.
* The Activity Series is potassium, sodium, calcium, magnesium, aluminium, zinc, iron, lead, hydrogen, copper, mercury, silver, gold.
* The metals at the top of the Activity Series are very reactive and those at the bottom are very unreactive.
* A metal higher up in the series will displace another metal which is below it from a solution of a salt of the latter.

Questions

Section A

1. The only common metal which is a liquid at room temperature is . . . .
2. The elements of Group I of the Periodic Table are commonly called the . . . .
3. Underline the non-metals in the following list: calcium, zinc, nitrogen, sodium, chlorine.

4. In all their chemical reactions the alkali metals tend to lose . . . .
5. Are the alkali metals more dense than water? . . . .
6. Which is the more reactive element, sodium or potassium? . . . .
7. Sodium is stored under oil to protect it from . . . . and . . . .
8. A list of elements in order of decreasing reactivity is called the . . . .
9. Arrange the following elements in decreasing order of reactivity: calcium, copper, sodium, aluminium . . . .
10. Arrange the following elements in increasing order of reactivity: silver, magnesium, zinc, potassium . . . .
11. A piece of magnesium metal is placed in a solution of silver nitrate. What would you expect to happen? . . . . . .
12. A metal in the Activity Series will displace another metal which is . . . . it from a solution of a salt of the latter.
13. If the iron blade of a penknife were left in copper sulphate solution for some time, what would you expect to happen? . . . .
14. Gold is suitable for making jewellery but sodium is not. Explain. . . . .
15. Underline the metal in the following list which would not displace hydrogen from dilute acids:

    Magnesium Zinc Copper Calcium

16. Which metal in the following list would you expect to be found free in nature: magnesium, zinc, silver, iron . . . .
17. Brass is an alloy of . . . . and . . . .
18. List two uses of the Activity Series. . . . .
19. The . . . . reaction was originally used to weld railway tracks together.
20. Copper does not react with dilute . . . . acid but does react with . . . . acid.

Section B

1. Give three similarities between the properties of the alkali metals and account for the similarities by reference to their electronic structures.

   Describe what happens when a piece of sodium is dropped into water. Name the two products and write a balanced equation for the reaction. State the effect of the products on moist litmus paper.

2. Compare the metals magnesium, copper and sodium under the following headings: (i) reaction with oxygen; (ii) reaction with water and (iii) reaction with dilute acids. Write a balanced equation in each case where reaction occurs.

   List these metals in decreasing order of chemical activity.

3. The metals copper, zinc and sodium are represented by the letters A, B, C but not necessarily in that order. The following table summarises some properties of A, B, C.

	Occurrence	*Reaction with water*	*Reaction with dilute acids*
Metal A	Never found free in nature.	Very vigorous — gas X liberated	Explosive — gas X liberated.
Metal B	Often found free in nature	No reaction.	No reaction.
Metal C	Rarely found free in nature.	When heated reacts with steam to liberate gas X.	X liberated.

From the information given in the above table, answer the following questions.
(a) Identify metals A, B and C.
(b) Name the gas X.
(c) Write a balanced equation for the reaction between A and water.
(d) Draw a labelled diagram of the apparatus used to react C with steam.

11 — Sulphur and Sulphur Dioxide

11.1 Introduction

The element sulphur is a yellow solid which is found in some parts of the world where there have been volcanoes e.g. Italy and Japan. In parts of France and Canada, sulphur compounds are removed from natural gas and crude oil. Some minerals and ores found in Ireland (e.g. iron pyrites, FeS_2) contain sulphur. However, the largest deposits of sulphur in the world are found in Texas, U.S.A. This source supplies over 90% of the world demand for sulphur.

The sulphur deposits in Texas cannot be mined in the normal way as they are covered by layers of fine sand and pockets of poisonous hydrogen sulphide gas. The sulphur is obtained by melting it with very hot water pumped underground. The molten sulphur is then forced to the surface with compressed air.

Sulphur is usually sold in one or two forms: yellow sticks of sulphur called **roll sulphur** or as yellow powder called **flowers of sulphur**. *Fig. 11.1.*

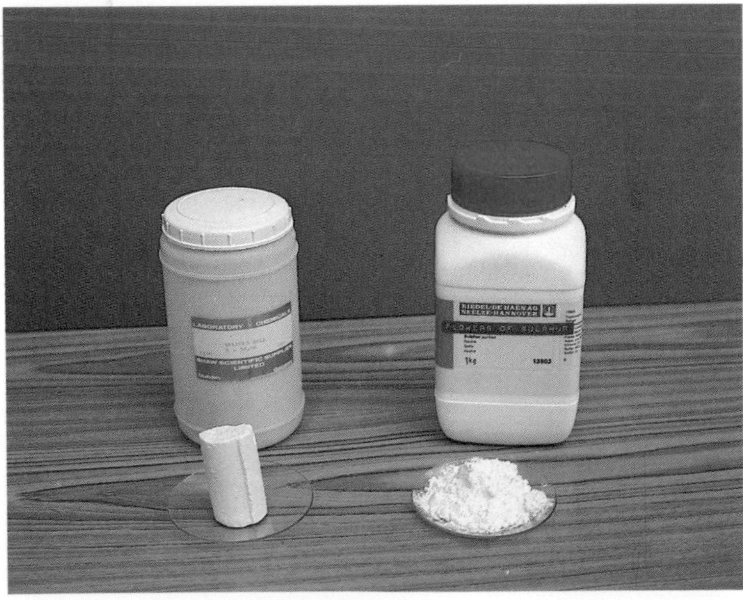

Fig. 11.1 The two forms in which sulphur is sold are roll sulphur and flowers of sulphur

11.2 Allotropes of Sulphur

Sulphur, like carbon, has a number of allotropes. There are two crystalline allotropes of sulphur: **rhombic sulphur** and **monoclinic sulphur**. These allotropes are so named because of the shapes of their crystals, *Fig. 11.2.*

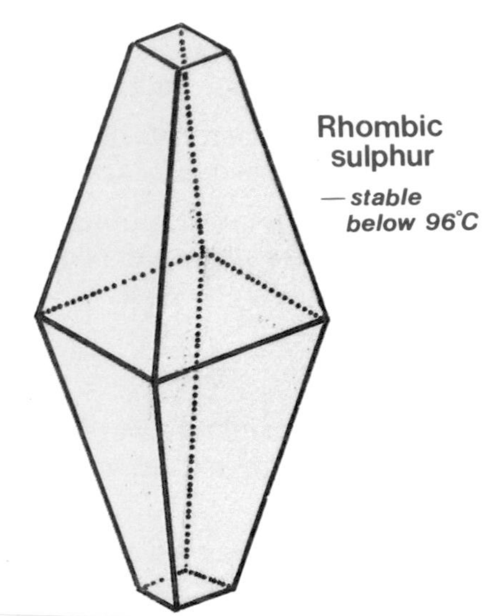

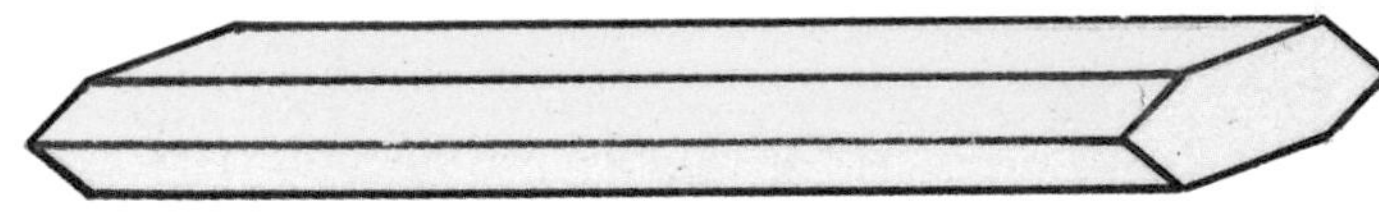

Fig. 11.2 The shapes of crystals of rhombic and monoclinic sulphur.

A molecule of sulphur consists of eight atoms arranged in a ring. These S_8 molecules pack together in a crystal in two different ways depending on the temperature. Below 96 °C the rings pack together to give the shape of the rhombic crystal. Above 96 °C the rings pack together to give the long needle-like shape of the monoclinic crystal. We make use of this fact when preparing these allotropes of sulphur.

Experiment 11.1 To Prepare Crystals of Rhombic Sulphur

Rhombic crystals are prepared by allowing a solution of sulphur to evaporate at a temperature below 96 °C. Sulphur does not dissolve in water but it does dissolve in methylbenzene.

Method

1. Fill a test-tube to about one third its volume with methylbenzene.
2. Stand the test-tube in a beaker of warm (not boiling!) water, *Fig. 11.3.*
3. Stir some powdered sulphur into the methylbenzene until no more will dissolve.
4. Filter the solution into an evaporating dish. Cover the evaporating dish with a filter paper in order to allow the methylbenzene to evaporate more slowly. Place the covered evaporating dish in a fume cupboard. In this way, rhombic crystals are formed which may be studied with a magnifying glass.

Note: Bigger crystals of rhombic sulphur may be prepared by filtering the solution into a test-tube which is insulated (using cotton wool, polystyrene, etc.) so that evaporation of methylbenzene takes place very slowly.

Experiment 11.2 To Prepare Crystals of Monoclinic Sulphur

Monoclinic crystals are prepared by allowing molten sulphur to cool.

Method

1. Fill a test-tube to about one third its volume with powdered sulphur.
2. Heat the sulphur *very gently* in a Bunsen flame until the sulphur *just* melts. The sulphur should melt to a pale yellow liquid. Withdraw it from the heat if it becomes orange or dark in colour — this means you are heating the sulphur too strongly.
3. Warm one side of the test-tube. Pour the molten sulphur along the warmed side of the test-tube into a filter paper cone in a funnel, *Fig. 11.4.*

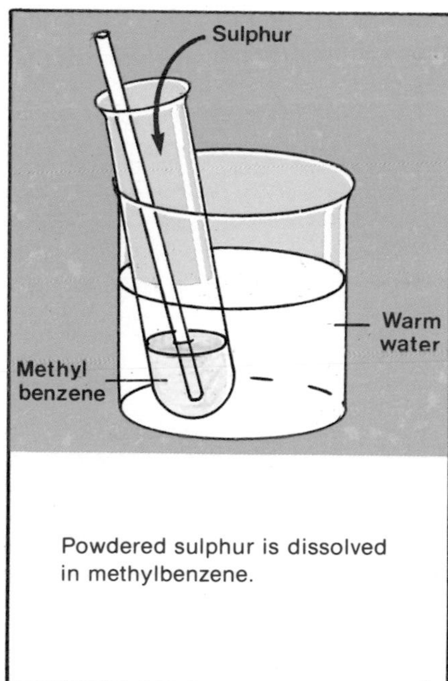

Powdered sulphur is dissolved in methylbenzene.

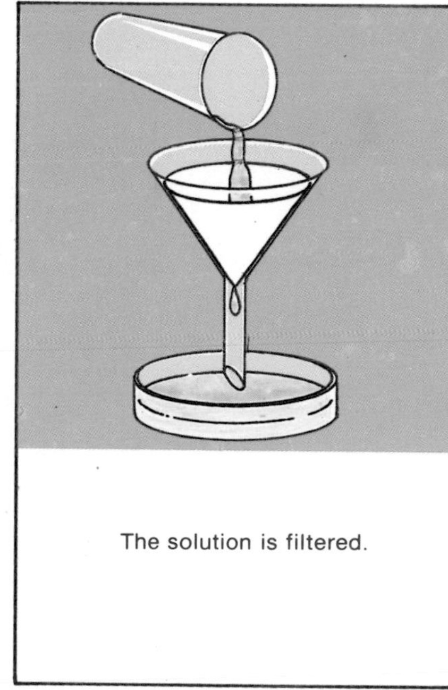

The solution is filtered.

The solution is partly covered and left to crystallise.

Fig. 11.3 The preparation of rhombic sulphur

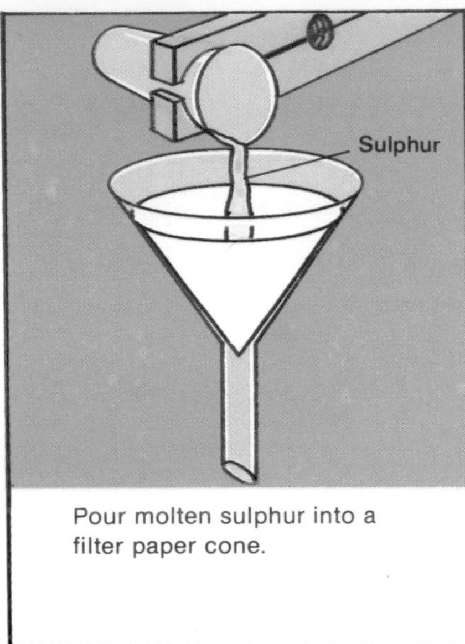

Pour molten sulphur into a filter paper cone.

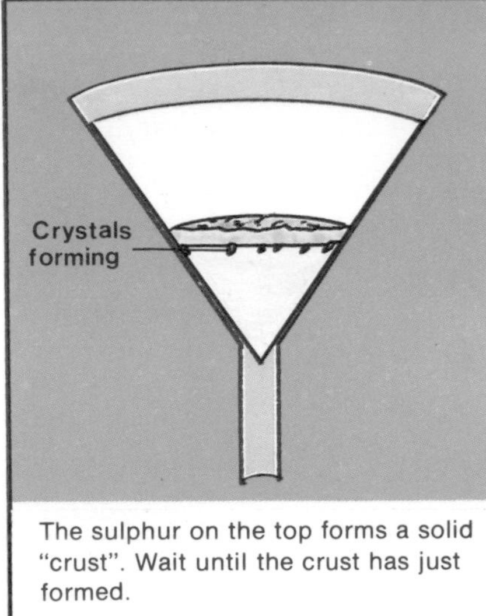

The sulphur on the top forms a solid "crust". Wait until the crust has just formed.

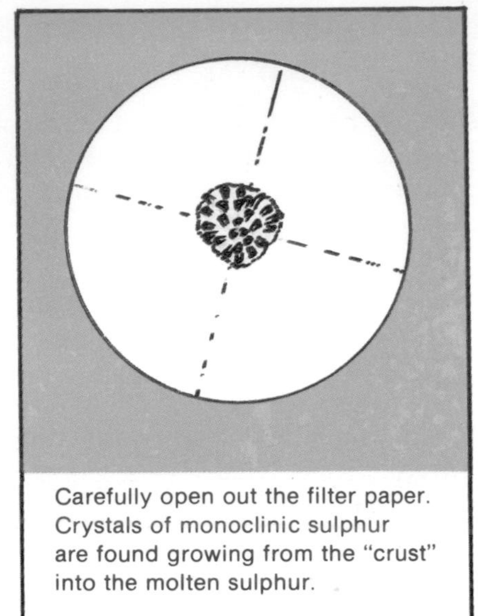

Carefully open out the filter paper. Crystals of monoclinic sulphur are found growing from the "crust" into the molten sulphur.

Fig. 11.4 The preparation of monoclinic sulphur

4. Wait until a crust has just formed on the top of the molten sulphur. Be careful as there is hot molten sulphur still underneath the crust. Open out the filter paper and you will find crystals of monoclinic sulphur growing from the crust into the molten sulphur. Examine these with a magnifying glass and you will clearly see the needle-like shapes of monoclinic sulphur.

Note: At room temperature, the long crystals of monoclinic sulphur break down into smaller rhombic crystals.

The best known non-crystalline allotrope of sulphur is **plastic sulphur**. This is so called because of its rubber-like properties.

Experiment 11.3 To Prepare Plastic Sulphur

Plastic sulphur is formed when boiling sulphur is rapidly cooled.

1. Fill a test-tube to about half its volume with powdered sulphur and heat it gently over a Bunsen flame. Note that the sulphur melts into a runny yellow liquid.
2. Continue heating and observe that the yellow liquid changes to red which gradually darkens until it becomes black. This substance is very viscous.
3. Continue heating and observe that the black, viscous material becomes runny again and finally begins to boil. When it is on the point of boiling, pour it into a beaker of cold water as shown in *Fig. 11.5*. Note that a soft elastic-type substance (rather like chewing gum) is formed. This is plastic sulphur. Plastic sulphur, like monoclinic sulphur, if allowed to stand, gradually changes to rhombic sulphur over a period of a few days.

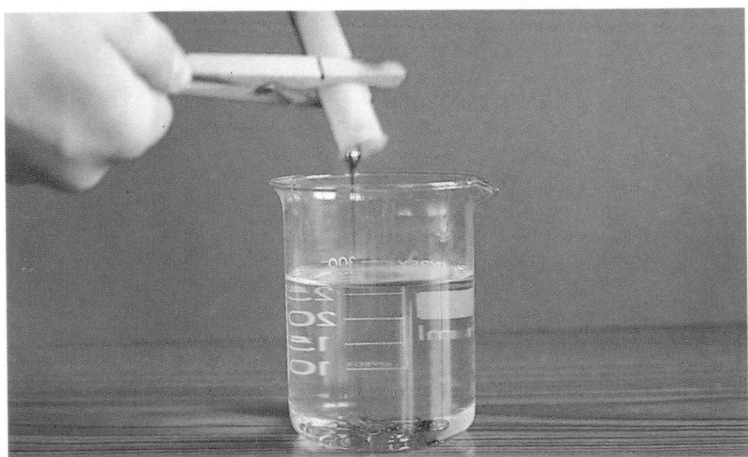

Fig. 11.5 The preparation of plastic sulphur

11.3 Properties of sulphur

1. Physical properties

As discussed in the previous section, each of the allotropes of sulphur has a distinct physical appearance. They also differ in other physical properties e.g. melting point, density, etc.

2. Chemical properties

As expected, all allotropes have the same chemical properties.

(a) Sulphur burns with a blue flame producing choking fumes of sulphur dioxide *(Book 2, Section 4.4)*

$$S_{(s)} + O_{2(g)} \rightarrow SO_{2(g)}$$

(b) Sulphur reacts with metals to form a salt called a sulphide e.g. iron reacts with sulphur to form iron II sulphide *(page 136)*

$$Fe_{(s)} + S_{(s)} \rightarrow FeS_{(s)}$$

11.4 Uses of sulphur

1. **Manufacture of sulphuric acid**: The main use of sulphur is in the manufacture of sulphuric acid. Sulphur is first burned in air to produce sulphur dioxide. This sulphur dioxide is then converted to sulphur trioxide (using a catalyst).

$$\underset{\text{sulphur dioxide}}{2SO_{2(g)}} + O_{2(g)} \rightarrow \underset{\text{sulphur trioxide}}{2SO_{3(g)}}$$

The sulphur trioxide is then dissolved in concentrated sulphuric acid and then diluted with water to form sulphuric acid. This is because the reaction of Sulphur trioxide and water is very dangerous.

$$SO_{3(g)} + H_2O_{(g)} \rightarrow H_2SO_{4(aq)}$$

2. **Vulcanising rubber**: Pure rubber is soft and sticky. Charles Goodyear discovered that it could be made hard and tough by adding sulphur. This process is called "vulcanising" rubber.

3. **Safety matches, fungicides, ointments, etc.**: Since sulphur melts easily and catches fire on heating, it was used in one of the first explosives — gunpowder. Safety matches contain a small amount of sulphur.

11.5 Laboratory preparation of sulphur dioxide

Most sulphur dioxide that is used in industry is made by burning sulphur in air. However, in the laboratory there is a more convenient method of preparing this gas. Sulphur dioxide is prepared by reacting dilute sulphuric acid with sodium sulphite in the apparatus shown in *Fig. 11.6.*

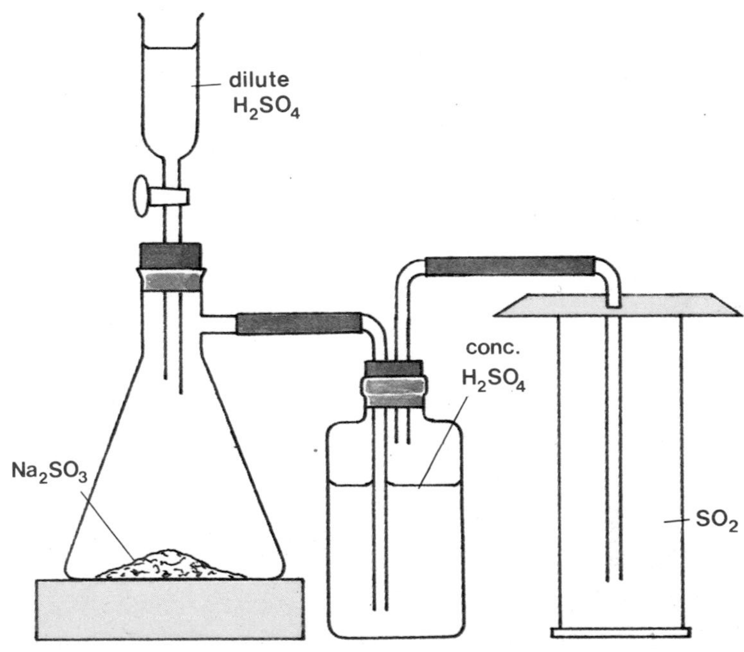

Fig. 11.6 The laboratory preparation of sulphur dioxide.

The following is the reaction which occurs:

$$\underset{\text{sulphuric acid}}{H_2SO_{4(aq)}} + \underset{\text{sodium sulphite}}{Na_2SO_{3(s)}} \rightarrow \underset{\text{sodium sulphate}}{Na_2SO_{4(aq)}} + \underset{\text{water}}{H_2O_{(l)}} + \underset{\text{sulphur dioxide}}{SO_{2(g)}}$$

If necessary, the reaction flask may be heated to speed up the reaction. The sulphur dioxide is dried by passing it through concentrated sulphuric acid. Since sulphur dioxide is soluble in water and heavier than air, it is collected by upward displacement of air.*

*An alternative method of preparing sulphur dioxide is to heat copper turnings and concentrated sulphuric acid.

$$Cu + 2H_2SO_4 \rightarrow SO_2 + CuSO_4 + 2H_2O$$

Extreme care is required when dealing with hot concentrated sulphuric acid.

11.6 Properties of Sulphur Dioxide

The main properties of sulphur dioxide are summarised in Table 11.1

Table 11.1

The properties of Sulphur Dioxide

Physical properties	*Chemical properties*
1. Poisonous gas with a choking smell.	1. Does not support combustion.
2. It is colourless.	2. Forms acidic solution when dissolved in water.
3. It is very soluble in water.	3. Good reducing agent.
4. It is heavier than air. Its density is over twice that of air.	4. Bleaches many damp materials, e.g. wool, paper, straw, etc.

1. **Sulphur dioxide is a poisonous gas with a choking smell.**
2. **It is a colourless gas but fumes in air** (due to the fact that it dissolves readily in water). This is observed when collecting the gas.
3. **The gas does not support combustion**. This fact is used to check when a gas jar is full.
4. **Sulphur dioxide is heavier than air**. This may be shown by inverting a full gas jar over an empty gas jar and removing the gas jar cover. After a short time, replace the gas jar covers on each gas jar and test each jar with a lighted taper. It is found that the taper is extinguished in the bottom jar.
5. **Sulphur dioxide dissolves in water and forms an acid called sulphurous acid.**

$$SO_{2(g)} + H_2O_{(l)} \rightarrow H_2SO_{3(aq)}$$

sulphur dioxide + water → sulphurous acid

This may be shown by adding some water to a gas jar of sulphur dioxide and shaking the water to dissolve the gas. Adding some blue litmus paper causes the paper to turn red.

6. **Magnesium burns in sulphur dioxide**. On placing some burning magnesium in a gas jar of sulphur dioxide, it is observed that a white powder is formed and yellow spots of sulphur are seen on the inside of the gas jar. (This reaction is similar to that of the reaction of magnesium with carbon dioxide).

$$Mg_{(s)} + SO_{2(g)} \rightarrow 2MgO_{(s)} + S_{(s)}$$

magnesium + sulphur dioxide → magnesium oxide + sulphur

7. **Sulphur dioxide is a good reducing agent**. This may be demonstrated by bubbling sulphur dioxide through an acidified solution of potassium permanganate (potassium manganate VII). The potassium permanganate (potassium manganate VII) solution turns colourless and this fact may be used to test for the presence of sulphur dioxide, *Fig. 11.7.*

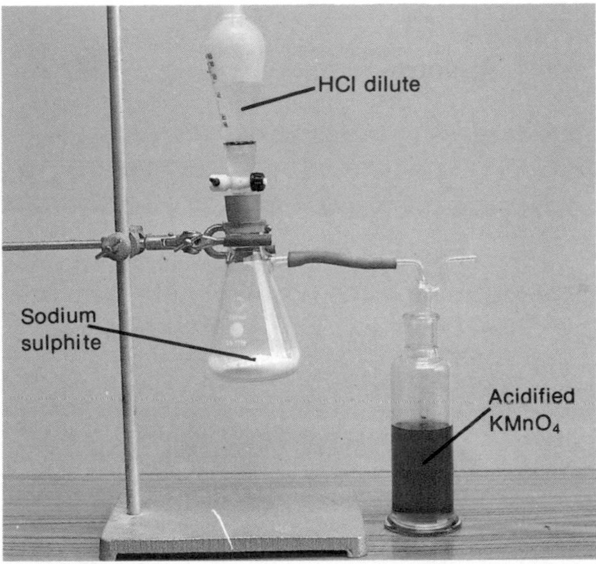

Fig. 11.7 When sulphur oxide is passed through acidified potassium permanganate solution, the solution loses its colour

Another reaction in which sulphur dioxide acts as a good reducing agent is with potassium dichromate or potassium dichromate paper (prepared by dipping a piece of filter paper into potassium dichromate solution).

Potassium dichromate is orange and when it comes in contact with sulphur dioxide it changes to green. This reaction is **generally used** as the test for sulphur dioxide.

8. **Sulphur dioxide is a good bleaching agent**. This may be shown by placing a piece of coloured cloth or straw or coloured paper in a gas jar of sulphur dioxide.

11.7 Uses of Sulphur Dioxide

1. Manufacture of sulphuric acid: this is the main use of sulphur dioxide.
2. Bleaching agent: sulphur dioxide is used in the paper-making industry to bleach paper.
3. Food preservative, wine making, etc.

Note: Most fuels contain small amounts of sulphur. When these fuels are burned, sulphur dioxide is formed and released into the atmosphere. Sulphur dioxide is the main cause of atmospheric pollution in industrial areas. This results in acid rain being formed *(Section 5.2), Fig. 11.8. (See also Book 2, Chapter 13)*

Summary

* The two crystalline allotropes of sulphur are rhombic sulphur and monoclinic sulphur.
* Crystals of rhombic sulphur are shaped like a rhombus; crystals of monoclinic sulphur are shaped like needles.
* Crystals of rhombic sulphur are prepared by allowing a solution of sulphur in methylbenzene to evaporate at room temperature.
* Crystals of monoclinic sulphur are prepared by allowing molten sulphur to cool.
* Plastic sulphur is a non-crystalline allotrope of sulphur.
* Plastic sulphur is formed when boiling sulphur is rapidly cooled.
* Sulphur burns in air to form sulphur dioxide and reacts with metals to form sulphides.
* Sulphur is used in the manufacture of sulphuric acid, vulcanising rubber, safety matches, etc.
* Sulphur dioxide is prepared in the laboratory by reacting dilute sulphuric acid with sodium sulphite (or by heating copper and concentrated sulphuric acid).
* Sulphur dioxide is dried by passing it through concentrated sulphuric acid and is collected by upward displacement of air.

Fig. 11.8 Sulphur dioxide is one of the main causes of atmospheric pollution in industrial areas

* Sulphur dioxide is a colourless gas, has a choking smell, does not support combustion and is heavier than air.
* Sulphur dioxide dissolves in water to form sulphurous acid.
* Magnesium burns in sulphur dioxide to form magnesium oxide and sulphur.
* Sulphur dioxide is a good reducing agent.
* Sulphur dioxide is used in the manufacture of sulphuric acid and for bleaching certain substances.

Questions

Section A

1. The two crystalline allotropes of sulphur are ....
2. Which one of these allotropes occurs in the form of long needle-shaped crystals? ....
3. Name one other element which exists in the form of allotropes. ....
4. The best known non-crystalline allotrope of sulphur is called ....
5. Below a temperature of 96 °C the most stable form of sulphur is .... sulphur.
6. Sulphur does not dissolve in water but does dissolve in ....
7. .... sulphur is formed when boiling sulphur is rapidly cooled.
8. Sulphur burns in air to form ....
9. Sulphur reacts with metals to form a salt called a ......
10. Sulphur is used to harden rubber. What is this process called? ....
11. Sulphur dioxide is prepared in the laboratory by reacting sulphuric acid with ....
12. Sulphur dioxide is dried by passing it through.........
13. Name two gases which are heavier than air ....
14. Sulphur dioxide dissolves in water to form ....
15. One of the few substances which burn in sulphur dioxide is ....
16. Sulphur dioxide decolourises potassium permanganate (potassium manganate VII) — this shows that sulphur dioxide is a .... agent.
17. Complete the equation: $SO_2 + H_2O \rightarrow$ ....
18. Give two uses of sulphur dioxide (i) ....
    (ii)..
19. Would you expect the bonding in sulphur dioxide to be ionic or covalent? ....
20. Give one method of distinguishing between carbon dioxide and sulphur dioxide.........................

Section B

1. What is an allotrope? Name two allotropes of carbon and two allotropes of sulphur.
   Describe carefully how you would prepare one of these allotropes of sulphur. List the principal properties of these allotropes of sulphur.
   Which of these allotropes is the most stable at room temperature?
2. Draw a labelled diagram to show the preparation of sulphur dioxide. List three of its physical properties and three of its chemical properties.
3. (a) What are allotropes?
   Name two allotropes of sulphur and two allotropes of carbon.
   Mention one common use of each of the allotropes of carbon you have named.
   (b) The diagram shows an apparatus for the preparation of sulphur dioxide.

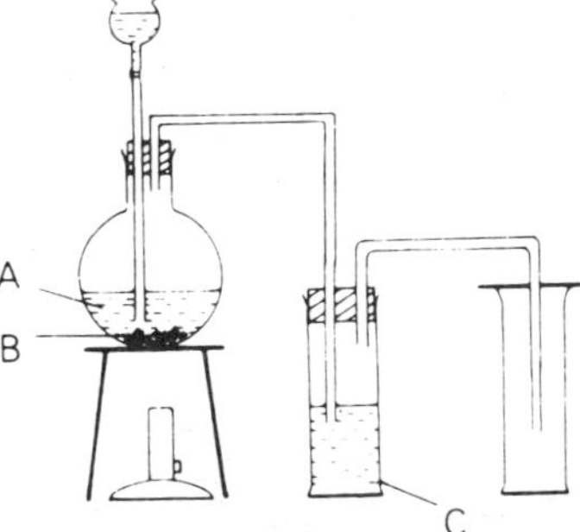

Give the names of (i) liquid A; (ii) solid B.
What is the function of the concentrated sulphuric acid in jar C?
List four properties of sulphur dioxide.

12 — Ammonia

12.1 Introduction

Ammonia is one of the most important compounds of nitrogen. It is manufactured in large quantities by I.C.I. *Fig. 12.1.* One of the main uses of ammonia is in the production of fertilisers — fertilisers are a source of nitrogen which is essential for plant growth. *(See Chapter 19)*

Fig. 12.1 Fertiliser plant

12.2 Laboratory Preparation of Ammonia

Ammonia is prepared in the laboratory by heating a mixture of ammonium chloride and calcium hydroxide (slaked lime) as shown in *Fig. 12.2.*

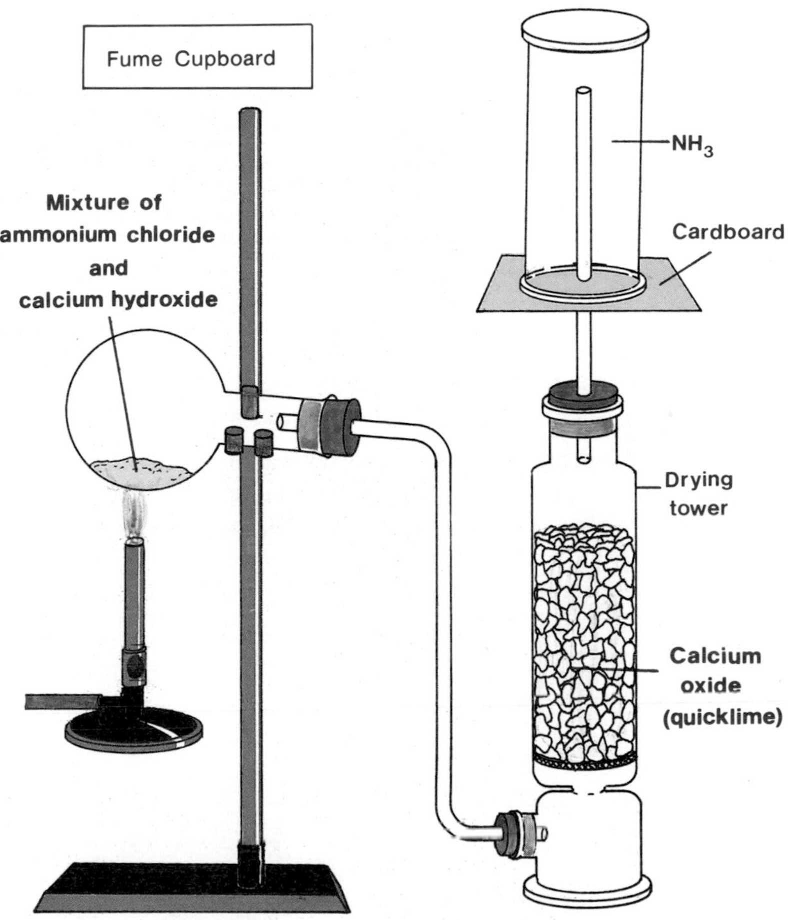

Fig. 12.2 Apparatus for laboratory preparation of ammonia

Balanced equation:

$$2NH_4Cl_{(s)} + Ca(OH)_{2(s)} \rightarrow 2NH_{3(g)} + CaCl_{2(s)} + 2H_2O_{(l)}$$

ammonium chloride, calcium hydroxide, ammonia, calcium chloride

If the gas is required dry, the water produced in the reaction must be removed. Calcium oxide (quicklime) is used to dry the ammonia as the usual drying agents (concentrated sulphuric acid, calcium chloride) react with ammonia.

Note: The reaction flask is sloped so that the steam produced will condense in the neck of the flask and not run back into the hot reaction mixture.

The gas cannot be collected over water as it is very soluble in water. It is collected by downward displacement of air since it is lighter than air.

12.3 Properties of Ammonia

The main properties of ammonia are summarised in *Table 12.1.*

Table 12.1 The Properties of Ammonia

Physical properties	*Chemical Properties*
1. Colourless gas with choking smell.	1. Does not support combustion. A lighted taper
2. Lighter than air. Note how it is collected.	plunged into an inverted jar of the gas is extinguished.
3. Extremely soluble in water.	2. Ammonia is an alkali. It the only common gas which turns moist red litmus paper blue.

Ammonia is colourless in the gas jar but fumes when the lid is removed. This is because the ammonia is reacting with the moisture in the air.

The Fountain Experiment

Ammonia is extremely soluble in water. It forms ammonium hydroxide when it dissolves in water.

$$NH_{3(g)} + H_2O_{(l)} \rightarrow NH_4OH_{(aq)}$$

These two properties of ammonia may be demonstrated by the *Fountain Experiment.*

Fill a flask with ammonia and fit it with a two-holed rubber stopper containing a jet as shown in *Fig. 12.3.* Close both clips and place the mouth of the flask under water. Add some litmus indicator to the water and a few drops of acid to colour it red. Keeping the mouth of the flask under water, open the clip leading to the jet. The water slowly rises up the tube and sprays into the flask with the colour changing from red to blue as it does so.

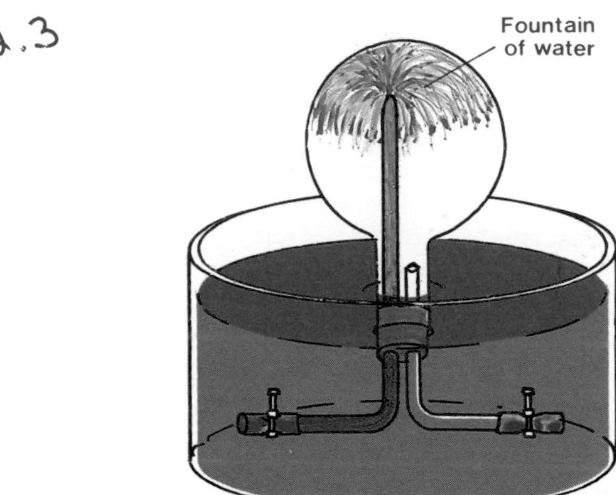

Fig. 12.3 The Fountain Experiment demonstrates the solubility and alkaline nature of ammonia

Ammonia reacts with hydrogen chloride to form dense white clouds of ammonium chloride.

$$NH_{3(g)} + HCl_{(g)} \rightarrow NH_4Cl_{(g)}$$

This may easily be demonstrated by holding the mouth of a bottle of concentrated HCl near that of ammonia solution, *Fig. 12.4.* (**Note**: A concentrated solution of ammonia in water is often called *880 ammonia* because its density is 0.88 g/cm³).

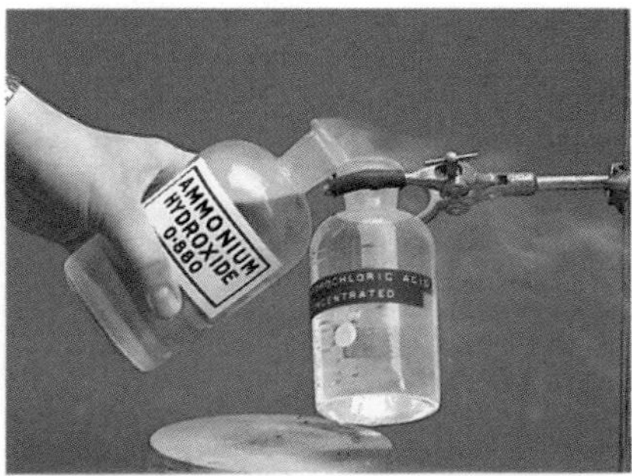

Fig. 12.4 The two gases, ammonia and hydrogen chloride, are reacting together to form ammonium chloride

Although ammonia does not support combustion and does not burn in air, it does burn in a stream of oxygen.

$$4NH_{3(g)} + 3O_{2(g)} \rightarrow 2N_{2(g)} + 6H_2O_{(l)}$$

12.4 Uses of Ammonia

1. In the production of fertilisers — ammonium nitrate, NH_4NO_3, and ammonium sulphate, $(NH_4)_2SO_4$, are commonly used fertilisers.

Fig. 12.5 Ammonia is used in the manufacture of fertiliser and in household cleaners

2. Household cleaners — ammonia is a good solvent for grease, *Fig. 12.5.*
3. Manufacture of nitric acid.

Summary

* The formula for ammonia is NH_3.
* Ammonia is prepared in the laboratory by heating a mixture of ammonium chloride and calcium hydroxide.
* Ammonia is dried by passing it through calcium oxide (quick lime).
* Ammonia is a colourless gas, has a choking smell, does not support combustion and is lighter than air.
* Ammonia is the only common gas which is alkaline.
* Ammonia is very soluble in water.
* Ammonia reacts with hydrogen chloride to form a white powder, ammonium chloride.
* The main uses of ammonia are in the manufacture of fertilisers, household cleaners and nitric acid.

Questions

Section A

1. The formula for ammonia is .... and the shape of the ammonia molecule is ....
2. Ammonia is prepared in the laboratory by heating a mixture of .... and ....
3. Ammonia is not collected over water because ....
4. Ammonia is dried by passing it through ....
5. Ammonia is lighter than air. True or False ....
6. Ammonia dissolves in water to form ....
7. Complete the equation: $NH_3 + HCl \rightarrow$ ....
8. Ammonia is the only common gas which is .... it turns litmus from .... to ....
9. Ammonia fumes in air because it reacts with the .... in the air.
10. Ammonia is used in the production of .... which are an important source of nitrogen for plants.

Section B

1. (a) Draw a clearly labelled diagram to show how you would prepare and collect dry ammonia. Give an account of the properties of ammonia under the following headings: colour, smell, density, solubility, reaction to moist litmus, reaction with hydrogen chloride.

   (b) Give the name and formula for any two salts of ammonia. Describe the shape of the ammonia molecule. How would you show experimentally that ammonia contains hydrogen?

13 — Chlorine

13.1 Introduction

The elements of Group VII are commonly called the **halogens** because they form salts so easily. (The word halogen means "salt maker"). Fluorine is a pale yellow gas which is far too dangerous to use in school laboratories; chlorine is a greenish-yellow gas; bromine is a dark-red liquid; iodine is a dark grey solid (a solution of iodine in alcohol is commonly referred to as *tincture of iodine*). Astatine is so rare that little is known about its chemistry. The halogens which are commonly encountered in the school laboratory are shown in *Fig. 13.1.*

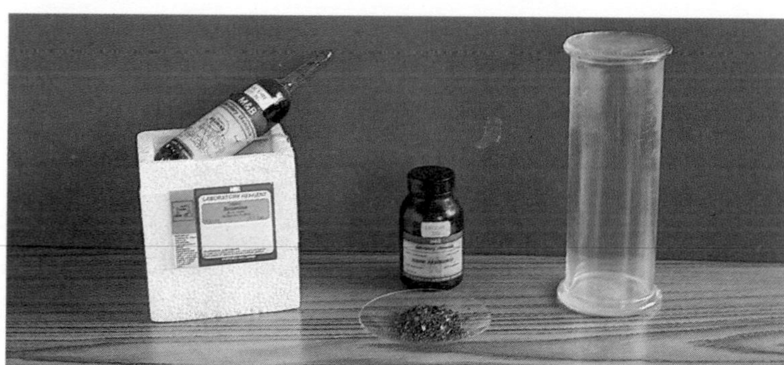

Fig. 13.1 The common halogens: chlorine, bromine and iodine.

In this chapter we shall study the chemistry of chlorine. Chlorine does not occur naturally as a free element. It occurs as chloride ions in rock salt which is impure sodium chloride. Chlorine gas is obtained from sodium chloride by electrolysis. Swimming pools always appear to have a special smell — this is because chlorine has been added to the water to kill any bacteria present. Only very small quantities of chlorine are required for this purpose. Large quantities of chlorine are very harmful and it is estimated that over 5,000 people died from chlorine gas poisoning during World War I.

13.2 Laboratory preparation of chlorine

Chlorine is prepared in the laboratory by the reaction of concentrated hydrochloric acid with potassium permanganate (potassium manganate VII). The potassium permanganate (potassium manganate VII), being an oxidising agent, removes electrons from chloride ions to give chlorine atoms which then combine to form chlorine molecules.

$$2Cl^- - 2e \rightarrow 2Cl \rightarrow Cl_{2(g)}$$

The gas is prepared using the apparatus shown in *Fig. 13.2.*

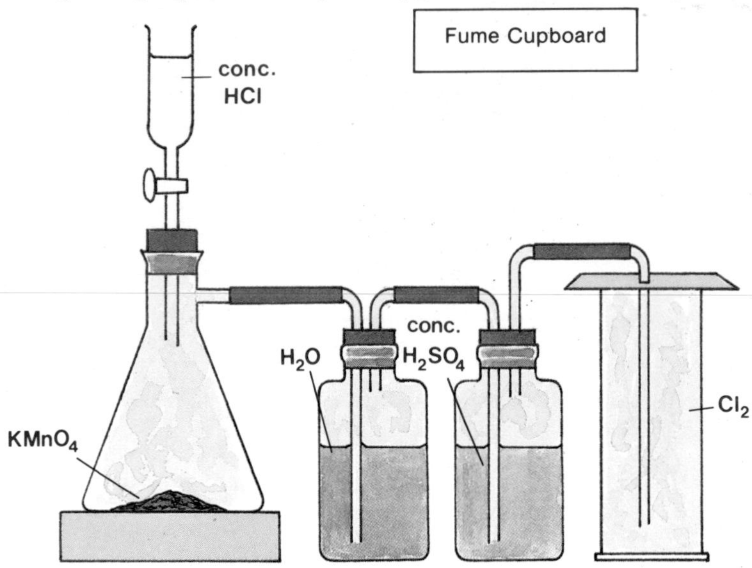

Fig. 13.2 The laboratory preparation of chlorine

Note that the chlorine is passed through water to remove HCl gas and through concentrated sulphuric acid to remove water vapour. The chemical equation for the preparation is:

$$2KMnO_{4(s)} + 16HCl_{(aq)} \rightarrow 2KCl_{(aq)} + 2MnCl_{2(aq)} + 8H_{2(l)}O + 5Cl_{2(g)}$$

(You are not expected to learn off this balanced equation).

WARNING: Since chlorine is a very poisonous gas its preparation should be carried out in a fume cupboard.

13.3 Properties of Chlorine

1. Chlorine is a **greenish-yellow gas** which is **heavier than air** and has a **choking smell.**
2. **Chlorine is fairly soluble in water**: When chlorine is bubbled into water a solution called "chlorine water" is obtained. The chlorine dissolves in the water and reacts with it to form two acids, HCl and HOCl (hypochlorous acid).
3. **Chlorine is a bleaching agent**: If a piece of damp grass is placed in a gas jar of chlorine it is found that it quickly turns white, *Fig. 13.3.* A similar reaction occurs with a piece of damp litmus paper.

Fig. 13.3 Chlorine does not burn but some substances burn in it

(a) **Chlorine reacts with practically all metals to form salts.**

$$\text{e.g. } 2Na_{(s)} + Cl_{2(g)} \rightarrow 2NaCl_{(s)}$$

(b) **Chlorine reacts with many non-metals.**
Phosphorus burns in chlorine to form white clouds of phosphorus pentachloride (phosphorus V chloride).

$$2P_{(s)} + 5Cl_{2(g)} \rightarrow 2PCl_{5(s)}$$

Also hydrogen reacts with chlorine to form hydrogen chloride.

$$H_{2(g)} + Cl_{2(g)} \rightarrow 2HCl_{(g)}$$

This reaction is explosive in the presence of sunlight.

5. **Chlorine is a very good oxidising agent** i.e. it has a great tendency to remove electrons from other substances.

$$Cl_2 + 2e \rightarrow 2Cl^-$$

This may easily be demonstrated by bubbling some chlorine through a solution of potassium iodide or potassium bromide, *Fig. 13.4.*

$$Cl_{2(g)} + 2KI_{(aq)} \rightarrow I_{2(s)} + 2KCl_{(aq)}$$

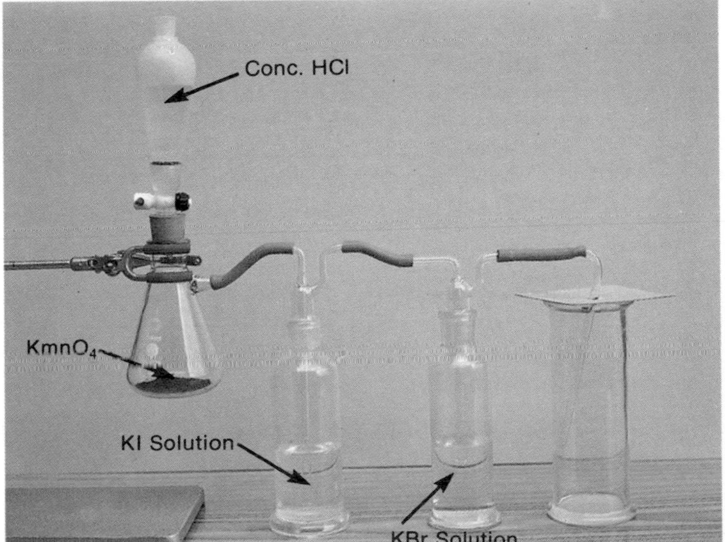

Fig. 13.4 The chlorine gas oxidises the I^- ions (colourless) to I_2 (dark brown/black) and the Br^- ions (colourless) to Br_2 (red)

The main properties of chlorine are summarised in *Table 13.1.*

Table 13.1 The Properties of Chlorine

Physical properties	*Chemical Properties*
1. Greenish-yellow gas with choking smell.	1. Does not burn but some substances burn in it.
2. Heavier than air. The density of chlorine is about 2.5 times that of air.	2. Very good oxidising agent.
3. Fairly soluble in water	3. Bleaches damp materials such as grass and litmus paper.

13.4 Uses of Chlorine

1. **Bleaching agent**: commercial bleaching solutions (e.g. *Parazone, Domestos,* etc.) contain chlorine in the form of NaOCl (sodium hypochlorite), *Fig. 13.5.*

Fig. 13.5 Chlorine is used in manufacturing bleaching agents and disinfectants

2. **Germicide**: A small quantity of chlorine is sufficient to kill almost all bacteria. Hence chlorine is put into swimming pools and into drinking water. Also, chlorine is used in the manufacture of antiseptics and sterilising fluids (e.g *Dettol, TCP. New Born, Milton,* etc.) insecticides and weedkillers (e.g. *Paraquat*).
3. **Manufacture of chemicals**: chlorine is mainly used in the production of a wide range of chemicals (e.g. hydrochloric acid, PVC (polyvinyl chloride), solvents for dry cleaning, anaesthetics, aerosol propellants, etc.).

Summary

* Chlorine is prepared in the laboratory by the reaction between concentrated hydrochloric acid and potassium permanganate (potassium manganate VII).
* Chlorine is passed through water to remove HCl gas and through concentrated sulphuric acid to remove water vapour.
* Chlorine gas has a greenish-yellow colour, a choking smell and is heavier than air. It is highly poisonous.
* Chlorine reacts with metals and non-metals.
* Chlorine is a very good oxidising agent.
* Chlorine is used as a bleach, as a germicide and in the manufacture of chemicals.

Questions

Section A

1. The elements of Group VII are commonly called the ....
2. One of the elements of Group VII is a dark red liquid. This element is called ....
3. X is a dark grey element which sublimes when heated. Name X. ....
4. Name two elements of Group VII which are gases at room temperature..............................
5. "Tincture of iodine" is a solution of iodine in ....
6. Chlorine gas may be prepared by dropping concentrated .... on to crystals of..........
7. X is a gaseous element. It reacts with hydrogen to produce another gas which dissolves in water to give the acid found in gastric juice (the digestive juice in the stomach). Name X ....
8. In the laboratory preparation of chlorine the gas is bubbled through water in order to remove ....
9. Give two uses of chlorine (i) .... (ii) ....
10. A moist red rose petal is placed in chlorine gas. What would you expect to observe?.......................

Section B

1. Chlorine, bromine and iodine from part of the same family of elements. What is this family called? Describe the physical appearance of each of these elements. Indicate how one of these elements will react with (a) a metal and (b) a non-metal. Describe in each case how the bond is formed and name the type of bond.

2. Draw a labelled diagram to show how you would prepare and collect dry chlorine. Mention any precautions which you would take when preparing this gas.
List three physical and three chemical properties of chlorine. Why is chlorine added to drinking water? Give one other use of chlorine.

---

14 — Thermochemistry

14.1 Exothermic and Endothermic Reactions

Thermochemistry is a branch of chemistry which studies the heat changes during chemical reactions. Nearly all chemical reactions involve heat being given out or taken in.

(**Note**: "ex" means "out" as in "exit".)

An exothermic reaction is one that gives out heat.

There are many examples of exothermic reactions. All reactions which involve the burning of fuel are exothermic, *Fig. 14.1.* We have met many examples of exothermic reactions in our study of chemistry. When a piece of sodium is added to water, heat is produced by the reaction and this heat melts the piece of sodium. How many other examples of exothermic reactions can you remember? *(See Chapter 5)*

Fig. 14.1 The burning of coal is an exothermic reaction

Instead of giving out heat, some chemical reactions can take in heat. Reactions of this type are called **endothermic reactions.**

An endothermic reaction is one that takes in heat.

An example of an endothermic process is dissolving ammonium nitrate in water, *Fig. 14.2.*

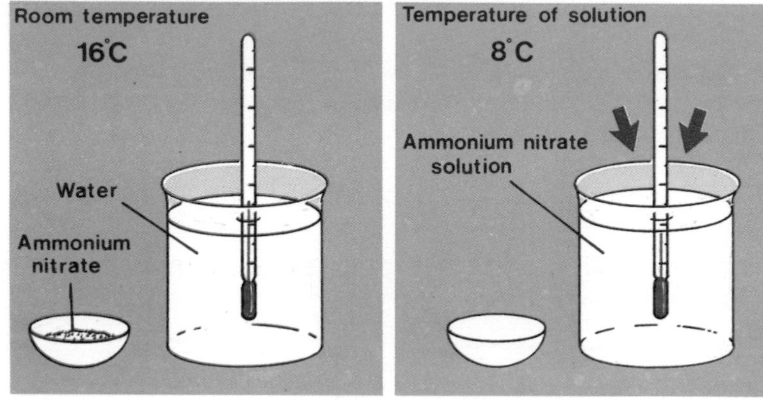

Fig. 14.2 When ammonium nitrate is added to water the temperature of the solution drops. Heat is taken in from the room as the solution warms up

14.2 Heat of Reaction

In order to indicate whether a reaction is exothermic or endothermic we use the symbol ΔH (pronounced "delta H"). ΔH is commonly referred to as the change of heat content or energy change of the reaction. ΔH is the heat given out or taken in during a reaction.

For an exothermic reaction Δ H is given a negative sign. For an endothermic reaction Δ H is given a positive sign.

Examples

(a) $CH_4 + 2O_2 \rightarrow CO_2 + 2H_2O$ $\Delta H = {}^{-}895$ kilojoules.

The negative sign of Δ H indicates that the burning of methane is an exothermic reaction. The 895 kilojoules is the heat obtained from burning 16 g (1 mole) of methane.

(b) $H_2O \rightarrow H_2 + 1/2\, O_2$ $\Delta H = +286$ kilojoules.

The positive sign of Δ H indicates that the conversion of water to hydrogen and oxygen is endothermic. The 286 kilojoules is the heat required to decompose 18 g (1 mole) of water into hydrogen and oxygen.

Note: A **mole** of a substance may be taken as its atomic mass or its molecular mass expressed in grams.

e.g. Atomic mass of carbon = 12

1 mole of carbon = 12 grams.

Molecular mass of water = 18 (O = 12; H = 1)

1 mole of water = 18 grams.

The idea of the mole is used in defining two particular types of heats of reaction. The use of the joule will be found in *(Chapter 30 and the use of kilojoule in Chapter 43)*

Heat of Solution

Heat of solution is the heat given out or taken in when one mole of a substance dissolves in water.

For example, when 1 mole of sodium chloride (23 + 35.5 = 58.5 grams) is dissolved in water 3.9 kilojoules of heat are absorbed. Therefore, the heat of solution of sodium chloride is 3.9 kilojoules/mole.

Heat of Neutralisation

Heat of neutralisation is the heat produced when an acid and a base react to produce one mole of water.

For example, if sufficient hydrochloric acid is mixed with sufficient NaOH to produce one mole of water, it is found that 57 kilojoules of heat are given out, *Fig. 14.3.*

Fig. 14.3

$HCl + NaOH \rightarrow BaCk + H_2O\ \Delta = {}^{-}57$ kilojoules.
The heat given out in this reaction is called the heat of neutralisation.

Thus, the heat of neutralisation of hydrochloric acid by sodium hydroxe is 57 kilojoules.

Summary

* An exothermic reaction is one that gives out heat.
* An endothermic reaction is one that takes in heat.

Remember: **Ex**it is for going out
Entrance is for coming in.

* ΔH is the heat given out or taken in during a reaction.
* For an exothermic reaction, ΔH is given a negative sign.
* For an endothermic reaction, ΔH is given a positive sign.
* Heat of solution is the heat given out or taken in when one mole of a substance dissolves in water.
* Heat of neutralisation is the heat produced when an acid and a base react to produce one mole of water.

Questions

Section A

1. A reaction which gives out heat is called ....
2. A reaction which takes in heat is called ....
3. An example of a reaction which takes in heat is ....
4. The symbol ΔH represents ....
5. For an exothermic reaction ΔH is given a .... sign.
6. Indicate whether the following reactions are exothermic or endothermic.

(a) $2H_2 + O_2 \rightarrow 2H_2O$ $\quad \Delta H = +573$ kJ.
(b) $CuSO_4.5H_2O \rightarrow CuSo_4 + 5H_2O$ $\quad \Delta H = 1508$ kJ.
(c) $S + O_2 \rightarrow SO_2$ $\quad \Delta H = -297$ kJ.

7. A mole of a substance may be described as ....
8. Neutralisation reactions are exothermic. True or False?
9. Heat of solution is defined as ....
10. Heat of neutralisation is defined as ....

Section B

1. Explain what is meant by the terms exothermic and endothermic. Give one example of an exothermic reaction and one example of an endothermic reaction. What is the significance of the symbol ΔH?
"The heat of solution of ammonium chloride is 15 kJ".
What does this statement mean?

Appendix: Summary of Gas Preparations and Properties

HYDROGEN	OXYGEN	CARBON DIOXIDE
Labelled Diagram dilute H_2SO_4 H_2 Water Zinc	**Labelled Diagram** Hydrogen peroxide O_2 Water Manganese dioxide	**Labelled Diagram** dilute HCl Cardboard CO_2 Marble chips Calcium chloride – to dry gas
Balanced Equation $Zn_{(s)} + H_2SO_{4(aq)} \rightarrow ZnSO_{4(aq)} + H_{2(g)}$	**Balanced Equation** $2H_2O_{2(aq)} \rightarrow 2H_2O_{(l)} + O_{2(g)}$	**Balanced Equation** $CaCO_{3(s)} = 2HCl_{(aq)} \rightarrow CaCl_{2(aq)} + H_2O_{(l)} + CO_{2(g)}$
Physical Properties 1. Colourless, odourless, tasteless gass. 2. Insoluble in water. 3. Lightest gas known.	**Physical Properties** 1. Colourless, odourless, tasteless gas. 2. Slightly soluble in water. 3. Slightly heavier than air.	**Physical Properties** 1. Colourless, odourless, tasteless gas. 2. Slightly soluble in water. 3. Heavier than air.
Chemical Properties 1. Burns in oxygen to form water. 2. Removes the oxygen from copper oxide. 3. No effect on litmus.	**Chemical Properties** 1. Supports combustion. 2. Reacts with most elements to form oxides. 3. No effect on litmus.	**Chemical Properties** 1. Does not support combustion. 2. Forms acidic solution. 3. Turns limewater milky.

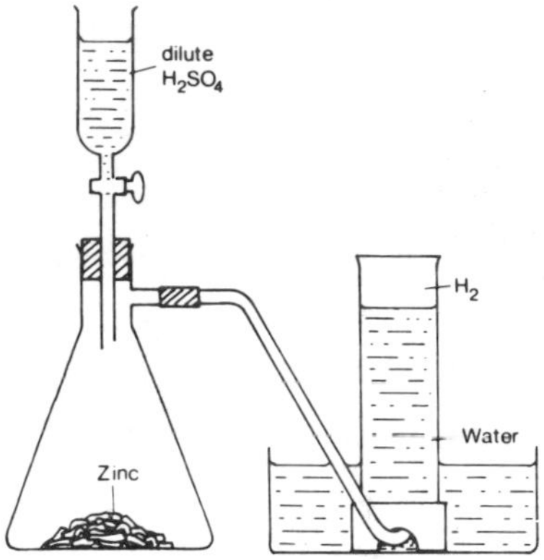

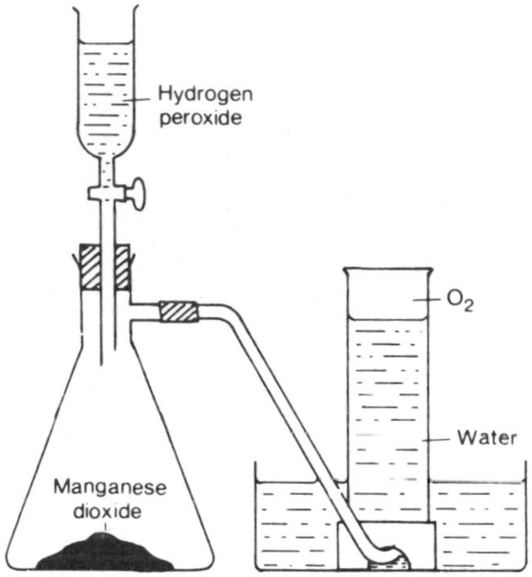

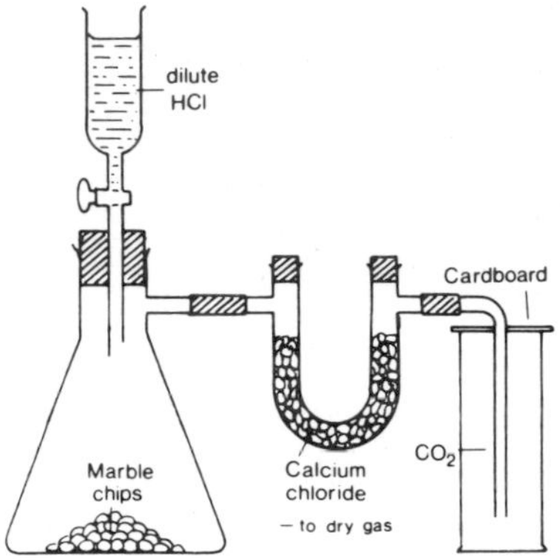

Appendix: Summary of Gas Preparations and Properties

CHLORINE

Labelled Diagram

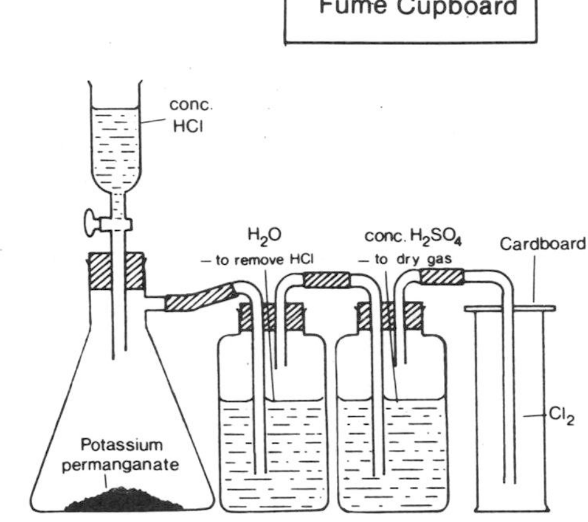

Balanced Equation

$$2KMnO_{4(s)} + 16HCl_{(aq)} + 2MnCl_{2(aq)} + 8H_3O_{(l)} + 5Cl_{2(g)}$$

Physical Properties

1. Greenish yellow gas with choking smell.
2. Fairly soluble in water.
3. Heavier than air.

Chemical Properties

1. Does not burn but some substances burn in it.
2. Good oxidising agent.
3. Bleaches damp materials, e.g. grass.

SULPHUR DIOXIDE

Labelled Diagram

(Heat may be necessary)

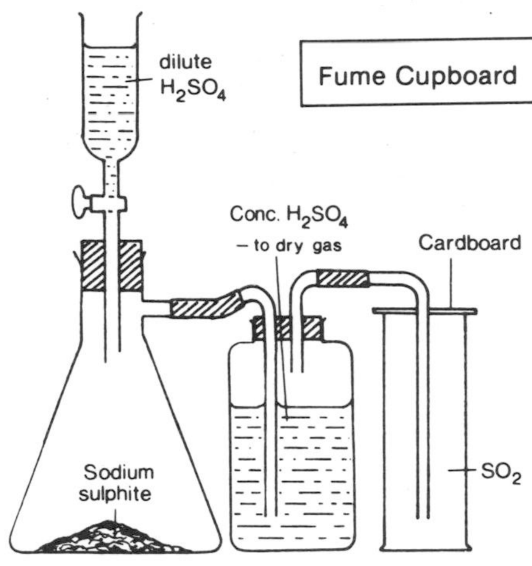

Balanced Equation

$$H_2SO_{4(aq)}\ Na_2SO_{3(s)} \rightarrow Na_2SO_{4(aq)}\ H_2O_{(l)} + SO_{2(g)}$$

or

$$Cu + 2H_2SO_4 \rightarrow SO_2 + CuSO_4 + 2H_2O$$

Physical Properties

1. Colourless, poisonous gas with choking smell.
2. Very soluble in water.
3. Heavier than air.

Chemical Properties

1. Does not support combustion.
2. Forms acidic solution when dissolved in water.
3. Good reducing agent.
4. Bleaches damp materials, e.g. wool, paper, etc.

AMMONIA

Labelled Diagram

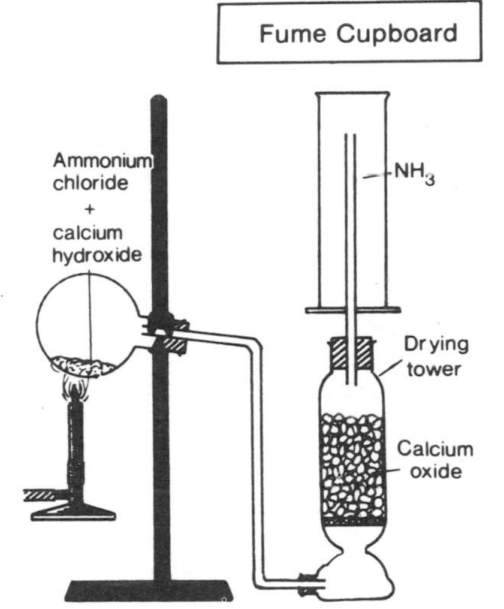

Balanced Equation

$$2NH_4Cl_{(s)} + Ca(OH)_{2(s)} \rightarrow 2NH_{3(g)} + CaCl_{2(s)} + 2H_2O_{(l)}$$

Physical Properties

1. Colourless gas with choking smell.
2. Very soluble in water.
3. Lighter than air.

Chemical Properties

1. Does not support combustion.
2. Forms alkaline solution when dissolved in water.

15 — Calculations in Chemistry

When an object is measured a standard is used as a comparison, for example if length is measured the standard is the metre and the length of the object is compared to the metre. In the same way the mass of an atom of the carbon – 12 isotope is used as the standard unit of mass on the atomic scale. It has a mass of 12 and all other atoms of elements are compared to it. Therefore the mass is known as the **Relative Atomic Mass** often abbreviated to R.A.M. or A_r. Relative Atomic Mass has **no units** because it is a ratio of two masses. *(see Chapter 1).*

Relative Molecular Mass (R.M.M.)

A molecule consists of a number of atoms joined together. The relative molecular mass can be found by adding together the relative atomic masses of all the atoms present.

Example

The formula of water is H_2O

2 atoms of hydrogen (R.A.M. = 1) = 2 x 1 = 2
1 atom of oxygen (R.A.M. = 16) = 1 x 16 = 16
Relative Molecular Mass = 18

Relative Formula Mass

Many compounds are made up of ions not molecules. For example it would not be correct to refer to a molecule of sodium chloride. For compounds made up of ions **formula unit** is used to describe the ions joined together to make the compound. The term relative formula mass is used for ionic compounds.

Relative formula mass is found by adding up the relative atomic masses of the elements in a compound.

Example 1

Find the relative formula mass of sodium chloride NaCl given R.A.M. sodium = 23, chlorine = 35.5.

Formula = NaCl
1 atom of Na = 1 x 23 = 23
1 atom of chlorine = 1 x 35.5 = 35.5
Total = 58.5

Relative formula mass of sodium chloride = 58.5

Example 2

Find the relative formula mass of magnesium hydroxide $Mg(OH)_2$, given R.A.M. magnesium = 24, oxygen = 16, Hydrogen = 1.

Formula is $Mg(OH)_2$
1 atom of magnesium = 1 x 24 = 24
2 atoms of oxygen = 2 x 16 = 32
2 atoms of hydrogen = 2 x 1 = 2
Total = 58

Relative formula mass of $Mg(OH)_2$ = 58.

Remember if atoms are in brackets, all the atoms are multiplied by the number outside the brackets.

Example 3

Find the relative formula mass of magnesium nitrate, $Mg(NO_3)_2$ given R.A.M. magnesium = 24, nitrogen = 14, oxygen = 16.

Formula is $Mg(NO_3)_2$
1 atom of magesium = 1 x 24 = 24
2 atoms of nitrogen = 2 x 14 = 28
6 atoms of oxygen = 6 x 16 = 96
Total = 148

Percentage Composition

If the formula of a compound is known the percentage by mass of each element in a compound can be found.

$$\text{Percentage of an element} = \frac{\text{R.A.M. of the element X number of atoms of that element}}{\text{R.M.M. of the compound}} \times 100$$

Example

Find the percentage of carbon in methane (CH_4) given R.A.M. carbon = 12, hydrogen = 1.

Formula is CH_4

Relative molecular mass is:—

1 atom of carbon = 1 x 12 = 12
4 atoms of hydrogen = 4 x 1 = 4
Total = 16

R.M.M. = 16

Percentage of carbon = $^{12}/_{16}$ x 100 = 75%

Summary

* The standard unit of mass on the atomic scale is the carbon – 12 isotope.
* Relative Atomic mass is often abbreviated to R.A.M. or A_r.
* Relative Molecular mass is the sum of all the relative atomic masses in a compound.
* Relative Formula mass is the mass of a unit of an ionic compound.

Questions

1. Find the relative formula masses of each of the following compounds. The relative atomic masses are given at the end of the question.

   (a) Carbon dioxide CO_2
   (b) Sulphur dioxide SO_2
   (c) Ammonia NH_3
   (d) Copper II sulphate $Cu\ SO_4$
   (e) Magnesium carbonate $Mg\ CO_3$
   (f) Calcium chloride $Ca\ Cl_2$
   (g) Zinc hydroxide $Zn(OH)_2$

   Given R.A.M. C = 12, N = 14, H = 1, 0 = 16, S = 32, Cu = 64, Mg = 24, Ca = 40, Cl = 35.5, Zn = 65.

2. Find the percentages by mass of:—

   (a) carbon and oxygen in carbon dioxide CO_2
   (b) sulphur and oxygen in sulphur trioxide SO_3
   (c) sodium and hydrogen in sodium hydroxide NaOH
   (d) magnesium and nitrogen in magnesium nitride Mg_3N_2
   (e) hydrogen and fluorine in hydrogen fluoride HF

   Given R.A.M. C = 12, 0 = 16, S = 32, Na = 23, H = 1, N = 14, Mg = 24, F = 19.

16 — Food Types

In *Chapter 8, Book 1* we learned that all living things need food to give them energy. Food is also needed for growth, to repair worn out or damaged parts and to help protect against disease.

The main types of food are grouped together according to the type and arrangement of the chemicals they are made up of. The **five** major groups of food (nutrients) are **carbohydrates, fats, proteins, vitamins** and **minerals**. We need to eat the right amounts of these nutrients regularly in order to stay alive and healthy.

In addition to the foods named above, we also need **water** and **fibre (roughage)** as part of our diet.

16.1 Carbohydrates

Carbohydrates are also known as the 'sugary and starchy' foods and are the main source of energy in the body. Carbohydrates contain the elements carbon, hydrogen and oxygen. They consist of single sugar units, such as glucose which join together to form long chains, *Fig. 16.2.*

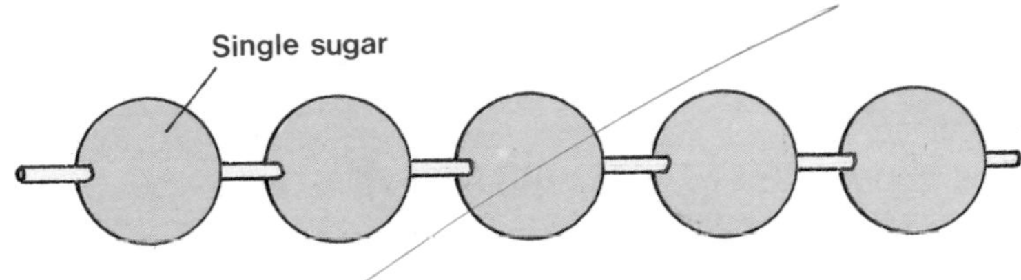

Fig. 16.2 Structure of carbohydrates.

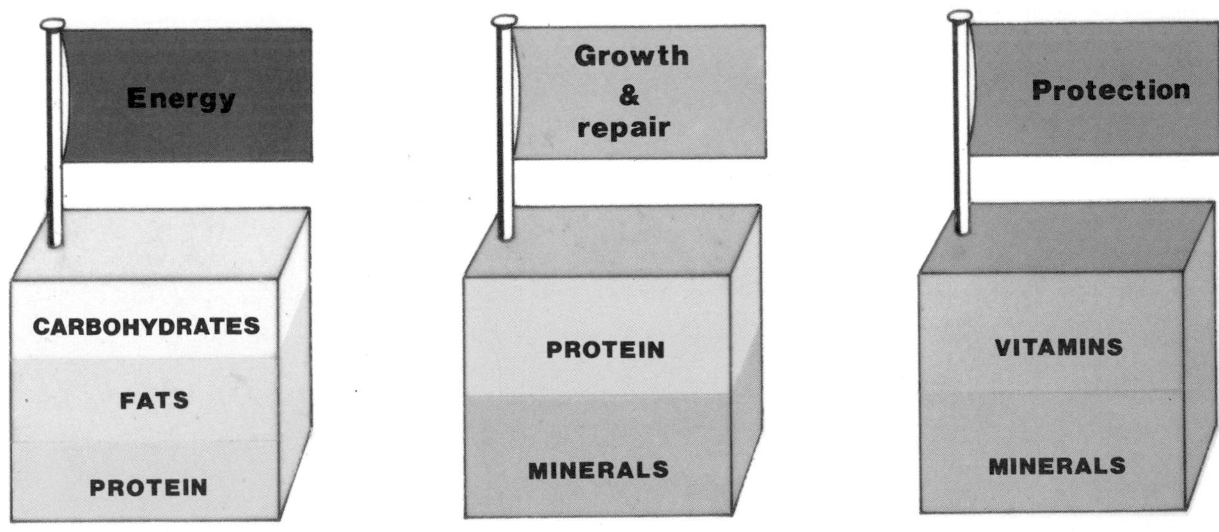

Fig. 16.1 Functions of the food.

Sources of Carbohydrates

Starch is found as the store of carbohydrate in most plants, so starchy foods include potatoes, flour and rice. **Sugar**-rich foods include jam, honey and table sugar. When we eat sugars and starches they are broken down (digested) into glucose. **Glucose** is the type of carbohydrate which is absorbed into the bloodstream.

Fig. 16.3 Sources of starch

Fig. 16.4 Sources of sugars

16.2 Fats

Fats contain the elements carbon, hydrogen and oxygen. Fats are made up of fatty acids and glycerol, *Fig. 16.5.*

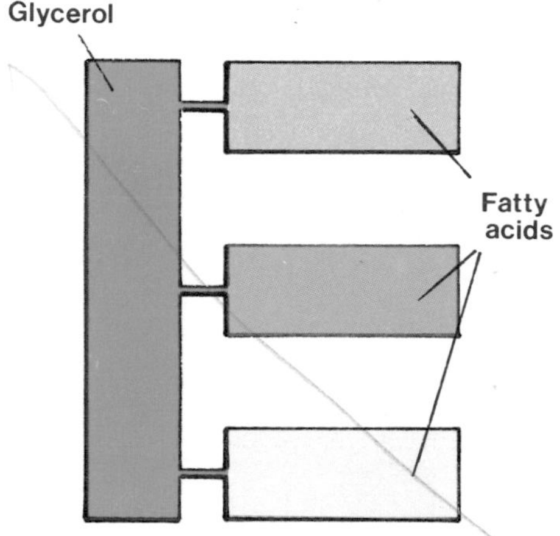

Fig. 16.5 Structure of fats

Sources of Fats

Fats can be found as liquids, e.g. sunflower oil, olive oil, or as solids, e.g. butter, margarine, suet.

Functions of Fats

1. Fats are a very important source of energy in the body.
2. Fats are made in the body and stored under the skin where they act as an insulating layer which helps to keep the body warm.
3. A layer of fat surrounds and protects the delicate organs of the body, e.g. heart, kidney.

But a word of warning! Too much fat in the diet can lead to obesity (being very overweight). People who are overweight run a high risk of suffering from heart attacks and other illnesses.

16.3 Protein

Proteins contain the elements carbon, hydrogen, oxygen and nitrogen. They differ from carbohydrates and fats in that they contain the element **nitrogen**. Proteins are made up of units called amino acids. Many amino acids join together in long chains to make protein molecules. There can be hundreds of amino acid molecules in a single protein molecule, *Fig. 16.6.*

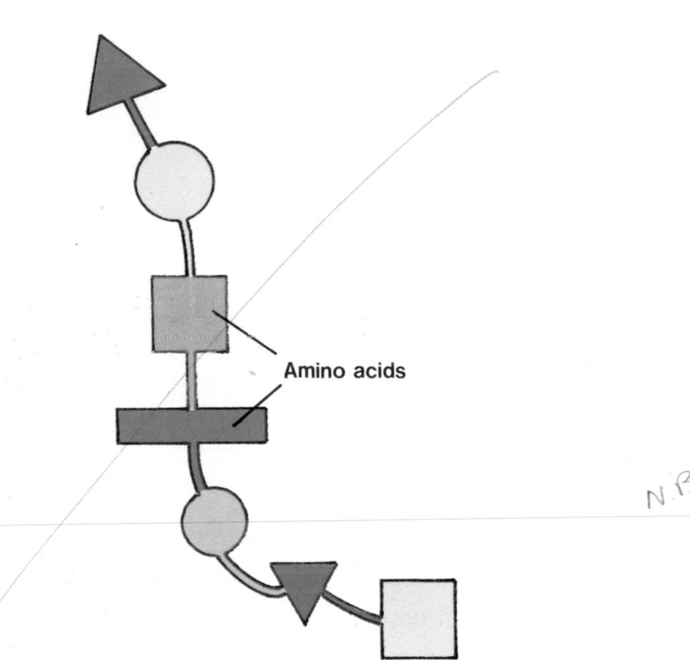

Fig. 16.6 Structure of proteins

Sources of Protein

Protein is found in lean meat, fish, egg(white) and milk. Protein is also found in plants such as peas, beans and nuts.

The main function of protein in the body is for growth and repair of damaged cells. For this reason protein is also known as the body-building food. Protein can provide a source of energy for the body but will only do so if no more is needed for body-building.

16.4 Vitamins

Vitamins are chemicals which the body requires for growth and to protect against diseases. Although vital for life, vitamins are only needed in tiny amounts.

Table 16.1 Vitamins

Vitamin	*Source*	*Function*	*Result of Deficiency*
A	Fish-liver oils, green vegetables, carrots.	Needed for healthy eyes.	Night blindness, poor skin.
B	Yeast, wholemeal bread	Controls the release of energy from food	Beri-beri, (disorder of the nervous system, wasting of muscles, weakness).
C	Citrus fruits, blackcurrants.	Needed for healthy gums.	Scurvy (bleeding of the mouth and gums).
D	Cod-liver oil, sunshine.	Needed for healthy bones and teeth.	Rickets (bones do not form properly).
K	Green vegetables, made by bacteria living in the human intestine	Needed for the clotting of blood.	Wounds heal very slowly.

16.5 Minerals

Minerals are chemicals which we need in small amounts for a variety of purposes.

Table 16.2 Minerals

Name	*Symbol*	*Good Source*	*Use*
Chlorine	Cl	Table salt (NaCl)	As part of stomach acid.
Sodium	Na	Table salt (NaCl)	Transport of messages along nerves.
Iron	Fe	Liver	Formation of the red blood pigment (haemoglobin).
Calcium	Ca	Milk, cheese	Formation of bones and teeth.
Phosphorus	P	Cheese	Formation of bones and teeth.
Potassium	K	Meat	Transport of messages along nerves.

16.6 Water

Although water itself has no nutritional value, it is vital for life. More than 70% of our body is made up of water and most of this is found as cytoplasm in our cells, and in our blood. The main functions of water are:—

1. To act as a medium in which the chemical reactions within the cells take place.
2. To help transport substances, because they dissolve so easily in water.
3. To help control body temperature by evaporation from skin.

16.7 Fibre

Dietary fibre used to be known as roughage. It is now realised that it plays an important part in our diet. It consists of plant cell material from foods such as wholemeal bread, vegetables and fruits. Fibre provides us with bulk, which assists our digestive system, and it is believed that a high fibre intake helps prevent a number of disorders of the digestive tract.

16.8 Balanced Diet

If our food provides us with all the carbohydrates, proteins, fats, minerals, vitamins, water and fibre that we need, we are said to have a balanced diet. This can easily be achieved by eating a mixture of the following foods:— wholemeal bread, fresh vegetables, fresh fruit, meat, fish, milk, cheese, eggs, etc.

Fig. 16.7 A balanced diet

16.9 Food Additives

Many foods are made more palatable or are preserved by the use of food additives. A large number of these are natural additives, such as vitamin C (E300), others are not naturally occuring substances, such as tartrazine (E102). Tartrazine is the yellow colouring, that is sometimes used in lemon squash, fizzy drinks, etc. As a result of unifying action by the European Economic Community, all food additives are to be given a number prefixed by the letter E.

Most additives are extremely useful, however, very occasionally a person may have an adverse reaction to a particular additive and it should be avoided.

16.10 Food Tests

Experiment 16.1 To Test for Starch

Iodine Test

Add **iodine solution** to a substance. If a **blue black colour** forms it means starch is present in the substance.

Method

1. Pour some starch solution into a test-tube to a depth of 2 cm.
2. Using a dropper, add 2-3 drops of iodine solution.
3. Gently shake the test-tube and note any colour change.
4. Record your result.
5. Repeat the test using milk, glucose solution and water instead of the starch solution.

Note: To test for starch, place a small bit of the solid, e.g. banana, on a dish and add 2-3 drops of iodine solution directly onto the surface of the solid.

Experiment 16.2 To Test for Sugars

Benedict's Test

Add **Benedict's Solution** (or Fehling's 1 + 2) to a substance, (e.g. glucose or maltose). Heat the mixture.

Result:	**Blue**	**Green**	**Orange/Red**
Conclusion:	No glucose	A little glucose	A lot of glucose

Method

1. Prepare a water bath.
2. Pour some glucose solution into a test-tube to a depth of 2 cm.
3. Pour some *Benedict's Solution* (or equal amounts of *Fehlings 1 + 2)* into a second test tube to a depth of 2 cm.
4. Add the *Benedict's Solution* to the glucose solution. Note the colour of the mixture.
5. Place the test tube in a beaker of boiling water (or a water bath at 100 °C) and leave for 3 minutes.
6. Remove the test-tube and note any colour change.
7. Record your result.
8. Repeat the test using milk, water or starch solution instead of the glucose solution.

Experiment 16.3 To Test for Protein

Biuret Test

Add **sodium hydroxide solution** to the substance.
Add **2-3 drops of copper sulphate solution**. If a **purple/violet** colour forms it means protein is present.

Method

1. Pour some milk into a test-tube to a depth of 2 cm.
2. Into another test-tube pour some dilute sodium hydroxide solution to a depth of 2 cm. **Care**: this solution is caustic. Add the milk solution to the sodium hydroxide solution and shake gently to mix the contents. Use a cork if necessary.
3. Add 3-4 drops of copper sulphate solution and shake the tube again.
4. Note any colour change and record the result.
5. Repeat the test using water, egg albumen, glucose solution or starch solution instead of the milk solution.

Experiment 16.4 To Test for Fats

Brown Paper Test

Rub the substance onto **brown paper**. Allow to dry. If a **translucent spot** appears it means the substance contains fat.

Method

1. Rub some margarine or butter on a piece of brown paper.

2. Put a drop of water onto a second piece of brown paper
3. Allow both to dry.
4. Compare the pieces of paper by holding them up to the light.
5. Record your result.
6. Repeat the test using glucose, starch or milk instead of the butter.

Experiment 16.5 To Show that Carbohydrates contain Carbon, Hydrogen and Oxygen

Method

1. Gently heat a small amount of sugar or glucose in a dry test-tube.
2. Continue heating for 2-3 minutes and notice the drops of liquid which form on the cool parts of the test-tube.
3. Test this liquid with a piece of blue cobalt chloride paper. The paper will turn pink, showing the presence of water. Water consists of the elements hydrogen and oxygen; therefore the carbohydrate must contain these elements.
4. Now look carefully at the substance which remains at the bottom of the test tube. This is carbon.

Experiment 16.6 To Show that Fats contain Carbon, Hydrogen and Oxygen

Method

1. Repeat the method as for carbohydrate testing above, using vegetable cooking oil instead of the sugar (or glucose).

Note: olive oil is not suitable, it spits violently when heated.

N.B. — test-tubes must be dry.

Experiment 16.7 To Show that Proteins contain Carbon, Hydrogen, Oxygen and Nitrogen

Note: Organic compounds containing nitrogen will give off ammonia gas when they are heated with soda lime. Ammonia gas is alkaline — it turns damp red litmus paper blue. *(See Chapter 12 — Ammonia)*

Method

1. Mix equal quantities of egg albumen and soda lime in a test-tube to a depth of about 1 cm.
2. Heat the mixture gently.
3. While still heating the test-tube, hold a piece of damp red litmus paper at the mouth of the test-tube. Note any colour change. If the litmus paper turns blue, it indicates the presence of ammonia gas, which has the formula NH_3.
4. Test the liquid which forms at the neck of the test-tube with blue cobalt chloride paper. If the paper turns pink this means that water (H_2O) is present.
5. The substance which remains at the bottom of the test-tube is carbon.

Summary

* Food is made up of chemicals called nutrients.
* A balanced diet consists of the following: carbohydrates, fats, proteins, vitamins, minerals, water and fibre.

Questions

Section A

1. Name three types of food (nutrient) commonly found in the diet. . . . .
2. Which of the following foods contain large amounts of fats or oils: jam, cake, lemons, margarine, carrots, suet, chocolate, olive oil, potatoes? . . . .

3. Name a vitamin found in:

   (a) liver ....

   (b) lemons and tangerines ....

   (c) wholemeal bread.................................

4. Roughage in the diet is not digested, but it is useful because (a) it supplies calcium; (b) it provides energy; (c) it helps prevent constipation; (d) it helps prevent scurvy ....

5. To test a substance for glucose you add .... to the mixture.

6. Name three minerals necessary for healthy growth.

   1..

   2..

   3..

7. Name a food which is rich in (a) starch...............

   (b) calcium ....

   (c) vitamin C ....

8. Name two uses our bodies make of the food we eat.

   1..

   2..

9. Which of the following mineral elements — Mg, Ca, Zn, Na, K, Fe is: (a) an important element in the composition of bone? ....

   (b) an important element in the composition of red blood cells? ....

10. Outline a simple test for the presence of water.........

    ....

11. Why is fibre a necessary part of our diet?

12. Name two food additives. State their function.

Section B

1. Milk is usually considered to be a complete food on its own. Name the types of nutrients you would expect to find in a completely balanced diet. Describe how you would show that a sample of milk contains protein.

2. Name three foods which an overweight person should avoid. List five mineral elements required by the body and for each one give a good source of the mineral in the diet.

3. Find out about the commercial production of milk or cheese. Write a short essay on your findings.

17 — Animal Nutrition

Animal nutrition involves four stages:

1. **Ingestion** — This is the taking in of food from outside the body. We ingest through the mouth.

2. **Digestion** — The pieces of food we eat are too big to pass into our bloodstream or our cells. For this reason we must digest (breakdown) the food into smaller soluble pieces. Digestion occurs in our **alimentary canal** or gut.

3. **Absorption** — Once the food has been made soluble, it can pass from the gut into the blood stream. This movement of food through the gut wall into the blood stream is called absorption.

4. **Assimilation** — This is the way in which the soluble food entering into the body cells is used for energy and for growth and repair.

5. A further process associated with nutrition is **egestion**. This is the name given to the process of removal of unused food, from the body, or defaecation.

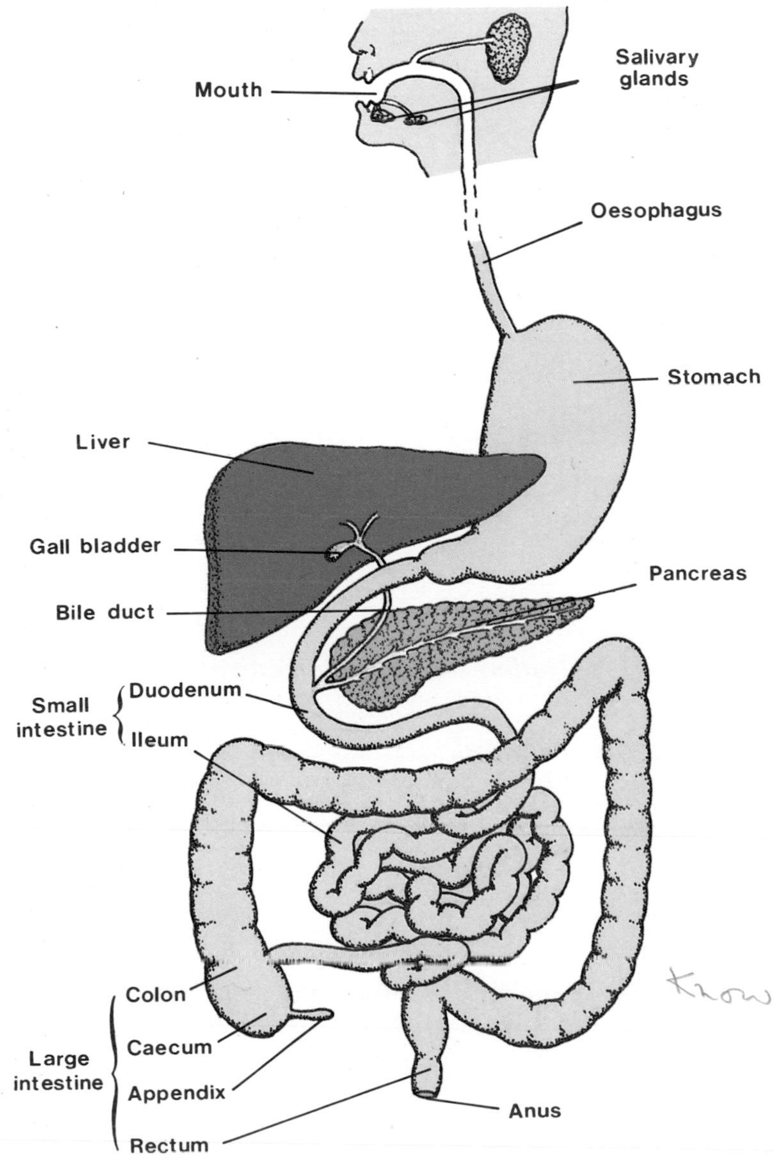

Fig. 17.1 The human digestive system

17.1 Digestion and Enzymes

The process of digestion involves the breakdown of large food molecules into their soluble components, e.g. proteins have to be digested into amino acids. To help this process, certain parts of the wall of the gut produce digestive juices which contain chemicals called **enzymes**. Enzymes are protein catalysts produced by living cells. They can help speed up a chemical reaction without themselves being changed by the reaction. In this way digestive enzymes enable the food we eat to be broken down intro soluble form faster than would otherwise be possible.

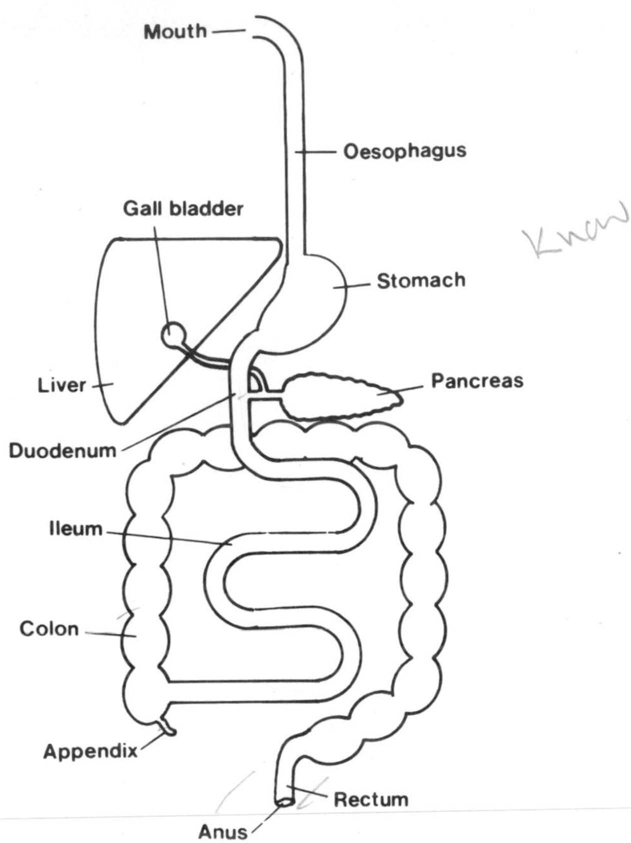

Fig. 17.2 Outline drawing of digestive system

The Alimentary Canal

The human alimentary canal, *Fig. 17.1*, is a long tube (approximately 10 metres) most of which is coiled to fit inside the body.

The Mouth

Digestion begins in the mouth. Firstly the teeth break up the food into smaller pieces (physical digestion).

Secondly saliva pours onto the food from the salivary glands (chemical digestion).

Saliva contains an enzyme called **salivary amylase** (ptyalin). Salivary amylase converts cooked starch (carbohydrate) to maltose. When the food is swallowed it passes down the oesophagus (food pipe) into the stomach. The food does not fall down to the stomach. It is actually pushed by waves of muscular contraction of the gut wall — **peristalsis.**

Experiment 17.1 To Show the Activity of the Enzyme Salivary Amylase

Method

1. Set up a water bath and heat the water to 37 °C (body temperature).
2. Label five test-tubes — A, B, C, D and E.
3. Collect saliva to a depth of 4 cm in tube E.
4. Pour starch solution to a depth of 2 cm in each of tubes A, B, and C or D.
5. Pour half the saliva collected into each of tubes B and C.
6. Shake the tubes to mix the contents.
7. Place all the tubes into the water bath at 37 ° C for 5 minutes.
8. Meanwhile copy *Table 17.1* into your class notebook.
9. After the 5 minutes, remove the tubes and then turn up the gas to get the water bath boiling.
10. Add 3 drops of iodine solution to tubes A and B. Note and record, in the table, any colour change.
11. Add 2 cm depth of *Benedict's Solution* (or equal volumes of *Fehling's 1 & 2)* to tubes C and D.
12. Place tubes C and D into the boiling water bath for 3 minutes.
13. Compare the colours which form and complete the table of results.

Table 17.1

Tube	*Contents*	*Tested with*	*Conclusion*
A			
B			
C			
D			

Answer the following questions:

1. Describe what happens when iodine solution is added to starch solution (tube A).
2. What seems to have happened to the starch in test-tube B?
3. Why were all the tubes kept at 37 °C during the experiment?
4. What food(s) does *Benedict's Solution* (or *Fehling's 1 & 2)* test for?
5. What does your result of the Benedict's test on tube C tell you?
6. Summarise the effect of saliva on starch.

The Stomach

The stomach is a muscular bag in which the food remains for 3-4 hours. Cells in the wall of the stomach produce gastric juice which contains hydrochloric acid (HCl) (see *Chapter 5, Acids and Bases)* and the enzyme **pepsin**. The acid helps to kill any bacteria (germs) which may have been swallowed with the food. It also provides an acidic environment in which the enzyme **pepsin** works best. You will remember that proteins are made up of long chains of hundreds of **amino acid molecules**. Pepsin breaks down protein molecules not into individual amino acids but into larger fragments of protein called **peptides**. During its time in the stomach the food is churned and mixed to form a semi-solid liquid called **chyme**.

The Small Intestine

When the chyme (food) passes from the stomach to the duodenum, it combines with secretions from the gall bladder and pancreas. Bile is made in the liver and stored in the gall bladder. Bile breaks up fats into tiny droplets which enables them to be more easily digested. Bile also helps to neutralise the stomach acid. This is important since the enzymes in the small intestine can only work properly in an alkaline environment.

The pancreas secretes pancreatic juice which is alkaline and contains three enzymes:

(a) **Pancreatic amylase** which breaks down starch to maltose;
(b) **Lipase** which breaks down fats to fatty acids and glycerol;
(c) **Trypsin** which breaks down protein into large fragments called peptides.

The wall of the intestine also produces enzymes. These include erepsin which converts peptides to amino acids and maltase which converts maltose into glucose. All the large food molecules (except cellulose) have now been digested. *See Table 17.3.*

Table 17.2

Food	*Final product of digestion*
Carbohydrate	glucose
Fat	fatty acids and glycerol
Protein	amino acids

Vitamins and minerals and the molecules of which water and alcohol are composed are small enough and do not need to be broken down. The digested food substances are absorbed into the blood stream through the wall of the **ileum.** *See below*. What remains is water and the undigested food, such as cellulose. This is pushed into the large intestine by peristalsis. It is very important that we include sufficient fibre or roughage in our diet. Fibre provides bulk which enables the muscles in the gut wall to function properly.

The Large Intestine

The main function of the large intestine is to reabsorb water into the bloodstream. This prevents the body becoming dehydrated. The solid waste material (faeces) which remains passes into the **rectum**, where it is stored before being released from the body through the **anus**.

Absorption

Absorption is the movement of digested and other soluble food through the gut wall into the bloodstream. Absorption mainly takes place in the **ileum**. The inner lining of the ileum wall is covered by millions of tiny finger-like projections called **villi**, *Fig. 17.3.* The villi greatly increase the surface area for absorption of digested food products.

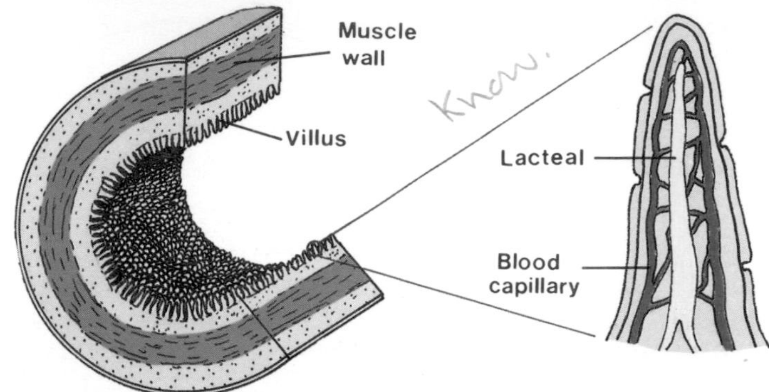

Fig. 17.3 Section of small intestine wall. A single villus.

Each villus consists of a network of **blood capillaries** surrounding a central blind-ending tube called a **lacteal**. Glucose, amino acids, minerals, vitamins and water pass from the ileum into the blood capillaries, and are then carried to the liver. Fatty acids and glycerol move into the lacteals and are carried away in the lymph vessels. Later the digested fats pass into the blood stream.

Assimilation

The absorbed food is eventually brought by the bloodstream to the liver and from there is it sent via the blood to the cells of the body when required, *Fig. 17.4.*

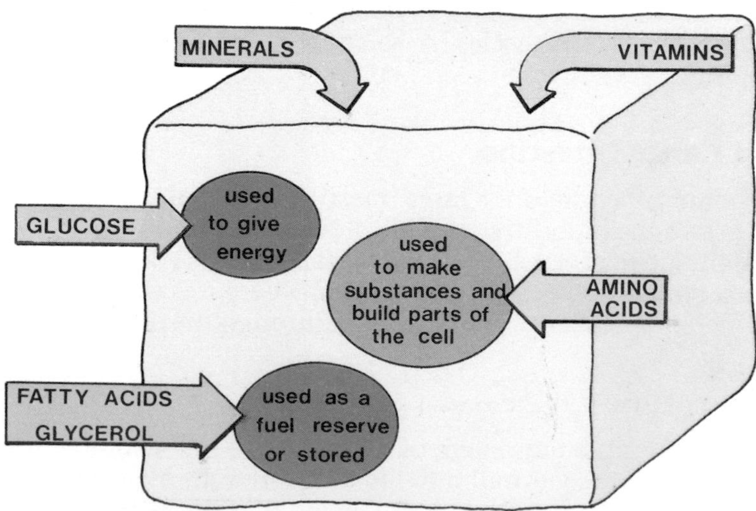

Fig. 17.4 Uses of food in cells.

Summary

* Food taken into the body (ingestion) must be broken down and made soluble (digestion) so that it can pass into the blood stream (absorption) and be taken to the body cells where it is either used or stored (assimilation). Unused food passes out of the body (egestion).
* Digestion takes place in our alimentary canal, *Table 17.4.*
* In the mouth there are four types of tooth: incisors, canines, premolars and molars. Each tooth-type has a particular function in helping to physically break up pieces of food into smaller pieces.
* *Table 17.3* shows the chemical digestion of food by ensymes in the different parts of the alimentary canal.
* Absorption of the digested food occurs in the ileum. The ileum is adapted for absorption because (a) it is very long and (b) the wall of the ileum is covered with villi which increase the area across which absorption can occur.

Table 17.3 Digestive Enzymes

Part of the Alimentary Canal	*Environ-ment Acid/alkaline*	*Enzyme*	*Food Sub-stance acted on*	*Products*
Mouth	Alkaline $pH>7$	Salivary Amylase	Starch	Maltose
Stomach	Acid $pH<7$	Pepsin	Protein	Peptides
Small Intestine	Alkaline			
Duode-num (enzymes secreted by the pancreas)	$pH>7$	Lipase Amylase Trypsin	Fats Starch Proteins & peptides	Fatty acids & Glycerol Maltose Amino acids
Ileum	Alkaline $pH>7$	Maltase Erepsin	Maltose Peptides	Glucose Amino acids

Table 17.4 Parts of the Alimentary Canal.

Region of the Alimentary Canal	*Function*
Mouth	1. Receives saliva. 2. Teeth break down food.
Oesophagus	Transports food to stomach by peristalsis.
Stomach	1. Adds pepsin. 2. Adds hydrochloric acid. 3. Churns and stores food. 4. Absorbs alcohol.
Duodenum	1. Receives bile. 2. Receives pancreatic enzymes.
Ileum	1. Secretes digestive enzymes. 2. Absorbs the products of digestion.
Large Intestine	Absorbs water.
Rectum	Stores faeces which are then removed through the anus.

Questions

Section A

1. What is the function of the incisor teeth? . . . .
2. Digestion of starch begins in the . . . .
   Name the enzyme concerned. . . . .
3. What is peristalsis? . . . .
4. Why is digestion necessary? . . . .
   . . . .
5. Name two enzymes involved in the digestion of protein.
   1. . . . .
   2. . . . .
6. Fats are substances containing the elements . . . .
7. Most human digestive enzymes work best at: (a) 27 °C; (b) 37 °C; (c) 17 °C; (d) 47 °C. . . . .
   . . . .
8. Where in the digestive system is the pH less than 7? . . . .
9. What is the main function of the large intestine? . . . .
   . . . .
10. Amino acids are produced as a result of the breakdown of: (a) fats; (b) sugars; (c) proteins; (d) minerals. . . . . . .
    . . . .
11. What is the function of a villus? . . . .
12. Lipase is an enzyme produced in the . . . .
    It acts on . . . . in the . . . .
13. State one function of the liver. . . . .

Section B

1. Draw a large labelled diagram of the alimentary canal. Mark on your diagram the region(s) of the canal (a) which are acidic; (b) where proteins are digested; (c) where bile is made; (d) where faeces are stored.
2. What is an enzyme? Name an enzyme and describe an experiment to show how it works.
3. Define the terms digestion and absorption. Describe briefly what happens to some starch from the time it enters the mouth until it is absorbed in the small intestine.

18 — Teeth

When an animal eats, it first of all cuts the food into small pieces using its teeth. This is known as 'mechanical digestion'. A **herbivore** e.g. a rabbit, eats grass and leaves, and so it must have teeth suitable for chewing these things. A **carnivore** e.g. a dog, eats meat and so its teeth must be adapted for tearing at the food. We are **omnivores**, we eat both meat and vegetables, and so our teeth must combine the action of a herbivore and a carnivore.

Fig. 18.1 Herbivore

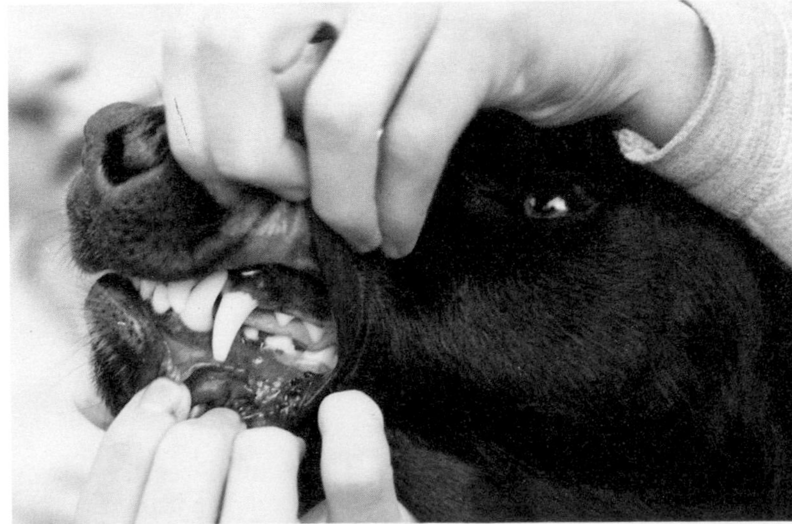

Fig. 18.2 Carnivore

18.1 Types of Teeth

There are four types of teeth, and each one has a slightly different function.

1. **Incisors** — these teeth are found at the front of the mouth, and are used for cutting and biting food. They are chisel-shaped and are sharp.

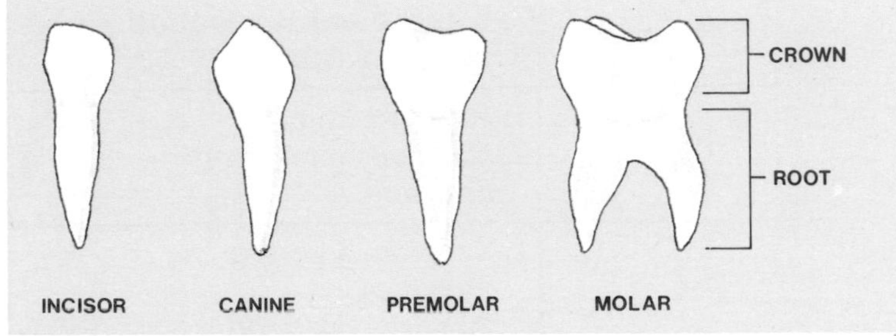

Fig. 18.3 Types of teeth

2. **Canines** — these are used for tearing and ripping food. They are very large in a dog, and can be seen easily. They have a pointed end, called a cusp, which helps them to sink deep into the food.
3. **Premolars** — these teeth have two cusps and are used partly to tear food and partly to grind food. They have one or two roots.
4. **Molars** — these are responsible for grinding and chewing food. For this reason they have four or five cusps, and they usually have two or three roots, e.g. the upper molars in man have three roots, whilst the lower molars have two roots.

18.2 Human Teeth

Man is an omnivore and so his teeth have developed to suit his mixed diet.

Infants begin their life feeding on milk, and so have no immediate need for teeth. Teeth begin to appear (although they have been growing without being seen), when a baby reaches about six months. The first set of teeth to develop are known as milk teeth. By the age of three, most children have a complete set of milk teeth.

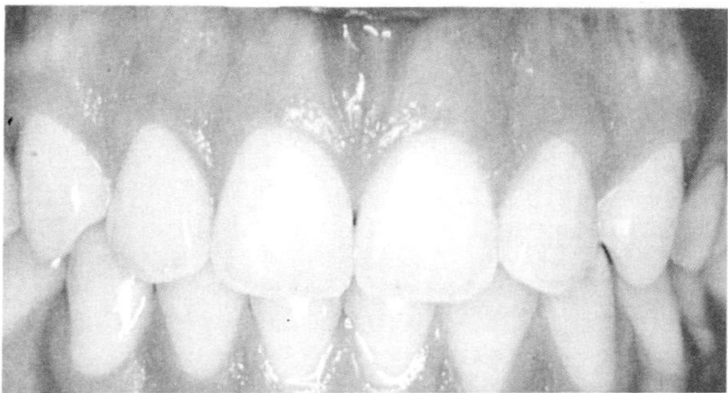

Fig. 18.4 Healthy teeth

These teeth are replaced by permanent teeth, which begin to appear at around the age of six. By the age of fourteen, twenty-eight permanent teeth should be present. Four more teeth, known as 'wisdom' teeth appear usually by the early twenties. When complete, a human will have four incisors, two canines, four premolars and six molars, in both his top jaw and his lower jaw.

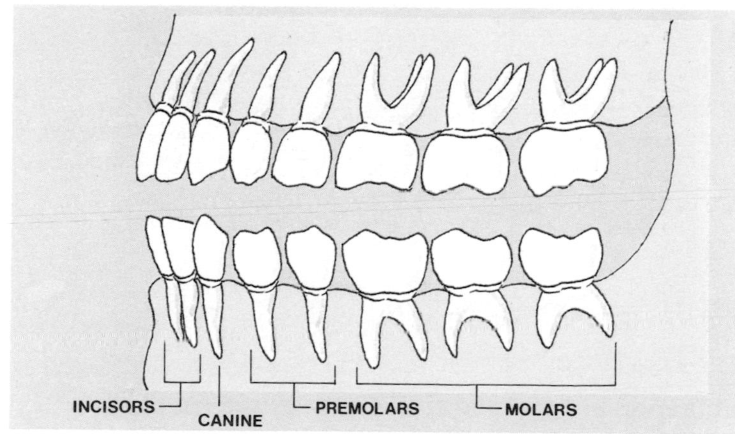

Fig. 18.5 A complete set of permanent teeth

18.3 Structure of a Tooth

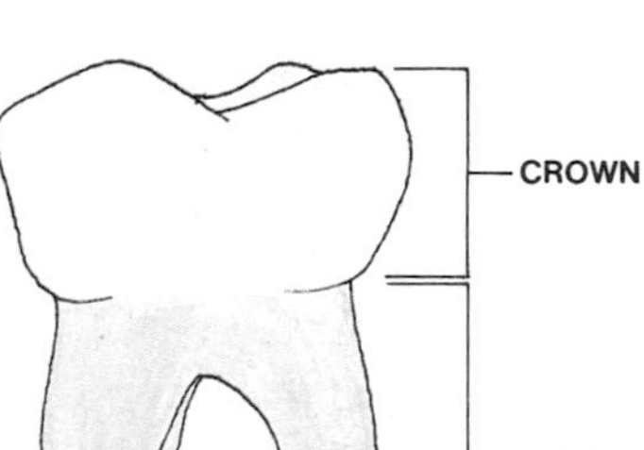

Fig. 18.6 Diagram of a tooth

All teeth have the same basic structure. The tooth can be divided into two sections:— the **crown**, which is the visible part of the tooth, and the **root**, which is embedded in the jaw.

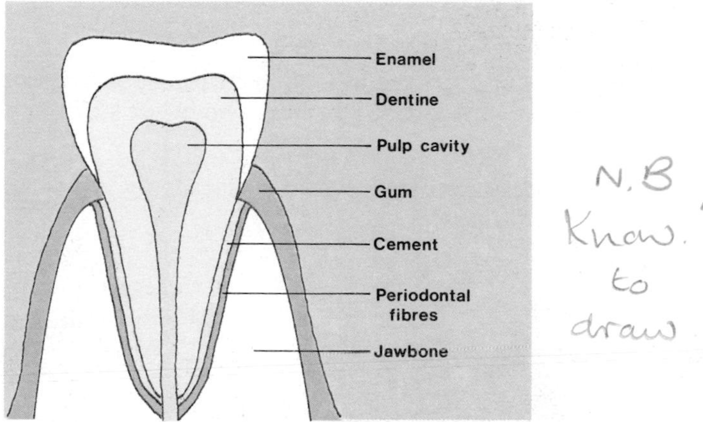

Fig. 18.7 Structure of a tooth

If you look at *Fig. 18.7*, you can identify the following regions:—

1. **Enamel** — this is the hardest substance in the body. It surrounds the crown, and protects it.
2. **Dentine** — this makes up the bulk of the tooth. It is softer than enamel, although it is still very hard.

3. **Pulp Cavity** — this is the 'living' part of the tooth. It consists of living cells, which make the dentine and it has blood vessels running through it, which supplies the cells with food and oxygen. There are also sensory nerves present, which cause pain when damaged.
4. **Cement** — this is found surrounding the root. It has a tough bone-like structure and it helps prevent root damage.

The root of the tooth is embedded deep into the jaw bone. This helps to anchor the tooth. This is also aided by thousands of periodontal fibres, which are found running between the cement and the jaw bone. The jaw bone and the roots are further protected by the gum (or gingiva).

18.4 Dental Health

Dental Decay

Experiment 18.1 To show Plaque on Teeth

Method

1. Work in pairs.
2. One student must clean his teeth thoroughly using toothpaste and a tooth-brush. The other student does not clean his teeth.
3. Both students must chew on a disclosing tablet, and then rinse their mouth.
4. Observe each others teeth.

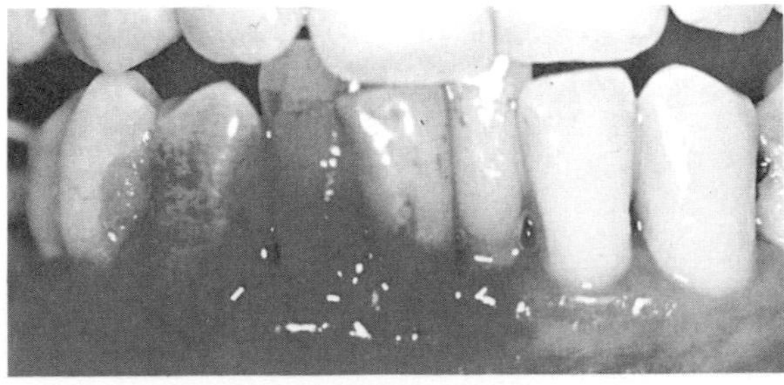

Fig. 18.8 Uncleaned teeth after use of a disclosing tablet

5. Both students should then brush their teeth thoroughly, until their teeth are clean. Note the time taken to clean their teeth.

The above experiment shows that unbrushed teeth are stained by the disclosing tablet. The disclosing tablet actually stains plaque. Plaque consists of a mixture of bacteria and remains of saliva, and plays an important role in tooth decay. The correct name for tooth decay is **caries**.

Tooth decay occurs as follows:—

1. The bacteria in plaque feed on sugary foods and produce an acid.
2. This acid collects on the enamel and begins to break it down.
3. If not prevented the acid will get through to the dentine, and eventually to the pulp cavity, causing pain.
4. Once the pulp cavity is open to the outside, bacteria can enter it, causing an infection, often leading to an abscess and subsequent loss of the tooth.

Plaque also plays a part in gum disease. Plaque formation close to the gums, leads to the resultant acid irritating the gums, causing them to become inflamed. This is known as gingivitis. If not treated, the disease will travel down the gum, surrounding the root, which will cause the tooth to become loose.

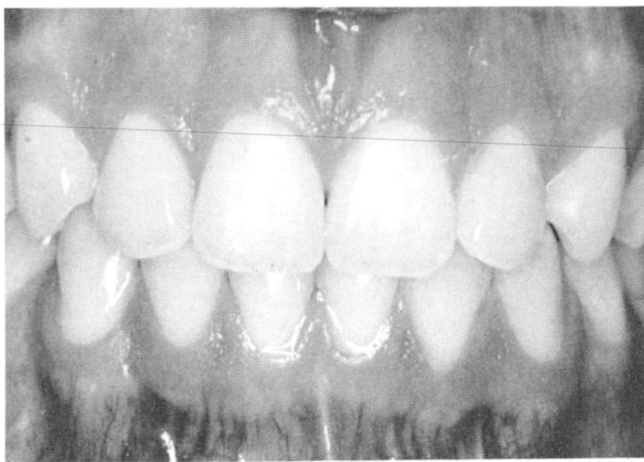

Fig. 18.9 Inflammed gums

Dental Hygiene

A combination of two conditions are required for tooth decay, or gum disease to occur:—

1. Formation of plaque — which contains the bacteria.
2. Presence of sugar — to feed the bacteria.

By altering our diet e.g. cutting out sweet and sugary food, we can decrease the amount of sugar available to the bacteria.

If we combine this with adequate brushing of the teeth to remove any plaque, as it forms, we can minimize tooth decay.

The Correct Way to Brush Teeth

You will probably have discovered, when you did the experiment, with the disclosing tablet, that it is difficult to remove plaque completely.

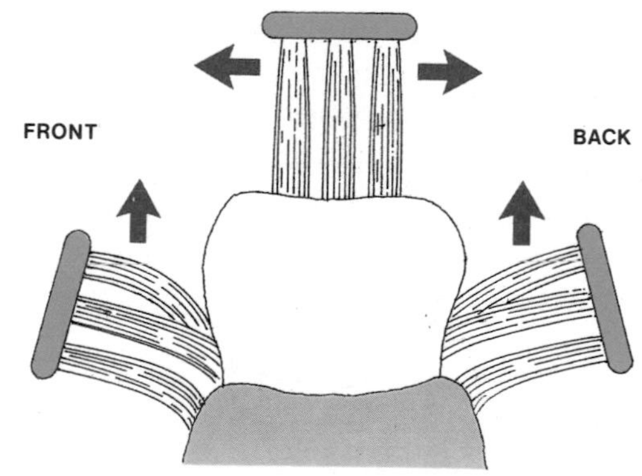

Fig. 18.10 Diagram showing how to brush a tooth

To do this, you must brush each tooth thoroughly, using a good toothpaste, and you should also brush in between your teeth. To complete the cleaning process, you should use dental floss. This is used to remove plaque from the sides and bottoms of the teeth.

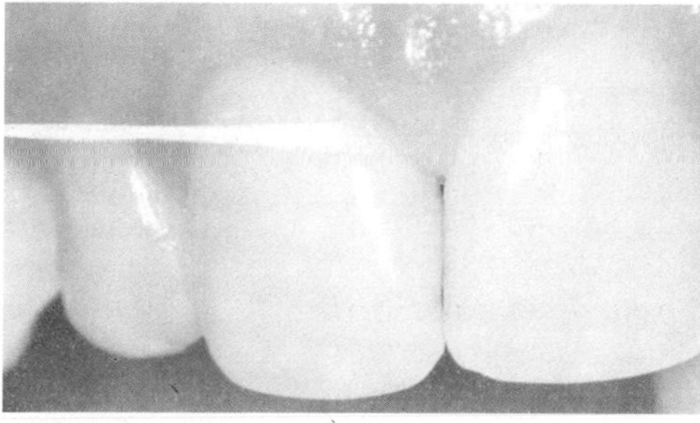

Fig. 18.11 Man using dental floss

Fluoride In Water And/Or Toothpaste

It has been discovered that if fluoride is available during teeth formation a tougher, more resistant enamel is formed.

For this reason some water authorities add fluoride to our drinking water, and many toothpastes contain fluoride.

Summary

* There are four types of teeth: — incisors for cutting, canines for tearing, premolars for chewing, and molars for grinding.
* A tooth consists of the visible crown and a root.
* Man has two sets of teeth 1) milk teeth; 2) permanent teeth.
* A cross section of a tooth consists of the following regions:—
  Enamel — for protection.
  Dentine — making up the bulk of the tooth.
  Pulp cavity — the 'living' part of the tooth, which contains cells, blood vessels and nerves.
  Cement — surrounding the root for protection and helping with anchorage.
* Dental decay is caused by acid, which is produced when the bacteria in plaque feed on sugar.
* Dental decay can be prevented by removing plaque and not eating sweet foods.
* Fluoride strengthens enamel and helps prevent tooth decay.

Questions

Section A

1. What is meant by mechanical digestion? . . . .
2. What is a herbivore? Give three examples. . . . .
. . . .
3. What is the function of the incisor teeth? . . . .
4. How many sets of teeth does man have? . . . .
5. What are 'wisdom' teeth? . . . .
6. The tooth is divided into two sections, the . . . . and the . . . .
7. Why is the pulp cavity known as the 'living' part of the tooth? . . . .
8. Where would you find cement in the body? . . . .
9. How is the tooth anchored to the jaw? . . . .
. . . .
10. A disclosing tablet is used to show up . . . . which is formed on the . . . . of a tooth.
11. What does plaque consist of? . . . .
. . . .
12. Two conditions are necessary for tooth decay. What are they? . . . .
13. What is dental floss used for? . . . .
14. How often should you clean your teeth? . . . .
15. Why is fluoride sometimes added to water? . . . .
. . . .

Section B

1. Describe the four different types of teeth. Indicate their function.
2. Describe, in detail, a programme of dental care, that you should adopt in order to maintain healthy teeth.
3. Plaque is involved in tooth decay. Explain how it is involved in bringing about this decay.

19 — Plant Nutrition

19.1 Photosynthesis

Green plants are able to make their own food in a process called **photosynthesis**. This process takes place in the leaves and other green parts of the plant. The food which the plant makes is in the form of glucose and is stored as starch in the cells of the leaf. To see if a plant has been photosynthesising (making food) we test its leaves for starch.

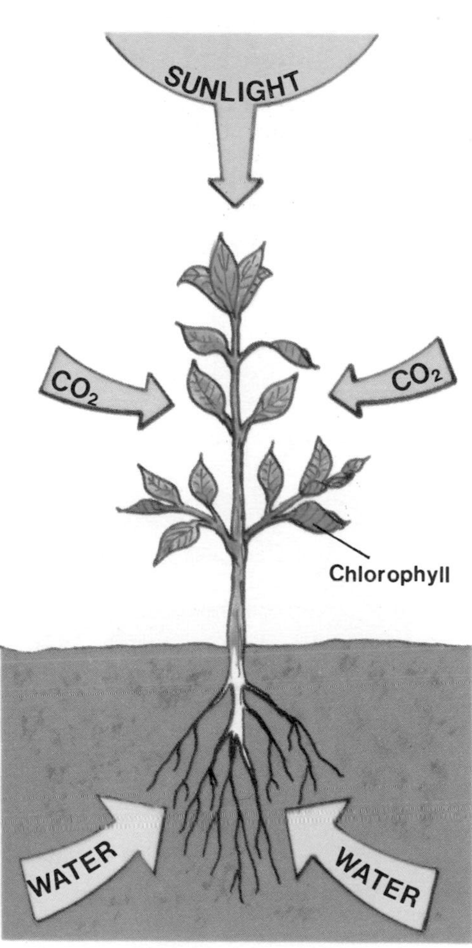

Fig. 19.1

Experiment 19.1 To Test a Leaf for Starch

Method

1. Set up a water bath and bring it to the boil.
2. Take a leaf from a plant that has been in the light and drop it into the boiling water for half a minute. This kills the leaf and makes it easier for iodine solution to pass into the cells.
3. Meanwhile, away from the Bunsen flame, half fill a test-tube with alcohol.
4. Remove the leaf from the water bath and gently push it into the tube of alcohol.
5. Turn off the Bunsen burner and transfer the test-tube containing the alcohol and leaf to the water bath. The alcohol removes the chlorophyll from the leaf and makes it easier to see the reaction of the starch and iodine solution.
6. After about 10 minutes, use a test-tube holder to lift the test-tube out of the water bath and set it in a test-tube rack.
7. Gently remove the leaf from the alcohol. If necessary, pour the alcohol off into a collecting jar (not down the sink) and then pick out the leaf.
8. The leaf is now a creamy white colour, but very brittle to touch. Soften it by dipping it gently into the warm water bath.
9. Spread the leaf carefully onto a white tile or clock glass.
10. Cover the leaf with dilute iodine solution and leave for a minute. Drain off any surplus iodine solution and look for the blue-black colour on the leaf which indicates the presence of starch. If starch is present, it means that the plant has been photosynthesising.

Factors Necessary for Photosynthesis

There are four factors needed by the plant for photosynthesis to take place. These are carbon dioxide, water, light energy and chlorophyll, *Fig. 19.1*.

1. Carbon Dioxide

Carbon dioxide comes from the air. It enters the plant through tiny openings in the leaves called **stomata**.

Experiment 19.2 To Show that Carbon Dioxide is necessary for Photosynthesis

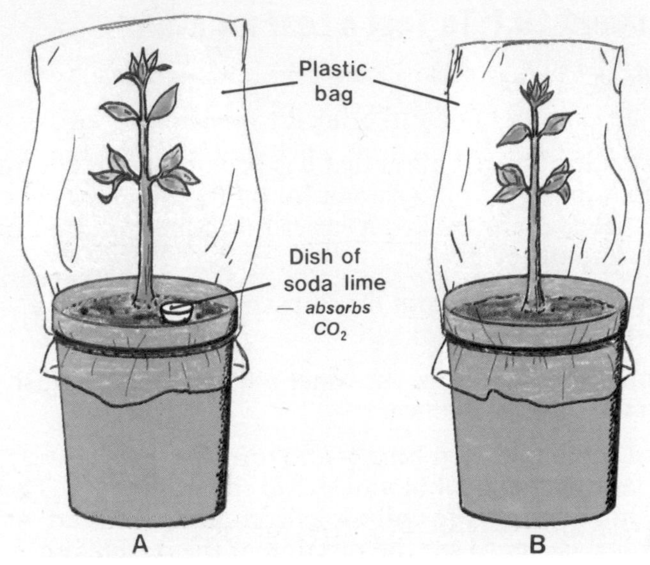

Fig. 19.2 Experiment 19.2

Method

1. De-starch two pot plants by placing them in darkness for 48 hours. In the dark, any starch in the plants will be used up, so that they are starch free at the start of the experiment.
2. Set up the apparatus as in *Fig. 19.2.* The soda lime (plant A) will absorb any carbon dioxide in the air surrounding the plant.
3. Leave the plants in good light for 6-8 hours.
4. Remove the plastic bags and pick a leaf from plant A and from plant B.
5. Test these leaves for the presence of starch by following the instructions in *Experiment 19.1* using a separate test-tube for leaf A and B.
6. Record the result of the starch test.
7. The leaf from plant B should turn blue-black showing that this leaf made food. The leaf from plant A should stay creamy white or iodine solution colour because this plant had no carbon dioxide and was therefore unable to make food.

2. Water Learn

Water comes from the soil. It is absorbed by the root hairs and travels up the leaves through the xylem tubes, *see Chapter 21 — Water and Transport in Plants.*

3. Light Learn

The light energy comes from the sun. It is absorbed by chlorophyll.

Experiment 19.3 To Show that Light is necessary for Photosynthesis

Fig. 19.3

Method

1. De-starch a plant, as described in *Experiment 19.2.*
2. Partly cover a leaf with light-proof paper, as shown in *Fig. 19.3.* Draw a diagram of your leaf to show the position of the cover.
3. Leave the plant in good light for 6-8 hours.
4. Remove the treated leaf and its cover. Test the leaf for starch by following the instructions in *Experiment 19.1.*
5. Record the result of the starch test. The area of the leaf that was covered by light-proof paper should not turn blue-black because this part received no light and was unable to make food. The uncovered areas of the leaf should turn blue-black indicating that in the presence of light the plant can make food.

Chlorophyll

Chlorophyll is the green pigment found in the leaves (and many stems) of plants. Its function is to trap the light energy.

Experiment 19.4 To Show that Chlorophyll is necessary for Photosynthesis

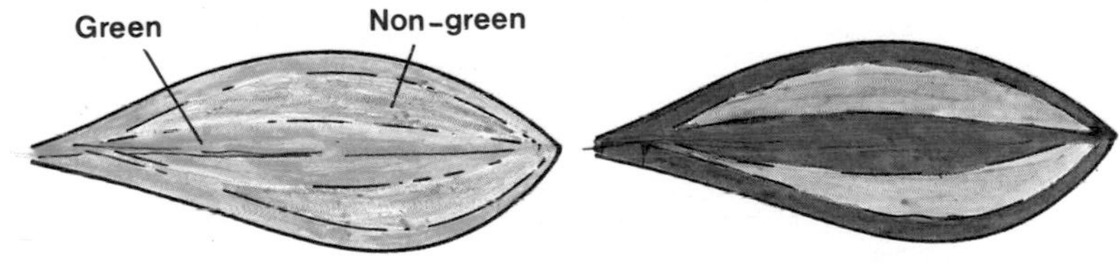

Fig. 19.4

Method

1. De-starch a plant, with variegated leaves such as *a Coleus* or *Tradescantia*, as described in *Experiment 19.2.* A variegated leaf is one which has only patches of green colour. It is not completely green, *Fig. 19.4.*
2. Into your class note book, draw the pattern of green areas on one leaf of the plant while it is still attached to the plant.
3. Leave the plant in good light for 6-8 hours.
4. Remove the leaf and test it for starch by following the instructions in *Experiment 19.1.*
5. Record the result of the starch test by re-drawing the leaf and indicating on the diagram the blue-black areas. The areas of the leaf which were originally green should be blue-black. The non-green areas should not be blue-black, indicating that chlorophyll is necessary for the plant to make food.

The Process of Photosynthesis

During photosynthesis, the light energy absorbed by chlorophyll is used to form sugars (carbohydrate) from carbon dioxide and water; oxygen gas is released as a by-product of the reaction, *Experiment 19.5.* Traditionally photosynthesis can be summarised by the following equation:

$$\underset{\text{carbon dioxide}}{6CO_2} + \underset{\text{water}}{6H_2O} \xrightarrow[\text{chlorophyll}]{\text{light}} \underset{\text{glucose}}{C_6H_{12}O_6} + \underset{\text{oxygen}}{6O_2}$$

While photosynthesis is taking place, glucose is transported around the plant in the phloem. Once it reaches the cells of the plant it can be:

1. Used to produce energy in respiration *(Chapter 20).*

$$C_6H_{12}O_6 + 6O_2 \rightarrow 6CO_2 + 6H_2O + \text{Energy}$$

2. Stored again in the form of starch.
3. Converted into protein by combining with some of the minerals, e.g. nitrates absorbed from the soil. (*See the Nitrogen Cycle, Chapter 27*).

Experiment 19.5 To Show that Oxygen is Released during Photosynthesis

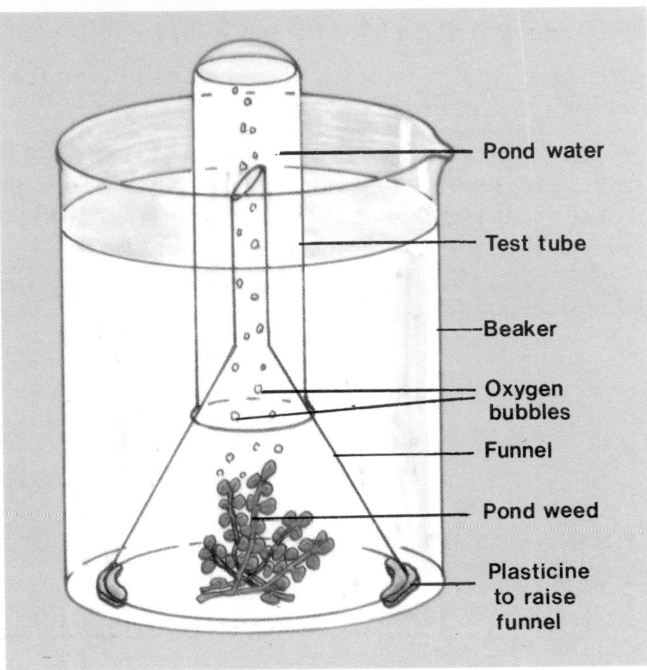

Fig. 19.5 Experiment 19.5

Method

1. Set up the apparatus, as in *Fig. 19.5.* The pond weed *Elodea* produces a colourless gas when light is shone on it.
2. Allow the gas to collect in the test-tube for a couple of days.
3. Test the gas with a glowing splint. If the gas is oxygen, the splint should re-ignite. (*See Chapter 4 — Oxygen*).

The Leaf and Photosynthesis

N.B. learn all 4

The leaves of plants are well suited to their role in photosynthesis. The main adaptations of the leaf for photosynthesis are:

1. The palisade layer which contains most of the chlorophyll (in the chloroplasts) is located on the upper side of the leaf. In this way it is exposed to the maximum amount of light.
2. The large air spaces of the mesophyll layer allow carbon dioxide to pass rapidly into the palisade cells and oxygen to leave.
3. The network of veins brings water from the soil into the leaf and carries the food away to all parts of the plant.
4. The leaf blade is usually broad and very thin — to allow maximum exposure to light.

19.2 Mineral Nutrition in Plants

Plants cannot live by photosynthesis alone. They also need minerals, which they absorb from the soil. Farmers usually add these minerals as chemicals, — either artificially (as fertilisers) or naturally (in the form of manure). The most important minerals required by plants are shown in the following table.

Table 19.1

Mineral	*Symbol*	*Absorbed as*	*Function*	*Deficiency Symptom*
Nitrogen	N	Nitrate ion NO_3^-	To make proteins	Stunted growth. Yellow leaves
Phosphorus	P	Phosphate ion HPO_4^-	To make cell membranes	Slow growth. Leaves dull green.
Sulphur	S	Sulphate ion SO_4^{2-}	To make some proteins	Yellowing of leaves.
Potassium	K	K^+	Increases hardiness	Yellow edges on leaves.
Magnesium	Mg	Mg^{2+}	To make chlorophyll	Yellowing of leaves.
Calcium	Ca	Ca^{2+}	Acts as a cement to bind cells together	Stunted growth of root or stem
Iron	Fe	Fe^{2+}	To make chlorophyll	Yellowing of leaves.

Experiment 19.6 To Demonstrate Mineral Deficiencies in a Plant using Water Cultures

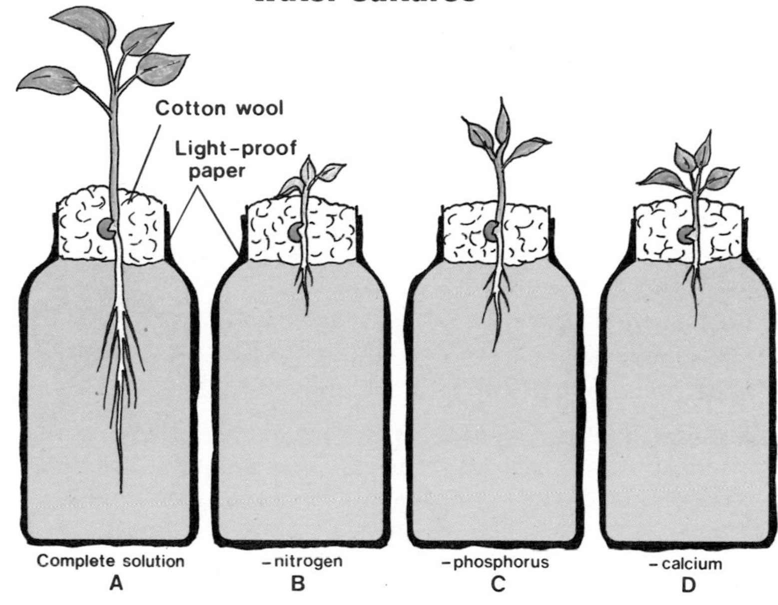

Fig. 19.6 Experiment 19.6

It is possible to grow plant seedlings in water solutions containing the necessary minerals. These solutions are known as water cultures. In this experiment a variety of culture solutions are used, some of which are lacking in a certain mineral. In this way the effect of the absence of a particular mineral on the growth of the seedling can be observed.

Method

1. Label four jars A, B, C and D.
2. 3/4 fill the jars with culture solutions as follows:
   A: Complete culture solution containing all the necessary minerals for growth.
   B: Culture solution lacking in nitrogen.
   C: Culture solution lacking in phosphorous.
   D: Culture solution lacking in calcium.
3. Place a seedling into each jar and wrap a small amount of cotton wool around the base of its stem.
4. Wrap a piece of light-proof paper around each jar (label on the outside) to prevent small algae growing in the solutions.
5. Leave the seedlings for 2-3 weeks with each jar receiving an equal amount of light.
6. After 3 weeks, compare the seedlings for length, number of leaves and colour. Copy and complete the table below.

Table 19.2 Results of Mineral Experiment

		Seedling	
Culture	*Length*	*Number of Leaves*	*Colour of leaves*
Complete			
Lacking N			
Lacking P			
Lacking Ca			

Summary

* Photosynthesis is the process by which plants make their own food.
* Photosynthesis is carried out in all green parts of a plant, e.g. leaves and stems.
* The equation for photosynthesis is:

$$\underset{\text{carbon dioxide}}{6CO_2} + \underset{\text{water}}{6H_2O} + \xrightarrow[\text{Chlorophyll}]{\text{Light}} \underset{\text{starch}}{6C_6H_{12}O_6} + \underset{\text{oxygen}}{6O_2}$$

* The factors necessary for photosynthesis are carbon dioxide, water, light and chlorophyll.
* Carbon dioxide enters the plant through stomata. Water is absorbed from the soil through the roots. The energy comes from sunlight. Chlorophyll is the green colour found in the chloroplasts of the leaf.
* Sugars made in the leaves are used by the plant as follows: (a) to produce energy; (b) to build parts of the plant body; (c) to form starch,protein, oils.
* In addition, plants need certain minerals for healthy growth. These minerals are absorbed by the plant roots from the soil. They include nitrates, sulphates, magnesium, calcium and potassium ions.

Questions

Section A

1. What is meant by photosynthesis? ....

   ....

2. Carbon dioxide together with light and .... are needed to make .... in a green plant.

3. Where would you find (i) stomata; (ii) a chloroplast?
   (i) ....
   (ii) ....

4. What is the function of the cuticle on a leaf? ....

5. Write an equation for the process of photosynthesis ....

   ....

6. What gas do green plants produce during photosynthesis? ....

   ....

7. A green leaf was tested with iodine solution and it turned a blue-black colour. What does this tell you? ....

8. Why are plants destarched before certain experiments on photosynthesis? ....

9. What is the function of soda lime in *Experiment 19.2*? Name another chemical which would perform the same function. ....

10. Which of the following mineral elements Fe, Ca, N, P:
    (a) is important in the formation of proteins? ....
    (b) is an important element in the composition of chlorophyll? ....
    (c) is important to prevent stunted growth of the root and shoot tips? ....

Section B

1. What do you understand by photosynthesis? Give two structural features of green leaves that enable them to carry out photosynthesis.

2. Describe an experiment to show that *one* of the following is necessary for photosynthesis to take place: (a) carbon dioxide; (b) light; (c) chlorophyll.

3. Describe an experiment to show that oxygen gas is produced during photosynthesis. Does the plant use the oxygen it produces in photosynthesis? If so, for what purpose is it used? Why do animals depend upon the oxygen produced by plants?

4. List five mineral elements required for healthy plant growth. For each of three of the elements you name give: (a) its function in the plant; (b) the symptoms shown by the plant when it is deficient. Describe an experiment to show the deficiency symptoms you have described in (b) above.

20 — Respiration

20.1 Respiration

Fig. 20.1

We already know that living organisms need energy to carry out their activities. For example, energy may be needed for movement or growth or to synthesise (make) essential chemicals. But how is this energy produced? Look at the photograph of a fire. *(Fig. 20.1)* To make the fire burn you need a supply of fuel and oxygen. The coal (fuel) reacts with the oxygen in the air to produce energy in the form of heat. Carbon dioxide gas is released in the process.

Coal + Oxygen → Energy(heat) + carbon dioxide

$$C + O_2 \rightarrow \text{Energy} + CO_2$$

Know

A similar reaction takes place in every cell of a living plant or animal. This reaction is called **cellular respiration**. Respiration is the process by which fuel in the form of food such as glucose, combines with oxygen to produce energy. The release of the energy is carefully controlled by means of enzymes. Respiration can be summarised by the following equation:

Glucose + Oxygen = Energy + Water + Carbon Dioxide

The chemical equation is

$$C_6H_{12}O_6 + 6O_2 \rightarrow \text{Energy} + 6H_2O + 6CO_2$$

Aerobic and Anaerobic Respiration

Know

There are two types of respiration:

1. Aerobic respiration involves the use of oxygen and is the normal method of respiration for most organisms.
2. Anaerobic respiration is the breakdown of sugar without the use of oxygen. This method is mainly used by bacteria and yeast, but it can also occur in the muscle cells of animals for short periods of time. For example, during vigorous exercise oxygen cannot reach the muscles fast enough to allow them to respire aerobically. When this happens, anaerobic respiration takes over temporarily and small amounts of energy and a substance called **lactic acid** are produced. Anaerobic respiration in yeast and bacteria is known as **fermentation**. Products of fermentations which have commercial importance include alcohol, citric acid and acetic acid.

Experiments on Respiration

If living organisms are respiring, then it should be possible to show that they (a) release energy, (b) release carbon dioxide.

Experiment 20.1 To Show that Respiring Seeds produce Heat Energy

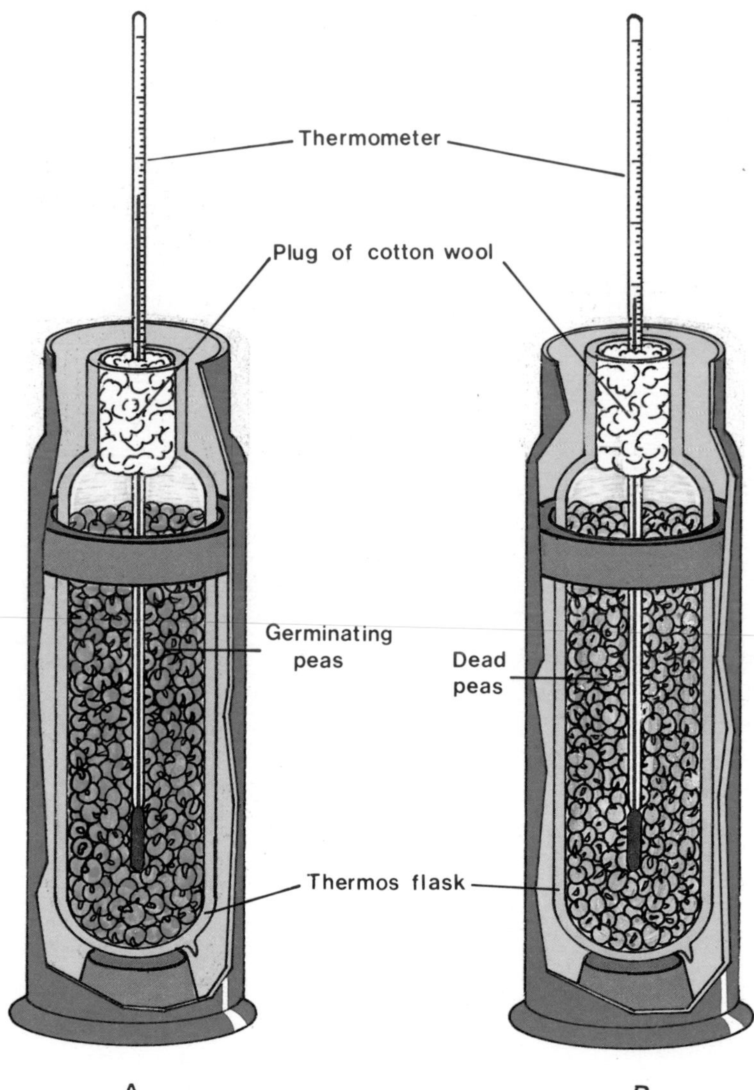

Fig. 20.2

Method

1. Set up the apparatus as shown in *Fig. 20.2.*
2. Read and record the temperature in both flasks.
3. Copy the table below into your notebook and record the temperature readings once a day for one week.
4. Plot a graph of time vs temperature (° C) for each flask.

Table 20.1

Day	*Flask A (° C)*	*Flask B (° C)*
1		
2		
3		
4		
5		
6		
7		

5. Note that the temperature of the flask with live peas rises but that of the dead peas does not. This is because the living peas produce heat energy when they respire.

Experiment 20.2 To Show that Respiring Seeds release Carbon Dioxide

Method

1. The apparatus is set up as shown in *Fig. 20.3.*
2. Turn on the tap or pump to draw air through the system.
3. Note that the lime water in flask D soon turns milky. This is because the respiring peas are releasing carbon dioxide. The lime water in flask B does not turn milky because all the carbon dioxide in the incoming air has been removed by the sodium hydroxide solution. Why do you think that has been done?
4. The experiment can be repeated using (a) a small animal such as a mouse or (b) a pot plant. If a pot plant is used, it must be covered by a black cloth to prevent photosynthesis occurring, as this would use up the carbon dioxide produced by the plant.

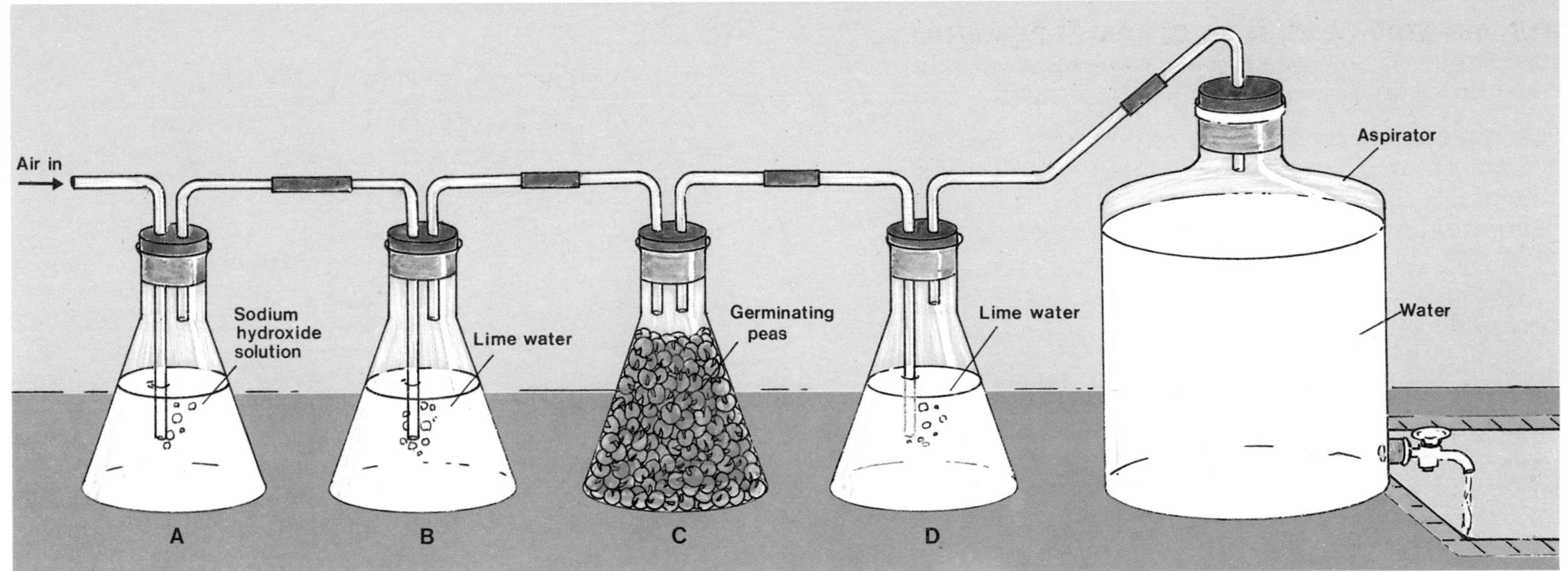

Fig. 20.3

20.2 Gaseous Exchange

In order to respire, organisms need to take in oxygen and the carbon dioxide produced must be removed. The exchange of oxygen and carbon dioxide is called **gaseous exchange**.

Gaseous Exchange in Plants

In plants, gaseous exchange takes place through the stomata, the tiny pores found on the leaves and stems. In woody stems, e.g. a rose bush, openings in the bark, called **lenticels**, are used for gaseous exchange.

Experiment 20.3 To Demonstrate that Gas is released from the Undersurface of a Leaf

Method

1. Fill a jar or beaker with very hot water.
2. Plunge a large hairless leaf, e.g. sycamore, into the hot water.
3. Note the presence of many tiny air bubbles forming on the undersurface of the leaf which demonstrate the presence of stomata.

The cells of a plant respire all the time, i.e. night and day. In the dark, the oxygen, needed for respiration, passes in

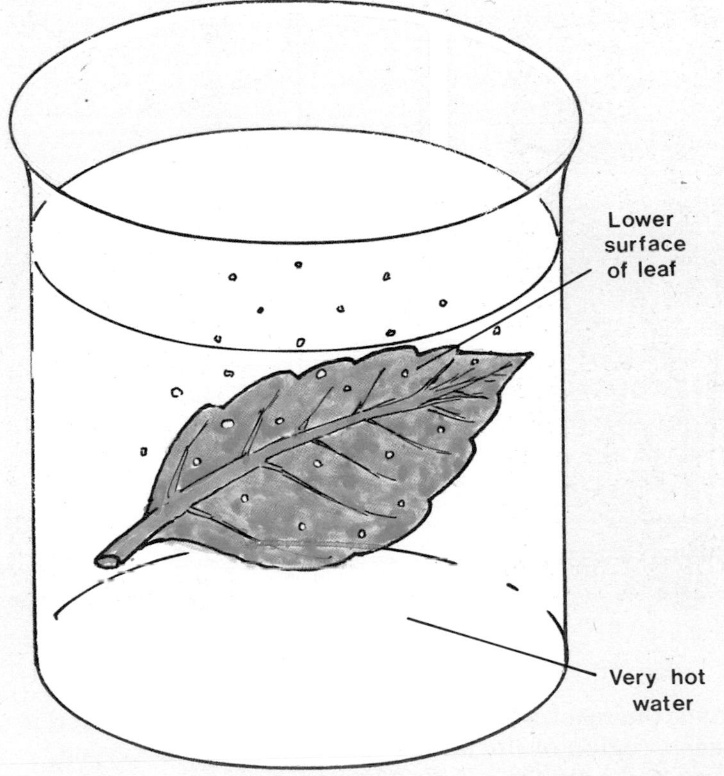

Fig. 20.4

from the air outside through the stomata and the carbon dioxide produced is released. But during the day (light), photosynthesis takes place as well as respiration.

The carbon dioxide produced by respiration is used up immediately to make sugars. In addition, more carbon dioxide passes into the plant from the air outside and the oxygen produced during photosynthesis passes out.

Gaseous Exchange in Animals

Most animals use respiratory organs to bring about an exchange of oxygen and carbon dioxide.

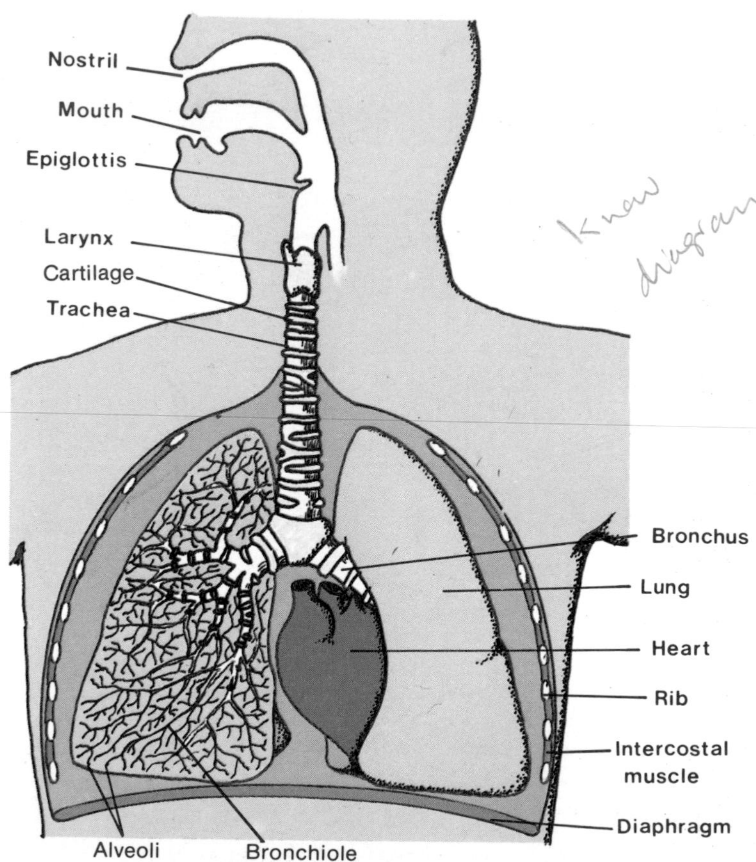

Fig. 20.5 Respiratory organs (breathing system)

In man, the respiratory or breathing organs are situated in the chest region of the body. They consist of the larynx, trachea and bronchi; a pair of lungs; the intercostal muscles and the diaphragm, *Fig. 20.5*.

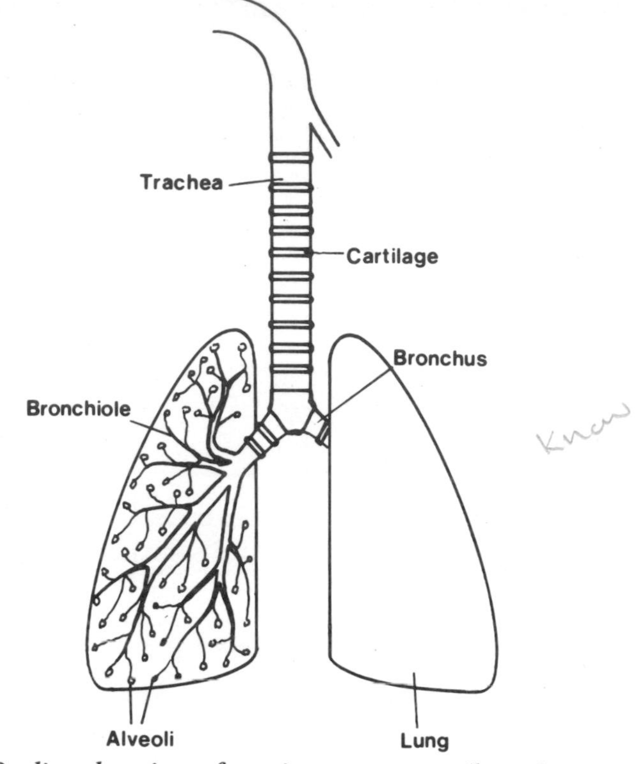

Fig. 20.6 Outline drawing of respiratory organs (breathing system)

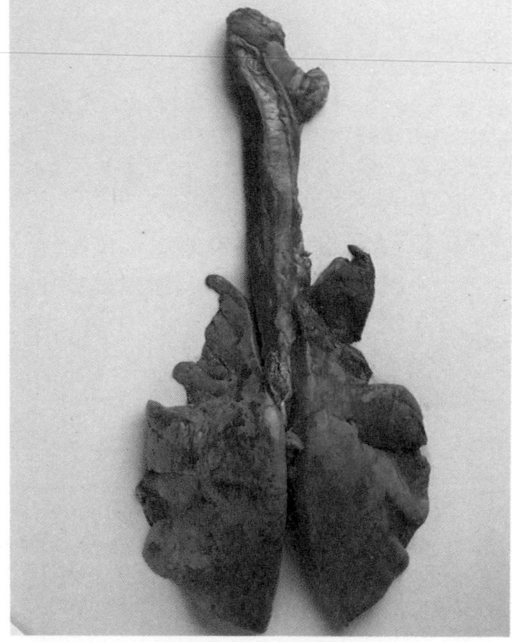

Fig. 20.7 Sheeps's breathing organs

1. The **larynx** is the voice-box which is responsible for making sounds.
2. The **trachea** or windpipe carries air to and from the lungs via the **bronchi**. There are two bronchi, one bronchus goes into each lung. The trachea and bronchi are protected by c-shaped rings of cartilage which keep the air tubes open.
3. The **lungs** are spongy organs lying one either side of the heart. Inside each lung, the bronchus divides many times into smaller tubes called **bronchioles**. The bronchioles end in bunches of tiny air sacs called **alveoli**, *Fig. 20.8.* There are millions of alveoli in each lung and each one is covered by a network of narrow blood vessels (capillaries). Carbon dioxide and oxygen are exchanged in the alveoli.

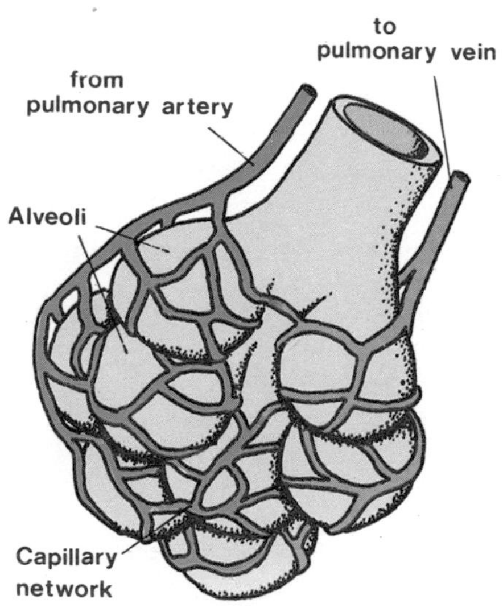

Fig. 20.8 Alveoli

4. The **intercostal muscles** lie between the ribs. The diaphragm is a sheet of muscle which forms the floor of the chest cavity. Both these muscles are used in the breathing movements.

Gaseous Exchange in the Alveoli

The walls of the alveoli are very thin and this allows gases to pass through quickly. Oxygen (in the air we breath in) diffuses across the wall of the alveolus into the blood where it is picked up by the red blood corpuscles. At the same time, carbon dioxide in the blood diffuses across into the alveolus and is breathed out of the body.

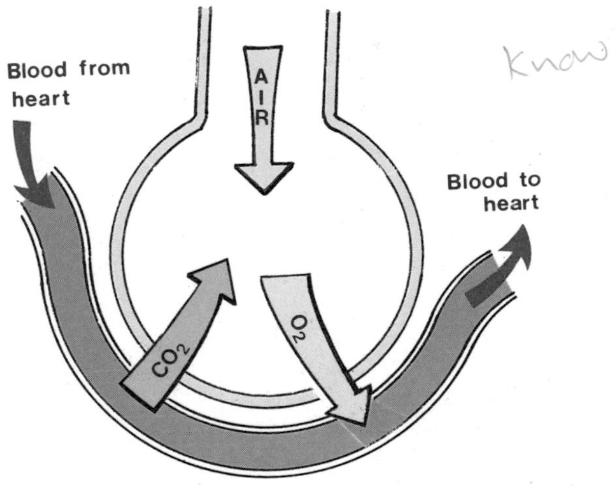

Fig. 20.9 Gaseous exchange in the alveoli

20.3 How Breathing Occurs (The Breathing Mechanism)

Breathing is caused by the contraction and relaxation of the intercostal muscles and the diaphragm.

Breathing air in is known as **inspiration** and breathing air out, as **expiration.**

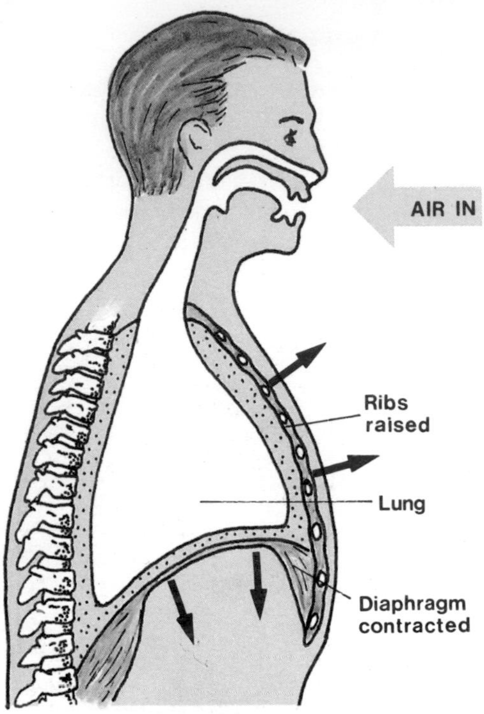

Fig. 20.10 (a) Inspiration

Inspiration

During inspiration, the intercostal muscles and the diaphragm contract. This causes the diaphragm to move down and the rib cage to move up and out. As a result, the volume (space) of the chest cavity increases, but the pressure of air inside it decreases. Air from outside is drawn into the lungs to balance the pressures, *Fig. 20.10 (a)*.

AIR OUT
Ribs lowered
Diaphragm relaxed

Fig. 20.10 (b) Expiration

Expiration

The diaphragm and intercostal muscles relax. This causes the diaphragm to move up (dome-shaped) and the rib cage to move down again. As a result, the volume of the chest cavity decreases, which increases the pressure inside it. Air is forced out of the lungs to balance the pressures, *Fig. 20.10. (b)*.

Experiment 20.4 To Demonstrate how Breathing occurs using the Bell Jar Model

Method

1. Draw the bell jar model *(Fig. 20.11)* in your class notebook.

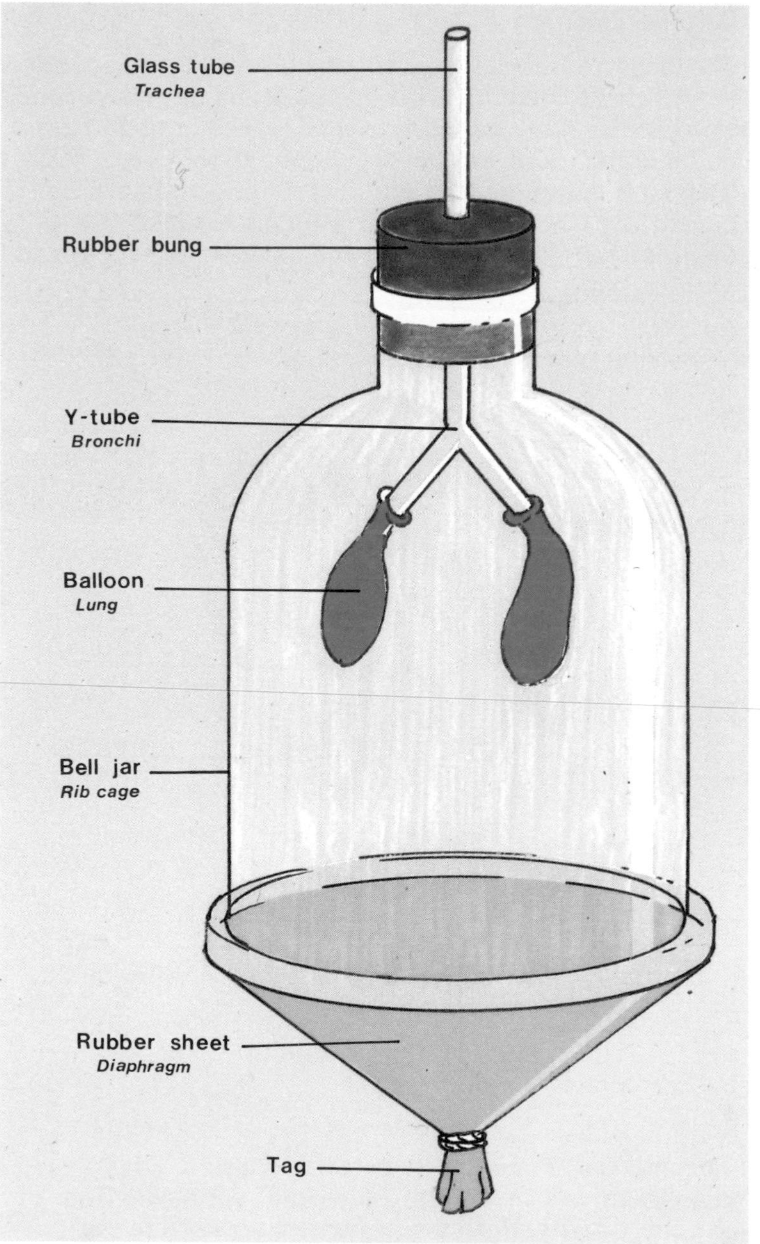

Fig. 20.11

2. Watch carefully as the tag is pulled gently downwards and then quite quickly pushed up again.
3. Watch what happens to the balloons as these movements are repeated.
4. As the tag is pulled downwards, the balloons inflate and when the tag is pushed up, the balloons collapse.

Table 20.2 The Differences between Inspired and Expired Air

	Composition (as % of volume)	
Gas	*Inspired*	*Expired*
Nitrogen	78%	78%
Oxygen	21%	16%
Carbon dioxide	0.03%	4%
Water Vapour	variable	saturated

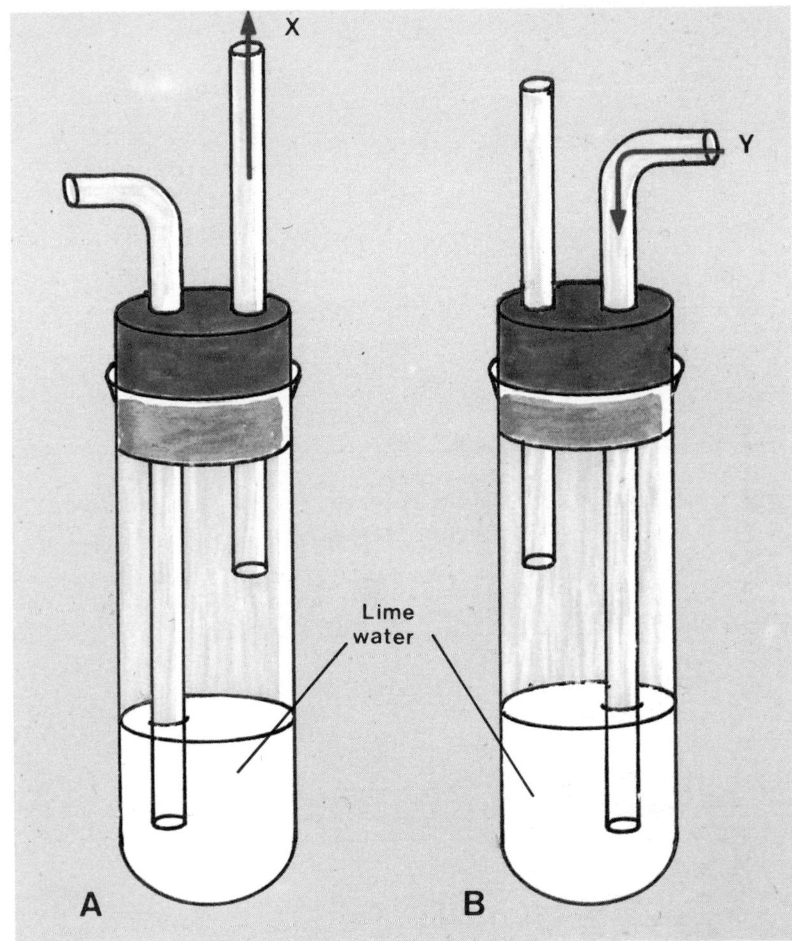

Fig. 20.12

Experiment 20.5 To Show that Expired Air contains more Carbon Dioxide than Inspired Air

Method

1. Collect two test-tubes, as in *Fig. 20.12.*
2. Place clear lime water in each tube.
3. Hold tube A in one hand and tube B in the other hand.
4. Breathe in through X of tube A (this represents inspired air). Hold this breath and breathe out through Y of tube B (this represents expired air).
5. Repeat stage 4 until the lime water in one of the tubes turns milky.
6. You should observe that the lime water in tube B goes milky first. This shows that expired air contains more carbon dioxide than inspired air.

Lung Capacity

Each lung in an adult man has a **total capacity** of approximately 2.5 litres. During normal breathing about 250ml of air passes in and out of the lungs. This is known as the **tidal air**. The **vital capacity** is the maximum amount of air that can be taken in, when taking a deep breath, and it is about 1.5 litres.

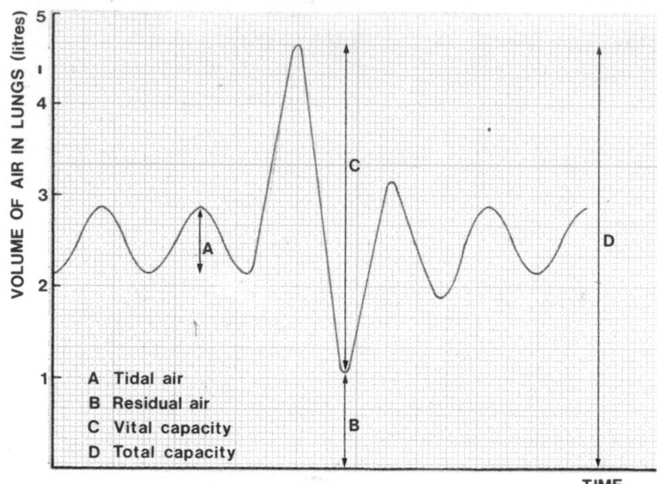

Fig. 20.13 Diagram to show volume of air within the lungs during breathing

Experiment 20.6 To Find The Vital Capacity

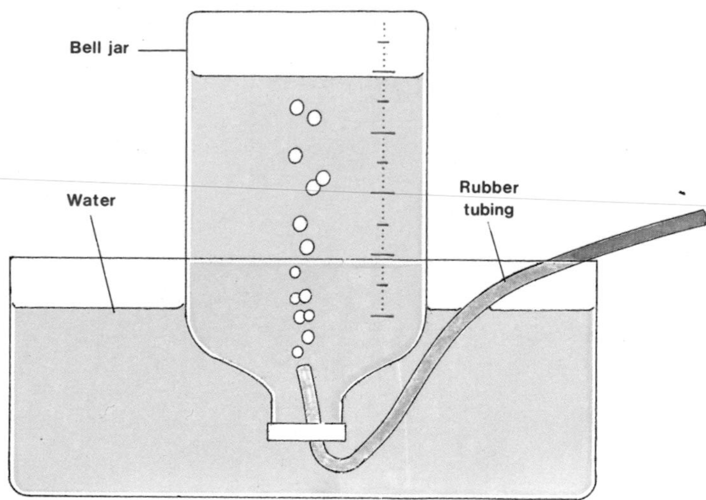

Fig. 20.14 Finding your vital capacity

Method

1. Set up the bell jar apparatus, so that the bell jar is full of water, as shown in *Fig. 20.14.*
2. Place a piece of rubber tubing, so that one end of the tube is under the bell jar.
3. Take a deep breath, hold your nose and then blow down the rubber tubing, until you cannot blow anymore.
4. Make a note of the volume of water, that has been displaced by your breath. This is equal to the amount of breath that you had in your lungs, i.e. it is your vital capacity.

Smoking and the Breathing Mechanism

Smoking is a harmful habit which can affect the breathing mechanism and your general health in the following ways:

1. Tobacco smoke irritates and damages the linings of the bronchioles.
2. Smoking can reduce the resistance of the lungs to certain diseases such as bronchitis and lung cancer.
3. Smoking during pregnancy reduces the oxygen available to the growing baby.
4. Carbon monoxide gas in cigarette smoke prevents red blood corpuscles from carrying oxygen. This may cause a smoker to breathe faster which can result in heart strain.

Summary

* Respiration is the release of energy from food.
* The equation for respiration is:
  $C_6H_{12}O_6 + 6O_2 \rightarrow \text{Energy} + 6CO_2 + 6H_2O$
* There are two types of respiration: aerobic and anaerobic.
* The exchange of oxygen and carbon dioxide during respiration is known as gaseous exchange.
* In plants, gaseous exchange occurs through the stomata and lenticels.
* In animals, gaseous exchange occurs by means of respiratory organs.
* The respiratory organs in man are the lungs and gaseous exchange occurs through the alveoli.
* The diaphragm and intercostal muscles are used in breathing. Inspiration is breathing in and expiration is breathing out.
* Expired air contains more carbon dioxide than inspired air. The extra carbon dioxide is made in the body cells during respiration.

Questions

Section A

1. Complete the following equation:
   Food + ...→ .... + carbon dioxide + water.
2. Define the term *respiration* ....
3. What is the difference between aerobic and anaerobic respiration? ....
   ....
4. List two similarities between respiration and a coal fire?
   1. ....
   2. ....
5. List two differences between respiration and a coal fire.
   1. ....
   2. ....
6. List four activities you do that need energy from respiration.
   1. ....
   2. ....
   3. ....
   4. ....
7. Name an organism that carries out fermentation. ......
8. The exchange of carbon dioxide and oxygen in organisms is known as ....
9. Where does gaseous exchange occur in (a) a buttercup?. ......; (b) a fish? ....; (c) a horse-chestnut twig in winter? ....
10. What is the function of the rings of cartilage on the trachea? ....
11. Where in the lungs does gaseous exchange take place? .
12. State two differences between the composition of inhaled and exhaled air.
    1. ....
    2. ....
13. Name the muscles involved in breathing ....
14. The approximate percentage of oxygen in expired air is (a) 0.03; (b) 21; (c) 16; (d) 4 ....
15. Air rushes into the lungs when the diaphragm is raised/flattened and the rib cabe is raised/lowered ....
16. Name a chemical, one in each case, to show the presence of (a) carbon dioxide and (b) water in expired air.
    (a) ....
    (b) ....

Section B

1. What is meant by the term respiration?
   Write an equation for respiration. Describe an experiment to show that respiring organisms produce carbon dioxide.
2. Draw a large labelled diagram of the human respiratory organs. Describe how breathing occurs.
3. (a) How does oxygen pass from the respiratory system into the bloodstream of the human body?
   (b) Give one function of each of the following: (i) stomata; (ii) diaphragm; (iii) trachea; (iv) alveoli.
4. (a) Label the parts A, B and C on *Fig. 20.15.*

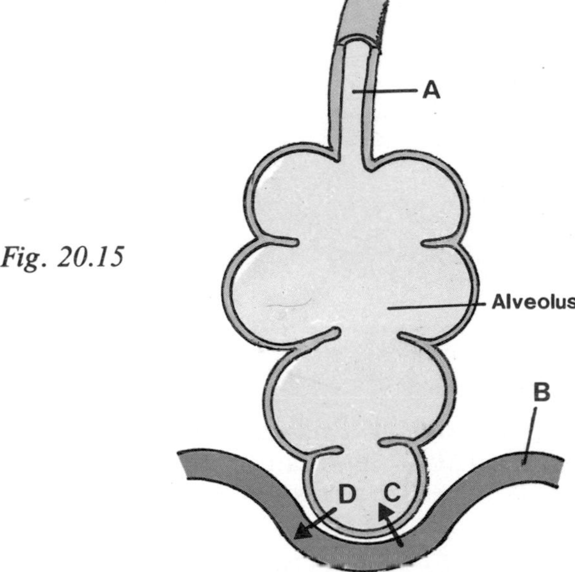

Fig. 20.15

   (b) Name the gas moving in the direction of the arrow shown at D and C.
   (c) List three structures, other than A, through which air will pass on its way from B to the mouth.
5. (a) Explain why the air we exhale contains more carbon dioxide than the air we inhale.
   (b) Describe an experiment to show that exhaled air contains more carbon dioxide than inhaled air.

21 — Water and Transport in Plants

21.1 Water

It is easy to see that water is a very important substance for living organisms. If you forget to water houseplants they wilt and may die. Humans and other animals cannot survive long without drinking some water, and for some other organisms — such as waterlilies, fish and tadpoles — water is their 'home'. The cells of plants and animals actually contain up to 90% water. So, if they are to work properly, these cells must receive a regular supply of water.

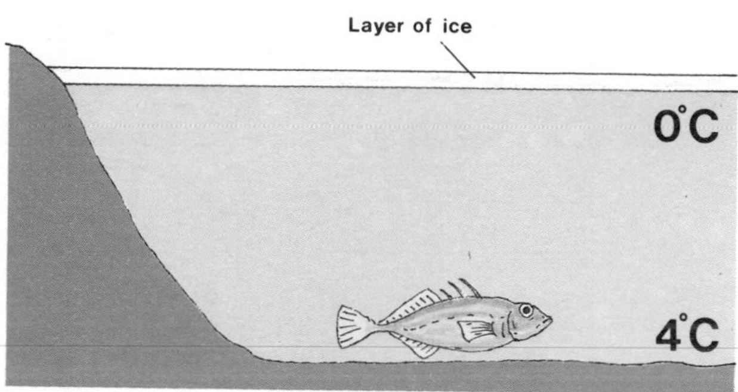

Fig. 21.1 A frozen pond

Important Facts about Water

1. Water is an excellent solvent. This means many things dissolve easily in it. This is important because the chemical reactions in cells, like respiration, take place in a liquid medium (environment).
2. Water acts as a transport medium by carrying dissolved substances. This occurs in the blood of animals and the xylem and phloem of plants.
3. When water freezes, its volume increases, and it becomes less dense. Water has a maximum density at 4°C. This means that ice tends to float to the top of a pond or lake. In this way animals that live at the bottom of the water are protected from freezing.

21.2 How Substances get in and out of Cells

There are a number of ways by which substances move into and out of cells. These include (1) diffusion; (2) osmosis.

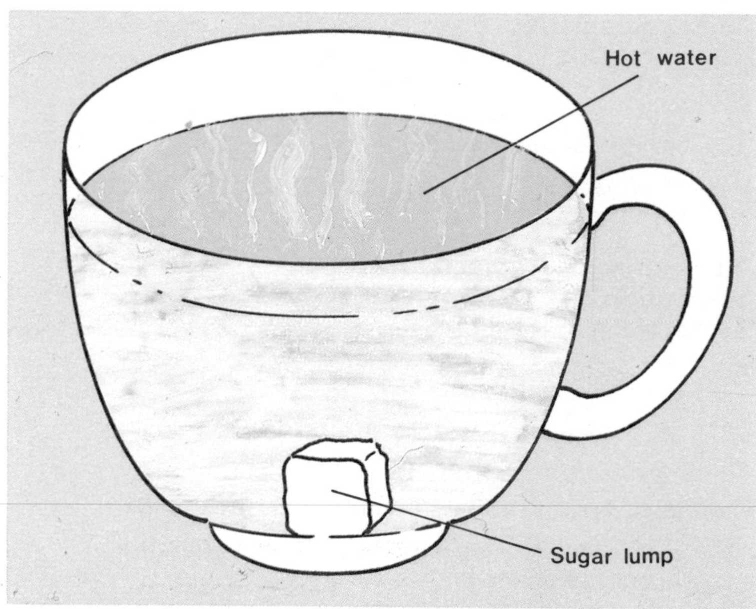

Fig. 21.2 Diffusion

1. **Diffusion** is the movement of molecules from a region of high concentration to a region of low concentration. Look at *Fig. 21.2.* Where is the greatest concentration of sugar molecules? What will happen after a while? We say that the sugar molecules gradually diffuse into the liquid, i.e. they move from where there are a lot of them to where there are less until they are spread evenly throughout the liquid. *(See Chapter 34. Exp. 34.1 Diffusion)*
2. **Osmosis** is the movement of water molecules across a semi-permeable membrane from a region of high water concentration to a region of low water concentration, i.e. from a weak solution to a strong solution.

Experiment 21.1 To Show Osmosis in an Artificial Cell

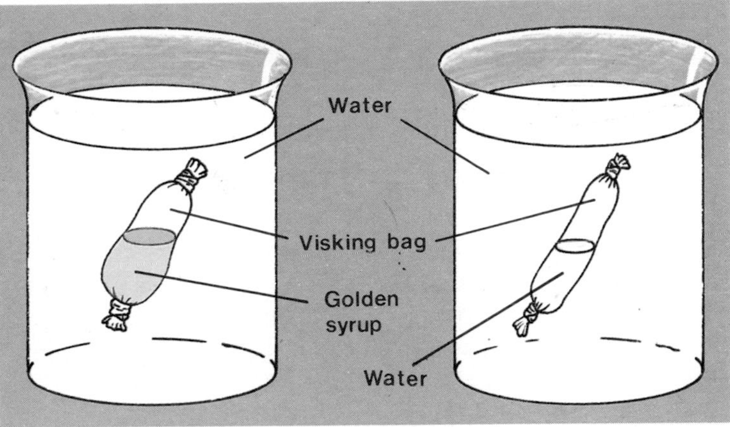

Fig. 21.3

Method

1. Cut a 12-15 cm length of visking tubing. Visking tubing acts as a semi-permeable membrane which lets small molecules through, but blocks larger molecules.
2. Wet the piece of tubing and tie a knot at one end.
3. Pour some golden syrup or diluted honey solution to half-fill the visking bag. Carefully squeeze the air out of the bag and then tie a knot to seal the bag.
4. Place the artificial cell in a beaker and cover with water.
5. Repeat steps 1-4, using water in the visking tubing and cover with water.
6. Label each beaker and set aside for 30 minutes.
7. Record the appearance of the two bags. This is best done by means of simple diagrams.
8. You should observe that the sugar bag has become swollen but that the water has moved from where it is in high concentration (outside the bag) to where it is in low concentration (inside the bag) across the visking membrane. In other words, osmosis has occurred. The water bag shows no change because there is no difference in the concentration of water either side of the membrane.

Experiment 21.2 To Demonstrate Osmosis Using the Thistle Funnel Method

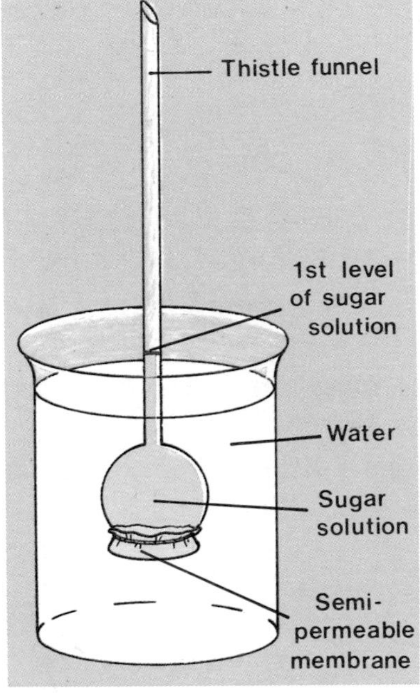

Fig. 21.4

Method

1. Set up the apparatus as shown in *Fig. 21.4.*
2. Mark the height of the sugar solution in the tube.
3. Leave for several hours.
4. Note the change in the level of the sugar solution. Mark this new level.
5. Explain in your own words the reason why the level of the sugar solution rises.

Experiment 21.3 To Demonstrate Osmosis in Living Cells.

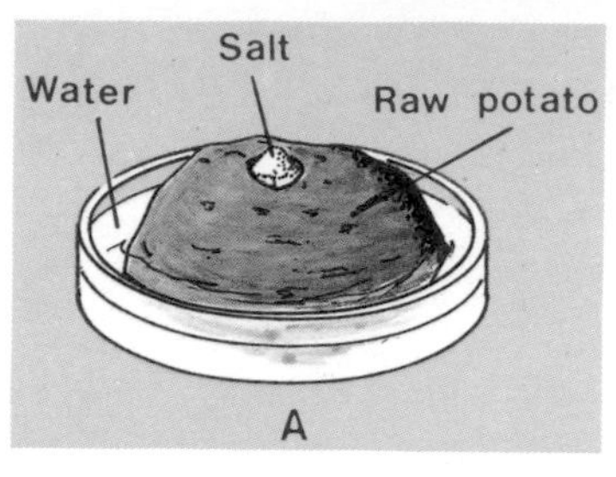

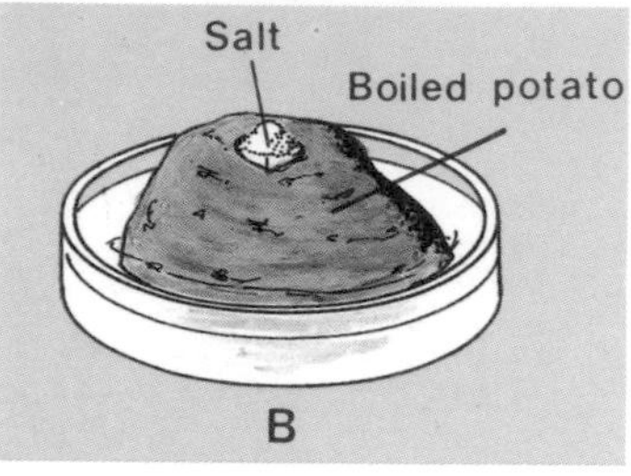

Fig. 21.5

Method

1. Half-fill a beaker with water and bring to the boil.
2. Cut a potato in half. Scoop a hollow in the top of the rounded end of each potato half.
3. Using a tongs, place one potato-half into the hot water. Boil gently for 10 minutes. This kills the potato cells.
4. Half-fill two petri-dishes with water. Label the dishes A and B.
5. Carefully remove the potato from the boiling water. Turn off the Bunsen burner.
6. Place the raw potato-half in dish A and the boiled potato-half in dish B.
7. Carefully fill the hollow in each potato-half with dry salt, *Fig. 21.5.*
8. Leave the dishes for 20 minutes.
9. After this time examine the appearance of the salt in each hollow.
10. You should observe that the salt is wet or dissolved in A but quite dry in B. In A the cells are alive and water is drawn through the potato cells from the dish, by osmosis, to dilute the salt in the hollow. In B the cells are dead and osmosis cannot occur because there are no semi-permeable membranes present.

21.3 Transport in Plants

If plant cells are to carry out their activities, they must be supplied with the raw materials for making energy and for growth. In addition, the wastes they produce must be

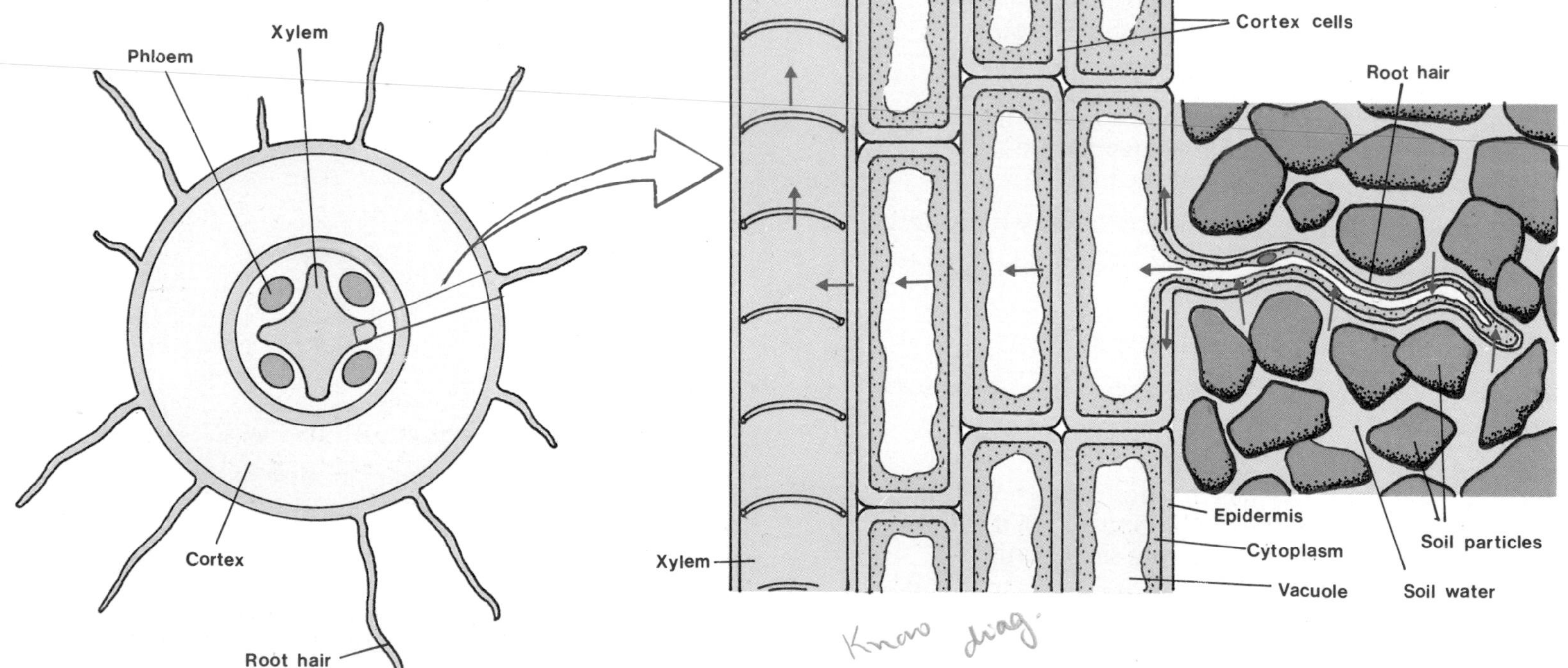

Fig. 21.6 Movement of water across root

removed. This means that plants must have a transport system.

In *Book 1, Chapter 11,* we learned that there are special cells in the plant for transporting substances. These cells are the **xylem** and **phloem**. Together they make up the vascular tissue in the plant. Xylem transports water and mineral salts from the root to the leaves. Phloem carries food made in photosynthesis, to all parts of the plant in a process called **translocation**.

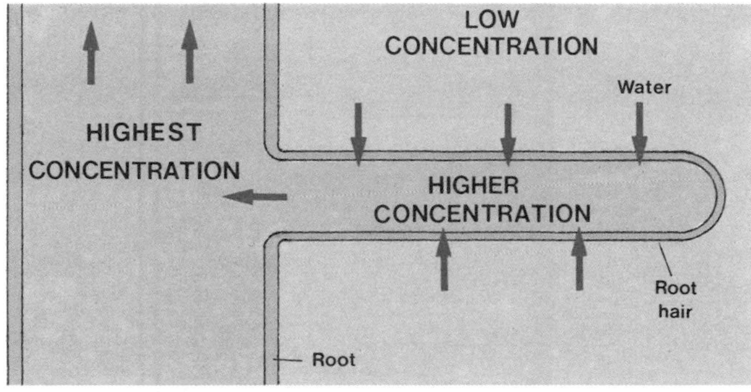

Fig. 21.7 Diagram showing concentrations in and around root

Absorption of Water by the Root

Water from the soil enters the root hairs by osmosis. The soil water surrounding a root hair is a weak solution of dissolved salts. The cytoplasm of a root hair cell contains a more concentrated solution of dissolved substances such as sugars. As a result, water molecules move from where they are in high concentration (outside of the root hair cell) to where they are in low concentration (inside the root hair cell). Mineral salts are taken in with the soil water, not by osmosis, but by a special method which uses energy from respiration. This is known as **active transport**.

Experiment 21.4 To Show the Absorption of Water by Roots

Method

1. Set up the apparatus as in *Fig. 21.8.*

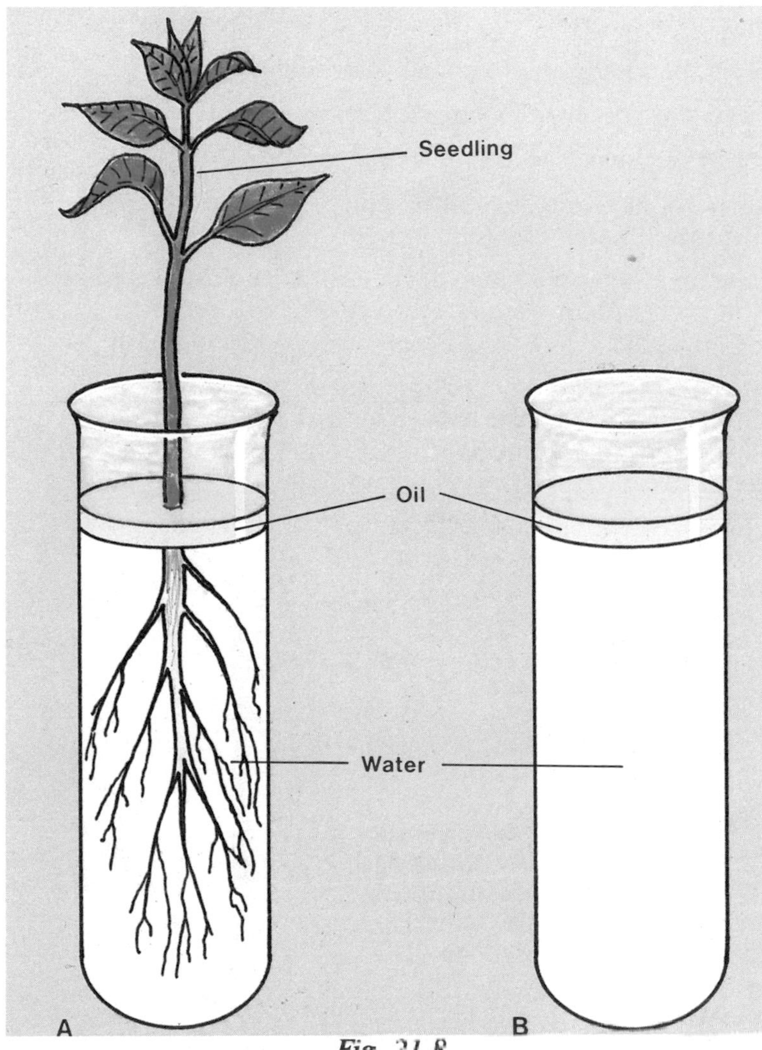

Fig. 21.8

2. Mark the level of the water on both tubes.
3. Set the tubes aside for 5-6 days.
4. Again mark the level of water in both tubes.
5. Note that the level of water in tube A has decreased but that in B it remains the same. This shows that the plant has absorbed water through its roots.

Experiment 21.5 To Show the Pathway of Water Movement in a Plant

Method

1. Gently remove a leafy seedling, e.g. groundsel or shepherd's purse, from the soil and wash its roots.
2. Place the seedling into a beaker or test-tube.
3. Cover the roots with a strong red ink solution.
4. Leave the beaker aside for a few days.
5. After 3-4 days remove the seedling from the ink solution and rinse its roots under a tap.
6. Describe the appearance of the leaves and the leaf veins. Can you explain why the leaf veins have a reddish colouration?
7. Place the seedling on a cutting tile and use a backed blade to cut across the root. Examine the cut surface with a hand lens. You should find that the red dye is at the centre of the root, i.e. in the xylem.
8. Cut across the stem in different places up to the top of the shoot. Examine the cut surfaces with a hand lens and make an outline sketch of one of them to show the position of the red dye.

This experiment shows that water moves upwards through the xylem of the plant.

Root Pressure

The water absorbed by the root hairs travels across the cortex of the root to the xylem as *Fig. 21.6* shows. In some plants, the water collecting in the xylem causes a pressure known as root pressure, which forces water a certain distance up the xylem tubes.

Experiment 21.6 To Demonstrate Root Pressure

Method

1. Cut the stem of a well-watered pot plant about 2 cm above soil level.
2. Push a piece of rubber tubing over the cut stump.
3. Attach a piece of glass tubing to the top of the rubber tubing.
4. Pour some water down the glass tubing to a depth of 5 cm.
5. Mark the level of the water using a rubber band or pen.
6. Notice an increase in the level of water over a period of days. The level rises due to root pressure.

21.4 Transpiration

Transpiration is the loss of water vapour from the plant. This loss of water usually takes place through the stomata of the leaves which are openings, that can be found on the underside of leaves.

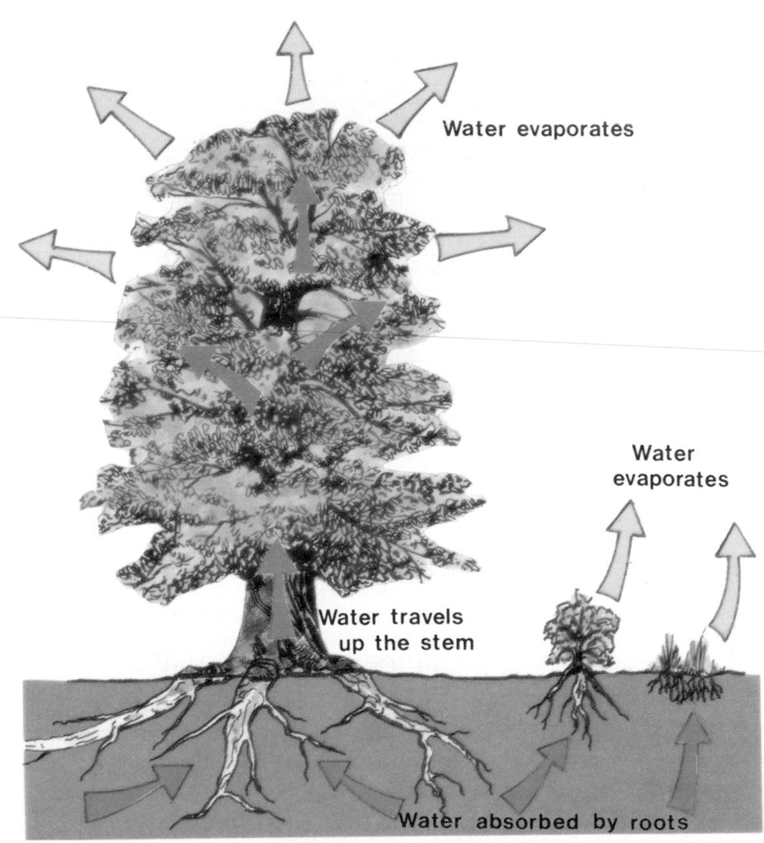

Fig. 21.9 Transpiration stream.

Experiment 21.7 To Demonstrate Transpiration

Method

1. Take a well watered pot plant and cover it with a plastic bag as shown in *Fig. 21.10.*

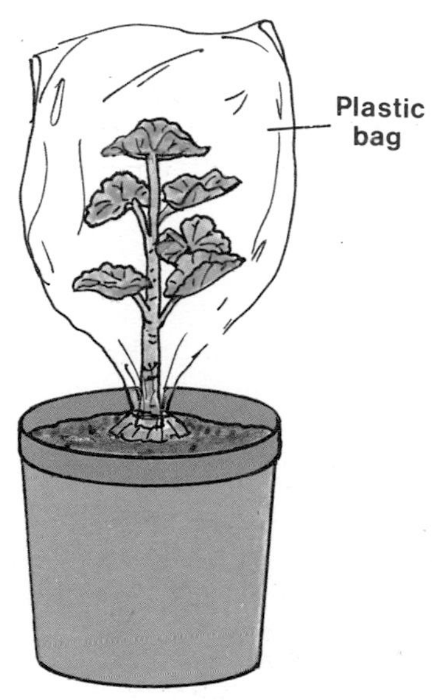

Fig. 21.10

2. Leave for several hours in a bright warm position.
3. Droplets of a colourless liquid condense on the inside of the plastic bag.
4. Test the droplets with blue cobalt chloride paper to show that the liquid is water. The cobalt chloride paper will turn pink.

An alternative method for this experiment is shown in *Fig. 21.11.*

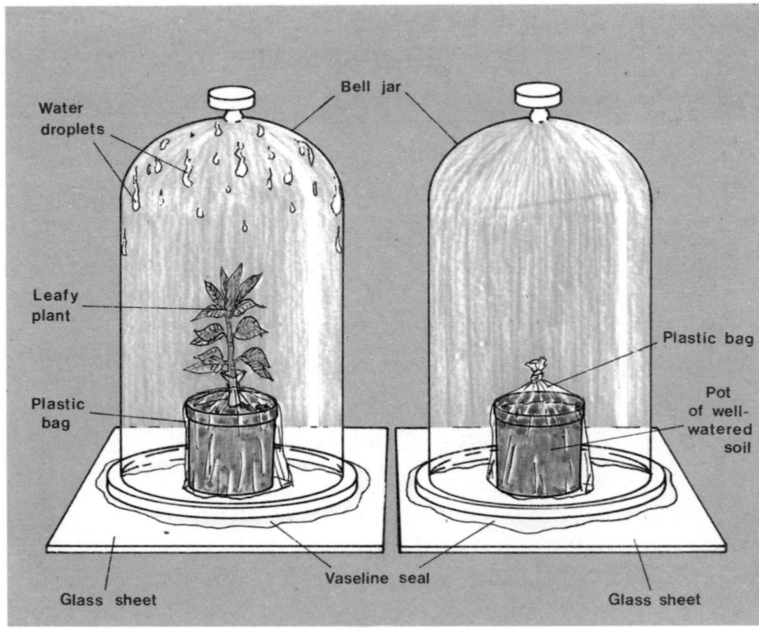

Fig. 21.11 To demonstrate transpiration

The effect of transpiration in the leaf is to cause water from the xylem vessels (in the veins) to pass into the leaf cells. This movement of water is to replace that which is evaporating out of the leaf. As a result, water is pulled up through the xylem from the root in what is known as the transpiration stream.

The functions of transpiration are:

1. To bring water, necessary for photosynthesis, from the roots to the leaves.
2. To carry mineral salts dissolved in the water up through the plant.
3. To cool the plant — in a similar way to that in which perspiring cools us down.

The rise of water from the roots to the leaves of plants is brought about by a 'push' from below (root pressure) and a 'pull' from above (transpiration).

Experiment 21.8 To Measure the Rate of Transpiration Using a Potometer

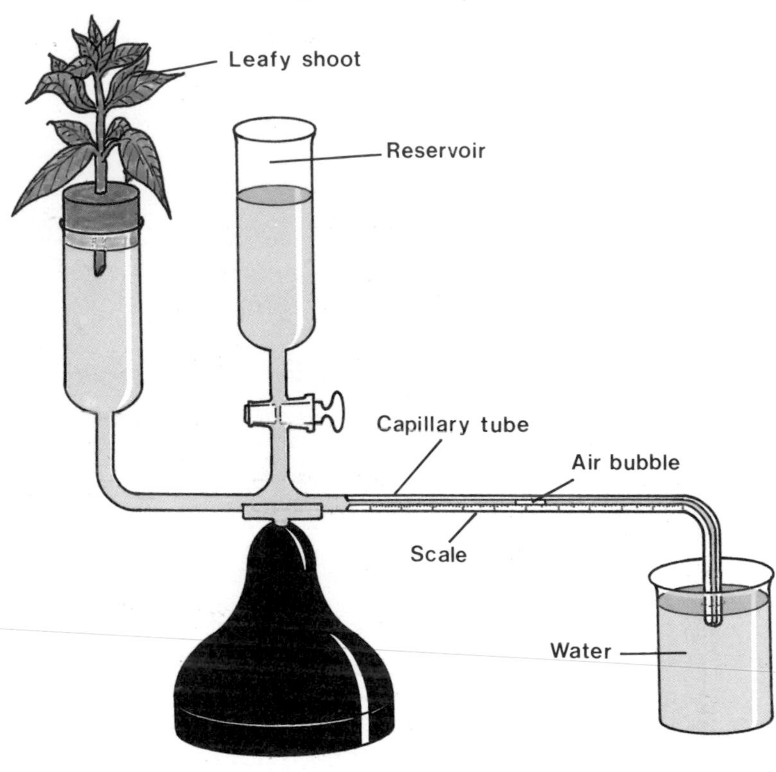

Fig. 21.12 Potometer

A potometer is an instrument which measures the rate at which a plant takes in water. Generally, the rate of water absorption is very nearly equal to the rate of transpiration, so we can use a potometer to measure the transpiration rate.

Precaution: It is necessary to keep the cut shoot stem in water from the minute it is cut, to prevent air entering the xylem vessels and so prevent movement of water.

Method

1. Cut a leafy shoot and place the cut end in water straight away.
2. Submerge the potometer, with its tap open, in a basin of water.
3. Cut the stem of the leafy shoot again, under water, and position the shoot in the potometer. Ensure that all the connections are airtight.
4. Close the tap and remove the potometer plus shoot from the basin.
5. Set up the potometer as in *Fig. 21.12*.
6. Introduce an air bubble into the capillary tube by removing the tube from the beaker for a few seconds, and then replacing it.
7. Note the position of the air bubble. The rate of transpiration (water uptake) can be seen by the rate at which the air bubble moves along the capillary tube.
8. Keep the potometer in a warm sunny position and measure the distance that the air bubble moves in 3 minutes. Take repeat measurements after 6 minute and 9 minutes and use these results to give you results for 3 consecutive 3 minute periods.
9. Calculate the average rate per minute by adding the three results together, and then dividing by 3.

Table 21.1

Reading	*Distance travelled by bubble in 3 minutes*	*Rate of water intake* = D/T
1		
2		
3		
Average		

Factors affecting the Rate of Transpiration

1. **Sunlight** — For transpiration to occur the stomata must be open. Generally stomata open during the day and close at night. So when light strength (intensity) increases, the rate of transpiration increases.

2. **Humidity** — Humidity refers to the amount of water vapour in the air outside the leaf. On a wet or damp day the air is full of water vapour, i.e. the humidity is high. In these conditions the rate of transpiration is low. Dry air increases the rate of transpiration.

3. **Air Movements** — Transpiration increases with a breeze. In still air the rate of transpiration is reduced.

4. **Amount of Water in the Soil** — If the amount of water available in the soil is very low, the rate of transpiration will decrease.

Summary

* Water is a good solvent and it acts as a medium for transport and chemical reactions.
* Diffusion and osmosis are two methods by which substances pass into and out of cells.
* Movement of food in the phloem of a plant is known as translocation.
* Water is absorbed through the root hairs by osmosis.
* Root pressure forces water a certain distance up the xylem vessels.
* Transpiration is the loss of water vapour from the plant.
* Transpiration occurs through the stomata.
* The transpiration stream causes water and mineral salts to be drawn up the plant from the roots to the leaves.
* A potometer is used to measure the rate of transpiration in a cut shoot.
* Factors which affect the rate of transpiration include (i) light intensity; (ii) humidity; (iii) air movements; (iv) available soil water.

Questions

Section A

1. Water is a good solvent. This means ....
   ....

2. List the ways in which a person gains water ....
   ....

3. Osmosis is ....
   ....

4. Diffusion is the movement of molecules from a region of .... to a region of ....

5. Translocation is the name given to the movement of ... . in the plant.

6. Food is carried in the .... and mineral salts in the ....

7. Describe a simple test to show that water is given off by the leaves of a plant. ....
   ....

8. Where does transpiration occur? ....

9. Describe the conditions which favour rapid transpiration. ....
   ....

10. The term used for the loss of water from the leaves of plants is included in the following list. Underline the correct term: expiration; perspiration; transpiration; translocation.

Section B

1. List the properties of water. Outline how any two of them are important for living things. Describe a simple test for water.

2. Consider the experiment shown in *Fig. 21.13.* State what could be observed after some time. Explain what happens during the experiment.

3. Describe an experiment to show that green plants transpire. List the factors which affect the rate of transpiration. State the conditions in which the rate of transpiration is greatest. Draw a labelled diagram of a potometer.

Fig. 21.13

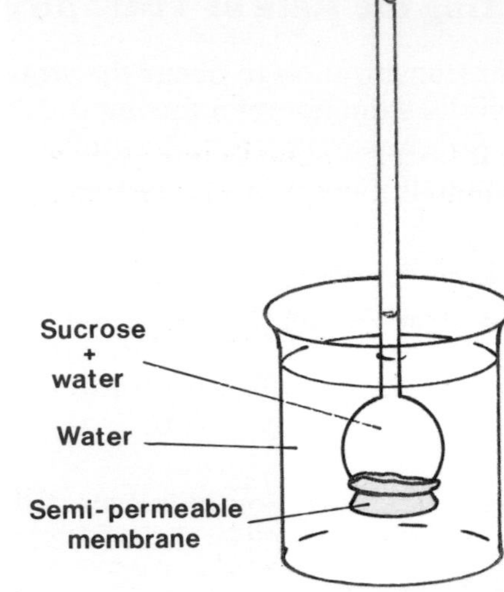

22 — Blood

The blood is the transport tissue in our body and the bodies of most animals. An adult human has 5 litres of blood.

22.1 Composition of Blood

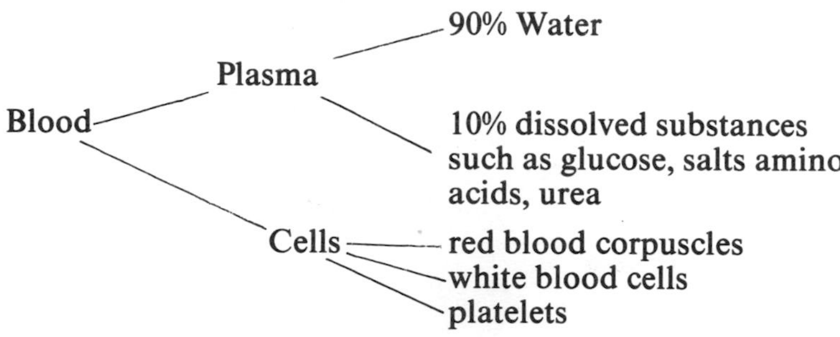

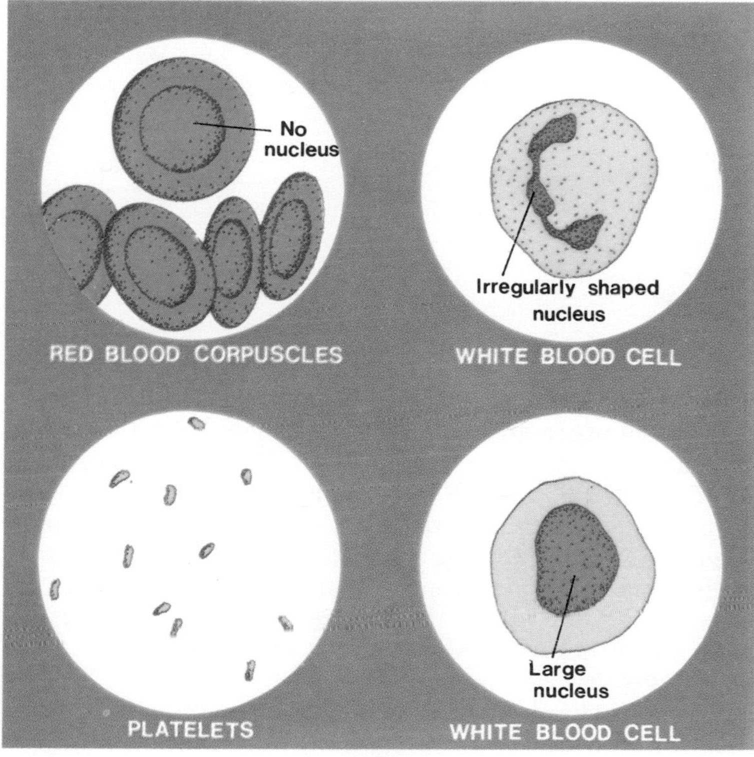

Fig. 22.1 Blood cells

Table 22.1 Facts about Blood Cells

	Red blood corpuscle	*White blood cell*	*Platelets*
Shape	round, biconcave* containing the red pigment haemoglobin	no definite shape — several types	fragments of cells
Nucleus	no nucleus	each type has a different shaped nucleus	no nucleus
Made in	bone marrow	bone marrow	bone marrow
Frequency	5 million/ mm^3	8,000 /mm^3	250,000/mm^3
Function	transport oxygen	1. protect against disease 2. produce antibodies	clotting of blood

* Biconcave means hollowed out on both surfaces.

Experiment 22.1 To Make a Blood Smear

Method

1. Your teacher will obtain a blood sample from an official source and will show you how to smear the drop of blood on the slide correctly.
2. Add 2-3 drops of *Leishman's Stain.* Leave for 5 minutes.
3. Gently wash off any excess stain under a slowly running tap.
4. Allow the slide to dry.

5. Examine the slide under the L.P. of the microscope. Blood cells are very tiny so look at the edge of the smear rather than in the middle.

6. Identify and draw a red corpuscle and a white blood cell under the H.P. magnification.

22.2 Functions of Blood

1. **Transport**

Blood carries many substances:

(a) Oxygen diffuses from the air in the lungs into the haemoglobin of the red blood corpuscles, forming oxyhaemoglobin. When these corpuscles reach the body tissues the oxygen diffuses from the haemoglobin into the cells.

(b) Carbon dioxide, produced during respiration in the cells, is carried back to the lungs, dissolved in the plasma.

(c) Excretory substances, such as urea from the liver, are carried by the blood.

(d) Digested food, such as glucose and amino acids, is transported to the cells.

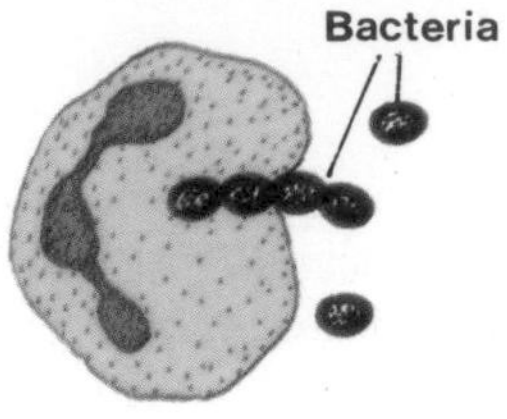

Fig. 22.2 (a)

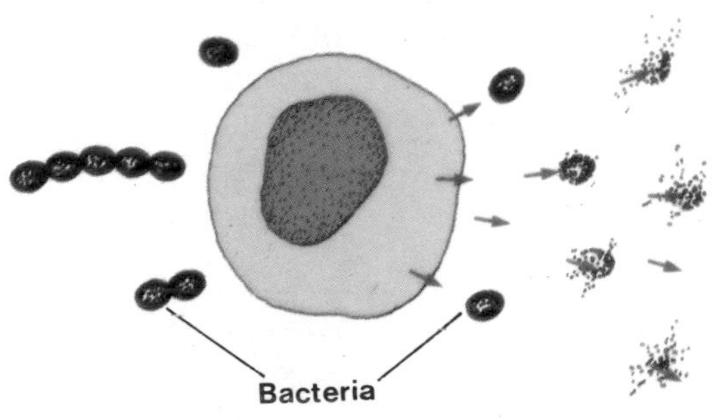

Fig. 22.2 (b)

2. **Defence against Disease**

(a) The white blood cells can engulf and destroy bacteria and other germs which invade the body, *Fig. 22.2 (a)*

(b) Some white blood cells produce chemicals called **antibodies**, which destroy harmful bacteria, *Fig. 22.2 (b).*

(c) Blood clotting: the platelets help in the process of blood clotting. This prevents loss of blood and protects the skin from invading bacteria or viruses.

3. **Distribution of Body Heat**

The chemical reactions which go on in cells produce heat energy. The muscles and liver are the main heat producing areas of the body. The blood carries the heat from the heat generating areas to parts of the body where little heat is produced.

22.3 Blood Groups

There are four main blood groups, known as A, B, AB, and O. If you belong to group A, this means you have a chemical called A in your blood. A group B person has a chemical called B, and AB person has both A and B present, whilst a person with group O has neither chemical present. In addition to this, a person may or may not have a chemical known as the rhesus factor. If they do have the rhesus factor, they will be rhesus positive, and if not, they will be rhesus negative. About one in seven people are rhesus negative.

In England, blood group O is the most common, followed closely by blood group A. A smaller proportion of people are blood group B, with group AB being the least common of all.

22.4 The Heart

The blood is carried around the body in blood vessels called arteries and veins. The heart is a pump which pushes the blood into the arteries. The human heart is about the size of your clenched fist and it lies between the lungs in the chest. The walls of the heart are made of cardiac muscle. This type of muscle never tires, it keeps working right throughout our lives. The structure of the heart can be seen in *Fig. 22.4.* Important points to note are:

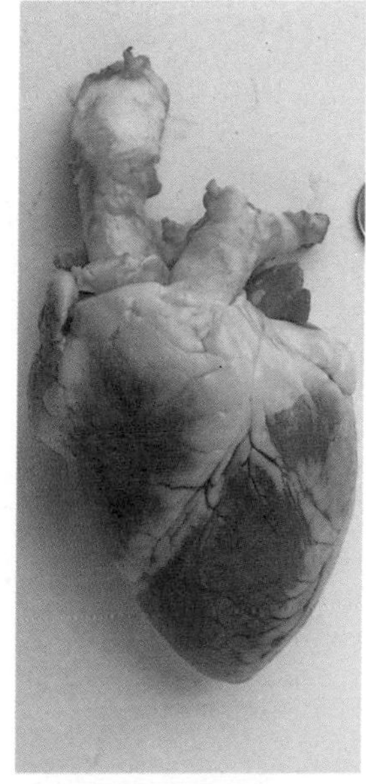

Fig. 22.3 Sheep's heart

1. The heart consists of four chambers, two atria at the top and two ventricles at the bottom. The ventricles are larger than the atria.
2. The left-hand side of the heart is separated from the right side by a muscular wall called the septum.
3. Valves in the heart stop a backflow of blood.
4. The muscular wall of the left ventricle is thicker than that of the right ventricle. This is because blood in the left ventricle has to be pushed all around the body whereas the blood in the right ventricle has only to be pushed a short distance to the lungs.

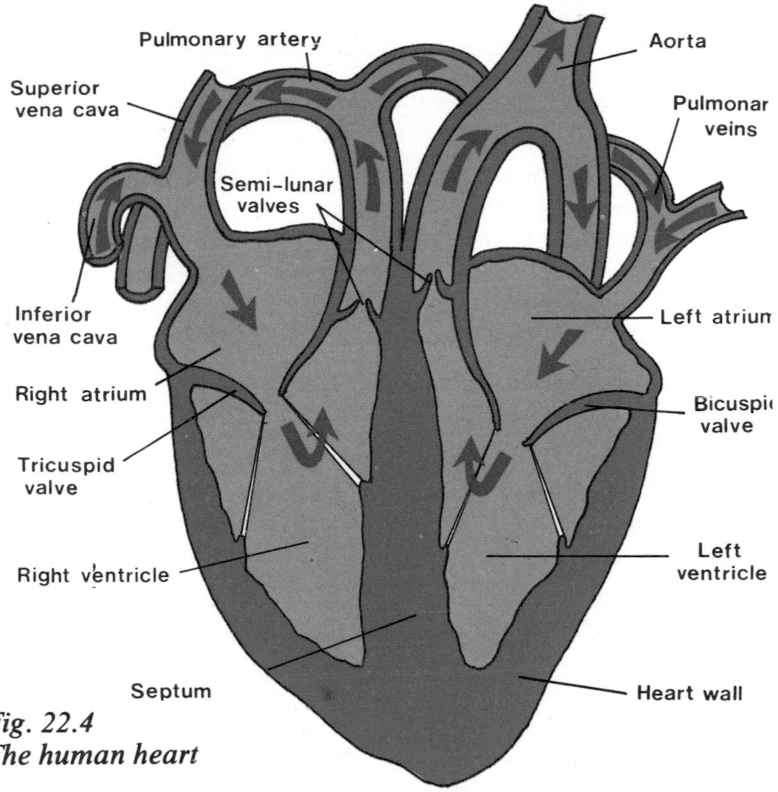

Fig. 22.4
The human heart

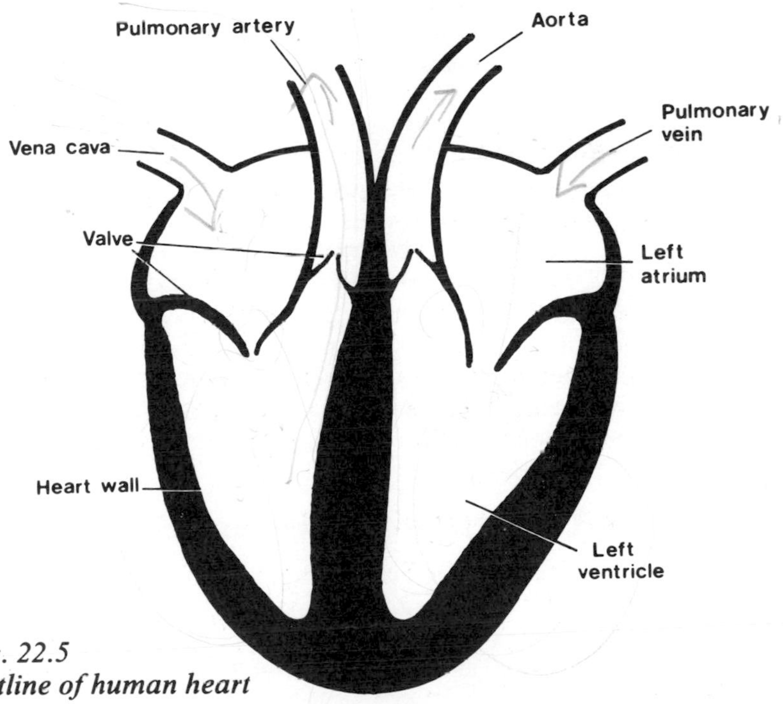

Fig. 22.5
Outline of human heart

The Pathway of Blood Through the Heart

Blood always enters the heart from the veins and leaves through the arteries.

1. Blood from the head, neck and arms enters the right atrium through the superior vena cava (the main vein of the body) and from the chest, abdomen and legs through the inferior vena cava. At the same time as the right atrium is filling with blood, the left atrium receives blood from the lungs through the pulmonary veins.
2. The muscles in the walls of the atria contract, the bicuspid and tricuspid valves open and the ventricles fill with blood.
3. Then the muscular walls of the ventricles contract, the bicuspid and tricuspid valves close, the semi-lunar valves open and the blood is forced into the arteries.
4. Blood from the right ventricle is pushed into the pulmonary artery and passes to the lungs. Blood from the left ventricle is pushed into the aorta and is pumped all around the body.

22.5 Heart Beat

The pumping of the blood through the heart can be felt as the heart beats. The average adult heart beats about 72 times per minute. It is possible to detect the heart beat in other parts of the body by taking a person's pulse. The pulse is when you feel the beat of the heart in an artery lying close to the surface of the skin. A pulse can be found at the wrist, temple, neck and groin. Take your pulse by counting the number of beats you can feel in 15 seconds and then multiply the number you get by four. Do this three times and then get an average. Is your pulse rate similar to the average of 72 beats per minute? What things do you think would (a) increase, (b) slow down, your pulse rate?

Factors Affecting The Heart Beat

When a person is walking or running, his muscles are working hard, and they require more oxygen and glucose than they did when the person was sitting down. The heart responds by beating faster, to maintain an adequate supply of these things.

Experiment 22.2

Method

1. Sit quietly for a few minutes, and then take your pulse for 15 seconds. Multiply this by 4 to find your resting pulse rate per minute.

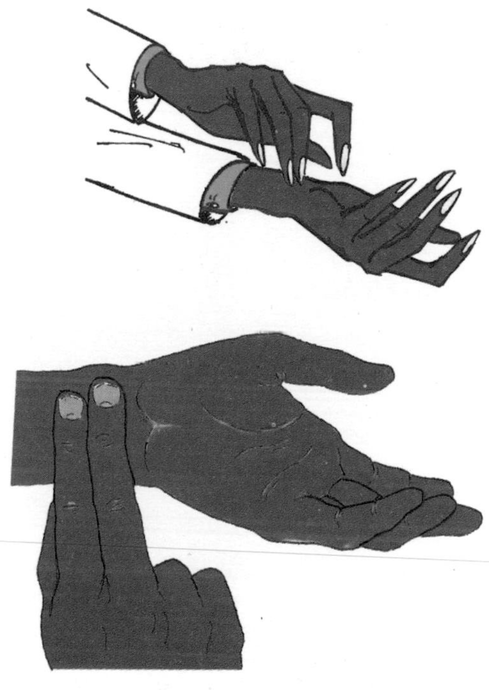

Fig. 22.6 Finding your pulse

2. Undertake some exercise for several minutes, e.g. running up and down stairs, or running on the spot, etc.
3. Take your pulse rate for 15 seconds, at the end of the exercise period, and at one minute intervals for 5 minutes (continue for longer, if necessary). Multiply each of your answers by 4 to find the pulse rate per minute.

Table 22.2

Time after exercise (minutes)	0	1	2	3	4	5
Pulses in 15 seconds						
Pulse rate per minute						

4. Plot your results on a graph of pulse rate per minute, against time in minutes. *Fig. 22.7*

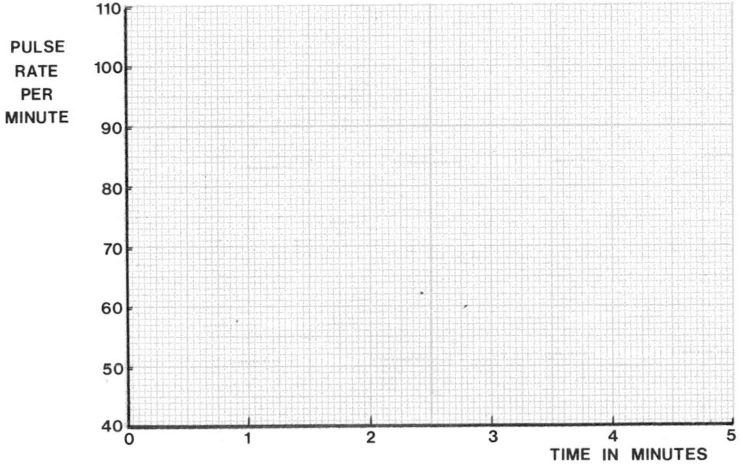

Fig. 22.7

You will have found that immediately after exercise, your heart beats faster, indicating that the heart is pumping more blood, and it takes a number of minutes for the heart beat rate to return to the resting stage.

Blood Pressure

Blood has to be pumped all round our body, sometimes against the pull of gravity, e.g. to the brain. This means that it must be pumped at great pressure. Sometimes people suffer from high blood pressure. This is often caused by thickening or hardening of the arteries, which makes the heart's job more difficult. Steps should be taken to ensure that no further damage occurs, for example by cutting down the amount of fat in the diet or by giving up smoking.

Table 22.3 The Blood Vessels of the Heart

Blood Vessel	*Function*
Aorta	The largest artery in the body. It carries oxygenated blood (blood rich in oxygen) from the left ventricle all around the body (except the lungs).
Vena Cavae	The main veins of the body. They carry deoxygenated blood to the right atrium from the rest of the body (except the lungs).
Pulmonary artery	Carries deoxygenated blood from the right ventricle to the lungs.
Pulmonary veins	Carry oxygenated blood from the lungs to the left atrium.

22.6 Blood Vessels

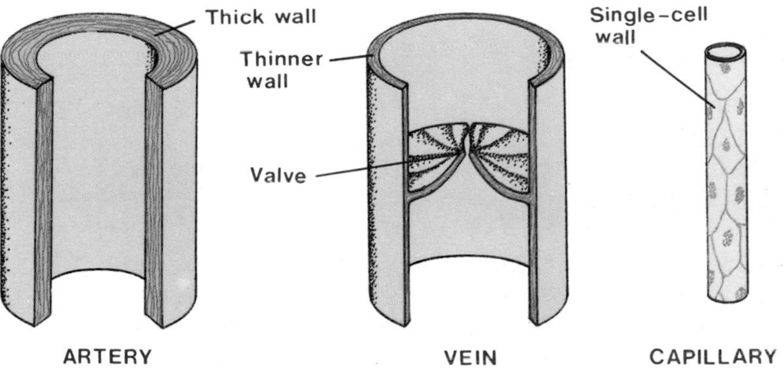

Fig. 22.8

Arteries — are blood vessels with thick elastic walls. They do not have valves and their internal diameter (lumen) is fairly small. Arteries carry blood under pressure **away** from the heart. With the exception of the pulmonary artery, all arteries carry oxygenated blood to all parts of the body. When the arteries reach the tissues of the body, the dissolved substances they carry must be able to pass out into the cells. To do this, the arteries branch into smaller vessels called arterioles which divide again into a network of tiny vessels called capillaries.

Capillaries — have walls which are only one cell thick. It is through the walls of the capillaries that substances such as oxygen and glucose can diffuse from the blood into the cells, where they are used. Wastes, such as carbon dioxide produced by the cells, pass back into the capillaries. These then join to form venules which unite to form veins. Veins carry blood back to the heart. Capillaries act as a link between the arteries and the veins.

Veins — are blood vessels with elastic walls. They have valves to prevent a backflow of blood and their lumen is fairly large. Veins carry blood **towards** the heart and all veins, except the pulmonary veins, carry deoxygenated blood. The blood flowing through the vein is not under pressure as it is in the arteries.

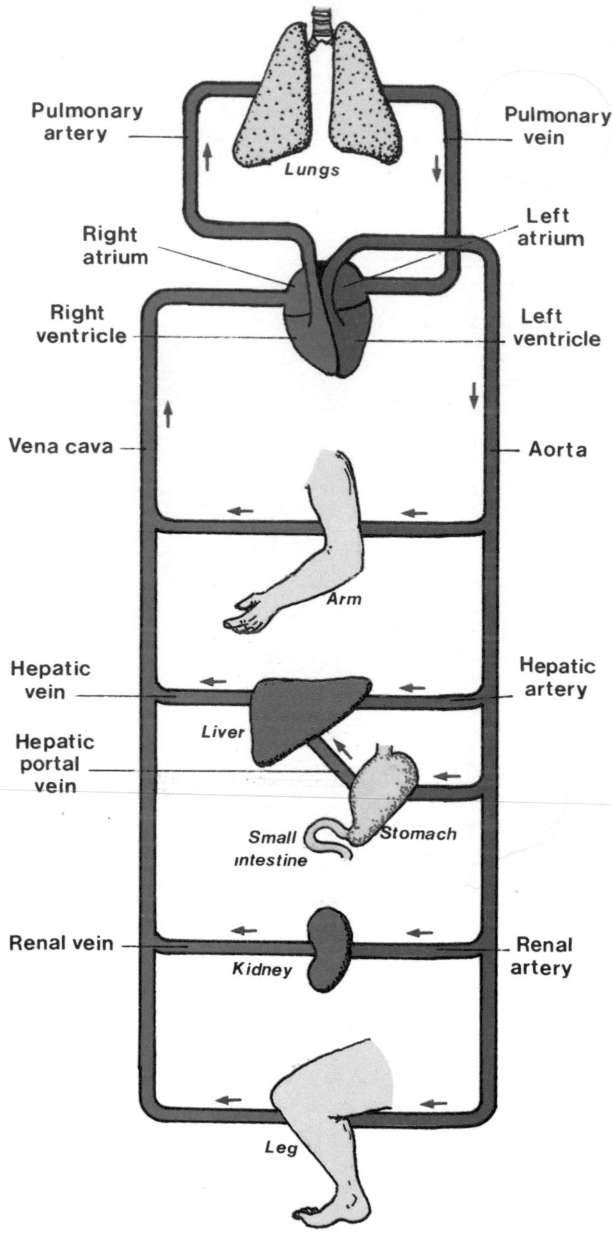

Fig. 22.9 Blood circulation

22.7 Circulation

The circulatory system consists of the blood, heart and blood vessels. The function of the system is to keep the blood moving in only one direction. This ensures that substances are transported from one place to another. For example, some glucose which has been stored in the liver is needed in the leg. Using *Fig. 22.9* let us trace the pathway that glucose must take to reach a muscle in the leg. The glucose leaves the liver in the hepatic vein and travels to the heart in the inferior vena cava. It passes down the right hand side of the heart and out to the lungs in the pulmonary artery. From the lungs, it passes back into the left hand side of the heart through the pulmonary veins and out of the heart again in the aorta. The glucose passes down the aorta until it reaches the leg artery by which it will arrive at the muscle cells in the leg. Quite a journey! But it shows the one-way direction of the blood flow.

22.8 The Lymphatic System

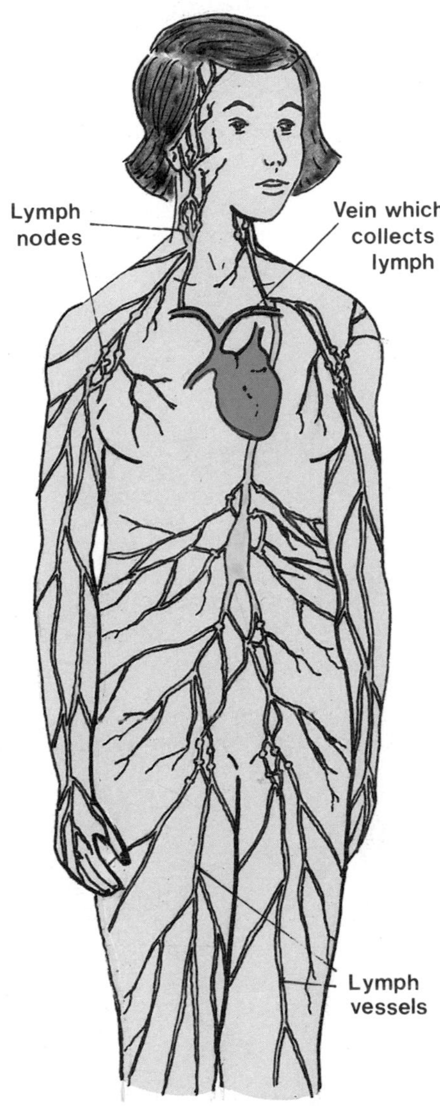

Fig. 22.10 The lymphatic system

All the cells of the body are bathed in a fluid called tissue fluid. This fluid is formed when blood plasma leaks from the blood capillaries.

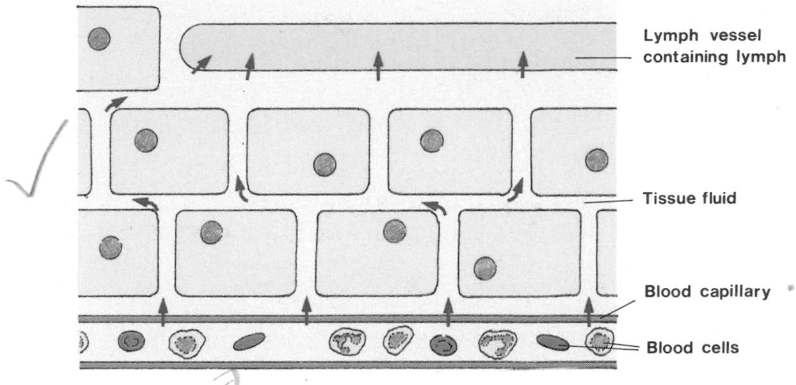

Fig. 22.11 Formation of lymphatic system

Substances needed by the cells of the body diffuse through the capillary wall into the tissue fluid and from there into the cells. Wastes produced by the cells, pass back into the blood via the tissue fluid. Any excess tissue fluid that does not drain back into the blood capillaries will drain into blind ending lymph vessels, where it is known as **lymph**. The lymph vessels join up with each other forming the **lymphatic system**. Eventually the lymph passes back into the veins near the collar bone. In this way leakages from the blood are collected so that the total volume of fluid circulating in the body remains constant.

Functions of the Lymphatic System

1. To absorb the leakages from the blood.
2. To assist the passage of substances into and out of the cells.
3. To transport fatty acids and glycerol from the villi of the small intestine to the blood stream.
4. To produce special white blood cells (lymphocytes) which help fight disease.

Summary

* Blood is composed of (a) a liquid called plasma; (b) red blood corpuscles which carry oxygen; (c) white blood cells which help fight disease; and (d) platelets which help the blood to clot.
* The functions of the blood are: (a) transport; (b) defence against disease; and (c) distribution of body heat.
* Blood travels around the body in arteries, veins and capillaries. The capillaries link the arteries and veins. Substances pass into and out of the blood through the walls of the capillaries.
* The heart is a hollow muscular organ which pumps blood around the body.
* Plasma which leaks from the blood forms tissue fluid.
* Tissue fluid drains into the lymph vessels and forms lymph.

Questions

Section A

1. List the constituents of blood. ....

   ....

2. State two functions of blood:

   1. ....

   2. ....

3. Where is the heart located? ....
4. All arteries carry blood rich in oxygen. True or False? . .
5. Blood flowing through the heart follows the pathway: vena cava → right .... → .... → lungs.
6. Where does blood go to when it leaves the left ventricle of the heart? ....
7. Name a type of blood vessel which has a thin wall and valves. ....

   ....

8. State the function of a valve ....
9. What is lymph? ....

   ....

10. Name a substance that lymph transports from the small intestine. ....
11. Name the main blood groups. ....
12. State 2 factors that could alter the rate of your heart beat. 1. ....

    2. ....

Section B

1. (a) Label the structures A-G on the following diagram of the external features of the heart.

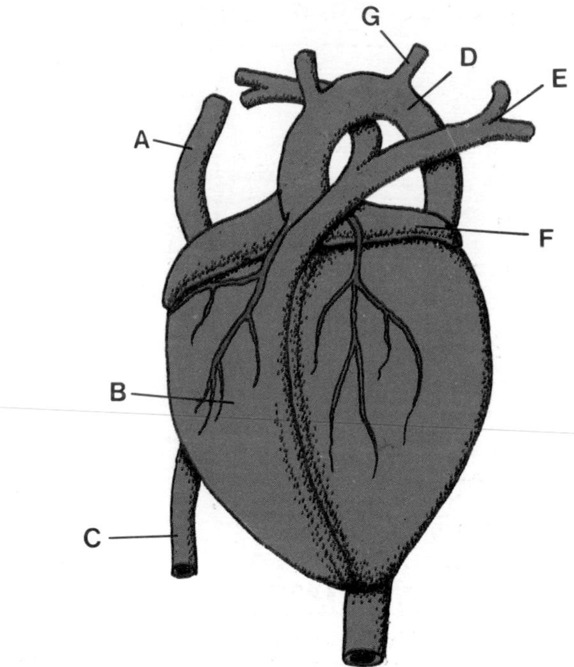

Fig. 22.12

   (b) State the part of the body supplied by blood vessel E.

2. Describe how a vein and artery differ in (a) function; (b) structure.
3. Draw a clearly labelled diagram of the internal structure of the heart and the main blood vessels entering and leaving it.
4. Describe the pathway that glucose must follow, when it travels from the intestines to a muscle in the arm.

23 — Excretion in Man

23.1 Introduction

The chemical reactions that go on inside the cells of plants and animals produce wastes in addition to useful substances. For example, respiration not only produces energy which is needed by the body, but also carbon dioxide and water which are waste products. Such wastes which result from metabolism* could become harmful and must be removed from the body of a plant or animal.

Excretion is the removal of the wastes of metabolism from the body of a plant or animal.

*** Metabolism is a word which summarises all the chemical reactions that go on inside living cells.**

23.2 Excretion in Man

Our waste products are removed from the body by excretory organs. *Table 23.1* summarises the major excretory organs and their waste products.

Table 23.1

Excretory Organ	*Waste product(s)*
Lungs	Carbon dioxide and water vapour
Kidneys	Urine (urea, water and salts)
Skin	Sweat (water and salts)

Carbon dioxide is produced during respiration:

$$C_6H_{12}O_6 + 6O_2 \rightarrow 6CO_2 + 6H_2O + \text{Energy}$$

Urea is produced in the liver from the break down of amino acids. When protein in the diet is digested, amino acids are produced which are used to build and repair cells. But if too much protein is eaten, the excess amino acids cannot be stored; they are broken down in the liver and urea is formed.

The Urinary System

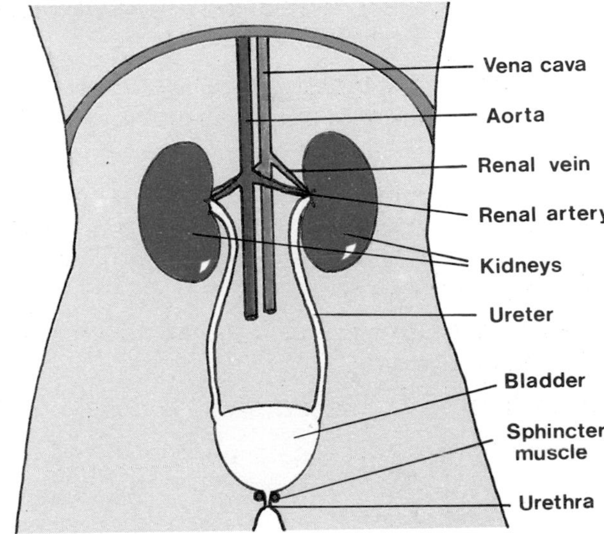

Fig. 23.1 Excretory organs (Urinary System)

The kidneys form part of the urinary system in man, *Fig. 23.1.* A pair of bean-shaped kidneys lie attached to the back of the abdominal wall. Each kidney is fed by a renal artery carrying blood rich in oxygen and urea and is drained by a renal vein. The ureter is a thin tube which connects the kidney to the bladder where urine is stored. The urine is released from the body through the urethra. A special muscle in the urethra controls the release of urine from the bladder.

Kidney Structure

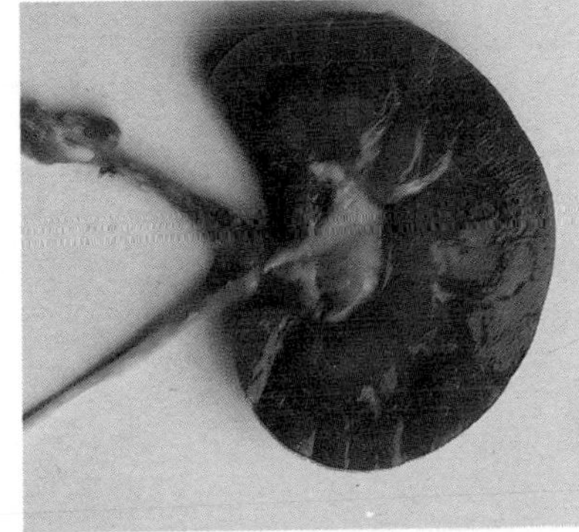

Fig. 23.2 Sheep's kidney

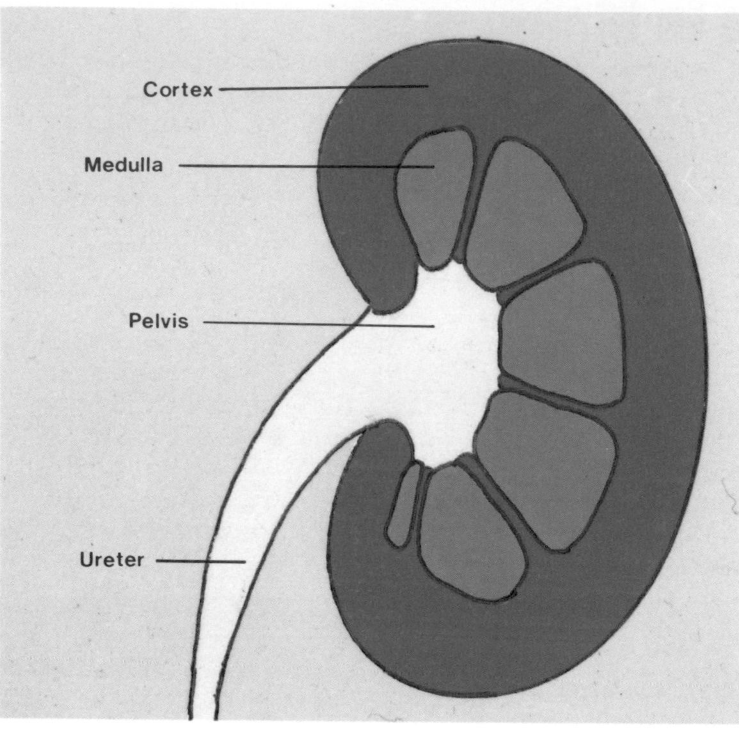

Fig. 23.3 L.S. of kidney

If a kidney is sliced open longitudinally, it can be seen to be made of three main parts, *Fig. 23.3*:

(a) The cortex on the outside.
(b) The medulla containing a number of pyramids.
(c) The pelvis, a white/creamy area.

You should try finding these parts in a sheep's or pig's kidney, *Fig. 23.2.*

The Functions of the Kidney

1. To make urine.
2. To regulate the water content of the body.

1. How the Kidney makes Urine

The cortex and medulla of the kidney are composed of millions of tiny tubules called **nephrons**. It is in the nephrons that urine is made. The blood coming to the kidney (in the renal artery) contains many useful substances such as glucose and amino acids in addition to the urea which is a waste. The body wants to get rid of its waste but to keep the useful substances. So the function of the nephron is to filter the blood. Glucose and other substances needed by the body are taken back into the blood stream through capillaries which later join to form the renal vein. The urea and excess water remain in the nephrons and combine to form urine. The urine passes from the kidney to the bladder where it is stored.

Nowadays, people who suffer from kidney failure can be attached to a kidney machine which will do the job of filtering the blood and producing urine. Usually a patient has to spend several hours about twice a week connected to a kidney machine. Yet, despite the inconvenience, these machines have helped many people live fairly normal lives.

2. Water Regulation

Another function of the kidney is to control the amount of water in the body. If you drink large amounts of water you will produce a lot of diluted urine. On the other hand, if you do not drink enough water, then you produce a small amount of very strong urine. In this situation, the kidney is helping to conserve or keep water in the body.

The Skin

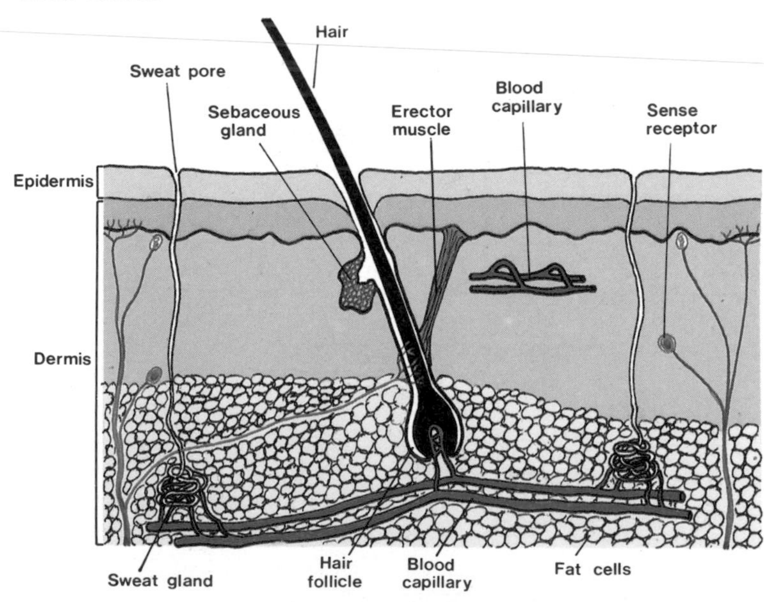

Fig. 23.4 V.S. of skin

The skin forms the outer covering over the whole body. The functions of the skin are shown in *Table 23.2.*

Table 23.2 Functions of the Skin

Function	*Explanation*
1. Excretion	The skin removes excess water and mineral salts through the sweat pores.
2. Sense Organ	The skin contains many sense receptors for detecting stimuli such as heat, cold, touch and pain.
3. Protection	The skin protects the organs below from damage and it prevents entry of bacteria and other harmful substances.
4. Temperature Regulation	The skin helps to control body temperature in a number of ways as *Fig. 23.5* shows.

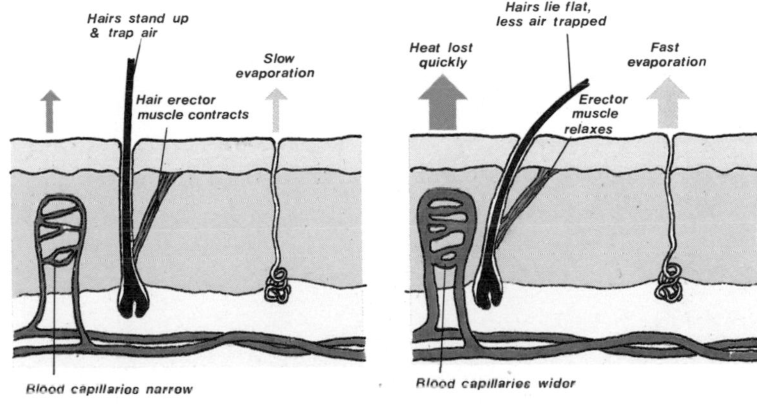

Fig. 23.5 Temperature regulation

The Lungs

The lungs are an excretory organ because they remove carbon dioxide and water vapour. Details of the structure and function of the lungs can be found in *Chapter 20 — Respiration.*

Excretion in Plants

Excretion in plants is simpler than that in animals and they do not have elaborate excretory organs. Plants release the waste gases from photosynthesis (oxygen) and respiration (carbon dioxide) through the stomata. Other wastes are made insoluble and stored inside cells without causing harm. In some deciduous plants (shrubs and trees), waste materials are deposited in the leaves during the growing season and then, when the leaves fall in the autumn, the wastes are removed as well.

Summary

* Excretion means getting rid of wastes made in the body of an organism.
* Excretory wastes include water, carbon dioxide and urea.
* The main excretory organs in man are the kidneys, skin and lungs.
* The functions of the kidneys are:
  1. Excretion of urine.
  2. Regulation of the water balance in the body.
* The skin excretes water and mineral salts in the form of sweat.
* The lungs excrete carbon dioxide and water vapour.
* Plants do not need complicated excretory organs. The stomata in the leaves allow excess carbon dioxide to be released.

Questions

Section A

1. Name three substances excreted by the human body.
   1. ....
   2. ....
   3. ....
2. Urea is made in the .... It passes to the kidney in the .... where it combines with water to form ....
3. The number of ureters in the human body is (a) one; (b) two; (c) several thousand; (d) millions ....
4. Name a substance you could use to prove that you excrete carbon dioxide from your lungs ....
5. The function of the nephron is to ....
6. When we are very cold the blood capillaries in the skin: expand; shrivel; contract; burst. ....
   ....
7. Name the main regions found in a cross section of a kidney ....
8. How does a deciduous plant use its leaves as a method of excretion? ....

Section B

1. Make an outline sketch of the human urinary system, including the blood supply. Give one function for each of the parts you label.
2. Explain how plants excrete their wastes. Draw a T.S. of a leaf and indicate on your diagram where excretion occurs.
3. List the functions of the skin. Outline how the skin carries out any two of the functions you list. Why is regular washing of the skin important in body hygiene?

24 — Movement

Movement is a characteristic of all living things. You know from experience that animals can move from one place to another in many different ways. Some animals have legs, e.g. humans, dogs, insects; others which do not have legs move by changing their body shape, e.g. worms. Movement from place to place, i.e. **locomotion**, in vertebrate animals, involves bones and muscles.

Plants, on the other hand, are unable to move from place to place, instead they remain anchored in the ground all their lives. Parts of their bodies are able to move although these movements are too slow to be noticed at the time. Plant parts move by growing in response to stimuli in the environment — such as light and water. The leaves of a plant grow towards light and roots grow towards water. Such movements in plants are known as **tropisms** *(Chapter 25, Sensitivity).*

24.1 Movement in Simple Cells

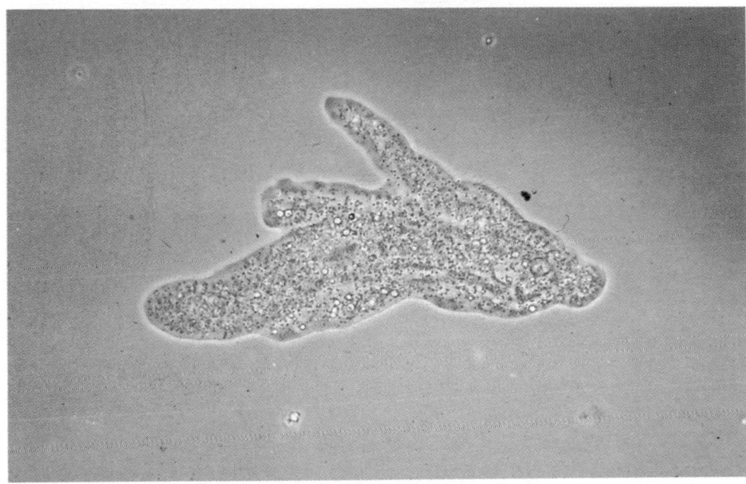

Fig. 24.1 Amoeba x 100

Unicellular organisms can move about freely. Some use tiny hair-like projections of the cell membrane called **cilia**; others use flagellae which cause the animal to move around. *Amoeba* produces false feet or pseudopodia in order to move around. When an *Amoeba* wants to move, it pushes out part of the cell membrane, and cytoplasm flows to form a temporary bulge (false foot), *Fig. 24.1.*

24.2 The Mammalian Skeleton

The human skeleton *(Fig. 24.2)* consists of 206 bones. Bone is a tissue. It is made up of living cells which are embedded in a hard non-living material containing a lot of calcium salts. The bones of the skeleton are held together by **ligaments** and the place where one bone meets another is called a **joint**.

Table 24.1 Parts and Functions of the Main Skeleton

Name	*Consists of*	*Function*
1. Skull	cranium jaws (upper and lower) sense sockets	Protect the brain. Hold the teeth. Protect the sense organs, e.g. eyes and ears.
2. Backbone (spine)	33 vertebrae 7 cervical (neck) 12 thoracic (chest) 5 lumbar (abdominal) 5 sacral (hip) (fused) 4 caudal (tail) (fused)	Protect the spinal cord. Allow nodding and shaking and other movements of the head. Allow attachment of ribs. Support the weight of the body. Support the pelvic girdle. No function.
3. Ribs	12 pairs attached to the thoracic vertebrae at the back and (except for the 2 pairs of floating ribs) to the sternum at the front.	Protect the lungs and heart. Involved in breathing.

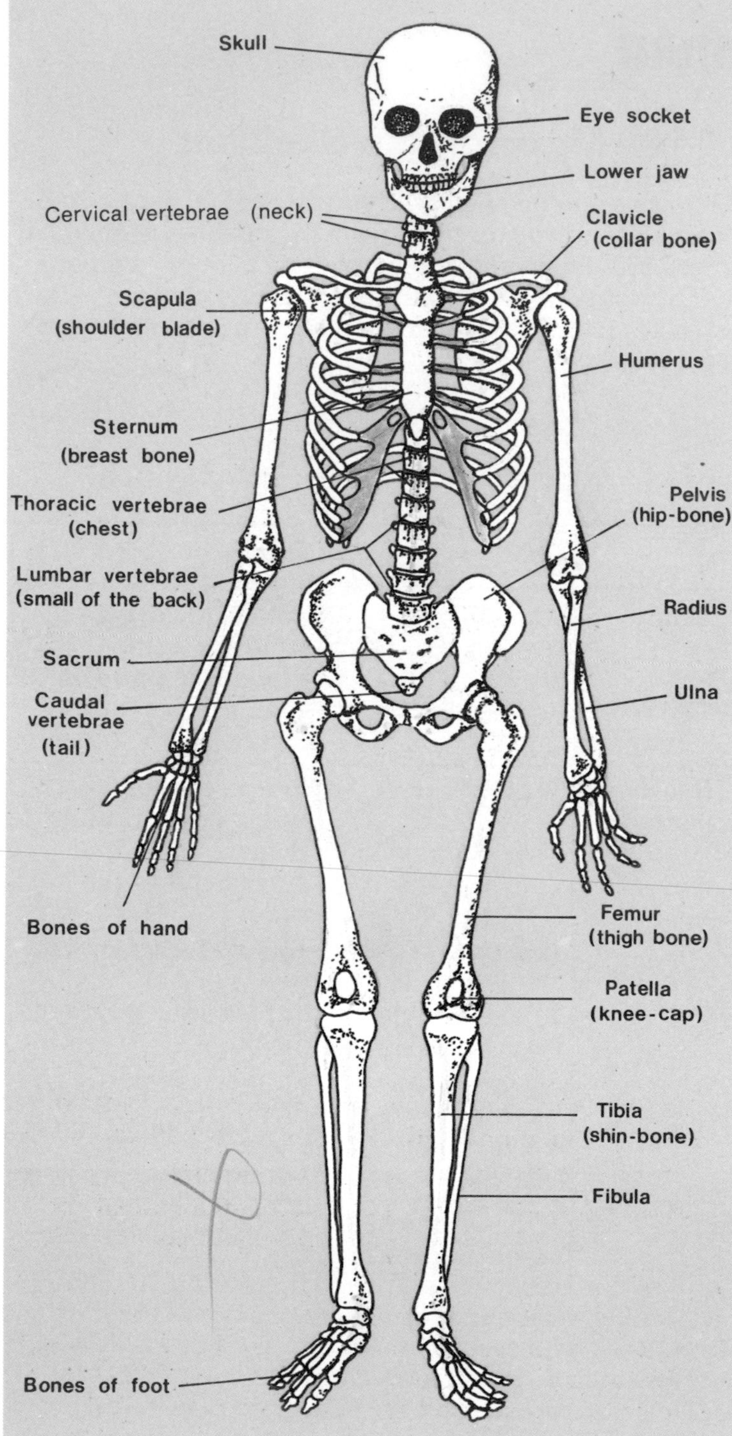

Fig. 24.2 Human skeleton

The Limb Girdles

The limb girdles are bones to which the limb bones attach. They are

1. The **shoulder girdle**, which consists of a pair of clavicles (collar bones) and a pair of scapulae (shoulder blades).
2. The **hip girdle**, which consists of a pair of hip bones.

Table 24.2 The Limb Bones

Limb	*Bone*	*Location*
Arm	Humerus Radius Ulna	Upper arm bone Lower arm bone Lower arm bone
Hand	Carpals Metacarpals Phalanges	Wrist Palm of the hand Fingers
Leg	Femur Patella Tibia Fibula	Thigh bone Knee cap Lower leg (thick) Lower leg (fine)
Foot	Tarsals Metatarsals Phalanges	Ankle Sole of the foot Toes

Functions of the Skeleton

1. **Protection** — Many of the bones act as a protection for the soft body organs; for example the cranium protects the brain and the ribs protect the lungs.
2. **Support** — The skeleton holds the body upright and gives it shape; for example, the backbone supports the spinal cord. Without its skeleton, the human body would be like jelly.
3. **Movement** — When the muscles attached to the bones contract (shorten), they pull on the bones causing movement.

Joints

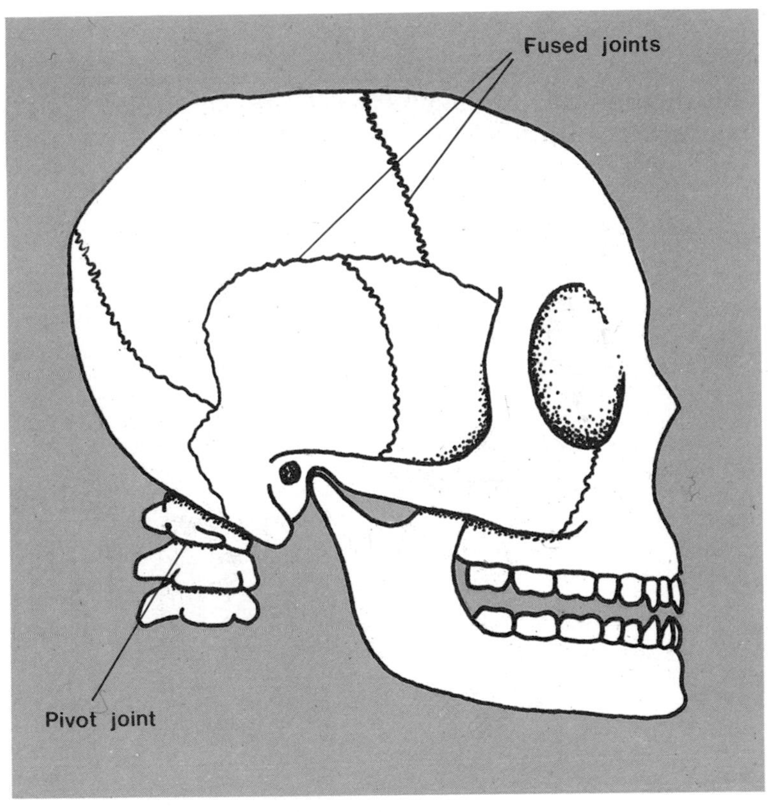

Fig. 24.3 Skull showing fused joints

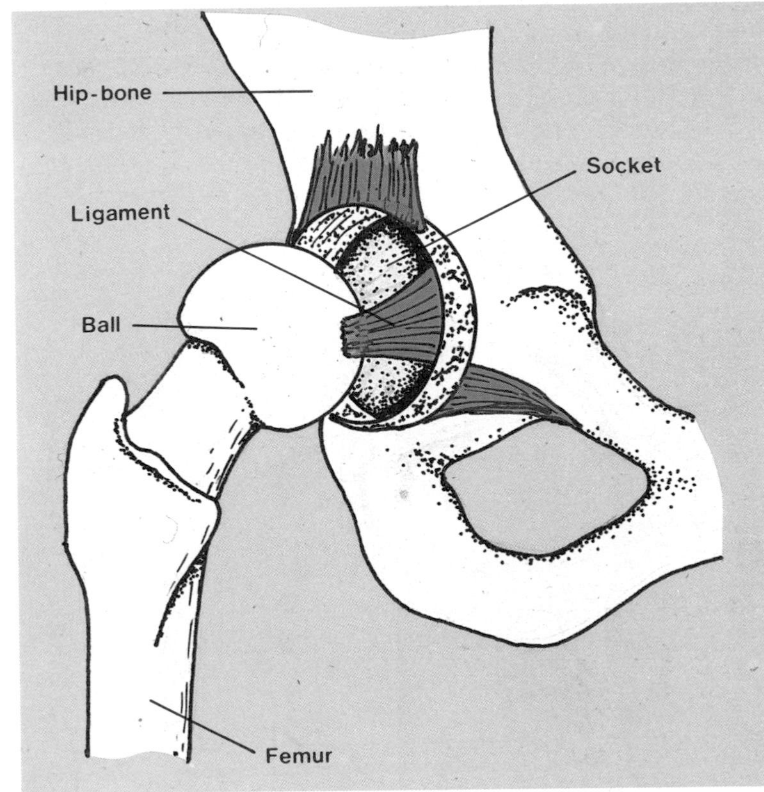

Fig. 24.4 Ball and socket joint

A joint is formed where one or more bones meet. Two types of joint are described here:

1. **Immovable or fused joints**: These occur when there is no movement between the bones, e.g. the bones of the skull, *Fig. 24.3.*

2. **Movable or Synovial joints**: These are freely movable joints.
   (a) *Ball and socket joint*: This type of joint allows movement in all directions. Ball and socket joints are found at the shoulder and hip, *Fig. 24.4.*
   (b) *Hinge joint*: This type of joint allows movement in one direction only. Hinge joints are found at the knee and elbow, *Fig. 24.5.*
   (c) *Pivot joint:* A pivot joint is found at the base of the skull. It allows you to move your head up and down and from side to side, *Fig. 24.3.*

In a movable joint, e.g. at the elbow, the bones are protected from rubbing off each other by a pad of cartilage or gristle and a lubricating fluid called *synovial fluid.* Together, the cartilage and synovial fluid help in the smooth movement of the joint. The bones at the joint are held together by tough fibres called **ligaments**.

Muscles and Movement

All movements of the body are caused by muscles, e.g. walking, breathing, swallowing and blinking. Muscle is a tissue made of muscle cells which work by contracting (getting shorter) and relaxing (returning to their original size). Muscle contraction is controlled by messages received from the brain.

There are three types of muscle:

1. **Voluntary Muscle** — found attached to the bones of our skeleton and also known as skeletal muscle. This type of muscle can be controlled by the will, i.e. it is under your conscious control. Voluntary muscle tires easily. You can see just how easily by clenching and unclenching your right wrist with your left hand for a minute.

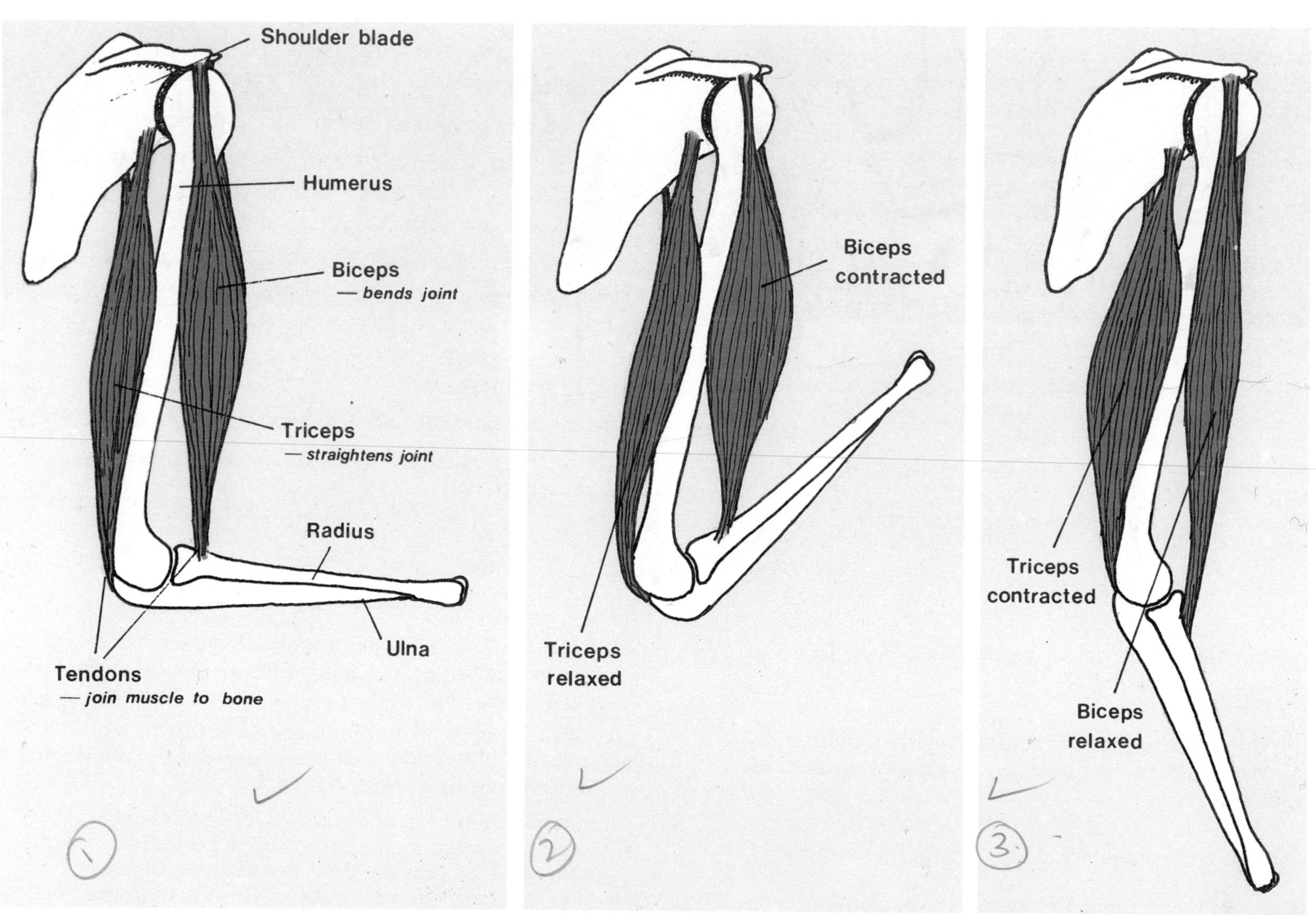

Fig. 24.5 Movement of the lower arm

Know sequence ie in correct order

2. **Involuntary Muscle** — found in the wall of the alimentary canal (digestive system) and the blood vessels. You cannot make this type of muscle contract and relax, it is controlled by the brain automatically.
3. **Cardiac Muscle** — found only in the heart. This is a special type of involuntary muscle which keeps the heart beating throughout one's lifetime.

Movement of Joints by Muscles

Muscles are attached to bones by non-elastic fibres called **tendons**. A tendon is really an extension of a muscle. When muscles contract, they pull on the skeleton and cause the bones at a joint to move, but muscles can only get shorter, they cannot get longer. This means that a muscle which causes a bone to move at a joint cannot straighten the bone again. There has to be another muscle which can pull in the opposite direction. Pairs of muscles which work opposite to one another are called **antagonistic muscles**. The biceps and triceps muscles of the arm are a pair of antagonistic muscles. They are the muscles which raise and lower the lower arm, as *Fig. 24.5* shows.

The biceps muscle is attached by tendons to the shoulder blade at the top end and, across the elbow joint, to the radius at the bottom end. The triceps muscle is attached to the shoulder blade at the top end and, across the joint, to the ulna at the other end.

To bend the arm, the biceps contracts and pulls on the radius causing the lower arm to bend upwards. To straighten the arm the triceps contracts and pulls on the ulna causing the lower arm to straighten out.

Summary

* The human skeleton consists of over 200 bones.
* The functions of the skeleton are: (a) to protect; (b) to give support; (c) to allow movement.
* When two or more bones meet, a joint is formed.
* There are four main joints: (a) fused (skull); (b) ball and socket (hip); (c) hinge (elbow); (d) pivot (neck).
* Bones are attached to other bones by ligaments.
* There are three types of muscle; (a) voluntary; (b) involuntary; (c) cardiac.
* Muscles can only contract and relax.
* Limb muscles usually work as antagonistic pairs, e.g. biceps and triceps.

Questions

Section A

1. Name two ways by which unicellular organisms can move. 1. . . . .
   2. . . . .
2. What is a tropism? . . . .
3. Bone is a living tissue. True or false? . . . .
4. What are bones made of? . . . .
5. Name three types of vertebrae: 1. . . . . ; 2. . . . . ; 3. . . . .
6. What is the function of the backbone? . . . .
7. The shoulder girdle consists of the . . . . and the . . .
8. Where is the patella located? . . . .
9. Ligaments connect . . . . to . . . .
10. Name two examples of a hinge joint.
    1. . . . .
    2. . . . .
11. Muscles cause limbs to move by a) expanding; b) contracting; c) relaxing; d) lengthening . . . .
12. Name the three types of muscle.
    1. . . . .
    2. . . . .
    3. . . . .
13. To raise the lower arm the . . . . contracts.
14. Give two places in the body where you find involuntary muscle.
    1. . . . .
    2. . . . .
15. What type of joint is found in the fingers? . . . .

Section B

1. What are the functions of the skeleton? List three different joints found in the human skeleton and give one example of each kind.
2. What functions, other than movement, has the skeleton of an animal.

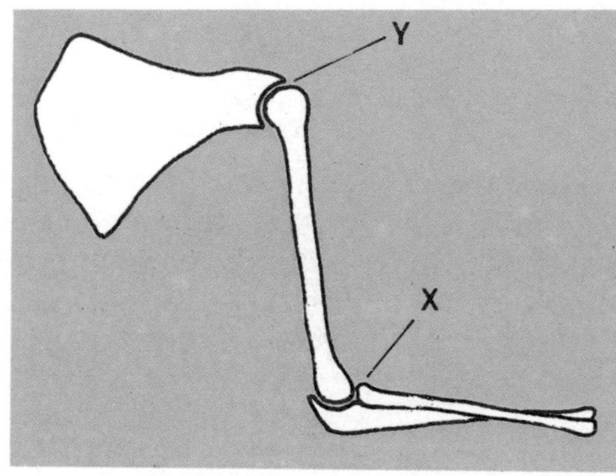

Fig. 24.6 represents the arm bones and shoulder joint of man

(i) What type of joint is shown at X?
(ii) What type of joint is shown at Y?
(iii) Explain how the movement of joint X differs from the movement of joint Y.
(iv) Name one other place in the body where a joint similar to X occurs and a place where a joint similar to Y occurs.
(v) Describe how the muscles raise and lower the forearm.
(vi) What is the chief difference between the way in which the muscles and the skeleton are arranged in mammals and the way they are arranged in anthropods (e.g. insects, crustaceans)?

3. Distinguish between voluntary and involuntary muscle. What is meant by the term 'antagonistic muscle pairs'?

25 — Sensitivity

25.1 Introduction

In order to survive, both plants and animals must be sensitive to change. Such change may come from outside their bodies or from within. Plant shoots for example, grow towards light. They need light to help them make food in photosynthesis. When acid food passes from the stomach to the small intestine, it causes (stimulates) the wall of the intestine to produce digestive juices. If you accidentally touch a hot iron, you immediately pull your hand away. In each of these cases the change that is reacted to is called the **stimulus** and the reaction is called the **response**.

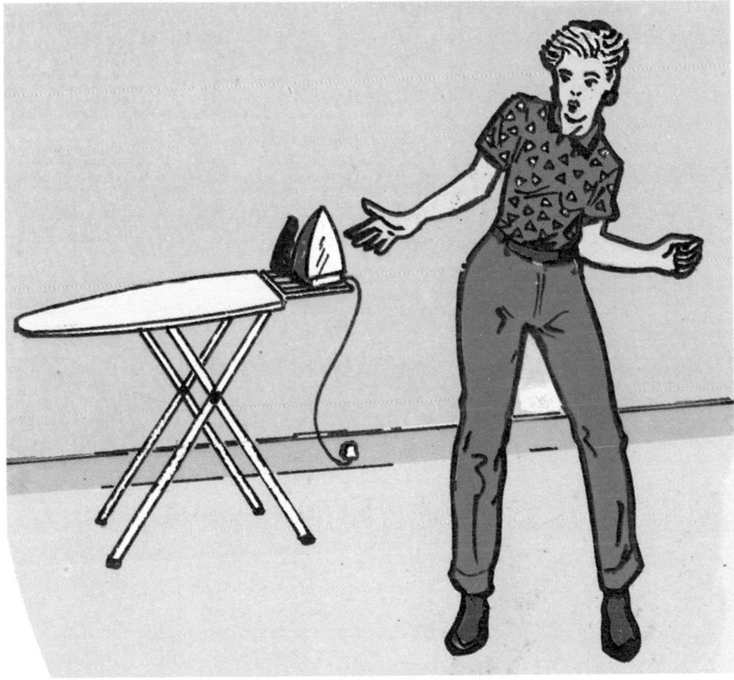

Fig. 25.1 Sensitivity

Stimulus	Response
1. Light	plant grows towards it
2. Acid food	release of digestive juices
3. Hot iron	hand pulled away

Many other examples in nature illustrate the importance of being able to respond to stimuli, such as plant roots growing towards water; the urge to drink water when thirsty; blinking when something is brought to the eye; many animals hibernate as the day length shortens in autumn. Try and explain the benefit each of the above responses has for the organism.

25.2 Plant Responses — Tropisms

Fig. 25.2 Plant bending towards light

Plants respond to light, the force of gravity, water, and some plants respond to touch. A potted plant growing on a window sill will bend towards the light. The growth of part of a plant in response to a stimulus is called a **tropism**. Tropisms can be either:

1. **Positive** — in which the response (growth) is towards the stimulus.
2. **Negative** — in which the response is away from the stimulus.

A number of different tropisms exist and these are summarised in *Table 25.1.*

Table 25.1 Tropisms

Stimulus	*Tropism*	*Examples*
Light	Phototropism	Shoots grow towards light; roots grow away from light.
The Force of Gravity	Geotropism	Roots grow towards the force of gravity; shoots grow away from the force of gravity.
Water	Hydrotropism	Roots grow towards water.
Touch	Thigmotropism	Sweet pea tendrils and other climbing plants are sensitive to touch.

Experiment 25.1 To Show Phototropism in Plants

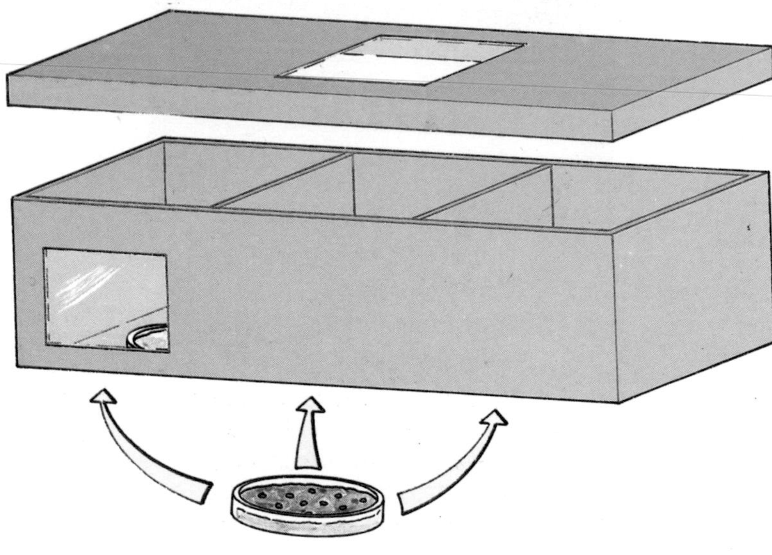

Fig. 25.3

Method

1. Construct a seed house, as shown in *Fig. 25.3,* using a shoe box, pieces of cellophane and sellotape.
2. Fill 3 petri dishes with wet cotton wool.
3. Cut 3 circles of blotting paper, big enough to cover each dish.
4. Place a piece of blotting paper on the wet cotton wool in each dish and place 10 mustard or cress seeds on top. The blotting paper should become dampened from the wet cotton wool.
5. Place one dish in each room of the seed house. Replace the lid of the box and leave it for 5-7 days in front of a window. Take care not to let the seeds dry out.
6. After a week, record the appearance of the seedlings in each dish.
7. Note that the seedlings in 'Room A' have grown towards the window (light). In 'Room B' the seedlings are green and have grown straight up. In 'Room C' the seedlings are a yellow colour and they have a straggly growth.

Conclusion

The effects of light on plants:

1. It causes the stems to grow towards the light, roots to grow away from light and leaves to arrange themselves at right angles to the light.
2. It is needed for photosynthesis *(Chapter 19).*
3. It is needed for the formation of chlorophyll (Room C).

Experiment 25.2 To Show Geotropism in Plants

Method

1. Line three jam jars or gas jars with blotting paper and label the jars A, B and C.
2. Fill the jars with damp peat moss.
3. Carefully position two soaked bean seeds in each jar between the glass and the paper, as shown in *Fig. 25.4.*
4. Leave in a dark place for one week. Take care to see that the peat moss does not dry out.
5. After a week, draw the appearance of one seed from each jar.

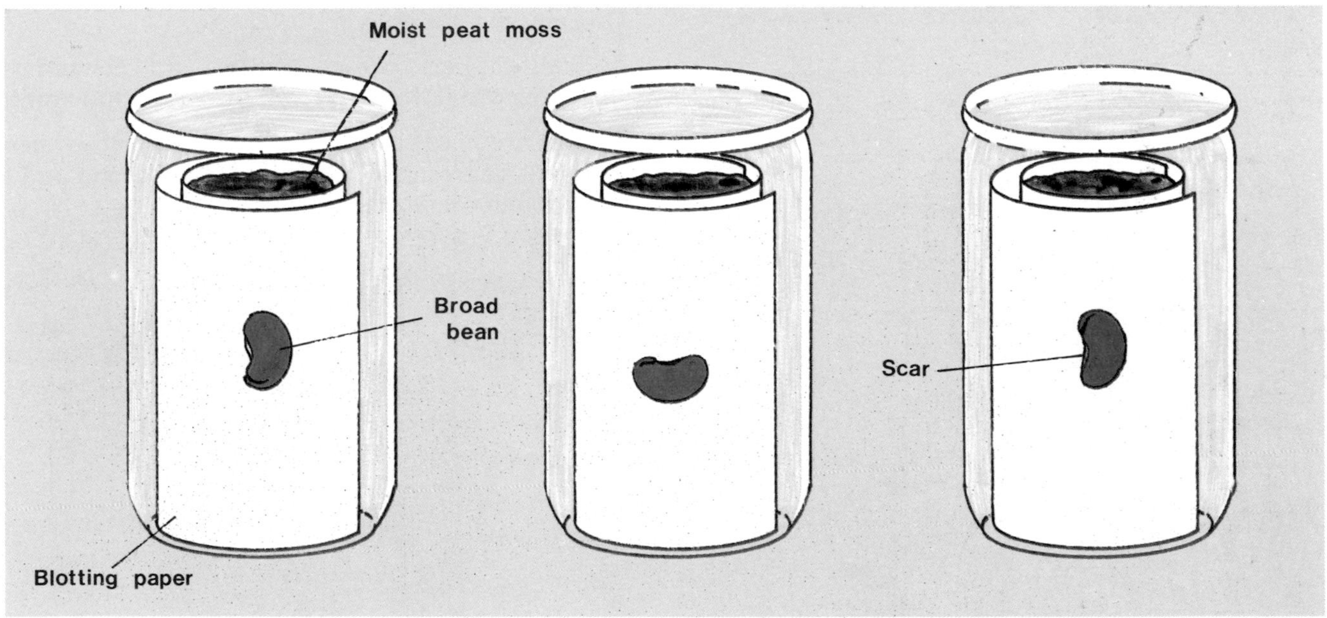

Fig. 25.4

6. The seeds in each jar will show the roots growing downwards and the shoots growing upwards, regardless of the position of the seed. This experiment shows that roots are positively geotropic while shoots are negatively geotropic.

Conclusion

The effects of the force of gravity on plants:

1. Main roots grow towards the force of gravity.
2. Shoots usually grow away from the force of gravity.
3. Most leaves grow at right angles to the force of gravity (exceptions include grasses and daffodils).

25.3 Animal Responses

In the body, stimuli are detected by special cells (**receptors**). These receptors are often found grouped together to form **sense organs**. Our eyes, ears, tongue and skin are examples of sense organs. Sensory receptors in the ear detect sound and taste buds in the tongue sense whether food is sweet or bitter. The parts of the body which respond to the stimuli are called **effectors**. Effectors can be muscles or glands.

In most animals, response to stimuli is co-ordinated by two body systems:

1. The Nervous System.
2. The Endocrine (hormone) System.

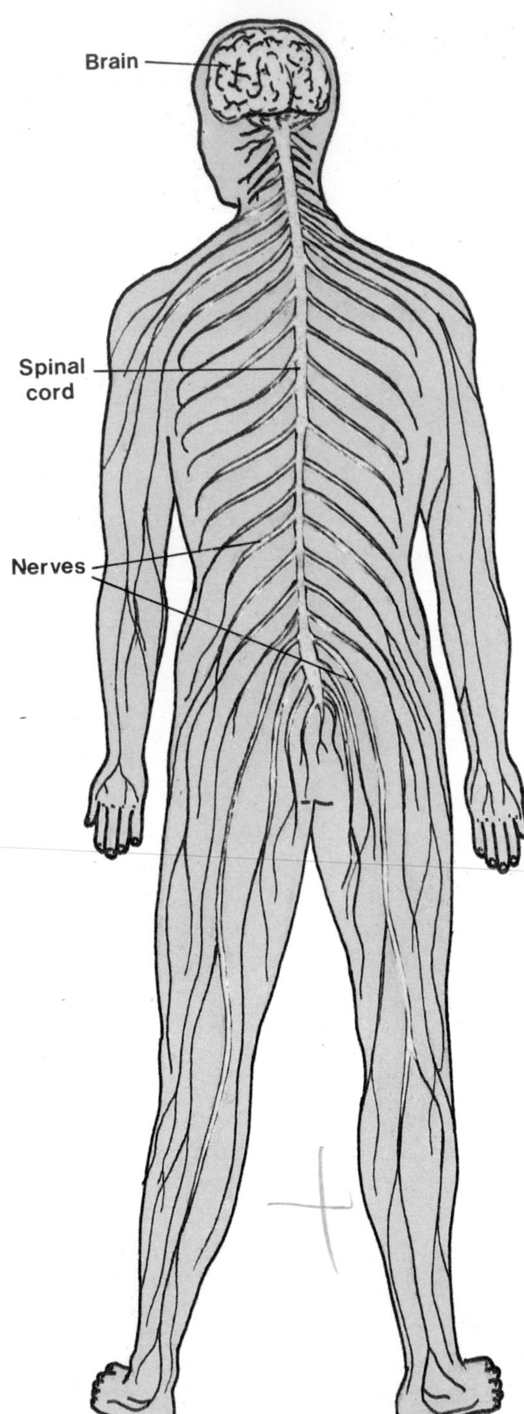

Fig. 25.5

1. The Nervous System

The nervous system has two parts *(Fig. 25.5)*:

1. The central nervous system (C.N.S) consisting of the brain and spinal cord.
2. The Peripheral nervous system (P.N.S.)made up of nerves which branch from the brain and spinal cord.

Nerves are made of bundles of nerve cells or **neurons**. Neurons carry messages called impulses to and from the central nervous system.

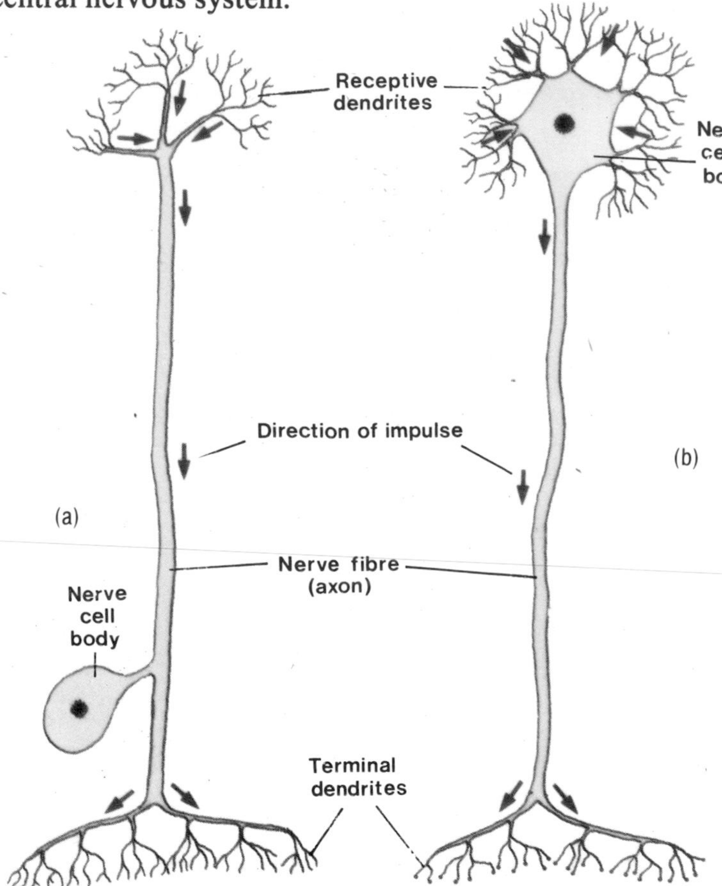

Fig. 25.6 (a) Sensory neuron; (b) Motor neuron

There are two types of neuron, *Fig. 25.6*:

1. Sensory neurons which carry impulses from a receptor to the CNS.
2. Motor neurons which carry impulses from the CNS to an affector.

Table 25.2 Neurons consists of the following parts:

Part	*(Notes)*
Cell body	Contains the nucleus.
Receptive dendrites	Branches of the cell body. Receive impulses from neurons nearby or stimuli at the receptors.
Nerve Fibre (axon)	Carries the impulse away from the cell body.
Terminal dendrites/ motor-end plate	Pass impulse on to the next neuron or to an effector.

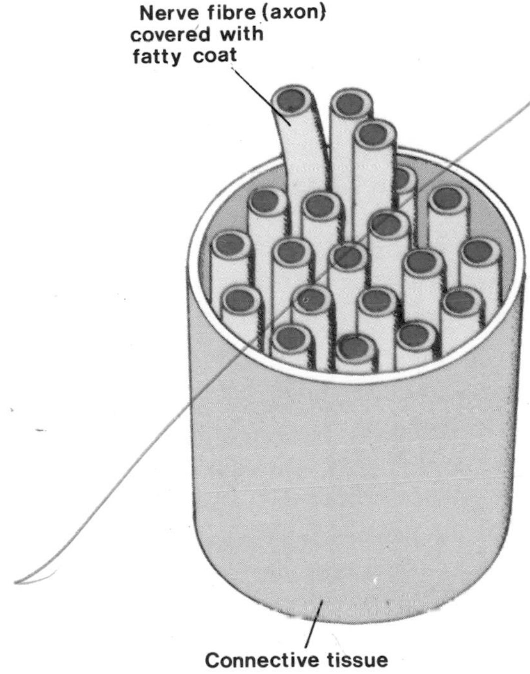

Fig. 25.7 Nerve structure

The Brain and Spinal Cord

The brain and spinal cord are covered by membranes called the meninges. The brain is protected by the skull and the vertebral column protects the spinal cord. The human brain is made up of about 10,000 million neurons all tightly packed together. The main parts of the brain and their functions are illustrated in *Fig. 25.8.*

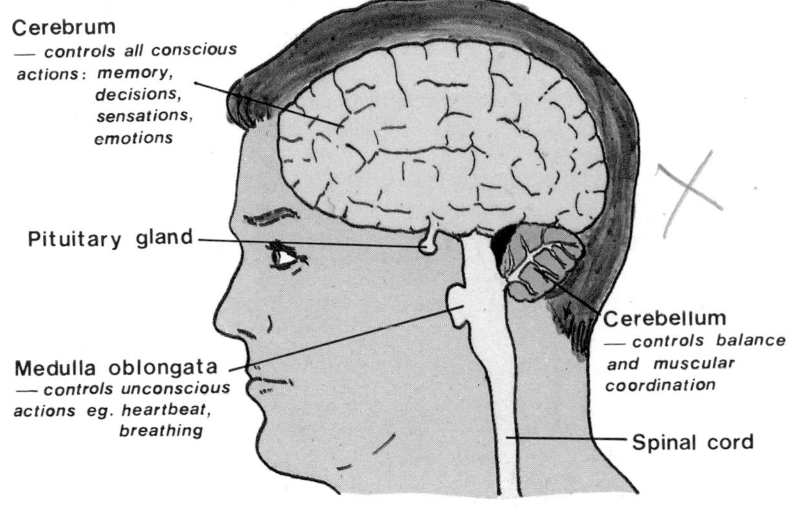

Fig. 25.8

The spinal cord is an extension of the medulla oblongata. It runs down through the bones of the spine. Pairs of spinal nerves leave the spinal cord at regular intervals along its length. These nerves contain both sensory and motor neurons, which feed messages to and from the brain to the rest of the body, *Fig. 25.9*

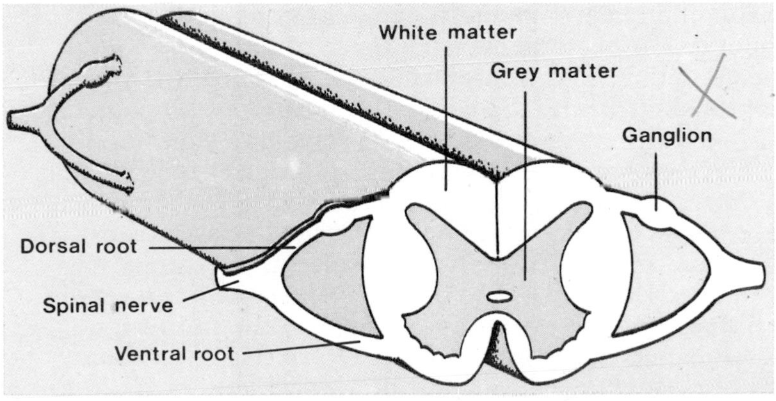

Fig. 25.9 Spinal cord

How the Nervous System Works

Voluntary Action

Most of the responses that the body makes are under the control of the will, these are known as voluntary or conscious actions. A good example of a voluntary action is running to catch a bus. It is an action that you think about and many inter-connecting neurons are involved in bringing about the action as described below:

(a) You see the bus — this is the stimulus.

(b) A message travels from the eye into the brain to the decision making area.

(c) From there, a message goes to the motor area which sends out impulses to various muscles in the legs, arms, heart and chest (intercostal muscles and diaphragm), causing responses which bring about the action, enabling you to run fast and catch the bus.

In summary, the voluntary action involves the following nerve pathway:

Stimulus (bus) → Receptor (eye) → Sensory neuron → Brain (decision taken) → Many motor neurons → Effectors (muscles) → Response (heart beats faster, arms move, running, breathing rate increases).

Reflex Action

A reflex action is one which happens when you respond to something automatically, i.e. without having to think about it. For example, when a speck of dust gets in your eye you blink. This is a reflex action. It is one that you cannot control with the will, i.e. you cannot stop yourself blinking. Other examples include removing your hand from a very hot object; coughing up food that goes down the 'wrong way'; swallowing, and the knee jerk. In each case, the action is carried out without a decision from the brain. In most cases, it is only after the response has happened that you aware of it. A reflex action is a very rapid response to a stimulus.It involves the shortest possible nerve pathway which is referred to as a **reflex arc** because it takes the shape of a curve. *Fig. 25.10* illustrates a simple reflex action.

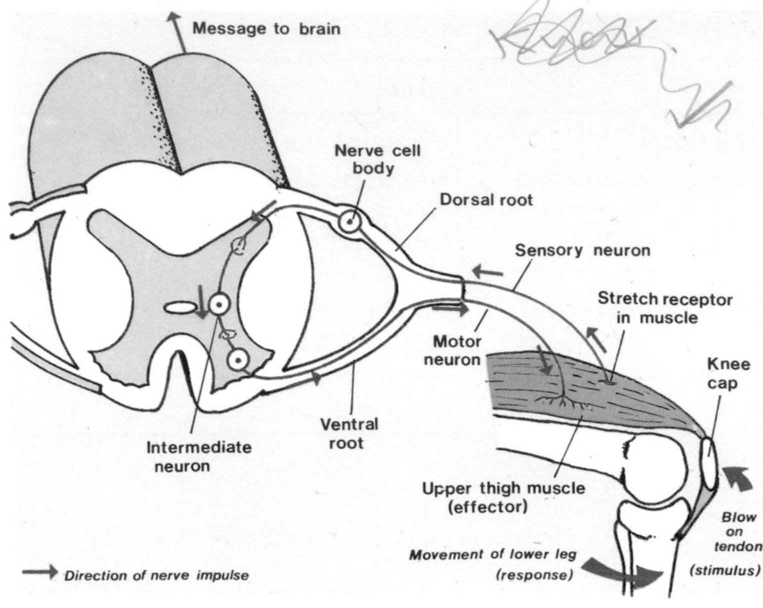

Fig. 25.10 Reflex arc

2. The Endocrine System

The endocrine system consists of a number of glands which produce hormones. A gland is a group of cells which make substances needed elsewhere in the body. Two types of gland are found in the body, **exocrine glands** and **endocrine glands**.

Exocrine glands have ducts or tubes. This means that the juices they secrete leave the gland through a duct, e.g. salivary glands, liver, pancreas.

Endocrine glands have no ducts. They produce hormones which are released directly from the gland into the bloodstream, e.g. pituitary, ovary.

A hormone is a chemical substance which is released by a ductless gland. Hormones are carried in the blood to many parts of the body where they control the activities of tissues and organs. Hormones are really chemical messengers which help in the co-ordination within the body. The main endocrine glands in men and women are shown in *Fig. 25.11* and further details can be found in *Table 25.3.*

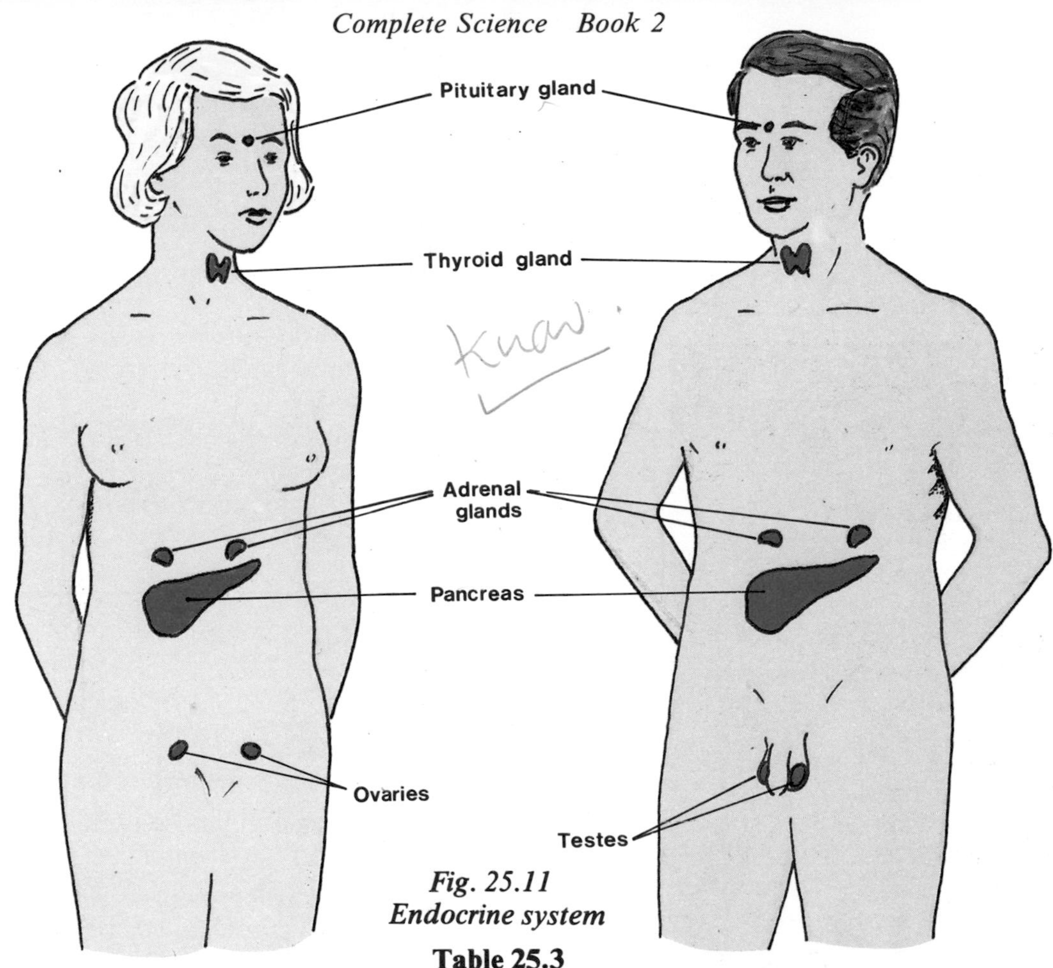

Fig. 25.11
Endocrine system

Table 25.3

Gland	*Location*	*Hormone Produced*	*Function*
Pituitary (master gland)	Base of brain *(see Fig. 25.8)*	Many — including growth hormone	Controls body growth
Thyroid	Neck	Thyroxine	Controls respiration in cells.
Pancreas	Under stomach	Insulin	Controls level of sugar in the blood.
Adrenal	Over each kidney	Adrenalin	Increases rate and depth of breathing; raises pulse rate.
Ovary (in female)	Abdomen	Oestrogen	Controls development of femaleness, e.g. body hair and shape.
Testis (in male)	Scrotal sac	Testosterone	Controls development in maleness, e.g. deep voice, beard.

Growth Hormone

Too little growth hormone can result in dwarfism; too much results in giantism.

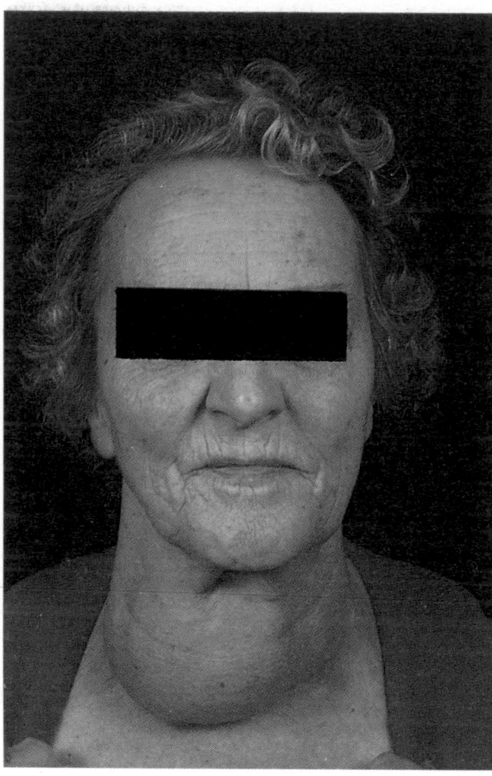

Fig. 25.12 An enlarged thyroid gland or goitre caused by either an overactive or underactive thyroid gland

Insulin

If too little insulin is produced, excess sugar is not stored in the liver but passes into the bloodstream. This causes the blood sugar level to rise — a condition known as diabetes.

A comparison between the Nervous and Hormonal Systems

Table 25.4

Nervous System	*Hormonal System*
1. The message is an electrical impulse.	The message is a chemical.
2. The message is carried by neurons.	The message is carried by the blood.
3. The response is usually very quick.	The response is usually gradual.
4. The effect is short-lived.	The effect can last a long time (over a period of years).

Summary

* Sensitivity means responding to a stimulus.
* Plants and animals respond to many stimuli such as light, temperature and water.
* A tropism is a growth response of a plant (or part of a plant) to a stimulus, e.g. phototropism.
* In animals, responses to stimuli are controlled by the nervous and hormonal systems.
* Stimuli are detected by receptors and responses are carried out by effectors.
* The nervous system links the receptors and effectors.
* The nervous system is made up of nerve cells called neurons. It consists of two parts — the CNS and the PNS.
* A reflex action is a fast automatic response to a stimulus.
* A hormone is a chemical messenger produced by an endocrine gland and passed directly into the bloodstream.
* The nervous and hormonal systems act together to co-ordinate the body.
* The pituitary is a master gland in that it controls the activity of a number of other endocrine glands.

Questions

Section A

1. A little boy jumped when he saw a mouse. What is (a) the stimulus, (b) the response?

   (a) ....

   (b) ....

2. What is a tropism? ....

   ....

3. The response of plant shoots to light is called ....
4. What is a nerve? ....
5. State three functions of the brain?

   1. ....

   2. ....

   3. ....

6. Sensory neurons carry impulses to the ....

   from the ....

7. Distinguish between exocrine and endocrine glands. ...

   ....

8. What is a hormone? ....
9. Why is the pituitary gland also known as the master gland? ....

   ....

10. The nervous system produces electrical/chemical messages which travel very slowly/fast and their effect lasts for a long/short time. Underline the correct terms.

Section B

1. What is a tropism? Outline how tropisms are of benefit to a plant. Describe an experiment to show the effect of either light or the force of gravity on a plant.
2. Redraw the diagram shown of a motor neuron. Label the following parts: the axon; dendrites; cell body; motor end plate. State two ways in which a motor neuron differs from a sensory neuron.

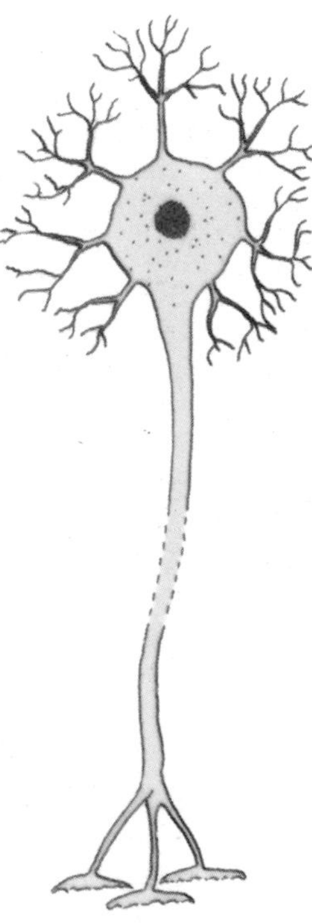

Fig. 25.13

3. Draw an outline diagram of the human female and include on it the position of the following glands: (i) pancreas; (ii) thyroid; (iii) ovaries.

   Give the name and function of a hormone secreted by each gland.

4. Describe the nerve pathway, when you catch a ball.

26 — The Sense Organs

Introduction

The main sense organs of the body are the skin, tongue, nose, eyes and ears. They are important as they give us information about our surroundings.

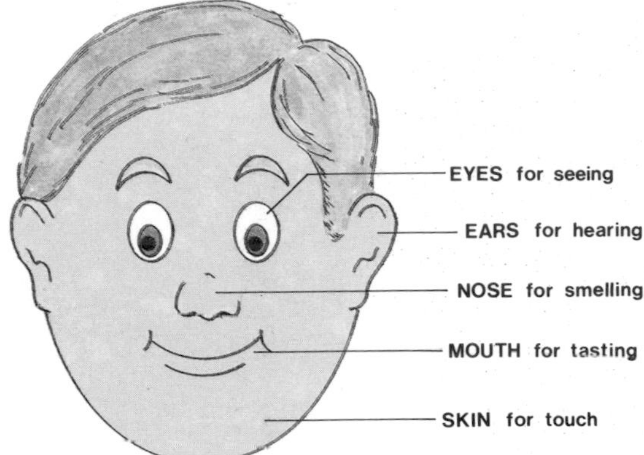

Fig. 26.1 The five sense organs

26.1 The Skin

Human skin contains four types of sensory receptor. These are the pain, pressure, touch and temperature receptors, *(Fig. 23.4)*. All four types of receptor are not necessarily evenly spread over the body. There are more touch receptors on the fingertips and tongue than on the back, and heat receptors are most abundant on the soles of the feet.

26.2 The Tongue

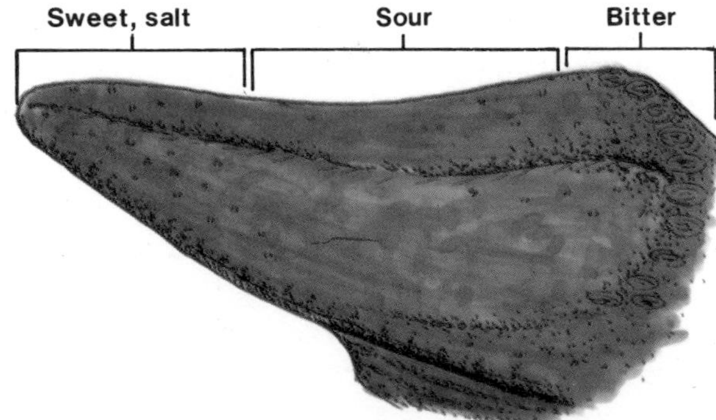

Fig. 26.2 The tongue

The tongue *(Fig. 26.2)*, contains about 10,000 receptors called taste buds. The taste buds are sensitive to four basic tastes — sweet, salt, sour and bitter. Most tastes are combinations of these four. *Fig. 26.2* shows the areas of the tongue sensitive to different tastes.

Only liquids can be tasted. This is because the taste buds are only stimulated when chemicals in the food are dissolved by saliva.

Experiment 26.1 To Map the Taste Receptors on the Tongue

Method

1. Draw an outline in your class note book of the human tongue. Decide on a key to represent each of the four tastes.

   Example: X = sugar; O = salt; o = bitter; * = sour.
2. Work in pairs, each member acting in turn as the subject and the experimenter. Blindfold the subject, using a scarf or tie.
3. Using a sterile glass rod, place drops of salt solution over the tip, sides and back of the subject's tongue. The subject should indicate each time the salt is tasted strongly.
4. These positions should be plotted on the diagram of the subject's tongue using the appropriate symbol.
5. The subject should rinse his/her mouth with water.
6. Repeat steps 3 or 4 using sugar solution.
7. Rinse the mouth and repeat steps 3 and 4 using a sour solution.
8. Rinse the mouth and repeat steps 3 and 4 using a bitter solution.
9. Compare the 'map' of the subject's tongue with *Fig. 26.2*, which gives the average positions for the taste buds.
10. Change places with your partner and begin again.

26.3 The Nose

The nose contains receptors which are sensitive to smells. Chemicals in the air dissolve in the moist lining of the nasal passages and are detected by the sensory cells.

Experiment 26.2 To Show that our Sense of Taste is Linked to our Sense of Smell

Method

1. Blindfold your partner using a scarf or tie.
2. Using a glass rod, place small drops of clove water and tap water at random onto your partner's tongue.
3. Make sure your partner can distinguish the two tastes.
4. Now ask your partner to hold his/her nose tightly. Repeat step 2, and ask your partner which taste he/she detects from each drop of liquid. Count the number of correct responses.
5. You should find that when the nose is blocked, your partner cannot tell the difference between the taste of water and clove water. This shows that our sense of taste to a large extent depends upon our sense of smell.

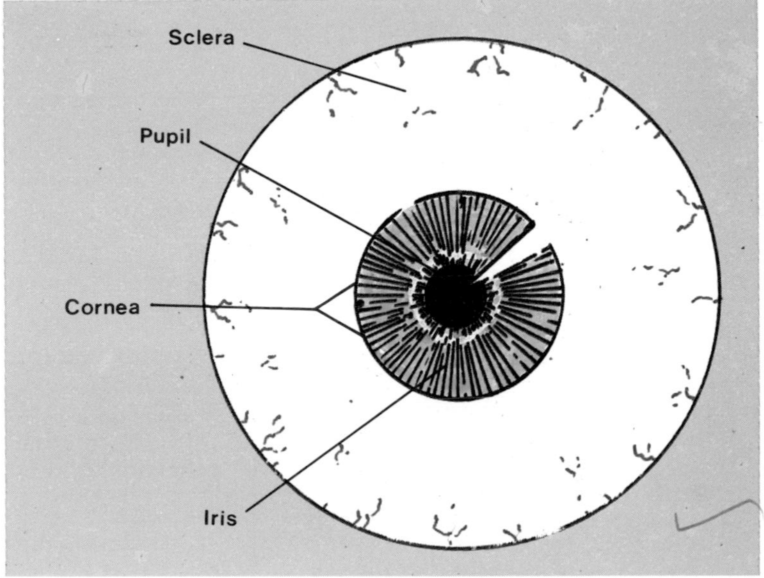

Fig. 26.3 Human eye

26.4 The Eye

The eyes are sensitive to light. The sensory cells are found on a part of the eye called the retina. They change light into nerve impulses which are then taken to the brain, along the optic nerve, and sorted out so that we see things. The structure of the eye can be seen in *Figs. 26.3* and *26.4*.

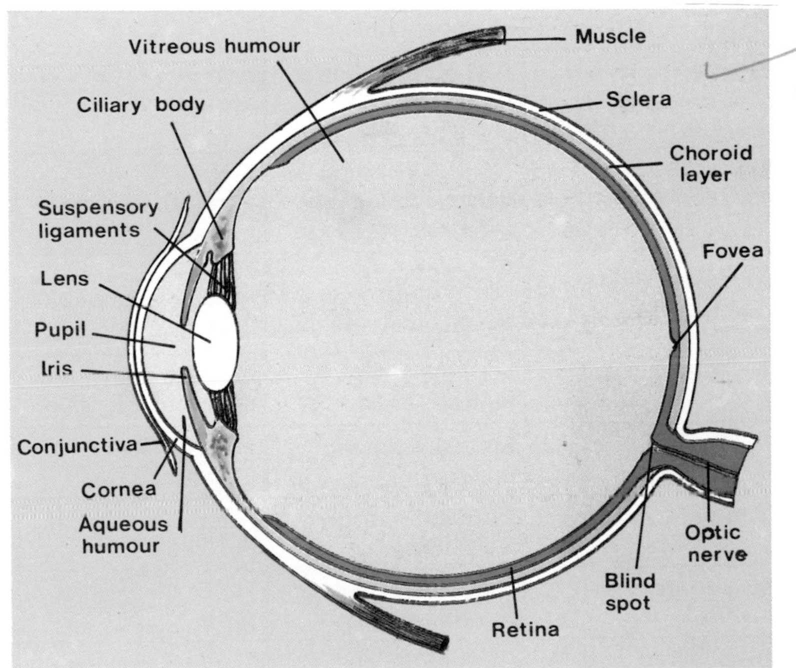

Fig. 26.4 Section through eye

Experiment 26.3 To Demonstrate the Pupil Reflex

Method

1. Look into a classmate's eyes. Note the size of the pupils.
2. Ask your friend to close his/her eyes and cover them with his/her hands for 15 seconds.
3. After 15 seconds, the hands should be taken away and the eyes opened. Watch carefully as the pupils of the

Table 26.1

Part	*Description/ Location*	*Function*
Sclera	Touch white outer coat	Protection
Cornea	Transparent layer of sclera, in front of the eye	Allows light to pass into the eye
Choroid	Dark coloured middle layer	1. Carries blood vessels 2. Prevents internal reflection of light
Iris	Circular pigmented muscle — 'the colour of the eye'	Controls the amount of light entering the eye
Pupil	A hole in the iris	Allows light into the eye
Retina	Light sensitive innermost layer. Contains the light receptors and nerves	Receives the stimulus of light
Blind spot	Part of the retina where the nerves leave the eye	Exit point for the optic nerve
Fovea	Part of the retina which contains the most sensory cells	Place of most accurate vision
Aqueous humour	A clear liquid between the iris and the cornea	Gives the front of the eye its shape
Vitreous humour	A transparent jelly behind the lens	Gives the back of the eyeball its shape
Lens	Soft transparent material	Focuses light onto the retina
Ciliary Muscle	Beside the suspensory ligaments	Alters the shape of the lens
Suspensory ligaments	Connect the lens to the ciliary muscle	Holds the lens in place
Optic nerve	Back of the eye	Carries nerve impulses to the brain

eyes contract (i.e. they get smaller). This is because the iris (coloured part) gets larger, thus narrowing the space through which light can pass. The pupils contract to prevent excess light entering the eye.

Experiment 26.4 To Demonstrate the Blind Spot

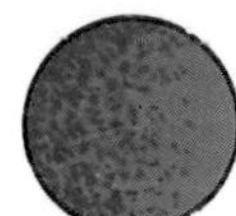

Fig. 26.5

Method

1. Hold this book in your right hand, with the diagram below at arms length.
2. Close the left eye and stare at the apple with your right eye. You should still be able to see the orange.
3. Keep staring at the apple and slowly bring the book towards your face. At a certain distance the orange will disappear. This is because the image of the orange has fallen on the blind spot.
4. If you continue to bring the book towards your face the orange will reappear.

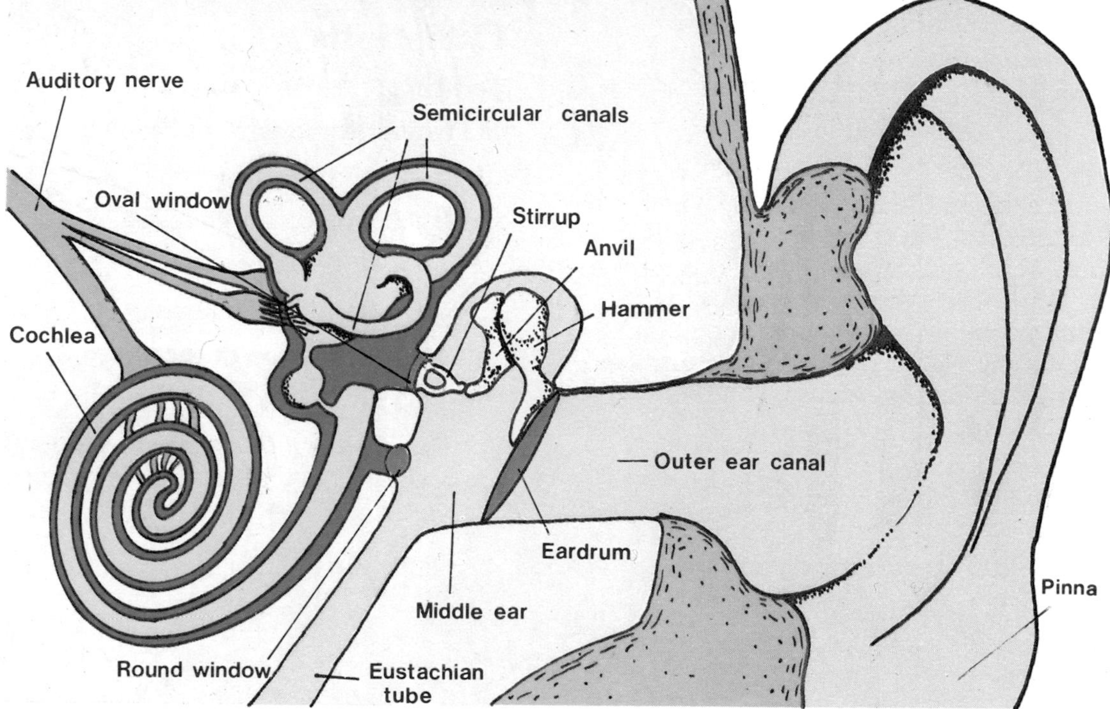

Fig. 26.6 The ear

26.5 The Ear

The ear is concerned with hearing and balance. Most of the ear is located deep inside the skull, for protection. The structure of the ear can be seen in *Fig. 26.6.*

Hearing

Sound waves entering the ear cause the ear-drum to vibrate. This vibration in turn causes the ear ossicles — the hammer, anvil and stirrup bones — to vibrate. The stirrup passes vibrations through the oval window into the

Table 26.2 The Parts and Functions of the Ear

Part	*Function*
Pinna	Gathers sound waves
Outer ear canal	Has cells with hairs. The cells secrete wax to trap dirt.
Ear-drum	Vibrates when in contact with sound waves.
Middle ear bones: (hammer, anvil, stirrup)	Carry vibrations from ear-drum to the oval window.
Eustachian tube	Equalises air pressure either side of the eardrum.

Part	*Function*
Oval window	Vibrates when the stirrup strikes it. Passes vibrations into the cochlea.
Cochlea	Fluid-filled tube. Contains receptor cells sensitive to sounds.
Semi-circular canals	Contain sense receptors which detect the position and balance of the body.
Auditory nerve	Transmits nerve impulses from the ear to the brain.

fluid-filled cochlea. Sensory cells in the cochlea detect vibrations in the fluid and pass the information to the brain, via the auditory nerve.

Balance

The three semi-circular canals are filled with fluid. When the head moves, the fluid moves. There are receptor cells at the bottom of each canal which pick up messages about the movement of the fluid. This information is then sent to the brain. Disease of the semi-circular canals causes a person to topple over when the eyes are shut. If you spin round quickly for some time and then stop suddenly, you feel dizzy and may lose your balance.

Summary

* The sense organs are the skin, tongue, nose, eyes and ears.
* The tongue detects tastes.
* The nose detects smells.
* The eyes detect light.
* The ears detect sounds and balance.
* The skin detects heat, cold, pressure, pain and touch.
* The light sensitive layer of the eye is the retina.
* The optic nerve carries impulses from the retina to the brain.
* The cochlea in the inner ear is sensitive to sound.
* The semi-circular canals are responsible for balance.
* The Eustachian tube helps to equalise air pressure either side of the ear-drum.
* The auditory nerve carries impulses from the cochlea and semi-circular canals to the brain.

Questions

Section A

1. Where would you find each of the following:
   (a) taste buds ....
   (b) heat receptors ....
   (c) smell receptors ....
2. The function of the iris is ....
   and the function of the choroid is ....
   ....
3. The nerve which carries impulses from the retina to the brain is called the .... nerve.
4. Name three bones in the middle ear.
   1. ....
   2. ....
   3. ....
5. What is the ear-drum for? ....
6. Name the part of the ear involved in
   (a) balance ....
   (b) equalising air pressure ....

Section B

1. Draw an outline diagram of the eye and mark on it the following labels: sclera, choroid; retina; blind spot; lens; iris; cornea; pupil.
2. Draw an outline diagram of the ear. Explain briefly how we hear sounds. What other functions does the ear have apart from hearing?

27 — Cycles in Nature

27.1 Introduction

Many substances are involved in a continuous circulation throughout nature. They may be taken in by plants and animals, and then released again as the organism dies, ready to be used in some other way. Substances involved in cycles are nitrogen, carbon and water.

27.2 The Nitrogen Cycle

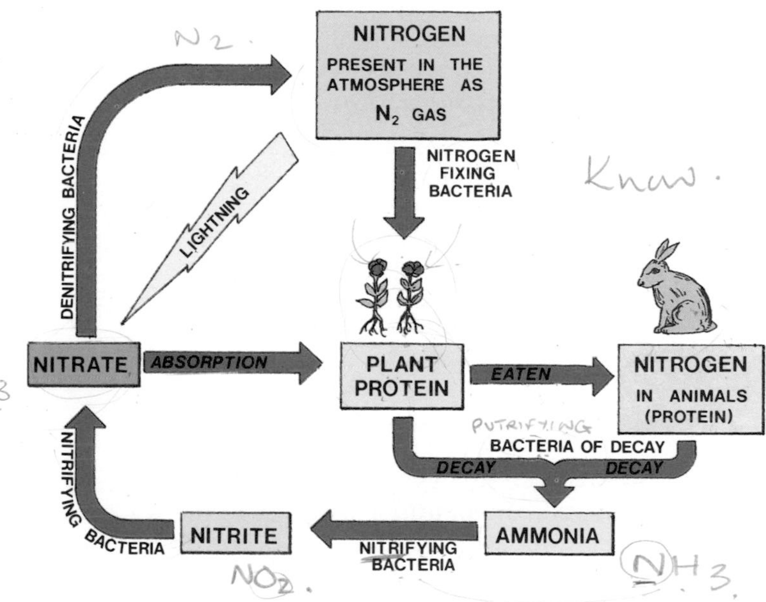

Fig. 27.1 The Nitrogen Cycle

The nitrogen cycle show nitrogen in the air becomes part of part of plants and animals and how it is constantly recycled in nature. Nitrogen makes up 78% of the air (*see Chapter 6, Book 1*). Nitrogen is needed by living organisms to make **protein** (remember, the basic elements in a protein are C, H, O and N). But plants and animals are unable to absorb nitrogen (N_2) directly from the air and they depend on bacteria to provide them with useable nitrogen from the soil in the form of nitrate (NO_3). The plants make protein and are in turn eaten by animals so the nitrogen eventually becomes part of the animal body. Bacteria play an important part in the circulation of nitrogen. Bacteria can live in many different environments, some live in the soil, some in the roots of plants and some live in dead and decaying matter. The involvement of bacteria in the nitrogen cycle is shown in *Fig. 27.1.*

Bacteria in the Nitrogen Cycle

1. **Nitrogen-fixing bacteria:** These bacteria live in tiny nodules on the roots of certain plants called legumes, e.g. clover, lupin and peas. Nitrogen-fixing bacteria are able to use nitrogen in the air and convert it into nitrate for the plant.
2. **Putrifying bacteria:** These bacteria are responsible for breaking down the remains of dead plants and animals. As a result ammonia (NH_3) is formed in the soil.
3. **Nitrifying bacteria:** These bacteria live in the soil where they convert the ammonia first to nitrite (NO_2) and then to nitrate (NO_3) which can be absorbed by the roots of the plants.

Fig. 27.2 Fertiliser adds nitrate to the soil in the form of Ammonium Nitrate, (see Chapter 12, Page 75)

4. **Denitrifying bacteria:** These bacteria re-convert the nitrate into atmospheric nitrogen, thus ensuring that the supply of free nitrogen in the air remains constant.

There is, however, another way in which nitrogen in the air can enter the nitrogen cycle. When there is a flash of lightning, an extremely high temperature is created. This is enough to bring about a chemcial reaction, between nitrogen and oxygen, both of which are present in the air. Oxides of nitrogen are formed, which will dissolve in rain water, and soak into the soil, where nitrates are formed.

27.3 The Carbon Cycle

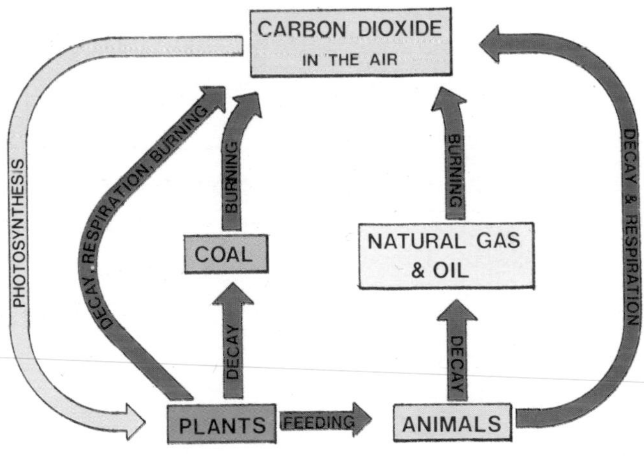

Fig. 27.3 The Carbon Cycle

The element carbon is important in all compounds found in plants and animals. Plant carbohydrate is a carbon compound. This may be eaten by an animal, and so the carbon compound appears in the animal. In turn the carbon may be released into the atmosphere, through the process of respiration. The carbon cycle is shown in *Fig. 27.3.*

Carbon is present in the atmosphere as carbon dioxide gas. Much less than 1% of the air is made up of carbon dioxide gas.

Loss of Carbon Dioxide in the Air

Plants make their own food, starch — a carbon compound, by photosynthesis. *(see Chapter 19).* Carbon dioxide is used in this process, and so the carbon cycle commences.

Gain of Carbon Dioxide in the Air

The carbon dioxide in the air is replenished by two processes. These are combustion and respiration.

1. **Combustion** — If certain conditions are present, when a plant dies, fossilization occurs and fuels, such as coal, gas, oil and peat may be formed. The carbon is trapped in these compounds, until they are burnt. When combustion of carbon compounds takes place, carbon dioxide is released, into the atmosphere. *(see Chapter 7 Carbon and Carbon Dioxide).*
2. **Respiration** — Carbon dioxide in the air may be replaced by the respiration of organisms, including plants, animals and decomposers e.g. bacteria *(see Chapter 20).* The animals obtain their carbon compounds by eating plants, and decomposers obtain their carbon compounds, by feeding on dead plants and animals.

27.4 The Water Cycle

Water is also involved in a cycle. It is important in every living organism, and so an understanding of the water cycle is essential. *(see Chapter 8 Hardness of Water)* in the Chemistry section. The water cycle shown in the Chemistry section, does not indicate the involvement of plants and animals in the cycle. This is a minor part of the cycle, but it is very important to the biologist.

Two important biological processes are involved in the water cycle.

1. Transpiration in plants. Water is carried from the roots, up the stem and out through the leaves. *(see Chapter 21 Water and Transport in Plants).*
2. Respiration in plants and animals. One of the by-products of respiration is water. This is released into the air, as the organism breathes out. This water vapour can be seen when you breathe out on a cold day.

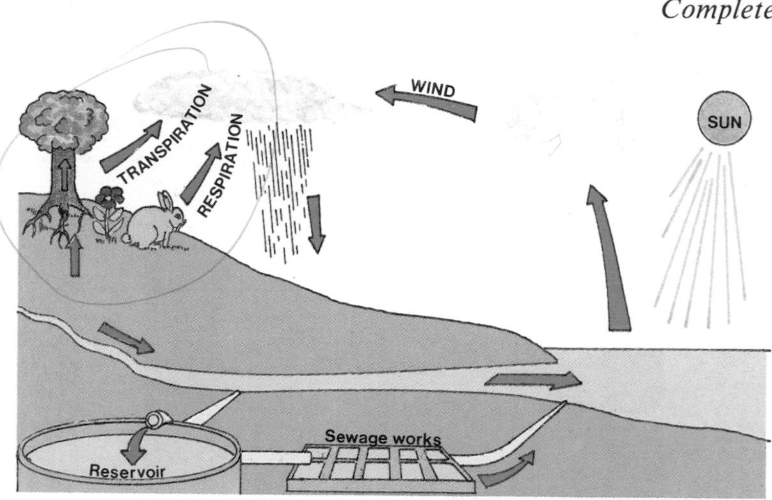

Fig. 27.4 The Water Cycle

Summary

* Nitrogen, carbon and water are substances, which are involved in cycles.
* Bacteria are involved in the nitrogen cycle.
* 78% of the air is nitrogen.
* Combustion and respiration are processes involved in the carbon cycle.
* Transpiration is involved in the water cycle.

Questions

Section A

1. Which substances are involved in cycles in nature? .....
2. Plants can only absorb nitrogen in the form of ....
3. Explain the term nitrogen fixation. ....
4. How does an animal obtain its protein supply? ....
5. How is lightning involved in the nitrogen cycle? ....
6. Plants make their food by .... which uses .... from the air.
7. What is fossilization? ....
8. What is transpiration? ....

Section B

1. Bacteria have an important part to play in the nitrogen cycle. Explain how they are involved in this cycle.
2. Find out, and write about the water cycle.

28 — Ecology

28.1 Introduction

Ecology is the study of plants and animals in relation to their environment. Ecology shows us how plants and animals depend upon each other and how they adapt to the surroundings. The place where a plant or animal lives is known as its **habitat**. Examples of habitats include woodland, pond, meadow, garden and hedgerow.

If we want to describe the place together with all its plants and animals then we are talking about an **ecosystem**.

The study of a habitat includes an examination of both the living and the non-living parts of environment. The living component is the community of plants and animals and the non-living part is the soil, or the water in a pond or the brick of a stone wall.

28.2 Interdependence

Interdependence is the way in which organisms depend on each other to stay alive.

1. Plants depend on animals for reproduction. Flowers depend on bees for pollination and on other animals for seed dispersal.
2. Animals depend on plants for food and shelter. Bees depend on flowers for pollen to make food; rabbits eat grass; birds nest in trees.

Fig. 28.1 Interdependence. Birds nest in trees

3. Some plants depend on other plants. For example, ivy with its weak stem grows up along other plants to gain height and to reach the light.
4. Animals sometimes live on other animals often causing damage to the host. The liver fluke (parasite) depends on a snail (host) to complete its life cycle.

Feeding Relationship in a Habitat

Green plants make their own food using the sun's energy in the process of photosynthesis. For this reason they are known as **producers**. All other organisms obtain their food either directly or indirectly from plants. These are known as **consumers**. There are four types of consumer:

1. **Herbivores:** animals which eat plants only, e.g. rabbit; sheep; greenfly; limpets. Herbivores are known as primary consumers.
2. **Carnivores:** animals which eat other animals only, e.g. fox; thrush; ladybird; sparrow hawk. Carnivores which feed on herbivores are called secondary consumers, e.g. ladybird. Carnivores which feed on other carnivores are called tertiary consumers, e.g. sparrow hawk.
3. **Omnivores:** animals which feed on both plants and animals, e.g. man; badger; acorn barnacles.
4. **Decomposers:** animals and non-green plants which feed on dead plant and animal material only, e.g. dung beetle; fungi; bacteria.

Food Chains

A feeding relationship between plants and animals is called a **food chain,** e.g. grass → rabbit → fox; rose leaves → greenfly → ladybird. In each case a herbivore eats a plant and then a carnivore eats a herbivore. Some food chains are longer and have four or five links in the chain, e.g. rose leaves → greenfly → ladybird → spider; plant plankton → animal plankton → mackeral → man.

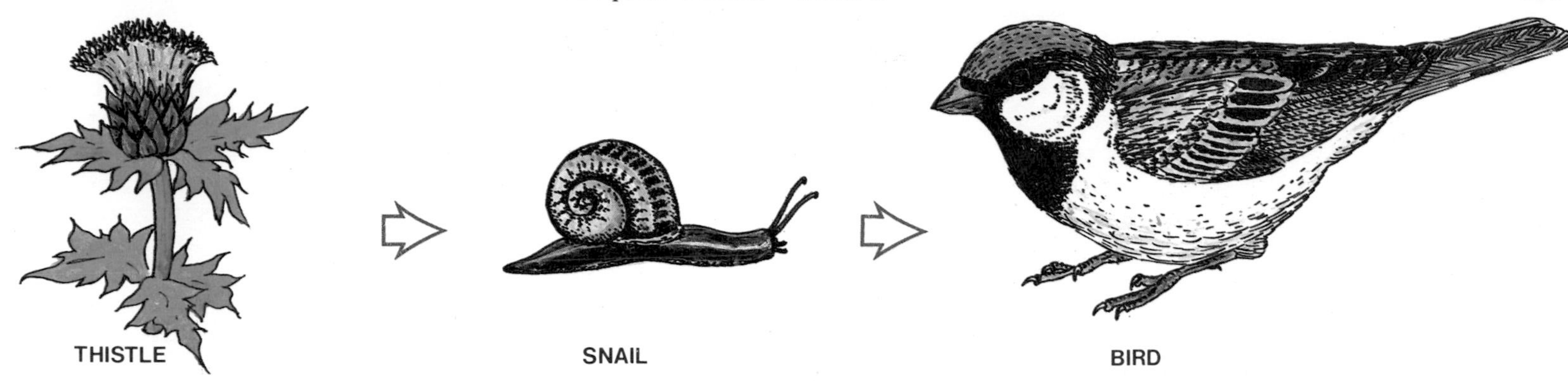

Fig. 28.2 Food chain

Pyramid of Numbers

The organisms at the start of a food chain are generally green plants and they are usually present in very high numbers. On the other hand, the animals at the top of the chain are far less numerous. This idea can be illustrated by a pyramid of numbers, *Fig. 28.3.*

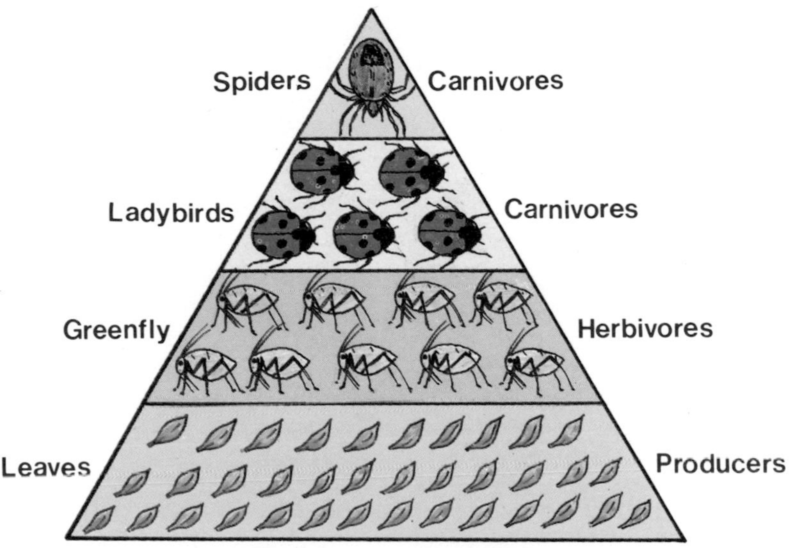

Fig. 28.3 Pyramid of numbers

The large number of organisms towards the bottom of the pyramid are needed to provide enough energy-containing materials (food) for the small numbers of organisms near the top. This is because the consumers in the chain either use up or waste nearly all of the energy containing materials they take in. Hence very few are left to be passed on to the next consumer and after two or three transfers there is only enough food to support a very small number of carnivores.

Food Web

In a habitat, the feeding relationships are rarely as simple as the ones described so far. Many food chains are interconnected forming a food web. Below, part of a woodland food web is illustrated. Pick out 4 simple food chains from this food web. List also a) the producers, b) the primary consumers, c) the secondary consumers and d) the tertiary consumers.

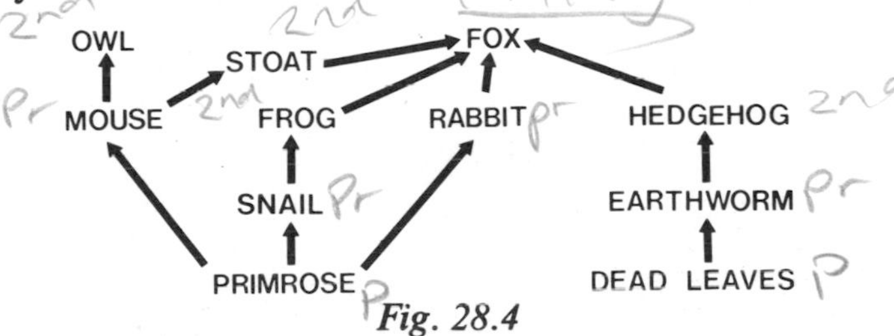

Fig. 28.4

Adaptation to the Environment

In order to survive in a habitat, plants and animals must be able to cope with and adapt to their surroundings. For example plants and animals living on the rocky shore must be able to cope with many changes within a 24-hour period. When the tide is in, they are covered with sea water; when the tide is out, they are exposed to the air or to fresh water when it rains. The dragging action of the waves means that plants and animals must have some method of clinging to rocks — otherwise they would be washed out to sea. Many of the animals have shells to prevent their soft bodies drying out when the tide goes out, and so on.

Fig. 28.5 Bull's eye moth — warning colouration and defensive attitude

Fig. 28.6 Insects showing adaptation using camouflage

Plants and animals living in terrestrial (land) habitat have many features which enable colouration, e.g. caterpillars are usually the colour of the plant they feed on; toads and frogs blend well with their background; stone coloured insects and spiders live on walls. Insects have developed has a long coiled tongue which allows it to collect nectar from deep inside the flower. Other animals use stings to stun their prey (food), e.g. jellyfish, or to frighten away attackers. Plants living in very dry habitats cannot afford to lose too much water. They are adapted by having tiny spines for leaves, e.g. the cactus. The roots of some plants are adapted for storing food, as in the carrot and turnip.

In your study of a habitat you will find many examples of adaptation. The ability of organisms to adapt to their enviroment is one of the most important principles of biology.

Environmental Factors affecting life in the Habitat

1. **Edaphic factors:** Factors related to the soil, e.g. the pH; porosity; capillarity; mineral holding capacity; humus and moisture content. All these factors are discussed and tested in *Book 1, Chapter 14 — Soil.* The type of soil present will determine the plant and animal life in the habitat.
2. **Climatic Factors:** These include light intensity; rainfall; temperature; wind and humidity.
3. **Physiographic Factors:** These include:
   (a) topography, i.e. whether the ground is flat or on a slope and whether it is sheltered or exposed;
   (b) aspect, i.e. whether the habitat faces north, south, east or west.
   (c) altitude, i.e. height above sea level.
4. **Biotic factors:** These are the factors caused by competition between plants and animals in the habitat. For example, plants compete with each other for light and water; animals compete for food, *see below.*

In the study of a habitat the environmental factors outlined above should be recorded and measured where appropriate.

Competition

Competition occurs between organisms when they are seeking the same raw materials (or resources) in the habitat. Such resources include water, food and shelter. Plants compete for light, water, minerals and space. Animals compete for food, shelter, territory and mating partners. Because animals can move around, they are able to overcome the problems of shelter, space and food shortage much easier than plants.

Colonisation and Succession

Colonisation occurs when plants and later animals move into and occupy a new environment such as cleared land or bare rock. The colonisation of new ground can take a long time and it occurs in stages to follow each other in sequence. The first organisms to inhabit the area would be lichens. The lichens would gradually begin to break up the surface of the rock allowing a foot-hold for mosses. Then, as the older mosses die, they begin to form humus which allows ferns and grasses to become established. Eventually flowers, shrubs and trees are able to survive and form a woodland. As soon as the plant life becomes established animals will inhabit the area. These will compete with each other for available food and shelter and those that cannot adapt to the environment will either leave or die.

28.3 Pollution

Fig. 28.5 Dead fish as a result of water pollution

To pollute means to dirty or contaminate the environment. Pollution can be caused by a variety of substances such as sulphur dioxide and carbon monoxide in the air, slurry from silage pits, fertilisers, pesticides, raw sewage, domestic waste, oil and litter. A new pollutant is radioactivity, as was seen after the nuclear accident at Chernobyl, Russia in April 1986, when many countries were affected by the fallout.

Two main types of pollution are water pollution and air pollution.

Water Pollution

This is caused by a variety of substances being dumped into our rivers, lakes and seas. These include sewage and slurry, fertilisers, poisons, oil and litter.

1. **Sewage and slurry** reduce the amount of oxygen available to fish and other aquatic organisms. This occurs because the decomposers, such as bacteria, which break down the sewage, use up the available oxygen in the water.
2. **Fertilisers** containing nitrogen and phosphorus, which wash into rivers from farm land, cause a sudden increase in the growth of microscopic algae known as an algal bloom. When the algae die, the decomposers use up the available oxygen and so prevent fish and other aquatic animals and plants from surviving.
3. **Oil** is a major pollutant of our seas and coastlines. The oil coats the feathers of sea birds preventing them from flying. Birds and fish are also poisoned as they swallow the oil. Oil on our seashores is unsightly and it ruins our beaches as a tourist amenity.

Water pollution can be prevented by the proper treatment of sewage and the careful disposal of agricultural wastes. It is an offence to pollute our water supplies and severe penalties and fines can be imposed on offenders. Individuals can play their part too by making sure they do not drop litter. It just takes a little thought and consideration.

Fig. 28.8 Litter pollution

Air Pollution

The main cause of air pollution is the burning of coal, oil and other fuels. As a result of combustion, smoke, dust, sulphur dioxide, carbon monoxide and lead are produced — all of which act as air pollutants.

1. **Smoke and dust** irritate the lines of the bronchial tubes causing bronchitis in humans. Dust particles in urban areas block light reaching plants and reduce their ability to photosynthesise.
2. **Sulphur dioxide gas** inhibits photosynthesis in plants and it also aggravates bronchitis in humans. When it combines with rain, sulphur dioxide forms sulphuric and sulphurous acids ('acid rain'), which wear away stonework of buildings and cause metals to corrode.
3. **Carbon monoxide and lead compounds** are produced by the burning of petrol and diesel by cars and lorries. Both of these substances are poisonous and unpleasant to inhale. However lead-free petrol became available for use in 1986, and is a step towards reducing lead pollution.

Industries, the government and individuals must become more aware of the hazards of pollution and take measures to combat the needless destruction of the environment.

28.4 Conservation

Conservation is the wise use of the environment. Man must be able to use his natural resources i.e. the land and sea, for both social and economic benefit and at the same time protect them for future generations.

We all know how much we depend upon agriculture to provide food crops and livestock which produce meat, milk and other dairy products. But many agricultural practices, including the drainage of land and the use of pesticides, must be carried out with caution and with the long term effects of such action always in mind. Drainage removes wetland habitats and, as a result, their characteristic flora and fauna, for instance the frog, become endangered.

Certain insecticides, used to kill insect pests on crops can have the effect of killing many useful insects as well. The spray from insecticides being applied to crops can destroy many plants and animals which inhabit the surrounding hedgerows. So the wise use of pesticides is necessary if the balance of nature is not to be upset.

The fishing industry is also dependant upon wise management for its survival. If fishermen and women use nets of too small a mesh size, they will catch young fish as well as the adults. These young fish are the adults of the future and they must be allowed free to breed and increase the fish stocks. Another problem is over-fishing which also results in a decrease in the number of breeding fish. To help conserve our fish stocks, special laws are enforced.

28.5 The Balance of Nature

In any particular habitat, there is an overall balance between the numbers of different plants and animals present. This balance of nature is due to the interdependence of the organisms in the habitat. The removal of any one type of organism can upset the balance of the entire habitat. For example, in the garden, greenfly are a serious pest of plants such as roses. Ladybirds feed on the greenfly and help to keep down the numbers of the pest. If some chemical were used to destroy the ladybirds, then the population of greenfly would get out of control and the plants on which they feed would be badly affected. In this way the balance of nature can be upset.

Conservation is the duty of all citizens. If we want future generations to benefit from nature we must ensure that the environment and its plants and animals are protected and conserved.

28.6 Fieldwork in Ecology

Introduction

Making a study of a habitat involves the following steps:

1. Make a map of the habitat to illustrate the main features of the area, e.g. pond, trees, paths, ditches.
2. Record the climatic, edaphic and physiographic factors.
3. Make a list of all the types of plants and animals in the habitat.
4. Estimate the numbers of plants and animals in the habitat.
5. Analyse the information collected. Draw graphs and diagrams to represent your data.

If you studied two habitats, or the same one during different seasons, compare the lists of plants and animals and note any differences. Try to explain any differences that occur.

Methods of Identifying and Collecting Plants and Animals

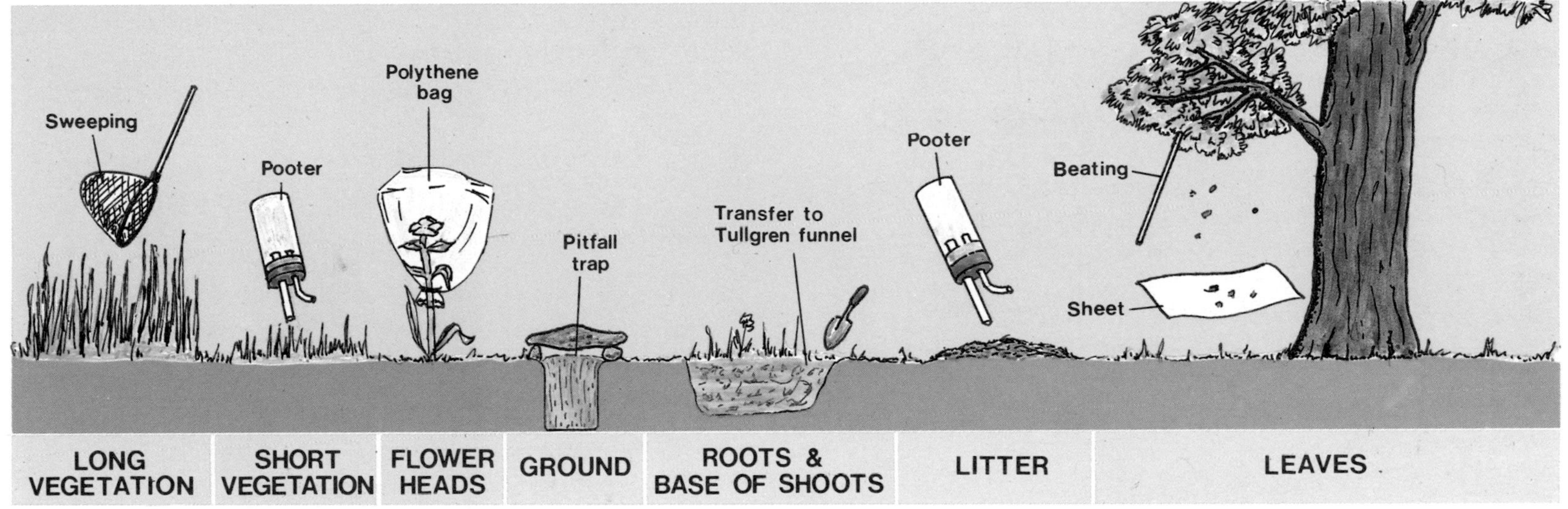

Fig. 28.9 Methods of animal collection

Plants

Since plants do not move around, it is easy enough to record which ones are present. A key, or a wild flower and tree-spotter's guide, can be used to identify many unknown plants in the ground. Sometimes unknown plants can be dug up using a trowel and placed in labelled plastic bags. These are taken back to the laboratory for identification. In the case of large shrubs or trees, a small twig with leaves and flowers (if possible) should be taken. Always remember that rare plants should never be collected.

Animals

1. Look under stones, on walls, under rotting pieces of bark; take water from a stream, pond or rock pool (for microscopic plants and animals); dig in the soil with a trowel; use a knife to dislodge animals such as limpets and whelks on rocks.

2. There are various types of **nets** which can be used to catch different animals:

   (a) *Plankton net* — used to collect plankton in streams, ponds, and seashore habitats.

   (b) *Butterfly net* — used to catch butterflies and moths on the wing.

   (c) *Sweep net* — used to catch insects by sweeping through grasses and tall vegetation.

3. A *beating tray* is used to collect insects and other small animals that live on the leaves and branches of trees. A tray/sheet is held under the leaves and the branches are beaten with sticks. This dislodges the animals and they fall onto the sheet from where they can be collected using a pooter *(see overleaf)*.

4. A *pooter* is used to collect insects and small animals from trees and bushes and also from the leaf litter in soil.

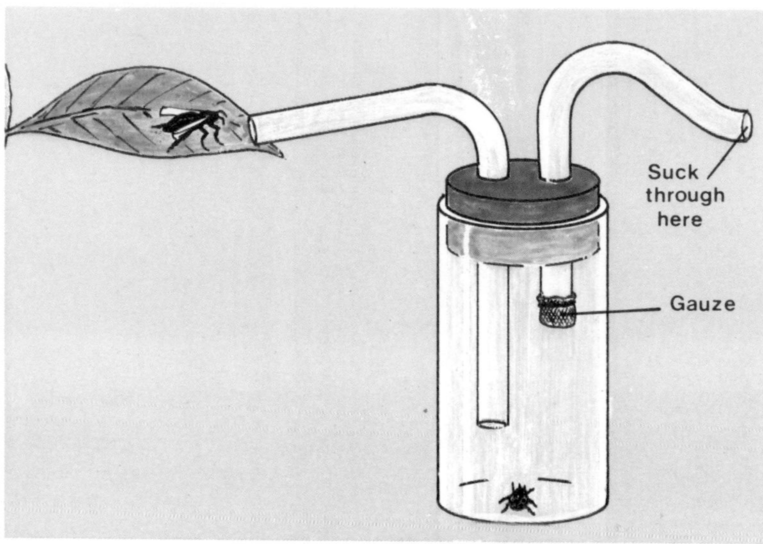

Fig. 28.10 A pooter

5. **Traps**

(a) *Pitfall Trap* — This type of trap is used to collect animals that walk along the surface of the ground. It consists of a jar sunk into the ground with its mouth level with the surface of the soil. Some bait such as meat, fruit or a preserving liquid can be placed in the bottom of the jar. The trap is set up and left for 8-12 hours (through the day/through the night). The animals which fall into the jar are unable to escape and can be identified later.

(b) *Cryptozoic Trap* — Cryptozoic traps are used to collect animals that are usually active at night (nocturnal), e.g. worms, slugs and woodlice. The trap consists of a flat piece of wood laid on the ground. The nocturnal animals will hide under the piece of wood during the day. If the trap is turned over, the animals can be easily seen and identified.

(c) *Mammal Trap* — Small mammals, such as mice, shrews and voles, can be caught using a mammal trap. Great care must be taken when opening these traps as small animals become very frightened if trapped and can give a nasty bite when being released.

6. A *Tullgren funnel, Fig. 28.11,* is used to extract small animals, especially insects, from leaf litter or soil. The warmth and light from the bulb cause small organisms to move down through the layer of soil through the gauze and down into the collecting fluid.

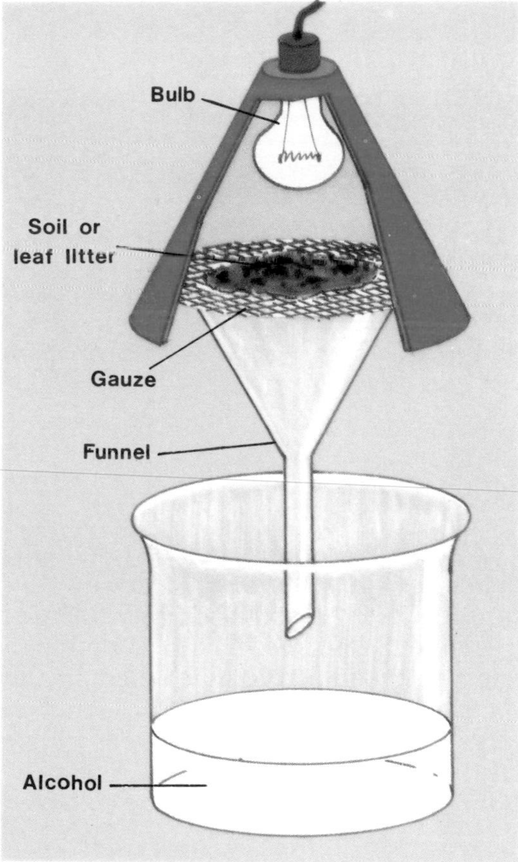

Fig. 28.11 A Tullgren funnel

Estimating the Numbers of Plants in a Habitat

It would be impossible to count and map all the plants present in a given habitat. Instead we count and map only a few of them, i.e. we take a sample which gives us some idea of the type of vegetation present as a whole.

Methods of Sampling

Fig. 28.12 Quadrat

1. *Quadrats:* A quadrat is a square area (usually 1 m²) which shows all the plants growing in that area. A quadrat can be marked out with wood, rope or metal. The quadrat frame, *Fig. 28.12*, is thrown at random (usually over the shoulder) in the habitat. The names of the types of plants present (the actual numbers of plants does not matter) in the quadrat should be recorded, as in *Table 28.1*. The quadrat frame should be thrown about 20 times at random in the area and the plants recorded each time.
   Total (add up) the number of times each plant has occurred and multiply the total by 5. This gives the percentage frequency (20 × 5 = 100) for the plant in the habitat. A bar chart of the frequency of plants can then be drawn. This makes your figures easier to understand and it also makes it simpler to compare with the vegetation from other habitats.

Table 28.1

Habitat: School garden — *Quadrat size: 1 m²*
Name: Elizabeth Sisk — *Date: 8-8-1986*
Number of quadrats thrown: 20

Species (Name)	*Quadratic Number* 1 2 3 4 5.... ....19 20	*T*	*Frequency T × 5*
Daisy	/ / /	6	30%
Fine-leaved grass	/ / / / /	19	95%
Medium-leaved grass	/ / / / / /- /	20	100%
Dandelion	/ /	8	40%
Yarrow	/	1	5%

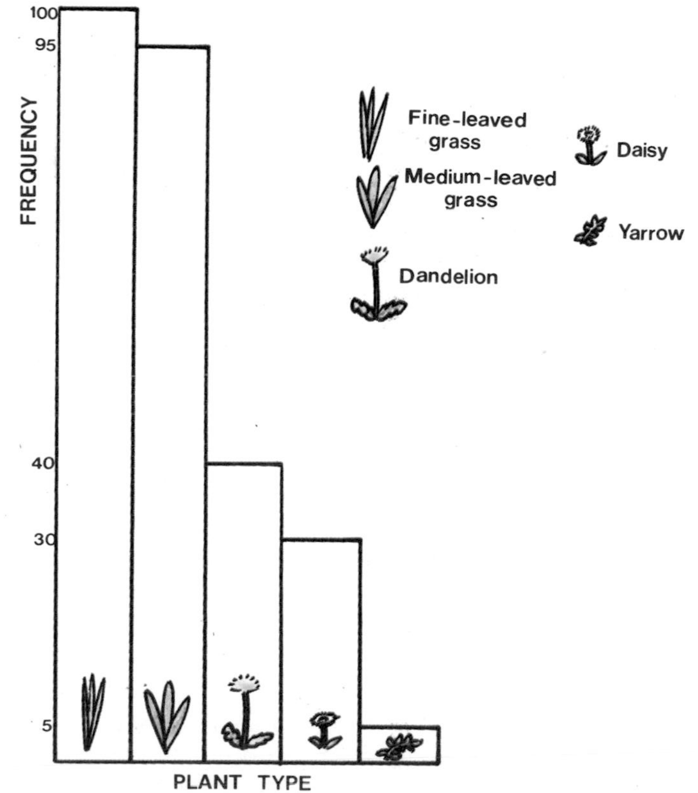

Fig. 28.13 Bar chart of plant frequency

2. *Transects:* The word transect means 'cut across'. A transect shows how the vegetation changes across an area, as for example across a path or seashore, or from a shaded area under trees to an exposed area of grass.

(a) A **line transect** consists of a rope which is laid across the habitat and staked at either end. The rope is marked off at regular intervals (1 m or 0.5 m) known as stations. The names of the plant(s), if any, which are touching the line at the stations are recorded and the height of each plant noted. A record like that in *Table 28.2* can be made.

Table 28.2 Recording Data for a Line Transect

Station Number	*Name of Plant*	*Height of Plant (cm)*
0	Nettle (n)	30
1	Goosegrass (g)	40
2	Chickweed (c)	8
3	Nettle (n)	28
4	— —	—
5	Buttercup (b)	15
6	Fine-leaved grass (fg)	5

A diagram to represent the line transect can then be drawn, *Fig. 28.14.*

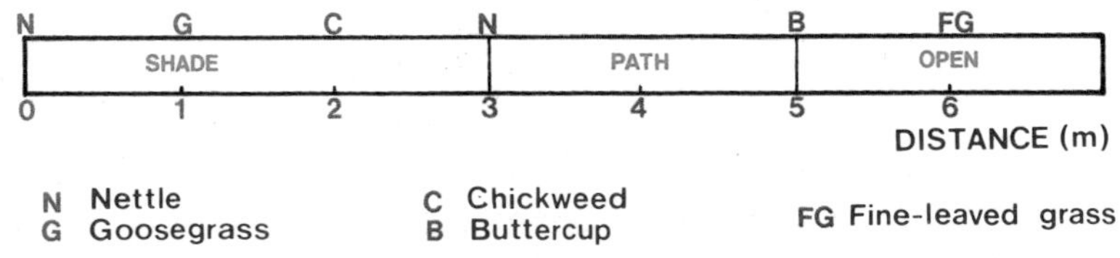

Fig. 28.14 Diagram of a line transect

(b) A **belt transect** consists of two ropes lying paralled to each other, 0.5 m or 1 m apart, and with cross strings at each station. This marks out a narrow belt of quadrats. The types of plant in each quadrat are recorded and a rough sketch of the transect can be made, *Fig. 28.15.*

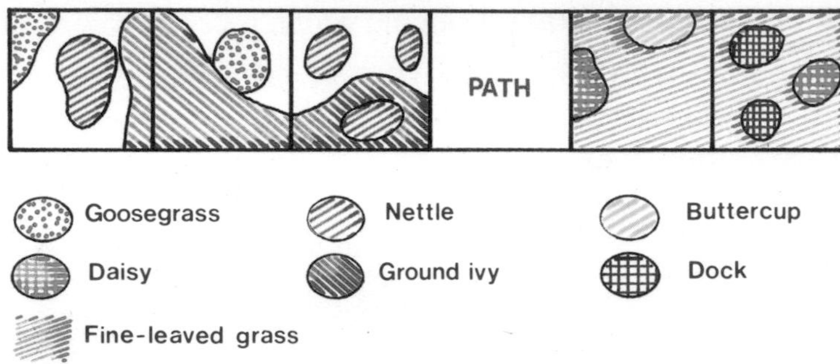

Fig. 28.15 Outline sketch of a belt transect

Table 28.3 Recording Data for a Belt Transect

Quadrat (1 m²)	*Plants present*
1	Nettle, goosegrass, ground ivy
2	Goosegrass, ground ivy
3	Nettle, ground ivy
4	Path/bare ground
5	Buttercup, fine-leaved grass, daisy
6	Fine-leaved grass, daisy dock

Experiment 28.1 A Habitat Investigation

Method

The study of the habitat should be written up as a report to cover the following steps:

1. Make a simple outline map of your habitat.
2. Record the climatic, physiographic and soil factors affecting the habitat.

3. Collect and identify the plants and animals in the habitat. Compile a list of organisms present. Classify to the phylum level.
4. Use quadrats to determine the percentage frequency of plants. Plot a graph (bar chart) of the result.
5. Make a transect (line or belt) across contrasting areas of the habitat, e.g. sunny to shade.
6. Use the information gathered to find examples of each of the following from the habitat: (a) food chains; (b) a food web; (c) competition; (d) adaptation; (e) interdependence.

28.7 The Rocky Sea-Shore

The rocky sea-shore is an interesting habitat to study with nearly every major group of animal represented. The tides have a very important role to play in the life of sea-shore plants and animals. When the tide is in, the organisms are usually submerged and, when the tide goes out, the plants and animals are exposed to the air. Sea-shore organisms have special adaptations to help them cope with their ever changing environment.

Table 28.4

Zone	*Plants and Animals on the Sea-shore*		
Upper Shore	*Plants*	sea pinks	Channel weed
	Herbivores	limpets, winkles	
	Omnivores	acorn barnacles	
	Decomposers/ scavengers	sand hoppers	
			Flat wrack marks the boundary
Middle Shore	*Plants*	sea lettuce, flat wrack, serrated wrack, bladder wrack, knotted wrack	
	Herbivores	periwinkles, top shells, limpets, smooth and edible winkles	
	Carnivores	mussels	
	Decomposers/ scavangers	crabs	
			Serrated wrack marks the boundary
Lower Shore	*Plants*	red seaweeds, e.g. carageen moss; oar weed	
	Herbivores	sea urchin	
	Carnivores	shanny, benny, starfish, sea anemones, brittle stars	
	Omnivores	sponges, mussels, shrimps	
	Decomposers/ scavangers	crabs	

Adaptations to Life on the Seashore

Plants

1. Seaweeds have strong root-like holdfasts to anchor them to the rocks. This helps the plant to withstand wave action.
2. Seaweeds are usually covered with a layer of mucilage which prevents them from drying out.

Animals

1. Many animals, e.g. limpets, barnacles and winkles, have a hard shell to prevent exposure when the tide goes out.
2. Sponges take refuge under the seaweeds on the sides of rocks facing away from the sea to protect their soft bodies.

28.8 Woodland

Fig. 28.16 Woodland habitat

Woodland can be divided into four zones or layers:
1. Tree or canopy layer.
2. Shrub layer.
3. Field or herb layer.
4. Ground layer.

Table 28.5

	Oak Wood pH < 5.5 (acid)
Tree	Oak
Shrub	Holly, mountain ash
Field	Ferns, wood sorrel
Ground	Mosses, leaf litter

Table 28.6 Plants and Animals of an Oak Wood

Plants	Birch, holly, ferns, mosses, bracken, bluebells, bramble, honeysuckle, mountain ash.
Herbivores	caterpillars, moths, butterflies, beetles, sawflies, mice, slugs, snails.
Omnivores	Blackbird, tits.
Decomposers	Earthworms.

Adaptations to Life in the Woodland

Plants

Light is the most important factor affecting plants. The tree layer uses maximum light. Once the leaves are on the trees, they form a canopy over the layers below, blocking most of the light. Plants of the field layer are either adapted to surviving on low light intensities, e.g. ferns, or to flowering and producing their seeds before the leaves form on the canopy layer, e.g. bluebell; primrose.

Animals

One of the main adaptations that woodland animals show is camouflage. Their colouration enables them to blend in with their surroundings so well that they are less likely to be eaten by predators. Animals showing camouflage include greenfly, birds, beetles, mice, shrews, and earthworms.

Fig. 28.17 Green brindled crescent moth, showing camouflage colouration

28.9 Freshwater Pond

A small pond is an ideal habitat to study. It is a more or less stable environment and it is less complicated than either the sea-shore or woodland habitats.

Table 28.7 Plants and Animals of a Pond

Plants		
Floating:	water lily; duckweed.	
Submerged:	water crowfoot; Canadian pond weed.	
At water's edge:	rushes; reeds; yellow iris; water plantain.	
Animals		
At the water surface:	mosquito larvae; ducks; various bugs; pondskater; springtails.	
In the water:	Herbivores:	pond snails.
	Carnivores:	water boatman, diving beetle, minnows, stickleback fish.
	Omnivores:	waterflea.
	Decomposers/ scavengers:	some water beetles, water shrimps.
On the bottom of the pond (on stones):	Herbivores:	pond snails.
	Carnivores:	mayfly, caddis fly, beetle and dragonfly larvae.

Adaptations to Life in a Pond

Plants

Light is an important factor for plant life. All green plants need light to photosynthesise. The deeper you go in the pond, the less the light can penetrate. So pond plants are adapted by either living at the water's surface or by having floating leaves which help them obtain maximum light.

Animals

Most pond animals are cold blooded and are therefore affected by temperature. In winter, a pond may freeze. To overcome this problem many pond animals are able to burrow into the mud at the bottom of the pond, e.g. water boatman. Pond animals obtain their oxygen supply either from the water around them or from the air above the surface. Some animals are adapted to taking in oxygen

Fig. 28.18 Fresh water pond.

from the water by diffusion, e.g. flatworms, or by gills, as fish do. Insects which must obtain oxygen from the atmosphere have developed special breathing tubes, e.g. mosquito larvae; water boatman. Others can come to the surface and trap air bubbles in different parts of their body and carry the air down with them under water, e.g. diving beetle.

28.10 Hedgerow

Hedges were used to enclose fields and protect crops from farm animals. As with woodlands, hedges vary greatly in the type of trees and shrubs they contain, depending upon the type of soil they are growing in.

Fig. 28.19 Aerial view showing hedgerows as boundary markers

Table 28.8 Plants and Animals of a Typical Hedgerow

Plants	
Trees and Shrubs:	Ash, elm (sometimes), hawthorn, blackthorn, elder.
Lower Edge:	Blackberry, honeysuckle.
Field Layer/ Bank:	Cow parsley, hog weed, nettle, 'Lords and Ladies', goosegrass.
Ditch (if present):	Rushes, plantain, yellow iris.
Verge:	Thistle, buttercup, poppies.
Animals	
Herbivores:	Caterpillars, greenfly, blackfly, chaffinch, butterfly, cranefly, slugs, snails, hoverfly, bee, mice, shield bug.
Carnivores:	Hoverfly larvae, thrush, shrew, ground beetle, hedgehog, spider, hedge sparrow.
Omnivores:	Blackbird, blue tit.
Decomposers:	Earthworms.

Adaptations to Life in the Hedgerow

The adaptations shown by hedgerow plants and animals are similar to those shown by organisms living at the edge of a woodland.

Summary

* Ecology is the study of the interrelationships between plants/animals and their environment.
* The habitat of an organism is the place where it lives.
* An ecosystem is the habitat together with the plants and animals living there.
* A feeding relationship between organisms is called a food chain.
* Two or more interconnecting food chains form a food web.
* Producers make their own food.
* Consumers include herbivores, carnivores, omnivores, decomposers and scavengers.
* Plants and animals compete with each other for raw materials in the habitat.
* Succession involves the building of a stable group of plants and animals in a habitat, e.g. the development of a woodland over many years.
* Pollution is caused by substances which make the environment unpleasant or dangerous for living things.
* Conservation is the way in which our natural resources (land, water and organisms) are protected for future generations.

Questions

Section A

1. Ecology is ....
2. Give one way in which (a) animals are dependent on plants .... and (b) plants depend on animals ...

   ....
3. What is a habitat? ....
4. A consumer is an organism that can/cannot make its own food.

   Name a consumer ....
5. Classify each of the following under the headings 'producer' and 'consumer': algae; fungi; earthworms; mosses; insects; ferns.

   Producers: ....

   Consumers: ....
6. What is the main source of energy in the world? ....
7. Why are there very few carnivores at the top of a food pyramid?

   ....
8. Give an example from the habitat you have studied, of how a named plant is adapted to life in the habitat.

   Plant ....

   Adaptation ....
9. What are edaphic factors? ....
10. List three climatic factors which can affect a habitat.

    1. ....

    2. ....

    3. ....
11. Give an example of competition in the habitat you have studied.

    ....
12. State two causes of water pollution. ....
13. The balance of nature refers to ....
14. Which of the following pieces of equipment would you use to collect animals that walk along the surface of the ground?

    quadrat; beating tray; transect; pitfall trap. ....
15. What would you use a pooter for? ....

Section B

1. Explain the terms (a) producer; (b) consumer; (c) food chain; (d) food web. The diagram represents part of a food web in an oak woodland.

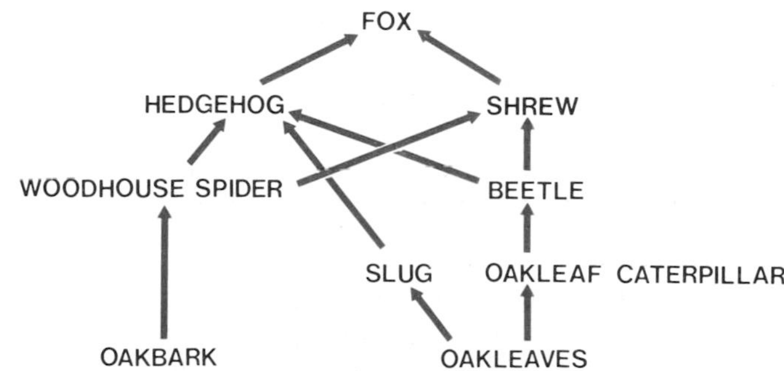

   From the diagram

   (a) Name (i) a producer; (ii) a primary consumer; (iii) a secondary consumer.

   (b) Pick out two food chains.

   (c) Draw a diagram to represent a pyramid of numbers.
2. Describe, under the following headings, a habitat you have studied:

   (a) Map or diagram to show the main features of the habitat.

   (b) Four plants and four animals commonly found in the habitat.

   (c) Two food chains that involve some of the above plants and animals.

   (d) An example, other than in food chains, of (i) the dependence of plants on animals; (ii) the dependence of animals on plants.

   (e) An example of (i) competition; (ii) adaptation.
3. (a) What is meant by the terms (i) pollution; (ii) conservation? Explain how each of the following water pollutants has a harmful effect on organisms living in a river; (i) raw sewage; (ii) oil; (iii) excess fertilisers.

   (b) Write a short essay entitled: *Conservation — the future in our hands.*

29 — Genetics

29.1 Introduction

Genetics is the study of heredity. It looks at the way characteristics (traits) are passed on from one generation to the next. For example, you, your family, classmates and teacher are all human beings. And, although we share certain characteristics (such as hair on the body and hands with grasping fingers) we are all different. Some of us have brown hair, some are blond; some have brown eyes, others have blue; some can roll their tongues, others cannot; and so on. In other words, human beings vary and it is these variations which make each of us an individual.

29.2 Types of Variation

Variations can be either inherited or due to the environment. Inherited variations include eye colour, hair colour and shape of nose, *Fig. 29.1.* Variations due to the environment are ones that are not passed on from parent to offspring but are acquired during the lifetime of the organism. The ability to play soccer or to ride a bicycle is not inherited but, as we all know, some people are able to play soccer better than others. Cress seeds grown in the light produce green stems and leaves. If grown in the dark, the seedlings are creamy white and grow straggly. Here the environment (light) determines whether the green colour is produced or not.

Experiment 29.1 To Look at Family Likeness

Method

1. Look at the eye colour of members of your family. Include your parents, brothers and sisters, and grandparents.
2. Fill your results into the following table.

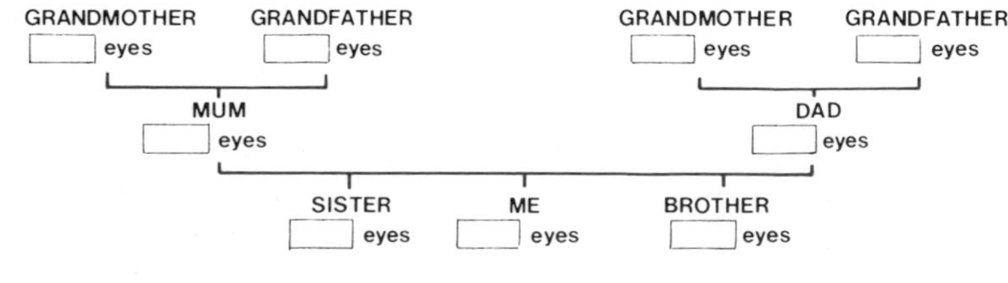

Table 29.1

Fig. 29.1 Inherited variations

Blue eye colour is known as a **recessive** character, whilst brown eye colour is **dominant**. A recessive character can 'miss' a generation, and appear in grandchildren. Did you find any example of this in *Experiment 29.1*?

Repeat this experiment using hair colour as your inherited characteristic.

29.3 Chromosomes and Genes

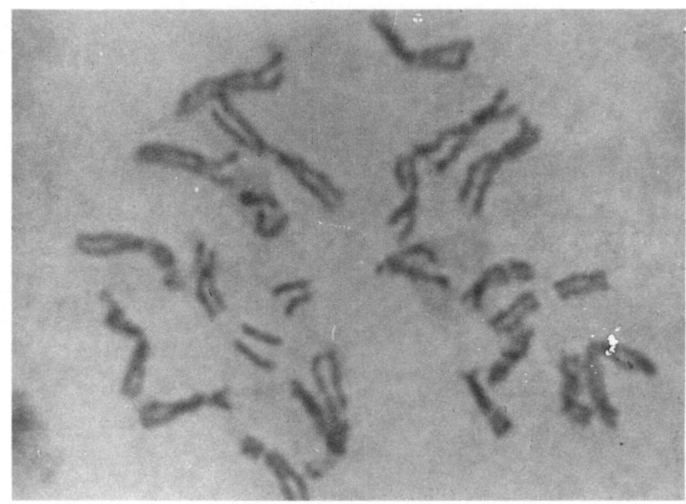

Fig. 29.2 Chromosomes in a cell

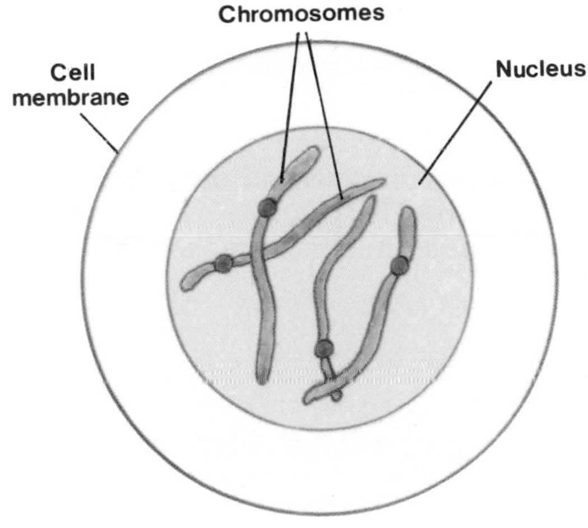

Fig. 29.3 Cell with nucleus showing chromosomes.

Every organism that is produced by sexual reproduction begins life as a single cell called a zygote. In man, the male sperm cell fuses with a female egg cell to produce the zygote from which the new individual grows. So the sperm and egg cells must carry all the instructions necessary to form the baby. These instructions are found in the nucleus of the cells. The nucleus of every cell contains a set of thread-like structures called **chromosomes**. The instructions necessary to form a new individual are carried on the chromosomes as a series of chemicals called **genes**, *Fig. 29.4.* Each gene is an instruction for making some part of the cell. For example, one gene may instruct the cell to make the hormone insulin which is found in the pancreas. Another gene might be responsible for the brown pigment of the hair and so on. It is thought that there may be over a thousand genes on each human chromosome.

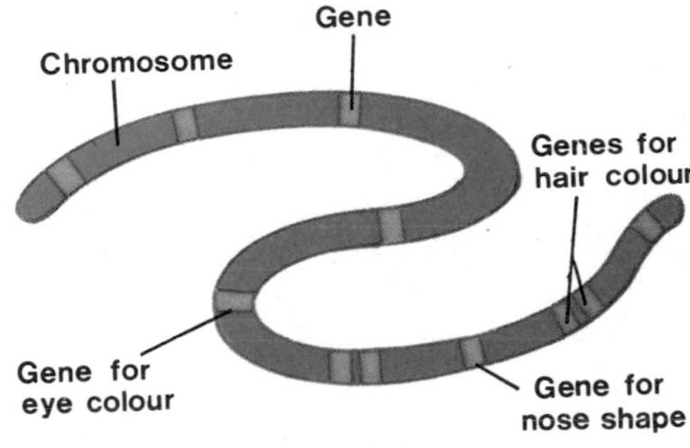

Fig. 29.4 Chromosome and genes

Chromosome Number

There is a fixed number of chromosomes in the cells of each species of plant or animal. In humans there are 46 chromosomes (23 pairs); in mice 40 (20 pairs); in the onion 16 (8 pairs). Every cell in the human body, except the egg and sperm, has the same 46 chromosomes on which are found the same set of genes. In a gamete (egg or sperm) there are only half the normal number of chromosomes. So in humans, the egg cell has 23 chromosomes and the sperm cell has 23 chromosomes. When the egg and sperm fuse together during fertilization the normal number of 46 chromosomes is restored, *Fig. 29.5.* The fertilized egg contains 46 chromosomes; 23 from the mother and 23 from the father. In this way, a new individual will have genes and therefore characteristics from both its father and its mother.

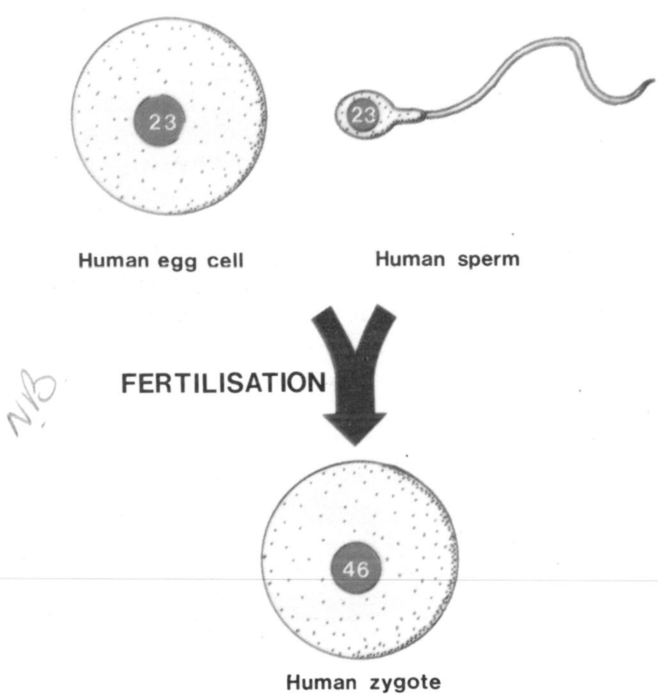

Fig. 29.5 Chromosome numbers in man

29.4 How Heredity Works

Let us take the example of hair colour in humans and see how it is inherited. In general, there is a tendency for more people to have dark hair than fair hair. We say that the gene for dark hair is **dominant** over the gene for fair hair, which is **recessive**.

When you look at a person's hair you do not see a gene, you see the colour that the gene for hair colour instructed the cells to make. The genes you have for a particular characteristic are known as the **genotype**. The appearance the genes produce is known as the **phenotype**, i.e. dark hair or fair hair.

We use letters of the alphabet to represent genes. The dominant gene is given a capital letter. The recessive gene is given the small letter of the dominant. For example, in hair colour, D respresents dark hair and d represents fair hair. In the sweet pea, tall plants are dominant over dwarf plants, so tall is labelled T and dwarf is labelled t. In humans, having freckles is dominant over not having freckles. Give letters to represent the genes involved.

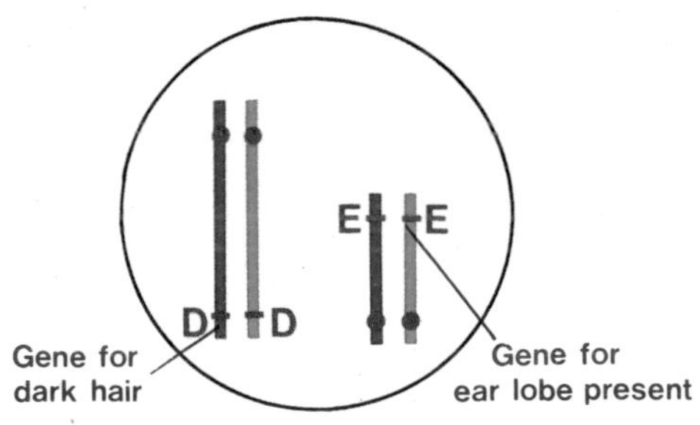

Fig. 29.6

Chromosomes in cells are found in pairs (one chromosome from each parent) and the genes are also in pairs. Genes for a particular characteristic are found in a corresponding position on the chromosomes, *Fig. 29.6.*

29.5 Homozygous and Heterozygous

When two dominant genes (DD) or two recessive genes (dd) appear on a pair of chromosomes, the organism is referred to as pure breeding or **homozygous**. When one dominant and one recessive gene combine (Dd) the organism is referred to as **heterozygous**.

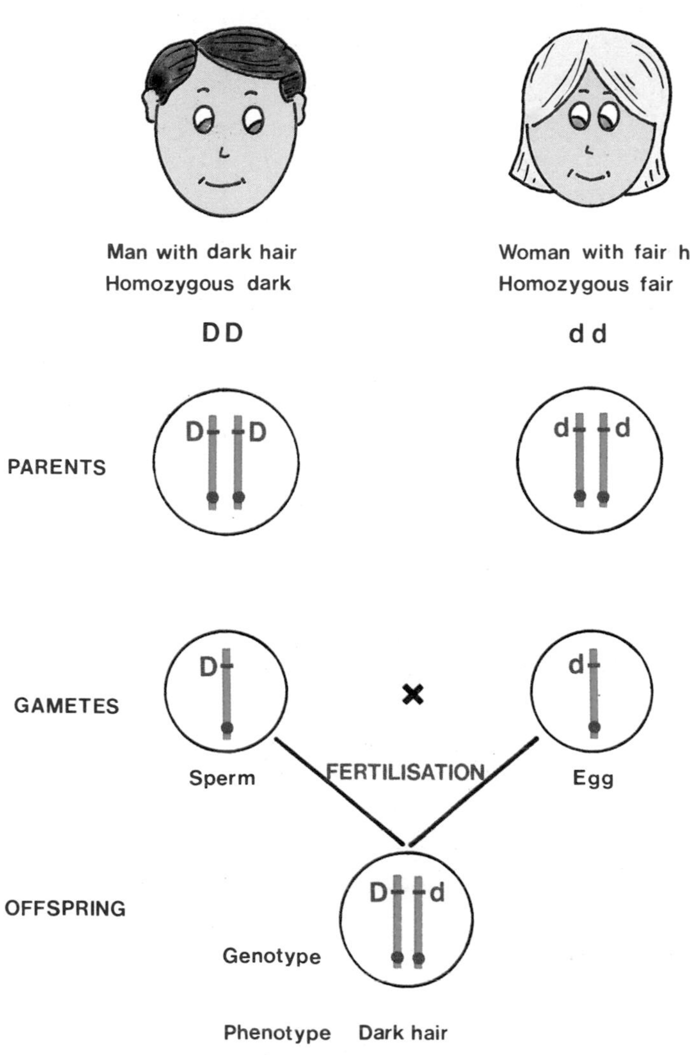

Fig. 29.7 Dark hair

In the heterozygous condition, e.g. Dd, the dominant gene wins out over the recessive gene and is expressed in the phenotype, i.e. Dd is expressed as dark hair. Now let us use all this information to see how hair colour is inherited.

If a homozygous dark haired man marries a homozygous fair-haired woman what is the possible hair colour of their children?

Fig. 29.7 shows how the result is obtained. This can be represented in a simpler fashion as follows:

Parents		DD	×	dd
Gametes		D	×	d
Offspring:				
	Genotype		Dd	
	Phenotype		Dark hair	

In other words, parents with the above genotypes for hair colour can only produce children with Dd or dark hair.

In another case, a heterozygous dark-haired man marries a heterozygous dark-haired woman. What hair colour would you expect their children to have?

Parents	Dd	×	Dd	
Gametes	D or d	×	D or d	
Off-spring:				
Genotype	DD	Dd	dd	Dd
Phenotype	dark	dark	fair	dark

The result of the above cross shows that it is more likely that the children will have dark hair. The result does not mean that four children are born at a time! It means that when these parents have a child there is a 3:1 chance that the child will have dark rather than fair hair. This ratio is true everytime they have a child.

The cross just described explains the inheritance of only one characteristic — hair colour. Such a cross is known as a **monohybrid cross**.

Problems

Here are some genetics problems for you to try yourself. It is important to set out the cross properly, labelling the parents, gametes and offspring and matching the phenotypes of the offspring to the corresponding genotypes.

1. In rabbits, black coat colour is dominant to golden. Describe the results of a cross between two rabbits heterozygous for coat colour. Clearly indicate the genotypes and phenotypes of the parents, gametes and offspring.
2. In humans, brown eyes are dominant to blue eyes. If a heterozygous brown-eyed woman marries a blue-eyed man, what will the genotypes and phenotypes of the possible offspring?
3. If a heterozygous tall sweet pea plant is crossed with (i) a homozygous tall sweet pea plant and (ii) a homozygous dwarf sweet pea plant, what will be the genotypes and phenotypes of the offspring?

Summary

* Genetics is the study of inheritance.
* Organisms show variation in their characteristics, variation can be due to the environment, or it can be inherited.
* Hereditary characteristics include eye colour, and hair colour.
* Chromosomes are found in the nucleus of a cell.
* Genes are chemicals which pass on information.
* A monhybrid cross investigates the inheritance of a single characteristic.
* Genotype — the type of genes an organism has.
* Phenotype — the physical expression of the genes.

Questions

Section A

1. What is the name given to the study of inheritance? .....
2. Give two charcteristics that can be inherited? 1..............; 2...............................
3. Where would you find chromosomes? ....
4. How many pairs of chromosomes are there in humans?..
5. The type of genes an individual has is described as its: offspring; gametes; genotype; phenotype. ....
6. Is a capital letter used to represent a dominant or a recessive characteristic? ....
7. The genotypes of the offspring from the cross Rr x Rr will be ....
8. In a cross between two mice FF and ff, the gametes produced are: Ff; all F; F and f; all f? ....

Section B

1. (a) The diagram represents a monohybrid cross:

Parents	Ee × ee
Gametes	E or e × e
Offspring	Ee ee

What letter(s) in the diagram represent

(i) the homozygous condition;
(ii) the hetrozygous condition;
(iii) a recessive gene
(iv) a dominant gene.

(b) In rabbits, long hair is dominant to short. Describe the results of a cross between two rabbits heterozygous for hair length. Clearly indicate the genotypes of the parents and offspring, the kinds of gamete formed and the phenotypes involved.

30 — Force

30.1 Force

All pushes and pulls are forces. When you peddle your bicycle you are applying a force to it. When you lift a cup or a book you are applying a force to it. A force, then, is something which can cause motion, i.e. make an object start to move or make it move faster than it is already moving. A force can also slow something down or change the direction in which it is travelling. So we can define force as follows:

A force is anything which causes a change in the speed or direction of an object.

There are many examples of forces in Nature. If you place two magnets near to each other they will either move closer together or move further apart. The magnets exert forces on each other. These forces, which were discussed in *Book 1*, are called **magnetic forces.**

If you hold a stone above the ground and let it go it will fall towards the ground with increasing speed; if you throw a stone up into the air it gradually slows down and stops and then falls back to the ground with increasing speed. These are examples of a force known as the **force of gravity**. You will learn more about this force in the next section.

Try this little experiment. Tear up some paper into small pieces. Now rub a plastic comb or biro on your sleeve and hold it near the pieces of paper. The pieces of paper move towards the comb or biro and, if everything is very dry, they may move away again. The forces in this case are known as **electric forces** and you will meet them again in *Chapter 11.*

Note: In Physics, the word **body** is often used to mean an object or a quantity of a substance.

Pairs of Forces

You may have noticed that in each of the examples given above there were always two objects associated with each force — the two magnets; the stone and the ground; the biro and the pieces of paper. From this we may conclude that:

Forces always occur in pairs.

Experiment 30.1 To Show that Forces always occur in Pairs

Method

1. Take a dynamics trolley and compress the spring by pushing in the rod. Fix the rod behind the metal plate on the end of trolley.
2. Put the trolley by itself on the bench and trigger the spring by striking the peg. Does the trolley move?

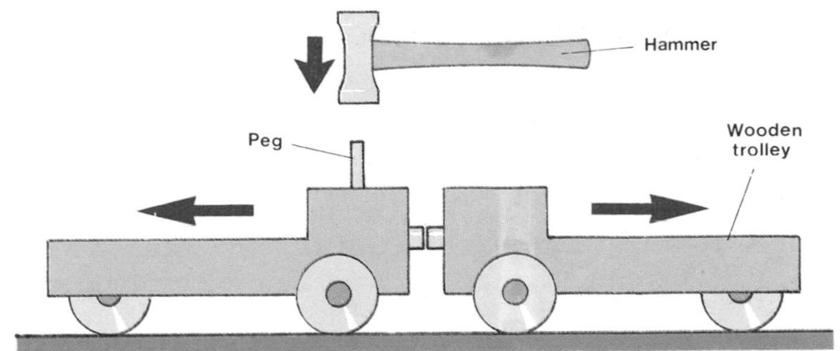

Fig. 30.1 Trolleys

3. Now take a second trolley and place the two trolleys end to end, having first compressed the spring again.
4. Trigger the spring and observe what happens this time. Push the rod back into the trolley.
5. Finally, using just one trolley, hold a small block of wood against the end of the rod and trigger the spring. What did you feel?

Conclusion

When one trolley is used, it does not move as it has nothing to push against. However when two trolleys are placed end to end, releasing the spring makes them move away from each other. The spring in the first trolley, A, exerts a force on the second trolley, B, and B exerts an equal and opposite force on A. This force is felt on your hand when the spring is released in the last part of the experiment.

The results of this experiment can be summarised in a statement known as **Newton's Third Law**.

To every action there is an equal and opposite reaction.

Note: Action is another word for force.
Reaction is an opposing force.

Measuring Force

Before we can measure any quantity we need a unit. The SI unit of force is called the newton (N), in memory of the English scientist, Sir Isaac Newton. What size of force is one newton (1 N)? Get some metal "weights" and find one which is marked "100g". When you lift this you are exerting a force of approximately 1 N. To lift two of these you must exert a force of 2 N, and so on. To lift one of your classmates would require a force in the region of 300 N to 500 N. A weightlifter, *Fig. 30.2*, can exert a force of over 4000 N. Forces can be measured with a spring balance *(see Section 30.3 below).*

Fig. 30.2

Effects of Forces

The effects that forces have on a body depend on the number, size and direction of the forces and on the shape and strength of the body. Thus, forces can cause compression (squeezing together), bending, torsion (twisting) or tension (stretching).
If a number of forces act on a body, the net force that results, changes the speed and direction of the body. Consider two people pushing a car, one with a force of 300N and the other 500N. If they push together the resulting force is 800N. However if they push against one another the resulting force is 200N in the direction of the 500N force.

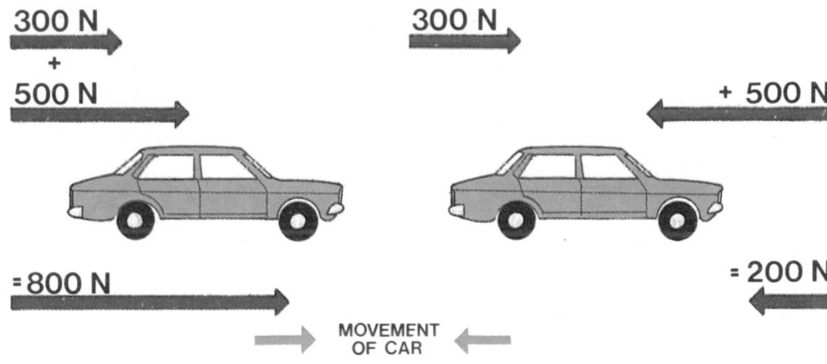

Fig. 30.3 Resultant forces

30.2 Weight

We noted in the last section that in order to lift something you have to exert a force on it. This is because the earth exerts a downwards force on all objects near to it. This force is called the **force of gravity**. The force of gravity on a body is called its **weight**.

The weight of a body is the force of gravity on it.

The weight of a body depends on its mass; the larger the mass, the larger the weight. On the surface of the earth it is found that the weight of a body in newtons is equal to its mass in kilograms multiplied by 10 (more exactly, 9.8). Thus, if your mass is 42 kg (about 6.5 stones) then your weight is 420 N.

The weight of a body also depends on its distance from the centre of the earth. The further it is from the centre of the earth, the smaller its weight. At a height of 2650 km above the earth, the weight of a body would be about one half of its weight on earth. The earth is not exactly sphericcal and so the weight of a body varies from one place to another on the surface of the earth, being greater near the Poles than near the Equator. It would also be slightly less on the top of a high mountain than at sea-level.

Remember that, although the weight of a body depends on its position, its mass is the same no matter where it is.

Note: The word "weight", as we have just seen, means *"force of gravity on a body"*. However, it is also used to mean an object of known mass (and therefore known weight), used for weighing things with the lever type of balance *(see next chapter).*

30.3 Springs

One of the effects of forces mentioned previously was the stretching effect. If you apply equal but opposite forces to both ends of a spring or a piece of elastic, it stretches. The following experiment shows how the increase in the length of a spring depends on the forces applied to it.

Experiment 30.2 To Investigate the Stretching of a Spring

Method

1. Hang the spring from a retort stand and attach a weight carrier to it, *Fig. 30.4.*
2. Measure the length of the spring. Place a weight on the carrier and measure the new length of the spring.
3. Repeat this procedure for about six different weights.
4. Record your results in the form of a table as shown below. Plot a graph of extension, i.e. increase in length (of spring) against weight, i.e. force applied or **load**.

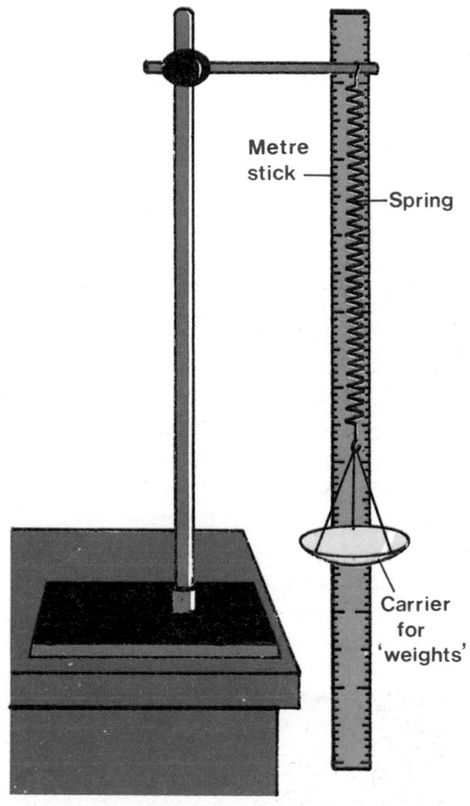

Fig. 30.4

Conclusion

The increase in the length of the spring is proportional to the weight added. That is, if a weight of 0.2N (20g mass) stretched the spring by 1 cm, a weight of 0.4N (40g mass) will stretch it by 2 cm. The graph of extension against weight added is a straight line through the origin, showing that the increase in length is proportional to the weight.

You should record your results for this experiment in a table like this:

RESULTS

Force/N	*Length/cm*	*Extension/cm*
0	20	0
0.2	21	1
0.4	22	2
etc.	etc.	etc.

The values in this table are given as a guide only. The values from your experiment may be quite different. If the weights which you are given are marked in grams rather than newtons (i.e. their mass is given rather than their weight), remember that "weight = mass × 10". So, a weight whose mass is 20 g (0.02 kg) has a weight of 0.2 N.

The conclusion of this experiment is known as *Hooke's Law*, after its discoverer, the English scientist Robert Hooke. Hooke's Law states that:

The extension of a stretched spring is proportional to the force (or load) applied to it.

Example

A spring is stretched 4 cm by a weight of 0.5 N. If the same spring is stretched 2 cm by a pencil hanging from it, what is the weight of the pencil?

4 cm extension caused by 0.5 N

1 cm extension caused by 0.5/4 N

2 cm extension caused by $\frac{0.5}{4} \times 2$ N

$$\frac{0.5}{4} \times 2$$

$$= 0.25 \text{ N}$$

Ans. 0.25 N

From this example we see how a spring can be used to find the weight of an object. First, we find how much the spring is stretched by a known weight. Then, as in the example, we can work out the weight of an object by attaching it to the spring and measuring the increase in the length of the spring. A spring balance has a scale beside the spring which measures the weight directly.

Elastic Limit

If you try to stretch a spring too far it will not return to its original length. The greatest length that a spring will stretch to and still return to its original length is called its **elastic limit**.

30.4 Work

When you say that you have work to do you may mean that you have an exercise to do or an essay to write, or you may mean that you have to cut the grass, do the shopping or some other such task. However, as in the case of other words which you have met, the word **work** has a much more definite meaning in Science than it has in everyday life. In Science, work is done only when a force moves a body.

Work is done when a force moves a body.

To calculate the amount of work done we multiply the force by the distance that the body moves.

Work = Force × Distance

Example

A boy pulls a sleigh with a constant (steady) force of 20 N for a distance of 40m. How much work does he do?

Work = Force × distance
= 20 N × 40 m
= 800 N m

The unit of work is called a joule (J), taking its name from the English physicist James Joule, who did much of the early work on energy and heating. So,

800 N m = 800 J

Ans. 800 J.

Notice from this last example that the mass of the sleigh does not matter. If the sleigh has a larger mass it will move over the distance more slowly but the total amount of work will still be the same.

Example 2

A spacecraft has a mass of 10 tonnes (10,000 kg). What work is done in launching it to a height of 2000 km?

Force required $= $ Weight of spacecraft
$= 10\,000 \times 10$
$= 100\,000$ N
$= 1 \times 10^5$ N

2000 km $= 2\,000\,000$ m
$= 2 \times 10^6$ m

Work $=$ Force $\times$ distance
$= 1 \times 10^5 \times 2 \times 10^6$
$= 2 \times 10^{11}$ J

Ans. 2×10^{11} J.

30.5 Power

In the first example above we calculated the amount of work done by a boy in pulling a sleigh a distance of 40 m without considering how long it took him to do the work. Let us suppose that it took him 20 s. The total amount of work he did was 800 J, so in each second he did 40 J. He was doing work at the rate of 40 J per second. We say that his power was 40 J/s.

Power is the rate at which work is done, i.e. the amount of work done per second.

The unit of power is the watt (W), called after the Scottish scientist and inventor, James Watt. 1 W is the same as 1 J/s, so the boy's power was 40 W.

Since work is the process of changing energy from one form to another, power may also be defined as:

Power is the amount of energy changed from one form to another in one second.

When we say that an electric light bulb is 100 W, we mean it changes electrical energy to radiant energy at a rate of 100 J/s. A 500 W motor changes electrical energy to kinetic energy at a rate of 500 J/s.

Summary

* A force is anything which changes the speed or direction of an object.
* Forces always occur in pairs — if A exerts a force on B, B exerts an equal but opposite force on A. (To every action there is an equal but opposite reaction.)
* The unit of force is the newton (N).
* The effects of forces include (as well as acceleration) compression, stretching, torsion (twisting) and bending.
* The weight of a body is the force of gravity on it.
* The weight of a body at a particular place depends on its mass. Weight (in newtons) = mass (in kilograms) × 10.
* The mass of a body does not change when it moves from one place to another but its weight depends on its distance from the centre of the earth.
* *Hooke's Law* states that the extension of a spring (the stretch) is proportional to the force (load) causing it.
* Work is done when a force moves a body. The unit of work is the joule (J).
* The amount of work done is equal to the product of the force and the distance moved.
* Work is the process of changing energy from one form to another.
* Power is the amount of work done in one second. The unit of power is the watt (W).

Questions

Section A

1. A force is anything which causes ....
2. The unit of force is the ....
3. What are the effects of a force? ....
4. If A exerts a force on B, B exerts an ....
5. The weight of an object is the ....
6. What is the unit of weight? ....
7. What is the weight of a body whose mass is 20 kg? .....
8. The weight of a body depends on its .... and on its ....
9. The weight of an object may be measured with a ......
10. The increase in the length of a spring is proportional to ....
11. What is the mass of a body whose weight is 420 N? ....
12. The .... of a body on the moon is less than it is on the earth but .... is the same.
13. If a spring is stretched beyond its .... it will not return to its original length.
14. Name four forces ....
15. To every .... there is an equal but opposite .... *(Newton's Third Law).*
16. Work is done when ....
17. The unit of work is the ....
18. The amount of work done per second is called ....
19. The unit of power is the ....
20. Work is the process of converting .... from one .... to another.

Section B

1. Given a spring, a metre rule, a 0.5 N weight and a small stone, describe how you would find the weight of the stone.
2. What is the weight of an object whose mass is (i) 35 kg; (ii) 5.2 kg; (iii) 500 g; (iv) 45 g?
3. What is the mass of an object whose weight is (i) 400 N; (ii) 25 N; (iii) 5 N; (iv) 1.2 N?
4. The length of a spring is 30 cm. When a 0.5 N weight hangs from it, its length is 35 cm. When a stone hangs from it, its length is 34 cm. What is (i) the weight; (ii) the mass, of the stone?
5. State *Hooke's Law* and describe an experiment to verify it.
6. Calculate the amount of work done when a man pushes a trolley with a force of 30 N over a distance of 40 m.
7. A woman whose mass is 50 kg wishes to climb a mountain which is 500 m high. How much energy must she use?
   If she spends five hours climbing the mountain what is her average power?
8. An electric fire is rated as 2 kW. How much electrical energy does it 'use' in one hour? What happens to this energy?

31 — Turning Forces

31.1 Moments

In the last chapter we looked at some of the effects of a force. One which we did not mention was the **turning effect**. When you push down on the handle of a door, the force you exert has a turning effect; when you pedal your bicycle, the force you exert on the pedals has a turning effect. The turning effect of a force is called the **moment** of the force.

Fig. 31.1 Turning effect of a force — opening a lock gate

The size of the turning effect of a force depends not only on the size of the force but also on where the force is applied. If you want to open a heavy gate, for example, it is easier if you hold the gate at the end furthest from the hinges. The line through the hinges of the gate is called the **fulcrum** (or pivot) around which the gate turns when it is being opened or closed. So, the further from the fulcrum that the force is applied, the greater the turning effect of the force. The line along which the force is applied is called the **line of action** of the force.

The moment of a force is equal to the product of the force and the perpendicular distance from the fulcrum to the line of action of the force.

Moment = Force × Perpendicular distance

Example

What is the moment of the force shown in Fig. 31.2?

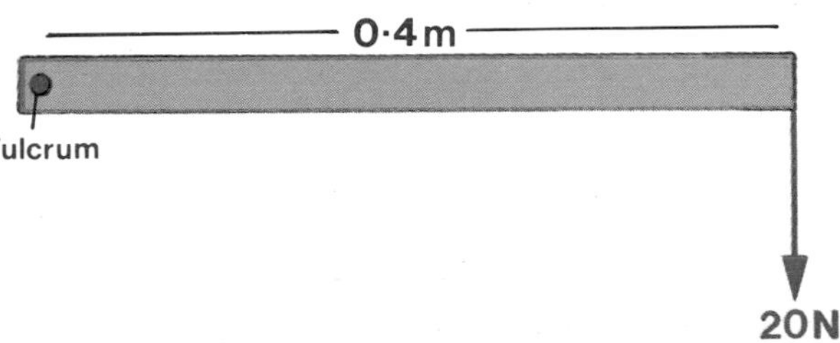

Fig. 31.2

Moment = Force × Perpendicular distance
= 20 N × 0.4 m
= 8 N m

Ans: 8 N m.

Experiment 31.1 To Investigate the Force required to open a Door

Method

1. Place a small piece of wood between the door and the jamb so that it cannot completely close.
2. Put a small sucker 10 cm away from the hinge. Then hook a spring balance onto the sucker and pull the door open. Record the reading of the spring balance as the door moves towards you.

Fig. 31.3 Measuring force required to open a door

3. Repeat step 2 at intervals of 10 cm across the breadth of the door.
4. Record your results in the form of a table as shown.

Distance from hinge d (cm)	Reading on spring balance, F (N)	F × d (N cm)

Conclusion

As the distance from the hinge increases the force required to open the door decreases. If the force and distance are multiplied together for each situation, the result is found to be constant.

31.2 Centre of Gravity

We saw in the last chapter that the weight of an object is the force of gravity on it. Where does this force act? Take a block of wood and try to balance it on the point of your finger. If the block falls, the weight of the block is acting beside your finger — the weight has a turning effect (moment) about your finger, *Fig. 31.4*.

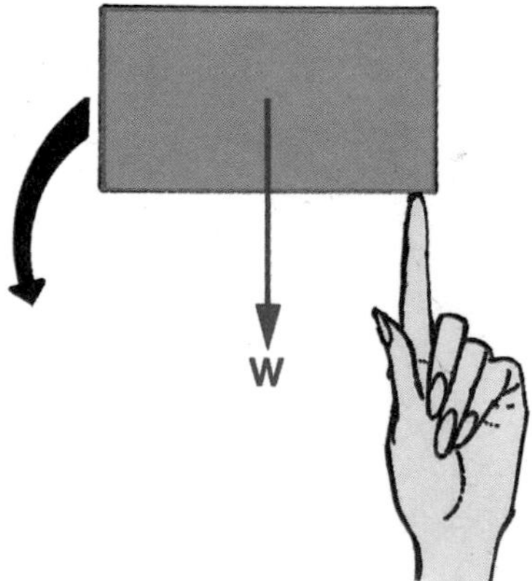

Fig. 31.4 The weight has a turning effect

When you have the block balanced on your finger, the weight has no moment, so the weight must be acting along the line AB, through your finger, *Fig. 31.5(a)*. Turn the block on its side and balance it on your finger again. The weight is now acting along the line CD, *Fig. 31.5(b)*. The point where the lines AB and CD cross is called the centre of gravity of the block.

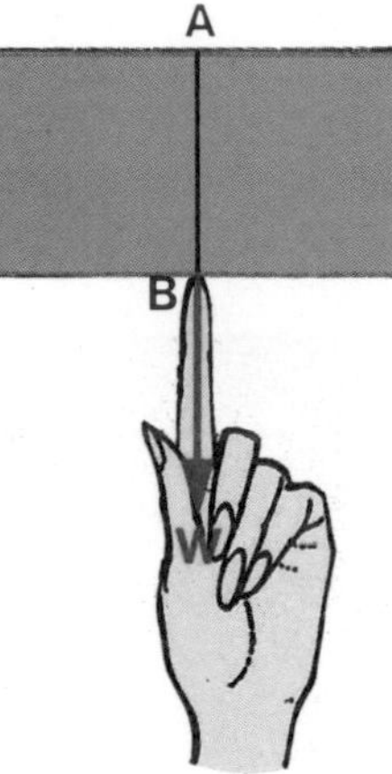

Fig. 31.5 (a)

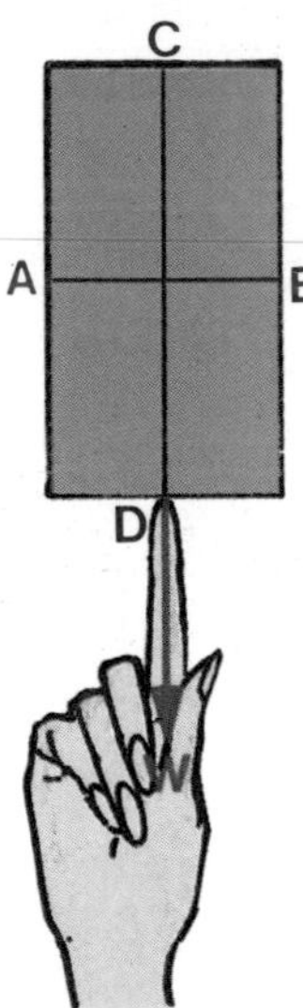

Fig. 31.5 (b)

The centre of gravity of a body is the point through which its weight acts no matter what position the body is in.

Experiment 31.2 To Find the Centre of Gravity of a Thin Sheet of Cardboard

Method

1. Fix a cork in the clamp of a retort stand.
2. Stick a pin through one corner of the cardboard and into the cork as shown in *Fig. 31.6.*

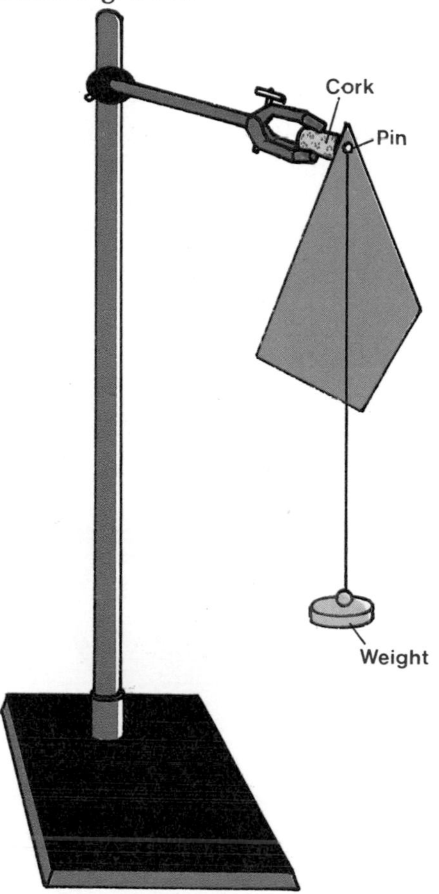

Fig. 31.6

3. Hang a plumb-line from the pin, making sure that the cardboard can swing freely on the pin.
4. When the cardboard is at rest, its centre of gravity must be directly below the pin. (If it were not the weight of the cardboard would have a turning effect about the pin and the cardboard would turn, *see Fig. 31.4.* Mark the position of the plumb line using two crosses.
5. Take down the cardboard and draw a straight line through the crosses. Stick the pin through the cardboard at a different point, not too close to the first one.
6. Push the pin into the cork and again mark the position of the plumb-line with two crosses. Remove the card and draw in the line. Where the two lines cross is the centre of gravity of the cardboard.
7. Repeat the whole procedure for at least two more points on the cardboard. All the lines should pass through the same point.
8. As a further check, you should be able to balance the cardboard on the position of the pin by placing the point of the pin at the point where the lines cross.

31.3 Equilibrium

When something is balanced we say that it is **in equilibrium**. When something is in equilibrium, all the forces acting on it cancel each other out. There are three different types, or **states of equilibrium**. These are: **stable** equilibrium; **unstable** equilibrium; **neutral** equilibrium.

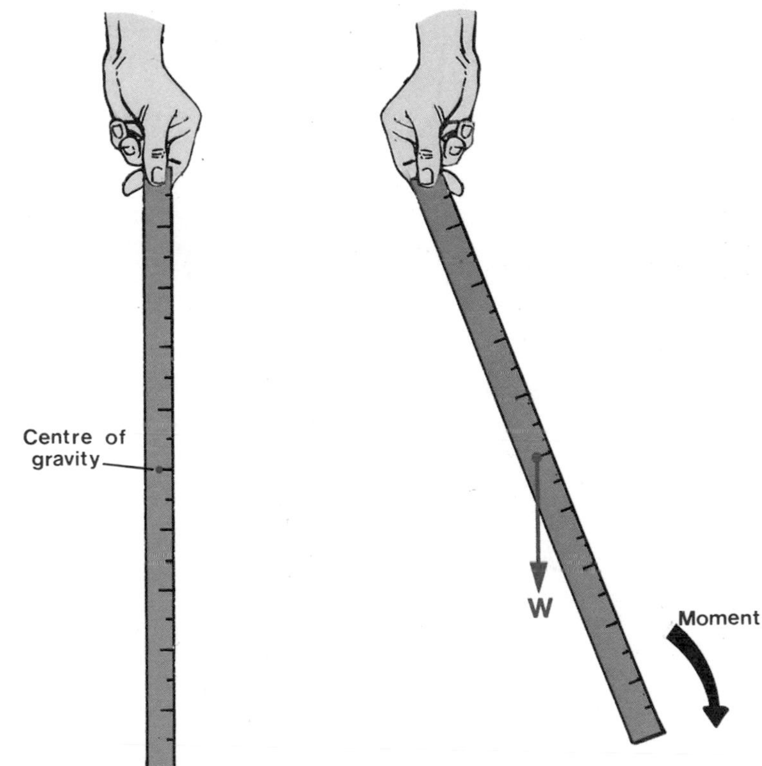

Fig. 31.7 (a) & (b) Stable equilibrium

Hold a metre rule between your finger and thumb as shown in *Fig. 31.7(a)*, so that it can swing freely. The metre rule is in equilibrium. If you now turn the metre rule by moving the bottom end to one side, it will return to its original position. For this reason, this type of equilibrium is called **stable equilibrium**. Note that moving the bottom of the rule to one side raises its centre of gravity. The weight now has a moment (turning effect) about the point at which the rule is supported, *Fig. 31.7(b)*, and so it falls back to its original position. Note that the centre of gravity of the metre rule is below the point at which it is supported. (This is not so for all examples of stable equilibrium, *see below*.)

Now balance the metre rule as shown in *Fig. 31.8(a)* (if you can!). The metre rule is now in **unstable equilibrium**. If the metre rule is turned slightly to one side, it will not return to its original position. In this case, moving the metre rule lowers its centre of gravity and the moment of the weight turns it away from its original position, *Fig. 31.8(b)*. Note also that the centre of gravity of the metre rule is directly above the point at which it is supported.

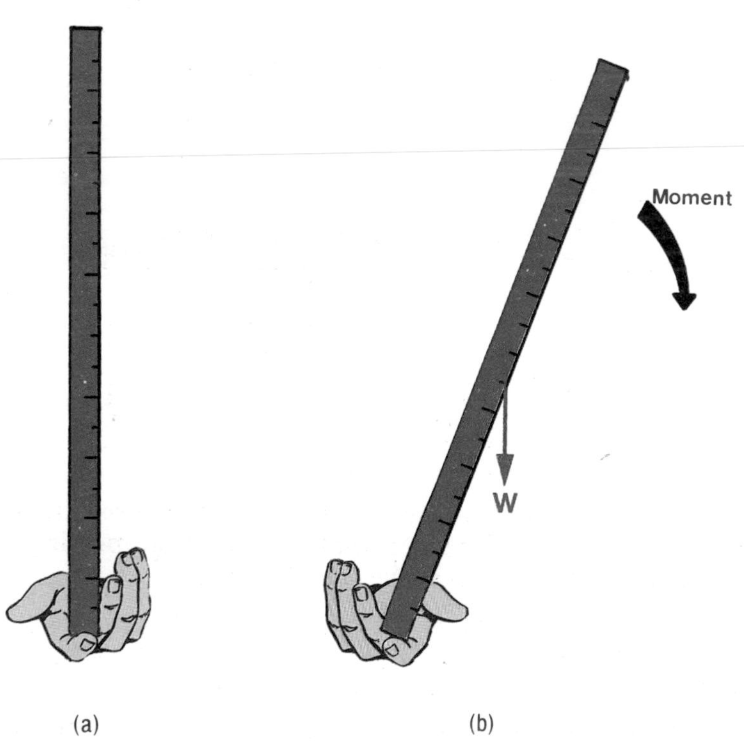

Fig. 31.8 (a) & (b) Unstable equilibrium

Finally, hold the metre rule at the 50 cm mark, that is, at its centre of gravity. No matter what position you move the metre rule to, it will stay in the new position. The metre rule is now in **neutral equilibrium**. Turning the metre rule does not change the height of its centre of gravity. In this example of neutral equilibrium, the centre of gravity is at the point of support but this is not always the case.

The stability of cars, buses, etc. is an important part of their design. Although the centre of gravity of a vehicle is always above the points at which it is supported, it is in stable equilibrium — up to a point! If a bus, for example, turns sharply to the left, the left hand side of the bus lifts up. Since this raises the centre of gravity, the bus tends to return to its original position — it is in stable equilibrium.

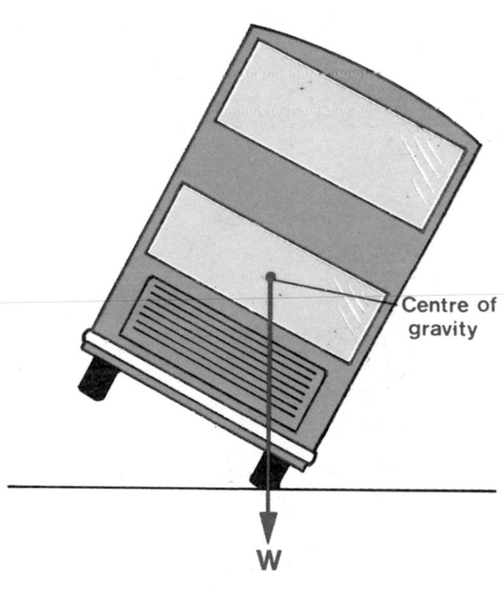

Fig. 31.9

However, if the left hand side lifts until the centre of gravity is above the right hand wheels, *Fig. 31.9*, any Further movement will lower the centre of gravity. The bus is now in unstable equilibrium and is on the point of toppling over.The lower the centre of gravity is in the first place, the less likely the bus is to topple over. For this reason buses and other vehicles, especially racing cars, are designed so that their centre of gravity is as low as possible.

Fig. 31.10 Racing cars have a low centre of gravity

31.4 Levers

When you use a spoon to take the lid off a jam jar or a screw driver to take the lid off a paint tin, you are using a lever. When you use nut crackers or a pair of scissors you are using a lever. Other examples of levers are: a crowbar, a door handle, the gear lever of a car, your arm. From these examples you can see that a lever is something which is rigid (does not bend easily) and which can turn about some fixed point.

A lever is a rigid body which is free to turn about a fixed point called the fulcrum.

Principle of Moments

Fig. 31.11 shows a metre rule supported at its centre of gravity. The metre rule is now an example of a lever with its fulcrum through its centre of gravity. There are two forces acting on the metre rule, one on either side of the fulcrum. Each of these has a moment about the fulcrum. The force on the left has an anticlockwise moment — it tends to turn the lever in an anticlockwise direction around the fulcrum.

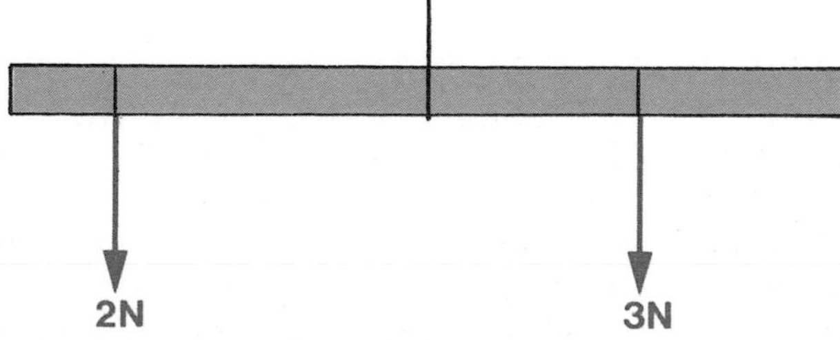

Fig. 31.11

The force on the right has a clockwise moment — it tends to turn the lever in a clockwise direction. If the metre rule is balanced (in equilibrium), these two moments must be equal in size. This is an example of the *Principle of Moments.* The *Principle of Moments* states:

When a body is balanced and not moving (in equilibrium), the sum of the clockwise moments acting on it is equal to the sum of the anti-clockwise moments.

Experiment 31.3 To Verify the Principle of Moments

Method

1. Hang the metre rule from a retort stand with a piece of thread.
2. Adjust the position of the thread until the metre rule is balanced. The thread is now over the centre of gravity of the metre rule.
3. Record the position of the centre of gravity.
4. Hang at least five weights from the metre rule at different points, *Fig. 31.12.*

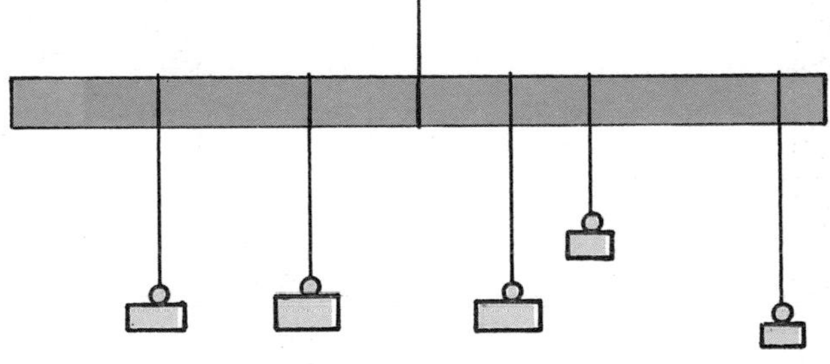

Fig. 31.12

5. Adjust the positions of the weights until the metre rule is again balanced, making sure that the thread supporting the metre rule is still over the centre of gravity.
6. Calculate the moment of each weight (moment = weight × perpendicular distance between thread supporting weight and centre of gravity of metre rule).
7. Record your results as shown below. Find the sum of the clockwise moments and the sum of the anticlockwise moments.

Conclusion

When the metre rule is balanced, the sum of the clockwise moments is equal to the sum of the anticlockwise moments.

RESULTS

Anticlockwise (Left side)			*Clockwise (Right side)*		
Weight (N)	*Distance (cm)*	*Moment (N cm)*	*Weight (N)*	*Distance (cm)*	*Moment (N cm)*

Example 1

A metre rule is suspended at its 50 cm mark. A 10 N weight is hanging from the 20 cm mark and a weight of X N is hanging from the 70 cm mark, Fig. 31.13. If the centre of gravity of the metre rule is at the 50 cm mark and the metre rule is in equilibrium, what is the value of X?

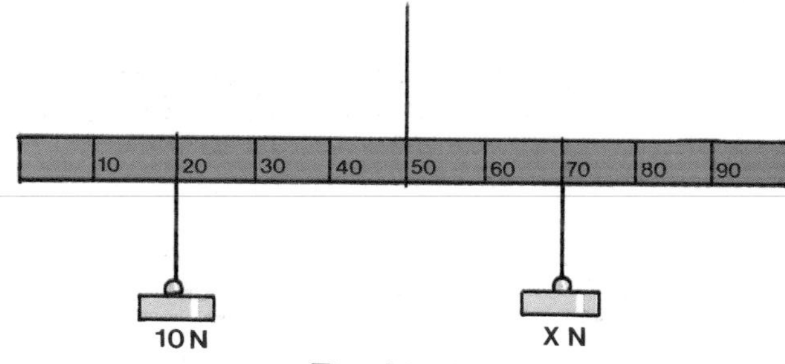

Fig. 31.13

$$\text{Anticlockwise moment} = 10 \times 30$$
$$= 300$$
$$\text{Clockwise moment} = X \times 20$$
$$= 20X$$

Since the metre rule is balanced

$$\text{Anticlockwise moment} = \text{Clockwise moment}$$
$$300 = 20X$$
$$X = \frac{300}{20}$$
$$= 15$$

Ans. 15

Example 2

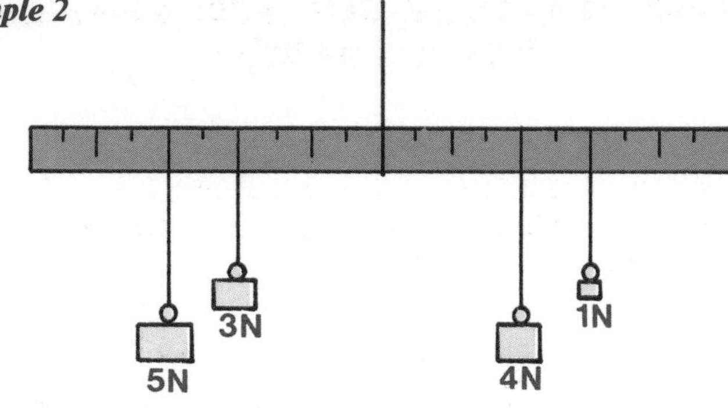

Fig. 31.14

The centre of gravity of a metre rule is at the 50 cm mark. Weights of 5N, 3N, 4N and 1N are hung from the 20 cm mark, the 30 cm mark, the 70 cm mark and the 80 cm mark, mark, the 30 cm mark, the 70 cm mark and the 80 cm mark, respectively (see Fig. 31.14). Where should a 2.5 N weight be hung to balance the metre rule?

Let the distance of the 2.5N weight from the centre of gravity be X cm.

$$\text{Anticlockwise moment} = (5 \times 30) + (3 \times 20)$$
$$= 150 + 60$$
$$= 210$$
$$\text{Clockwise moment} = (4 \times 20) + (1 \times 30) + (2.5 \times X)$$
$$= 80 + 30 + 2.5X$$
$$= 110 + 2.5X$$

When the metre rule is balanced:

$$\text{Anticlockwise moment} = \text{Clockwise moment}$$
$$210 = 110 + 2.5X$$
$$100 = 2.5X$$
$$X = \frac{100}{2.5}$$
$$= 40 \text{ cm}$$

The 2.5 N weight is 40 cm from the fulcrum, i.e. at the 90 cm mark.

Ans. At the 90 cm mark.

Experiment 31.4 Using a Metre Rule to Find the Weight of an Object

Method

1. Find the centre of gravity of the metre rule.
2. Suspend the metre rule at its centre of gravity and hang a 1 N weight on one side of the centre of gravity and the object on the other side of it.
3. Adjust the positions of the weight and the object until the metre rule is balanced.
4. Using the *Principle of Moments*, calculate the weight of the object.

The method used in this experiment is basically the principle used in various types of balance, for example the lever balance. While most lever balances in shops and laboratories have been replaced by electronic balances, some are still used. *Fig. 31.15* shows one such balance.

Fig. 31.15 A steelyard balance

This type of lever balance is called a steelyard and it has been known since Roman times.

Experiment 31.5 To Find the Weight of a Metre Rule Using a I N Weight

Method

1. Find and record the position of the centre of gravity of the metre rule as in the last experiment.
2. Move the thread supporting the metre rule to a point around the 30 cm mark.
3. Hand the 1 N weight from the metre rule and move it around until the metre rule is balanced.
4. Record the position of the weight and of the thread supporting the metre rule. Calculate the weight of the metre rule as shown in the following example.

Example

In an experiment to find the weight of a metre rule, it was supported at the 40 cm mark. The metre rule was balanced when a 0.5 N weight was hung from the 20 cm mark. If the centre of gravity of the metre rule was at the 50 cm mark, what was the weight of the metre rule? What was its mass?

In this case the anticlockwise moment is the moment of the 0.5 N weight and the clockwise moment is the moment of the weight of the metre rule itself. We shall let the weight of the metre rule be *W*, *Fig. 31.16.*

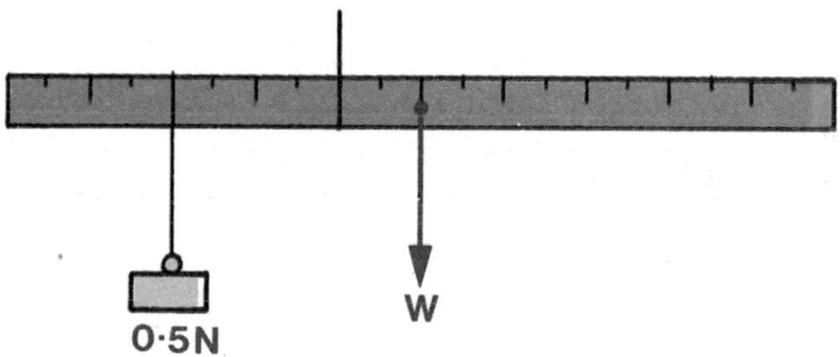

Fig. 31.16

(Remember: The weight acts through the centre of gravity, which is at the 50 cm mark). Thus:

$$\begin{aligned} \text{Anticlockwise moment} &= 0.5 \times 20 \\ &= 10 \\ \text{Clockwise moment} &= W \times 10 \\ \text{Anticlockwise moment} &= \text{Clockwise moment} \\ 10 &= W \times 10 \\ W &= 1 \end{aligned}$$

The weight of the metre rule is 1 N.

Since weight = mass × 10, the mass of the metre rule is 0.1 kg or 100g

Ans. 1 N; 100g.

Classes of Lever

As we noted earlier, there are many types of lever in use in everyday life. These are generally divided into three classes, depending on the positions of the forces applied to them. The two forces which are of most importance are the load and the effort. When you use a spoon to take the lid off a tin, the force which you apply to the spoon is the **effort**, while the force on the other end due to the lid is the **load**. In general, the load is greater than the effort. In other words, a lever is a machine which magnifies the force which we can apply to something. When the fulcrum is between the load and the effort, as it is when you use a spoon to remove a lid, the spoon is a **Class 1** lever. When the load is between the effort and the fulcrum, the lever is a **Class 2** lever. An example of this type is a nut cracker, *Fig. 31.18.* In a **Class 3** lever, the effort is between the load and the fulcrum. Your forearm, *Fig. 31.19*, is an example of a Class 3 lever.

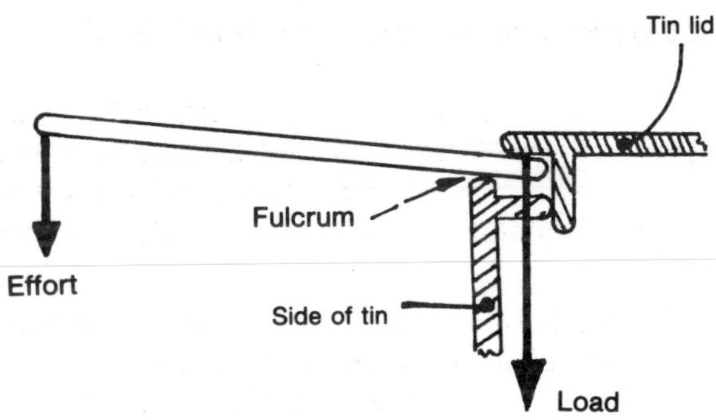

Fig. 31.17 Removing a tin lid — Class 1 lever

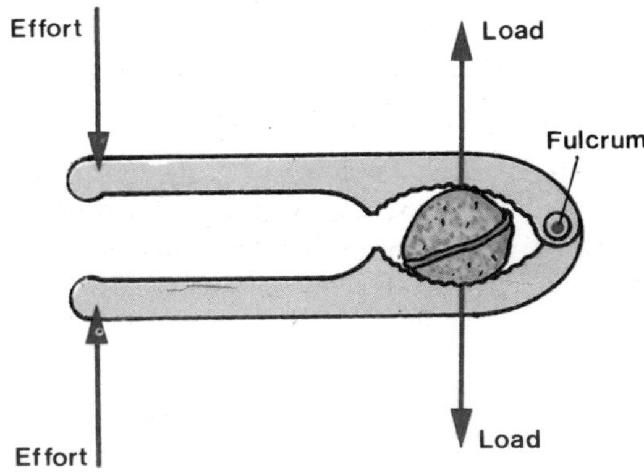

Fig. 31.18 Nutcrackers — Class 2 levers

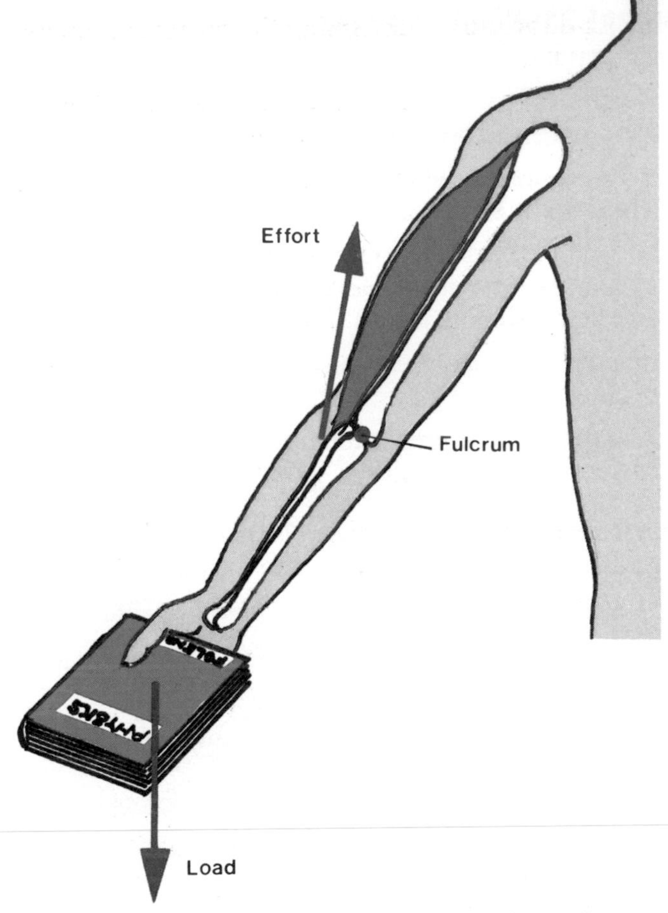

Fig. 31.19 The forearm is a Class 3 lever

Summary

* The turning effect of a force is known as the moment of the force.
* The moment of a force is equal to the product of the force and the perpendicular distance from the fulcrum to the line of action of the force.

  Moment = Force × Perpendicular distance
* The centre of gravity of a body is the point through which its weight acts no matter what position the body is in.
* When an object is balanced and not moving, it is in equilibrium.
* Stable equilibrium — disturbing the object raises its centre of gravity.

* Unstable equilibrium — disturbing the object lowers its centre of gravity.
* Neutral equilibrium — disturbing the object does not change the height of its centre of gravity.
* A lever is a rigid body which is free to turn about a fixed point called the fulcrum.
* The Principle of Moments states that when a body is in equilibrium, the sum of the clockwise moments acting on it is equal to the sum of the antilockwise moments.

Questions

Section A

1. The turning effect of a force is called a ....
2. The moment of a force is equal to ....
3. What is a lever? ....
4. When a lever is balanced we say that it is in ....
5. List six examples of levers ....
6. The centre of gravity of an object is the point ....
7. Name the three states of equilibrium ....
8. What is the Principle of Moments? ....
9. In a Class 2 lever the .... is between the effort and the ....
10. Explain the terms: Load; Effort; Fulcrum ....
11. When a body is hanging freely from a point, its .... must be directly below the point of support.
12. In a Class 1 lever the .... is between the effort and the ....
13. Give two examples of objects in each of the three states of equilibrium.................................. ....
14. In a Class 3 lever the .... is between the and the fulcrum.
15. Why are racing cars very low, with wheels which are far apart? ....

Section B

1. Describe how you would find the centre of gravity of an irregularly shaped sheet of cardboard. How would you check that the point you had found was the centre of gravity?
2. Describe an experiment to verify the *Principle of Moments.*
   A metre rule is supported at its 50 cm mark. A force of 12 N is applied at the 20 cm mark and a force of X N at the 60 cm mark. If the metre rule is balanced what is the value of X? (Assume that the centre of gravity is at the 50 cm mark.)
3. The centre of gravity of a metre rule is at its 50 cm mark. The rule is supported at its 40 cm mark and is balanced when a weight of 0.3 N is hung from the 10 cm mark. What is the weight of the metre rule? What is its mass?
4. A metre rule is suspended at its centre of gravity (the 50 cm mark). Weights are hung from it as follows: 2 N from the 10 cm mark; 3 N from the 30 cm mark; 8 N from the 40 cm mark; 6 N from the 60 cm mark. Where must a 4 N weight be hung to balance the rule?
5. What is meant by the centre of gravity of a body? How would you find the centre of gravity of a metre rule? Describe an experiment to find the mass of a metre rule using one weight of mass 100 g.

32 — Motion

32.1 Displacement

The distance between Sheffield and Newcastle, in a straight line is 176 km. This information alone will not allow you to get to Newcastle from Sheffield, because it does not tell you in which direction to go. We need the extra information that Newcastle is approximately North of Sheffield. Then we can say that the displacement of Newcastle from Sheffield is 176 km due North.

Fig. 32.1

Displacement is distance in a given direction.

32.2 Velocity

If it takes a car two hours to travel 60 miles we say that the average speed of the car is 30 miles per hour. The speed of the car is the distance that it travels in one hour. So we define speed as:

The speed of an object is the distance that it travels in unit time.

Example

A girl cycles 800 m to school in 200 s. What is her average speed?

Speed is the distance travelled in one second. The girl travels 800 m in 200 s, in one second, she travels 4 m. From this we see that:

$$\text{Average Speed} = \frac{\text{Distance travelled}}{\text{Time taken}} = \frac{800\text{ m}}{200\text{ s}} = 4\ \frac{\text{m}}{\text{s}}$$

$\frac{\text{m}}{\text{s}}$ is usually written as m/s and read as metres per second. (It may be written as m s^{-1}.)

From this example we can see that speed may also be defined as:

$$\textbf{Average Speed} = \frac{\textbf{Distance travelled}}{\textbf{Time taken}}$$

In the last example we did not consider the direction in which the girl was travelling. Suppose the school is due South of her home. Then, as she goes to school, she travels at 4 m/s southwards. We say that her velocity is 4 m/s southwards. Thus, velocity means *'speed in a given direction'.*

The velocity of an object is the distance that it travels in a particular direction in unit time.

32.3 Acceleration

You have probably heard the expression *'the car accelerated quickly'*, meaning *'the speed of the car increased quickly'.* In Science, the word acceleration refers to any change in the velocity of an object. It can refer to an increase, a decrease or even a change in direction. It is defined as follows:

The acceleration of an object is the change in its velocity in unit time.

Example

The velocity of a car changes from 10 m/s northwards to 18 m/s northwards in 4 s. What is its acceleration?

The velocity of the car changes by 8 m/s northwards in 4 s. Therefore the change in velocity in 1 s is 2 m/s northwards. In other words:

$$\text{Acceleration} = \frac{\text{Change in Velocity}}{\text{Time taken}} = \frac{8\ \text{m/s}}{4\ \text{s}} = 2\ \text{m/s/s}$$

m/s/s is usually written as m/s^2 or as $m\ s^{-2}$ and is read as metres per second squared.

From this example we can see that acceleration may also be defined as:

$$\textbf{Acceleration} = \frac{\textbf{Change in Velocity}}{\textbf{Time taken}}$$

Vectors and Scalars

We have already seen in this chapter that it is sometimes necessary to know the direction of something. Quantities which have a direction are called **vector quantities.** Examples are displacement, velocity and acceleration. Quantities which have no direction are called **scalar quantities**. Examples are length, area, volume, distance and speed. You will meet more examples of both vector and scalar quantities in later chapters.

Summary

* Displacement is the distance travelled in a particular direction.
* Speed is the distance travelled in unit time:

$$\text{Average Speed} = \frac{\text{Distance travelled}}{\text{Time taken}}$$

* Velocity is the distance travelled in a particular direction in unit time.
* Acceleration is the change in velocity in unit time:

$$\text{Acceleration} = \frac{\text{Change in Velocity}}{\text{Time taken}}$$

* A vector quantity is one which has a direction, e.g. velocity, acceleration.
* A scalar quantity is one which has no direction, e.g. length, area, time.

Questions

Section A

1. Displacement is ....
2. Speed is defined as..............................
3. When a car travels 600 m in 30 s its average speed is ...
4. The speed of an object in a particular direction is called its ....
5. Acceleration is defined as ....
6. Give three examples of vector quantities ....
7. When a body is accelerating it means that its velocity is either ....
   or changing ....
8. Give five examples of scalar quantities. ....
9. The speed of a car changes by 10 $m\ s^{-1}$ in 20 s. What is its accleration? ....

Section B

1. A car travels 500 m northwards in 25 s. What is the average speed? What is its average velocity?
2. A car travels 18 km in 30 minutes. What is its average speed in (i) km/h; (ii) m/s?
3. The speed of a train changes from 10 $m\ s^{-1}$ to 15 $m\ s^{-1}$in 10 s. What is its acceleration? Why is the acceleration of a train usually much less than the acceleration of a car?
4. A car starts from rest with a constant acceleration of 2 m/s. What is its speed after 8 s? How long will it take the car to travel 2.4 km at this speed?
5. The speed of a car is 20 m/s when the brakes are applied. If the car comes to rest in 4 s, what is its acceleration?
   What is the average speed of the car during this 4 s period?
   What is the distance covered by the car while it is slowing down?

33 — Pressure

33.1 Pressure

It is easier to crack an egg by striking it on the edge of a basin than on a flat surface; if you carry a heavy bag by a piece of string it may cut your hand but if you carry it by a wide strap it is quite comfortable. When two surfaces come into contact they exert forces on each other — the egg exerts a force on the basin and the basin exerts an equal but opposite force on the egg, for example. The effect that these forces have on the surfaces depends not only on the size of the forces but also on the area of the surfaces which are in contact with each other. Thus the egg breaks easily on the edge of the basin where the areas in contact are small; it is more difficult to break the egg when the areas in contact are large.

When we wish to consider the effect of force and area together we talk about pressure. The pressure due to a force is equal to the force divided by the area of the surfaces in contact.

$$\textbf{Pressure} = \frac{\textbf{Force}}{\textbf{Area}}$$

This definition may also be stated as:

Pressure is the force per unit area.

Thus, as suggested in the first paragraph, the smaller the area over which a force acts, the greater the pressure; the larger the area, the smaller the pressure.

Example

The weight of a block of wood is 12 N. What is the pressure under the block if the area of the side on which it is resting is 0.2 m²?

$$\text{Pressure} = \frac{\text{Force}}{\text{Area}}$$
$$= \frac{12\text{ N}}{0\ 2\text{ m}^2} = 60\text{ N}/\text{m}^2$$

Ans. 60 N/m²

From this example we see that pressure is measured in N/m² (newtons per metre squared). This unit is also called the pascal (Pa). So, 60 N/m² could also be written as 60 Pa.

Example

Fig. 33.1 shows a block of metal weight of 6.4 N. What is (i) the least possible pressure; (ii) the greatest possible pressure, under the block?

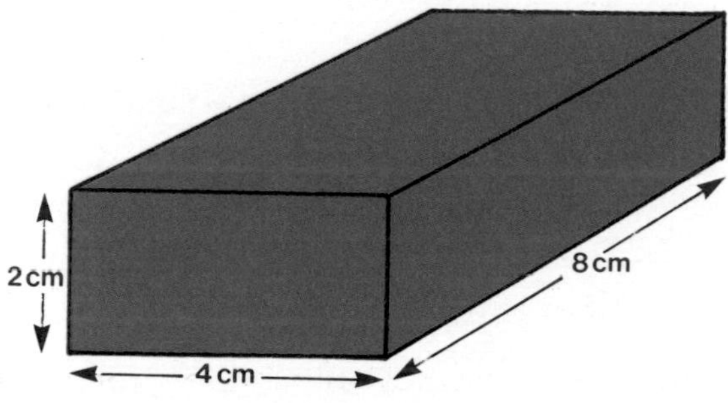

Fig. 33.1

(i) The pressure is smallest when the block is resting on the face of the largest area. The largest area is given by 8 cm x 4 cm = 32 cm²

$$\text{Pressure} = \frac{\text{Force}}{\text{Area}}$$
$$= 6.4\text{ N}/32\text{ cm}^2$$
$$= 0.2\text{ N}/\text{cm}^2$$

(ii) The pressure is greatest when the block is resting on the face of the smallest area. The smallest area is given by 2 cm x 4 cm = 8 cm²

$$\text{Pressure} = \frac{\text{Force}}{\text{Area}}$$
$$= 6.4\text{ N}/8\text{ cm}^2$$
$$= 0.8\text{ N}/\text{cm}^2$$

Ans. (i) 0.2 N/cm²; (ii) 0.8 N/cm².

Note that these answers have been given in N/cm² rather than in N/m². The N/cm² is a more convenient unit for many measurements. However, it is not the standard unit and it must be converted to N/m² before calculations involving other units are done.

Fig. 33.2

In cases where small pressures are required, forces (or loads) are spread over large areas. Thus vehicles which must travel on soft gound have very wide tyres or caterpillar tracks, *Fig. 33.2.* For walking on soft snow large snow shoes are used, and so on. On the other hand, when large pressures are required, the forces are applied to as small an area as possible. The most common examples of this are knives, pins, nails, etc., which have sharp (narrow) edges or points so that when a force is applied to them, the pressure under them is very great.

Pressure due to a Column of Liquid

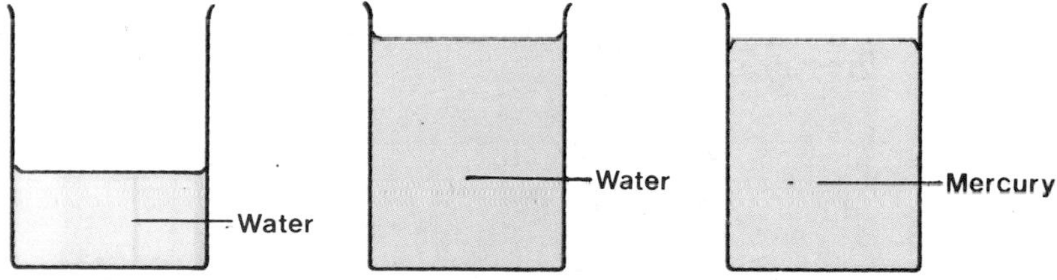

Fig. 33.3

Just as there is pressure under a solid block due to its weight, there is also pressure at the bottom of a column of liquid due to its weight. *Fig. 33.3* shows three beakers. The first contains water to a depth of 10 cm, the second contains water to a depth of 20 cm and the third contains mercury to a depth of 20 cm. How do you think the pressure will differ from one beaker to the next?

All the beakers are the same size so the area is the same in each case. The second beaker contains twice as much water as the first, so the force on the bottom of the second (due to the weight of water) will be twice as great as in the first. Since the areas are the same, the pressure at the bottom of the second will also be twice the pressure in the first. Thus pressure in a liquid depends on **depth** — the greater the depth the greater the pressure.

Fig. 33.4 A diver is fitted with a special diving suit

The depth of mercury in the third beaker is the same as the depth of water in the second. The density of mercury is 13.6 times that of water. Therefore, the force on the bottom is 13.6 times greater in the third beaker. Again, since the areas are the same, this means that the pressure is 13.6

times greater in the third beaker. Thus, pressure in a liquid also depends on **density** — the greater the density the greater the pressure.

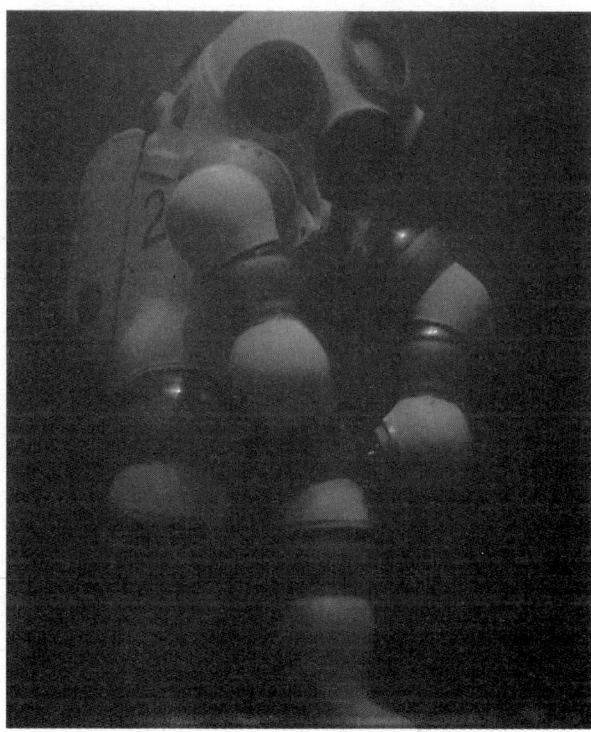

Fig. 33.5 In deep water, the suit protects the diver's body from the pressure of the body

We have now seen that the pressure in a liquid depends on the depth and the density. It can be shown that the exact relationship between pressure, depth and density is:

Pressure = Depth × Density × 10

The increase of pressure with depth can be demonstrated by using a tall can with three equal holes punched in the side.

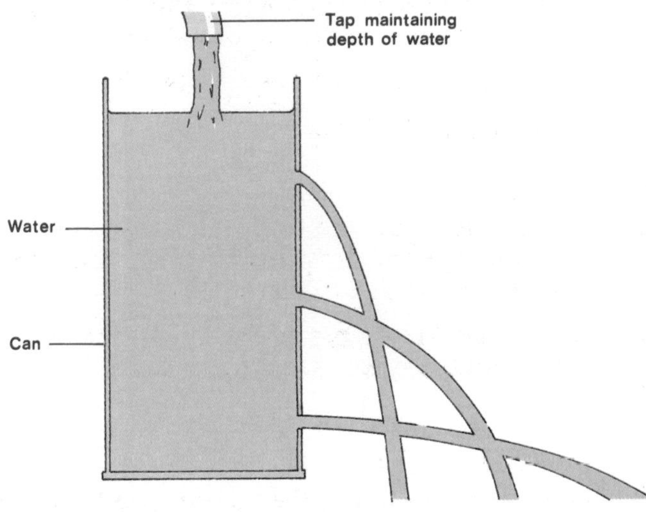

Fig. 33.6 (a) & (b)

The water from the bottom hole travels the greatest distance, so it must be experiencing the greatest force. As all the holes have the same area, pressure is therefore greatest at the bottom of the can.

This equation applies not only to the bottom of the beaker but to all points in the liquid. For example, the liquid in the bottom half experiences a force due to the weight of the liquid in the top half and so on.

33.2 Atmospheric Pressure

The earth is surrounded by a layer of gases called the atmosphere. There is no definite upper limit to the atmosphere but most of it lies below a height of about 150 km. The force of gravity on the atmosphere causes pressure which is known as **atmospheric pressure**. Normal atmospheric pressure is taken to be 1×10^5 Pa. The value varies with weather conditions and with height above the surface of the earth — the greater the height the lower the atmospheric pressure.

Experiment 33.1 To Demonstrate the Effect of Atmospheric Pressure

Method 1

1. Completely fill a gas jar with water and slide a light piece of cardboard over the top of it, holding it in place.
2. Gently turn the gas jar upside down and take your fingers off the card.

Conclusion

The water does not come out of the jar, so the pressure on the outside, atmospheric pressure, is greater than the pressure on the inside due to the water.

You should repeat this experiment with other vessels of different sizes and shapes.

Method 2

1. Put about 2 cm of water in the bottom of a 5 litre can and put it on a tripod stand.
2. Heat the can until the water has boiled for several minutes and the can is full of steam.
3. Lift the can off the stand and quickly screw the cap on tightly.

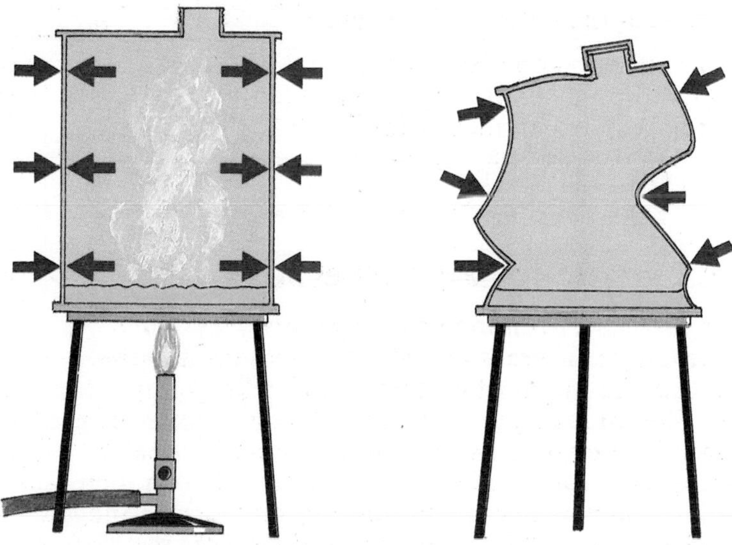

Fig. 33.7 (a) & (b)

Conclusion

When the can cools, the steam condenses and the sides of the can collapse inwards. *Fig. 33.7* shows the forces on the sides of the can before the cap is screwed on, *(a)*, and after *(b)*. The red arrows are the forces due to the steam and the blue arrows are the forces due to the atmosphere.

> **Note**: *This experiment is best done as a demonstration by your teacher.*

Measuring Atmospheric Pressure

In the last section, we saw that the atmosphere could support a column of water in different sizes of vessel. Note from the equation on *page 200*, that the width or shape of the vessel does not matter. The pressure in a given liquid, in this case water, depends only on the depth. So, just what height of water column could the atmosphere support? Experiments, first carried out by the German physicist, Otto von Guericke, show that the atmosphere can support a column of water approximately 10 m high. This fact gives us a means of measuring atmospheric pressure. However, working with columns of water 10 m high would be rather awkward, so we use mercury instead. Mercury is 13.6 times as dense as water, so a column of mercury 76 cm high will produce the same pressure as a column of water 10 m high. ($0.76 \times 13.6 = 10$ approximately). An instrument used for measuring atmospheric pressure is called a **barometer**.

The Mercury Barometer

A simple mercury barometer can be made with a long glass tube, a basin and some mercury. The tube should be about 80 cm long and have fairly thick sides. The mercury must be clean and dry.

The tube is first filled to within less than a centimetre of the top. The open end of the tube is covered* and the tube is turned upside down. This causes the bubble of air from the open end to travel up the tube, collecting any little bubbles of air which were trapped in the mercury. (This may be repeated a number of times if necessary. Tapping the side of the tube helps to move the small air bubbles.) The tube is now turned with the open end up and is completely filled with mercury. When it is full it is turned

*Great care should be taken with this experiment as mercury is poisonous.

upside down again and the cover is removed from the open end while it is under the surface of the mercury in a basin. The mercury falls down the tube until the pressure due to the mercury is equal to the atmospheric pressure, *Fig. 33.8(a)*. This leaves a vacuum at the top of the tube. This vacuum is known as the **Torricellian vacuum**, after the Italian physicist, Evangelista Torricelli, who first performed this experiment. As stated above, the height of the mercury column is normally 76 cm.

Fig. 33.8(b) show the type of mercury barometer normally found in laboratories. It is known as a Fortin barometer and it can be used to measure atmospheric pressure very accurately.

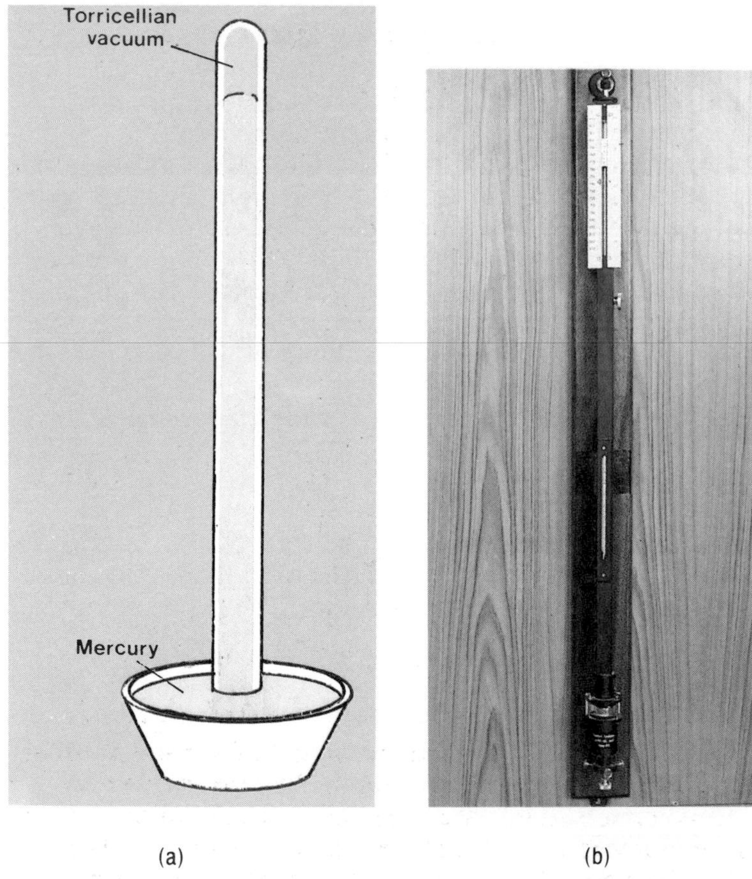

Fig. 33.8 (a) A simple mercury barometer; (b) A Fortin barometer

While atmospheric pressure, like other pressures, is properly measured in pascals (Pa) or newtons per metre squared (N/m^2), it is often given in centimetres of mercury (cm of Hg) because of the way in which it is measured. Normal atmospheric pressure is taken as 76 cm of Hg, which is equal to 1.013×10^5 Pa. Another unit used by weather forecasters is the millibar. 1 millibar equals 100 Pa, so normal atmospheric pressure is 1013 millibars.

The Aneroid Barometer

While the mercury barometer is very accurate it is also very expensive and fragile. The aneroid barometer is much cheaper and more robust, although it is less accurate. It consists essentially of a flat metal box with corrugated sides, *Fig. 33.9*. Most of the air is removed from the box before it is sealed. An increase in the atmospheric pressure causes the sides of the box to move inwards, a drop in the pressure allows them to spring out again. This movement is very small and it has to be magnified by a system of levers attached to a pointer and arranged so that movements by the sides of the box cause the pointer to move around a scale.

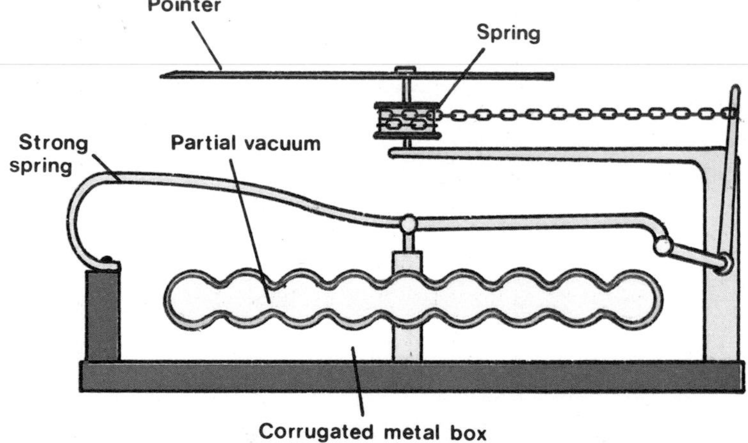

Fig. 33.9 An aneroid barometer

As mentioned before, atmospheric pressure decreases with height above the earth. In fact, the atmospheric pressure decreases by about 1% for every 100 m increase in height. A barometer can thus be used to measure height above the earth. The aneroid barometer is particularly suited to this purpose since it is much more portable than the mercury barometer. An instrument used for measuring height, for example of an aircraft, is called an altimeter. It is simply an aneroid barometer with the scale converted to read height rather than pressure.

Pressure and Density

We saw earlier in this chapter that pressure depends on depth and density. We will now make use of this fact to measure the density of a liquid.

Experiment 33.2 To Compare the Densities of Two Liquids Using a U-Tube

Method

1. If the liquids will mix with each other, first pour some mercury into the tube. Pour the two liquids into the tube until the highest one is about 2 cm from the top, *Fig. 33.10* and the mercury is at the same level on both sides of the tube.

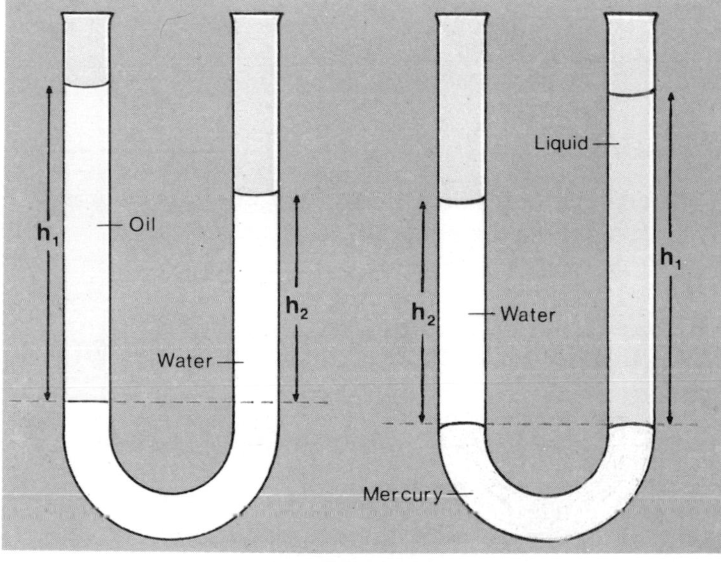

Fig. 33.10

2. Mark the level where the two liquids meet (or the level of the mercury if using liquids which mix).
3. Measure the height of each liquid above the marked level. At the level marked in either case the pressure in the two limbs of the tube is the same. Therefore as atmospheric pressure acts on the top of each column:

Pressure due to water column = pressure due to liquid column

Using the equation for pressure due to a column of liquid

$$h_1 \times d_1 \times 10 = h_2 \times d_2 \times 10$$

$$\frac{d_1}{d_2} = \frac{h_2}{h_1}$$

33.3 Archimedes' Principle

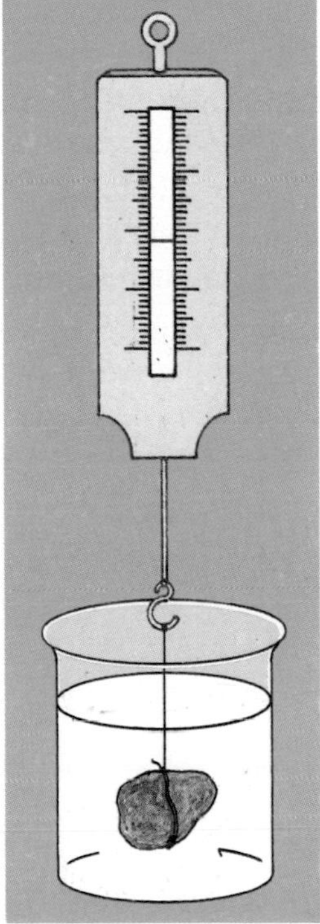

Fig. 33.11

Using a spring balance, find the weight of a stone or other object. Now note the reading on the balance when the stone is immersed in water, *Fig. 33.11.* The reading is now less than it was when the stone was hanging in air. The water is pushing the stone upwards. That is, the water is exerting an upward force on the stone. This upwards force is called the **upthrust**. (The upthrust is also sometimes called the **bouyancy force**.) When the stone is lowered into the water it displaces its own volume of water. (Remember how you measured the volume of a stone in *Book 1*). Archimedes discovered that the upthrust was equal to the weight of water displaced. This fact is now known as *Archimedes' Principle*. It applies not only to water but also to all other liquids and to gases. (Liquids and gases are called **fluids**).

Archimedes' Principle states that, when a body is immersed in a fluid, the upthrust is equal to the weight of the fluid displaced.

Experiment 33.3 To Verify Archimedes' Principle

Method

1. Weigh a dry beaker and then fill the eureka can with water to overflowing. Allow the excess water to run away.
2. Tie a stone to a spring balance and note the reading on the balance when the stone is hanging in the air.
3. Place the beaker under the spout of the eureka can and then completely immerse the stone in water. Note the reading on the balance, making sure that the stone does not touch the sides or bottom of the can.
4. When the water has ceased to flow, weigh the beaker and displaced water. Find the weight of the displaced water by subtraction.
5. Record your results as shown below.

Conclusion

The upthrust on the stone is equal to the weight of water displaced.

RESULTS

Weight of stone in air	= N
Apparent weight of stone in water	= N
Upthrust on stone	= N
Weight of beaker	= N
Weight of beaker + displaced water	= N
Weight of displaced water	= N

33.4 Flotation

Fig. 33.12 shows a cork floating in water. Since it rests on the surface of the water, the upthrust must be equal to its weight. According to *Archimedes' Principle* the upthrust is equal to the weight of water displaced. Putting these two facts together we have the *Law of Flotation*.

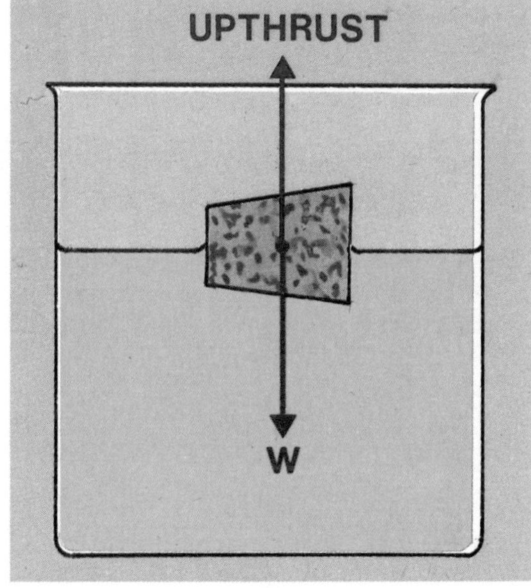

Fig. 33.12

When a body floats in a fluid the weight of the body is equal to the weight of fluid displaced.

Experiment 33.4 To Verify the Law of Flotation

Method

1. Find the weight of a test-tube with some sand in it.
2. Find the weight of a dry beaker. *
3. Gently float the test-tube in an eureka can so that the displaced water flows into the weighed beaker.
4. Weigh the beaker and the displaced water and by subtraction find the weight of the displaced water.

*The spring balance could be used to find the weight of the beaker but it is more convenient to find the mass of the beaker using a top pan balance and then convert the mass to weight.

Conclusion

The weight of the the test-tube and sand is equal to the weight of water displaced.

You should repeat this experiment for other liquids.

Flotation and Density

While we have considered only objects floating in water, the same applies to an object floating in any fluid (liquid or gas). If an object floats in a fluid its density must be less than the density of the fluid in which it is floating. Look at the table of densities and see which substances will float in water and which will float in mercury.

Substance	*Density / (g/cm³)*
Osmium	23.5
Gold	19.3
Mercury	13.6
Lead	13.6
Copper	8.9
Aluminium	2.7
Glass	2.5
Water	1.0
Paraffin Oil	0.8
Meths.	0.8
Wood	0.6 to 1.1
Polystyrene	0.02

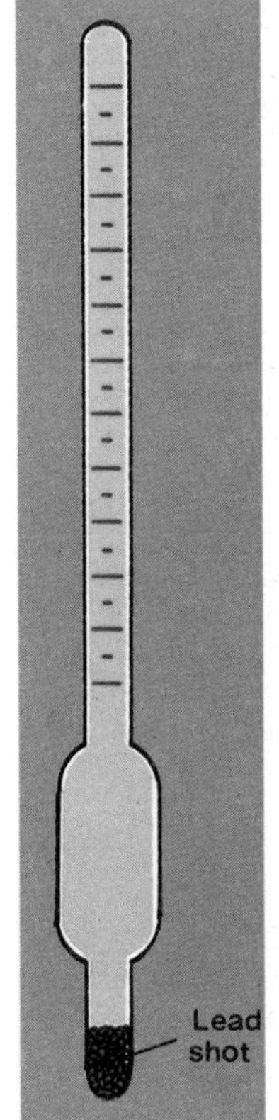

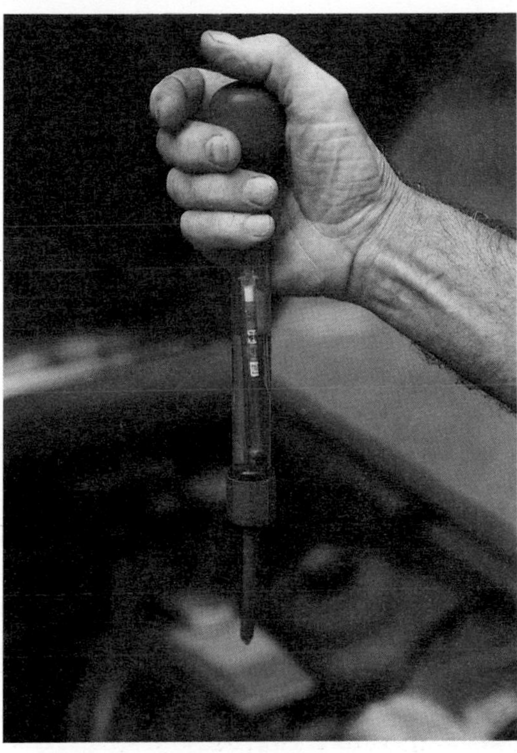

Fig. 33.13 (a) A hydrometer; (b) Hydrometer being used to check density in a car battery

The Hydrometer

The hydrometer is a device for measuring the densities of liquids. It is based on the *Law of Flotation.* It consists of a glass tube, *Fig. 33.13(a)*, generally with a bulb in the middle and with a smaller bulb at the end. The small bulb is usually filled with lead and it helps to make the hydrometer float upright. The long stem above the bulb contains a scale which reads from top to bottom.

For the hydrometer to float in a liquid, it must displace its own weight of the liquid. The more dense the liquid is, the smaller the volume of it required to be equal to the weight of the hydrometer. Thus, when the hydrometer is placed in a dense liquid, it displaces only a small volume of the liquid. In other words, it will not sink very far into the liquid. On the other hand, if the density of the liquid is small, a large volume of it will be required to equal the weight of the hydrometer and so the hydrometer will sink further into the liquid to displace its own weight. Thus, the distance which the hydrometer sinks in a liquid is a measure of the density of the liquid. When the hydrometer is floating in a liquid, the mark on the scale opposite the surface of the liquid gives the density of the liquid (usually in kg/m³).

Hydrometers are used in dairies (where they are called **lactometers**) to find the density of the milk. The density of the milk gives a measure of the percentage of water in it. (Hydrometers are now being replaced for this purpose by more efficient electrical methods.) They are used in the making of wine and beer where the density gives a measure of the alcohol content. Special hydrometers are used in garages to measure the density of the acid in car batteries. In this case, the density gives a measure of the amount of charge in the battery. The acid in a fully charged battery has a density of 1280 kg/m^3 while a density of 1150 kg/m^3 means that the battery must be recharged to prevent the possibility of permanent damage.

Submarines and Balloons

Ships float because the weight of water they displace is equal to their own weight. When a ship is loaded, it displaces more water, and so the upthrust increases to equal the new weight. The safe depths to which a ship may be loaded are indicated on its side.

A submarine can float either on the surface or at a given depth in the sea. A submarine is fitted with ballast tanks which can be filled with either air or water. When the tanks are filled with air, the submarine floats on the surface. When the tanks are filled with water, the weight of water displaced by the submarine becomes less than the total weight of the submarine and so it sinks. It is brought to the surface again by pumping the water out of the ballast tanks.

Fig. 33.14

There are two main types of balloon — those filled with hot air and those filled with gas, *e.g.* helium. The hot-air balloon floats because hot air is less dense than cold air. Helium is less dense than air, so again a balloon filled with helium will float in air.

Summary

* Pressure is the force per unit area.

$$\text{Pressure} = \frac{\text{Force}}{\text{Area}}$$

* The unit of pressure is the newton per metre squared (N/m^2) or the Pascal (Pa).
* The pressure in a column of liquid depends on the depth and the density.

$$\text{Pressure} = \text{Depth} \times \text{Density} \times 10$$

* Atmospheric pressure is the pressure caused by the weight of the atmosphere. Normal atmospheric pressure is 76 cm of Hg (1×10^5 Pa or 1013 millibars).
* Atmospheric pressure is measured with a barometer. A mercury barometer consists of a long glass tube in a container of mercury. It is very accurate but it is expensive and fragile.
* The aneroid barometer consists of a partly evacuated box attached to a system of levers and a pointer. An aneroid barometer may be used as an altimeter.
* The densities of two liquids may be compared using a U-tube.
* *Archimedes' Principle* states that when a body is immersed in a fluid, the upthrust on it is equal to the weight of fluid displaced.
* The law of flotation states that the weight of a floating body is equal to the weight of the fluid displaced.
* When a body floats in a fluid, the density of the body must be less than, or equal to, the density of the fluid.
* A hydrometer is an instrument, based on the *Law of Flotation*, for measuring the densities of liquids.

Questions

Section A

1. Pressure is defined as . . . .
2. The unit of pressure is the . . . .
   or the . . . .
3. The pressure in a liquid depends on the . . . . and the . . . .
4. Why do deep-sea divers require protective suits? . . . . . .
   . . . .
5. What causes atmospheric pressure? . . . .
6. Why is the atmospheric pressure less on top of a high mountain than at sea-level? . . . .
7. An instrument used for measuring atmospheric pressure is called a . . . .
8. Normal atmospheric pressure is . . . . . cm of Hg or . . . . Pa.
9. Name three units which are used to measure atmospheric pressure . . . .
10. Why does an object appear to weigh less when it is hanging in a liquid than when it is hanging in air? . . . . .
    . . . .
11. When an object is immersed in a fluid the upthrust on it is equal to . . . .
12. What are the two forces which act on a floating body? . .
    . . . .
13. When a body floats in a fluid the . . . . is equal to the . . . .
14. A hot air balloon floats because . . . .
    . . . .
15. A hydrometer is used to measure . . . .
16. In order to make a submarine dive, its . . . . tanks are filled with . . . .
17. What is the density of the liquid shown in *Fig. I*? . . . . . .

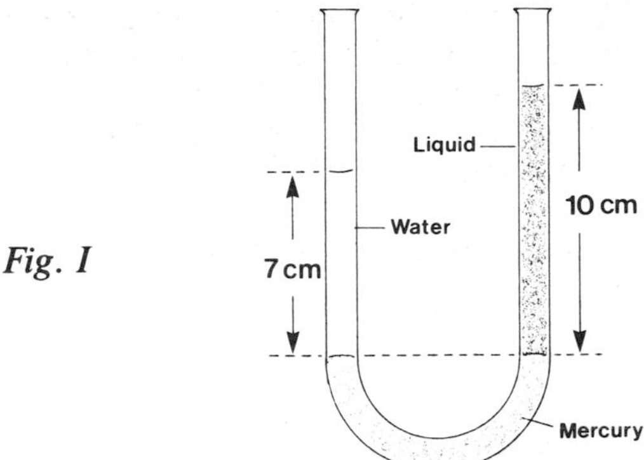

Fig. I

18. A hydrometer used in a dairy is called a . . . .
19. An instrument used for measuring height (of an aircraft, etc.) is called . . . . and it is based on the . . . .

Section B

1. A metal cylinder has a weight of 8.4 N. If the area of its base is 12 cm^2, what is the pressure under it in (i) N/cm^2; (ii) N/m^2; (iii) Pa?
2. Explain the following: (i) Earth movers have very wide wheels; (ii) Snow shoes make it easier to walk in snow; (iii) It is very difficult to break an egg by squeezing it in the palm of your hand; (iv) It is easier to carry a suitcase by the handle than by a piece of string; (v) It is easier to cut something with a sharp knife than with a blunt one.
3. Describe how you would demonstrate the effect of atmospheric pressure.
4. Describe, with the aid of diagrams, two types of barometer and give the advantages and disadvantages of each.
5. State *Archimedes' Principle.* The weight of an object is 12 N. The apparent weight of the object when it is hanging in water is 10 N and when it is hanging in another liquid its apparent weight is 8 N. Calculate (i) the weight of water displaced; (ii) the weight of liquid displaced; (iii) the upthrust in the water; (iv) the upthrust in the liquid.

34 — The Gas Laws

34.1 States of Matter

There are three states of matter, solid, liquid and gas in which any substance can exist. We are all familiar with ice, water and steam which are the three states for water but for most other substances we are aware of only one or two states. Consider **aluminium**; we are familiar with its solid form because of its use for pans and as a wrapping foil in everyday use. Also we know that to have formed these objects it must have been liquid at some stage in their manufacture. However we do not think of it in the gaseous state — but this is precisely how very thin coatings of aluminium are achieved. So what are the differences between these states? As the substance passes through all the states, the basic units of which it is made do not change. That is to say; all matter is made of atoms and molecules, but it is the way in which they are held together which changes.

In a solid the forces between the atoms are very strong so the solid has a definite shape and size. The atoms however are able to vibrate or shake and this movement increases when the substance is heated. A point is reached when the strong bonding between the atoms will break down and a liquid is formed.

In the liquid state the atoms can slide around one another but they are still weakly held together. This means that although a liquid has a definite volume it can take up any shape. If more energy is supplied to the substance, the atoms can become completely free of one another and a gas is formed. The atoms in the gaseous state have a large kinetic energy compared with those in a solid. They move with a range of velocities, the average velocity of the air molecules in this room being around 1600 km/hr (1000 mph).

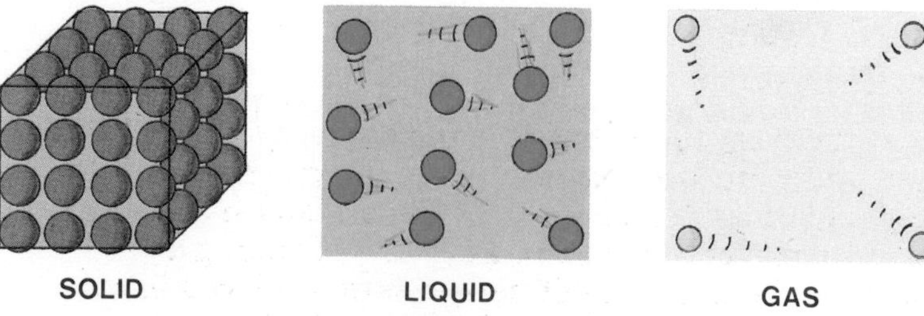

Fig. 34.1 States of Matter

Boiling Point and Melting Point

The boiling point of a substance is the temperature at which it changes from the liquid state to the vapour state. The boiling point depends on the pressure; the higher the pressure, the higher the boiling point. This is because the higher the pressure, the more difficult it is for the molecules to escape from each other. Thus, the boiling point of water at normal atmospheric pressure (76 cm of Hg) is 100° C. At twice normal atmospheric pressure the boiling point is approximately 120° C. Use is made of this fact in the pressure cooker. This is a special saucepan which can be sealed. When the water in it boils, the steam cannot escape, and so the pressure increases and the boiling point also increases. A valve in the lid releases the steam when the pressure reaches a certain value. The advantage of the pressure cooker is that it cooks food at a higher temperature, usually around 120° C, and so it cooks much more quickly, thereby saving energy.

Fig. 34.2 A Pressure Cooker

We saw in *Chapter 33* that pressure decreases with height above sea-level. This means that the boiling point of water, and other substances, also decreases with height. On a very high mountain, for example, the boiling point of water could be as low as 80° C, making it very difficult to cook food. The lowered boiling point may be demonstrated as follows.

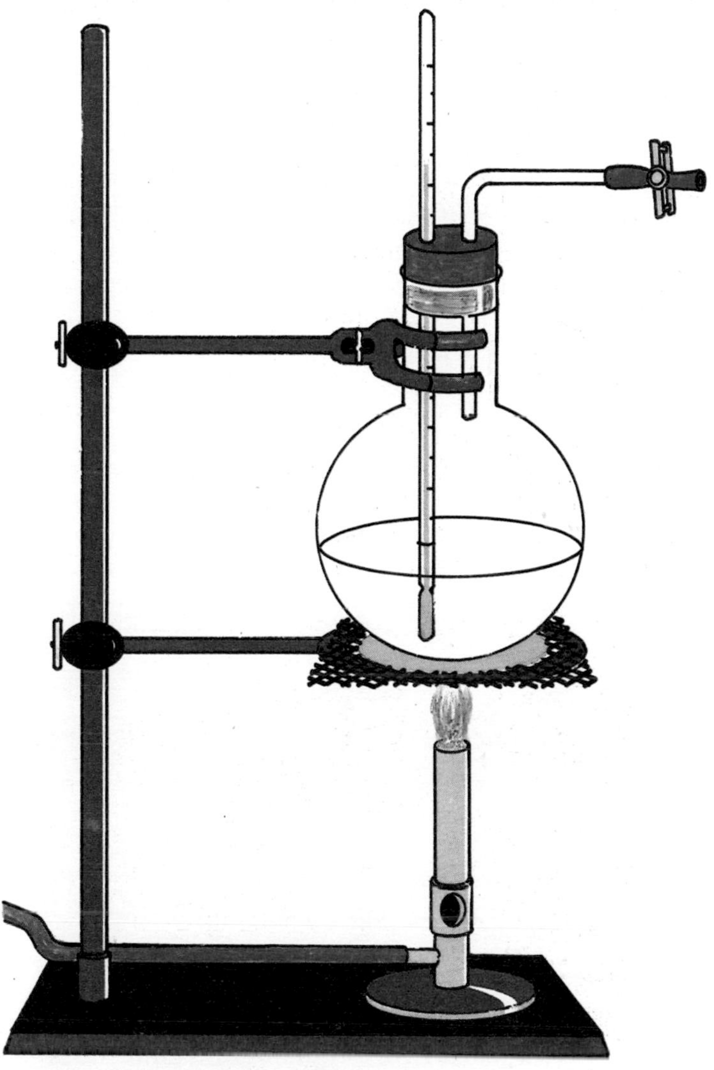

Fig. 34.3

A round bottomed flask is arranged as shown in *Fig. 34.3.* With the clip open, the water in the flask is boiled until the flask is full of steam. The Bunsen is then removed, the clip closed and the flask cooled under the cold tap. When the flask cools, the steam condenses, so the pressure inside the flask is lowered. When this happens the water can be seen to start boiling again.

The melting point of a substance is the temperature at which it changes from being a solid to being a liquid. We saw above that this occurs when the molecules are given enough energy to break the bonds which hold them together in the solid state. The melting point, or freezing point, of a substance, depends on its purity. Thus, pure water, for example, freezes at 0° C. When salt is added to it, its freezing point falls, that, is, it is still liquid at temperatures below 0° C. The more salt is added, the lower the freezing point becomes. This is why, in some countries, salt is spread on icy roads in winter.

Viscosity

We have just seen that liquids are made up of atoms, or molecules, which can "slide" around each other, while still being weakly attracted to each other. (It should be noted that atoms can also repel each other if they are brought too close together — it is almost impossible to squeeze a liquid into a smaller volume than it normally occupies.) In some liquids, the forces attracting the atoms to each other are stronger than in others. The effect of this is that such liquids cannot flow as easily as those in which the forces are weaker. Liquids which do not flow easily are said to have a high **viscosity** or to be very **viscous**. Examples of such liquids are syrup, engine oil and tar. Liquids which do flow easily are said to have a low viscosity — water and mercury are good examples. The viscosity of a liquid varies with its temperature. The hotter it is, the lower its viscosity.

Capillarity

Just as there are forces between the atoms or molecules of a liquid, there are also forces between the molecules of a liquid and those of its container. Thus, water rises up the sides of a beaker or measuring cylinder, forming a meniscus. If a glass tube of narrow bore is placed in a beaker of clean water, the level of water in the tube may rise several centimetres above the level in the beaker, as

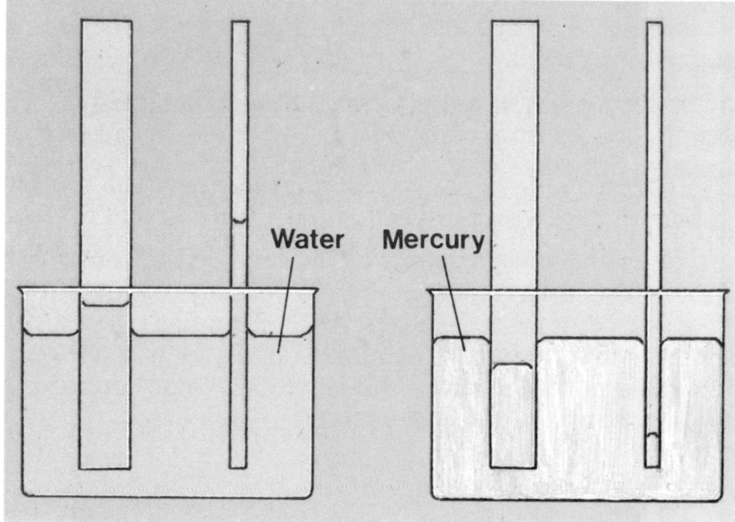

Fig. 34.4 Demonstrating capillary action (a) water in glass; (b) mercury in glass

shown in *Fig. 34.4(a)*. This happens because the water molecules are more strongly attracted to the glass molecules than they are to each other. The narrower the tube, the further the water rises. This is known as **capillary action**. If the experiment is repeated with mercury instead of water, the reverse happens, the level of the mercury in the tube goes down, *Fig. 34.4(b)*.

Capillary action can be responsible for the movement of a liquid through any substance which contains small gaps or holes. For example, a sponge or cloth can soak up water due to capillary action. Sap rises in plants partly due to capillary action and chromatography also depends on capillary action. Bricks and concrete absorb water by capillary action and this can cause "rising damp" in houses unless a "damp course" (a layer of plastic) is laid between the wall and the foundation.

Diffusion

We saw above that the molecules of a gas are completely free of each other. A number of observations lead us to the conclusion that gas molecules travel at quite high speeds. For example, if someone opens a bottle of perfume at one end of a room, it can be smelled throughout the room in a very short time. The process by which gases travel through each other in this way is called **diffusion**. The following experiment shows how different gases diffuse. This experiment can, if necessary, be used to measure the rate at which gases diffuse and, if this is done, it will be found that the more dense the gas the more slowly it diffuses. This fits in with our picture of gases being made up of molecules moving around at high speeds. The denser the gas, the closer the molecules are together and therefore the more likely they are to bump into each other and the longer it will take them to get from one place to another.

Experiment 34.1 To Investigate Diffusion

Method

1. Soak a piece of cotton wool in ammonia and another piece in hydrochloric acid.
2. Take a long wide glass tube and place the pieces (at the same time) in opposite ends of the tube, *Fig. 34.5*.

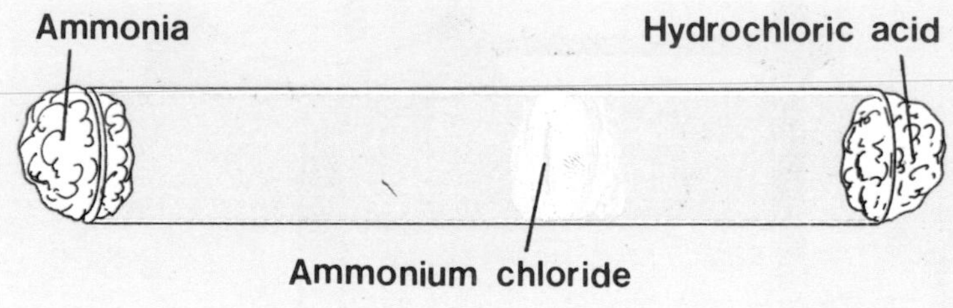

Fig. 34.5

Conclusion

In a short time a white ring of ammonium chloride is formed in the tube, showing that ammonia vapour and hydrochloric acid vapour have travelled along the tube — the ammonium chloride is formed when the ammonia reacts with the hydrochloric acid. The ring is nearer the end with the hydrochloric acid, showing that the ammonia vapour is the less dense.

Diffusion does not only occur in gases but also in liquids and solids.

Experiment 34.2 To Demonstrate Diffusion in Liquids

Method

1. Fill a measuring cylinder one third full with water and then pour some concentrated copper sulphate solution down a thistle funnel to form an equal layer below the water.
2. Remove the funnel very carefully so that the two liquids do not mix and leave the apparatus for several days.

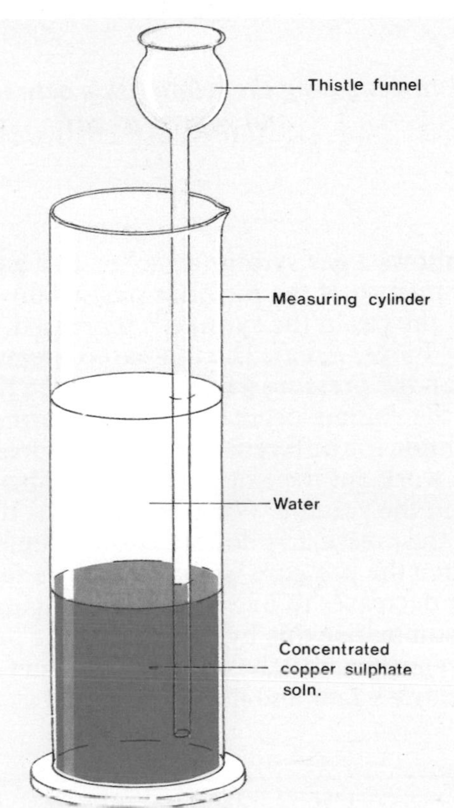

Fig. 34.6 Diffusion in liquids

Conclusion

After a few days the blue colour will have moved into the water layer. If left longer the boundary between the two liquids disappears as they have now mixed completely.

Experiment 34.3 To Demonstrate Diffusion in Solids

Method

1. Half fill a test-tube with melted gelatine and allow it to set.
2. Pour some (yellow) potassium chromate solution into the tube and cork it securely. Clamp the tube so that it slopes upwards as shown in *Fig. 34.7.* Leave it for several days.

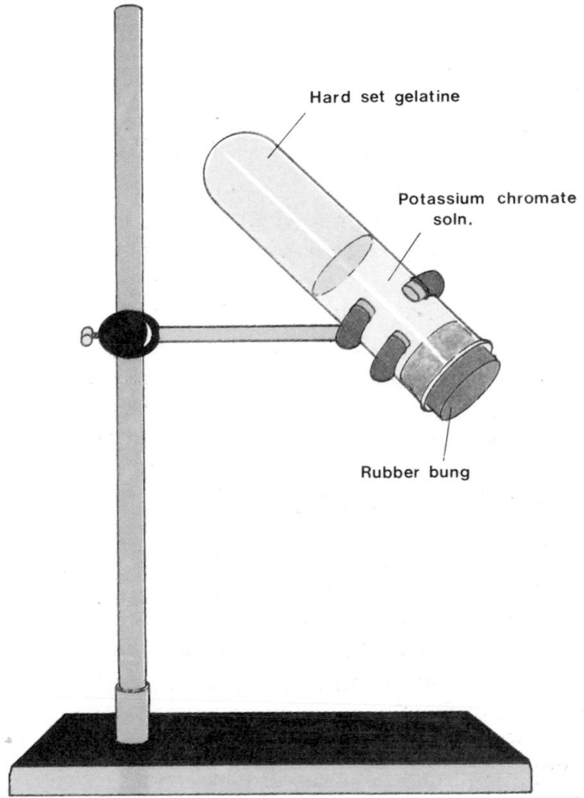

Fig. 34.7 Diffusion in solids

Conclusion

After a few days the yellow colour can be seen to be moving (diffusing) slowly into the gelatine.

These three experiments show that although molecules move very easily in gases, they move more slowly in liquids and solids.

Compression of Solids, Liquids and Gases

Compression means squeezing something into a smaller space. So how easy is it to compress solids, liquids and gases? For a solid this is a very easy question to answer. At present you are sitting on a stool or a bench made of metal or wood. When you sat down did it get smaller? Perhaps it bent a little but did the space it occupies become smaller? The answer is NO!, because solids are very difficult to compress.

In order to find an answer to the question for liquids we must try a simple experiment.

Experiment 34.4 To Find How Easily Water can be Compressed

Method

1. Collect a plastic syringe and fill it with water. Hold it upright so that any trapped air will rise to the nozzle end. Get rid of the air by gently pushing in the plunger.
2. Now put your finger tightly over the nozzle and try to force in the plunger of the syringe.

Conclusion

It is very difficult to push the plunger in and probably your finger will be forced away from the nozzle. It is best to do this experiment over a sink!

A similar experiment can be used to investigate the compression of gases. The syringe is emptied and air drawn in. A finger is placed over the nozzle and the plunger pushed in. This time the plunger moves easily to begin with but then it stops.

From these experiments it is clear that gases are fairly easy to compress, but liquids and solids are not.

34.2 Boyle's Law

The relation between the volume and pressure of a gas was first investigated by the Irish scientist, Robert Boyle in 1662. (Boyle was also the first to demonstrate the effect of atmospheric pressure.)

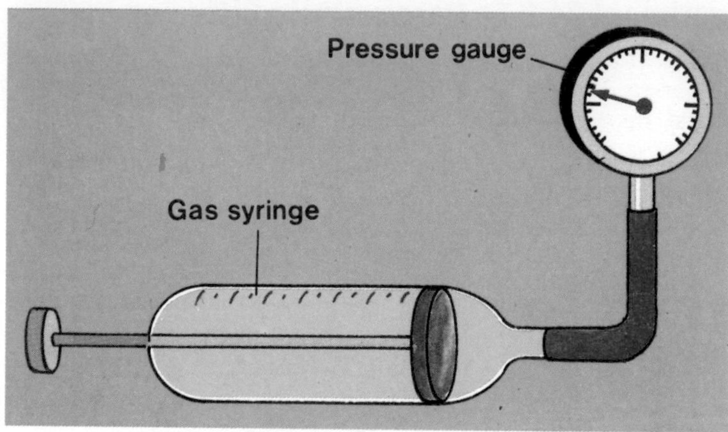

Fig. 34.8 Investigating the relationship between the pressure and volume of gas

Fig. 34.8 shows a gas syringe attached to a gauge which measures pressure. If the piston is pushed down, the pressure of the gas in the syringe is increased. (Remember: Pressure = Force/Area). The increased pressure can be measured on the pressure gauge. Thus when the pressure is increased, the volume decreases. By measuring the pressure and the volume for different values of the pressure, it is possible to work out the exact relationship between the pressure and the volume. When this is done, it is found that, when the pressure is doubled, the volume decreases by half; when the pressure is increased by a factor of three, the volume decreases to one third of its original value, and so on. We summarise this by saying that the pressure is **inversely proportional** to the volume. This fact is now known as *Boyle's Law* and it may be stated as:

> **The volume of a fixed mass of gas is inversely proportional to its pressure if the temperature is kept constant (i.e. does not change).**

Note that the law refers to a **fixed mass** of gas. If there were a hole in the syringe, the volume could decrease without any change in the pressure. So, for the law to hold, the mass of gas must be kept the same (constant).

Note also that the law refers to the **temperature** being kept constant. If a gas is heated it will expand and the volume will change. If we wish to study the effect of pressure on volume, the temperature effect must be eliminated from the experiment, therefore it must be carried out at constant temperature.

Boyle's law may be verified using the apparatus shown in *Fig. 34.8.* An apparatus more commonly found in school laboratories, *Fig. 34.9*, is used in the following experiment.

Experiment 34.5 To Verify Boyle's Law

(Description of apparatus: A fixed mass of air is trapped in a glass tube by a quantity of oil. The volume of air in the tube is read on a scale behind the tube. The pressure of the air is increased by pumping more oil into the tube and the pressure is read on a pressure gauge.)

Fig. 34.9 Boyle's Law Apparatus

Method

1. Using the pump, increase the pressure to the maximum value on the gauge. Close the tap.
2. Read the pressure and the volume. Record the values in a table as shown below.
3. Slowly open the tap until the pressure falls 2 or 3 divisions on the scale. Read and record the new pressure and volume.
4. Repeat stage 3 until the pressure has fallen to atmospheric pressure.
5. Plot a graph of pressure against the inverse of the volume.

Conclusion

A graph of pressure against the inverse of the volume (1/V) is a straight line through the origin, showing that pressure is inversely proportional to volume.

RESULTS

Pressure (p) *(Pa x 10^5)*	*Volume (V)* *(cm^3)*	$\frac{1}{\text{Volume}}$	$p \times V$

In column 4 of the above table you worked out the product of the pressure and the volume and you should have found that p x V was the same in each case. (Because it is impossible to take any reading completely accurately you probably found that *all* the values of p x V were not *exactly* the same. This is known as experimental error.) The fact that pressure multiplied by volume is constant is just another way of saying that pressure is inversely proportional to volume. *(See box on page following).*

Thus, *Boyle's Law* may also be stated as:

For a fixed mass of gas at constant temperature, pressure multiplied by volume is constant.

Example

A certain mass of gas has a volume of 200 cm³ when its pressure is 2 × 10⁵ Pa. If the pressure is increased to 4 × 10⁵ Pa, while the temperature is kept constant, what is the new volume of the gas?

Let P_1 and V_1 be the pressure and volume to start with and let P_2 and V_2 be the pressure and the volume after the pressure is increased.

Then, since:

$$p \times V \text{ is constant}$$

$$p_1 \times V_1 = p_2 \times V_2$$

$$2 \times 10^5 \times 200 = 4 \times 10^5 \times V_2$$

$$400 = 4V_2$$

$$V_2 = 100 \text{ cm}^3$$

Ans. 100 cm³

Example

The volume of a fixed mass of gas is 400 cm³ when its pressure is 70 cm of Hg. What is the pressure of the gas when its volume is reduced to 250 cm³, the temperature being kept constant?

$$p_1 \times V_1 = p_2 \times V_2$$

$$70 \times 400 = p_2 \times 250$$

$$\frac{70 \times 400}{250} = p_2$$

$$p_2 = 112 \text{ cm of Hg}$$

Ans. 112 cm of Hg.

To help you understand how we were able to write *Boyle's Law* as "pressure multiplied by volume is constant (pV = a constant)", consider the following example.

The price that you pay for sugar is proportional to the mass of sugar that you buy — if you buy twice as much, you pay twice as much. Suppose 1 kg of sugar costs 20p. Then:

1 kg	costs	20p
2 kg	costs	40p
3 kg	costs	60p
.....	.....	.....
10 kg	costs	200p

In each case, the priced divided by the mass equals 20 — the price divided by the mass is constant. So we see that the fact that price is proportional to mass means that price/mass is constant.

In the case of *Boyle's Law* pressure is proportional to the inverse of V. i.e. p is proportional to $1/V$. Therefore, p divided by $1/V$ is constant. But p divided by $1/V$ is the same as p multiplied by V, so we have pV = a constant.

In general, if A is proportional to B then A/B is constant and a graph of A against B is a straight line through the origin.

34.3 Charles Law

While Boyle investigated the relationship between the volume of a gas and its pressure, the French scientist, Jacques Charles, investigated the relationship between the volume and temperature of a gas. It had been shown earlier that all gases expand at the same rate for a given increase in temperature. Charles was able to work out the exact relationship between volume and temperature and this relationship is now known as *Charles' Law*. *Charles Law* states:

All gases expand by 1/273 of their volume at 0° C for each degree Celsius rise in temperature if the pressure is constant.

This means that if a gas has a volume of 546 cm^3 at 0° C, its volume at 1 °C will be 548 cm^3, i.e. 546 + 546/273. Similarly, its volume at 10 °C would be 566 cm^3, i.e. 546 + (546/273) × 10. The volume of the gas increases by 1/273 of its volume at 0 °C for each degree Celsius rise in its temperature.

Just as the volume increases by 1/273 for each degree *rise* in temperature, it decreases by 1/273 of its volume at 0 °C for each degree *fall* in temperature. Thus, if a gas has a volume of 546 cm^3 at 0 °C it will have a volume of 544 cm^3 at −1 °C and a volume of 526 cm^3 at −10 °C.

Since the volume of a gas decreases by 1/273 for each degree fall in temperature, it follows that the volume of all gases at −273° C will be zero. Since the volume of something cannot be less than zero, this means that there can be no temperature below −273 °C.

The fact that there is no temperature lower than −273 °C led to the invention of a new scale of temperature, known as the Kelvin scale. Zero on the Kelvin scale is −273 °C. The unit of temperature on this scale is equal in size to the Celsius degree and is called the **kelvin (K)**. Thus:

−273 °C	= 0 K
−272 °C	= 1 K
−263 °C	= 10 K
0 °C	= 273 K
100 °C	= 373 K

and so on. In other words, to convert temperatures in degrees Celsius to kelvins you simply add 273. (Note that the unit of temperature on this scale is the kelvin and not the *degree* kelvin.)

When temperatures are measured in kelvins, the volume of a gas is proportional to the temperature when the pressure is constant. This means that volume divided by temperature (measured in kelvins) is constant when the pressure is constant.

At constant pressure, V/T is constant, where T is temperature in kelvins.

Example

The volume of a certain mass of gas is 600 cm^3 at 27° C. What is the volume of the gas at a temperature of 127° C and at the same pressure?

First, we must change the unit of temperature of °C to K.

$$T_1 = 27\ °C = (27 + 273)\ K = 300\ K$$

$$T_2 = 127\ °C = 400\ K$$

$$\frac{V_1}{T_1} = \frac{V_2}{T_2}$$

$$\frac{600}{300} = \frac{V_2}{400}$$

$$2 = \frac{V_2}{400}$$

$$V_2 = 800\ cm^3$$

Ans. 800 cm^3

34.4 Kinetic Theory of Gases

We saw at the beginning of this chapter that all substances are made up of atoms and molecules and that, in gases, the molecules move around freely at high speeds in a random fashion. This model of gases which is called the *Kinetic Theory of Gases*, can help us to understand how the volume of a gas changes with changes in its temperature and pressure.

Fig. 34.10 Kinetic Theory model

Fig. 34.10 shows a model used to demonstrate the kinetic theory of gases. A number of small ball bearings represent the gas molecules. A piston at the bottom, driven by a small motor, moves up and down, supplying energy to the molecules (this corresponds to heating the gas). The top of the tube is closed by a very light piston which is free to move up and down. The pressure of the gas can be increased by placing cardboard discs on top of this piston.

To investigate *Boyle's Law* the motor is run at a constant speed (this corresponds to constant temperature) and the pressure is changed by adding cardboard discs to the top piston. As the pressure is increased, the volume occupied by the ball bearings is reduced. To investigate the effect of changing the temperature the motor is run at different speeds while the pressure is kept constant. As the motor speeds up, the "molecules" gain energy and move faster, and so occupy a larger volume.

Diffusion and Brownian Motion provide further experimental evidence in support of the kinetic theory of gases.

Summary

* All substances are made up of tiny particles called atoms.
* In solids atoms are fixed in position; in liquids they can slide over each other; in gases they are completely free of each other.
* Liquids which do not flow easily have a high viscosity.
* Water in a narrow tube rises; mercury in a narrow tube moves down. This is called capillary action.
* Diffusion is the movement of one kind of molecule through a volume already occupied by another kind.
* *Boyle's Law* states that the volume of a fixed mass of gas is inversely proportional to its pressure if the temperature is constant.
* *Boyle's Law* may also be stated as: For a fixed mass of gas, volume multiplied by pressure is constant if the temperature is constant.
* *Charles' Law* states that all gases expand by 1/273 of their volume at 0 °C for each degree Celsius rise in temperature, if the pressure is constant.
* −273 °C is the lowest temperature possible. This temperature is zero on the Kelvin scale of temperature.
* To convert degrees Celsius to kelvins add 273.
* When temperature is measured in kelvins, the volume of a gas is proportional to its temperature if the pressure is constant, i.e. V/T is constant at constant pressure.

Questions

Section A

1. A cloth soaks up water by ....
2. Water moves up a narrow tube due to ....
3. The process by which gases mix through each other is called ....
4. In a solid, molecules are .... but in a liquid they are ....
5. Tomato ketchup has a very high .... while milk has a low ....
6. There are three states of matter ...., ... and ....
7. The .... a body is, the faster its .... vibrate.
8. Name the law which relates pressure to volume ....
9. The volume of a fixed mass of gas depends on its ...... and ....
10. When the pressure of a gas is increased at constant temperature its volume ....
11. *Boyle's Law* states.. ....
12. According to *Boyle's Law* the pressure multiplied by the volume of a fixed mass of gas is .... when the ....is constant.
13. When the temperature of a gas is increased at constant pressure its volume ....
14. *Charles Law* states ....
15. The lowest possible temperature is ....
16. Zero on the Kelvin scale is equal to .... on the Celsius scale.
17. The unit of temperature on the Kelvin scale is the .....
18. The freezing point of water on the Kelvin scale is ...... and the boiling point is ....
19. When temperature is measured in .... the volume of a gas is................ to its temperature when the pressures is constant.

Section B

1. Describe an experiment which verifies *Boyle's Law*.
2. A certain mass of gas has a volume of 240 cm^3 at a pressure of 1×10^5 Pa. What is its volume when the pressure is 3×10^5 Pa and the temperature remains the same?
3. A given mass of gas has a volume of 380 cm^3 when its pressure is 78 cm of Hg. What is the pressure of the gas when its volume is 390 cm^3 at the same temperature?
4. What is the relationship between the volume of a gas and its temperature at constant pressure?

   A certain mass of gas has a volume of 500 cm^3 when its temperature is 27 °C. If the temperature changes to −23 °C at the same pressure, what is the new volume of the gas?
5. A given mass of gas has a volume of 160 cm^3 at a temperature of 17 °C. What is its temperature when its volume is 200 cm^3 at the same pressure?
6. A fixed mass of gas has a volume of 400 cm^3 at a temperature of 27 °C and a pressure of 80 cm of Hg. What is the volume of the gas at normal temperature and pressure?
7. Convert the following to kelvins: (i) 20 °C; (ii) −40 °C; (iii) 150 °C.
   Convert the following to degrees Celsius: (i) 300 K; (ii) 123 K; (iii) 563 K.

35 — Heat Transfer

35.1 Conduction

Heating means the transfer of energy from a place at high temperature to a place at a lower temperature. (Energy transferred in this way is sometimes referred to as heat.) One of the ways in which this process occurs is called **conduction.**

If you hold the end of a metal rod in a flame it will soon become too hot to hold. This is an example of heating by conduction. When heating by conduction is taking place in an object, energy moves through the object from one point to another without any part of the object itself moving between the two points. Conduction, then, can be defined in this way:

Conduction is the movement of energy through a substance without any movement of the substance.

Conduction normally takes place in solids. Fluids (liquids and gases) are generally very poor conductors *(see Experiment 35.3)*. The process of conduction can be explained in terms of the kinetic theory. The hotter a substance is the faster its atoms vibrate (shake). When the end of a metal rod is heated the atoms at the end move faster. Since the atoms are very close together in a solid, the movement of the atoms at the end causes nearby atoms to move faster. This process is repeated along the length of the rod until all the atoms are vibrating faster. In this way energy is transferred along the rod and it becomes hotter. (You can picture this as the atoms passing the energy from one to the other without moving from their own position.)

Experiment 35.1 To Show that some Metals are better Conductors than Others

Method

1. Take four different metal strips (e.g. iron, copper, brass and steel), of equal length, arranged as shown in *Fig. 35.1.*

Fig. 35.1

2. Melt a little candle wax onto the outer end of each piece of metal and stick a matchstick into the candle wax.
3. Place the metals over the Bunsen burner as shown in the diagram, making sure that the point where the four metals meet is directly over the middle of the Bunsen flame.

Conclusion

Energy from the Bunsen flame is conducted along the pieces of metal to the candle wax. When the wax melts, the matchsticks fall. They fall at different times showing that some of the metals are better conductors than others.

Make a list of the metals in your notebook, putting the best conductor at the top of the list and the worst conductor at the bottom.

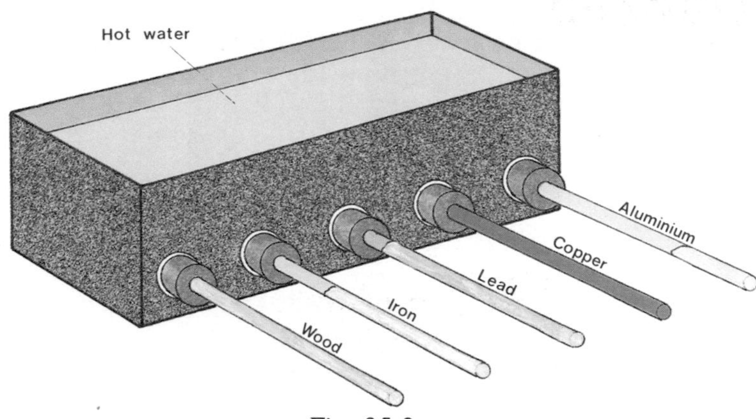

Fig. 35.2

A different method of carrying out *Experiment 35.1* uses the apparatus shown in *Fig.35.2.* Rods made from different materials are first coated with candle wax and then stuck through the stoppers in the side of the box. (The rods need not all be metals. Glass and wood, for example, can also be used.) The box is then filled with boiling water. As the rods are heated the wax on them melts. It is thus possible to see which are heating faster, that is, which are the best conductors.

Experiment 35.2 To Show that Copper is a better Conductor than Wood

Method

1. Get a piece of copper pipe and a piece of wood which will just fit into the end of the pipe.
2. Fit the wood into the pipe and cover the join with a piece of paper as shown in *Fig.35.3.*
3. Warm the paper very gently with a Bunsen flame.

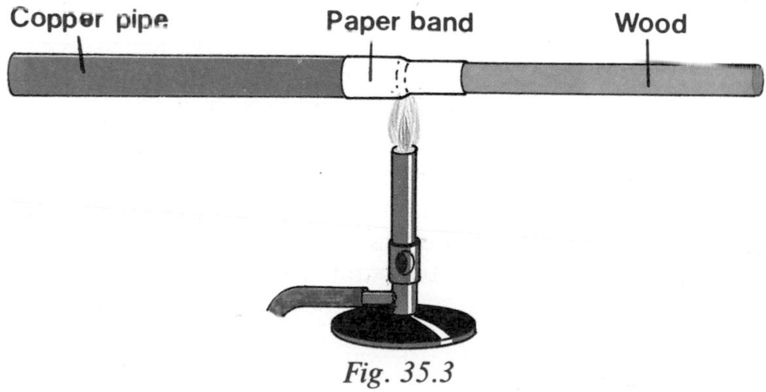

Fig. 35.3

Conclusion

The paper becomes charred where it covers the wood but not where it covers the copper pipe. This shows that the copper is able to conduct the energy away from the paper before it can become hot enough to char. The wood is a poor conductor and so the wood under the paper becomes hotter more quickly.

Experiment 35.3 To Show that Water is a Poor Conductor

Method

1. Put a piece of ice in a test-tube and place a weight on top of it.
2. Fill the test-tube with cold water and place it in the clamp of a retort stand.
3. Heat the water at the top of the test-tube.

Conclusion

The water at the top of the test-tube soon boils while the ice remains at the bottom. Thus, even though there is a temperature difference of 100 Celsius degrees, energy does not travel from the top of the test-tube to the bottom. This shows that water is a very poor conductor.

If a substance is a poor conductor it is called an **insulator**. While metals are good conductors, substances like cotton wool, fibre glass, polystyrene, asbestos, etc., are good insulators. To investigate this carry out the following experiment.

Experiment 35.4 To Investigate the Effect of Insulation

Method

1. Place a metal can in a larger can or beaker and surround it with cotton wool or fibre glass (insulated).
2. Fill the can with boiling water.
3. Put the same volume of boiling water in another can (uninsulated) and in an polystyrene cup and cover them.
4. After about half an hour record the temperature of the water in each of the containers.

Conclusion

The water in the uninsulated can is coldest, showing the effect of insulation. Which of the two containers is the colder will depend on the thickness of the insulation around the metal can.

Insulators are widely used in everyday life. Now that the various fuels used for home heating are so expensive, house insulation is particularly important. The outer walls of houses are often made up of two separate walls. The gap between the two walls is full of air (which, like all fluids, is a very poor conductor), or, in newer houses, it may be filled with polystyrene foam. The amount of energy escaping through the windows is reduced by double glazing — each pane has two sheets of glass with air between them. To prevent energy escaping through the roof, the floor of the loft is covered with a layer of insulation several centimétres deep. This insulation may be fibre glass or polystyrene in one form or another.

Fig. 35.4 Putting down insulation in a loft

Other examples of the use of poor conductors or insulators are the handles of kettles and saucepans, the grips on the handlebars of a bicycle, oven gloves, etc.

35.2 Convection

In *Experiment 35.3* above we saw that water is a very poor conductor — the water at the top of the test-tube boiled while the ice at the bottom remained frozen. If you repeat that experiment with the ice at the top of the test-tube while you heat it at the bottom, you will find that the ice quickly melts. So, if water is such a poor conductor, how is the energy travelling from the bottom of the tube to the top? Carry out the following experiment and you will see the answer to this question.

Experiment 35.5 To Demonstrate Convection Currents in Water

Method

1. Fill a round bottomed flask with cold water.
2. Using a thistle funnel, place a few crystals of potassium permanganate at the bottom of the flask.
3. Warm the bottom of the flask under the permanganate crystals gently with a Bunsen burner.

Conclusion

The water, coloured by the permanganate, rises up the centre of the flask and then falls down by the sides. This process continues until all the water is coloured. At this point it is no longer possible to see anything happening although the process continues until the water boils. What is happening is explained as follows.

When the water at the bottom of the flask is heated it expands and therefore becomes less dense. Because it is less dense than the surrounding water it "floats" to the surface and its place is taken by denser, colder water. This water in turn is heated, becomes less dense and rises. This process is repeated until all the water is hot. This method of heating is called convection and the moving currents of water are called **convection currents**.

> **Convection is the movement of energy through a substance by the movement of the molecules of the substance.**

It should be clear from this that convection can take place only in fluids. It cannot take place in solids since the atoms of a solid cannot move around each other. (When a substance is being heated by convection you can picture the molecules of the substance moving and carrying the energy with them.)

Experiment 35.6 To Demonstrate Convection Currents in Air

Method

1. Set up the apparatus shown in *Fig. 35.5*

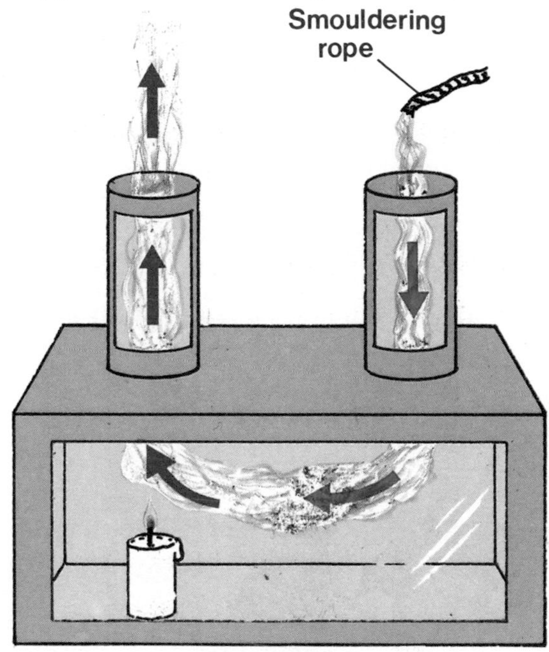

Fig. 35.5

2. Light the candle and place it in the box under one of the holes as shown in the diagram.
3. Light the end of a piece of string for a moment and then blow it out.
4. Hold the smoking end of the string over the other hole in the box.

Conclusion

The smoke from the string is drawn down into the box and then rises up again through the hole above the candle. This is another example of a convection current and may be explained as follows. When the air above the candle is heated it expands, becomes less dense, and therefore rises. The surrounding cold air and the smoke take the place of the warmed air. They, in turn, are heated and rise and so a convection current is set up.

There are many everyday examples of heating by convection. In a domestic central heating system, a boiler, heated by burning coal, oil or gas, is situated on the ground floor or in the basement. The hot water from the boiler is then circulated around the house. In practice, convection currents alone would be rather slow, so a pump is included in the system to improve the circulation of the water.

One way of providing domestic hot water is in a hot water cylinder fitted with a dual immersion heater *Fig. 35.6.* This is really two separate electric heaters. One heats only the top of the cylinder and provides enough water for washing dishes, etc. The other heats the whole cylinder when water is required for baths. (This system would not work if water were a good conductor. Why?) Note that the pipe carrying hot water to the taps comes out of the top of the cylinder while the cold water enters at the bottom.

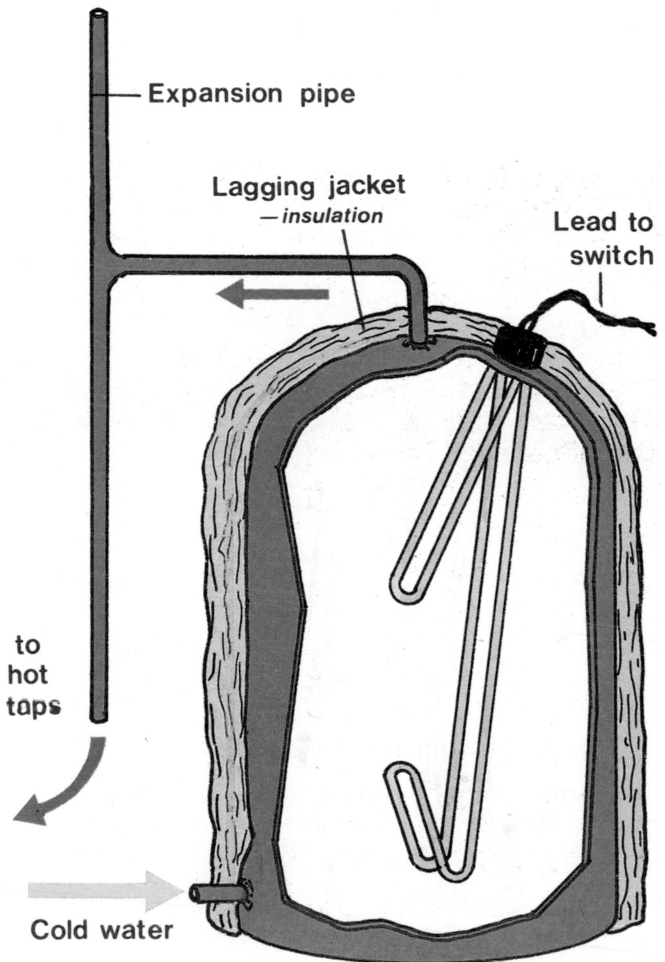

Fig. 35.6. Water tank with dual immersion heater

Note also the expansion pipe to allow for the increase in the volume of the water when it is heated. Any water which expands out of the cylinder is returned to the storage tank in the loft.

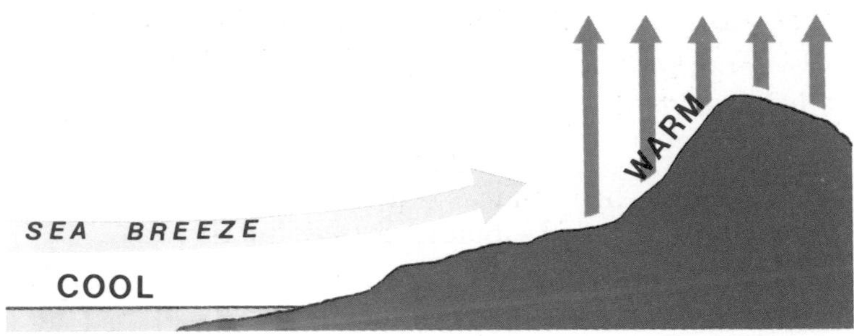

Fig. 35.7

Convection currents in the atmosphere and in the oceans are responsible for most changes in weather conditions. Clouds are formed when convection currents over the earth's surface carry warm, moist air upwards, where it expands and cools. During hot summer days cool breezes sometimes blow in from the sea, *Fig. 35.7.* These sea breezes are formed when hot air over the land rises and is replaced by cooler air from over the sea. At night this situation is reversed, *Fig. 35.8.* The ground cools more quickly than the sea and as a result land breezes are formed.

Fig. 35.8

35.3 Radiation

The earth is warmed by energy from the sun. This energy travels mostly through space so the process can be neither conduction nor convection. This method of heating in which energy is "thrown" outwards from a hot object is called **radiation**.

> **Radiation is the method by which energy travels out from a hot object in straight lines in all directions.**

Unlike conduction and convection, radiation can take place in a vacuum as well as in a fluid. The rate at which energy is radiated from a hot object depends not only on how hot it is but also the type of surface which it has. The following experiment demonstrates this.

Experiment 35.7 To Show that a Dull Black Surface is a Better Radiator than a Bright Surface

Method

1. Take two similar flasks and blacken one of them, either by holding it in a candle flame or painting it with matt black paint.
2. Fill each of the flasks with boiling water, and fit stoppers (rubber bungs) with thermometers. Note down the readings on the thermometers.
3. Record the temperature of the flasks at 10 minute intervals.

Conclusion

The temperature of the water in the blackened can falls more quickly than the temperature of the water in the other can. This shows that a dull, black surface radiates energy faster than a bright surface.

The last experiment showed that a dull black surface radiates better than a bright surface. The reverse is also true, as the next experiment shows.

Experiment 35.8 To Show that a Dull Black Surface is a Better Absorber of Radiated Energy than a bright Surface

Method

1. Take two sheets of metal, e.g. biscuit tin lids, and blacken one of them with a candle flame or matt black paint.
2. Using candle wax, stick a penny to the back of each of the metal sheets.
3. Clamp the metal sheets vertically in retort stands and place them at equal distances on either side of a Bunsen flame.

Conclusion

After a few minutes the wax on the black sheet melts and the penny falls off. The other penny does not fall off, even after several minutes heating. This shows that the dull black surface absorbs the energy radiated from the Bunsen flame much faster than the bright surface does.

Fig. 35.9 Oven insulation. Note use of shiny surface to reduce energy losses due to radiation

All bodies radiate and absorb a certain amount of energy. If the temperature of the body is the same as its surroundings it absorbs energy at the same rate as it radiates it. If the temperature of the body is higher than the temperature of its surroundings it radiates more energy than it absorbs. The higher the temperature of a body the more energy it radiates. Central heating radiators in buildings actually radiate very little energy because their temperature is quite low — less than 60 °C. For this reason it matters little what colour radiators are painted. Most of the heating caused by radiators is by convection and so radiators should always be placed as near the floor as possible.

The Thermos Flask

The thermos flask, *Fig. 35.10*, is a vessel which is used for keeping liquids hot or, sometimes, cold. It consists of a double walled glass vessel. The air is removed from between the walls and the insides and outsides of the walls are silvered. (Because of the vacuum between the walls the flask is sometimes known as a vacuum flask. It is also known as a Dewer flask, after the Scottish scientist, James Dewer, who invented it in 1892.)

Energy cannot pass between the inside of the vessel and the outside by any of the three methods of heating. Conduction cannot take place because there is no solid connection between the inside and outside except for the stopper which is made of material which is a poor conductor. Convection cannot take place because there is no fluid between the walls. Finally, very little energy is radiated because the walls are silvered. Thus, if the flask is filled with something hot it stays hot and if it is filled with something cold it stays cold.

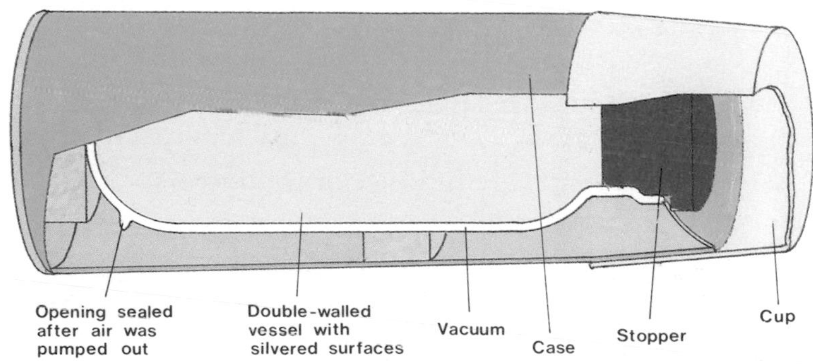

Fig. 35.10 A thermos flask

Summary

* Heating in solids takes place by conduction. This is the transfer of energy through a substance without the atoms of the substance moving from one place to another.
* Metals are good conductors. Substances like polystyrene and cotton wool are poor conductors and are called insulators.
* Convection is the transfer of energy through a substance by the movement of the molecules of the substance. Convection takes place in fluids.
* Energy is "thrown" outwards in straight lines from hot objects. This method of heating is called radiation.
* Dull black surfaces are good radiators and also good absorbers of radiated energy. Bright surfaces are poor radiators and also poor absorbers of radiated energy.
* The thermos flask is a double walled glass vessel which keeps substances inside it either hot or cold because energy cannot travel between its two walls by means of conduction, convection or radiation.

Questions

Section A

1. Heating takes place through solids by ....
2. Substances which are poor conductors are called ......
3. .... are generally good conductors while fluids are .... conductors.
4. Give three uses of good conductors and three uses of insulators. ....
   ....
5. Heating in fluids takes place by means of............
   .... currents.
6. Why, do you think, are fluids poor conductors? ....
   ....
7. Why are central heating radiators placed near the floor of a room? ....
8. Why is polystyrene, or similar material, spread on the floor of the loft of a modern house? ....
   ....
9. A bright surface is a better .... than a ....surface.
10. Why are the walls of a thermos flask silvered?.........
    ....
11. Why is bright clothing worn in tropical countries? .....
    ....
12. Why is the element of an electric kettle at the bottom rather than at the top? ....
    ....
13. Why do the metal parts of a bicycle feel colder on a cold day than the plastic hand grips? ....
    ....
14. Changes in weather conditions are mainly due to ......
    .... in the atmosphere.
15. Why is the ice box at the top of the refrigerator rather than at the bottom? ....

Section B

1. What is meant by conduction? Describe how you would show that some materials are better conductors than others.
2. Explain how fluids are heated by convection.

   Describe an experiment which demonstrates convection currents in water.
3. Describe an experiment which shows that water is a poor conductor. Since water is a poor conductor, explain why it is not used as an insulator, for example around a hot water cylinder?
4. What name is given to the process by which energy travels from the sun to the earth?

   Describe an experiment which shows that a dull black surface is a better absorber of radiated energy than a bright surface.

36 — Reflection

36.1 Types of Reflection

When a ray of light strikes an object some of the light is reflected. If the surface is very smooth, then regular reflection occurs and an image is seen in the surface. The surface acts like a mirror.

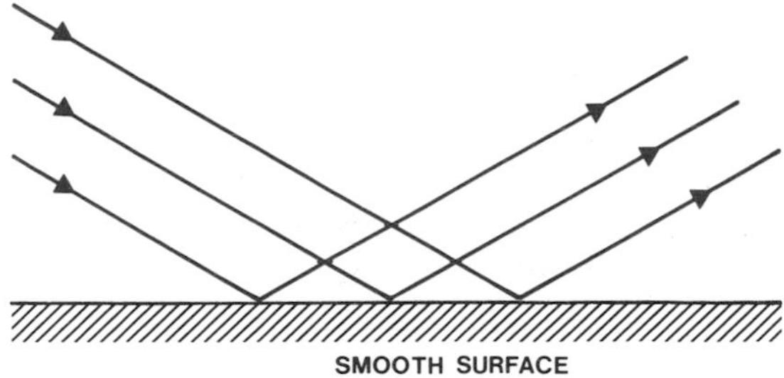

Fig. 36.1 Regular reflection

If the surface is rough then irregular or diffuse reflection occurs and no image is seen. This is the type of reflection that usually occurs.

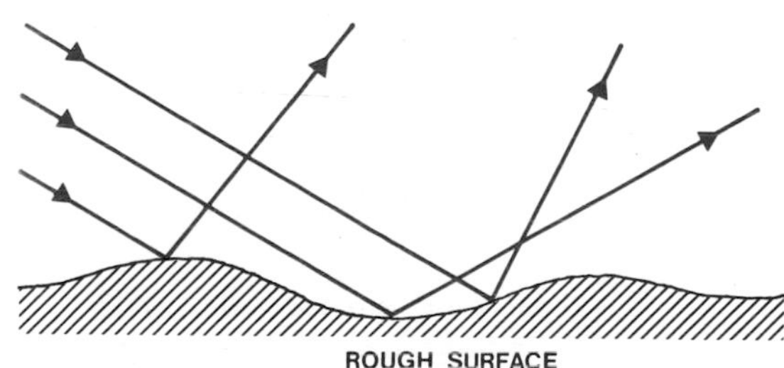

Fig. 36.2 Diffuse reflection

36.2 Laws of Reflection

There are two laws which explain the way in which the light is reflected.

They are:

> **1. The angle of incidence is equal to the angle of reflection.**
> **2. The incident and reflected rays lie in the same plane as the normal.**

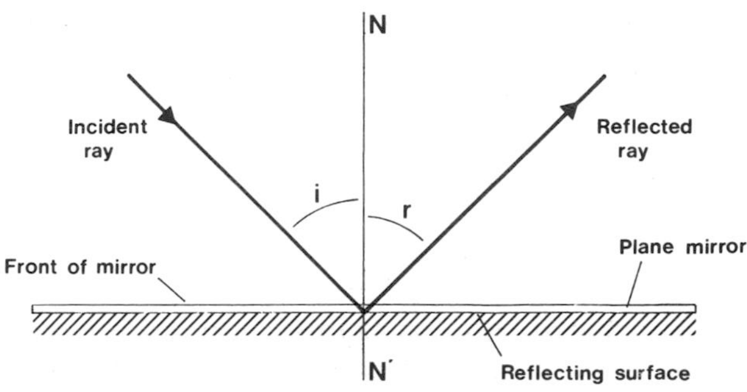

Fig. 36.3 Laws of reflection

////// shows the back of the mirror.
NN' — Normal — a line drawn at 90° to the mirror surface at the point where the incident ray strikes the mirror.
i — Angle of incidence
r— Angle of reflection

In order to study light we need to use a very narrow beam called a ray. To obtain a ray, a piece of equipment known as a ray box is used. It consists of a lamp situated inside a box which has one end closed and a lens at the other end. The position of the lens can be adjusted to give a parallel beam of light — this is one in which the width of the beam does not alter. A slotted screen can be placed beyond the lens to give one or three parallel rays of light.

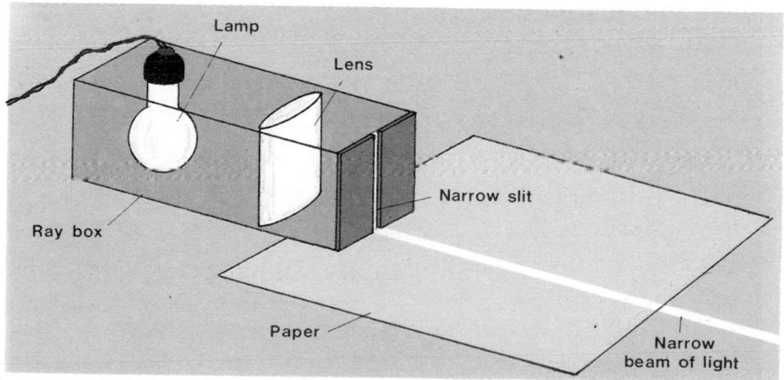

Fig. 36.4 Ray box

Experiment 36.1 To Demonstrate the Laws of Reflection

Method

1. Place a plane mirror, on edge, on a piece of plain paper.
2. Draw along the back of the mirror.
3. Using a ray box, direct a single ray of light towards the mirror.
4. Mark the path of the incident ray and the reflected ray using pencil dots.
5. Remove the mirror and using a ruler draw in the rays through the marks. Where they touch the line drawn along the back of the mirror, construct a normal using a protractor.
6. Mark in the angles *i* and *r* and then measure them using a protractor.
7. Replace the mirror in its original position on the plain paper and repeat the experiment once more using a different incident angle.

Conclusion

When *i* and *r* are measured they are found to be the same size, therefore demonstrating the first law to be correct. Since we were also able to draw both rays and the normal on the piece of paper, they must lie in the same plane. Therefore the second law is also shown to be correct.

36.3 Mirrors

There are three types of mirror:—

Fig. 36.5 Types of mirror

When we look into a mirror we see a reflection of ourselves. This reflection is called an **image**. Different mirrors produce different images. There are **two** kinds of images:—

Real — these are produced when the rays of light actually cross, the image can be shown on a screen.

Virtual —these are produced when the rays of light only appear to cross. They can not be shown on a screen.

Fig. 36.6 Kinds of images Real & Virtual

Parallax

If you look out of a moving car you will see that fixed objects appear to move relative to each other. The spire of a distant church may appear to move from one side of a nearby tree to the other. We know this is an illusion, due to the movement of the car and the distances of the church and tree. It is an effect known as parallax and can be demonstrated by the following experiment.

Experiment 36.2 To Observe Parallax and No-parallax

Method

1. Hold your hands out in front of you with only the first finger extended. Have one finger point upwards and the other downwards with the tips of your fingers level.
2. Place the 'downward' finger behind the other, close one eye and line them up. Now move your head to one side and then the other, without moving your fingers. Your fingers appear to move apart and together as you move your head (parallax).
3. Alter the distance between your fingers and repeat step 2. The only time that there is no motion between your fingers is when they are one above the other (no-parallax).

Plane Mirror

When we look into a plane mirror the image we see is formed behind the mirror. This can be shown by the following experiment.

Experiment 36.3 To Find the Position of the Image formed by a Plane Mirror

Method

1. Pin a piece of plain paper on a soft board using drawing pins. Place a mirror, on edge, on the paper and draw along the back. Put a small pin in front of the mirror.
2. Place a piece of plasticine or coloured paper on the pin, this is the **object** pin.
3. Place a large pin behind the mirror, this is the search pin.
4. Look into the mirror and move the search pin until it is in no-parallax with the image of the object pin. (i.e. the search pin and the image do not move apart when you move your head.)

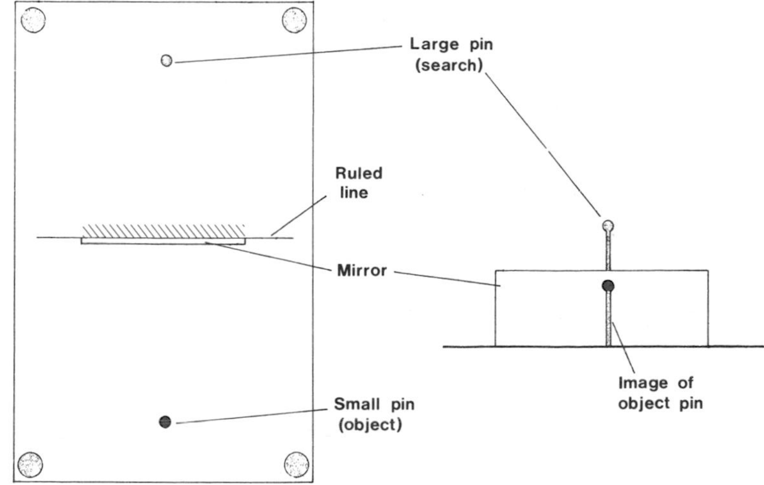

Fig. 36.7 Position of image in plane mirror

5. Mark the positions of the object pin and the search pin. Remove the mirror and draw a straight line between the marks.
6. Measure the distances from the object to the mirror line and from the image (search pin) to the mirror line.
7. Using a protractor measure the angle between the line joining the object position to the image position and the mirror.

Conclusion

The image is found to be formed as far behind the mirror as the object is placed in front. It is also a virtual image. The angle between the line joining the image to the object and the mirror is found to be 90 °.

The image formed by a plane mirror is as far behind the mirror as the object is in front.

Lateral Inversion

Experiment 36.4 To Investigate the Image Formed by a Plane Mirror

Method

1. Take a mirror and look into it. What do you see?
2. Now look at your hair parting, what do you notice?
3. If the image was another person standing in front of you, would they have a parting on the left or right hand side? What side is your parting?
4. Put up one hand to your face, which hand did you use and which hand did the image use?

Conclusion

You will notice that left becomes right and right becomes left. The image formed by a mirror is back to front. This effect is known as **Lateral Inversion.**

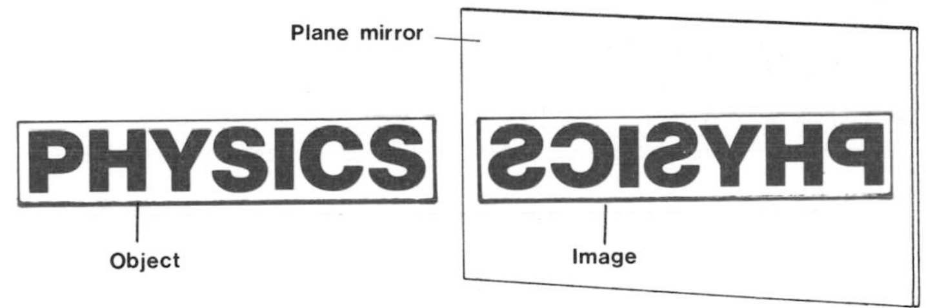

Fig. 36.8 Lateral Inversion

Now write ƎꓛAMI on a piece of paper and hold this up to the mirror. It appears the correct way round. This is known as mirror writing and can be used for secret messages!

Properties of the image formed by a plane mirror

Virtual
Laterally inverted
Same size as the object

Multiple Images

Experiment 36.5 To Show the Effect of Using Two Mirrors at 90 °

Method

1. Place two mirrors at 90° to one another and between them place an object.

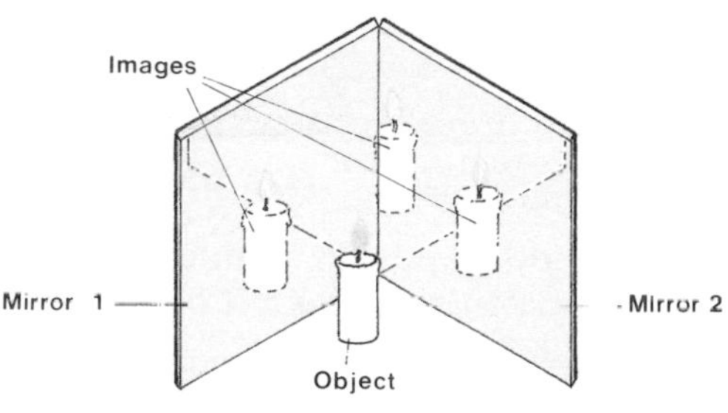

Fig. 36.9 Mirrors at 90°

2. Look into the mirrors, how many images can you see?
3. Now alter the angle between the mirrors, first making it larger and then smaller. What do you observe to happen?

Conclusion

When the mirrors are at 90°, **three** images are observed plus the object. If however the angle is changed, the number of images seen also changes. The smaller the angle, the greater the number of images produced. A kaleidoscope works on this principle.

A **kaleidoscope** consists of two strip mirrors placed at 60° in a tube. At the bottom of the tube is a piece of ground glass on which is sprinkled small pieces of coloured plastic or glass. Looking down the tube a symmetrical pattern of six sectors is seen.

Experiment 36.6 To Show the Effect of Two Parallel Mirrors

Method

1. Place two plane mirrors facing one another and between them place an object.
2. Look into one of the mirrors, what do you see? Check that the same thing happens when you look in the other mirror.

Conclusion

When two mirrors face one another, an infinite number of images are formed. All the images lie on a straight line drawn through the object and at 90 ° to the mirrors.

Uses of a Plane Mirror

Make-up or shaving mirror.
Driving mirror.
Optically increase the size of a room by covering a wall with a mirror.
In theatrical productions to produce a ghost.
In a periscope.
On a dangerous corner.

The Periscope

A periscope allows us to look over peoples heads, round a corner or over a wall without being seen. It is used in submarines so that they can see what is happening on the surface when they are submerged.

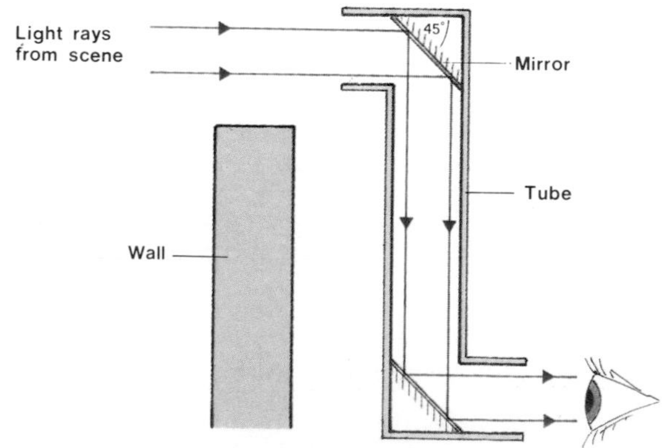

Fig. 36.10 The Periscope

Experiment 36.7 To Make a Simple Periscope

Method

1. Collect two mirrors and a plastic bottle (e.g. washing-up liquid bottle).
2. Cut two slots in the bottle at an angle of 45° and also two openings *(Fig. 36.11)*.
3. Slip the mirrors into the slots so that they face one another and tape in place.
4. Hold up the periscope and look into one of the mirrors as shown in *Fig. 36.11.*

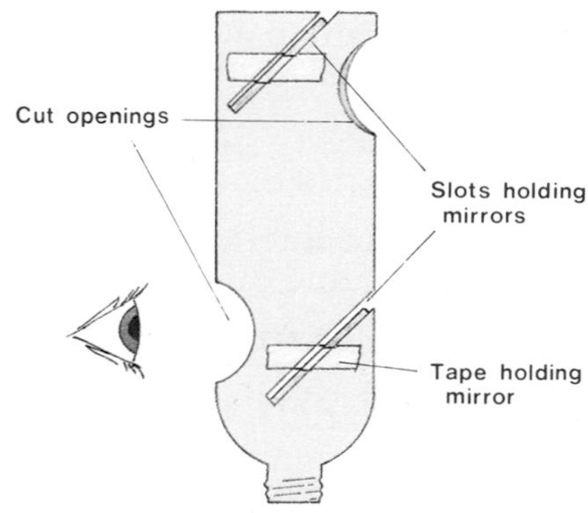

Fig. 36.11 Simple periscope to make

Curved Mirrors

There are many examples of curved mirror like surfaces around us. One which we use everyday is the spoon. A spoon has both concave and convex surfaces.

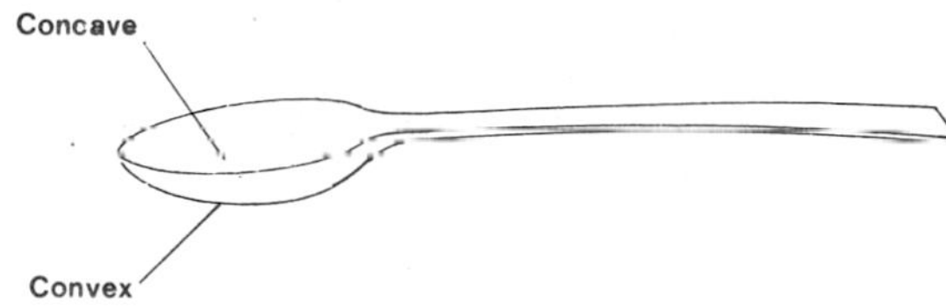

Fig. 36.12 Spoon (Concave & Convex surfaces)

A Concave mirror curves inwards (like a cave).
A Convex mirror curves outwards.

If you look into a polished spoon you will see that the front and back surfaces give different images.
Another example of curved surfaces which you may have seen at the fairground, is the hall of mirrors. Here concave and convex mirrors are combined on one piece of glass. A very distorted image is produced.

Experiment 36.8 To Observe the Effect of a Concave Mirror on Parallel Rays of Light

Method

1. Use a soft board with a piece of white paper pinned to it. Place a concave strip mirror on it and draw a line along the back of the mirror.
2. Using a ray box with three slits, direct the rays towards the mirror as shown in *Fig 36.13.*

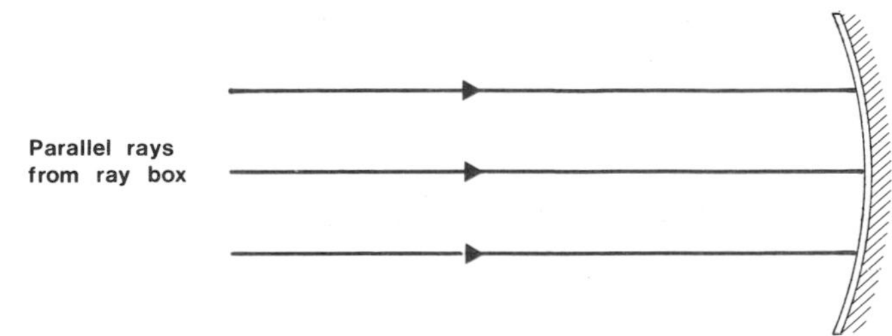

Fig. 36.13 Parallel rays striking concave mirror

3. Mark the positions of the rays before they strike the mirror and after they have been reflected.
4. Draw in all the rays; what has happened to the parallel rays of light?

Conclusion

When the parallel rays reflect from the concave mirror, they are brought together (converge) and all pass through one point. The distance of this point from the mirror changes with the curvature of the mirror.

A concave mirror is a converging mirror

36.4 Focal Length

A line drawn at right angles to the centre of the mirror is called the **Principal Axis**. If the incident rays are parallel to this line, the point where they come together is called the **principal focus** of the mirror and the distance from the mirror to the principal focus is the **focal length**.

The more curved the mirror, the smaller the focal length.

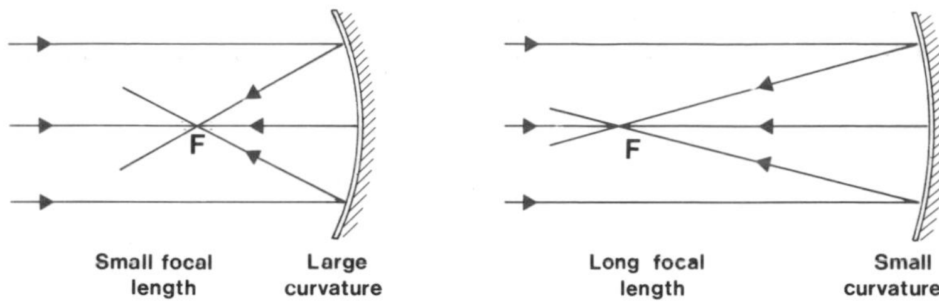

Fig. 36.14 Effect of curvature (focal length)

If *experiment 36.8* is repeated with a convex strip mirror the rays are observed to spread out (diverge). They all appear to have come from a particular point behind the mirror. This is the focal point (focus) of the mirror.

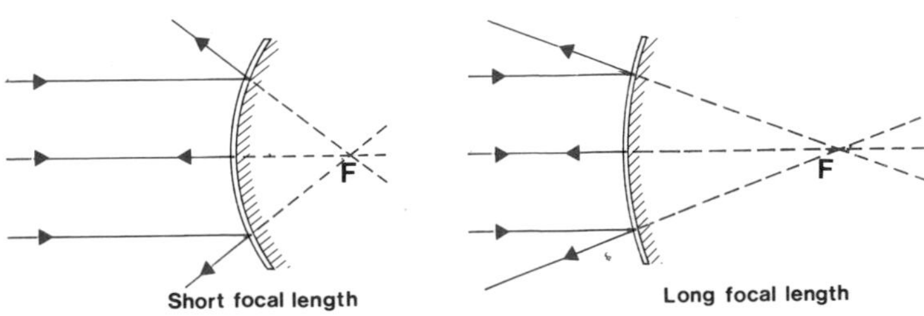

Fig. 36.15 Effect of curvature (convex mirror)

A convex mirror is a diverging mirror

Images Produced By Curved Mirrors

Concave

A concave mirror can produce two types of image, a virtual but magnified image — such as in the make-up or shaving mirror — or a real image as in a reflecting telescope.

Convex

A convex mirror **always** produces an upright (erect) and diminished (smaller) image. This property of the mirrors is used in:—

security mirrors in supermarkets
driving mirrors
mirrors in buses, where the driver can see the upper deck from downstairs.

Summary

* When light strikes a surface it reflects. There are two types of reflection, regular and diffuse.
* The angle of incidence is equal to the angle of reflection.
* The incident and reflected rays lie in the same plane as the normal.
* A ray box is an enclosed lamp with a lens and a slotted screen which produces parallel rays.
* A ray is a very narrow beam of light.
* There are three types of mirror; plane, concave and convex.
* There are two kinds of image; real and virtual.
* Parallax is when two fixed objects appear to move relatively to each other.
* The image formed by a plane mirror is as far behind the mirror as the object is in front, virtual and the same size as the object.
* The image formed by a plane mirror is laterally inverted (back to front).
* Mirrors at 90° and parallel to one another produce multiple images.
* A concave mirror curves inwards (like a cave).
* A convex mirror curves outwards.
* A concave mirror is a converging mirror.
* A convex mirror is a diverging mirror.

Questions

Section A

1. When light strikes a surface it is ....
2. The Normal is a line drawn at ....to the mirror surface at the point where the .... strikes the mirror.
3. A ray box produces a .... beam of light.
4. The ....is equal to the ....
5. The ray of light which strikes the mirror is called the ... .
6. The angle of reflection, *r* is the angle between the .... and the ....
7. Name three types of mirror ....
8. When we look into a mirror we see an ....
9. Which kind of image can be formed on a screen? ....
10. The image formed by a plane mirror is ...., ... and ....
11. If a card with the word HELP written on it is held up to a plane mirror, what would you see? ....
12. Two plane mirrors are placed at 90° to one another, how many images do you see? ....
13. Name the instrument used by a submarine to observe action on the surface while it is submerged ....
14. A concave mirror curves .... while a convex mirror ....
15. Another name for a concave mirror is a .... mirror.
16. The line drawn at 90° to the centre of the mirror is called the ....
17. The distance between a concave mirror and the point where the rays come together is called the ....
18. A ....image is formed by a shaving mirror.
19. Two uses for a convex mirror are .... and ....

Section B

1. Describe an experiment to prove that the angle of incidence is equal to the angle of reflection.
2. Do you think that a concave mirror would be any use as a driving mirror? If not, why not?
3. Parallax is the relative movement of one fixed object to another due to the observer moving. Describe an experiment which demonstrates this effect.
4. Explain how you think a piece of plate glass could be used to produce a ghost in a theatrical production. (**Hint**: Remember that all smooth surfaces reflect a certain amount of light.)
5. Devise an experiment to measure the focal length of a concave strip mirror.

37 — Refraction

37.1 Laws of Refraction

If a straw is placed in a glass of lemonade, it appears to bend as it enters the liquid. A pond or swimming bath also appear shallower than they actually are. This effect is due to refraction. Refraction is the bending of the rays of light as they pass from one medium to another.

In these examples the media involved are water and air, but similar effects have been observed when a piece of glass is placed on some writing. The writing appears nearer. So what is happening?

Experiment 37.1 To Find the Effect of A Glass Block on A Ray of Light.

Method

1. Pin a sheet of plain paper to a soft board.
2. Place a glass block on the paper and draw round it.
3. Using a ray box, direct a ray of light towards the glass block as shown in *Fig. 37.1.*

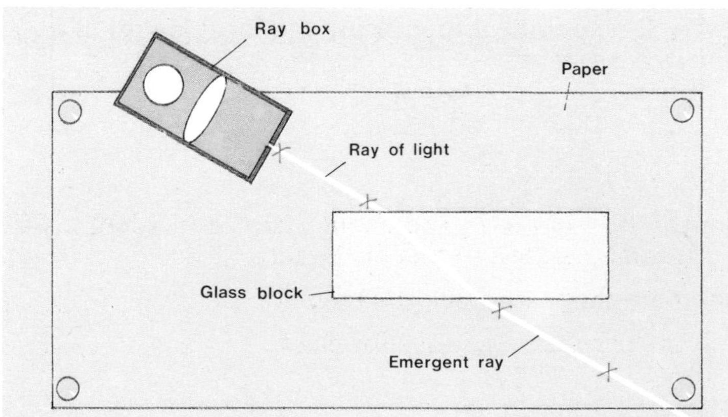

Fig. 37.1 Plotting path of a ray through glass block

4. Mark the path of the ray before it enters the glass and when it emerges, using pencil crosses.
5. Remove the ray box and glass block.
6. Draw a straight line through the crosses as far as the outline of the block as shown in *Fig. 37.2.*

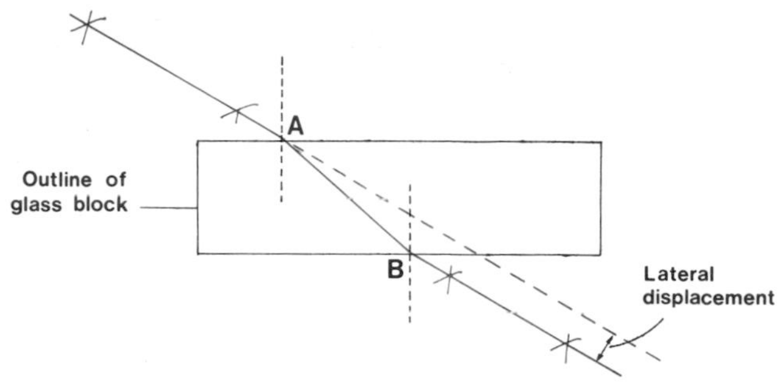

Fig. 37.2 Plotting path of a ray through glass block

7. Draw a line from A to B, using a ruler.
8. At A and B construct a dotted line at 90° to the surface of the block using a protractor. These are **normals.**
9. Look carefully at the way in which the light changes direction as it enters and leaves the glass.

Conclusion

As the light ray enters the glass it bends **towards** the normal. As it leaves the glass it bends **away from** the normal. It is also **laterally displaced**. When other materials are used, it is found that the general rule is:—
When light enters a denser material (medium), it bends **towards** the normal, and when it enters a less dense medium, it bends **away from** the normal. This change in direction is called **refraction**.

Laws of Refraction

There are two laws which explain the way in which the light is refracted. They are:—

1. The incident and refracted rays are on opposite sides of the normal at the point of incidence and all three are in the same plane.
2. The ratio of the sine of the angle of incidence to the sine of the angle of refraction is a constant for a given pair of media —

$$n = \frac{\text{Sin } i}{\text{Sin } r.}$$

n is called the refractive index.

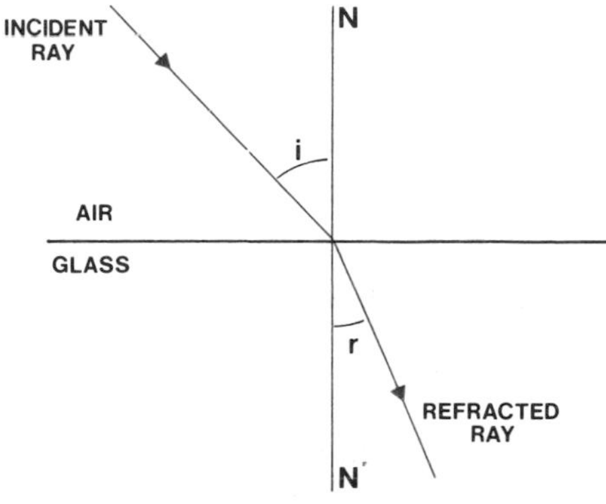

Fig. 37.3 Bending of light ray (laws of refraction)

NN' — Normal (a line drawn at 90° to the surface at the point where the incident ray strikes it).
i — angle of incidence.
r — angle of refraction.

Experiment 37.2 To Find the Refractive Index of Glass

Method

1. Repeat the previous experiment. *(Expt. 37.1)*
2. Mark on your results sheet the incident angle *(i)* and the refracted angle *(r)*.

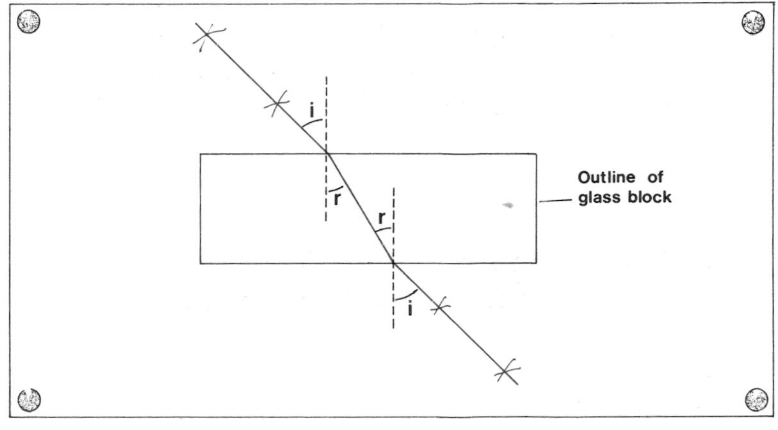

Fig. 37.4 Measuring i & r

3. Measure *i* and *r* and place the values in Snell's equation.

$$n = \frac{\text{Sin } i}{\text{Sin } r}$$

4. Work out n.
5. Repeat the complete experiment with the incident ray in a different position so that *i* is larger.
6. Compare the two values you have for n.
7. This is the refractive index for glass.

Conclusion

The value of n for glass is found to be 1.5.

37.2 Total Internal Reflection

When a ray of light passes from a denser medium (glass) into a less dense medium (air) it moves away from the normal. This means that the angle in the air is always larger than that in the glass.

The maximum angle possible in the air for the emerging ray is 90°.
So, what happens when this angle is reached?

Experiment 37.3 To Observe the Effect of Increasing the Angle Inside The Glass

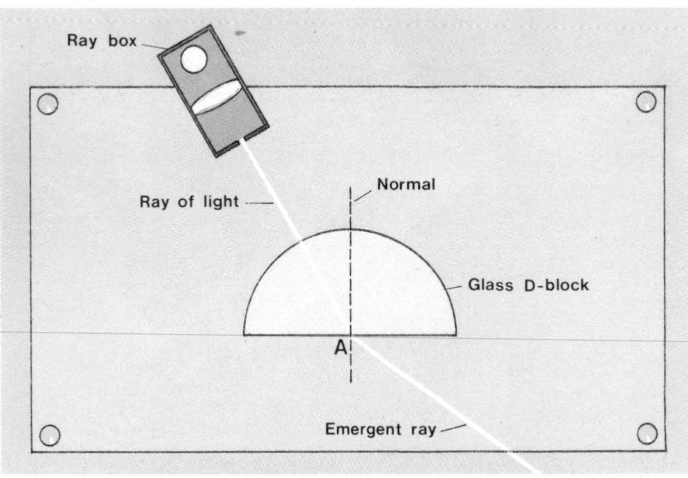

Fig. 37.5 Ray passing through D-block

Method

1. Place a glass D-block on a sheet of paper and draw round it.
2. Remove the glass block and mark the centre of the straight side, A. At this point draw a line at 90° to the straight side of the D-block (a normal).
3. Replace the block and using a ray box, direct a ray of light through the block to A, along the normal.
4. Observe the ray passing through both surfaces without bending.
5. Now, keeping the ray passing through A, increase the angle between it and the normal. Observe what happens to the emergent ray. At the point where the emergent ray just skims the surface of the block, mark the position of the incident ray.
6. Remove the block and draw in the ray, measure the angle, C, between the ray and the normal.
7. Replace the block and increase the angle. Observe what happens to the ray.

Conclusion

The four diagrams below show the effects observed.

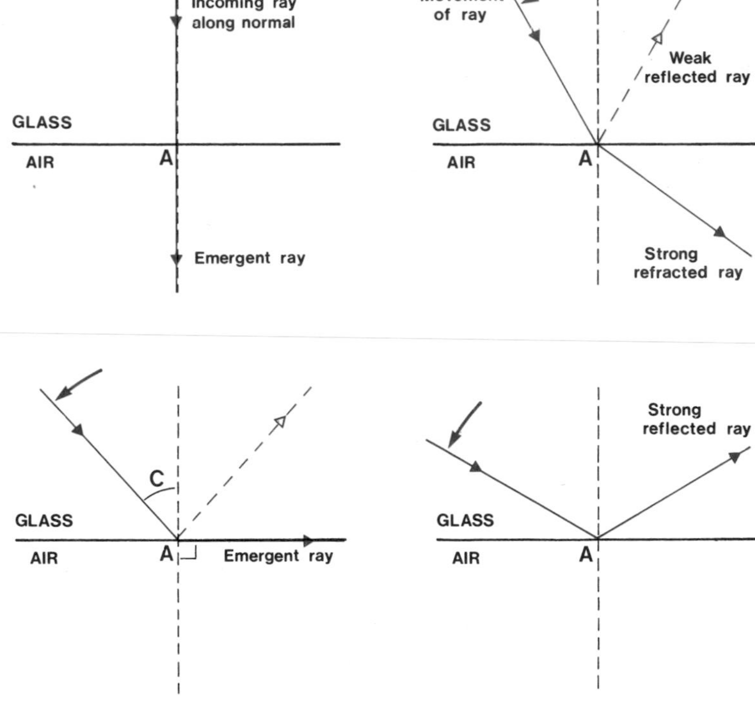

Fig. 37.6 Effect of increasing internal angle

The results of the experiment tell us that once a certain angle, C, has been reached in the glass the light is **totally internally reflected**.
The angle C is known as the **critical angle** and has the value 42° for glass.

The Prism Periscope

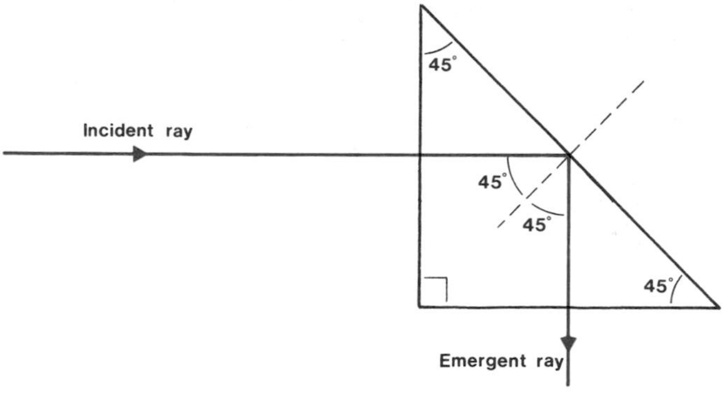

Fig. 37.7 Ray turned through 90°

If a ray of light is directed towards a prism as shown in the diagram above, it will pass through the first surface without being deviated. Inside the glass it meets the second surface with an angle of incidence of 45°. As this is greater than the critical angle of 42° for glass, total internal reflection occurs.

The ray then leaves the 45° prism through the third side without deviation.

In this situation the ray of light has been turned through 90°. This arrangement is used in the prism periscope.

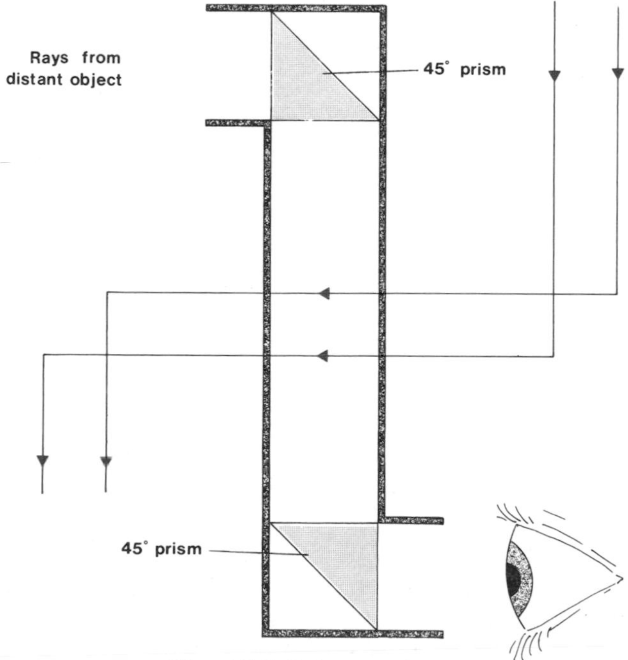

Fig. 37.8 Prism periscope

45° prisms can also be used to turn a light ray through 180°. The prism is arranged as shown below.

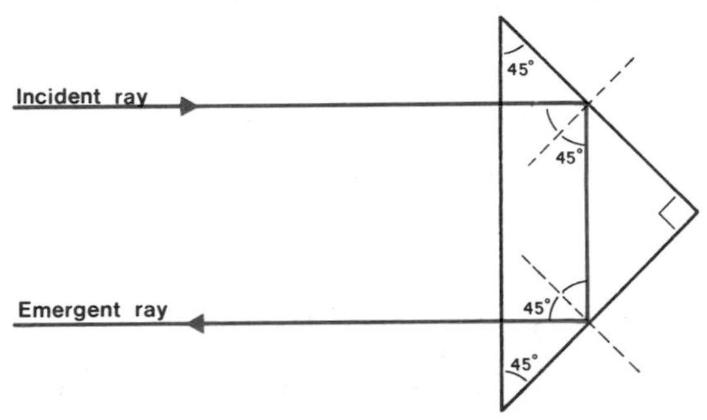

Fig. 37.9 Ray turned through 180°

This arrangement is used in prism binoculars, 'cats eyes', and bicycle reflectors.

The Prism Binoculars

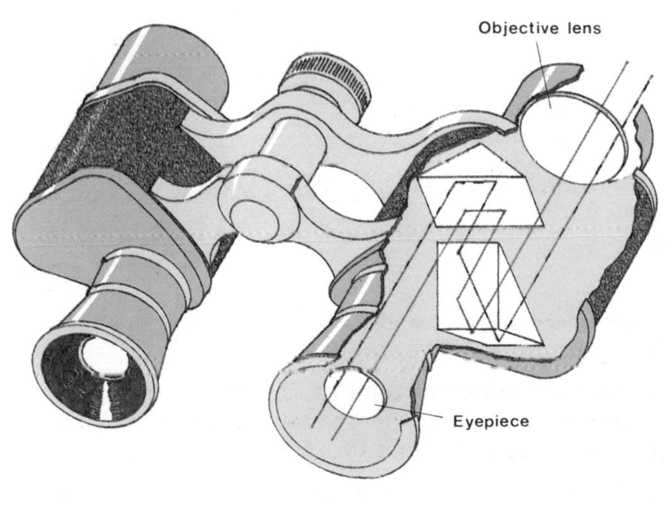

Fig. 37.10 Prism binoculars

Other Examples of Total Internal Reflection

1. The Light Pipe

If a lamp is shone into one end of a curved glass or perspex rod and a piece of card placed near the other end; a bright spot is observed on the card. This is because the light has been internally reflected as shown below.

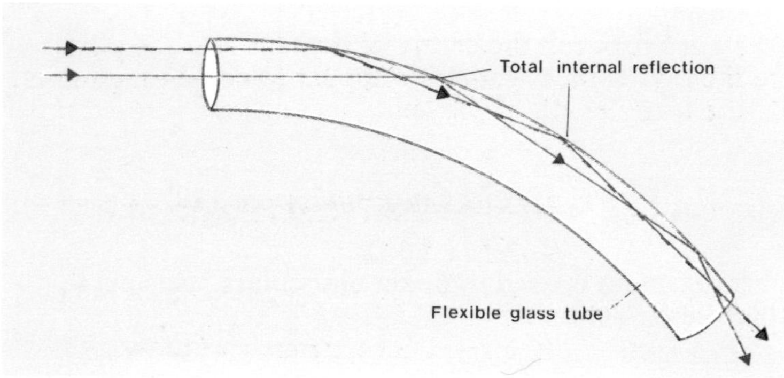

Fig. 37.11 Light-pipe

Uses of the Light Pipe

Microscope slide illuminator
Illumination of dials on radios and cars
Decorative fibre optics lamps

And if the rod is thin and flexible enough it can be used to inspect various channels in the body — **the fibrescope**.

2. The Mirage

Sometimes when driving along a road on hot days, pools of water appear on its surface. This is because light rays from the sky are being refracted as they move through the air layers near the ground. The air near the ground is less dense than that above it because it is hotter. At one point the light rays are totally internally reflected and come up towards our eye. The water is not really there, it is an image of the sky. This effect is known as a mirage.

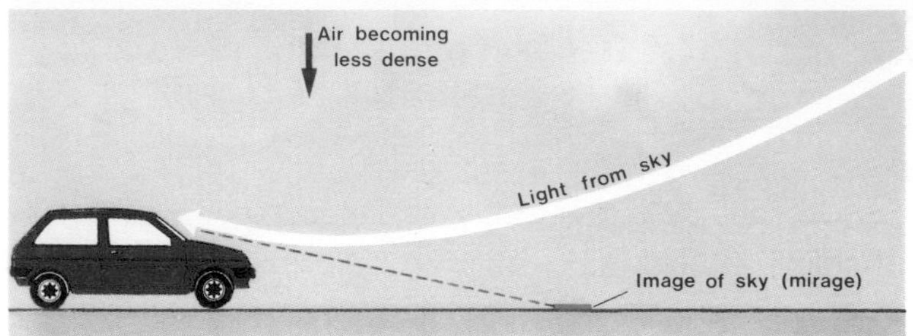

Fig. 37.12 Mirage

37.3 Lenses

Lenses are specially shaped pieces of glass or perspex which have at least one surface shaped like part of a large sphere. There are two main types of lens.

Convex
Concave

A convex lens converges light (brings it closer together) and is fatter in the middle than at its edges.

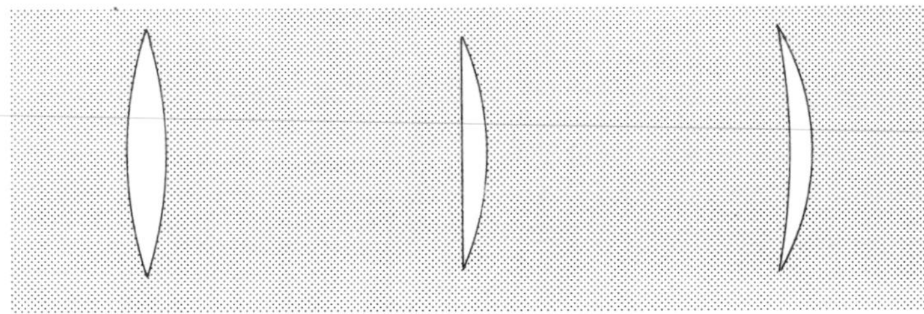

Fig. 37.13 Sections through some common convex lenses

A concave lens diverges the light (spreads it out) and is thinner in the middle than at the edges.

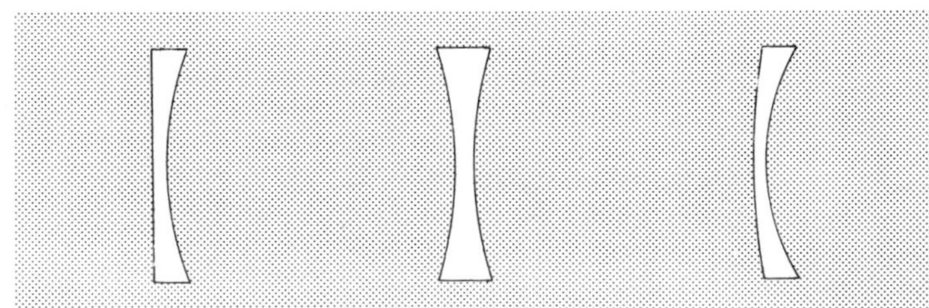

Fig. 37.14 Concave lenses

Experiment 37.4 To Observe the Effect of a Lens on a Parallel Beam of Light

Method

1. Place a sheet of plain paper on a soft board and draw a straight line on it.
2. Put a cylindrical convex lens centrally on the line and at 90° to it, and draw round it.
3. Using a ray box and three slits, direct three parallel rays of light towards the lens so that the central one lies on the pencil line.
4. Mark the positions of the rays before and after they pass through the lens, using a pencil.
5. Remove the ray box and the lens from the paper and draw in the light rays.
6. Repeat the experiment using a cylindrical concave lens.

Conclusion

a) Convex lens

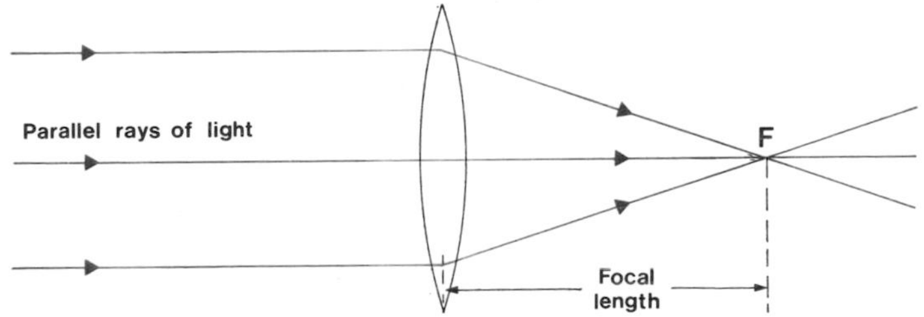

Fig. 37.15 Focal length convex

b) Concave lens

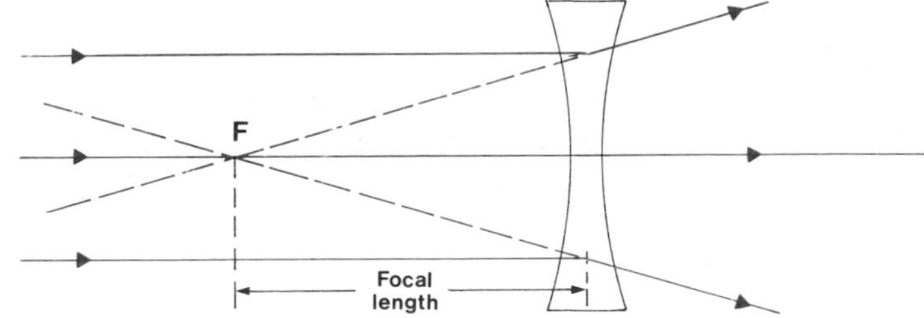

Fig. 37.16 Focal length concave

The distance between the centre of the lens and the point where the rays come together or appear to come together is called the focal length of the lens.

Experiment 37.5 To Find the Focal Length of a Convex Lens

Method

1. Set up a vertical screen well away from a window.
2. Hold a convex (converging) lens so that rays of light from a house or tree outside are being focussed on the screen and a clear image is formed.
3. Measure the distance between the lens and the screen. Record your result.

Conclusion

As the house or tree is distant, the rays of light coming from it are considered to be parallel. Therefore the distance from the lens to the screen is equal to the focal length of the lens.

Summary

* The substance through which the light is travelling is called the medium.
* When light passes from one medium to another it changes direction. This effect is called refraction.
* Light bends towards the normal, when it passes into a denser medium and away when it moves into a less dense one.
* The angle between the normal and the incident ray is called the angle of incidence.
* The angle between the normal and the refracted ray is called the angle of refraction.
* The laws of refraction are:
  The incident and refracted rays are on opposite sides of the normal at the point of incidence and all three are in the same plane.
  The ratio of the sine of the angle of incidence to the sine of the angle of refraction is a constant for a given pair of media.
* Total internal reflection can only occur when light is moving from a dense medium to a less dense medium (i.e. glass to air, water to air).
* When the angle of incidence is 0°, the light does not bend as it passes through the surface.
* A prism can be used to turn a ray of light through 90° or 180°.
* A thin flexible light pipe used in medicine is called the fibrescope.
* A mirage is formed when light rays from the sky are bent as they pass from denser air into less dense air near the ground.
* Lenses are specially shaped pieces of glass. There are two main types: Convex and Concave.
* A convex lens brings rays of light together (converges) and a concave lens spreads them out (diverges).
* The distance between a convex lens and the point where originally parallel rays of light are brought together is called the focal length of the lens.

Questions

Section A

1. When light passes from water into air it is . . . .
2. Refraction is the . . . .
3. The refractive index n = ...
4. Rays of light travelling from glass into air bend . . . . the normal.
5. Rays travelling from air to glass bend . . . .
6. The angle in glass beyond which total internal reflection occurs is called the . . . .
7. A 45° prism can turn a ray of light through . . . . and . . . .
8. A light pipe used in hospitals is called a . . . .
9. There are two types of lenses . . . . and . . . .
10. A concave lens . . . . a light beam.

Section B

1. When a ray of light passes through a glass block it is laterally displaced. Describe an experiment to show this.
2. In an experiment to find the refractive index of a substance, the angle of incidence was measured as 65° and the angle of refraction as 30°. What was the refractive index?
3. Describe an experiment to find the critical angle for glass. Can you find a relationship between this and the refractive index.
4. Explain with diagrams how 45° – 45° – 90° prisms can be used to reflect light through (i) 90° (ii) 180°.
5. You are given a convex lens to make a simple camera. How can you find the distance needed between the lens and the film. (**Hint**: Remember that for the lens, most objects are distant.)

38 — Optical Instruments

38.1 Magnifying Glass

The magnifying glass is a large convex lens. The lens, when held close to the object, will give a magnified (larger) and upright image. This is because the object is closer to the lens than the focal point (focus).

If the lens is moved so that the object lies outside the focal length, an upside down (inverted) image will be produced. This varies in size depending on how far away the lens is. You can check these effects by holding a 10 cm or 15 cm lens above the writing on this page. First move it closer to the page and then further away.

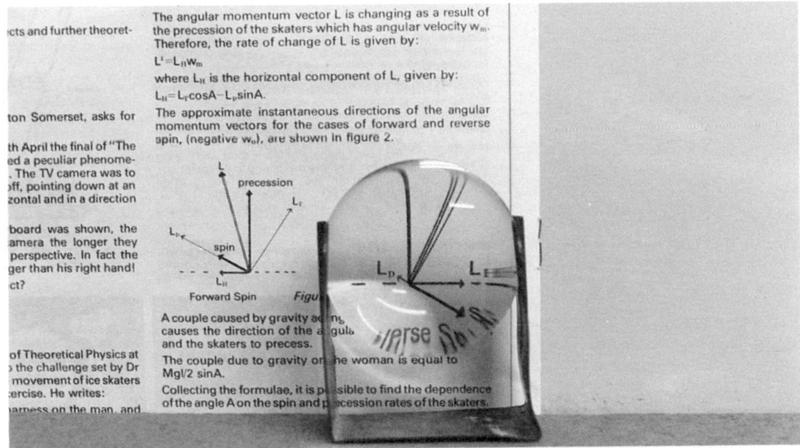

Fig. 38.1 Effect of magnifying glass

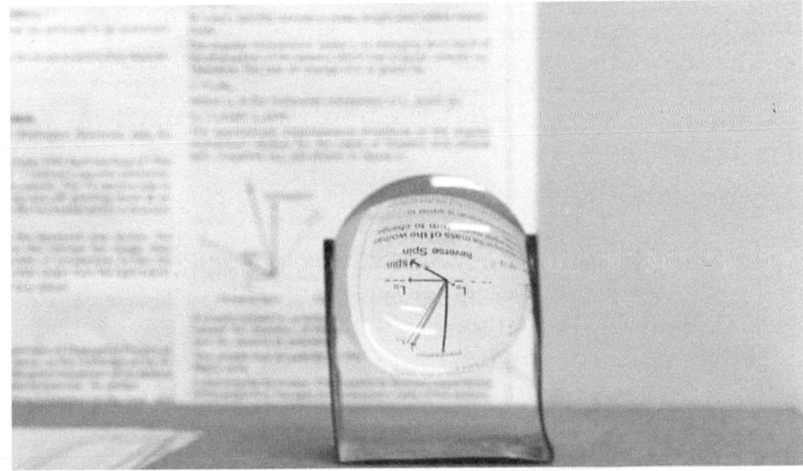

Fig. 38.2 Object outside the focal point of convex lens

38.2 The Lens Camera

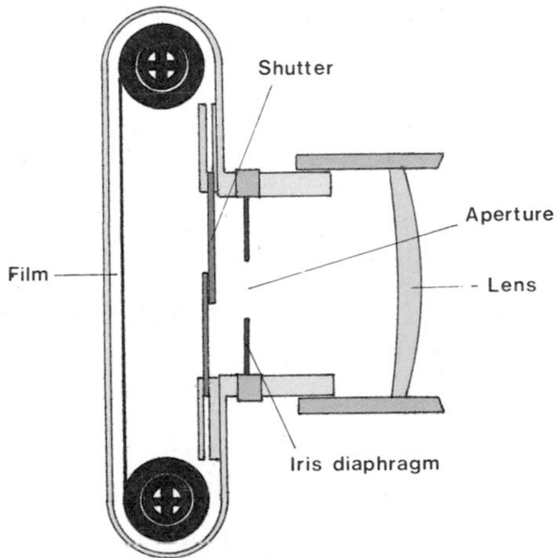

Fig. 38.3 (a) Section diagram of Camera

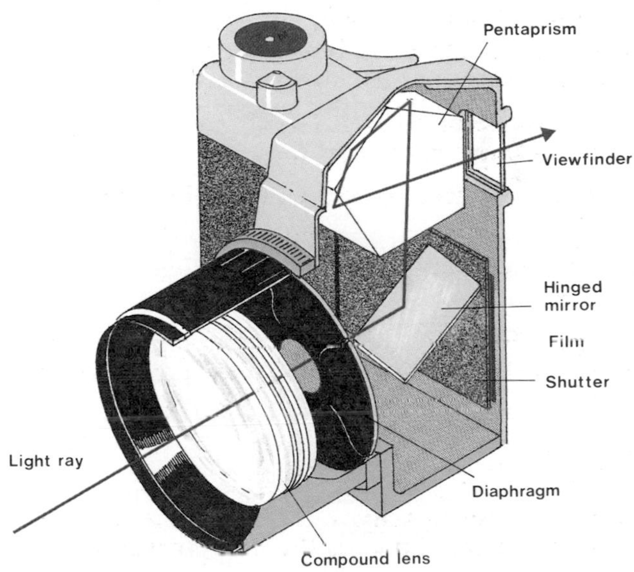

Fig. 38.3 (b) Cut away diagram of S.L.R. camera

The camera consists of a light-tight box which contains a converging lens and a light sensitive film. An adjustable aperture (opening) and a shutter allow the amount of light entering the camera to be controlled. The camera is focused by altering the distance between the lens and the film.

38.3 The Eye

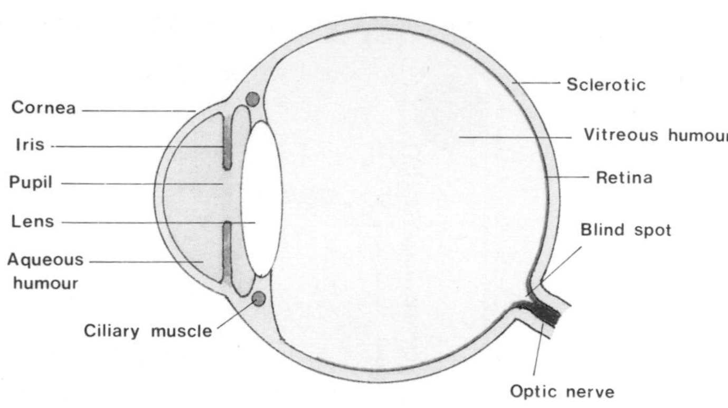

Fig. 38.4 The Eye

There are many similarities between the camera and the eye. (The function of each part of the eye is given in *Chapter 26*).

When the eye focuses, the majority of the bending of the light is done by the curved cornea, but the lens changes its shape to alter its focal length slightly and so focus the image. This adjustment is known as accommodation. The closer the object, the fatter the lens becomes.

Comparison of Eye and Camera

Similarities

Both have: Light tight containers
A lens which can be focused
A light sensitive screen
An iris (stop)
A variable aperture (pupil)
Inverted image produced
Black inside

Differences The eye is a living organ
Different mechanisms for focusing
— the eye focuses by altering the shape of the lens, whereas in the camera the distance of the lens from the film is changed.
In the camera images are easily stored on film (permanent record)
The camera takes one picture at a time, the eye continually scans the scene.
The eye has a blind spot.

Reaction of the Pupil to Varying Light Conditions

When you walk from bright sunshine into a dark building you will be aware that you cannot see clearly for a short time. This is because the pupil has to adjust its size to allow just the right amount of light onto the retina. Too much light and the light sensitive cells of the retina are all sending maximum signals to the brain and there is no variation from which the brain can produce a picture. Too little light and none of the cells respond so that nothing is seen. In very bright light the pupil becomes very small but as the brightness or intensity of the light decreases the pupil slowly opens up. In a very dark room the pupil will be very large.

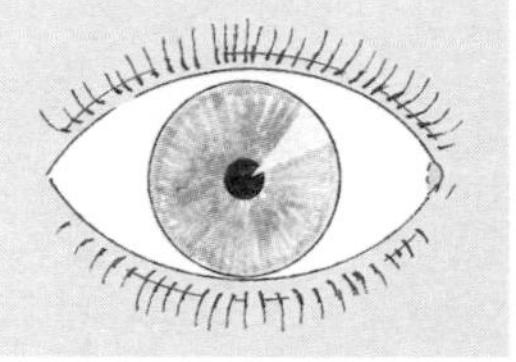

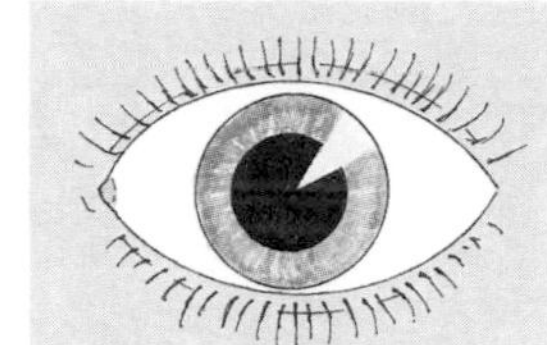

Fig. 38.5 Size of pupil in bright and dark conditions

You can check this working with a partner. Have your partner cover their eyes for a short time and then look carefully at the pupils when they uncover them. You should observe that they are very large initially and then close down quickly.

Defects of Vision

There are a number of defects, which include long-sight, short-sight, and colour blindness.

If your eyesight is normal you should be able to focus on both distant objects and those 25 cm from the eye. This 'near point' can be even less for teenagers. However, there exists a large number of people who have difficulty in seeing objects in one of these positions.

Long-Sight

A person who is able to see objects at a distance but is unable to focus near objects is said to be **long-sighted**. This is because the eye-ball is too short or his eye-lens is too thin, when fully squeezed and therefore the rays from the object are focused behind the retina.

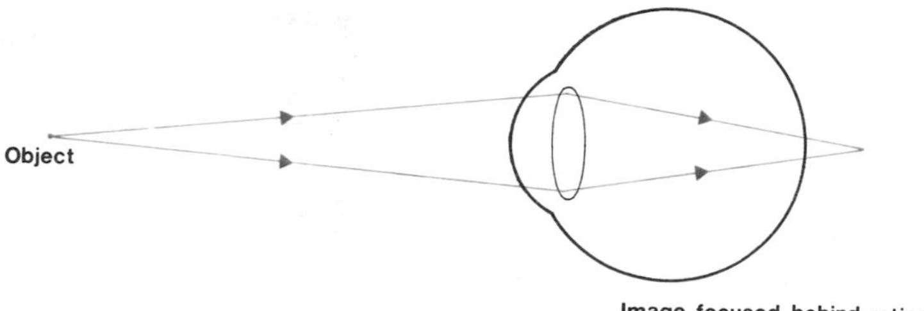

Fig. 38.6 Long-sight

To correct this condition a convex lens must be placed in front of the eye. This converges the rays a little so that the eye lens is now able to focus them on the retina.

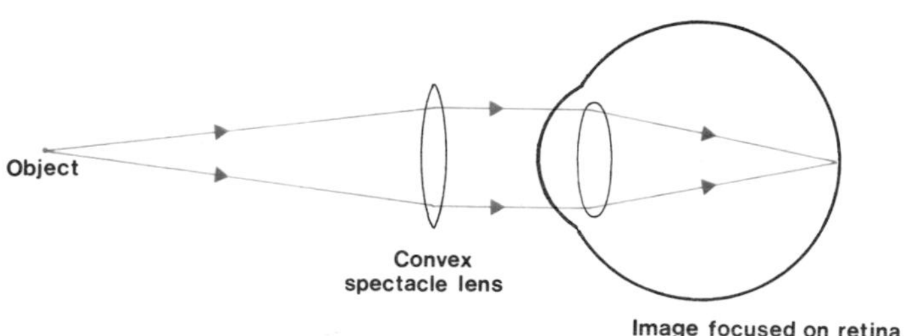

Fig. 38.7 Correction for Long-sight

Short-Sight

A person who can see near objects clearly but cannot focus distant objects is said to be **short-sighted**.
This is because the eye-ball is too long or the lens too curved. The rays from a distant object are brought to a focus in front of the retina.

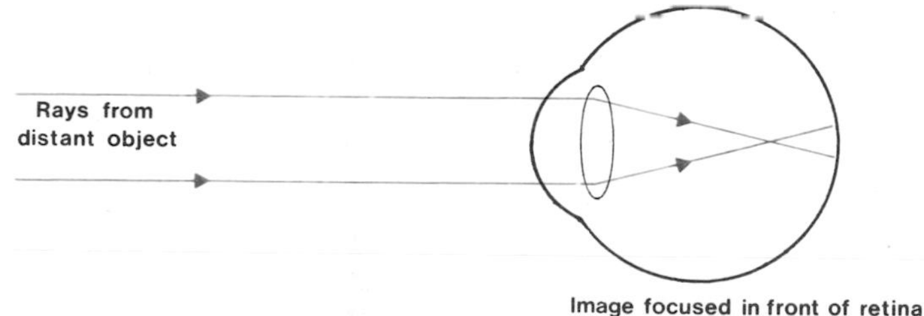

Fig. 38.8 Short-sight

To correct this defect a concave lens is placed in front of the eye.

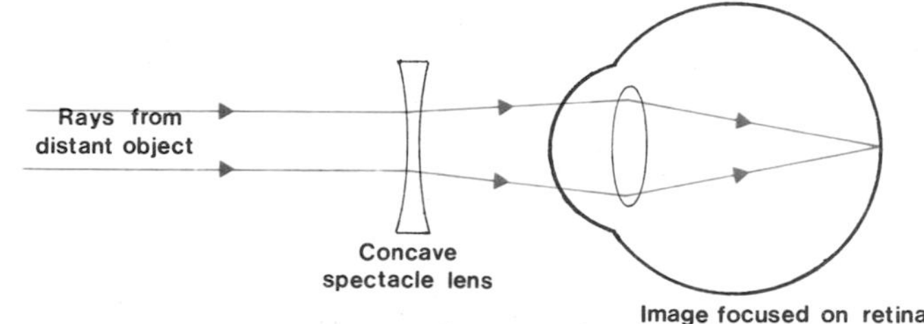

Fig. 38.9 Correction for Short-sight

The rays are diverged by this lens so they appear to come from the farthest point on which the eye can focus.

Experiment 38.1 To demonstrate Long and Short Sight and its Correction

Method

1. Fill with fluorescent solution a special round-bottomed flask, which has three lenses of different focal length attached to it.

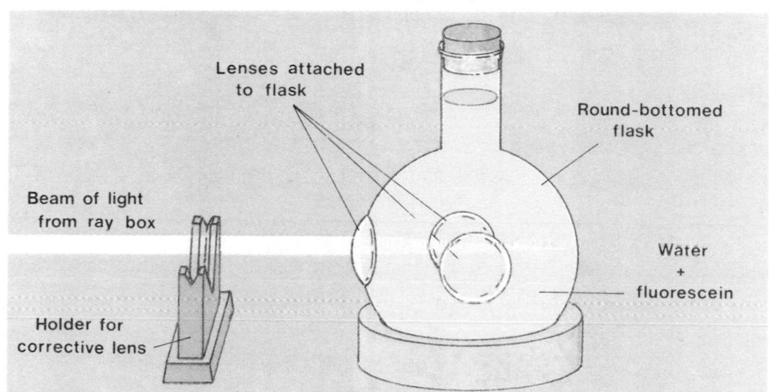

Fig. 38.10 Flask and lenses as model eye

2. Using a ray box shine a parallel beam of light onto each lens in turn. How does each lens affect the beam of light?
3. Now place a lens holder between the ray box and the flask. First place a convex lens in the holder and find which situation this corrects. Then replace the convex lens by a concave and repeat this step.
4. What do you observe to happen?

Conclusion

The flask and lens acts as a model eye. The side of the flask opposite the lenses acting as the retina. One of the lenses should focus the light onto it. Another should bring the light to a focus inside the flask — demonstrating short-sight while the final lens focuses the light outside the flask showing long-sight.
When a convex lens is placed in the lens holder it is found to correct the focusing in the case of long-sight. The concave lens achieves a similar effect for short-sight.

Colour Blindness

There are two types of cell in the retina which are sensitive to light. These are called rods and cones. The rods are there to distinguish between light and dark, whereas the cones are responsible for colour vision. There are three sets of cones, one set sensitive to blue light, one sensitive to red and the other sensitive to green light. These are the primary colours and any colour can be produced by mixing these in the correct proportions. Colour blindness is due to one of the sets of cones not working properly and the person therefore having difficulty in distinguishing between colours. There are over 2 million people in Great Britain who are colour blind and it is more common in men; one in twelve of whom are colour blind.

Judgement of Distance

If you only have one eye, it is difficult to judge distance. To test this have a partner stand about five paces away from you holding their hand out with the first finger pointing upwards. Now cover one of your eyes and stretch out a hand with your finger pointing downwards. Walk towards your partner and try to place your finger over theirs. Did you succeed? Try it again! Now move away and repeat the experiment with both your eyes uncovered.

You probably found that it was very easy to place your finger over your partners the second time but when you had one eye closed it was very difficult. This judgement of distance is very important to predatory animals, so they have both eyes directed forwards.

Persistence of Vision

A reel of cine film consists of thousands of still pictures which are flashed on a screen at 24 pictures per second. Our eyes then blend them together as the nerve endings retain the light signal for a short time. This retention of the image is called persistence of vision.

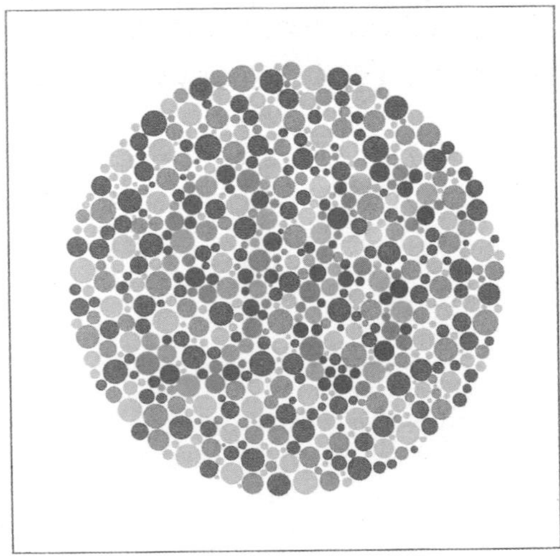

Fig. 38.11 Card for testing colour-blindness. With full-colour vision you should be able to see a number. The answer is on *page 253*

Fig. 38.12

It can be demonstrated by cutting a piece of stiff card about 10 cm square and drawing a bird or wild animal on one side and a large cage on the other. Attach a knitting needle vertically to the centre of one side and then spin the card. The bird or animal appears to be inside the cage.

Summary

* A convex lens can be used as a magnifying glass.
* A camera consists of a light-tight box which contains a converging lens, adjustable aperture, shutter and sensitive film.
* The camera focuses by changing the distance between the lens and the film.
* The eye focuses by altering the thickness of the lens.
* In bright light the pupil of the eye is very small, but in poor light it becomes much larger.
* A person who can see distant objects clearly but cannot focus near objects is said to be long-sighted.
* A person who can see near objects clearly but cannot focus distant objects is short-sighted.
* The eye contains two types of light sensitive cells, cones and rods. The cones provide the colour vision and the rods distinguish between light and dark.

Questions

Section A

1. The magnifying glass gives an image which is .... and ....
2. The .... and .... control the amount of light entering the camera.
3. The camera is focused by ....
4. The eye focuses by ....
5. The light sensitive material in the eye is called ....
6. Three similarities between the eye and the camera are .. .., ... and ....
7. If you walk from a dark room into sunlight, your pupil becomes ....
8. If you are short-sighted, the rays of light are brought to focus .... retina.
9. The two types of light sensitive cells in the eye are .... and ....
10. Colour blindness is caused by ....

Section B

1. Draw a diagram of a camera and write about the similarities between the camera and the eye.
2. Describe an experiment to demonstrate the correction of long and short-sight.
3. How could you prove the existence of persistence in vision. Describe fully the method you would use.

39 — Waves and Sound

39.1 Waves

If you throw a stone into a pond when the water is still, waves, spread out in all directions from the point where the stone hits the water, *Fig. 39.1.* If you take a length of rope which is fixed to something at one end and shake the other end back and forth, a wave moves up and down the rope. These are only two examples of waves, there are many more. These include microwaves, radio waves, light, X-rays and sound waves. All of these waves have one thing in common — they result in the transfer of energy from one place to another. To see that this is so, consider the following examples.

Fig. 39.1 Waves on water

A small boat is floating on a pond. A boy holds a stone above the water. The stone has potential energy. If the boy now drops the stone into the pond the stone loses its potential energy. A few seconds later the boat starts to move up and down — it has gained kinetic energy. This energy must have come from the stone and it is carried from the point where the stone hits the water to the boat by a wave. Note that the water does not move from the stone to the boat, it only moves up and down and eventually comes to rest where it was before the stone was dropped.

Fig. 39.2 shows a small box resting beside a long spring, e.g. a "Slinky". When one end of the spring is moved back and forth a wave travels down the spring and the box moves. Energy is transferred along the spring to the box. When the wave has passed, the spring comes to rest in the same position it was in to start with. Try this experiment in the laboratory, making certain that the slinky is stretched before moving one end quickly sideways and back to the original position.

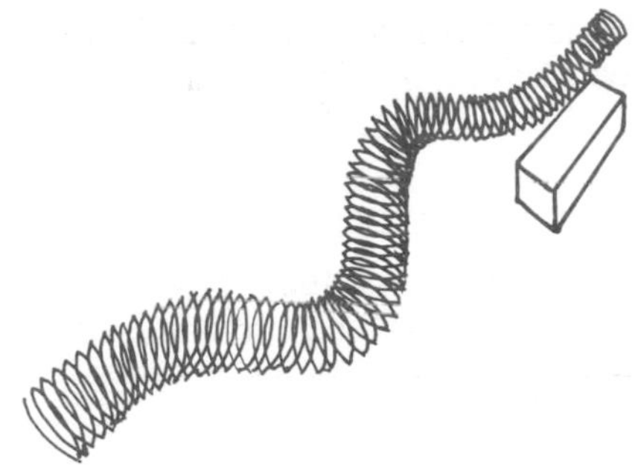

Fig. 39.2 Wave in a slinky

A wave is a means of transferring energy from one point to another.

The substance through which the wave is travelling is called the medium. For example, for waves on the sea the medium is water.

Types of Wave

There are two types of wave. The type we have just been considering is called a **transverse wave**. In this type of wave the substance through which the water is travelling vibrates at right angles to the direction in which the energy is travelling. In our first example the water moves up and down while the energy moves horizontally.

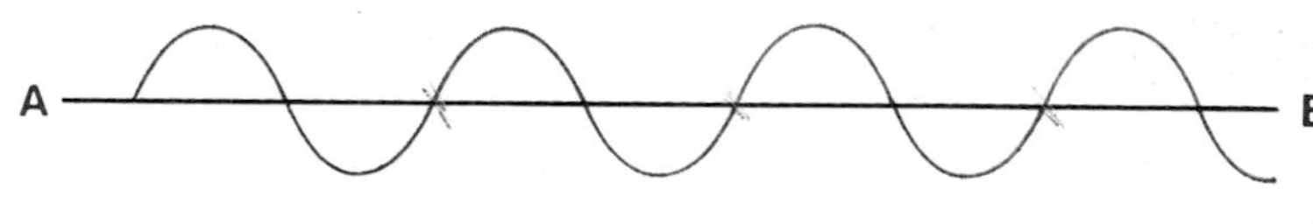

Fig. 39.3

A transverse wave, in a spring or in water for example, may be represented by a diagram like the one shown in *Fig. 39.3.* The straight line AB represents the spring or the surface of the water when they are not moving. The highest part of the wave is called the **crest** and the lowest part is called the **trough**. The distance from the crest of one wave to the crest of the next is called the **wavelength** of the wave. The wavelength is represented by the Greek letter λ (lambda). Since wavelength is a distance it is measured in metres.

Wavelength, λ, is the distance from the crest of one wave to the crest of the next.

The number of complete waves which pass a particular point in one second is called the **frequency**. Frequency is represented by the letter f, and is measured in hertz (Hz). If a wave of frequency 2 Hz is spreading across a lake it means that there are 2 waves passing any particular point on the surface of the lake in each second.

Frequency, f, is the number of waves passing a particular point in one second.

The height of a crest or the depth of a trough is called the **amplitude** of the wave. It is represented by the letter a, and is measured in metres. The amplitude is the greatest distance that the medium moves when a wave passes through it.

Amplitude, a, is the maximum displacement of the medium.

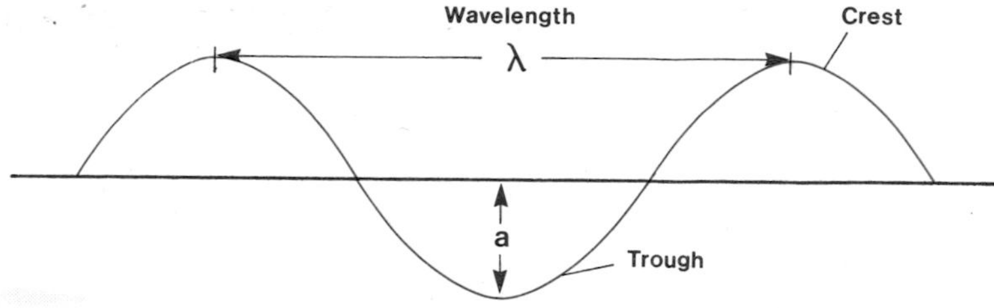

Fig. 39.4 Diagram illustrating wave definitions

The speed at which the wave is travelling from one place to another is the distance travelled in one second *(see Chapter 32).* Speed is represented by the letter v, and is measured in metres per second (m/s). The speed of a wave may also be said to be the distance travelled by the energy in one second. The velocity of a wave is its speed in a particular direction *(see Chapter 32).*

The speed of a wave is the distance travelled by the wave in one second.

Suppose the wavelength of a wave is 10 m, i.e. one full wave occupies 10 m, and suppose the frequency of the wave is 5 Hz, i.e. 5 full waves pass any particular point in one second. Then the total distance travelled by the wave in one second is 50 m. In other words, the speed of the wave is 50 m/s. From this example we see that the speed of a wave is equal to its wavelength multiplied by its frequency. This is true of all waves and is a very important relationship.

Speed = Frequency × Wavelength

or

$$v = f \times \lambda$$

The second type of wave is called a **longitudinal wave**. In this type of wave the substance through which the wave is travelling vibrates in the same direction as the energy is moving. This type of wave can also be demonstrated using a “Slinky”. In this case the end of the spring is moved in the direction of the length of the spring. In other words, the spring is first stretched and then compressed (squeezed together). When this process is repeated a longitudinal wave is set up in the spring and the spring looks as shown in *Fig. 39.5*. The parts of the spring where the coils are squeezed together are called **compressions** and the parts where the coils are further apart than normal are called **rarefactions.** Thus, a longitudinal wave is made up of a series of compressions and rarefactions.

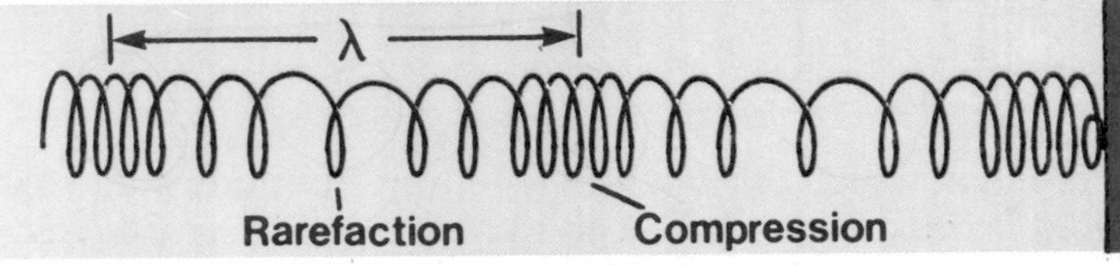

Fig. 39.5 A longitudinal wave

A longitudinal wave has similar properties to a transverse wave. The wavelength of a longitudinal wave is the distance from one compression to the next, *Fig. 39.5.* Frequency and speed are defined in the same way as for a transverse wave.

Example

The speed of a wave on a spring is 0.5 m/s and its frequency is 2 Hz. What is the wavelength of the wave?

$$v = f \times \lambda$$

$$0.5 = 2 \times \lambda$$

$$\lambda = \frac{0.5}{2}$$

$$= 0.25 \text{ m}$$

$$= 25 \text{ cm}$$

Ans. 25 cm.

Example

A radio wave has a wavelength of 200 m and a frequency of 1.5 MHz (MHz = megahertz. 1 MHz = 1 x 10^6 Hz). What is the speed of the radio wave?

$$v = f \times \lambda$$

$$= 1.5 \times 10^6 \times 200$$

$$= 1.5 \times 10^6 \times 2 \times 10^2$$

$$= 3 \times 10^8 \text{ m/s}$$

Ans. 3×10^8 m/s

The radio wave in the last example travelled at a speed of 3 x 10^8 m/s. In fact all radio waves travel at this speed. Indeed, all the different types of radiation which make up the electromagnetic spectrum are waves and travel at the same speed.

The speed at which electromagnetic waves travel is very large — 300 000 000 m/s or 1 080 000 000 km/h! Radiation from the sun takes only 8.3 minutes to reach the earth, a distance of 150 million kilometres. In astronomy, distances are often measured in **light years**. A light year is the distance that light travels in one year. There are just under 9000 hours in one year, so one light year is equal to approximately 9×10^{12} km. The nearest star to earth, apart from the sun, is 4 light years away and the Milky Way galaxy, of which our solar system is a part, is approximately 100 000 light years across.

39.2 Sound

Like light, sound is a form of energy. All sounds come from something which is vibrating. When a drum is struck, the skin vibrates; when a guitar string is plucked, it vibrates; when you speak your vocal chords vibrate. In each case you can feel the vibration if you place your fingers lightly against the drum skin, the guitar string or your larynx.

Since sounds come from vibrating objects we would expect that sound is a wave motion and this is so. When the skin of a drum moves outwards the surrounding air molecules are squeezed together and so a compression is formed. When the skin moves back the molecules have space to spread out and so a rarefaction is formed. This process is repeated continuously and so a series of compressions and rarefactions spread out from the drum. When a compression reaches our ear it causes our ear-drum to move in; when a rarefaction reaches our ear the ear-drum springs out again. The ear-drum vibrates at the same frequency as the drum skin from which the sound came. Thus, we can see that **sound is a wave** — a longitudinal wave in fact.

The fact that sound is a wave motion can be demonstrated with an oscilloscope and a microphone. An oscilloscope is a piece of equipment, rather similar to a television, which can be used for displaying waves on a screen. First the microphone is connected to the oscilloscope. When a vibrating tuning fork is held near to the microphone, a pattern like that shown in *Fig. 39.6* appears on the screen of the oscilloscope.

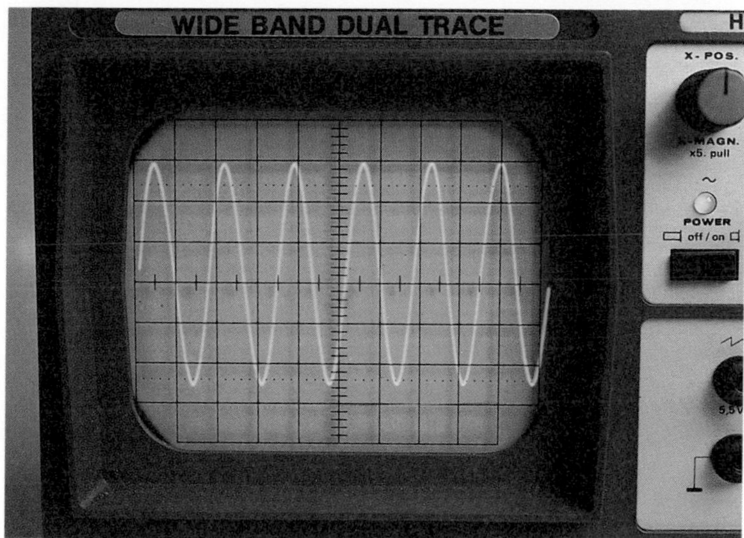

Fig. 39.6 Displaying a wave on an oscilloscope

Noise and Notes

Most people know the difference between the sound of a noise and of a musical note. To see how the waves differ in the two cases we can again use the oscilloscope and a microphone. If you make a noise, for example by banging a book on the bench or by talking, a pattern like that shown in *Fig. 39.7* will appear on the screen.

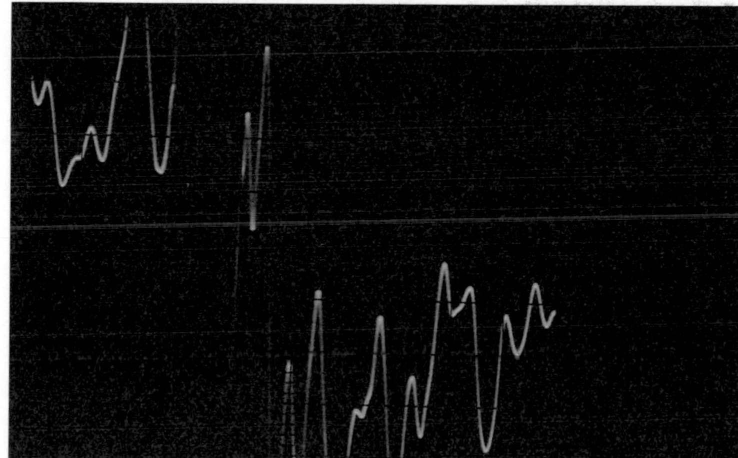

Fig. 39.7 Oscilloscope pattern of a noise

The pattern is made up of a jumble of waves of different wavelengths and amplitudes. If you now hold a vibrating tuning fork in front of the microphone or whistle into it, a pattern like that shown in *Fig. 39.6* will appear. In this case the pattern is a regular wave of only one wavelength. To summarise then, a noise is a random collection of waves of different wavelengths while a musical note is a regular wave of only one wavelength.

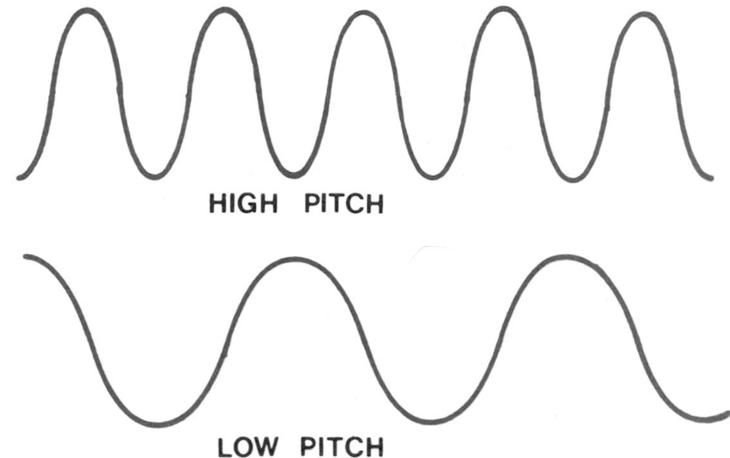

Fig. 39.8 Pitch depends on frequency

The pitch of a note depends on the frequency of the wave. The higher the frequency the higher the pitch, *Fig. 39.8*. The loudness of a note depends on the amplitude of the wave. The larger the amplitude the louder the note, *Fig. 39.9*.

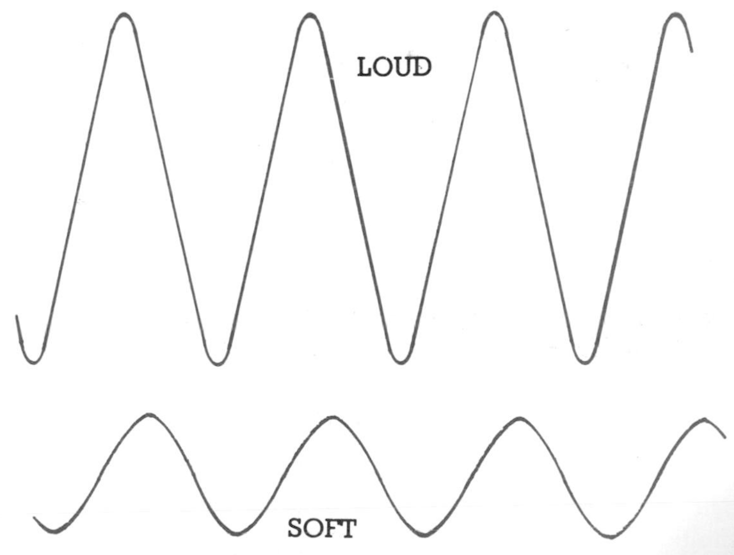

Fig. 39.9 Loudness depends on amplitude

While the loudness of a note depends on the amplitude, it also depends on the frequency. The human ear works best at a frequency of 1000 Hz. At frequencies above and below 1000 Hz the efficiency of the ear decreases. It does not respond at all to frequencies below about 20 Hz or above about 20 000 Hz (20 kHz). These two frequencies are called the limits of audibility. The upper limit falls with age and most adults cannot hear sounds of frequency above about 15 kHz. The ears of some animals, dogs and bats for example, can respond to much higher frequencies than human ears. A dog's ears are sensitive to frequencies of up to 35 kHz, hence, the use of "silent" dog whistles which emit notes with frequencies between 20 kHz and 35 kHz. Pure notes are produced by musical instruments. The most common types of which are:—

(i) stringed instruments (e.g. violin, guitar, piano & cello)
(ii) wind instruments (e.g. flute, clarinet, trumpet, recorder)

All stringed instruments are more complex versions of a sonometer. A sonometer consists of a piece of polished wood on which a wire is stretched over two bridges. The tension of the wire is altered by turning a peg at one end and its value is read from a spring balance at the other.

If you have heard a guitar being played you know that each string produces a different note. How is this achieved? The following experiment explains.

Experiment 39.1 To Find the Factors which Affect the Note Emitted by a String

Method

1. Set up the sonometer so that the string (wire) is just taut. Place the bridges underneath the string near each end. Pluck the string.
2. Now tighten the string so that the reading on the spring balance at the end has doubled. Pluck the string again. What has happened to the note? Repeat this step once more.
3. Adjust the tension of the string so that the reading of the spring balance is in the middle of the scale.
4. Pluck the string and listen to the note. Now move the bridges closer together and pluck the string (do not alter the tension). What has happened to the note? Repeat this step once more.

Conclusion

As the tension of the string is increased the frequency (pitch) of the note also increases. When the length is altered, the shorter the length of the string the higher the note it emits. If the string had been changed for a thicker one, the note it emitted would have been lower than that of the present one.

Therefore the note emitted by a string is found to depend on:—

Length of the string
Tension of the string
Thickness of the string

Wind instruments consist of a tube made out of wood or metal which can be open at one end or both ends. The pipe opened at both ends is known as an **open pipe** and that closed at one end is a **closed pipe**.

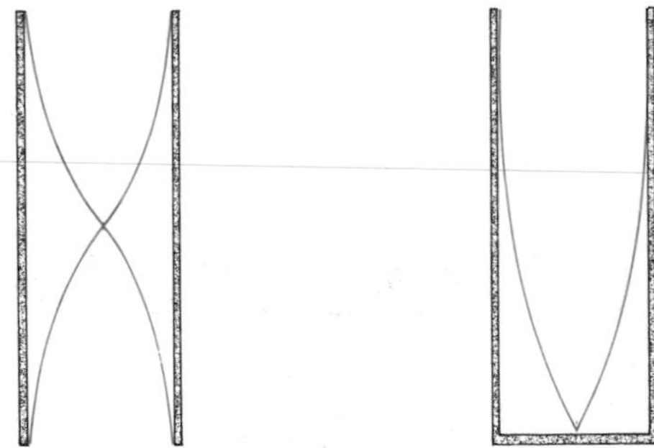

Fig. 39.10 Open and closed pipes for producing notes

Each pipe has a reed (sharp edge) near one end and air blown across it, begins to vibrate. A closed pipe has a frequency half that of an open pipe of the same length. The largest of all wind instruments, is the organ which has many pipes of various sizes which enable it to provide a wide range of notes. The following experiment demonstrates how it works.

Experiment 39.2 To Make a Bottle Organ

Method

1. Collect 8 identical bottles and fill each with water, to a different level.
2. Arrange them in order so that the bottle with the least water is at the left hand side.
3. Now blow across the top of each bottle in turn. Adjust the water levels until you have a scale. A little light music perhaps!

Conclusion

As the column of air in the bottles becomes shorter a higher note is produced.

Transmission of Sound

Sound travels better through some types of material than others. Sound will not travel through cotton wool or similar materials for example, and such materials are therefore used to provide sound insulation. On the other hand, sound travels well through water and through solids like wood and steel. If you hold your ear to the bench while someone taps the other end of the bench very gently you will hear the sound quite clearly. You can make a simple string "telephone" which illustrates that sound can travel through a string.

To make a string telephone get a length of string and two empty cans. Make a hole in the bottom of each of the cans and thread the string through the holes. Tie a knot on each end of the string so that it cannot be pulled out of the cans. Now get a partner to take one of the cans and move away until the string is taut. If you now speak quietly into your can your partner will be able to hear you by holding his can to his ear.

Experiment 39.3 To Show that Sound cannot Travel through a Vacuum

Method

1. Set up the apparatus, *Fig. 39.11*, with the bell sealed inside the bell jar.
2. Connect the bell to a battery or low voltage power supply and connect the vacuum pump to the apparatus.
3. Switch on the bell and note that it can be heard clearly.
4. Start the vacuum pump and note that the sound quickly dies away although the bell can be seen to be still working.

Conclusion

Sound cannot travel through a vacuum. It requires a material to travel through. (Note that this is one way in which sound differs from light. Light *can* travel through a vacuum. You can still see the bell ringing after the air has been removed from the bell jar.)

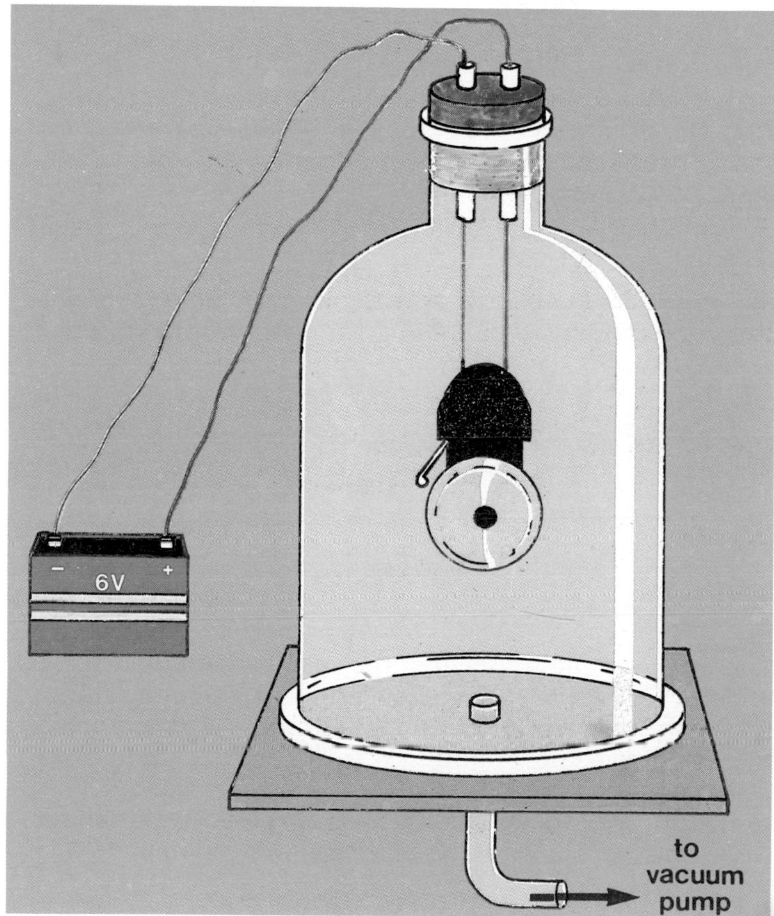

Fig. 39.11

Speed of Sound

There are many ways of measuring the speed of sound, some more accurate than others. We shall describe two methods here, one of which is very simple but which must be performed out-of-doors and another which may be done in the laboratory.

The first method requires two people, one with a pistol and the other with a stopwatch, to stand several kilometres apart and within sight of each other. The first person fires the pistol. When the second person sees the flash he starts the stopwatch and when he hears the bang he stops the stopwatch. The time taken for the light to travel from one person to the other is extremely small (about a hundred thousanth of a second!) and so it may be ignored. In other words we can take it that the second person sees the flash as soon as it occurs. So the time on the stopwatch is the time taken for the sound to travel from one person to the other. The distance between the two is then measured accurately and the speed of sound found by dividing the distance by the time.

Example

In an experiment to measure the speed of sound the distance between two people was 3.4 km. If the time recorded by the stopwatch was 10 s, what is the speed of sound?

$$\text{Speed} = \frac{\text{distance}}{\text{time}}$$

$$= \frac{3400}{10}$$

$$= 340 \text{ m/s}$$

Ans. 340 m/s

From this example we see that the speed of sound, in air, is 340 m/s (1224 km/h). This is only an approximate value because the speed of sound depends on the temperature and humidity of the air and so it varies from place to place and from time to time. The speed of sound in water is about 4 times its speed in air and its speed in steel is about 4 times its speed in water or 16 times its speed in air.

The second method is based on a very important phenomenon which is known as resonance. To help you understand this phenomenon, make up two simple pendulums of equal length by tying equal lengths of thread to two small weights. Tie the two pendulums to a length of string stretched between the tops of two retort stands as shown in *Fig. 39.12*. Now start one of the pendulums swinging. Soon, the second pendulum starts to swing with the same frequency — the same number of swings per second. The amplitude of the swing builds up until the first pendulum has stopped. Then the process is reversed — the first starts to swing again and the second stops — and so on. This is an example of resonance — energy is transferred between two objects which have the same frequency and one swings (vibrates) in sympathy with the other.

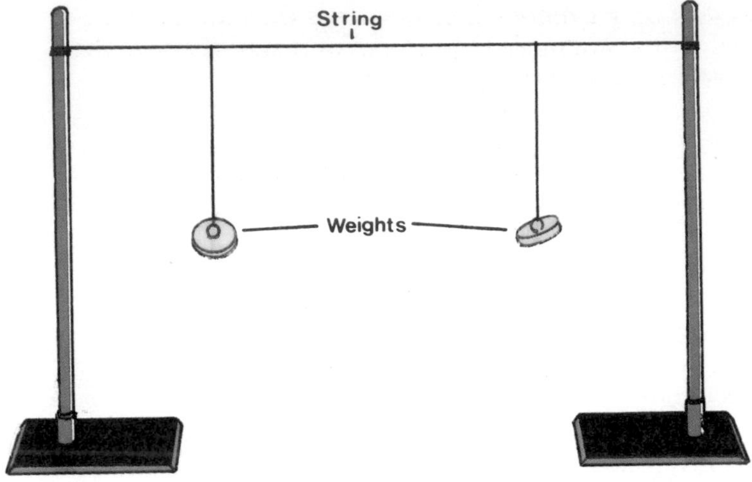

Fig. 39.12

As a second example of resonance get two identical tuning forks. Strike one of the forks and hold it close to the second. In a short time the second will have started vibrating and the first one will have stopped. Another well known example of resonance is that of a glass being shattered by a singer singing a high note. The glass starts to vibrate in sympathy with the note and is shaken to pieces.

Experiment 39.4 To Measure the Speed of Sound in Air using a Resonance Tube

Method

1. Fill a large measuring cylinder nearly to the top with water.
2. Place a glass tube or plastic pipe loosely in the clamp of a retort stand so that it rests on the bottom of the

measuring cylinder. The length of the tube should be such that not more than 15 cm of it stands above the surface of the water, *Fig. 39.13*.

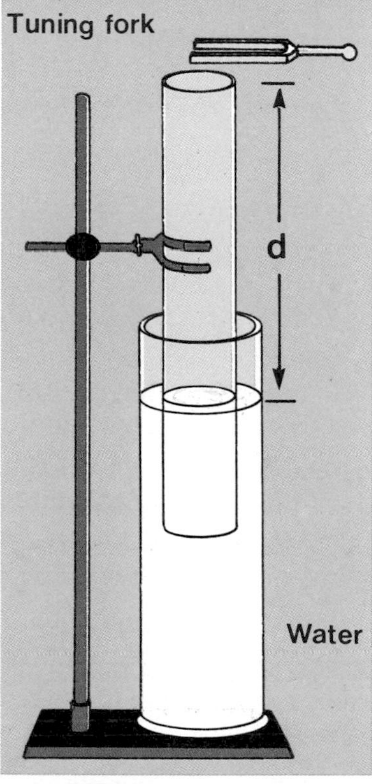

Fig. 39.13

3. From a selection of tuning forks take the tuning fork of highest frequency and strike it on a block of wood held in your other hand. Hold the vibrating tuning fork over the top of the tube.
4. Slowly raise the tube until it resonates with the tuning fork. When this happens the note will sound loudest. Tighten the clamp gently to hold the tube in this position.
5. Measure the distance, *d*, from the top of the tube to the surface of the water.
6. Multiply this distance by 4. This is the wavelength of the sound wave. Multiply the wavelength by the frequency (marked on the tuning fork) to get the speed. Make out a table for your results as shown below.
7. Repeat the procedure for tuning forks of different frequency and work out an average value for the speed.

RESULTS

f/Hz	d/m	λ/m	v/(m/s)

For accurate results the diameter of the tube should be small — less than 2 cm. If the diameter is not small, the following correction may be made. Measure the diameter and multiply the result by 0.3. Then add this to *d* before multiplying by 4 to get the wavelength in each case.

Example

In a resonance tube experiment the length of the tube above the water was 16.5 cm when it was resonating with a tuning form of frequency 512 Hz. Calculate the speed of the sound.

$$\begin{aligned} \text{Wavelength} &= \text{Length} \times 4 \\ &= 0.165 \times 4 \\ &= 0.66 \text{ m} \\ v &= f \times \lambda \\ &= 512 \times 0.66 \\ &= 338 \text{ m/s} \end{aligned}$$

Ans 338 m/s

Echoes

If you stand in a large empty room or some distance from a tall cliff and shout you will hear the sound of your voice being repeated, perhaps several times. This is called an **echo** and it is caused by the sound being reflected from the walls or the cliff.

Use is made of echoes in a process which is known as echo sounding. This is a method of measuring the depth of the sea or of a shoal of fish by sending down a high frequency wave and measuring the time take for the echo to return. Then, knowing the speed of sound in water, it is possible to work out the distance travelled by the wave.

Example

A ship sends down a high frequency wave and 3 s later receives the echo from the sea bed. If the speed of sound in the water is 1500 m/s what is the depth of the sea at that point?

$$\text{Distance travelled by wave} = \text{Speed} \times \text{Time} = 1500 \times 3 = 4500 \text{ m}$$

This is the distance from the ship to the sea bed and back again.

Therefore, the depth of the sea is

$$4500/2 = 2250 \text{ m}$$

Ans. 2250 m

The speed of sound can also be determined using an echo method.

Experiment 39.5 To Find the Speed of Sound using Echoes

Note This experiment requires two people, one to make the sound and the other to do the timing. A clear space in which you can stand about 100 m from a high wall is best.

Method

1. Stand a measured distance from the wall and clap together two small wooden blocks and listen for the echo.
2. Once you hear the time interval, clap the blocks continuously so that the claps coincide with the echo.
3. The person timing must now time 20 or 30 claps. Record the time, number of claps and distance from the wall.

Conclusion

The time between each clap is that taken for the sound to reach the wall and return. If 20 claps are timed then the total distance of the sound travelled in that time is

$$20 \times 2d$$

where d is the distance from the wall.

If this has taken a time, t secs

The velocity of the sound is given by:—

$$\frac{\text{distance travelled}}{\text{time taken}} = \frac{20 \times 2d}{t} \text{ metres/sec.}$$

Summary

* A wave is a means of transferring energy from one point to another.
* In a tranverse wave the medium vibrates at right angles to the direction in which the energy is travelling.
* In a longitudinal wave the medium vibrates in the same direction as the energy is travelling. A longitudinal wave consists of a series of compressions and rarefactions.
* The wavelength, λ, is the distance from the crest of one wave to the crest of the next. It is measured in metres.
* The frequency, f, is the number of waves passing a particular point in one second. It is measured in hertz (Hz).
* The amplitude, a, is the maximum displacement of the medium. It is measured in metres.
* The speed (or velocity) of a wave is equal to its frequency multiplied by its wavelength, $v = f \times \lambda$.
* Sound is a form of energy. All sounds come from vibrating objects and are carried by longitudinal waves.
* A noise is a jumble of unrelated waves of different wavelengths. A musical note is a regular wave of a single wavelength.
* The pitch of a note depends on its frequency; the loudness of a note depends on its amplitude.
* The note emitted by a string depends on the length of the string; the tension in the string and its thickness.
* An open pipe has a frequency double that of a closed pipe of the same length.
* Sound requires a material medium. It cannot travel through a vacuum.
* The speed of sound can be measured by finding the time taken for the sound of a pistol shot to travel a measured distance. In the laboratory it is measured using a resonance tube.
* An echo is a reflected sound.

Questions

Section A

1. A wave is a means of transferring ....
2. The substance through which a wave is travelling is called the ....
3. What is the difference between a transverse wave and a longitudinal wave ....
4. The distance from the crest of one wave to the crest of the next is called the .... and it is measured in...................................
5. The frequency of a wave is .... and it is measured in ....
6. What is the relationship between the speed, frequency and wavelength of a wave? ....
7. Sound is a form of ....
8. What type of wave is a sound wave? ....
9. What is the difference between a note and a noise? ....
10. The pitch of a note depends on its ....
11. The note emitted by a sonometer depends on the ...., ... and .... of the string.
12. The speed of sound in air is approximately ...... m/s.
13. What is meant by resonance? ....
14. Give two differences between sound waves and light waves. ....
15. If the speed of a wave is 40 m/s and its frequency is 0.4 Hz, what is its wavelength ....
16. Sound requires a .... medium. It cannot travel in a..
17. An echo is ....
18. The loudness of a note depends on its...............
19. Name two materials through which sound will not travel. Give two uses for such materials ....
20. Why do you think the speed of sound in air is much less than in steel?....................................
21. What is meant by the amplitude of a wave? ....

Section B

1. What evidence is there to suggest that sound is a wave? Describe an experiment which demonstrates the wave nature of sound.
2. The speed of radio waves is 3×10^8 m/s. What is the frequency of a radio wave whose wavelength is 200 m?

   What is the wavelength of a radio wave whose frequency is 30 kHz?
3. Describe an experiment which shows that sound cannot travel through a vacuum. Explain why this should be so.
4. Describe an experiment to measure the speed of sound in the laboratory.
5. What is meant by saying that the frequency of a wave is 500 Hz? If the frequency of a wave on the sea is 0.2 Hz how many waves will pass a particular point in one second?
6. Thunder and lightning occur at the same time yet the lightning is nearly always seen before the thunder is heard. Explain.

   If the time between seeing the lightning and hearing the thunder is 5 s how far away is the thunder storm?
7. In an experiment using echoes to find the velocity of sound, an observer standing 100 m from a high wall, times 30 claps in 18 seconds. What is the speed of sound?

Answer to colour test on Page 242, *Fig. 38.11* is 96.

40 — Static Electricity

40.1 Electric Charges

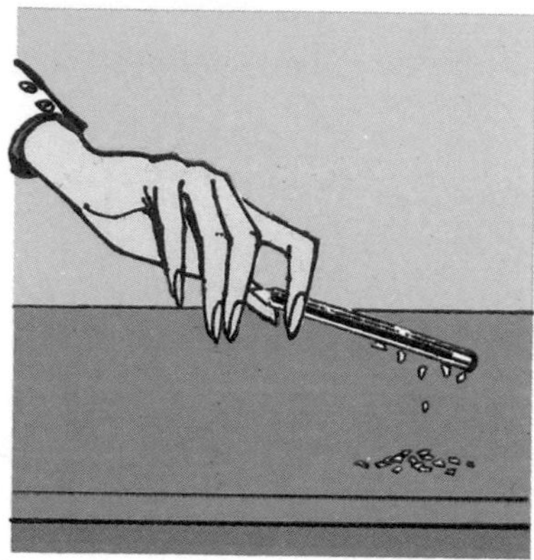

Fig. 40.1 A charged body attracts uncharged bodies

If you rub a plastic comb or pen on your sleeve it is then able to pick up small pieces of paper, *Fig. 40.1*. We say that the comb or pen has become electrically charged or that the comb or pen has an electric charge on it. As well as attracting bits of paper a charged body will attract most other things, even water, *Fig. 40.2*. To investigate further the forces exerted by charged bodies, set up the following experiment.

Fig. 40.2 Water is attracted to a charged body

Experiment 40.1 To Investigate the Forces between Charged Bodies

Method

1. Attach a paper stirrup to a retort stand with some thread and place a perspex rod in the stirrup, *Fig. 40.3*.

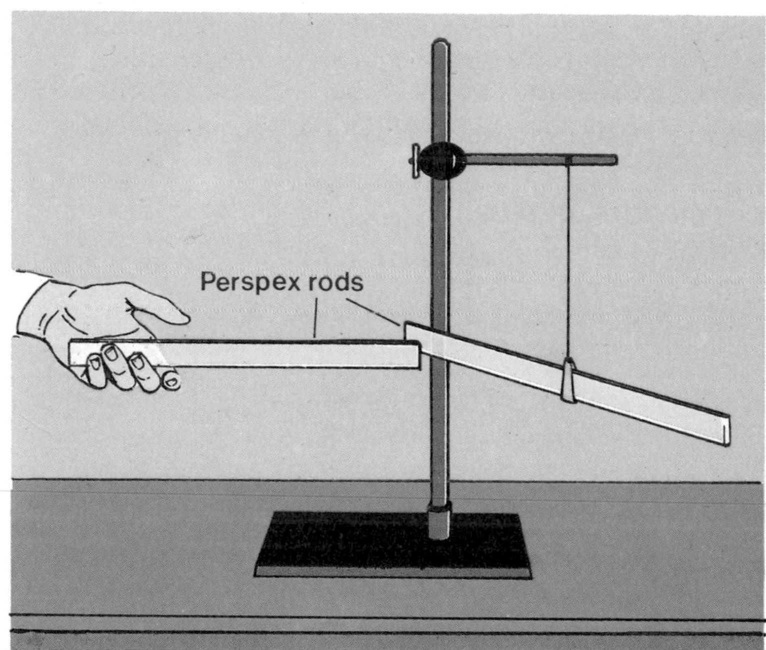

Fig. 40.3 Charged bodies exert forces on each other

2. Charge another perspex rod by rubbing it on a cloth and hold it near the rod in the stirrup. Note the result.
3. Charge a polythene rod and hold it near the rod in the stirrup. Note the result.
4. Remove the perspex rod from the stirrup, charge it and return it to the stirrup.
5. Charge the other perspex rod and hold it near the one in the stirrup. Note the result.
6. Charge a polythene rod and hold it near the rod in the stirrup. Note the result.

Conclusion

The uncharged perspex rod is attracted to both types of charged rod. The charged perspex rod is attracted to the charged polythene rod but is repelled by the other charged perspex rod.

From this experiment we see that the charge on the perspex is different from the charge on the polythene rod. In other words, there must be two types of charge. These two types of charge are called **positive charge** and **negative charge**. (In this case the perspex rod carries a positive charge and the polythene rod carries a negative charge.) Thus, we can say that positive and negative charges attract each other while two positive charges repel each other. Likewise, two negative charges repel each other. You should check this last statement by charging a polythene rod and placing it in the stirrup and then charging another polythene rod and bringing it near to the one in the stirrup. These facts concerning the forces between charges may be summarised as:

Like charges repel each other; unlike charges attract.

Here are some more ways in which you can demonstrate the forces between charges:

1. Get a strip of polythene and rub it with a cloth. It should now "stick" to the wall.
2. Rub a balloon on your jumper and hold it against the wall.
3. Rub a perspex rod and hold it near your hair or near a friend's hair.
4. Charge two strips of polythene and hold them up together so that they hang parallel to each other. Do they, in fact, hang parallel to each other?

Note: For experiments involving electric charges, everything must be very dry. It is a good idea to dry everything with an electric heater or a hair dryer.

Atomic Theory

We saw in *Chapter 34* that all substances are made up of tiny particles, called atoms. Atoms, in turn, are made up of even smaller particles. There are three types of particle in an atom — **protons, neutrons** and **electrons**, *Fig. 40.4*.

Protons and neutrons are about the same size and make up the central part of the atom which is called the **nucleus**. Electrons are much smaller and they travel around the nucleus.

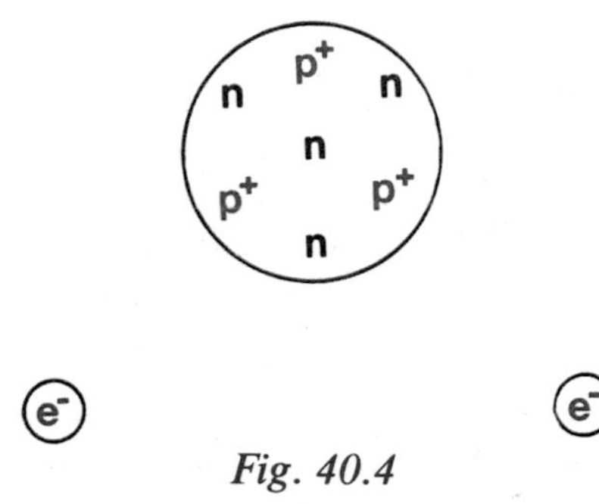

Fig. 40.4

You will learn more about the structure of atoms in *Chapter 1*. What is of most interest to us here is that electrons have a negative charge while protons have a positive charge of equal size. Normally an atom has equal numbers of protons and electrons so that the charges cancel each other and the atom is electrically neutral, or uncharged.

When two bodies are rubbed together, electrons can be rubbed off one and onto the other. The body which gained the electrons now has more electrons than protons and so has a negative charge. The body which lost the electrons now has more protons than electrons and so has a positive charge.

40.2 The Gold-Leaf Electroscope

A simple instrument which is very useful for learning more about electric charges is the gold-leaf electroscope, *Fig. 40.5*. It consists of a metal case which has a glass front and back. A metal cap (sometimes called the plate) on top is connected by a metal rod to two metal leaves. These leaves were originally made of gold, hence the name of the instrument, but are now usually made of Dutch metal (an alloy of copper and zinc). The leaves are very light and are free to move. (In some types of electroscope only one of the leaves is free to move.) At the point where the rod enters the case it is surrounded by a piece of plastic so that the rod does not touch the metal of the case.

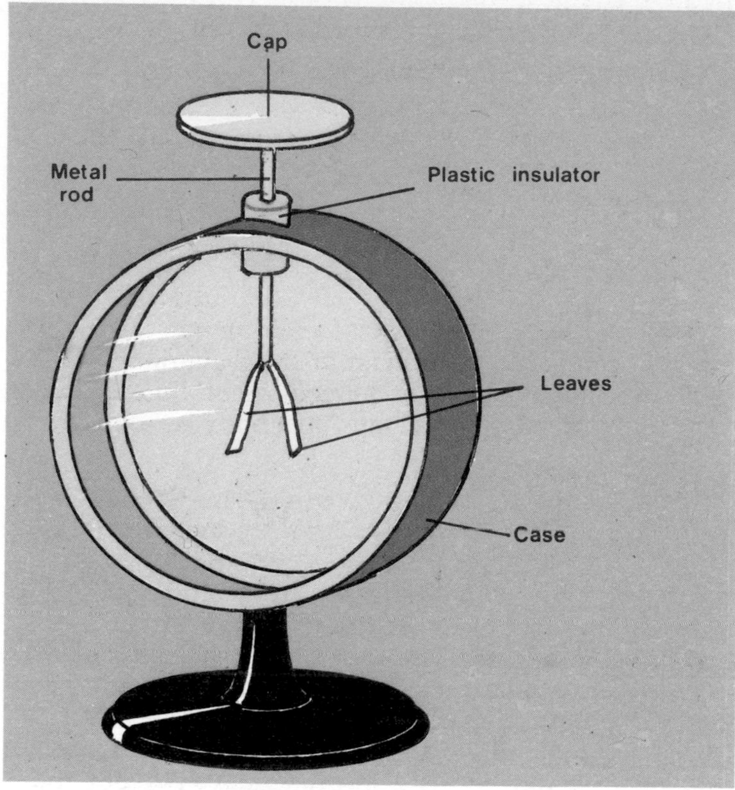

Fig. 40.5 A gold-leaf electroscope

When a charge is placed on the cap it spreads down to the leaves. Since both leaves have the same charge, they repel each other and move apart. In general, the more charge is placed on the cap the further the leaves move apart.

Charging by Induction

If you charge a perspex rod by rubbing it on a cloth and place it on the cap of an electroscope, the leaves rise. When you take away the rod again, the leaves fall. In other words, the electroscope does not stay charged. In order to place a charge on the electroscope, so that it stays there, the following method is used. It is called charging by induction. It consists of four steps:

1. Charge a polythene rod by rubbing and hold it near the cap of the electroscope, *Fig. 40.6(a)*. The result of this step is that the negative charges in the electroscope are repelled by the negative charges on the rod. The negative charges thus gather on the leaves, leaving the cap with a positive charge. As a result of the negative charges on the leaves they move apart (repel each other).

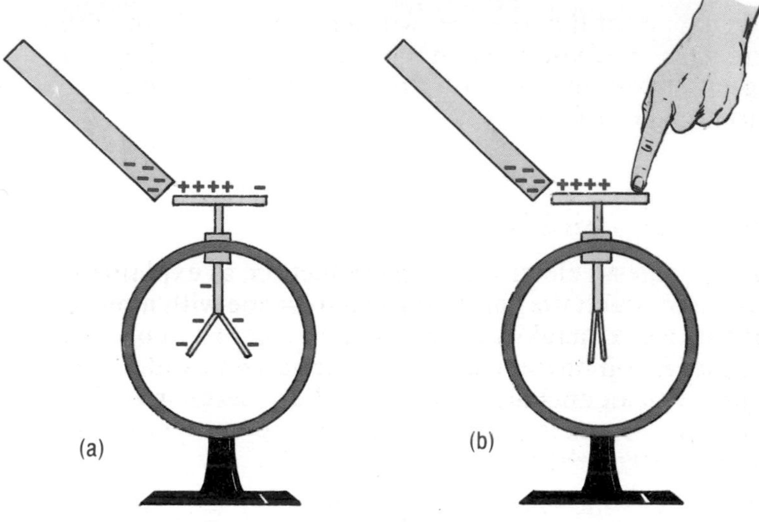

Fig. 40.6 (a) & (b)

2. Touch the cap with your finger, *40.6(b)*. This allows the negative charges on the leaves to flow to the ground through your body and is called **earthing** the electroscope. The positive charges remain on the cap because of the attraction of negative charges on the rod.
3. Remove your finger while still holding the rod in place, *Fig. 40.7(a)*.

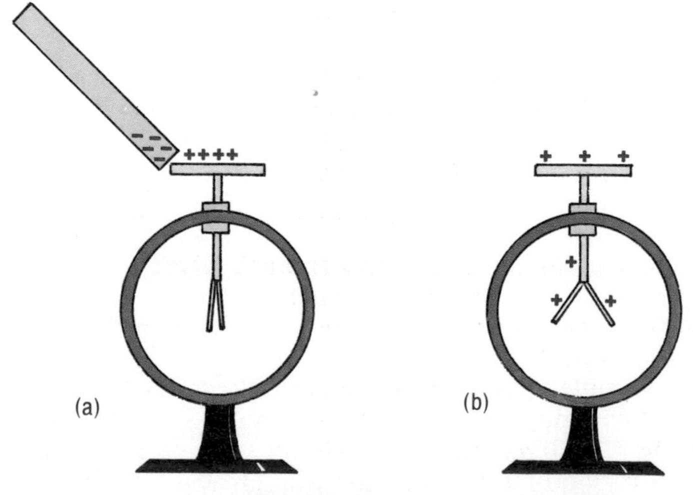

Fig. 40.7 (a)& (b)

4. Finally, remove the rod. Negative charges move up from the leaves and cancel some of the positive charges on the cap. the leaves now have a positive charge and so they move apart, *Fig. 40.7(b).*

It is important that the last two steps be carried out in the correct order. If you remove the rod before removing your finger, negative charges will flow up from the earth and cancel the positive charges on the cap.

Conductors and Insulators

If you charge an electroscope by induction, as explained above, and touch the cap of the electroscope with a piece of metal, e.g. a metal ruler or a coin, the leaves immediately collapse. If you now recharge the electroscope and touch the cap with an uncharged plastic rod, the leaves remain apart. It is clear that the metal allowed the charge to flow through it while the plastic did not.

Substances which allow charge to flow through them are called **conductors**. Metals are good conductors, silver and copper being the best. Graphite (carbon) is also a good conductor. Substances which do not allow charge to flow through them are called **insulators**. Plastics are generally good insulators, as are glass, rubber, mica, etc. Pure water is an insulator but ordinary tap water is a conductor due to impurities dissolved in it. Try the following experiment.

Charge an electroscope and touch the cap with a wooden ruler. The leaves immediately fall, showing that the ruler is a conductor. But, is wood a conductor? Now test the ruler again to see if it is a conductor. If the ruler is completely dry, you should find that it is now an insulator. Wet the ruler under the tap and you should again find that it is a conductor. This experiment shows that tap water is a conductor and, most importantly, that even an insulator — when it is damp — becomes a conductor.

Conductors allow charge to flow through them; insulators do not.

It is not possible to charge an insulator by induction. the process of charging a body by induction involves the movement of charges through the body and this can only happen if the body is a conductor. Similarly, it is very difficult to charge a conductor by rubbing it since any charges which are produced immediately flow off it.

It should be remembered that, in metals, it is only electrons which are free to move — protons cannot move *(see Chapter 1)* So all movement of charge in metals is caused by moving electrons.

Uses of an Electrosope

We have just seen how an electroscope can be used to tell us whether a body is a conductor or an insulator. It will also tell us whether a body is charged or not. Further, we can use it to find out if the charge on a body is positive or negative.

The electroscope is first charged positively. This may be done by charging it by induction from a polythene rod or by connecting the cap to the positive terminal of a high voltage power supply *(see next chapter)*. The charged body to be tested is now brought near the cap of the electroscope. If the leaves move further apart, then the body is positively charged. If the leaves move closer together, the body is either negatively charged or it is uncharged. If this happens, the electroscope is recharged negatively by charging it by induction from a perspex rod or by connecting it to the negative terminal of a high voltage power supply. The body being tested is again brought close to the cap and if the leaves go further apart, then the body has a negative charge; if the leaves go together, the body is uncharged. The uses of an electroscope can be summarised thus:

An electroscope is used to show if a body is charged or not; to show if a body is charged positively or negatively; to show if a body is a conductor or an insulator.

Charges Produced by Rubbing

We can use the electroscope to show that rubbing two bodies together produces the same amounts of positive and negative charge on each, as predicted by the atomic theory described above.

Experiment 40.2 To show that Rubbing Produces Equal Amounts of Positive and Negative Charges

Method

1. Wrap a cloth around a perspex rod and then wind some silk thread around it about 5 times. Place them in a tall metal can. Now place the can on the cap of an electroscope.
2. Keep the rod and cloth in the can and pull the silk. This will rub the cloth on the rod.
3. Remove the rod, leaving the cloth in the can. Note the result.
4. Replace the rod and remove the cloth. Note the result.
5. Remove both the rod and the cloth. Note the result.

Conclusion

When both the rod and the cloth are in the can, the leaves do not rise, *Fig. 40.8(a)*, showing that the total charge in the can is zero. When either the rod or the cloth is removed, *Fig. 40.8(b)* and *(c)*, the leaves rise by the same amount, showing that both carry the same amount of charge. Since the charges on the rod and the cloth cancel each other when both are in the can, it follows that one must be positive and the other negative.

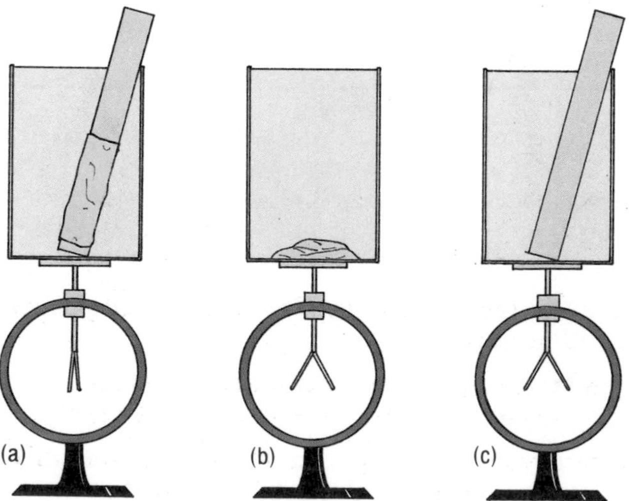

Fig. 40.8 (a) (b) (c)

Examples of Static Electricity

There are many examples of static electricity in everyday life. The best known and most spectacular of these is lightning. In thunder clouds, huge charges build up. Generally, the top of the cloud has a positive charge and the bottom has a negative charge. The negative charge on the bottom of the cloud induces a positive charge on the ground underneath the cloud.

Fig. 40.9

Although air is normally an insulator, if the charge is big enough, the air may become a conductor and the charge then flows through it. It is this flow of charge through the air which produces the flash of lightning and it can take place either between a cloud and the earth or (much more frequently) between one cloud and another or (occasionally) between one part of a cloud and another part which has the opposite charge. As well as producing light (the flash of lightning) the flow of charge also heats the air very rapidly to very high temperatures. This causes the air to expand and it is this expansion of the air which produces the sound we call thunder. If lightning strikes a building, the flow of charge through the building to the earth may cause great damage. To prevent this happening, most tall buildings have lightning conductors attached to them. A lightning conductor is simply a metal rod which is attached to the highest part of the building. The top end of the rod has a sharp point and the other end is connected to a thick copper strip which runs down the outside of the building and is connected to a long metal rod which is buried in the ground. If lightning strikes the lightning conductor, the charge can thus flow harmlessly to earth through the copper strip. Because the lightning conductor is higher than the highest part of the building and because it has a sharp point, lightning is more likely to strike the conductor than to strike any part of the building.

Fig. 40.10 Lightning conductor

An electric charge can sometimes build up on a car when it is moving. When the car stops, a person stepping out of the car may feel a slight shock as the charge from the car flows through her/him to earth. In a similar way, a person who has walked on a nylon carpet may get a shock when he/she touches a metal object which is earthed.

As well as dangers and discomforts, electric charges also have many practical uses. Among these are electrostatic photocopying, spraying paint on car bodies and removing ash from the smoke in the chimneys of coal-fired power stations.

Electrostatic Machines

The amounts of charge which can be produced by rubbing are very small and a number of machines have been invented to produce large static charges. One of these, commonly found in school laboratories, is the **Van de Graaff generator**, invented by the American physicist, Robert Van de Graaff in 1931. It consists of a rubber belt running on two rollers, *Fig. 40.11*, the top roller being inside a metal dome. The belt is charged by rubbing on the bottom roller. This charge is carried upwards on the belt and is transferred to the dome by a "brush" near the top roller. In this way, large charges can build up on the dome and large sparks can be produced by bringing an earthed metal object (or even your finger!) near to the dome.

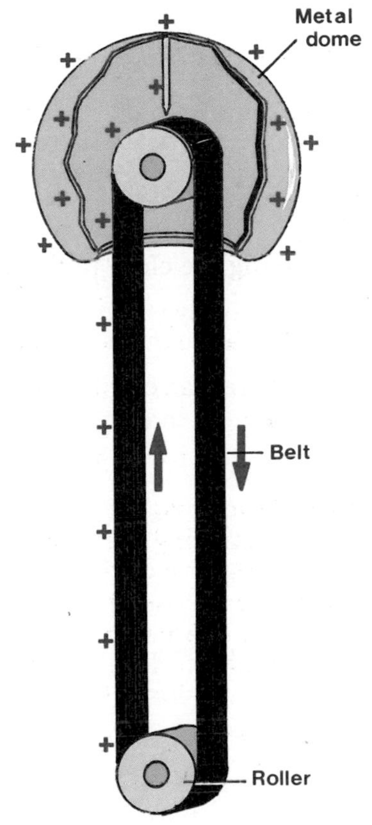

Fig. 40.11 Van de Graaff generator

Summary

* When a piece of plastic is rubbed with a cloth it can attract pieces of paper and it is said to be electrically charged.
* There are two types of charge. These are called positive charge and negative charge.
* Like charges (two positives or two negatives) repel each other; unlike charges (a positive and a negative) attract.
* All substances are made up of atoms. Atoms normally contain equal numbers of electrons and protons. Electrons have a negative charge; protons have a positive charge of equal size.

* Rubbing two bodies together transfers electrons from one to the other so that one gains a negative charge while the other is left with an equal positive charge.
* Substances which allow charge to flow through them are conductors. Metals are good conductors.
* Substances which do not allow charge to flow through them are insulators. Plastics are good insulators.
* A gold-leaf electroscope consists of a metal case, with a metal cap which is attached to two metal leaves by a metal rod. The rod is insulated from the case.
* An electroscope is used for showing if a body is charged or not; showing if a body is charged negatively or positively; showing if a body is a conductor or an insulator.
* Thunder and lightning result from the passage of charge between a cloud and the earth or between two clouds.

Questions

Section A

1. When a plastic rod is rubbed with a cloth both become . ...
2. The two types of charge are called .... and .....
3. Like charges ....; unlike charges ....
4. Substances which allow charge to flow through them are called .... Those which do not are called ....
5. It is not normally possible to charge a .... by rubbing it.
6. It is not posible to charge an insulator by ....
7. If a positively charged rod is used to charge an electroscope by induction the charge on the electroscope is ....
8. If a .... perspex rod is brought near to a ..... polythene rod they attract each other.
9. Why are the hoses used to refuel aircraft usually earthed?.. ....
10. Why is a shock sometimes felt when touching an earthed object after walking on a nylon carpet? ....
11. Why does dust collect on a record? ....
12. A positively charged body has lost .... A negatively charged body has gained ....
13. An uncharged body has equal amounts of ....
14. Name four parts of an electroscope ....
15. During a thunder storm what causes the thunder? ....

Section B

1. Explain, in terms of electrons, how a perspex rod becomes charged when it is rubbed with a cloth. Describe an experiment which shows that the rod and the cloth carry opposite charges and that there is the same amount of charge on each.
2. Explain how a body may be charged by induction.

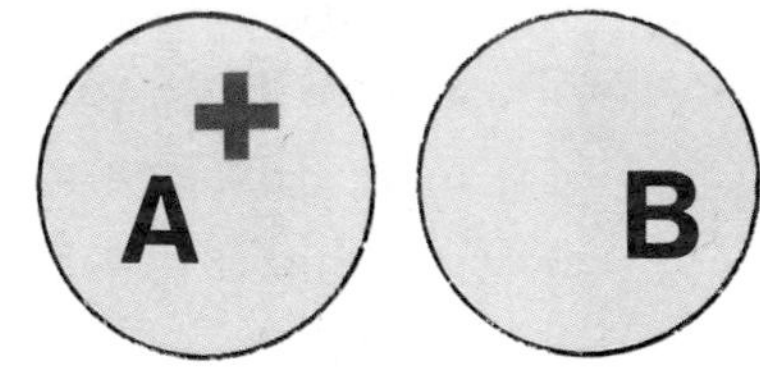

Fig. I

Fig. I shows two metal spheres close to each other. Sphere A carries a positive charge. What charge will be on B if it is first earthed and then removed from A? Explain, in terms of electrons, how B comes to have this charge.

3. Draw a labelled diagram of a gold-leaf electroscope. Explain how an electroscope may be used to show (i) whether a body is a conductor or an insulator; (ii) whether a body is positively charged or negatively charged.

41 — Current Electricity

41.1 Electric Currents

In the last chapter we dealt with electric charges at rest. In this chapter we shall learn what happens when charges are moving from one place to another.

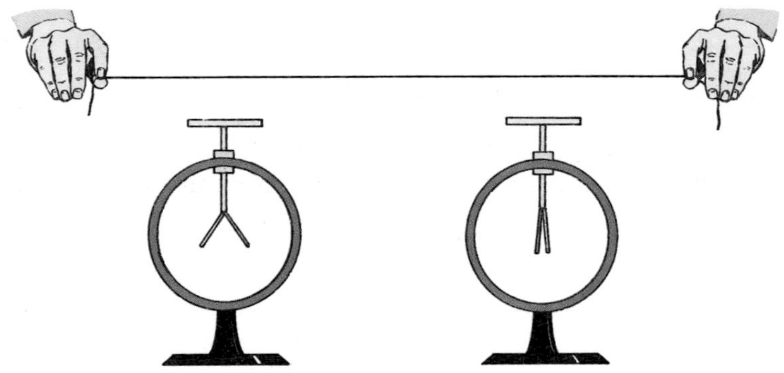

Fig. 41.1

Take two electroscopes. Place them side by side and charge one of them by induction. Now, drop a thread across the caps of both electroscopes, *Fig. 41.1.* Result: the leaves of the charged electroscope fall slowly while the leaves of the other electroscope rise. This continues until the leaves of both electroscopes are approximately the same height. It is clear from this that charge has flowed from one electroscope to the other through the thread. The flow of charge from one place to another is called an electric current. The symbol for current is *I.*

An electric current is a flow of charge.

Electric current is measured in amperes, in honour of the French physicist, André Marie Ampère, who did much of the early work on current electricity. The ampere is often referred to as the amp. and the symbol for it is A.

You will remember from the last chapter that charge cannot flow through an insulator. That is, current can only flow in conductors. Most conductors are metals and in these the charge is carried by electrons. We say that the **charge carriers** in a metal are electrons.

Potential Difference

Fig.41.2 shows two tanks of water connected by a pipe with a tap on it. The water in tank A is deeper than the water in tank B. Since pressure depends on depth *(see Chapter 4)*, the pressure at the end of the pipe in A is greater than the pressure at the end of the pipe in B. There is a pressure difference between the two ends of the pipe. If the tap is opened the water will flow from A into B and it will continue to flow until the water is the same depth in both tanks. In other words, the water flows until there is no pressure difference between the two ends of the pipe. Thus, water flows from one place to another if there is a pressure difference between them.

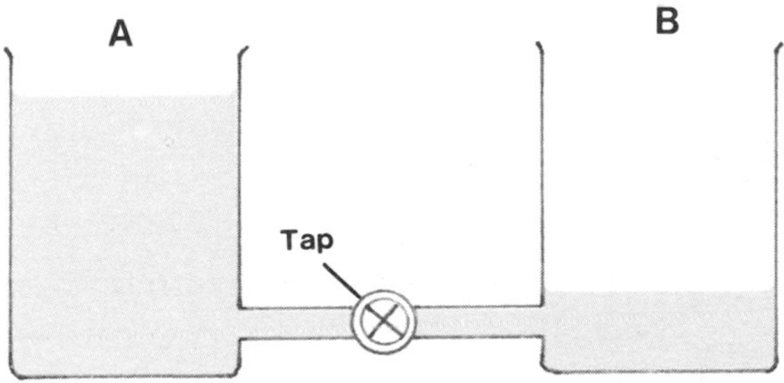

Fig. 41.2

The experiment above with the two electroscopes is similar to the two tanks of water. The electroscopes are two "tanks" of charge. When we connect one to the other with a "pipe", charge flows from one to the other. In this case we say that there is a **potential difference** between the two electroscopes. You can think of potential as a sort of "electrical pressure". Thus, if there is a potential difference between two points, charge will flow from one to the other and it will continue to flow until there is no potential difference between the two points. Of course, just as water cannot flow from one tank to the other if there is no pipe joining them, so charge cannot flow from one body to another unless there is a conductor joining them.

Potential difference is measured in **volts**, in honour of the Italian scientist, Alesandro Volta. The symbol for the volt is V. Because of the unit in which it is measured potential difference is sometimes referred to as voltage.

41.2 Cells and Batteries

One way of producing a potential difference between one body and another is to charge one of them, either by rubbing or by induction. While it is possible to generate quite large potential differences in this way, the amounts of charge produced are extremely small and so any currents which flow are also extremely small. Nevertheless, these were the only known ways of producing electricity for around two thousand years.

The Simple Cell

A simple cell is a device for generating a potential difference between two points by means of a chemical reaction. The first such cell was invented by Alesandro Volta in 1794.

Experiment 41.1 To Make a Simple Cell

Method

1. Fill a beaker approximately half full with dilute sulphuric acid.

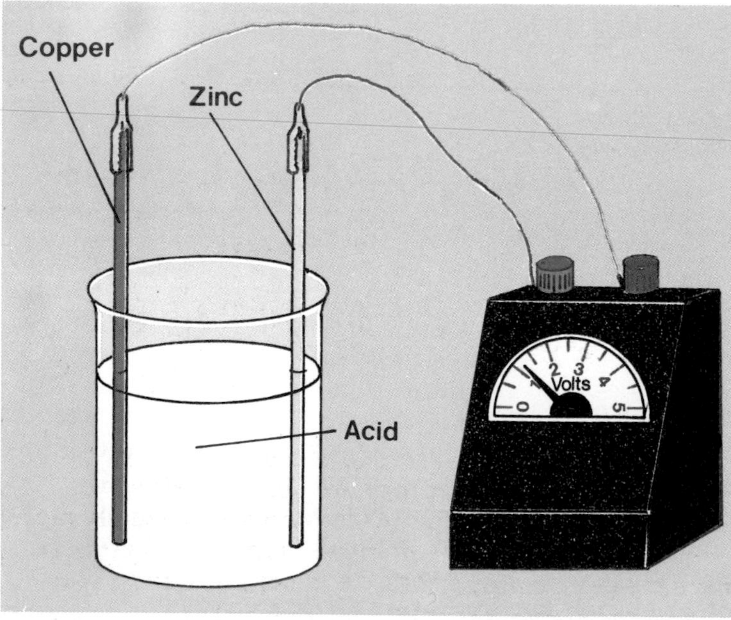

Fig. 41.3 A simple cell

2. Connect a voltmeter to two carbon rods using leads and crocodile clips and place the carbon rods in the acid. (Note: A voltmeter measures the potential difference between two points.) Note the reading on the voltmeter.
3. Replace one of the carbon rods with various metals, e.g. iron, copper, zinc. Record the voltmeter reading in each case.
4. Repeat for pairs of metals, e.g. copper and iron, iron and zinc, etc. Record your results in the form of a table.

Conclusion

When two different metals are placed in the acid a potential difference is produced. The size of the potential difference generated depends on the pair of metals used. (Note: Where electricity is concerned, carbon behaves in a similar way to metals.)

This arrangement of two metals, or one metal and carbon, in an acid is a **simple cell**. The metals are called **electrodes** and the acid is an **electrolyte**.

The Dry Cell

The modern dry cell, *Fig. 41.4*, is very similar to the original simple cell invented by Volta.The electrodes are carbon and zinc and the electrolyte is ammonium chloride. To prevent the ammonium chloride spilling, it is made into a paste by mixing it with flour and gum. The zinc electrode also serves as the case. Manganese dioxide is added to remove the hydrogen which is produced around the carbon electrode. If this hydrogen were not removed it would quickly reduce the potential difference between the electrodes.

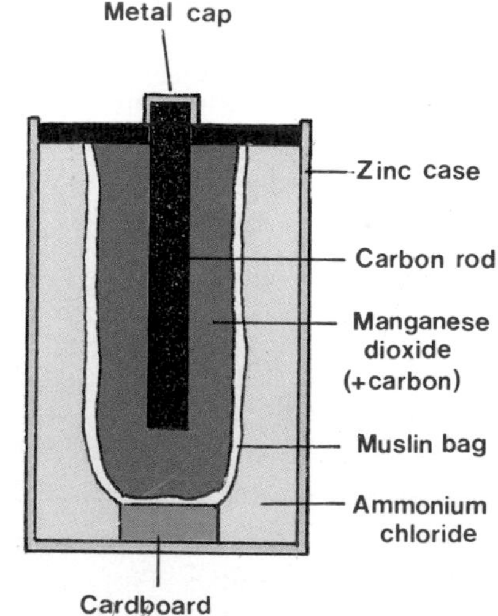

Fig. 41.4 A dry cell

The maximum potential between the terminals of a zinc/carbon cell is 1.5 V.

Primary and Secondary Cells

The cells described so far are called **primary cells.** The chemical reactions which produce the current cannot be reversed. Therefore, when the electrolyte is used up, the cell cannot be recharged. It is dangerous to attempt to recharge a primary cell.

Cells in which the chemical reactions are reversible are called **secondary cells.** (They are also called **accumulators** or **storage cells.**) These may be recharged by driving a current through them in the opposite direction to the direction in which they supply current. This type of cell is used in car batteries and in the rechargeable batteries in calculators, etc.

Batteries

There are many different types of cell. However, the largest potential difference which can be obtained from a single cell is little more than 2 V. To obtain larger potential differences a number of cells may be connected together. This is usually done by connecting the positive terminal of one cell to the negative terminal of the next and so on. Such an arrangement of cells is called a battery. Since the potential difference between the terminals of a single carbon/zinc cell is 1.5 V, a 6 V battery consists of 4 cells connected in this way, a 9 V battery consists of 6 cells, and so on.

Fig. 41.5 A 9 V battery containing 6 cells

Experiment 41.2 To Investigate the Effect of Connecting Cells in Series

Method

1. Collect four cells and label them A. B. C. & D. Connect a voltmeter, which will measure 6 V, across each cell in turn and record the reading in your book. (The red terminal of the voltmeter should be connected to the positive side of the cell).
2. Now connect the negative side of A to the positive side of B so they make a battery of 2 cells. Connect the voltmeter to the positive side of A and the negative side of B. Record the reading.
3. Repeat step 2 with (i) C & D (ii) A, B & C (iii) B, C & D and (iv) A, B, C, & D always connecting the negative side of one cell to the positive side of the next. The cells follow one another and are said to be in **series**. Record all your readings in a table (as shown below). Can you see any relationship between the values you have?

Cells	A	B	C	D	A & B	C & D	A, B & C	B, C & D	A, B C & D
Voltage (Volts)									

Conclusion

When the voltage of each cell is measured they are very similar. However when A & B are connected together the total voltage is the sum of A plus B. All other arrangments also give the sum of the individual voltages for the cells involved.

You might like to see what happens when one of the cells is turned round in each of the above arrangements.

Power Supplies

Batteries are a convenient source of electrical energy, their main advantage being that they are portable. However, they are also expensive. In the laboratory it is usually more convenient to use low voltage power supplies. These take current from the mains at 240 V and supply current at low voltages, usually in the range 1 V to 24 V. They also convert the alternating current from the mains to direct current. (The current obtained from a battery is direct current (d.c). It flows in one direction only — from the positive terminal to the negative terminal. The current supplied by the

Fig. 41.6 A generating station

Electricity Board is alternating current (a.c.). It flows in one direction for one hundredth of a second and then it flows in the opposite direction for one hundredth of a second.) A power supply has thus two main parts – a **transformer** to change the voltage and a **rectifier** to change the current from a.c. to d.c.

41.3 Electrical Circuits

When you connected the voltmeter to the simple cell in *Experiment 41.1* above, you were making a simple electrical circuit. An electrical circuit consists of a number of electrical devices connected by conductors, usually wires, to a battery or power supply. When drawing a diagram of an electrical circuit it is normal to use symbols for the different parts. If you consider that the radio or a television may have hundreds of parts you will realise that it would

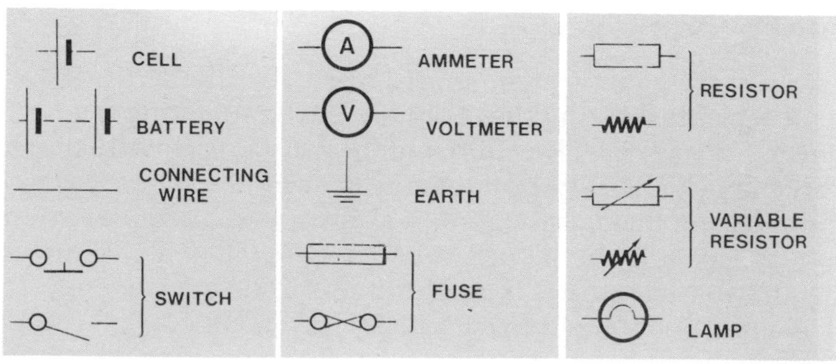

Fig. 41.7 Electrical symbols

be impossible to draw a circuit diagram containing a 'picture' of each part. *Fig. 41.7* shows the symbols for some of the more common components.

A circuit must always consist of a continuous conducting path from one terminal of the battery to the other. If there is any break in the circuit or if any part of the circuit is not a conductor, a current cannot flow.

Experiment 41.3 Making a Circuit

Method

1. Connect a cell to a light bulb using loose wires or a circuit board. What do you see happen?
2. Now make a gap in the circuit by removing one of the connectors. Does the bulb still light?
3. Replace that connector and remove another. What happens? Does it make any difference which connector you remove?

Conclusion

When the cell and light bulb are connected, the bulb lights but as soon as a connector is removed it goes out.

When the lamp lights, we say an electric current is flowing around the circuit. This current is said to flow from the positive side of the battery to the negative side. For a current to flow we must have a complete circuit with no gaps.

The circuit you made can be recorded by drawing a diagram using the symbols. *(see Fig. 41.8)*

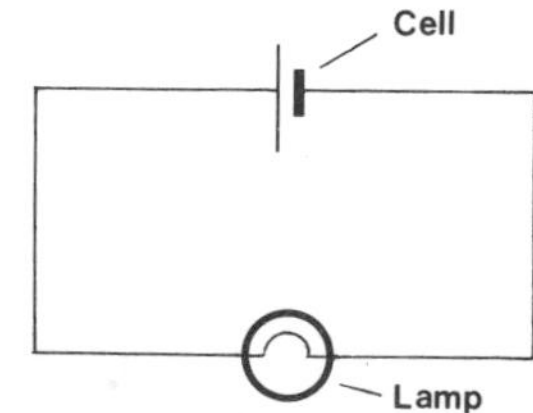

Fig. 41.8 Simple circuit

In the experiment above you were making the lamp light and go out by creating a gap in the circuit and then closing it again. You were in fact controlling when the bulb was alight by switching the current on and off. *Fig. 41.9* shows some light switches found around the home.

Fig. 41.9 Photograph of switches, a timer switch, and old style fuses

The bulb in the circuit only tells us if a current is flowing but it does not tell us how large the current is. To do that we need a special meter called an **Ammeter**.

Current

Using the ammeter we can investigate where the current flows, the size of the current and what may affect its value. When a current flows in a circuit, it must flow through all the circuit not just part of it.

Experiment 41.4 Movement of Charge in a Circuit

Method

1. Connect up the circuit shown in *Fig. 41.10 (a).* Close the switch and the lamp will light.

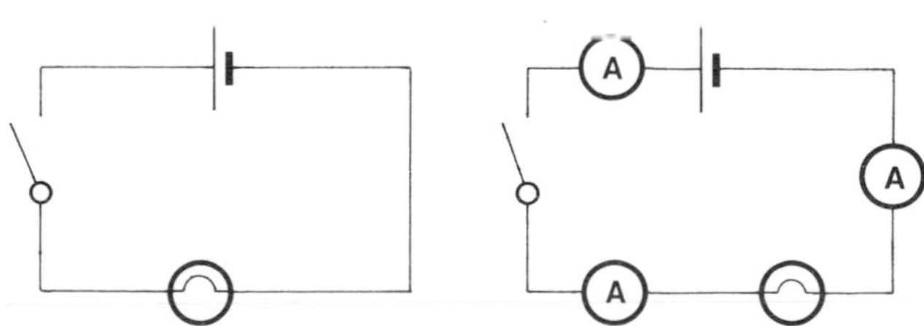

Fig. 41.10 (a) & (b) Circuit containing Ammeters

2. Switch off the lamp and add to the circuit three identical ammeters in the positions shown in *Fig. 41.10 (b).*
3. Now close the switch again and take the reading of each ammeter.

Conclusion

When the switch is closed all the ammeters have the same reading. Thus the **same current** flows through the circuit. Now we need to know how the value of the current can be changed. If we look at the circuit there are only two things which can be altered, (i) the number of cells, (ii) the number of bulbs. We only need one ammeter in our new circuit as the current is the same in all parts of the circuit.

Experiment 41.5 To Observe the Effect of Changing the Number of Cells

Method

1. Set up the circuit shown in *Fig. 41.11.* Close the switch and record the ammeter reading.

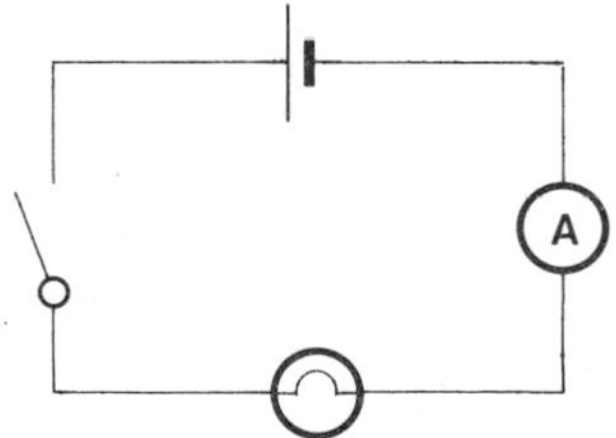

Fig. 41.11 Circuit diagram

2. Open the switch and then connect a second cell in the circuit. Make sure that the positive terminal of one is connected to the negative terminal of the other. Close the switch and note the reading on the ammeter.
3. Place a third cell in the circuit, again connecting it so that it increases the voltage of the battery. Close the switch and record the ammeter reading.

Conclusion

As the number of cells is increased the reading on the ammeter becomes larger. Adding cells to the circuit increases the voltage (electrical push) in the circuit and this means that a larger current will flow.

Experiment 41.6 To Observe the Effect of Changing the Number of Bulbs

Method

1. Set up the circuit shown in *Fig. 41.11.* Close the switch and record the ammeter reading.
2. Switch off the light and connect another bulb in the circuit. Close the switch and record the ammeter reading.
3. Repeat step 2 twice, then switch off the circuit.

Conclusion

When the number of bulbs is increased, the ammeter reading decreases, that is the current becomes smaller. The reason for this, is that each bulb has a resistance and increasing the number of bulbs increases the resistance.

Resistance

Current is the flow of electrons through the material. This flow is always opposed to some extent by forces between the moving electrons and the stationary atoms, of which the material is made. It is also limited by the number of electrons which can move.

This opposition to the movement of the electrons is called the resistance of the material. The greater the opposition, the smaller the current which flows.

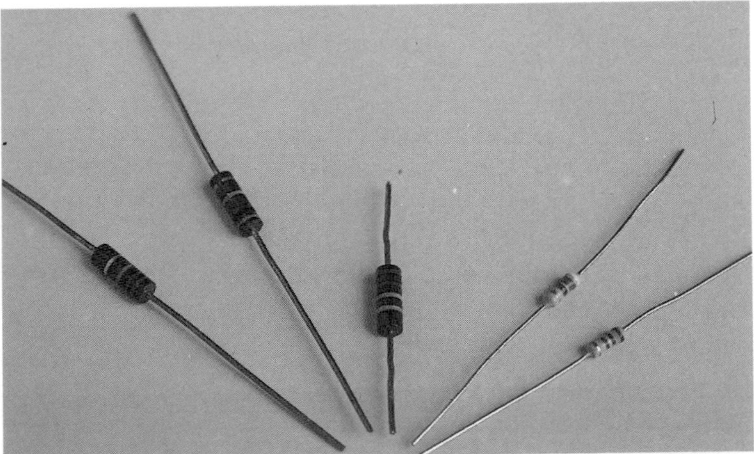

Fig. 41.12 A selection of resistors

Metals generally have a low resistance while insulators have an extremely high resistance — so high that, for most practical purposes, no current can flow through them. Resistance is measured in ohms, after the German physicist, Georg Simon Ohm. The symbol for the ohm is Ω.

Resistors are used in radios, televisions, record players, etc. to control the current flowing in various circuits. Resistors can have resistances as low as a few ohms or as high as millions of ohms. They are usually made of either wire (those which have to carry large currents) or carbon. Resistors whose resistance is variable are also available. These are called **rheostats** or **potentiometers**. The volume control of a radio or telvision, for example, is a potentiometer.

Voltage, Current and Resistance

It should be clear from what we have said so far in this chapter that there is a connection between voltage, current and resistance in a circuit.In general terms, the larger the voltage the larger the current and the larger the resistance the smaller the current. The exact relationship between voltage and current was first established by Ohm in 1827 and is now known as *Ohm's Law.* This states that, at constant temperature, voltage is proportional to current. In other words, voltage divided by current is constant. This constant is, in fact, the resistance. So, we have:

$$\textbf{Resistance} = \frac{\textbf{Voltage}}{\textbf{Current}}$$

Therefore,

$$\textbf{Voltage} = \textbf{Current} \times \textbf{Resistance}$$
$$V = I \times R$$

Example 1

A 9 V battery is connected to a resistor whose resistance is 2 Ω. What is the current flowing in the circuit?

$$V = I \times R$$
$$9 = I \times 2$$
$$I = 4.5\ A$$

Ans. 4.5 *A*.

Example 2

Calculate the current flowing in the circuit shown in Fig. 41.13.

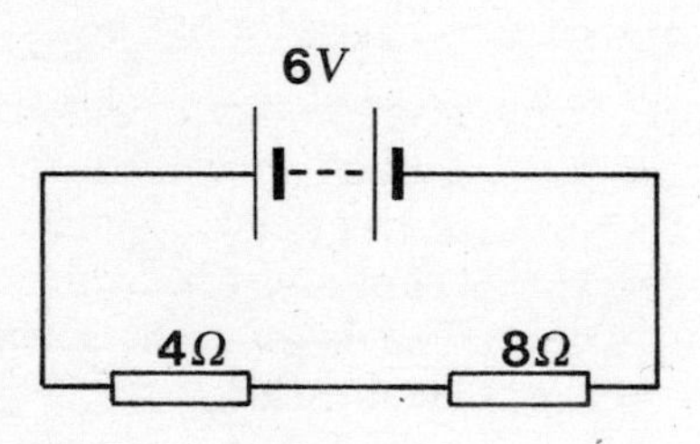

Fig. 41.13

The total resistance is

$$R\ 13 = 4 + 8$$
$$= 12\ \Omega$$
$$\text{Using } V = I \times R$$
$$6 = I \times 12$$
$$I = 0.5\ A$$

Ans. 0.5 *A*.

Experiment 41.7 To Measure the Resistance of a Length of Wire

Method

1. Connect up the circuit as shown in *Fig. 41.14*, with the length of wire in a beaker of water so that it will not get warm.

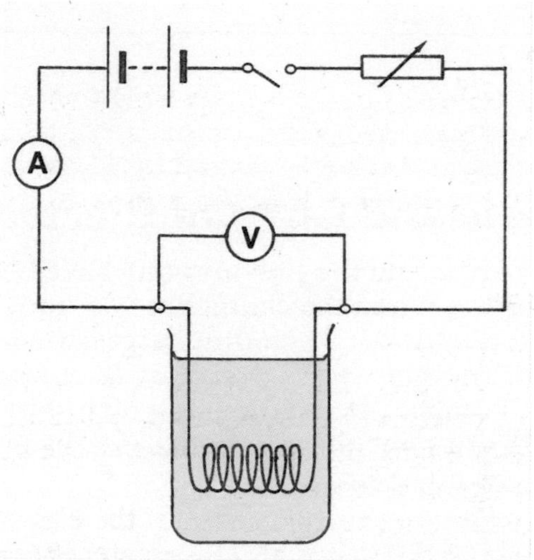

Fig. 41.14

2. Switch on the current and adjust the rheostat to give a current of 0.1 A. Read the potential difference between the ends of the wire. Record the voltage and current in a table as shown below.
3. Using the rheostat, increase the current. Record the new voltage and current.
4. Repeat Step 3 five or six times.
5. Calculate the resistance for each value of the voltage and current.
   Calculate the average value of the resistance.
6. Draw a graph of voltage against current.

Conclusion

The graph of voltage against current is a straight line through the origin showing that the voltage is proportional to the current.

RESULTS

V/volts	I/amps	$V/I = R$/ohms

41.4 Static and Current Electricity

Both this chapter and the previous one have been all about electric charges. When the charges are not moving we talk about static electricity; when the charges are moving from one place to another we are dealing with current electricity. There are a number of experiments which show that we are dealing with the same thing in both cases, even though the effects may be different.

Experiment 41.8 To Show that Static Electricity and Current Electricity are Equivalent

Method

1. Connect a sensitive current-measuring meter between the dome of a Van de Graaff generator and earth. When the generator is running the meter registers a current. This shows that the charge flowing from the dome of the generator to earth is in fact a current.
2. Hold a tube from a fluorescent lamp near the Van de Graff generator and it will light. Hold the tube near a charged rod and it will light briefly. Again, this shows that charges, when they move, have the same effect as a current.
3. Connect a high voltage power supply to a gold-leaf electroscope. The leaves move apart, showing that current from a power supply can charge an electroscope in the same way as charge from a plastic rod.

Conclusion

State electricity and current electricity are essentially the same (equivalent).

Summary

* Electric current is the flow of charge from one place to another. The symbol for current is I and it is measured in amperes (A).
* The charge carriers in metals are electrons.
* A current will flow from one point to another if there is a potential difference between them. Potential difference is measured in volts (V) and is also called voltage.
* A simple cell consists of two metals (or one metal and carbon) in an electrolyte.
* A dry cell consists of carbon and zinc in ammonium chloride.
* The resistance of a conductor is a measure of its opposition to the movement of charge through it.
* Voltage = Current × Resistance: $V = I \times R$.

Questions

Section A

1. An electric current is a flow of ....
2. The charge carriers in a metal are ....
3. If there is a potential difference between two points a .... will flow from one to the other provided that they are joined by a ....
4. Potential difference is sometimes called ....
5. The unit of potential difference is the ....
6. Potential difference is to .... as .... is to flow of water.
7. What are the essential parts of a simple cell? ....
   ....
8. What are the electrodes in a dry cell made of? ....
   ....
9. What is a battery? ....
   ....
10. When a battery is connected in a circuit, current flows from the .... terminal to the .... terminal.
11. If a conductor has a low .... current flows easily through it.
12. The unit of resistance is the ....
13. .... = Current × ....
14. When a 12 V battery is connected to a 4 ohm resistor the current flowing in the circuit is ....
15. In a .... cell the chemical reactions cannot be reversed and so the cell cannot be ....
16. A cell which can be recharged is called a .... cell, an .... or a .... cell.
17. The amount of current flowing in a circuit depends on the .... and the ....
18. How many cells are in a 22.5 V zinc-carbon battery? ...
    ....
19. Why is there manganese dioxide in a dry cell? ....
    ....

Section B

1. What is meant by the terms: current; potential difference; resistance?
   What is the unit of each of these quantities?
   What is the relationship between them?
2. Describe, with the aid of a labelled diagram, a simple cell.
3. What is the resistance of the resistor in the circuit shown in *Fig. I*, if the current flowing is 0.75 A?

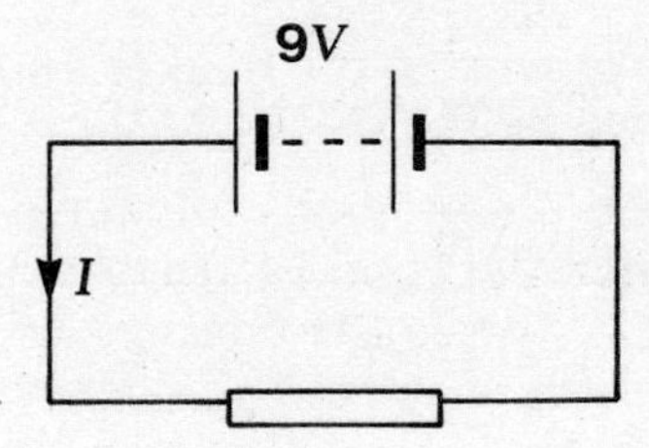

Fig. I

4. What is the current flowing in the circuit shown in *Fig. II?* What is the potential difference across the 4 Ω resistor?

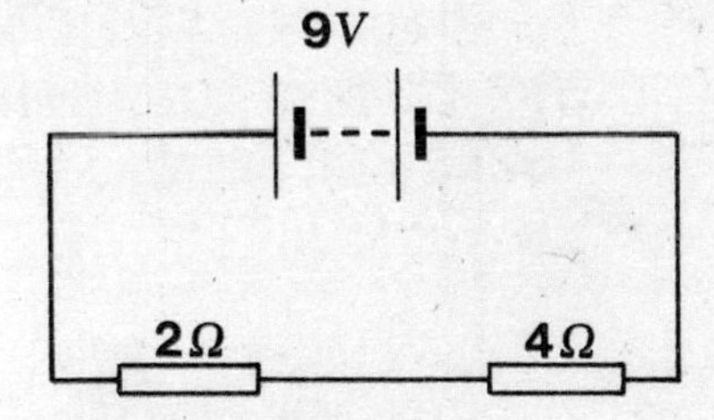

Fig. II

42 — Effects of Electric Current

42.1 Heating Effect

That an electric current has a heating effect should be obvious when you think of the number of devices which use electricity for heating in your home. These may include an electric fire, an electric kettle, an iron, an immersion heater, an electric cooker, etc. The heating effect of an electric current may be demonstrated in the laboratory as follows.

Experiment 42.1 To Demonstrate the Heating Effect of an Electric Current

Method

1. Half fill a beaker with cold water. Note the temperature of the water.
2. Place a small coil of wire in the beaker and connect up the circuit as shown in *Fig. 42.1.*

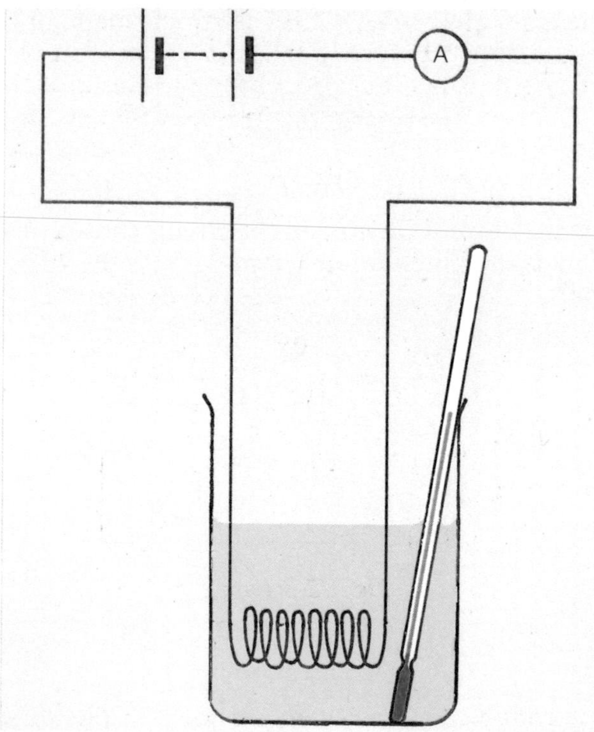

Fig. 42.1

3. Note the current flowing and the temperature at 5 minute intervals.

Conclusion

While the current is flowing, the temperature of the water rises steadily. Therefore, an electric current has a heating effect.

The arrangement used in this experiment is really a simple electric kettle or immersion heater. All the electrical devices referred to above work on the same principle. The coil of wire which carries the current in each case is known as the element and it is usually wrapped on a ceramic former and surrounded by a metal case.

When an electric current flows through a wire, electrical energy is converted to internal energy in the wire. As a result the temperature of the wire rises and heating of the surroundings then takes place by one of the three methods described in *Chapter 35.*

The rate at which this energy is converted is known as the power and is measured in watts. It can be calculated using the following equation:—

$$\text{Watts} = \text{Amps} \times \text{Volts}$$

Example 1

Calculate the power of a heater which when connected to a 240 V supply draws 5A.

Using the equaion:

$$\begin{aligned}\text{Power (watts)} &= \text{Amps} \times \text{Volts}\\ &= 5 \times 240\\ &= 1200 \text{ watts } (1.2\text{kW})\end{aligned}$$

Ans. 1200 Watts (1.2kW)

The equation can also be used to find the current flowing in a device.

Example 2

Find the current flowing through the element of a 2 kW fire when it is connected to the mains.

$$\begin{aligned}\text{Power} &= \text{Amps} \times \text{Volts}\\ 2000 &= \text{I} \times 240\\ \text{I} &= \frac{2000}{240}\\ &= 8.3 \text{ A}\end{aligned}$$

Ans. 8.3 A

The Kilowatt-Hour

When your parents receive a bill from the Electricity Board essentially what you are being charged for is the amount of energy converted from electrical to other forms in your home over the three month period. The unit of energy is the joule. However, the joule is a rather small unit so the Electricity Board uses a unit called the **kilowatt-hour (kWh)**.

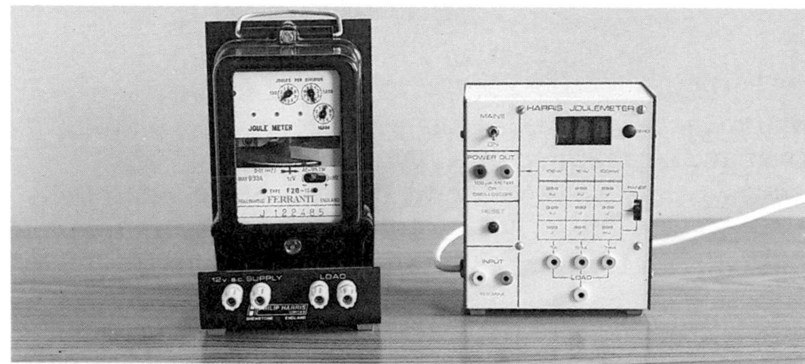

Fig. 42.2 Joulemeters (a) similar to the type used by the Electricity Board; (b) a digital type used in laboratories

> **The kilowatt-hour is the amount of electrical energy converted to other forms in one hour when the rate of working is one kilowatt, i.e. 1000 J per second.**

Thus, if you use a 1 kW electric fire for 1 h you will have used 1 kW h or 1 **Unit** of electricity. Similarly, a 2 kW fire used for half an hour uses 1 Unit as does a 100 W bulb for 10 hours.

Example

Calculate the total cost of using a 100 W bulb for 5 h; a 2 kW fire for 3 h; a 5kW immersion heater for 2 h and a 50 W TV for 10 h if 1 Unit costs 5½p.

100 W for 5 h = 0.5 kW h
2 kW for 3 h = 6.0 kW h
5 kW for 2 h = 10.0 kW h
50 W for 10 h = 0.5 kW h
Total = 17.0 kW h
17 Units at 5½p = 93½p

Ans. 93½p

Fuses

When a current flows through a wire it becomes warm. How warm it will become depends on its resistance and on the current flowing through it. When wires are used for connecting electrical appliances to the mains it is important that they do not become too warm, otherwise a fire might result. The current flowing in a particular circuit depends on the appliance (or appliances) connected in the circuit. (In *example 2*, we saw that a 2 kW fire draws a current of 8.3.A.) Thus, the only way of keeping the connecting wires from becoming warm is to keep their resistance as low as possible. The larger the current which has to flow in the wires the lower their resistance must be. Thus, wires to an electric cooker, for example, are very thick and are made of copper.

A fuse is a device which is designed to switch off the current in a circuit if, for whatever reason, the current flowing in the circuit becomes larger than the circuit was designed to carry. A fuse consists of a short length of wire in a porcelain holder, *Fig. 42.3*. The wire is made of a special alloy which melts at a fairly low temperature. When current flows through the wire it becomes warm. If the current is larger than a certain value the wire becomes so hot that it melts.

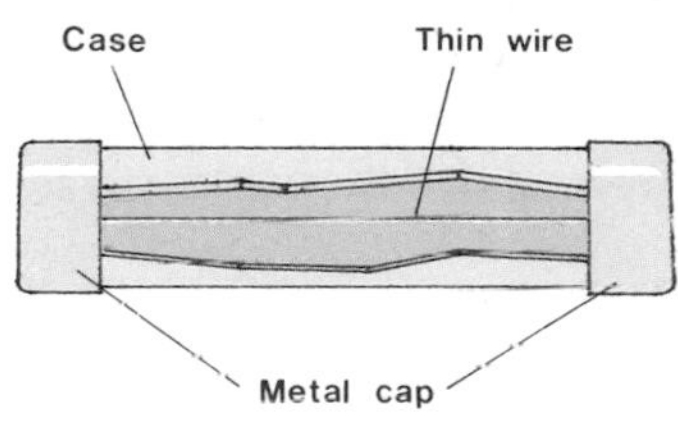

Fig. 42.3 Fuse

A fuse is connected in a circuit as shown in *Fig. 42.4* so that when the fuse wire melts no current can flow in the circuit. Fuses are available with various ratings, e.g. 3 A, 5 A, 42 A, and so on. This means that they will melt if currents greater than these flow through them.

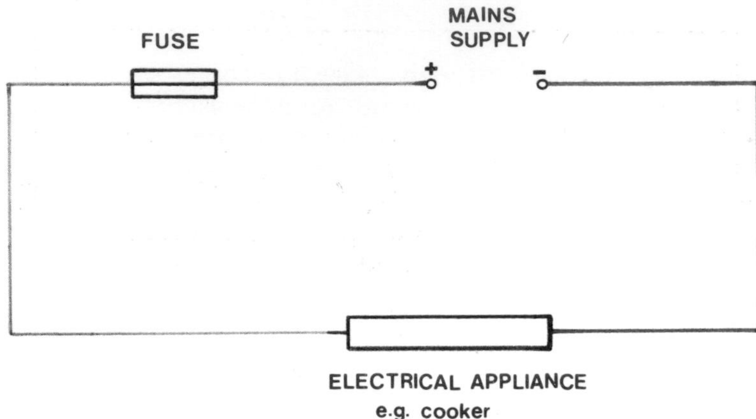

Fig. 42.4

It is very important that a fuse of the correct rating be fitted in a circuit. If a fuse of a higher rating is fitted a current may flow in the circuit which will cause some part of the circuit to overheat and perhaps start a fire. Under no circumstances should a fuse ever be replaced with a piece of ordinary wire or with a piece of tinfoil.

While a fuse greatly reduces the risk of fire it does not give any protection against electric shock. Most household fuses will carry at least 1 A, while a current of a few thousandths of an ampere is sufficient to kill. In any case, a fuse would not melt quickly enough.

There are generally two types of circuit in a house — a lighting circuit and a power circuit. A lighting circuit will have a number of lights connected in it and is usually protected by a 15 A fuse at the distribution board near the meter. A power circuit has a number of sockets connected in it and is usually protected by a 30 A fuse at the distribution board. In addition, appliances connected to a power circuit by plugs *(see below)* are protected by smaller fuses in the plugs. The rating of the fuse to be used with a particular appliance can be calculated from a knowledge of the power rating of the appliance.

Example

What fuse should be used in a plug which is to be connected to a 750 W vacuum cleaner?

First, we must calculate the current which will be drawn by the vacuum cleaner.

$$\text{Power, } P = V \times I$$
$$750 = 240 \times I$$
$$I = 750/240$$
$$= 3.1 \text{ A}$$

The current drawn by the cleaner is 3.1 A. The correct fuse is rated 5 A, the next highest rating above 3.1 A.

Ans. 5 A fuse.

Earthing

Two wires lead from your local transformer sub-station to your home. One of these is called the neutral and is connected to the earth. The other is called the live or phase wire and it is at a voltage of 240 V relative to the neutral. That is, there is a potential difference of 240 V between the two wires. Therefore, if one wire is connected to the other by a conductor a current will flow, the size of the current depending on the resistance of the conductor. As the neutral is connected to earth, any conductor which connects the live wire to earth will experience a current. The human body is a conductor, so if you touch a live wire a current will flow through you to earth. In most cases, the size of this current will be enough to kill you.

If a fault occurs in an electric kettle, for example, such that the body of the kettle comes in contact with the live wire, anyone touching the kettle would get an electric shock and could be killed. To prevent this happening, all appliances which have a metal body must be earthed. This means that the body of the appliance must be connected to the ground with a length of copper wire. Now if the body comes in contact with the live wire the resulting current will flow directly to earth. Since the earth connection is of low resistance copper wire the current will usually be large enough to blow the fuse in the plug.

Plugs

Most electrical appliances are connected to the mains by means of plugs. Most of these plugs have three terminals as shown in *Fig. 42.5* and it is essential that each terminal be connected to the proper wire. Looking into the plug with the cover removed, the right hand terminal (with the fuse) is the live(L), the left hand terminal is the neutral(N) and the central terminal is the earth(E). The live terminal must be connected to the brown wire, the neutral to the blue wire and the earth to the wire with the yellow and green stripes. (On older appliances the corresponding colours were red (live), black (neutral) and green (earth).)

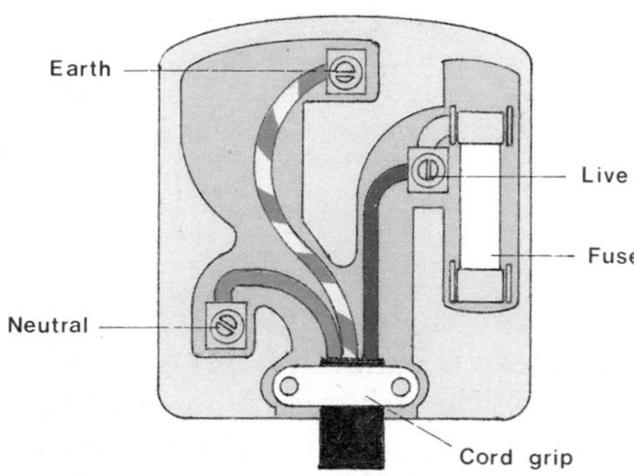

Fig. 42.5 A three-pin plug

Two-pin plugs should only be used on appliances which do not require an earth connection, in general, those which do not have a metal body *(see above)*. Some appliances are "double-insulated". This means that the metal body is doubly insulated from all live parts of the appliance. Such appliances do not require an earth connection. (An older type of two-pin plug, still in use, has an earth terminal on its side. This type of plug is the equivalent of the modern three-pin plug. In this type of plug the yellow/green wire should be connected to the side terminal.)

42.2 Magnetic Effect

In 1819 the Danish physicist, Hans Christian Oersted, noticed that a compass needle, placed near a wire, was deflected when a current flowed in the wire. Further experiment showed that there is always a magnetic field around a wire in which a current is flowing.

Experiment 42.2 To Demonstrate the Magnetic Effect of a Current

Method

1. Connect a length of wire to a battery or low voltage power supply through an ammeter, *Fig. 42.6*, and hold the wire parallel to a compass needle.

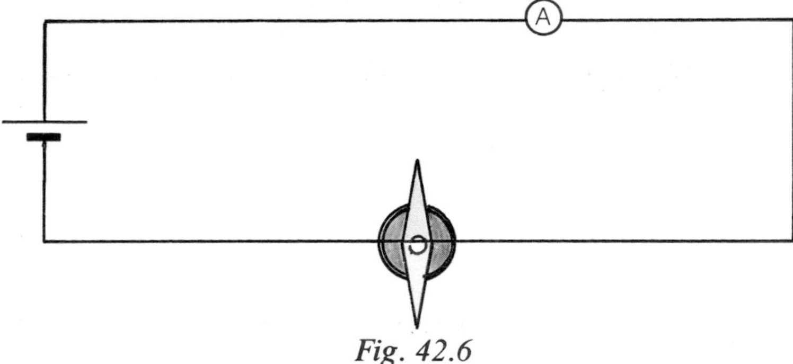

Fig. 42.6

Conclusion

When a current flows in the wire the compass needle turns until it is at right angles to the wire. This shows that a current has a magnetic effect.

The shape of the magnetic field lines depends on the shape of the wire and the direction of the lines depends on the direction in which the current is flowing.

Field Due to a Straight Wire

A straight length of wire is passed vertically through a horizontal sheet of cardboard as shown in *Fig. 42.7*. A current is then passed through the wire by connecting it to a battery or low voltage power supply. The resulting magnetic field may be plotted using iron filings or plotting compasses.

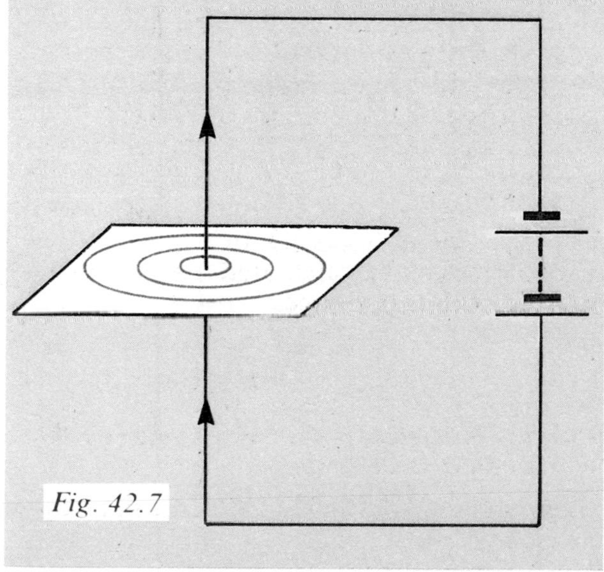

Fig. 42.7

It is found that the magnetic field lines are concentric circles with the wire as centre and are in the directions shown in *Fig. 42.8*.

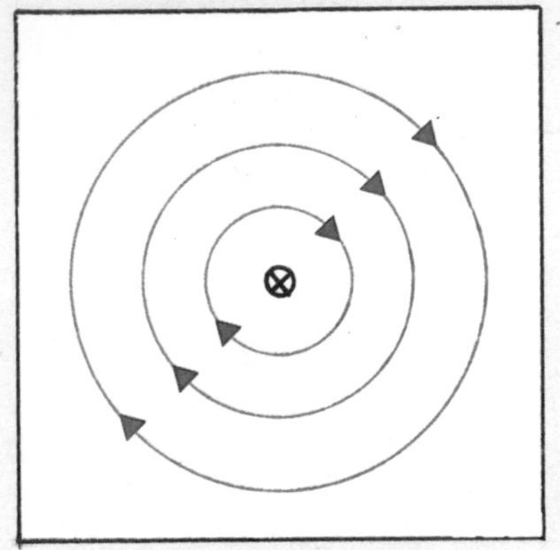

Fig. 42.8 Magnetic field due to current in a straight wire

In *Fig. 42.8* the X represents the current flowing at right angles into the page. If the direction of the current is reversed, the directions of the magnetic field lines are also reversed. An easy way of remembering the directions is illustrated in *Fig. 42.9*. Hold your right hand with the fingers curved as shown and the thumb extended. When the current is flowing in the direction of your thumb the magnetic field lines are in the directions indicated by your fingers.

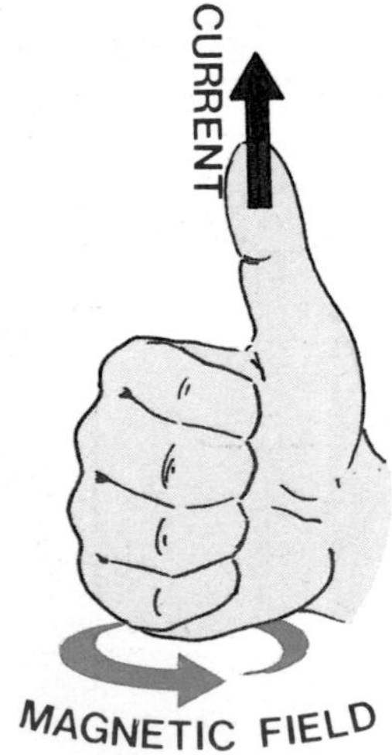

Fig. 42.9 Right hand rule

Magnetic Field Due to a Coil

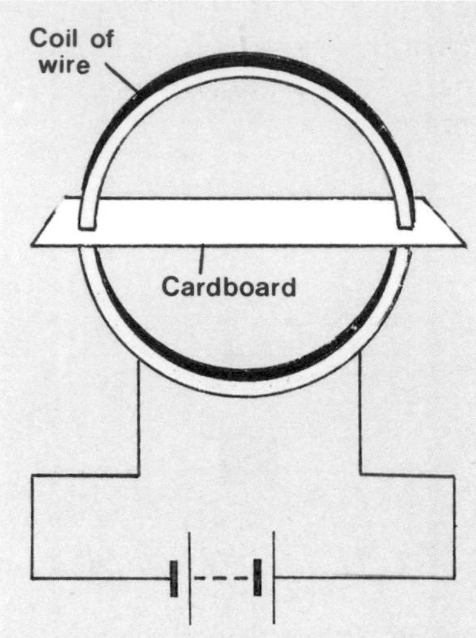

Fig. 42.10

A coil is a length of wire wrapped around in the shape of a circle a number of times. The magnetic field due to a coil may be plotted in a similar way as was done for a straight wire. *Fig. 42.10* shows a vertical coil passing through a horizontal sheet of cardboard. The resulting pattern on the cardboad when a current flows through the coil is as shown in *Fig. 42.11*. The current is flowing vertically into the page at ⊗ and vertically out of the page at ⊙.

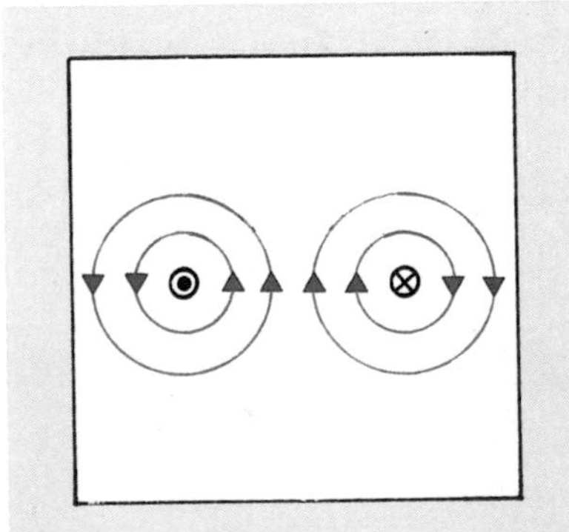

Fig. 42.11 Magnetic field due to current in a coil

Magnetic Field Due to a Solenoid

A solenoid is simply a long coil. The magnetic field due to a solenoid may be plotted as in the two previous cases and the result is as shown in *Fig. 42.12.* Note the similarity between the magnetic field pattern due to a solenoid and that due to a bar magnet.

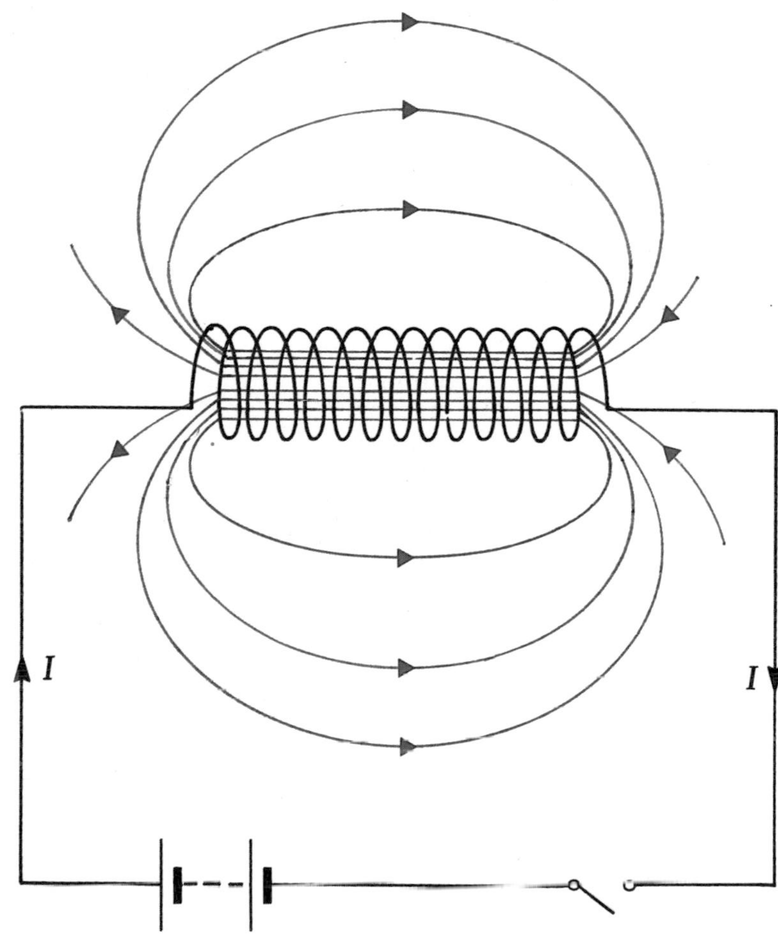

Fig. 42.12 Magnetic field due to current in a solenoid

The Electromagnet

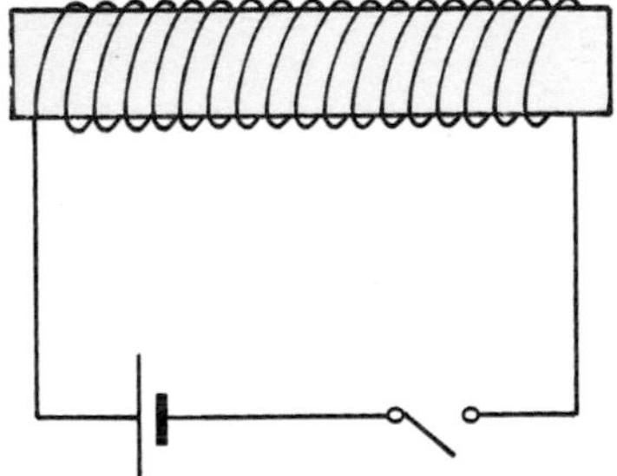

Fig. 42.13

An electromagnet is a solenoid with a piece of iron at its centre, *Fig. 42.13.* The effect of the iron is to increase the strength of the magnetic field by up to 1000 times. When the current is switched off, the iron quickly loses its magnetism. In effect, it is only a magnet while the current is flowing.

Electromagnets have many uses. Large ones, attached to cranes, are used in scrapyards for moving scrap iron and steel. Most electric motors contain electromagnets and they are the basis of the electric bell *(see next section).* They are also the basis of the electromagnetic relay — a device in which a current flowing in an electromagnet is used to switch on or off a current in another circuit.

Fig. 42.14 An electromagnet in a motor

The Electric Bell

The electric bell, *Fig. 42.15* is really an electromagnet in which the current is switched on and off automatically. When the circuit is not switched on the contacts are closed. When the bell push is pressed, the circuit is complete and a current flows through the electromagnet. The magnet attracts the iron bar, causing the hammer to strike the gong and, at the same time, opening the contacts. With the contacts open, current no longer flows through the electromagnet and it ceases to be a magnet. The spring then pulls the iron bar back and re-closes the contacts. The whole cycle of events is then repeated with the result that, while the bell push is pressed, the hammer repeatedly strikes the gong.

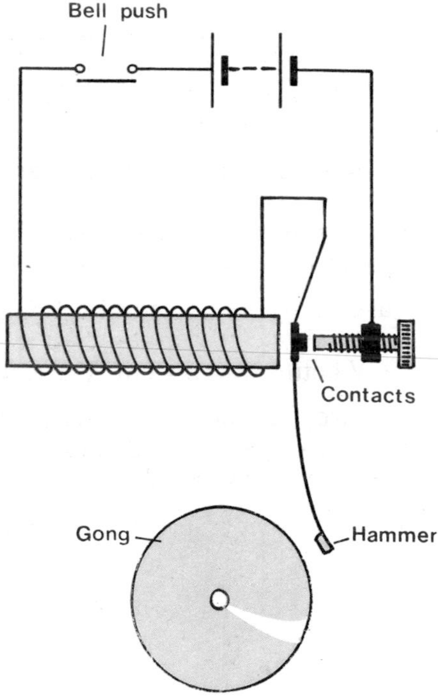

Fig. 42.15 An electric bell

An electric current also has a chemical effect. When it flows through certain liquids, chemical reactions take place. For example, if a current flows through water with a little acid added, it splits up the water into **oxygen** and **hydrogen**. This effect is known as **electrolysis**. The liquid involved is called an **electrolyte**.

Summary

* An electric current has a heating effect. Electric kettles, fires, cookers, immersion heaters, etc. are based on the heating effect of an electric current.
* Power = Voltage × Current. $P = V \times I$. Watts = Volts × Amps.
* 1 kilowatt-hour (1 unit of electricity) is the amount of electrical energy converted to other forms in one hour when the rate of working, i.e. the power, is 1 kW, i.e. 1000 J per second.
* A fuse is a device for switching off the current in a circuit if the current becomes too large. It consists of a piece of wire which melts when the current reaches a certain value.
* Electrical appliances with metal bodies should be earthed. This ensures that a person touching the appliance cannot get a shock from it in the event of a fault.
* The colour code for wiring a plug is: brown — live; blue — neutral; yellow and green — earth.
* A wire carrying a current has a magnetic field around it. The shape of the field lines depends on the shape of the wire and their directions depend on the direction of the current.
* The magnetic field of a solenoid (long coil of wire) is very similar to the magnetic field of a bar magnet.
* An electromagnet is a solenoid with an iron core. It is only a magnet while a current is flowing in the solenoid.
* When a current flows through certain liquids, chemical reactions take place. Such liquids are called electrolytes and the process is called electrolysis.

Questions

Section A

1. Electric kettles, cookers, etc. are based on the .... effect of an electric current.
2. The rate at which energy is converted in a resistor depends on the current .... and on the ....
3. Power =............. × ....
4. The unit of electrical energy used by the Electricity Board is called the ....
5. A fuse consists of ....

   It is used to protect against ....
6. .... = Volts × ....
7. In a three-pin plug the brown wire is connected to .....

   the blue wire to .... and the yellow/green wire to ....
8. What is the cost of using a 3 kW heater for 4 hours if one unit costs 5½p? ....
9. When a current flows through a wire the surrounding space is a ....
10. What is an electromagnet? ....

    ....
11. Which metal is used for the core of an electromagnet? Why? ....

    ....
12. Why would steel not be a suitable material for the core of an electromagnet? ....
13. The kilowatt-hour and the .... are both units of

    ....
14. At what voltage is electricity supplied in (i) your home; (ii) a car?

    ....
15. Which would draw a larger current, a 60 W bulb in a car headlamp or a 60 W bulb in a house? ....
16. The yellow and green wire connects the .... of an appliance to the ....

Section B

1. Describe an experiment which shows that an electric current has a heating effect.
   Calculate the current flowing through a 720 W vacuum cleaner connected to the mains.
2. What is meant by saying that the power of an electric heater is 3 kW?
   What is the current flowing in the element of a 3 kW heater when it is connected to the mains?
3. The following fuse ratings are available: 1 A, 5 A, 13 A. Which should be used in a plug connected to (i) 100 W lamp; (ii) a 2.3 kW kettle; (iii) a 1500 W toaster?
4. Describe how you would plot the magnetic field due to a current in a straight wire. Sketch a diagram of the pattern you would expect to obtain.
5. Draw a labelled diagram of an electric bell and explain how it works.

43 — Energy and Heating

43.1 Heat Capacity

We learned in *Chapter 35* that heating a substance increases its internal energy, that is, it increases the kinetic and potential energy of its molecules. In general, this causes the substance to become hotter — its temperature increases. In this chapter we want to discover if heating always raises the temperature and if the same amount of heating — supplying the same amount of energy — always produces the same increase in temperature.

Suppose we take two identical beakers, one containing 100 g of water and the other containing 200 g of water and we heat both at the same rate for the same length of time. You would probably guess, correctly, that the first beaker would become hotter than the second beaker. In fact, the rise in the temperature of the first beaker would be exactly twice the rise in temperature of the second. Thus, the change in temperature of a body depends not only on the amount of energy transferred to it but also on the mass of the body. If we were to repeat the experiment with 100 g of water and 100 g of copper we would find that the rise in temperature of the copper would be almost eleven times greater than the rise in temperature of the water. From this we see that not only does the rise in temperature depend on the mass of a body it also depends on the type of substance from which the body is made. In order to compare the abilities of different substances to absorb energy we define a quantity called **specific heat capacity**.

The specific heat capacity of a substance is the amount of energy required to change the temperature of 1 Kg of the substance by 1° C.

Example

Calculate the amount of energy required to raise the temperature of 500 g of water from 20° C to 50° C.

The amount of energy required to change the temperature of 1 kg by 1 °C = 4180 J

Therefore, the energy required to change the temperature 0.5 kg by 1 °C = 4180 × 0.5 J

Thus, the energy required to change the temperature of 0.5 kg by 30 °C = 4180 × 0.5 × 30 J
= 62700 J
= 62.7 kJ

Ans. 62.7 kJ.

Energy supplied = Specific Heat Capacity × Mass × Rise in Temperature

This equation also applies when something is cooling. If X J are required to heat a body by 10 °C then X J will be given out when that body cools by 10 °C.

Experiment 43.1 To Measure the Specific Heat Capacity of Paraffin Oil

Method

1. Find the mass of a copper calorimeter.
2. Half-fill the calorimeter with paraffin oil and find the mass of the calorimeter and oil. Subtract to find the mass of the oil.
3. Place the calorimeter in a beaker surrounded by insulation. Place a heating coil in the calorimeter and connect up the circuit as shown in *Fig. 43.1.*

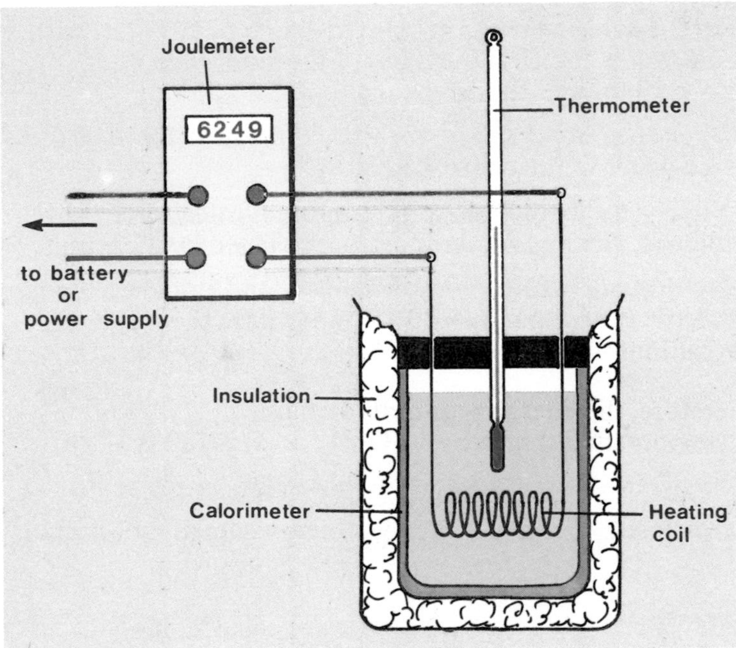

Fig. 43.1

4. Note the temperature of the oil. Zero the joulemeter and switch on.
5. Allow the temperature of the oil to rise by about 10 °C. Switch off the current, note the final temperature of the oil and the number of joules supplied.
6. Record your results as shown below and calculate the specific heat capacity of the oil from the formula:
(Energy supplied = (S.h.c. of copper × Mass of calorimeter × Rise in Temp.) + (S.h.c. of oil × Mass of Oil × Rise in Temp.)

$$E = M_c \times C_c \times (\theta_2 - \theta_1) + M_o \times C_o \times (\theta_1 - \theta_2)$$

RESULTS

Mass of Calorimeter .... = M_c kg

Mass of calorimeter + oil .... = M_t kg

Mass of oil .... = M_o kg

Initial temp. of oil and calorimeter.... = θ_2 °C

Rise in temp. of oil and calorimeter... = θ_2 °C

Energy supplied .... = EJ

Specific heat capacity of copper..... = 390 J/(kg °C)

Specific heat capacity of oil .... = C_OJ/(kg °C).

Note: If a joulemeter is not available the energy supplied can be found by measuring the current flowing, the voltage across the heating coil and the time for which the current flows. The energy supplied is then given by:
(Energy supplied = Current × Voltage × Time.)
The circuit diagram for this method is shown in *Fig. 43.2.*

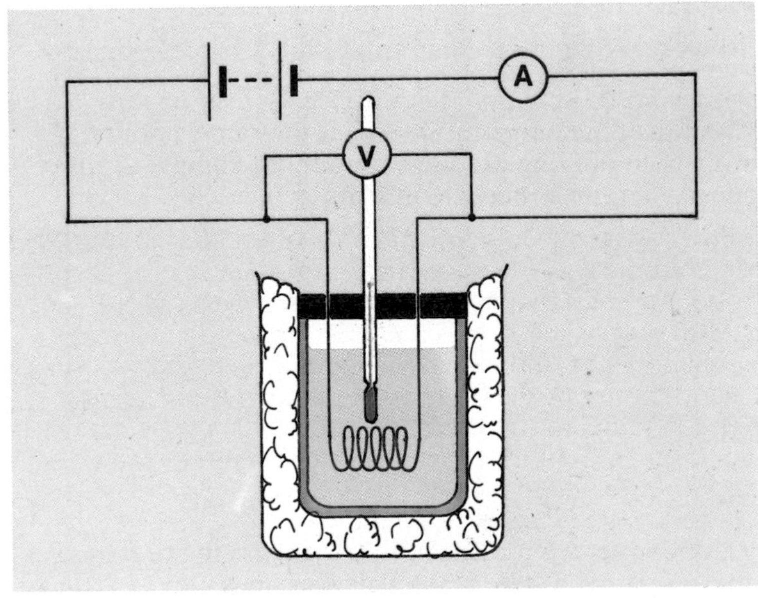

Fig. 43.2

Example

In an experiment to measure the specific heat capacity of a liquid it was found that 8.8 kJ were required to raise the temperature of 400 g of the liquid by 10° C. What was the specific heat capacity of the liquid?

Energy supplied = S.h.c. × Mass × Rise in Temp.

8800 = S.h.c. × 0.4 × 10

= S.h.c. × 4

S.h.c. = 8800/4

= 2200 J/(kg °C)

Ans. 2200 J/(kg °C).

Experiment 43.2 To Measure the Specific Heat Capacity of Copper by the Method of Mixtures

Method

1. Find the mass of some copper rivets and put them in a test-tube.
2. Fill a beaker with water and place the test-tube in it, *Fig. 43.3.*

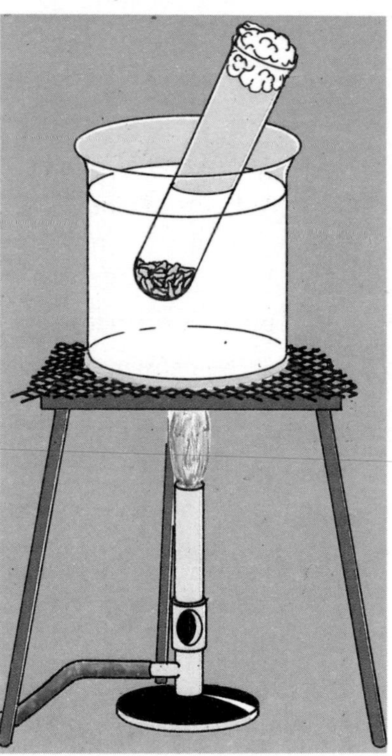

Fig. 43.3

3. Heat the beaker until the water boils. Turn down the gas and allow the water to boil for 10-15 minutes. You may now assume that the temperature of the copper is 100°C.
4. Find the mass of a copper calorimeter.
5. Fill the calorimeter approximately one quarter full with cold water and find the mass of the calorimeter and water. Subtract to find the mass of the water.
6. When the copper is hot, measure the temperature of the cold water in the calorimeter.
7. Quickly empty the hot copper into the calorimeter, stir and note the highest temperature reached by the water.
8. Record your results as shown below and calculate the specific heat capacity of the copper from the following equations.

Energy lost by copper $= M_{Cu} \times C_{Cu} \times (100 - \theta_2)$

Energy gained by water $= M_w \times 4180 + (\theta_2 - \theta_1)$

Energy gained by calorimeter $= M_c \times C_{Cu} \times (\theta_2 \times \theta_1)$

Energy lost by copper = Energy gained by water and calorimeter.

RESULTS

Mass of copper rivets	$= M_{Cu}$ kg
Mass of calorimeter	$= M_c$ kg
Mass of calorimeter + water	$= M_T$ kg
Mass of water	$= M_w$ kg
Temp. of hot copper	= 100 °C
Temp. of cold water and calorimeter	$= \theta_1$°C
Final temp. of water, copper and cal.	$= \theta_2$°C
Specific heat capacity of copper	$= C_{Cu}$ J/kg °C).

43.2 Latent Heat

If you heat some ice in a beaker its temperature gradually increases until it reaches 0 °C. If you continue to heat it, its temperature will remain at 0°C until all the ice has melted. The energy supplied during this period is called **latent heat**. It does not cause a rise in the temperature of the ice. Instead, the energy is used to break the bonds which hold the molecules together in the solid state.

If you continue to heat the melted ice the temperature will begin to rise again and will continue to rise until it reaches 100 °C. If you still continue heating, the temperature will remain at 100 °C until all the water has been turned into steam. *Fig. 43.4* shows, in a general way, how the temperature would change with time.

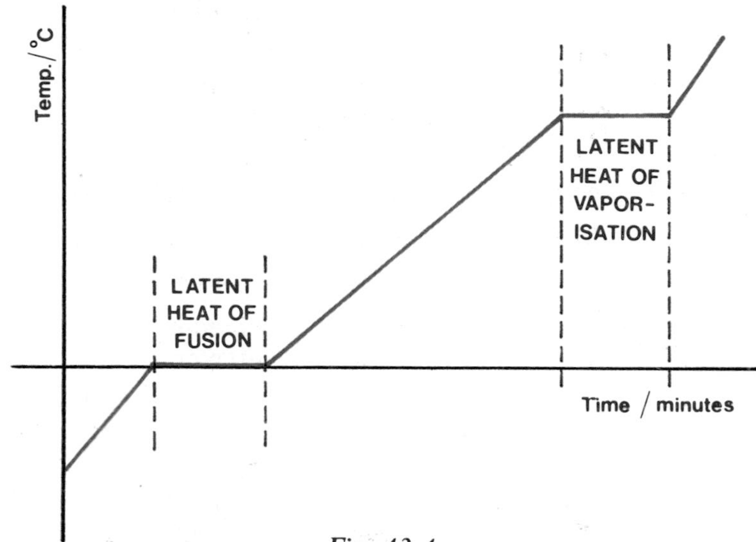

Fig. 43.4

The amount of energy required to change the state of 1 kg of a substance is called the **specific latent heat** of that substance.

The specific latent heat of a substance is the energy required to change the state of 1 kg of the substance without change in temperature.

When the change of state is from solid to liquid the specific latent heat is called the **specific latent heat of fusion**. When the change is from liquid to vapour it is called the **specific latent heat of vaporisation**.

Example

The specific latent heat of vaporisation of steam is 2240 kJ/kg. How much energy is required to change 200 g of water to steam?

The energy required to change 1 kg

= 2240 kJ

Therefore, the energy required to change

0.2 kg = 2240 × 0.2 kJ

= 448 kJ

Ans. 448 kJ.

From this example we see that the energy involved in a change of state is given by:

Energy supplied = Specific latent heat × Mass

Experiment 43.3 To Measure the Specific Latent Heat of Fusion of Ice

Method

1. Find the mass of a copper calorimeter.
2. Approximately half fill the calorimeter with warm water (at about 25 °C). Find the mass of the calorimeter and water and by subtraction find the mass of the water.
3. Place the calorimeter in a beaker surrounded by insulation and note the temperature of the water.
4. Crush some ice and dry it with blotting paper or filter paper.
5. Add the ice to the water, a little at a time, stirring with the thermometer until the ice is melted. Continue until the temperature of the water has fallen to about 10 °C. Note the final temperature of the water.
6. Find the mass of the calorimeter and water and by subtraction find the mass of ice added. Record your results as shown below and calculate the specific latent heat of fusion of ice from the following equations.

Energy gained by ice $= M_I L + C_{Cu} \times (\theta_1 \times \theta_2)$

Energy lost by calorimeter $= M_c \times C_{Cu} \times (\theta_1 \times \theta_2)$

Energy lost by water $= M_w \times C_w \times (\theta_1 \times \theta_2)$

Energy gained by ice = Energy lost by calorimeter and water.

RESULTS

Mass of calorimeter......	$= M_c$ kg
Mass of calorimeter + water	$= M_1$kg
Temp. of warm water	$= \theta_1$°C
Temp. of ice	$= \theta$ °C
Final temp. of water and calorimeter	$= \theta_2$°C
Rise in temp. of ice water....	$= \theta_2$
Fall in temp. of water and cal.....	$= (\theta_1 - \theta_2)$°C
Mass of cal. + water + melted ice ...	$= M_2$kg
Mass of ice	$= M_1$kg
Specific Latent heat of fusion of ice ..	= L J/kg.
Mass of water ...	$= M_w$ Kg.

Effects of Latent Heat

You may have noticed that the specific latent heat of vaporisation of steam is very large; it is 2240 kJ per kilogram. This is more than five times the amount of energy required to heat a kilogram of water from 0 °C to 100 °C. This explains why a scald from steam is much more painful than one from boiling water. When the steam touches the skin large amounts of energy are released as the steam turns to water.

The body's cooling mechanism depends on the large specific latent heat of vaporisation. Your body secretes sweat from glands just under the skin. On the surface of the skin the sweat evaporates, taking the necessary latent heat from the skin and therefore cooling it.

Experiment 43.4 To Determine the Melting Point for Naphthalene

Method

1. Put some naphthalene in a test-tube and put the test-tube in a beaker of water.
2. Arrange the beaker and the test-tube on a retort stand as shown in *Fig. 43.5*.
3. Heat the water in the beaker until it boils.
4. Switch off the Bunsen burner. Note the temperature of the naphthalene.

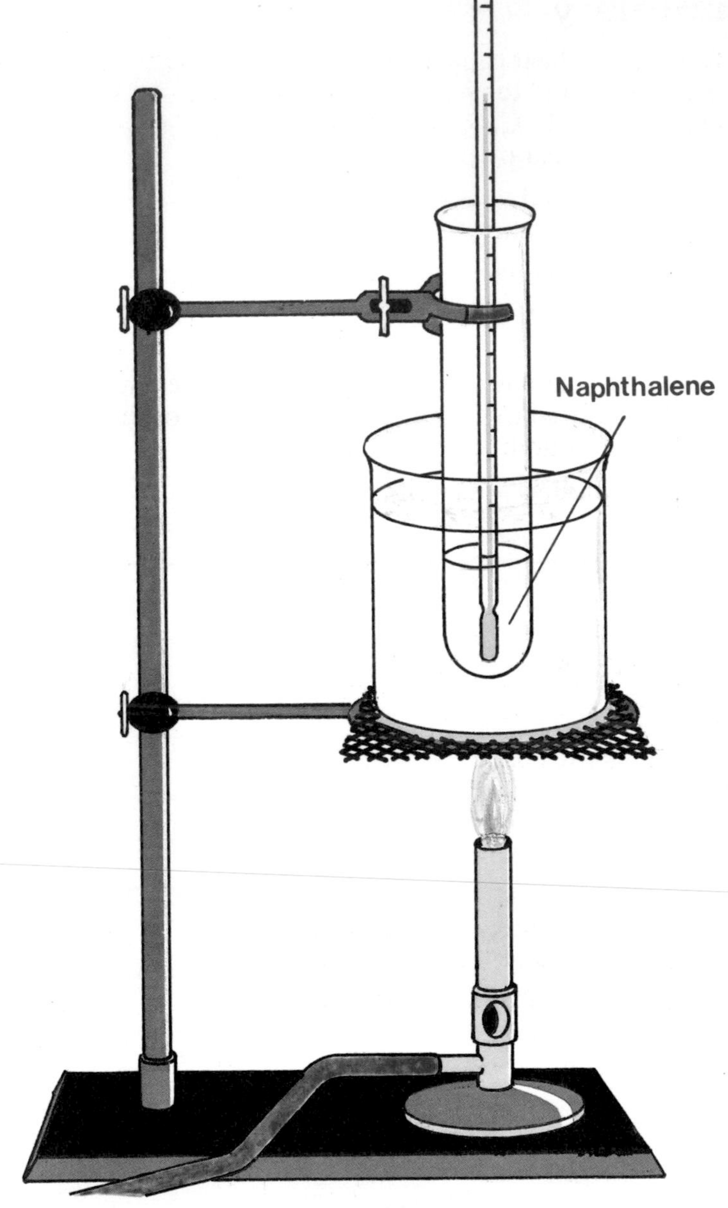

Fig. 43.5

5. Record the temperature of the naphthalene at one minute intervals until it solidifies and then continue for a further 5 minutes.
6. Record your results in the form of a table and then plot a graph of temperature against time.
7. From the graph calculate the freezing point/melting point of naphthalene.

Summary

* The specific heat capacity of a substance is the amount of energy required to change the temperature of 1 kg of the substance by 1 °C. Specific heat capacity is measured in joules per kilogram per degrees Celsius, i.e. J/kg °C).
* Energy supplied = Specific heat capacity × Mass × Rise in Temperature.
* The energy involved in a change of state is called latent heat. At a change of state the temperature remains constant.
* The specific latent heat of a substance is the amount of energy required to change the state of 1 kg of the substance without change in temperature.
* Energy supplied = Specific latent heat × Mass

Questions

Section A

1. The specific heat capacity of a substance is ....

   ....
2. The unit of specific heat capacity is ....
3. The specific heat capacity of water is 4180 J/kg °C). How much energy is required to heat 100 g of water from 10 °C to 50 °C? ....
4. When 200 g of water cools from 80 °C to 20 ° How much energy is given out? ....
5. Why is water used in central heating systems? ....

   ....
6. The energy involved in a change of state is called ......

   ....
7. The energy required to change 1 kg of water into steam at the same temperature is called the ....
8. Why does it usually feel colder when snow is thawing than before it starts to thaw? ....

   ....
9. If you spill some ether on your hand it feels cold. Why?

   ....
10. The energy required to change 1 kg of ice to water at the same temperature is called the ....

Section B

1. What is meant by specific heat capacity? Describe how you would measure the specific heat capacity of a liquid.
2. If 7.8 kJ of energy are required to raise the temperature of 2 kg of copper from 20 °C to 30 °C, what is the specific heat capacity of copper?
   How much energy would be required to raise the temperature of 400 g of copper from 15 °C to 65 °C?
3. The specific heat capacity of a solid is 400 J/(kg °C) and the specific heat capacity of a liquid is 2000 J/(kg °C). If 200 g of the solid at 80 °C are placed in 400 g of the liquid at 20 °C, what is the final temperature of the mixture?
4. What is meant by specific latent heat?
   Describe an experiment to measure the specific latent heat of fusion ice.
5. Calculate the total amount of energy required to change 2 kg of ice at 0 °C to steam at 100 °C, given the following information:

   Specific latent heat of fusion of ice = 334 kJ/kg

   Specific heat capacity of water = 4180 J/(kg C)

   Specific latent heat of vaporisation of steam = 2240 kJ/kg.
6. When 20 g of ice at 0 °C are added to 300 g of a liquid at 30 °C the final temperature of the liquid and melted ice is 10 °C. What is the specific heat capacity of the liquid? (Use the data given in the last question).

Index